From Burke to Beckett

From Burke to Beckett
Ascendancy, Tradition and Betrayal
in Literary History

W. J. Mc Cormack

CORK UNIVERSITY PRESS

First published in 1985 as
Ascendancy and Tradition in Anglo-Irish
Literary History from 1789 to 1939

Revised and enlarged edition
published in 1994 by
Cork University Press
University College
Cork
Ireland

British Library Cataloguing in Publication Data
A CIP catalogue record for this book is available from
the British Library.

ISBN 0 902561 94 4 paperback

Typeset by Tower Books of Ballincollig, Co. Cork
Printed by ColourBooks, Baldoyle, Co. Dublin

Contents

Acknowledgements

This book has had two distinct period of composition. In relation to the first, I would refer readers to *Ascendancy and Tradition* (1985) where a list of people to whom I was indebted for information, assistance or friendship can be found. To repeat that list here would simply render mechanical an act of appreciation which I believe was well-judged at the time. In relation to the second, I was particularly glad to have the use of certain facilities in the School of English, Trinity College, Dublin, even though I was not a member of the academic staff there. To successive heads of department – Nicholas Grene, John Scattergood, Richard McCabe and Thomas Docherty — I want to express a refugee's warm gratitude.

Personal thanks, of at least the same warmth, are due to the following: Ciaran Brady, Terence Brown, Marilyn Butler, Peter Connell, Alan Downie, Antony Farrell, Rachel Finnegan, Tom Garvin, Selina Guinness, Jeremy Hawthorn, Patrick Healy, Louise Kidney, Fred Lowe, Fiona Macintosh, Lucy Maddox, Geraldine Mangan, Stephen Matterson, Ferenc Takács, Lucinda Thomson, Tim Webb, Wolfgang Wicht and Stephen Wilson.

For more than twenty years, my family have tolerated books in the bathroom, footnotes in the fridge, and other intrusions. Domestically, the freelance writer can be indistinguisable from the free-booter. Now that I am able to use the address which appears below, the prospect of clearing the table for regular celebrations is real.

W. J. Mc Cormack
Goldsmiths' College
London
July 1994

Introduction

> The last thing one discovers when writing a work is what one
> should put first.
>
> (Blaise Pascal)[1]

A FEW PREFATORY REMARKS

In this twinkling-of-an-eye, post-modern age, books generally have a story
to tell or a thesis to defend; that is to say, they still resist instant capitula-
tion, sometimes by doing two things at the same time. In some ways, *From
Burke to Beckett* is argued at a level of generalization familiar to historians
who, however, probably regard the mass of directly cited matter as a crude
survival from some pre-historic methodology. Fans of the quote-and-dote
approach to Irish literary studies will, by an unpleasing symmetry, deplore
the abstractions and the exotic allusions. Yet the mix of history-writing and
literary criticism is done on the basis of their strong categorical resemblance.
   What kind of book is this? It narrates no thesis, it 'theorizes' no meta-
narrative. Instead, it makes terms between a predominating concept of an
essentially political kind and a corpus of writing which is largely but not
exclusively literary. Ultimately, the relations of 'concept' to 'corpus' should
be seen as fully reciprocal, though the emphasis here must for the moment
fall upon exchanges in which the work of literature is still thought to occupy a higher, though secondary, position. Such a description does not hold
out much prospect of hilarity nor even of spiritual uplift, but it is better
to be honest. The area of concern is predominantly Irish, but William

1

Godwin and Thomas Mann gain admittance; national pride may not be much flattered as a consequence.

Resemblances properly implicate differences; otherwise we should have to surrender to that barby-doll of recent debate – identity. Only when a means of establishing two-way traffic between concept and corpus has been elaborated might the construction of non-identical thinking be overcome. Meanwhile, this book continues – now in its second version – to 'make terms'; that is, to negotiate a critical idiom through which quotation and abstraction might comprehend each other.

AGAINST DEFINITIONS

The emergence of Anglo-Irish literature lies close to the heart of European romanticism. The Anglo-Irish Renaissance is central to modernist literature in the English language. With these two perspectives in mind I have tried here to describe the functioning of two crucial concepts in my own cultural heritage – the sociological formation of 'Protestant Ascendancy', and the Yeatsian elaboration of an Irish literary 'tradition'.

The task has not been easy. If all the books ever written on the subject were laid end-to-end in a straight line they would on the instant curl into the shape of a question-mark. On the one hand venerable and respectable, on the other a kind of post-war phenomenon not unconnected to Marshall Aid, Anglo-Irish literature slips between the categories to defy definition, indeed perhaps to question the very notion of definition in this area. The bibliography is exhausting and it grows annually, yet the subject is as much obscured as clarified by these additional studies: bright lights cast dark shadows. Every speculative study of Joyce throws Yeats into isolated relief; every close analysis of a poem by Yeats is eloquently silent on the totalities in which the poem may properly be seen; every account of the Abbey Theatre raises unspoken questions about the Renaissance and its coolness towards the novel. In *Ascendancy and Tradition* I attempted to deal with Yeats and Joyce as mutually defining figures within the totalities which historical as well as literary critical analysis depends upon.[2] Yet while committed to a whole view of Anglo-Irish literature, a view which acknowledges its social existence, I resist the pressures which would establish the Anglo-Irish 'thing' as not just a literature but a national literature – if not indeed a culture or even a civilization.[3] With such an escalation of dignity comes a concomitant intensity of feeling, feeling often prescribing rules of exclusion – 'Robert Graves (or Samuel Beckett) is not Irish' – or turning into elegiac celebrations of a dubious past – Yeats as a young boyo in his 'native' Sligo.

This tendency to become personal about the subject is not merely a sign of the critic's individual attachment, it is an indicator of a deeply rooted problem at the centre of the Anglo-Irish phenomenon. 'The time is coming fast, if it isn't already here, when the question, "Is So-and-So really an Irish writer?" will clear a room in seconds.'[4] In this manner did Derek Mahon commence an assessment of Louis MacNeice some years ago. The significant feature of this characteristic self-scrutiny is not Mr Mahon's very proper contempt for the naivety of such inquiries, it is the evidently social occasion on which they arise – clear a room in seconds. For, if Anglo-Irish literature is a difficult animal to classify, it has also long been the subject of wondering conversation, anecdote, and gossip, the locus of an advanced tourism. Here again, the implications are not simply of innocent vulgarity or the bar-room availability of a provincial wisdom; in a larger context, the argument in favour of an Anglo-Irish civilization leads towards specific attitudes to sectarian violence in Ulster and its place in the politics of the United Kingdom. Like Shakespeare, Yeats is full of quotations, and too many of them have been employed as the titles of novels and improving tracts on Irish sociology. Doubtless, a high proportion of these works have dealt with 'the Ulster question', but too often the apt quotation and the beguiling cadence are not employed to do more than confirm a satisfying eccentricity in the topic. Investigating my own cultural heritage (as I suggested at the outset), I have found it more illuminating to see it as part of what Theodor Adorno has termed 'the culture industry' than of Celtic–Anglican civilization. Nor is there summer school but singing monuments of its own magnificence.

The literature itself incorporates much conversation and gossip, the exploits of ward politicians, society belles, 'what the butler Said to a drunken game-keeper In mid-October', the careers of real statesmen, 'strong men, and thieves, and deacons' whose names may be traced in *Who's Who*, *Stubb's Gazette*, or some similar directory.[5] There is an important difference to be drawn between Standish O'Grady and Madame Sosostris as they are rendered in poems by Yeats and Eliot respectively: to declare them both figures of poetic mythology is to impose a blanket term on the unique processes of composition of each poet and, perhaps more damagingly, on the very different social relations within the United Kingdom which locate the work of the two writers. It is not enough simply to remark, as a characteristic of Irish society, that it abounded in 'characters' who required no invention. Such notions take on a different tone if we reflect that it is only with this assimilation into art that O'Grady acquires a degree of coherence. Is not *Toryism and the Tory Democracy* (O'Grady's tract of 1886) effectively read

through the prism of 'Beautiful Lofty Things' whereby the significance of
that conjuncture of Celticism, contempt for 'the Protestant Ascendancy',
and violent rhetoric is refined to 'high nonsensical words'.[6] In the Irish experience, art does not exploit reality; it completes, perhaps concludes it.
The dealings between these hypostasized values, art and reality, are prominent and complex in Anglo-Irish literature: each is at times evidently obliged to masquerade as the other. Here indeed is a central problem which lures
the scholar-pilgrim towards Sligo – the works he has chosen to read and
celebrate, while they are intensely concerned with society and politics, with
conversation and rhetoric, are also deeply secretive, arcane, and (in some
people's view) wilfully obscure. The Irish, or the Ulster, experience is a
cave-drama of considerable popularity in recent years, but attempts to define
it strongly resemble attempts to authenticate it. Professor Denis Donoghue,
to whom I shall be indebted continuously in the pages that follow, illustrated
in a penetrating exercise in defining this experience the attendant risks. There
are two significant moments:

> The real trouble in Ireland is that our national experience has been too limited
> to be true. Since the Plantation of Ulster there has been one story and one
> story only in Irish feeling: the English, how to get rid of them, or, failing
> that, to circumvent them, cajole them, twist their tails. Our categories of feel-
> ing are therefore flagrantly limited; our history has been at once intense and
> monotonous. We have had no industrial revolution, no factory acts, no trade
> union movement: hence the frail basis upon which our Labour Party exists,
> by contrast with the two major parties which still define themselves in terms
> of our civil war. A limited history, a correspondingly intimidating mythology,
> a fractured language, a literature of fits and starts and gestures: no continuity
> from one age to the next. Irish novelists, the few who survive, feel the anxiety
> of influence but not the incitement or the challenge of a tradition.[7]

Denis Donoghue's distinctive skills are not engaged here. That is, the historical summary he offers is not really the product of the mind which elaborated
his masterly account of Yeats.[8] The assumptions he makes, however, have
a representative status. 'National experience' indiscriminately labels semi-
feudalism in pre-plantation Ulster and romantic politics in the nineteenth
century, as if the word 'nation' had not changed greatly in the intervening
centuries. To argue that Ireland had no industrial revolution, it is necessary
to ignore Belfast and the Lagan valley, to go no further. To deny factory
laws, you deny Belfast and the statute books of the United Kingdom.[9] The
truth is that such a view of Irish history is itself a mythology, not simply
because it gets specific facts wrong, but because it reads back into the past
the truncated success of bourgeois nationalism in twenty-six counties of

Ireland, cavalierly ignoring the historical actuality of the United Kingdom of Great Britain and Ireland in the nineteenth century, and compensating for the 'loss' of Belfast and Ulster by a denial of their previous existence.

The second moment from Professor Donoghue's essay comes near the end of the piece:

> It is common to have the experience and miss the meaning . . . it is my impression that Irish writers sense a rift between experience and meaning, but in reverse: the meaning is premature, already inscribed by a mythology they have no choice but to inherit, and the experience is too narrow to be entirely natural and representative.[10]

Here I find the narrowness of the earlier passage entirely enlightened and accepted, and a number of consequences can be noted. The priority of meaning over experience for Irish writing is one way of observing a tendency towards allegory in certain large areas of nineteenth-century fiction. The same proposition might be stated conversely as the tendency towards abstract experience in this colonial fiction, a tendency we shall trace in some work by Sheridan Le Fanu, and – to a lesser extent – Charles Lever.

From Burke to Beckett is not intended to rival the various sequential histories and personal guides to Anglo-Irish literature recently published.[11] Basically, what follows takes its bearing from the development of modernism out of the break-up of the romantic proposition in the nineteenth century. Nineteenth-century realism lent credence to the theory of literature as an imitation of reality. The mass of Irish writing in this period, however, rested upon a confusion of romantic assumption and naive reportage. Politics, saturated in such assumptions, took its shape from a concern with the past: the past, conceived in terms of expropriation, legitimized a growing obsession with land. Thus, the increasingly bourgeois nature of Irish political activity could yet be presented as the driving home of ancient rights, the reassertion of some Gaelic nobility in revenant form. The novel took the fundamental shape of this view of history and rendered it fabulous.

Historians have a rather different story to tell, indeed they have many stories to tell, not all of them reconcilable one with another. Oliver MacDonagh has indicated a number of important areas in which early nineteenth-century Ireland saw the commencement of an experiment in administration conducted ultimately from Westminster and through Dublin. In local and municipal government, public order (policing), and social welfare Ireland was for much of the century at least formally more advanced than Britain.[12] No doubt the vision of Ireland as a social laboratory might become as cloudy as the nationalist stereotype or the fictional convention. But if we add to

MacDonagh's argument some consideration of the complex organization of land purchase and the growth of joint stock company investment later in the century, we begin to see that Ireland was not metaphysically different from the West Country or Wolverhampton.[13] If this sounds like latter-day historical revisionism, we should note how, in 1837, an anonymous critic seeking to define what Anglo-Irish literature might be, lamented the necessity of Irish participation in the changes determined by the more advanced economy of Britain – and this in the columns of the *Dublin University Magazine*, flagship of that cultural conservatism which nurtured Samuel Ferguson, Isaac Butt, and Sheridan Le Fanu.[14] Unionism which resents Union is not simply a demonstration of Irish incorrigibility; it is, as my first chapter aims to demonstrate, a fundamental romantic dichotomy in the political structure of the United Kingdom between 1801 and 1920. Indeed, in the United Kingdom as modified in 1920 by the Government of Ireland Act, the dichotomy persists with a modernist aura of violence and indifference.[15]

If nineteenth-century Ireland is fundamentally relatable to England, and to Britain generally, why is it that in the area of cultural production the relationships are suppressed more often than expressed? The central issue here concerns Ireland's complex role as metropolitan colony within the United Kingdom. In relation to the Empire overseas – the army in India is an instance in point – Ireland was part of the metropolitan 'home country'; in relation to that home economy it was in significant ways itself colonial. Much might be written on that issue in political, social, and economic terms; but in a basically cultural context, answers to the question of suppressed relations between Ireland and the rest of the United Kingdom may be gathered under three headings. The first of these is the nationalist mythology of a historical uniqueness, a proposition which might have achieved validity if the fate of the Gaelic language in the past one hundred and fifty years had been other than it was. The second emphasizes the distinctive Catholicism of the Irish population within the British Isles – Daniel Corkery is the chief advocate here – and this sectarian difference can only strain belief if it is also employed to isolate Irish culture from Europe.

A third, more specifically literary answer absorbs these two and effectively sets them up as a mutual cancellation – the third answer may be called Yeatsian tradition. Yet while Yeats's theoretical constructions use the bricks and mortar of literary terminology, they serve to house diverse ideological interests. In rather more *ad hominem* terms, this third answer lies in the extent to which critics of Anglo-Irish literature have derived their historiography from W. B. Yeats. Yeats, of course, was only one of several late nineteenth-century voices who propounded a view of Ireland as more venerable, traditional, and spiritual than degenerate England – though all were perhaps laggard in acknowledging their debt to British exemplars such as Carlyle and Arnold. The proposition that Yeatsian tradition has unacknowledged British debts might be rewritten as a measure of the extent to which Yeats is the concentrated statement – significantly in literary terms – of a dominant historiography rooted in both British and Irish aspects of nineteenth-century experience. The Anglo-Irish Renaissance, the Irish genius for words, is not solely a product of native soil.

Of the figures besides Yeats, Standish James O'Grady is taken here to mediate between this Victorian wisdom and the imminent 'Cuchullainoid' mythology of the Renaissance.[16] Beyond anything which might be ascribed to Yeats's influence there lies a further and more pervasive force – the notion that, whatever the stock exchange or the statistics of food production and exports might say, Ireland had a distinctive if not unique social structure, the crowning feature of which was the Protestant Ascendancy. The mysteries of the Protestant Ascendancy, to which J. M. Synge, Lady Gregory, and W. B. Yeats variously adhered, were such that outsiders could do no better than take it on trust. And essential to the viability of this concept was the complementary notion that Ireland had no middle class. In Victorian England, when the aristocracy was adopting bourgeois ways, and the labouring classes were urged to adopt the mores (but not the financial expectations) of their betters, this alleged absence of an Irish middle class effectively silenced a comparative study of Irish and British culture. Moreover, while Irish industrialization and urban development should not be written off as non-existent, it is still true that in Britain middle-class behaviour was increasingly associated with the life of the towns while Ireland saw itself as a rural community with incidental conurbations.

In the second part of chapter two, I analyse at length the emergence of the term 'Protestant Ascendancy' in the context of revolutionary alarm in the 1790s. In due course Yeats's use of it is to indicate the governing élite in Ireland from the Williamite Settlement (1697) onwards. This is only one anomalous aspect of Protestant Ascendancy, its being back-dated before the moment of its coinage as a phrase to provide an encapsulated history of the eighteenth century *in toto*. There is another, even more striking, anomaly between the quasi-aristocratic connotations of the Yeatsian usage and the distinctly mercantile and urban surroundings of the concept's minting in the vicinity of the Common Council of Dublin Corporation. Some stages of the evolution of the 1790s neologism into the timeless language of Augustan élitism are provided in the chapter called 'Ascendancy and Cabal': this evolution, though important in itself, is less significant than the negotiation between the sociological formation calling itself 'The Protestant Ascendancy' and the ideological construction of an eighteenth-century hegemony of the same name. From this contradiction, rather than from any mechanical causality in the families of Yeats and Synge and Lady Gregory, derives the modernist, valorized tradition associated with their names.

Joyce stands apart. Or at least, that is the traditional placing of Joyce *vis-à-vis* Yeats and the Protestant Ascendancy. Here, an attempt is made to relate Joyce's *petit-bourgeois* inheritance to the suppression of middle-class evidences in Irish Protestantism. Ironically, some attention to the development of the novel in nineteenth-century Ireland can uncover a fictional prologue to Joyce's great innovations. For example, though the absence of a middle class was accepted tacitly on the western shore of the Irish Sea, in the 1840s (when Anthony Trollope was as productive of novels set in Ireland as Sheridan Le Fanu) the author of *The Kellys and the O'Kellys* (1848) perceived a more recognizably bourgeois Ireland than any of his Irish contemporaries, Charles Lever included. Later, it is true that Lever (in such a novel as *Barrington*) did attend to the life of the Irish bourgeoisie but he evidently needed the security of German *biedermeier* sentiment to feel at ease in his task. Lever, it might be observed in passing, is a proto-modernist at least in his choice of prolonged exile on the Continent. His novel of 1865, *Luttrell of Arran*, provides us with an early instance of the Irish modernist concern with 'Celtic' primitivism. Whereas these Irish novelists of the Victorian period – Le Fanu, Lever, Kickham, Moore, Somerville and Ross – employed structures in which a polarization between castle and cabin characterized their reflection of society, the fiction of Maria Edgeworth (who is so much closer in time to the origins of Protestant Ascendancy ideology) would show how this polarization is shaken with irony, energized more by desire than achievement.

Irony and desire – these are terms more usually conjoined in discussion of James Joyce's fiction than in, say, an account of that neglected novel, *The Absentee*. But the political function of Protestant Ascendancy in the first decades of the nineteenth century was specifically sectarian – the granting of priority to a sectarian sociology over and above reformist administration and incipient democracy. The paradox of this development rests mainly on the very limited mobilization of the term Protestant Ascendancy, and the complementary nervous concern with rival, putative 'ascendancies' — popish, biblical and the like. The sectarian strategy soon articulated rival statements of Irish history which together constituted the romantic reformulation of the past. In Joyce we discover manifestly one of these histories, that of the Irish Catholic lower middle classes, urbanized, yet still traumatized by the devastation of the countryside in mid-century. The Joyce we discover will be the inheritor of that disaster, the passing of the Gaelic language, which he is so often thought to have discounted. It is with Joyce that we encounter the ironies of tradition in that he therapeutically enacts in his life's work those repressions which otherwise would have remained repressed, untreated, ascendant. For the violence of a bifurcated history has its sexual as well as political register; and Joyce's *oeuvre* (for all the celebrated fissures and discontinuities of his individual texts) offers a vision of an ultimate, if historically postponed, wholeness. For this reason, Joyce is the only author here whose work is treated in all its major textual forms.

A contrast between Joyce and Yeats is generally understood: a sustained comparison is less often encountered. If Joyce posits a psychic wholeness (qualified by the historical determinants of his time) Yeats offers Unity of Being. The former lies ostensibly in the future, the latter ostensibly in the past. In the case of Yeats, the drama offers particular advantages for this inquiry – the explicitly multi-vocal form of expression, the accessible fissures between set and dialogue, setting and allusion, etc. Yeatsian tradition ought to lead one to *The Words upon the Window-Pane*, in which the playwright's predilection for cultural heroes made Jonathan Swift manifest through a spiritualist medium in latter-day Dublin. It is doubtless true that *The Words upon the Window-Pane* draws Yeats's Augustan constructs into play with the filthy modern tide, yet in detailing the late eighteenth-century origins of Protestant Ascendancy I find *Purgatory* to be the more revealing drama. If, as I argue, *Purgatory* is not only based on what Donald Torchiana has called Yeats's 'theory of the symbolic tragedy of the eighteenth century' but is directly related to that dangerous intersection of modernist aesthetics and totalitarian politics, then an analysis of the play may serve to indicate – however briefly – an area for further inquiry, the place of Protestant Ascendancy ideology in the broader field of European racism.[17]

I take Protestant Ascendancy to be the central cultural assumption of Yeats's meditation on his own inheritance. By it he measured the politics of the Irish Free State, having earlier he performed in his *Autobiographies* remarkable transformations of his social experience of the nineteenth century; by celebration of it he brought his own late work into creative relationship with that of Jonathan Swift, George Berkeley, Oliver Goldsmith, and Edmund Burke. However, an examination of articles in the *Catholic Bulletin* in the early 1920s suggests that Yeats was no *primum mobile* in the matter. In his exhaustive and valuable study of these relationships, Donald Torchiana has paid tribute to T. R. Henn's account of the Anglo-Irish background in *The Lonely Tower*. Henn, however, is more exegete than critic and nothing better illustrates the debt owed to (or distortion traceable to) Yeats's own reading of history: looking at once at the nineteenth century *in toto* and the early 1920s in isolation, Henn saw that

> everywhere the Big House, with its estates surrounding it, was a centre of hospitality, of county life and society, apt to breed a passionate attachment, so that the attempt to save it from burning or bankruptcy became an obsession (in the nineteen twenties and onwards) when that civilization was passing . . . To this society, in the main Protestant, Unionist, and of the 'Ascendancy' in character, the peasantry was linked. The great demesnes had their tenantry, proud, idle, careless, kindly, with a richness of speech and folklore that Lady Gregory had been the first to record. The days of *Castle Rackrent* were, in the main, over; the relationship between landlord and tenant varied, but was on the whole a kindly one, and carried a good deal of respect on either side.[18]

From the notion of the 'the Big House', Henn is led on to evoke idyllic social relations in which matters of estate management, rates of interest, toil itself, do not intrude. It is true that taxes imposed from Westminster are accorded a measure of responsibility for the decline of the estates, but burning and bankruptcy remain magisterially unaccounted for. The idyll existed before the 1920s, and this is a recurrent Anglo-Irish complaint – the Golden Age always existed before some moveable disaster, before the Union, before the Famine, before the Encumbered Estates Court, the Land War, Parnell, the Rising, the Troubles, an accelerating succession of unfortunate falls each one briefly inaugurating some (retrospectively acknowledged) idyll which is itself soon dissolved by the next disaster. Ascendancy is the principal medium by which this fleeting vision of a stable, pre-lapsarian order is imposed on the insolence of fact and circumstance. Expanding on the theme of *Purgatory*, Yeats pointed with approval to Nazi legislation which allowed (certain, Aryan) families to go on living where their ancestors had lived – the background to such approval is not exclusively non-Irish.

But the staccato of mere legislated disaster in Ireland was insufficient for Yeats's imagination; in place of Land Acts and political demagogues, Yeats saw as the principal barrier to the past the nineteenth century itself, beyond which lay – he was to claim – the Irish Augustan age, 'that one Irish century that escaped from darkness and confusion'.[19] Much of the material discussed in the succeeding chapters focuses on that barrier, but here we can note briefly a few details of Yeats's Augustan age. Having escaped from darkness and confusion, it was necessarily fated to end in, return to, some such condition, darkness and confusion, the filthy modern tide – it is important to record this qualification of Yeats's exemption. The energies of his cyclical history generate a dual perspective: with reference to the eighteenth century Goldsmith is not only presented 'deliberately sipping at the honey-pot of his mind', in 'The Seven Sages' his serene response to the countryside is also gravely qualified:

> Oliver Goldsmith sang what he had seen,
> Roads full of beggars, cattle in the fields,
> But never saw the trefoil stained with blood,
> The avenging leaf those fields raised up against it.[20]

This return to violence, breaking down of order into disorder, is the acknowledgement of historical process by which Protestant Ascendancy is born – not among the pastoral beggars – but with avenging leaves and stained trefoils as its symbolic paraphernalia.

Despite this dual function which Goldsmith performs in Yeats's poem, the eighteenth-century figures of Yeats's mythology are too often read simply as heroes. One frequently hears that Swift (or Burke, or Yeats himself) is 'the father of Anglo-Irish literature', though in truth Walter Scott or Goethe may well have an equally valid claim at times to the title. Biological metaphors of this kind have an insidious effect in that they generate notions of a legitimizing family tree which distinguishes the Anglo-Irish writer from a larger context instead of locating him in it. Swift himself, writing about the Anglo-Scottish Union, drew attention to the absurdities which can arise from a metaphor which has supplanted, instead of moved, reality:

> Henceforward let no stateman dare
> A kingdom to a ship compare;
> Lest he should call our commonweal
> A vessel with a double keel.[21]

Such eighteenth-century sense should be applied drastically to the conceit of stormy love affair or unhappy marriage so often employed of Anglo-Irish relations, from the days of Swift himself to those of Seamus Heaney. Indeed the first step in defining Anglo-Irish literature must be to challenge such dominant metaphors. Once alerted to this unconscious tendency towards organicist assumptions, our critical debate may find it easier to admit that 'the Anglo-Irish writer' is a rhetorical shorthand for written texts which, in turn, stand in positive and potent relation to wider cultural structures.

In that wider context Tradition is of course a familiar enough concept. Having denied any crudely causal influence of the Protestant Ascendancy on Yeatsian tradition, I should also make it clear that the idea of tradition I associate with Yeats is not simply that of sanctified continuity. The modernist interest in tradition is self-evidently ironic, and the complexities of that interest may be traced in figures as diverse as T. S. Eliot and Martin Heidegger as well as in the fossil-history of the word's etymology. Hermeneutics, I should immediately concede, lies well beyond the range of the present inquiry, which will deal with the issue of tradition strictly in its Yeatsian form. This is not to suggest that Yeats's thought on this topic is of merely local interest, nor to insinuate that it is merely a piece of obfuscating ideology peddling distortions of an otherwise accessible and unsullied past. It is a statement of certain continuities – in the nineteenth century crucially – which Yeats elsewhere denied. And this contradiction between tradition and its material is a further statement of the disjunction between an Irish local literature and the European culture into which it cries out for reinsertion.

We shall have need, therefore, of Eliot's wry comment that 'in English writing we seldom speak of tradition, though we occasionally apply its name in deploring its absence.'[22] Nowadays, the Anglo-Irish tradition is cited so often that its existence must be seriously in doubt. However, the notion of Anglo-Irish literature is given an excessive stability by the acceptance of tradition as accumulated and accumulating succession. Just as ascendancy emerges to assert a condition which is longed for protectively rather than possessed confidently, so (Eliot reminds us) tradition is a negative marker in many of its citations. If we think spatially about Anglo-Irish literature as the meeting ground of various directions and forces – Gaelic culture and Celticism, English romanticism and revolutionary alarm, bourgeois compensation and subversive allegory – we should consider tradition historically as the (sometimes contradictory and violent) convergence of readings, not of texts. Tradition as the convergence of readings, tradition as involving a 'Thou' – in Hans-Georg Gadamer's terms – is necessarily an active element in literary history. Less abstractly, the epigraph to my second-last chapter states the proper corollary of this position.

An introduction should not only introduce to the readers the material which follows, it should also advise them of possible difficulties or surprises lying ahead. In this connection two particular problems will arise in the course of the present argument. First the accepted canon of Anglo-Irish literature will be subjected to new pressures, not only by the attention given to relatively unfamiliar books but by the deliberate fracture of the canonical text as such, a fracture embarked upon to release the covert readings within. For the Anglo-Irish enthusiast, both of these tactics may be uncomfortable, while the reader whose primary interest lies in literary history as a methodology may feel the time and space given to individual texts excessive. The first category of reader will lament the absence of George Moore and Seán

O'Casey, while deploring the presence of Theodor Adorno, Walter Benjamin, and György Lukács. If both parties thought hard about their differences they might find common ground in the striking non-appearance of the great English critics – Leavis, Empson, Williams, and their disciples – who have had so remarkably little to say on the subject of Anglo-Irish literature.

The specifically literary history uncovered here can be summarized as romanticism and its transformation into modernism. The specifically political element of Anglo-Irish history is the Union and its modification after 1921. These are not hermetically separate. Romanticism adopts Union as symbolic, not so much of its transactions as of its aspirations, its desire; and that desire grows among the fragmented ruins of romanticism itself. Indeed, the symbol itself, with its transcendental, numinous harmony of object and meaning, becomes symbolic of the romantic aspiration. Thus, allegory, which Coleridge declared untenable for the English-speaking world, is particularly significant in the detection of those aspirations and desires in the cultural politics of the United Kingdom of Great Britain and Ireland. Allegory lays bare the absences, distances, and differences which constitute the only ground of desire. To speak of 'desire' in such a large context is not simply to invoke a particular school of continental philosophy, it is to draw attention to the pervasive language of sexuality which underpins conventionally accepted metaphors for Anglo-Irish relations, Anglo-Irish conflict, from Swift's 'Injured Lady' to Heaney's 'Act of Union'. Allegory is not a simple alternative to this violent romanticism: while it stresses division, it is found repeatedly to be a mode through which a series of radically alternative readings of texts suggest themselves. Those readings, of course, will not restrict themselves to the canonical texts *per se*, or even to literature conceived in symbolic terms; they are necessarily historical, uncompleted. And, in its incompleteness, Ireland itself may be found to be a larger arena than its entrenched defenders had realized.

WEARY OF THEORY OR ITS MALPRACTICE?

In an introduction which serves also as preface to a new edition of a work very substantially revised, it may be permitted to add a few words of comment on changes which occurred between the original moment of publication and the issuance of the revision. I find that, in an essay on Oliver Goldsmith written in 1983, I deplored the 'neglect . . . of Anglo-Irish literature generally, by Marxist critics specifically' and went on to complain of 'a surprising silence on the colonial or neo-colonial status of the Yeatsian or Joycean context, and a complementary excision of the colonial and

imperialist dimension to that "English" culture upon which the New Left
intermittently concentrates.'[23]

Yet when the essay came to be synopsized in *Ascendancy and Tradition*,
this passage (like others, less pregnant with omens) was omitted. *The Battle
of the Books* (1986) sought to elicit some kind of order among the increasing
number of participants in what was emerging as a 'debate', but the omission complained of remained largely unaddressed. Since 1986 there has been
a plethora of 'interventions' by persons deeming themselves radical (if not
Marxist, for the latter term is sparingly invoked since 1989) in one fashion
or another. 'Colonial Discourse Analysis' has won a degree of popularity
on the international conference circuit which the dull old chestnut of base-
and-superstructure never enjoyed. In Ireland it diversified into 'The Colonial Question' (formerly trading as The National Question). Consequently, it is difficult to decide whether one is a prophet honoured in his own
country or a veritable Dermot MacMorrough of Critical Theory, a bringer-
in of alien notions from Frankfurt and Budapest. Certainly, Woman is central (cf. the legendary Dervorgilla) for the 'Colonial Question' goes hand
in hand with feminism, as at a memorable conference in University College, Galway in the summer of 1992.[24] It is with a genuine sense both of
relief and comradeship that one finds in Janet Todd's *Gender, Art, and Death*
(1993) a cautionary note sounded by one of the most important of feminist
critics.

More personally, one reserves the right not to be bowled over by the success of one's complaint or prophecy. Much of what declares itself post-
colonialist in its concerns is readily detectible as Irish nationalism,
unreconstructed yet occasionally garnished with the *origami* of notable house-
Trotskyites in the Dublin newspaper world. Two academic commentators
on the role of political economy in nineteenth-century Ireland treat the social
divisions of 1832 as 'the result of a sustained policy of colonization, begun
in the twelfth century.'[25] (One awaits in trepidation a decision against the
Irish, at the bar of revolutionary justice, for colonizing Scotland and exter-
minating the Picts.) The urge to associate Ireland with the Third World has
many virtues to recommend it, but a clear conception of Ireland's relation
to the first is not always assisted. Irish support for the Boers is well known,
but it is hardly reflected intelligently in a prominent historian's reference
to the 'colonial apartheid Dublin' of 1888.[26]

Automatic, even automatonic, anti-English feeling may be 'understandable'
in certain quarters but it sheds little light on the complex and pervasive actualities of Irish society within the United Kingdom. In a searing indictment of the flaccid reinscriptions which resulted from the success of Edward

Said's *Orientalism* in 1978, Aijaz Achmad has given prominence to the contradictions of so-called cultural nationalism, 'not to speak of the professional petty bourgeoisie's penchant for representing its own cultural practices and aspirations, virtually by embodying them as so many emblems of a unified national culture.' [27] Achmad's argument of course relates to 'the Third World', a notion he finds all too homogenized and lacking in analytical specificity. He conducts his questioning of Said with something of the lofty radicalism of the Marxist and communist movement in the Indian subcontinent. Yet, given Said's indulgent analysis of W. B. Yeats's politics, the point may be properly domesticated to the Irish situation. For the maintenance of hyper-responsive anti-English attitudes after 1921 might again be understandable in persons of fastidiously republican principles: in Yeats it raises questions about the complicity of post-colonial sensibilities in the emotional economy of the old enemy, a complicity which is displaced into tacit or overt support for some other aggressive power. If Britain was imperialist, was not the Reich at least its equal in this regard?

The consequences of anti-colonial *ressentiment* are rarely contained within the frontiers of the home country, and uncomfortable truths may still be gleaned from W. H. Auden's celebrated observation that those to whom evil is done, do evil in their turn. Of course those words are taken from '1 September 1939'. Auden suppressed the poem as if to demonstrate that even the wise can stoop to folly.[28] Ethical categories are suspect in radical circles, though it is likely that the Women's Movement carried more genuinely intellectual and political clout before it converted itself into feminism. Theological categories – and Auden's Evil is bigger than any ethical negative – are even less politically correct, for all that political correctness is itself Manichean in its language, ritual, and retributiveness. Silence alone mollifies its zealotry. Substantial Irish participation in the near-genocidal wars waged by the United States against the native population is rarely mentioned in radical conferences nor is it easy to remind post-colonial theorists that Irish missionary zeal in Africa might be considered as a form of ideological imperialism. Now that the Second World (the Soviet bloc) has disappeared, this kind of self-deception may decline. And once again we shall have to pray for the conversion of Russia.

Historical revisionism is everywhere spoken against; as is empiricism, identified (oddly enough) as the philosophical basis of the revisionist 'programme'. Given this hostility towards research among the new theorists, it should be promptly declared that the present book, considered as a revision of *Ascendancy and Tradition*, has opted for more, not less, documental analysis in the historical domain. As a consequence, two chapters on the fiction of Maria Edgeworth have been replaced by an extensive tracing of Protestant Ascendancy in a number of nineteenth-century political contexts. No offence to Edgeworth or to feminism is intended, for the material removed will feature in revised form in a full-length study of the novelist. The new chapter is 'Ascendancy and Cabal, 1800–1840' already referred to: if the material under examination is less exciting than anti-phallocentrism, let it be pointed out that – its terminal dates notwithstanding – the chapter begins with Yeats and ends with Nietzsche. Further pages are divided among György Lukács, Thomas Mann, and T. W. Adorno, not simply as representatives of a particular continental tradition to which the present writer is attracted, but as readers (or prismatic reading devices) through whom the betrayal inherent in consolidated tradition can be detected at its Irish task. Finally, the book's original terminal date of 1939 (Yeats died in January 1939) is now removed so as to allow discussion of Samuel Beckett and Elizabeth Bowen.

Vigilant readers will also have noted that the conceptual emphasis of the original title (Ascendancy and Tradition) has been relegated to sub-titular status, whereas personal names (Burke and Beckett) are elevated to replace it. It is probably futile to insist that no ideological shift of ground should be detected here, for theorists who glory in spelling Marxism with a small *m* (even to begin a sentence) or see themselves as a post-contemporary intervention, are possessed of a visionary *éclat* against which I offer nothing. Yet the reversing of title and subtitle has been carried out for a purpose. Indeed, it is done precisely to remind the visionary that, pending the re-integration of the national territory or second coming of the transcendental signifier, cultural production in western societies has generally been mediated through the agency of individual persons. This is not – he adds wearily – to argue for the autonomy of the bourgeois individual but merely to point out the blindingly obvious existence of that mediatory process.

On the question of Protestant Ascendancy and its origins, a great deal has been written since 1985. It would have been possible to incorporate in the present book a summary of work by Jacqueline Hill, James Kelly and others in this area. In practice, however, any adequate account of these recent discussions arising from the topic of ascendancy was found to require a bibliographical approach not readily assimilable to the overall shape and mood of the revised *Ascendancy and Tradition*. Consequently, readers of the pages still devoted to Edmund Burke are referred to *The Dublin Paper War of 1786-1788* (1993), where I have provided a more specialized treatment of events culminating in the conceptualization of Protestant Ascendancy in 1792 than would be proper in the context of a broadly based literary history.

The concepts invoked in the title of 1985 have now been augmented by the inclusion of Betrayal. I am aware that this is open to misunderstanding, as if it were suggested that Beckett and Bowen (also now included) are to be aligned with this newly admitted term. Nevertheless, the recollection that 'terrorism' now signifies (amongst other things) 'a type of writing which refuses to make use of the "flowers of rhetoric" and which entails a refusal of many of the traditional supports and devices of literature' reconciles me to betrayal.[29] I considered – and rejected – revisionism as an alternative new term, meaning the theory or theories underpinning a writer's strong engagement with the work of an earlier writer deemed an ominous precursor. Though revisionism, in this sense of Harold Bloom's, and involving various processes of poetic misreading, might be conceptually aligned with betrayal, the possibilities for confusion with the Leninist doctrine of some traditionalist historians advised against its use.

In any case, for reasons which continue to be pressing, ascendancy continues to require more comment than tradition, though the two might valuably be considered together, especially in so far as tradition constitutes a specialized form of treason.[30] Indeed, the changes enacted in the distinctive words betrayal . . . tradition . . . treason . . . should at one and the same time remind us of the folly to which Heideggerian etymological analysis can lead and of the common root which they have in the Latin verb *tradere* (to give up). Erich Heller, in a tribute to Thomas Mann delivered in the year of the novelist's death, observed that 'to live within a tradition means to enjoy once again, if only in some small measure, the privileges of innocence.' This may sound benign, even reassuring, but it is immediately followed by the definition that tradition is 'the wise agreement not to ask certain questions'.[31] Such agreement only flows after the formulation of the questions in question, and so constitutes an instance of Freudian sublimation ('a displacement under the control of the ego') or, in a broader context, a form of what Jürgen Habermas calls 'cultural renunciation'.[32]

Betrayal, in conventional present-day discourse, implicates the giving up of something (or somebody) which rightly claims the loyalty or protection of the betrayer. But, as Mann was acutely aware in his own person and nationality, such claims are often made oppressively, and the right to make them appropriated falsely, by monstrous powers keen to legitimize themselves precisely through the successful imposition of claims masquerading as rights. The phenomenon is restricted neither to the political nor the aesthetic spheres. In the ironic German's terrifying masterpiece, a novel relating musical composition and the course of the Second World War, the narrator secretly confesses to himself that he not only wishes for German defeat, and not German victory, but that he *longs* for defeat and does so in 'perpetual torments of conscience'.[33] What he fears in victory is the suppression of the work of his composer-friend, though readers are left in no doubt but that the modern Faustus has compacted with the same Devil which drove Germany into fascist barbarism. Betrayal of such a polity is, therefore, an obligation, and by no means an easy one. Though Nazi Germany remains a unique obscenity, *mutatis mutandi* a similar crisis of loyalties – similar in kind, related in its concerns, but incomparable in scale – afflicted Samuel Beckett in Paris in 1940 and Elizabeth Bowen in London throughout the war. Primarily, what Beckett betrayed was neutral Ireland or, in a preferable formulation, Irish neutrality. Bowen's position was more complex, personally and politically; the novel central to it, *The Heat of the Day* (1948), has been exhaustively analysed elsewhere.[34]

To convict Beckett and Bowen of treachery towards their native land would be woefully simpleminded. Indeed, she looks set to follow him into a latter-day pantheon of the Anglo-Irish redeemed, figures whom an intelligent tourist industry is prepared to rehabilitate with no questions asked. What Beckett and Bowen betrayed was not Ireland, but a tradition. Specifically, they gave up that latter-day and far from antique tradition of Ireland which W. B. Yeats had enunciated in those writings of the 1930s where he synthesized an obsession with death as an aesthetic event, an authoritarian politics, and a fabulous past articulated through his rhetoric of Protestant Ascendancy. Confronted, as he by virtue of his death in January 1939 was not, by the consequences of this synthetic tradition, they refused 'not to answer certain questions'.

Little or none of the extensive wordage devoted in recent years to the matter of Yeats's politics has considered this betraying alternative tradition, not even Conor Cruise O'Brien's detonating essay, 'Passion and Cunning' (1965).[35] In so far as this debate extends that already initiated by W. H. Auden, Louis MacNeice and George Orwell, it has been concerned with the issue of relating literary style and political tendency, an issue which Orwell felt Marxist criticism had failed to illuminate. But the post-colonialists, taking their bearings from Elizabeth Cullingford Butler's exculpatory *Yeats, Ireland and Fascism* (1981), have hitched their wagons to his star. Ignoring evidence of his endorsing Nazi legislation, his indifference to the fate of concentration camp victims, his seeming ignorance of German expansionism in eastern Europe, and his virtually monosyllabic response to the Italian invasion of Abyssinia – ignoring such dully archival trivia, they have succeeded in making Yeats safe for the Third World. This at least seems to be the conclusion reached in three Field Day pamphlets published simultaneously by Terry Eagleton, Fredric Jameson and Edward Said.[36] Though David Lloyd is neither the terrorist nor fascist he is alternately cast as by some observers, his *Anomalous States* (1993) does manage to avoid most of the tricky questions: purporting to examine Yeats's 'later poetry', he concentrates in practice on *The Winding Stair and Other Poems*, a volume containing no work written later than June 1932. This opting for a pre-Hitler selection of the poems, together with the exclusion of Yeats's drama and his avowedly political writing, makes a full examination of the poet's fascist sympathies unlikely.[37] Similarly, the dodging of Yeats's work after mid-1932 is particularly regrettable in that Lloyd, invoking the Frankfurt School's concept of 'administered society', asks whether 'fascism, in all its specificities, represents an end or a beginning'.[38] However, the specificities of Nazism having been excluded by the critic's *terminus ad quem*, we are still in the dark.

Why should this be? Are we condemned to breakfast on Weetabix Theory as the lights go on all over Europe and Hegel's owl falls from its perch? Not the Hotel Catastrophe, in which Lukács imagined Adorno as cultural commissionaire, but rather Henry Miller's air-conditioned nightmare promises to accommodate our deliberations, and at conference rates. An omission from Lloyd's analysis, complementary to his suppression of 1933 – 1939 in accounting for Yeats, is a statement of attitude towards contemporary Irish nationalism. In a distinction which sits oddly in the work of a self-proclaimed revolutionary, this is relentlessly subdivided into 'cultural nationalism' and 'militant nationalism'. Perhaps we are intended to see the problem resolved in such a sentence as this – 'the acts of militant nationalism are always more significant as symbols than as pragmatic deeds.'[39] The first adjective deftly avoids being military, lest we should suspect nationalism of engaging in the gross empiricism of the car-bomb; the second begs the question as to who commands the right to determine what is significant. For deeds, even 'pragmatic' ones, are not the sole property of the doer, they involve a done-to also, or – as seems implicit in this scenario – a done-in. Dialectic appears to have fallen out of the younger Marxists' kit-bag. As its replacement one might suspect a vein of violent sentimentality, not least in the illogical assumption that an Algerian analogy (itself highly doubtful) will, at every hypothetical point of contact, legitimize a comparability of colonial situations. There is something touching in the popularity accorded to Frantz Fanon and Albert Memmi in recent Irish debates, not least where the former excoriates the narcissism of a colonialist bourgeoisie as 'expounded by members of its universities'.[40] One is not wearied of theory, but rather of its simulacrums, the schoolboy debater's recitation of names, of the big words which make us happy, and the profitable disguise of nationalist rhetoric as cosmopolitan chic.

If I have concentrated disproportionately on David Lloyd's most recent publication, it is principally because I respect the practice of continuing debate. But his invoking of Memmi's 'colonizer who refuses' in Yeats's connection renders meaningless any definition of colony and colonization, so plentiful are the distinctions (as well as resemblances) between Irish history and that of most Third World countries. Ironically, the Algerian analogy was bequeathed to the post-colonialists by one whom they hold in bizarre contempt – the author of *To Katanga and Back* (1962). Of course, the version preferred is not that to be found in Cruise O'Brien's study of Albert Camus, but rather the cinematic epic *Battle for Algiers*.[41] Despising Cruise O'Brien partly for his altered attitudes towards Northern Ireland and partly for his pro-Israeli stance, they fail to ask the relevant questions about the context in which a figure like Cruise O'Brien changes his mind. George Orwell, struggling to account for Jonathan Swift's reprehensible politics, blamed 'the follies of the progressive party of the moment' for driving him into a perverse Toryism.[42] Confronted with the mixture of sloganizing and self-delusion deployed to obliterate evidence of exactly what 'militant nationalism' has been doing for the past twenty-five years, one might be forgiven for embracing anything – short of the North Down Conservative Association.

One feature of this intellectual abdication of responsibility has been what could be called tit-for-tat thinking. Both David Lloyd and Seamus Deane have proposed that nationalism makes a grievous error in reproducing the ideological and cultural structures of the imperialism it opposes. Of course, only imperialism is subjected to detailed condemnation in this regard, and the reader is encouraged to wait for the day in which nationalism will overcome its dependence on the enemy – though not retrospectively. As a local consequence, IRA terrorism is either equated with the (earlier, and so more culpable) atrocities of loyalist gangs or explained in terms of a state violence which has provoked it. Here again, Franco-Algerian debts are being paid off in the Irish market, in the 'dumping' or 'remaindering' of Parisian sophistication – Althusser's anti-humanism, Sartre's contempt for ethics – by importers indifferent to the divergent conditions effective in each area. In short, the debates surveyed in *The Battle of the Books* should be more rigorously traced to the same argument so brilliantly analysed in E. P. Thompson's *The Poverty of Theory*.[43]

Essentially, Thompson was concerned to defend the historical method against what was increasingly presented simply as Theory. The notion of

Theory is more theoretically vacuous than an empty sack of potatoes. Indeed, if Tom Bottomore's definition of materialism in one of its philosophical aspects retains any validity – 'a methodological commitment to concrete historiographical research, as opposed to abstract philosophical reflection' – then the Althusserian Theory which Thompson opposed is so naked that even the sack appears to have disappeared. Fredric Jameson has demonstrated that Althusser's attack on historicism should be contextualized within the internal struggles of the French Communist Party to be appreciated as an 'offensive' against Stalinism: this will greatly console the kulaks of South Fermanagh.[44]

What has all this to do with ascendancy and tradition? In so far as the former term has come to name (or rather postulate) an eighteenth-century ruling élite, quasi-aristocratic in kind and yet somehow unique to Ireland, then 'The Peculiarities of the English', the second essay in *The Poverty of Theory*, is closely relevant. Responding vigorously to early work by Perry Anderson and Tom Nairn, Thompson rejected their identification of classes so epochal in scale and (static) duration that 'the bourgeoisie' embraces William de Pole, Oliver Cromwell and Edward Heath.[45] Though even the most traditional usage of Protestant Ascendancy has declined to push it back much earlier than 1690, it is clear that Yeats's Protestant Ascendancy shares certain features with the aristocracy of Nairn and Anderson.[46] Thompson, in reply, argued that the governing élite of eighteenth-century England was not an example of some classic category of class analysis but more nearly resembled a system of brigandage. It was

> nothing but itself. A unique formation. Old Corruption. It could scarcely have seen the eighteenth century out if the French Revolution had not occurred, providentially, to save it. If it commanded immense influence, it raised also immense resentments.[47]

One should not mistake the claim of uniqueness as a defence of English exceptionalism, any more than one would encourage the view that Protestant Ascendancy was simply and solely a phenomenon special to Ireland, like shamrock. What is unique is the concept not the brigandage, though the concept participates in the brigandage: it is closer to resembling whiskey spelled with an *e*, something immediately recognizeable in Scotland as both similar and different. Thompson is at pains to establish that historical work attends to particular social and economic processes involving actual human participants. If English historians had suffered from a certain 'conceptual lethargy', the answer lay in the renewed definition of appropriate questions, the elaboration and testing of hypotheses and the exposure of ideological attributes in the existing historiography. Such arduous intellectual labour constituted a valuable conceptual engagement through historical method, and was not to be upstaged by theoretical virtuosity *in vacuo*. Thompson's efforts of 1965 did not save the New Left from Althusser; the events of 1968 enhanced his appeal by adding the mirage of heroic insurrection. If Althusser's personal tragedy has taken him off the reading lists, Paris continues to dominate much radical debate through Foucault, Lacan and Derrida.

All in all post-war France has exercised a profound, even imperial, influence on Irish intellectual debate. Much of this influence was mediated through specific academic agencies – conferences devoted to the sociology of literature at Essex University throughout the late 1970s, increased mobility among American professors, incorporation of the Women's Movement (as feminism) into the curriculum, and the turning of James Joyce's work into a dispenser of twenty-minute papers. All of this lucrative activity has generated a suitably impressive series of theoretical covering positions – post-colonialism, post-contemporary interventionism, post-modernism, post-structuralism. All of these come under the general heading of Theory, though it might be more theoretically acute to note the tenurial continuity inscribed with longing in the iterated *posts*, each of them a certificate of professional survival in the American academy. Contrary to the naive belief of a few, Theory is not short-hand for Critical Theory, as practiced by Adorno or Marcuse. It is an Althusserian gesture, originally deployed to neutralize the historical method, and now appropriated as a career move.

Whether as a consequence of this development or not, the historical profession has become less confident of its own ability to justify intellectually the work which it does.[48] Denouncers of revisionism have contributed little of substance to Irish history, for their first principle must establish that the vision defended is replete. Yet they have had the effect – as yet only partly measurable – of forcing some practitioners to question the value of what they are doing. It is not implicit here that adoption or adaption of E. P. Thompson will see off the strong men, and thieves, and deacons who desire to re-read Irish history with the innocence of those who dwell in perpetual Edenic self-righteousness. (Not a dead Indian in sight, and hence no need to bewail the misdemeanours of General Philip Sheridan.) Yet some response is required to see off what Tom Garvin, borrowing from a source close to Thompson, has characterized as the Dublin-lumpen-intelligentsia.

One notable practitioner of Irish history, S. J. Connolly, has taken on the exponents of the colonial explanation. In *Religion, Law and Power*, he makes a case for considering eighteenth-century Ireland (at least till 1760) as a kingdom in its own (admittedly peculiar) right, and that 'such a perspective . . . does more to make sense of the central characteristics of post-Restoration Ireland than the alternative label of a colonial society, so casually yet so persistently applied.'[49] The implications of this argument have yet to be followed through to their ultimate conclusions; but the author offers one uncomfortable example. If Ireland did gradually come to function as an English colony, it was as a consequence of the Stuart monarchy's inability to resist parliamentary government.[50] An intersection of Thompson's dispute with Anderson and Nairn, with Connolly's rebuttal of the assumption of Ireland as colony, appears when one considers changes occurring later in the eighteenth century. The French Revolution preserved Old Corruption in England, and the same paradox extended its sway to Ireland by provoking the conceptual consolidation of a Protestant Ascendancy rhetoric on which the ink was still wet. It is gratifying to note that Seán Connolly largely endorses the thesis first consolidated in *Ascendancy and Tradition*, further documented and analysed in *The Dublin Paper War*, and now augmented through the pursuit of the concept in the years after the transfer of Old Corruption to Dublin Castle.[51]

In addition, however, to the point of intersection between the historians' concern with the eighteenth century *in extenso* and the present inquiry into Protestant Ascendancy, there is the possibility that literary history may provide specific occasions on which the historical method can recover confidence. By a pleasing corollary, investigation of a concentrated political event in the 1780s has facilitated the refinement of concept analysis. Literary history requires this kind of sophisticated equipment. Theoretical engagement does not consist in the carrying of placards and the waving of little red signifiers. And behind most of the Theory erected on or about the material of Irish literature, one discovers the discarded dust-jackets of someone else's empirical research. To suggest that the proponents of Theory are engaged in such malpractices is to indicate the need for a betrayal of Theory in the name of praxis.

NOTES AND REFERENCES

1 See Blaise Pascal, *Pensées* (London: Dent, 1960), No. 8, p. 3; I have preferred the translation provided by Philip Thody in his translation of Lucien Goldmann, *The Hidden God: A Study of Tragic Vision in the Pensées of Pascal and the Tragedies of Racine* (London: Routledge and Kegan Paul, 1964), p. 6.

2 It may help the reader if I point to the concept of totality as employed by György Lukács in *History and Class Consciousness*, trans. Rodney Livingstone (London: Merlin Press, 1971), as underpinning much of the argument that follows.

See, in particular, 'Whatever the subject of debate, the dialectical method is concerned always with the same problem: knowledge of the historical process in its entirety. This means that "ideological" and "economic" problems lose their mutual exclusiveness and merge into one another . . . The approach of literary history is the one best suited to the problems of history' (p. 34).

3 This escalation is quite explicit in T. R. Henn's writings on Anglo-Irish literature, which are deeply coloured by the experience of his own family. It is more surprising to find it at work in F. S. L. Lyons, *Culture and Anarchy in Ireland 1890–1939* (Oxford: Clarendon Press, 1979), pp. 20, 94, etc. Of course, this book virtually announces a political programme for Ulster based on the 'cultures' of denominations and quasi-national groups.

4 Derek Mahon, 'MacNeice in England and Ireland', in Terence Brown and Alec Reid eds., *Time was Away: The World of Louis MacNeice* (Dublin: Dolmen Press, 1974), p. 113.

5 J. M. Synge, 'Preface', in Robin Skelton (ed.), *Collected Works*, vol. i, *Poetry* (London: Oxford University Press, 1962), p. xxxvi.

6 W. B. Yeats, 'Beautiful Lofty Things', *Collected Poems* (London: Macmillan, 1963), p. 348. Note that all of Yeats's work – I use the poetry as an example – prior to *The Tower* (1928) was written while he lived in the United Kingdom of Great Britain and Ireland.

7 Denis Donoghue, 'Being Irish Together', *The Sewanee Review*, vol. 84 (Winter 1976), p. 131.

8 Denis Donoghue, *Yeats*, Modern Masters Series, (London: Fontana, 1971).

9 Some legislation in this area was restricted by region and hence excluded Ireland, but there were specific acts relating to Ireland also. This tendency to legislate for industry on a regional basis was probably more characteristic of the first half of the nineteenth century rather than the years 1850–1921.

10 'Being Irish Together', pp. 132-3.

11 Roger McHugh and Maurice Harmon, *Short History of Anglo-Irish Literature from its Origins to the Present Day* (Dublin: Wolfhound Press, 1982); A. Norman Jeffares, *Anglo-Irish Literature* (London: Macmillan; Dublin: Gill and Macmillan, 1982); Alan Warner, *A Guide to Anglo-Irish Literature* (New York: St Martin's Press; Dublin: Gill and Macmillan, 1981); Seamus Deane, *A Short History of Irish Literature* (London: Hutchinson, 1986).

12 Oliver MacDonagh, *Ireland: The Union and its Aftermath* (London: Allen and Unwin, 1977), esp. the second chapter, pp. 35-52.

13 For Ireland as 'social laboratory' see W. L. Burn, 'Free Trade in Land: An Aspect of the Irish Question', *Transactions of the Royal Historical Society*, 4th series, vol. 31; also MacDonagh and Lyons, op. cit., pp. 9-10.

14 'Past and Present State of Literature in Ireland', *The Dublin University Magazine*, vol. 9, No. 52 (March 1837), pp. 365-76. I discuss some aspects of this anonymous article (which I believe was written by Isaac Butt) and its attempt to define Anglo-Irish literature in 'J. Sheridan Le Fanu's "Richard Marston" (1848): The History of an Anglo-Irish Text', in Francis Barker et al. (eds.), *1848. The Sociology of Literature* (Chelmsford: University of Essex, 1978), pp. 107-25, esp. pp. 108-11. The article itself is reprinted in S. Deane (ed.), *The Field Day Anthology of Irish Writing* (Derry: Field Day, 1991), vol. I, pp. 1200-12.

15 In a sense this work relates to southern Ireland rather than to all of Ireland in the period after 1921; in this respect, it postpones the issue of relating partition to cultural production. For the background see Liam de Paor, *Divided Ulster* (Harmondsworth: Penguin, 1970); Michael Farrell, *Northern Ireland: The Orange State* (London: Pluto Press, 1976); Henry Patterson, *Class Conflict and Sectarianism* (Belfast: Blackstaff Press, 1980).

16 'A purely fantastic, unmodern, ideal, breezy, springdayish, Cuchullainoid National Theatre' – in a draft of a letter from J. M. Synge to Stephen MacKenna, c.1904; see Ann Saddlemyer (ed.), 'Synge to MacKenna: The Mature Years', *Massachusetts Review*, vol. 5, No. 2 (Winter 1964), pp. 279-95, at p. 281.

17 I use 'racism' to cover all those ideologies which utilize differences of inheritance or belief to create valorized social categories, usually to the end of obliterating or suppressing class interests and conflicts. Nazism is not only the most obvious example but also possesses an articulate intellectual apologetics, for an analysis of which see George L. Mosse, *The Crisis of German Ideology: Intellectual Origins of the Third Reich* (New York: Grosset and Dunlap, 1964; repr. Schocken Books, 1981). For an immediate British context in which the ideology of Irish sectarianism may be read, see Martin Barker, *The New Racism: Conservatives and the Ideology of the Tribe* (London: Junction Books, 1981).

18 T. R. Henn, *The Lonely Tower: Studies in the Poetry of W. B. Yeats* (London: Methuen, 1965), 2nd rev. edn, p. 7.

19 W. B. Yeats, *Explorations* (New York: Macmillan, 1962), p. 345.

20 W. B. Yeats, *Collected Poems*, op. cit., p. 237.

21 'On the Union', in Jonathan Swift, *Poetical Works* (London, 1866), vol. i, p. 68.

22 'Tradition and the Individual Talent', in *Selected Prose of T. S. Eliot*, ed. Frank Kermode (London: Faber, 1975), p. 37.

23 W. J. Mc Cormack 'Goldsmith, Biography and the Phenomenology of Anglo-Irish Literature' in Andrew Swarbrick (ed.), *The Art of Oliver Goldsmith* (London: Vision Press, 1984), pp. 168-9.

24 See below pp. 324-8 for the treatment of Goldsmith; see also Mc Cormack *The Battle of the Books: Two Decades of Irish Cultural Debate* (Mullingar: Lilliput Press, 1986).

25 Thomas A. Boylan and Timothy P. Foley, *Political Economy and Colonial Ireland: the Propagation and Ideological Function of Economic Discourse in the Nineteenth Century* (London: Routledge, 1992), p. 17.

26 John P. Duggan 'C. H. Bewley: a Tribute' in *Columbanus: Journal of the Knights of St. Columbanus*, vol. 77, No. 1 (1992), p. 10. As Bewley supported the Nazis enthusiastically, it is ironic to find him celebrated in a journal devoted to the memory of the sixth-century saint who brought Celtic Christianity to many parts of France, Germany and Italy. See Charles Bewley, *Memoirs of a Wild Goose*, (W. J. Mc Cormack, ed.) (Dublin: Lilliput Press, 1989).

27 Aijaz Achmad, *In Theory: Classes, Nations, Literatures* (London: Verso, 1992), p. 8. See also below pp. 225-239 for my revised comment on Said's *Orientalism* and the concept of Celticism.

28 In my particular case, they are taken from a un-footnotable samizdat copy picked up in Budapest in the 1980s. Not communist censorship but the author's latter-day American Christianity drove me to this underground resource.

29   Jeremy Hawthorn, *A Concise Glossary of Contemporary Literary Theory* (London: Arnold, 1992), p. 108.
30   See below p. 408.
31   Erich Heller, *Thomas Mann: the Ironic German* (Cambridge: Cambridge University Press, 1981), p. 14.
32   Jürgen Habermas, *Knowledge and Human Interests* (Boston: Beacon Press, 1971), pp. 245, 276.
33   Thomas Mann, *Doctor Faustus: the Life of the German Composer Adrian Leverkühn* (Harmondsworth: Penguin, 1949), p. 34.
34   See W. J. Mc Cormack, *Dissolute Characters: Irish Literary History Through Balzac, Le Fanu, Yeats and Bowen* (Manchester: Manchester University Press, 1993), pp. 208-31.
35   Collected in Conor Cruise O'Brien, *Passion and Cunning and Other Essays* (London: Weidenfeld, 1988), pp. 8-61. I single out Cruise O'Brien simply because his expertise in French literature might have led him to make the comparison with Beckett. For an extended discussion of Yeats's politics in its inherited historical context, see my Introduction in W. B. Yeats, *Prose Writings on Politics and Irish Literature* (London: Penguin, 1995).
36   All three pamphlets bore the title *Nationalism, Colonialism and Literature;* the following subtitles distinguished the individual contributors, *Irony and Commitment* (Eagleton), *Modernism and Imperialism* (Jameson), and *Yeats and Decolonization* (Said). All published Derry: Field Day, 1988.
37   David Lloyd, *Anomalous States: Irish Writing and the Post-Colonial Moment* (Dublin: Lilliput Press, 1993), pp. 59-87.
38   Ibid., p. 60.
39   Ibid., p. 70.
40   Frantz Fanon, *The Wretched of the Earth*, trans. Constance Farrington, (Harmondsworth, 1967), p. 36.
41   I am grateful to Liam de Paor for pointing out the calamitous impact of the film on Irish attitudes towards insurgency. For another perspective see Hugh Roberts, *Northern Ireland and the Algerian Analogy: a Suitable Case for Gaullism?* (Belfast: Athol Books, 1986).
42   George Orwell 'Politics vs. Literature; an Examination of Gulliver's Travels', see A. N. Jeffares (ed.), *Swift: Modern Judgements* (London: Macmillan 1969), p. 192. The essay appeared in 1950, the year of Orwell's death.
43   E. P. Thompson, *The Poverty of Theory and Other Essays* (London: Merlin Press, 1978). The title-essay occupies pp. 193-406.
44   Tom Bottomore (ed.), *A Dictionary of Marxist Thought* (Oxford: Blackwell, 1983), p. 324. Fredric Jameson, *The Political Unconscious: Narrative as a Socially Symbolic Act* (London: Methuen, 1981), p. 27, n12.
45   Thompson, op. cit., p. 86. The essay first appeared in 1965. Achmad (op. cit., p. 177) makes a similar point against Said; 'Who . . . had ever thought that Lamartine and Olivia Manning . . . the anonymous composers of El Cid and the Chanson de Roland . . . [and] Henry Kissinger – all belonged in the same archive and composed a deeply unified discursive formation!'
46   For commentary on Yeats and Protestant Ascendancy, see Mc Cormack, *Dissolute Characters*, pp. 187-8, 196-203; also Mc Cormack, *The Dublin Paper War of 1786-1788* (Dublin: Irish Academic Press, 1993), pp. 16-7.

47 Thompson, op. cit., p. 49. 'Old Corruption' was a coinage of William Cobbett; Thompson suggests that 'Old Corruption transplanted its flag, after 1832, to Dublin Castle' (p. 53).
48 See the introductions to successive volumes of papers read to the Irish Conference of Historians, Tom Dunne (ed.), *The Writer as Witness* (Cork: Cork University Press, 1987) and Ciaran Brady, *Ideology and the Historians* (Dublin: Lilliput Press, 1991).
49 S. J. Connolly, *Religion, Law and Power: the Making of Protestant Ireland 1660–1760* (Oxford: Clarendon Press, 1992), p. 2; see also pp. 106-14.
50 Ibid., p. 106.
51 Ibid., pp. 103-4. Colonial Theorists will be disturbed, however, and rightly so, by a 'best of possible worlds' tonality audible in an earlier observation of Connolly's – 'beliefs and attitudes that were shared by all or most of the members of a particular society cannot, by definition, have been either stupid or immoral.' (p. 4) What one should hear in this sentence is a warning of the limits within which reconstruction of a mentality can sensibly proceed without requiring the kind of historical reflexivity which Connolly provides elsewhere.

1

Romantic Union:
Wordsworth, Ireland, and *Reflections on the Revolution in France*

> There have been many antirevolutionary books written in favour
> of the Revolution. Burke has written a revolutionary book against
> the Revolution.
>
> (Novalis)[1]

One of the few generalizations in literary history which stands up to scrutiny
is that romanticism is a European rather than an English or a French
phenomenon. Given the close association of romanticism and nationalism,
it is also a generalization which helps to broaden the basis of literary history
from any self-defining local integrity. But if critics and commentators have
learned that Goethe can shed light on Scott, and that Chateaubriand is not
wholly irrelevant to an interest in Keats, the result has too often been a
cosmopolitan indifference to the particular interactions of social and aesthetic
concerns in Germany, France, and Britain. In place of the spurious relating
of literature to social life which characterized the various national histories,
the various literatures are subordinated to a Great Code which excludes all
social life. It is not intended here to replace the well-worn legend that Anglo-
Irish fiction is about the Big House and Anglo-Irish poetry about 'the
discovery of the Gaelic past' with a synchrony in which Lady Morgan tangos
with William Blake. The dynamics of literary history do not accept the empirical distinction between concrete detail and abstraction, and text is not
regarded as an inviolable sanctuary. If we subject *Reflections on the Revolution
in France* to a species of stylistic analysis this is not to deny its political

28

material but rather to extend our concern with that material to aspects which have too often been regarded as secondary. If metaphor is treated as a form of politics, it goes without saying that the self-contained entity known as Ireland necessarily is reinserted in the complex relations of the romantic age.

Renowned from the outset for its influence in changing opinion, Burke's *Reflections* (1790) came to embody a fixed star in conservative ideology in the nineteenth century. Burke's impact on figures as diverse as Benjamin Disraeli and Alfred Tennyson and Matthew Arnold is but a further indicator of the continuity of that influence which is first measurable in the literary world through the novels of Jane Austen and Walter Scott. Augustan, romantic, Victorian . . . the fixity which Burke came to represent for generations of British thinkers is itself a movement of immediate political and cultural significance. Disraelian imperialism and Arnoldian visions of the Celt are alike indebted to the author of the *Reflections*. And the apparently opposed scales and proportions of these areas of development – global policy, domestic policy, India, and Skibbereen – are already present in the terms of Burke's politics, Burke's aesthetics.

For politics and aesthetics come together in Burke in a conjunction of the most profound significance. There is a line of development between ideas explored by Burke as early as 1756 in his *Philosophical Inquiry into the Origins of our Ideas on the Sublime and the Beautiful* and the famous apostrophe to Marie Antoinette in the *Reflections*. But the biographical line of consistency or development is less pertinent than the extensive links which locate the *Reflections* in the context of Wordsworth's 'Prelude', Coleridge's *On the Constitution of the Church and State*, and Jane Austen's *Mansfield Park*. Nor is this to invoke influence as some personal, biographical debt which the poets and novelists owe to the politician – Wordsworth's own employment of the term in such poems as 'Tintern Abbey' and 'Michael' should suggest a more complex relationship – rather it is to point to the intensively literary priorities and preoccupations of the *Reflections* and the mediate access thus afforded us to the politics of fiction and poetry. For a radical such as Paine, of course, Burke's lingering upon the frailties of the queen's position was an evasion of the real – attention to the plumage and neglect of the dying bird. Yet it is that dichotomy between ornament and use, the illusory and the real, the literary and the political which Burke's work drastically challenges.

From the outset, the *Reflections* attracted attention to its language, and much of the evidence marshalled in James Boulton's *Language of Politics in the Age of Wilkes and Burke* is critical of Burke's use of imagery and metaphor. Doubtless, Burke's style – so conceived – is massively and energetically effective, but it would be mistaken to assume that stricter notions of literary form, and considerations of contemporary literary practice, can be separated from personal style. Polemic, narrative, and metaphor in the *Reflections* contribute to a synthesis which at once enacts and exposes certain preoccupations which run deep in English romanticism and in what we have learned to call Anglo-Irish literature. Indeed, the politics of Burke's sublime and beautiful, as enforced in the epoch of the French Revolution, constitutes one statement – others are available in economic or social terms – of the principles of that essentially fragmentary and separatist 'tradition' of romantic nationalism. Tradition will come to imply, virtually to impose, a unitary concept of continuity and unity, but its romantic origins attest – as does the Irish politics of Union – to the characteristically divided and reciprocal (to go no further) nature of such a movement. One's interest in Anglo-Irish literature, or in the Irish language, or in the velleities of De Valera's Constitution, is determined not by some endearing merit dormant in such material but by the necessity of a material history which incorporates Europe and India and America. The Anglo-Irish novel is launched by Maria Edgeworth and we have come to acknowledge that unremarkable truism; what remains crucially to be achieved is the demonstration of that 'fragmentary union' which is Burke's contribution to the aesthetics of Anglo-Irish fiction.

The thrust and tone of Burke's *Reflections* are well known. And yet the important task before us is not economically to summarize the agreed argument of that familiar work but rather to seize upon the distinctions between its past significance and present meaning with especial reference to the trajectory in literary history we call Anglo-Irish literature. In time we shall refer in some detail to the particular narratives and pervasive metaphors of the work, but for the moment a reminder of its ostensible form is needed. The *Reflections* is a letter addressed to a young French gentleman in Paris and written as one continuous sequence of sentences. This specific form is crucial in Burke's tactic of adopting the role of political sage, of the master addressing his pupil.[2] Here, it shares many characteristics of pamphlet propaganda in the eighteenth century. This has not prevented a recent editor from dividing the text in two 'Parts', the first further divided into ten chapters and the second into five, chapters which are then given titles such as 'A Defense of the French Monarchy and Aristocracy'.[3] What is significant here is not any sacrilegious interference with the seamless text of 1790; on the contrary, we are watching the dissemination of a latter-day 'Burke as methodical political scientist' in the context of American public education. Arguments deployed against the introduction of innovative, deliberate government to the detriment of ancient custom are thus rendered serviceable in defence of custom-less *laissez-faire* economics. Burke's 'own' contempt for political theory and abstract argument is theorized in defence of the historical descendants of his enemies. Nor is this instance an isolated one; the application of Burke's ideas to the cause of American conservatism in the age of the Cold War, though happily a temporary phenomenon, has its Victorian precedents. Burke as the founder of the modern Conservative Party is of course an anachronism, and yet Walter Bagehot's *English Constitution* (1865) had, in the words of one sober historian, 'translated the almost mystical celebrations of Burke and Coleridge into inspired commonplaces'.[4] The celebrations referred to here were Burke's defence of prescription as the fundamental principle of a landed society. And landed property, with its prescriptive rights attached inviolably, forms the central concern of Burke's polemic in the *Reflections*. Nevertheless, as Novalis and others recognized, this was no serene, classic statement of unshakeable truth. It partook of the nervous, innovative, revolutionary circumstances into which it intervened.

If we take the broad binary division of the argument into a statement of 'British Tradition' and 'French Enlightenment', we note different narrative strategies within each. The account of British history is present in reverse-chronology; that is, we are taken back from the present occasion and a specific addressee through the adjustments of 1688 and the Glorious Revolution, the vicissitudes of the Great Rebellion, back ultimately to Magna Carta. British constitutional history is thus taken up to its original fountain-head where it is emblemized in a statement of historical guarantee. French constitutional history, in contrast, is traced downwards from 'your old states . . . your ancient states' to 'the last generations of your country [which] appeared without much lustre in your eyes'.[5] This contrast in narrative method is entirely at one with Burke's placing of the present generation – 'People will not look forward to posterity, who never look backward to their ancestors.'[6]

Other local instances of specific narrative method could be analysed for their political direction, whether unconscious or otherwise. For example, the early introduction of the Revd Dr Price as stalking-horse is subsequently absorbed in the allusion to the Revd Hugh Peters, who mocked Charles I and was then executed at the Restoration, a narrative strategy which looks forward fearfully to the fate of those who side with Price and the British friends of the revolution. The resemblance of this device to the tactics of the historical novelist prompts thoughts of other points of comparison. Like *Waverley*, the *Reflections* advances two rival views of history, and like the

Scott novel generally there is both a preference for the organic unity of the
past and a recognition of less totally satisfactory circumstances in the present. The device of addressing the *Reflections* to a very young Frenchman
produces an emotional force-field not unlike that generated by Scott's
unremarkable heroes, who in their ordinariness stimulate in the reader a
participating sympathy even in their errors. The difference between Scott
and Burke as historical fictionalist is essentially that Scott does not relish
the tragic denouement. Burke, in characteristic self-division, reluctantly does
relish it.

It was Schopenhauer, Nietzsche's erstwhile master, who suggested that
all art aspires to the condition of music. The particular version of romanticism which we find in Burke's historical narratives suggests that all history
aspires to the condition of eternity. In the fusion of the Revds Price (died
1791) and Peters (executed 1660), Burke comments that the two differ 'only
in place and time'.[7] Such an aspiration to transcend history is offset constantly in Burke by his awareness of the purely negative terms in which
transcendence is available to modern man. The conclusion to that famous
passage in the *Reflections* which begins 'Society is indeed a contract' ends
with a rhetorically heightened meditation on the consequence of human
choice succeeding ordained necessity:

> if that which is only submission to necessity should be made the object of
> choice, the law is broken, nature is disobeyed, and the rebellious are outlaw-
> ed, cast forth, and exiled, from this world of reason, and order, and peace,
> and virtue, and fruitful penitence, into the antagonist world of madness,
> discord, vice, confusion, and unavailing sorrow.[8]

The myth of the Fall is only invoked here at one remove; this world, albeit
presented as peaceful and virtuous, is also one of fruitful penitence. The
rhetorical emphasis falls upon a more immediate, if officially hypothetical,
world of unavailing sorrow. The world of the Revolution is post-lapsarian,
known and yet unexperienceable except in the most arithmetical formulae,
the most abstract relations. This sense of cosmic desolation, detectable in
different forms in Wordsworth and Shelley (for whom the political lessons
are also drastically different), also suggests affinities between Burke and
Hegel, Burke and the early Marx, Burke and Nietzsche. So broadly defined
an affinity is perhaps insufficiently fine to be really useful in argument, and
the closer, localized context of English romanticism now requires consideration.

What Wordsworth dreaded in Jacobin abstraction and Jacobin social engineering, Shelley and Blake condemned in the society defended by Burke –

Hanoverian Britain with its coercive Church and imperial aggression, The consistency of English romanticism does not lie in any political agreement, though English romantics of various political views shared common animosities and sympathies. Dealing in primarily biographical (and psychological) terms, Thomas McFarland has located Wordsworth's psyche between the extremes of severe egotism and universal benevolence: 'Impelled toward but at the same time retreating from both isolation and community, Wordsworth came to be as it were suspended in an emotional force-field between them.'[9] For McFarland, the resolution of these tensions lay in the poet's increasing commitment to 'the significant group'; not humanity at large nor the untrammelled ego, but a significantly intimate and yet extensive group of individuals earned his loyalty and emotional commitment. In the solitaries of Wordsworth's great poems – 'Resolution and Independence', 'Michael', and of course 'The Prelude' itself – there is more concrete and accessible evidence of a dialectical process incorporating solitude and relationship, integrity and integration, in a constantly renewing and sustaining pattern. If one were to turn to the case of Shelley and his reputation, then E. T. Webb and other recent commentators have shown how a comprehensive idealism competed positively with a practical commitment to specific social projects and political causes.[10] In place of Augustan antithesis, romantic dialectics focused on the objective contradictions of a rapidly developing society experienced in its full European breadth and in the recesses of its common people. The Revolution, and the Grand Alliance against it, made the experience of politics and the experience of war public property.

For comparison with Burke, Wordsworth offers greater scope than Shelley. And the crucially significant group in his work is not the actual family circle but the 'statesmen' of the Lake District:

> The domestic affections will always be strong amongst men who live in a country not crowded with population, if these men are placed above poverty. But if they are proprietors of small estates, which have descended to them from their ancestors, the power which these affections will acquire amongst such men is inconceivable . . . Their little tract of land serves as a kind of permanent rallying point for their domestic feelings, as a tablet upon which they are written which makes them objects of memory in a thousand instances when they would otherwise be forgotten. It is a fountain fitted to the nature of social man from which supplies of affection, as pure as his heart was intended for, are daily drawn.[11]

Less particularly, Burke draws on the same powerful sources of imagery in the *Reflections*, and in defending 'the method of nature in the conduct of the state'   that is, hereditable property – he identifies the state with the home:

> In this choice of inheritance we have given to our frame of polity the image of a relation in blood; binding up the constitution of our country with our dearest domestic ties; adopting our fundamental laws into the bosom of our family affections; keeping inseparable, and cherishing with the warmth of all their combined and mutually reflected charities, our state, our hearths, our sepulchres, and our altars.[12]

Not only does Burke give to the state the emotive connotations of intimate family life, he argues that citizenship and social action have their origin in domestic experience:

> We begin our public affections in our families. No cold relation is a zealous citizen. We pass on to our neighbourhoods, and our habitual provincial connections. These are inns and resting-places. Such divisions of our country as have been formed by habit, and not by a sudden jerk of authority, were so many little images of the great country in which the heart found something which it could fill. The love to the whole is not extinguished by this subordinate partiality.[13]

There is another, more renowned statement of a similar sentiment in the *Reflections*, but it is one which requires attention in the context of its preceding sentences:

> Turbulent, discontented men of quality, in proportion as they are puffed up with personal pride and arrogance, generally despise their own order. One of the first symptoms of a selfish and mischievous ambition, is a profligate disregard of a dignity which they partake with others. To be attached to the subdivision, to love the little platoon we belong to in society, is the first principle (the germ as it were) of public affections. It is the first link in the series by which we proceed towards a love to our country and to mankind. The interests of that portion of social arrangement is a trust in the hands of all those who compose it; and as none but bad men would justify it in abuse, none but traitors would barter it away for their own personal advantage.[14]

The assault on turbulent men of quality is noteworthy, for it is Burke's version of that repression of egotism which Wordsworth found it necessary to exercise throughout his career. In general terms Burke condemns, or at least is exceedingly wary of, 'separate insulated private men' but the thrust of the *Reflections* is directed more specifically against 'literary caballers, and intriguing philosophers; with political theologians and theological politicians'.[15] In short, 'Men of Letters, fond of distinguishing themselves, are rarely averse to innovation.'[16] The articulation of caballers or writers is explicitly contrasted to the silent virtue of a rural image of society in its organic continuity:

> Because half a dozen grasshoppers under a fern make the field ring with their importunate chink, whilst thousands of great cattle, reposed beneath the shadow of the British oak, chew the cud and are silent, pray do not imagine, that those who make the noise are the only inhabitants of the field; that of course, they are many in number; or that, after all, they are other than the little shrivelled, meagre, hopping, though loud and troublesome insects of the hour.[17]

Burke does not identify his 'significant group' so clearly as Wordsworth but the extremes between which he seeks such a human locus are immediately evident and interconnected. On the one hand, there are the multitudes who are regimented in the newly conceived divisions of Jacobin France, or 'a swinish multitude',[18] a society judged by mathematical criteria. On the other, there are insulated men. If this looks like another version of Wordsworthian polarities, we should note in Burke that insulated men contribute to the establishment of schematic societies, departments, communes, and cantons. Historically speaking, one should observe that Wordsworthian fulmination against manufactories and Burkean denunciations of Jacobinism represent the old antithesis of city and country (*urbs et rus*) in crisis.

In a rather stricter historical sense, the Irish background to Burke's thought in the 1790s cannot be neglected. Dying in 1797, he did not have to face the decisions of 1799 and 1800 in relation to the proposed Union between Britain and Ireland. While speculation as to whether he would have been unionist or anti-unionist is largely pointless in so far as the altered political circumstances arising between 1797 and 1800 are concerned, the metaphoric implications of union *per se* directly relate that issue to Burke's devotion to 'the little platoon'. The romantic age aspired to wholeness and unity and yet was characterized by a profound sense of fragmentary human existences in a disintegrating world. If we accept that the union between Britain and Ireland was sought for conscious, specific political reasons, or if we go beyond this to argue that the union was determined by economic necessity, we do not invalidate the relevance of the intense romantic investment in union as a value. Politically, there was a precedent by which the initiative might be measured – the union with Scotland in 1707. But the Scottish union was generally referred to as resulting from a Treaty of Union, and the implication was that, in the early eighteenth-century sense of the word, this was a union between two nations. This implication of official parity was facilitated in that a king of Scotland (James VI) had become king of England (James I),

and that the palpable superiority of England in *Realpolitik* was balanced
by a Scottish dignity in the line of succession. The Irish union enjoyed no
such Augustan balance: the means whereby the king of England was also
king of Ireland was memorably warlike, and the union was (and is) universally referred to as the Act of Union, that is, a parliamentary decision doubly
ratified at Westminster and College Green.

As we shall see, the parliament was by the 1790s felt at least by some
to be gravely anomalous, not only in relation to the middle-class wealth of
Ireland but also in relation to the intrusive power of the London administration. The Irish government, so to speak, operated independent of the Irish
parliament, and the existence of the Lord-Lieutenant and Chief Secretary
added a further stratum of complexity. If the real motive behind the union
was a need to close the gap in British defences by drawing Ireland closer
to England, then the uniting of the parliaments (the principal means by
which the Union proper was effected) was singularly beside the point, for
Ireland as symbolized in its parliament and its military arrangements had
never been effectively independent. If there was a serious intention to reconcile Catholics to the house of Hanover by means of a union which dissolved
the intransigent Protestant element so active in the Dublin parliament, then
the immediate abandonment of such an intention in 1801 sabotaged the
primary base upon which a union of palpable social import might have been
achieved. Yet, bearing these unsatisfactory propositions in mind, we can
see that the romantic ideology of wholeness and union is enacted in the very
incompleteness of the union. Leaving aside the absence of parity between
the elements officially joined in the Act of Union (as they were open to observation in the preceding century), and passing over the immediate question
of motivation or intention, we find that the administration of Ireland after
1801 was characterized both by newly created 'union' features – the united
parliament, the united Established Church, and so forth – and by the survival of pre-union features, the lord-lieutenancy, the legal system, etc. Oliver
MacDonagh has described these arrangements as producing 'a curious
dualism in Irish government, the effects of which were hardly understood,
still less allowed for, in the nineteenth century'.[19] The Scottish union had
preserved to Scotland a popular church and a distinctive legal system; the
Irish union perpetuated into an age of increasingly democratic feeling a
minority establishment and a professional élite in which sectarian pride took
consolation. If all this seems momentarily remote from a discussion of
Burke's *Reflections*, let us recall that the French Revolution was undoubtedly the active occasion of all Anglo-Irish discussions from 1790 onwards, and
that one little platoon to which Burke might have had to advise loyalty

was the 'Junto of jobbers', soon to announce itself as 'the Protestant Ascendancy'.[20]

Burke's dual concentration on the violent pretensions of the ascendancy party in Ireland and the innovations of the Jacobins in France is itself an example of the fragmentation of the argument for a comprehensive view of things. Protestant Ascendancy is unable to see that Catholics are valuable allies in the counter-revolutionary struggle; Whigs like Fox are unable to see that they are the imminent victims of the revolution they espouse. Burke employs the revolution as a metaphor ironically imposed upon the ascendancy jobbers, and the Jacobins are cast in the role of ultra-Protestants, but the employment of metaphor both draws together and distinguishes the objects cited. From the outset the *Reflections* was acknowledged as possessing an intimate conjunction of style and content, as being in effect a literary work. But to say this is not simply to establish an unproblematic virtue in the book. James Boulton argues that 'Burke's veneration for stability, dignity, and a cultural tradition is transmitted through the image of the noble country-house or castle.'[21] Success in conveying this to the reader depends not solely on the rigour of the argument or the aptness of the tropes, but on the reader's prior assent to the identification of dignity with country houses. To say that style and content in the *Reflections* are at one is to mark the limitations of the book's potential as well as to measure its drawing of aesthetics and politics into harmony. Once again, the inherent division within the vision of a longed-for wholeness is acknowledged. The apostrophe to the queen in its absence of detail recalls Burke's own judgement in the *Enquiry* (1756) that readers of Homer are impressed by Priam's account of Helen for the very reasons that he does not specify (and so limit) her beauty; the Burkean evocation of a latter-day *reine fatale* is similar:

> It is now sixteen or seventeen years since I saw the queen of France, then the dauphiness, at Versailles; and surely never lighted on this orb which she hardly seemed to touch, a more delightful vision. I saw her just above the horizon, decorating and cheering the elevated sphere she just began to move in, – glittering like the morning-star, full of life, and splendour, and joy. Oh! What a revolution! and what an heart must I have, to contemplate without emotion that elevation and that fall! . . .[22]

Surely the most effective analysis of this passage is William Blake's verse paraphrase:

> The Queen of France just touched this globe,
> And the pestilence darted from her robe;
> But our good queen quite grows to the ground,
> And a great many suckers grow all around.[23]

The central metaphor (of elevation) is maintained but, by being stripped of its sonorous repetitions and cast in brutal doggerel, is shown to reveal callous remoteness. Beyond this, of course, the crucial difference between Blake and Burke is that Blake moves to concentrate on the actuality of a present tense scene in which meaning is a potential to be drawn out by stylistic emphasis, whereas Burke insinuates a second object of consideration into his evocation of the queen – the effects of time doubly upon her and upon his altered sentiments towards her. If we read elsewhere in the *Reflections* that society becomes 'a partnership not only between those who are living, but between those who are living, those who are dead, and those who are to be born',[24] this 'eternal contract' is in keeping with the mediation of time between the object and subject (so to speak) of the *Reflections*.

Incompleteness, sentiment, the passage of time – the dominant metaphor which draws these concerns together in Burke is *ruination:*

> one of the first and most leading principles on which the commonwealth and the laws are consecrated, is lest the temporary possessors and life-renters in it, unmindful of what they have received from their ancestors, or of what is due to their posterity, should act as if they were the entire masters; that they should not think it amongst their rights to cut off the entail, or commit waste on the inheritance, by destroying at their pleasure the whole fabric of their society; hazarding to leave to those who come after them a ruin instead of an habitation . . .[25]

Addressing his young French gentleman, Burke directs the same metaphor towards the same conclusion:

> Your constitution, it is true, whilst you were out of possession, suffered waste and dilapidation; but you possessed in some parts the walls, and in all the foundations of a noble and venerable castle. You might have repaired those walls; you might have built on those old foundations.[26]

As James Boulton points out, this use of the great house as an image of the state or of society has a distinguished ancestry including Ben Jonson, Marvell, and Pope. The flourishing house of Jonson's 'To Penshurst' is a model of an orderly society, with the active bountiful garden contributing emblems of human generosity and so forth. In Burke, by way of contrast, the house spatially occupies a large place in his imagery, even when the house itself is ruined or damaged. Continuity, expressed through legal concepts such as entail or prescription, is to be preferred to temporary well-being. The ruin is a characteristic romantic metaphor in that a form of incompleteness is reconciled to a form of wholeness, incompleteness of physical space assimilated to the evidence of wholeness in time. No doubt Gothic and

antiquarian enthusiasms contribute to the romantic interest in ruins, but
the evidence of the fragmentary text (e.g. 'Kubla Khan', 'The Prelude', etc.)
and of the poets' sense of their own lives as ruins amid ruins confirms the
centrality of the romantic metaphor.

The legislatures of Britain and France are contrasted implicitly through
this imagery. The National Assembly is treated simply as that – an assembly
of persons speaking as the nation; the English parliament, however, can be
referred to as 'the two houses', and the sense of a house as a social entity
with its continuous life sanctions the decisions of parliament.[27] Speaking
of British liberty, Burke insists that 'it has its gallery of portraits', and the
architectural metaphor is significant for its insinuation of the ancestral and
generational human material of portraiture as displayed in galleries of a great
house.[28] This device of employing the static architectural metaphor in order
to introduce a covert implication of a (quasi-)dynamic history has other
related applications; having emphasized 'grounds of hope and fear . . . a
solid ground on which any parent could speculate . . .', Burke draws his
paragraph up to an explicit topographical trope in which Jacobin in-
dividualism is identified with the process of architectural ruination:

> Barbarism with regard to science and literature, unskilfulness with regard to
> arts and manufactures, would infallibly succeed to the want of a steady educa-
> tion and settled principle; and thus the commonwealth itself would, in a few
> generations, crumble away, be disconnected into the dust and powder of in-
> dividuality, and at length dispersed to all the winds of heaven.[29]

'Disconnected into the dust' enacts its sense in the very tenuousness of its
verbal structure, and this harmony of style and content mocks ironically
at the ruination of the commonwealth. The young György Lukács launched
his *Theory of the Novel* (1914-15) from an intense longing for Greek completeness, and declared that 'irony is a negative mysticism to be found in
times without a god'; recalling the affinities between the *Reflections* and the
emergent form of the historical novel, we note also that, in such circumstances, 'irony is the objectivity of the novel.'[30]

If the great house is a dominant metaphor of the *Reflections*, with the attendant imagery of gardens and grounds and picture-galleries, its recurrent
citation is ironic and objective in that Burke uses it primarily as an image
of ruination contrasted with a wholeness which historical community may
afford:

> Is it then true, that the French government was such as to be incapable or
> undeserving of reform; so that it was of absolute necessity the whole fabric
> should be at once pulled down, and the area cleared for the erection of a
> theoretic experimental edifice in its place?[31]

Or again,

> The French builders, clearing away as mere rubbish whatever they found,
> and, like their ornamental gardeners, forming every thing into an exact level,
> propose to rest the whole local and general legislature on three bases of three
> different kinds . . .[32]

This use of the 'great good place' in contexts where ruination or damage
is taking place is one form of paradox which Burke employs; perhaps the
most striking instance of it is the single sentence which begins and ends
with reversal and oxymoron:

> The *fresh ruins* of France, which shock our feelings wherever we can turn our
> eyes, are not the devastation of civil war; they are the sad but instructive
> monuments of rash and ignorant counsel in time of *profound peace*.[33]
> (emphasis added)

Reflections on the Revolution in France is not so much an Augustan account,
or refutation, of the political philosophy and practice of Jacobinism as it
is a literary enactment of fundamentally romantic assumptions. In the context of Anglo-Irish literature it is worth noting how its treatment of history
occasionally anticipates the devices of the historical novel, and how its sense
of history involves the collaboration of a metaphysic of eternity with the
psychology of recollection. Metaphor, by means of a related subjectivity,
is recurrently ironic. Many of these features of the *Reflections* are echoed
in the subsequent sporadic writings on Protestant Ascendancy. The degree
of public attention which Ireland earned in the 1790s – and especially from
1798 onwards – ensured that the new romantic mode of expression came
to be applied to its political affairs. With the exception of Keats, all the
great romantic writers concerned themselves with Irish affairs. One
background to this romantic interest in Ireland could be summarized in
William Blake's friendship with James Barry, another in Shelley's support
for Catholic Emancipation. The first of these links the argument to that
band of Irish adventurers – Burke himself, Goldsmith, Sheridan, and so
on – who left home to make their way in the larger arena of London and
whom Yeats subsequently and selectively declared to be part of an Irish
Augustan tradition; the second touches upon one major theme in the
nineteenth-century liberal concern with Irish vicissitudes.

   This development is part of a broader alteration of relations between Britain and Ireland in the transition from the eighteenth to the nineteenth century. No magical quality resides in the precise date of 1800 or 1801, though
the Union clearly marks one major element in this alteration. Using it as
an indicator of change, we see that the nominal independence of the

pre-Union parliament in Dublin (and, less obviously, of the pre-Union kingdom of Ireland) is absorbed into a united parliament and a united kingdom. We see also, however, that this Union was built on powerful contradictions and dislocations. One index of this contradiction lies in the reports of travellers – whether from Britain or the Continent – who visited Ireland in the late eighteenth century or the early decades of the nineteenth century. No generalized conclusions on this topic could be attempted here, but one or two isolated elements may be briefly noted. In the 1790s, for example, when Ireland was nominally independent, its political affairs were seen as far more thoroughly interwoven with those of Britain than was the case for long periods in the nineteenth century when the official relationship between the islands was one of Union.

In June 1794, William Wordsworth wrote to the bookseller Mathews in London about a projected dissident journal:

> I entirely approve of what you say on the subject of Ireland, and think it very proper that an agent should be appointed in Dublin to disseminate the impression. It would be well if either of you have any friends there, to whom you could write soliciting their recommendation. Indeed it would be very desirable to endeavour to have, in each considerable town of Great Britain and Ireland, a person to introduce the publication into notice . . . If you think that by going over to Dublin I could transact any business relative to the publication in a better manner than it could be done by Letter, though I have no friends there I would willingly undertake the voyage, which may be done at any time from this place.[34]

Wordsworth did not make this proposed trip to Ireland, and indeed his encounter with the island did not occur until September 1829, when he stayed with Maria Edgeworth in the course of a five-week tour. Much had changed between 1794 and 1829 – Wordsworth's own political attitudes, the events of 1798 which included *Lyrical Ballads* and the United Irishman rebellion, Union, the growth of reaction in Britain during the Napoleonic wars, frustration in Ireland at delay in the emancipation of Catholics, an agricultural slump, two Irish Tory prime ministers of the United Kingdom (George Canning and the Duke of Wellington), the rise of Daniel O'Connell.[35] Neither these developments nor the postponement of his own visit prevented Wordsworth from propounding his views on Ireland in the intervening years. It is a measure of the extent to which Ireland was becoming a topic upon which Englishmen spoke confidently that the contradictions of Union did not inhibit such assertions. The terminology of these assertions is, however, explicitly revealing of the romantic base of this ideological confidence. In the case of Wordsworth, two instances may be significantly related.

Writing to Henry Crabbe Robinson in July 1826, the poet apologized for once again having to abandon plans to visit Ireland. He was, on the other hand, happy to provide advice to intending travellers:

> Of Ireland I can say nothing but that every body sees Killarney there are some fine ruins of monasteries, etc not far from Limerick the Vale of the Dargle and the Wicklow Mountains would lie in your way from Killarney to Dublin supposing you to start from Dublin you would go by Limerick and return by the Wicklow country but to one who should leave Wales out the best way of seeing Ireland from London would be to go from London to Bristol and thence to Cork Killarney and Dublin and the Giants Causeway. From Belfast there will no doubt be a Steam Boat to Glasgow . . .[36]

Given that this paragraph is written in his daughter's hand at Wordsworth's dictation, perhaps the breathless lack of punctuation should not be attributed to the poet himself. There is none the less a comprehensive confidence that Ireland is a romantic itinerary, a succession of picturesque scenes with priority given to ruined monasteries. It was just the previous year which had brought Maria Edgeworth and Sir Walter Scott to Killarney for the first time, and the comparison between Maria Edgeworth's attitude to scenery in literature and that evinced by Scott and Wordsworth illustrates the extent to which she retained pre-romantic attitudes generally. This distinction between the romantics' delight in Irish scenery, and the Irish novelist's willingness to rely on handbooks for what descriptions of landscape her novels required, has another dimension. Wordsworth and Scott are primarily looking at a foreign landscape, from which the continuous buzz of mundane social activity – boats, hotels, the state of dress of the people – has been filtered. We note the irony of this Irish foreignness in the attitude of two British romantics whose devotion to the institutions of the United Kingdom of Great Britain and Ireland was without rival. But we add to it a more intensely romantic counter-proposition – that the foreignness of Ireland is related to its pastness, its emblematic depiction in ruination. The ruin, in romantic poetry from Wordsworth's Grasmere to Holderlin's Patmos, is a metaphor uniting incompleteness and completeness, the fragmentation of human domicile and the continuity of memorized landscape. The 'Gothick ruin' of a Wicklow villa garden, which Maria Edgeworth focuses upon in *The Absentee*, is for her a superficial imitation of metaphor, romantic longing reduced to sentimental fabrication. Maria Edgeworth's travels in France in 1820 offer an illuminating comparison to Wordsworthian Ireland. As always, she is concerned to relate the familiar and the unfamiliar, but in comparing French and Irish social occasions she unwittingly reveals her own tendency to identify the foreign and the romantic:

In the evening we were at a *fête de village* at La Celle, to which Mme de Vindé
had invited us, as like an Irish pattern as possible, allowing for the difference
of dress and manner. The scene was in a beautiful grove on each side of a romantic road leading through a valley. High wooded banks: groups of gaily-dressed
village belles and beaux seen through the trees, in a quarry, in the sand-holes,
everywhere where there was space enough to form a quadrille. This grove was
planted by Gabrielle d'Estrées for whom Henry IV built a lodge near it. Fanny and Harriet danced with two gentlemen who were of our party, and they
all danced on till dew-fall, when the lamps, little glasses full of oil and a wick
suspended to the branches of the trees were lighted, and we returned to La
Celle, where we ate ice and sat in a circle, playing *trouvez mon ami* – mighty
like 'why, when, and where' – and then played loto till twelve. Rose at six,
had coffee, and drove back to Paris in the cool of the delicious morning.[37]

The most pertinent comment on this passage is that provided by the editor
of Maria Edgeworth's correspondence, in a footnote – 'Mme. de Genlis
. . . speaks of the post-Revolution changes in *fêtes champetres*; the gentry
no longer danced with the lower classes and their gardens were opened to
cabaretiers and *traiteurs* etc.'[38] Maria Edgeworth, the foreigner in La Celle,
sees a veritable vision of social harmony, dancers in the quarry, Marvellian
lamps in the trees; the disenchanted memorialist sees the hired caterer, class
tension, 'la morgue des dames de chateaux, qui, dans ces rejouissances, ne
vouloient point danser avec les paysans'.[39] This observation of bourgeois
encroachment on previous complex distinctions and interactions relies of
course on celebration of a past which is less than fully real; as Madame de
Genlis expresses it, she works 'pour reparer le temps perdu'.[40] Yet, to the
Irish visitor, the evidence of latter-day decline has its own timeless charm.

Wordsworth on Irish landscape and Irish ruination constituted the first
instance of the romantic ideology lying behind the confident assertions of
English opinion on the subject of Ireland. The second illustrates the extent
to which the sectarian tensions excited in the 1790s gave birth to a sociology
which continues to colour political debate in Ireland. That Wordsworth's
views changed drastically between 1794 and the 1820s is well known, but
that fact should not deter us from seeing in the change (and its specific continuities) a more than biographical significance. Writing to Sir Robert Inglis on 11 June 1825, he deplored George Canning's speech on Catholic
Relief 'attempting to reconcile us to Papacy, by endeavours to prove that
in points of Faith and practice, Protestantism stands pretty much upon a
par with it'.[41] If Canning seems to echo a broad inclusive theology, Wordsworth's language follows closely strict formulations:

Were we to abandon the hope of gaining upon the Romanists, we must be
prepared to admit the evil of their gaining upon us. Protestant Ascendancy

must be renounced, and sooner or later will be substituted Catholic domination – the two religions cannot coexist, in a Country free as our's upon equal
terms. For my own part while I condemn as founded in ignorance, I reprobate
as of the most injurious tendency, every Measure that does not point to the
maintenance of Protestant ascendancy, and to the diffusion of Protestant principles: and this doctrine I hold not more as a friend to Great Britain, than
to Ireland.[42]

Wordsworth (like Coleridge) came to hold views upon the sanctity of Church
and State with which Edmund Burke, in so many ways their mentor, could
not have sympathized. Yet the differentiation cannot be attributed simply
to galloping reaction on the individual level. The Coleridgean notion of a
'clerisy', an intellectual class devoted to aims at once religious and cultural,
may certainly be related to the desire of finding 'a significant group' upon
whom the future of the nation could safely depend, but the conditions upon
which such a proposition relied were not available in Burke's lifetime.
Burke's practical experience as eighteenth-century parliamentarian qualifies
any romantic description of him. Yet here we find that the consistency of
romanticism is what sceptics must regard as its inconsistency; the divergence
of Wordsworth from Burke on the question of 'the Protestant religion' is
a historical statement of their unanimity. This romantic contradiction informs much of the subsequent development of Anglo-Irish literature in the
nineteenth century, and it is entirely in keeping with such dialectical procedures that Burke's role, Burke's significance, should be suppressed or
denied by the ultimately crowning notion of an Augustan tradition. Successive stages, or seismic registers, of that development can be traced in the
fiction of Maria Edgeworth, Sheridan Le Fanu, and Charles Lever; in the
emergence of nineteenth-century Celticism; and climactically, in the polarized productions of Anglo-Irish modernism whose terms we can simply call
Joyce and Yeats.

Reflections on the Revolution in France is not advanced here as a proto-
novel upon which Maria Edgeworth subsequently models the real thing. As
against such merely sequential notions of influence in literary history a more
dynamic alternative must be now developed which, while immersing itself
in the actuality of history, also acknowledges the full interaction of reader
and text, subject and object. In this sense, consequently, we draw attention
to certain novelistic features of the *Reflections*; but the *Reflections*, thus read,
is as much influenced by *Castle Rackrent*, the Act of Union, and Yeats's
Collected Poems as they are influenced by it. To see an unbridgeable distance
between the France Burke lamented in the *Reflections* and the Irish Protestant jobbers he mocked in his letters is to travesty their historical and

ideological setting. In the words of Thomas McFarland, the modalities of romanticism are fragmentation and longing, ruination and wholeness: the completely romantic poem is, like those *magna opera* upon which Wordsworth and Coleridge so long laboured, incomplete. Among Edmund Burke's writings it may appear futile to search for such a paradigm of the romantic metaphysic – once again the practical demands of a public career would appear to discourage that kind of imitative form. Nevertheless, if we have yet to look at the particular political circumstances in which Burke's letter to his son, Richard, was written – commencing between mid-February and 10 May 1792, in the weeks running up to the publication of a *Collected Works* – we can still take a full measure of *Letter to Richard Burke*.

The letter is indeed unfinished, and was most ostentatiously published as an unfinished text. Bibliographical facsimulation could confirm instantly that the text 'ends' in a series of asterisks, but what is considerably more significant is the fact that, in the five years remaining to him, Burke did not attempt to replace those asterisks. Admittedly, his most dearly beloved son – no biographer can hope to convey the devastation Richard Burke's death in 1794 wreaked upon Burke – was dead within a poignantly shorter time. In turn, this totally unexpected bereavement lends a special poignancy to the 'final' paragraph of *Letter to Richard Burke*: 'All titles terminate in prescription; in which (differently from Time in the fabulous instances) the son devours the father, and the last prescription eats up all the former.'[43] We shall read the *Letter* thoroughly for its scathing analysis of Protestant Ascendancy – 'A word has been lately struck in the mint of the Castle of Dublin.' The fiscal metaphor, the exploitation of commercial idiom, is not limited to the letter to his son, but is repeatedly employed in the *Reflections* where the financial system of the Republic is condemned for its 'continual transmutation of paper into land, and land into paper':

> By this means the spirit of money-jobbing and speculation goes into the mass of the land itself, and incorporates with it. By this kind of operation, that species of property becomes (as it were) volatized; it assumes an unnatural and monstrous activity . . .[44]

Of course, finance is a central concern of Burke's in his polemic against republican France, and his use of fiscal metaphor is apt: it counterbalances in its aptness the irony of his great-house images of contemporary ruination. In *Letter to Richard Burke*, the coinage 'Protestant Ascendancy' is ferociously analysed precisely because Burke is aware of the dangers of its currency. In other words, his account of Protestant Ascendancy is closer to his ironic use of the great house than to the analysis of republican finance.

Burke's account of Protestant Ascendancy, therefore, is intimately related to his writings on France, and indeed *Letter to Richard Burke* incorporates both formal and tonal aspects of his romanticism. Its concluding image of prescription, as the son devouring the father, reverses the classical notion of time (Cronus) swallowing up its children. And this introduces a motif which will persist in Anglo-Irish literature from *Castle Rackrent* to *Purgatory*: that is, the symbiosis of Oedipal conflict and social *mésalliance*. In the former, blood relationship is both under- and over-valued. In the latter, class is at once stridently invoked and travestied.

As we approach the modernist period a third element becomes more prominent – a metaformal self-consciousness in the work of art by which it expresses its revolt against the author, its Oedipal assault upon its own creator. That such themes originate in the romantic period can be confirmed by reference to areas of literary production other than Ireland. Burke's condemnation of the volatility, the monstrous activity of the Revolution is a muted expression of a drastically new element in human consciousness, recognized by the German poet Novalis:

> Most observers of the Revolution, especially the clever and fashionable ones, have declared it to be a dangerous and contagious disease. They have gone no further than the symptoms, and have interpreted these as being in many ways haphazardly confused. Many have regarded it as a merely local evil, but the most inspired opponents have urged castration for they have noticed that this alleged illness is nothing other than the crisis of imminent puberty.[45]

If the Revolution is the onset of adult sexuality, and its repression drastically symbolized by castration, then the persistence in Anglo-Irish literature of various forms of sexual redirection in covert guise – incest, homosexuality, the anti-Oedipal violence of fathers upon sons – signals larger collocations of cultural, political, and economic interest. Such a vocabulary does not miraculously begin *ex nihilo* with the romantic age, but has its earlier, simpler (and ultimately redundant) manifestation in the Augustan antitheses of the eighteenth century.

Novalis' estimate of Burke lay dormant for a century, until the German constitutional lawyer and theorist of dictatorship, Carl Schmitt, reactivated it for deeply reactionary purposes. In 1919 Schmitt published a high diatribe under the title, *Politische Romantik* (Political Romanticism). Burke, Joseph de Maistre, and Friedrich von Gentz were its recurring points of reference. In the name – initially – of a new conservatism, the appropriation of revolution (*pace* Novalis) to fascism was underway. The task of literary history is to demonstrate how genesis and value, in relation to any complex written work, effect each other. The *Reflections*, upon which Yeats will reflect in his last decades, cannot simply be dated to 1790.[46]

NOTES AND REFERENCES

1 Novalis (F. von Hardenberg), 'Fragmente', *Gesammelte Werke* (Zurich: Buhl, 1945), vol. ii, p. 36.
2 Although it is not primarily concerned with the *Reflections* Chris Reid's article 'Language and Practice in Burke's Political Writing', *Literature and History*, vol. 6, (Autumn 1977), pp. 203-18, has been most helpful in developing this discussion. See also his *Edmund Burke and the Practice of Writing* (Dublin: Gill and Macmillan, 1985).
3 *Reflections on the Revolution in France*, edited with an introduction by Thomas H. D. Mahoney with an analysis by Oskar Piest (Indianapolis: Bobbs-Merrill, 1955; 13th printing 1978).
4 Richard Shannon, *The Crisis of Imperialism 1865–1915* (London: Paladin, 1976), p. 26.
5 *Reflections on the Revolution in France*, ed. Conor Cruise O'Brien (Harmondsworth: Penguin, 1970), p. 122. All subsequent references to the *Reflections* relate to this edition.
6 *Reflections*, p. 119.
7 Ibid., p. 158.
8 Ibid., p. 195; some of his strictly fallacious arguments invoking 'law' are discussed by Herbert J. Muller in *The Uses of the Past: Profiles of Former Societies* (New York: Oxford University Press, 1952), pp. 316 etc.
9 Thomas McFarland, *Romanticism and the Forms of Ruin: Wordsworth, Coleridge, and Modalities of Fragmentation* (Princeton: Princeton University Press, 1981), p. 152.
10 See in particular Timothy Webb, *Shelley: a Voice not Understood* (Manchester: Manchester University Press, 1977), pp. 75-98 *et passim*.
11 *The Letters of William and Dorothy Wordsworth: The Early Years 1787–1805*, ed. Ernest de Selincourt, rev. Chester L. Shaver (Oxford: Clarendon Press, 1967), pp. 314-15; quoted by McFarland, p. 173.
12 *Reflections*, p. 120.
13 Ibid., p. 315.
14 Ibid., p. 135.
15 Ibid., pp. 91, 93.
16 Ibid., p. 211.
17 Ibid., p. 181.
18 Ibid., p. 173; for some important comments on this phrase see Cruise O'Brien's annotations, pp. 385-6.
19 Oliver MacDonagh, *Ireland: The Union and its Aftermath*, (London: Allen and Unwin, 1977; rev. edn.), p. 17.
20 See below, pp. 75-89 ff., for Burke's use of these phrases.
21 James Boulton, *The Language of Politics in the Age of Wilkes and Burke* (London: Routledge and Kegan Paul, 1963), p. 111.
22 *Reflections*, pp. 169-70; Boulton, op. cit., discusses the apostrophe on pp. 127-33; for Burke on Priam and Helen see *A Philosophical Enquiry into the Origin of our Ideas of the Sublime and the Beautiful*, ed. James T. Boulton (London: Routledge and Kegan Paul, 1958), p. 171.
23 William Blake, *Poems*, ed. W. H. Stevenson, text by David V. Erdman (London: Longman, 1971), p. 168; for a discussion of Blake's rewritings of Burke

see David V. Erdman, *Blake: Prophet against Empire*, (Princeton: Princeton University Press, 1969; rev. edn), pp. xi, 11, 184, 219, 469.

24 *Reflections*, pp. 194-5.
25 Ibid., p. 112.
26 Ibid., p. 121.
27 Ibid., p. 102.
28 Ibid., p. 121.
29 Ibid., pp. 193-4.
30 György Lukács, *Theory of the Novel*, trans. Anna Bostock (London: Merlin Press, 1971), p. 90.
31 *Reflections*, p. 230.
32 Ibid., p. 285.
33 Ibid., pp. 126-7.
34 *The Letters of William and Dorothy Wordsworth: The Early Years*, pp. 126, 128.
35 George Canning was of course born in London, but, to adapt Wellington's comment on such matters, to be born in a stable does not entail one's being a horse. Canning's family came from Garvagh in County Derry.
36 *The Letters of William and Dorothy Wordsworth: The Later Years, Part I, 1821–1828*, edn Alan G. Hill, from the 1st edn of Ernest de Selincourt (Oxford: Clarendon Press, 1978), p. 478.
37 *Maria Edgeworth in France and Switzerland: Selections from the Edgeworth Family Letters*, ed. Christina Colvin (Oxford: Clarendon Press, 1979), p. 187.
38 Ibid., n1.
39 Stephanie Félicite, comtesse de Genlis, *Mémoires inédits* (Paris, 1825), vol. v, p. 109.
40 Ibid., vol. v, p. 107.
41 *The Letters of William and Dorothy Wordsworth; The Later Years, Part I*, p. 359.
42 Ibid., pp. 359-60.
43 'Letter to Richard Burke', *Writings and Speeches of Edmund Burke*, vol. 9, R.B. McDowell ed. (Oxford: Clarendon Press, 1991), p. 658.
44 *Reflections*, p. 308.
45 Novalis, loc. cit.
46 See Carl Schmitt, *Political Romanticism*, trans. Greg Oakes (Cambridge, Mass.: MIT Press, 1986), esp. pp. 112 and 113.

2

Edmund Burke
and the
Imagination of History

> My failing to have a nice ear for vowel sounds, and the Anglo-Irish slurred, hurried way of speaking, made me take the words 'Ireland' and 'island' to be synonymous.
>
> (Elizabeth Bowen)[1]

In the eighteenth century Ireland and England were different from each other. At the end of the nineteenth century they were different – different from each other and from what they had been. Moreover, the means and effects of their alteration were far from identical. Finally, the Irish and the English differed in how they described and accounted for these various differences.

Such a cat's cradle of tense parallels could be made more solid simply by a few references to industrialization, trade, social infrastructure, education, religious policy. Indeed, the history of Ireland's relations with England, England's relations with Ireland, is most familiar in the forms of such extensive differentiation. With a treaty of independence in 1921 the two gave the most concrete institutional recognition to this state of affairs. Yet, at least until 1921, and arguably afterwards too, there should be added to our model a higher level of relation in which Ireland and England, so to speak, concurred, a level at once ideological and effective in which the two were contained on terms of some extensive comparability and equity. In the eighteenth century this can be identified principally as the Monarchy or, more abstractly,

49

the Protestant Succession. the king of England was also the king of Ireland. In the nineteenth century, we speak of the United Kingdom, and the significant alteration is not simply the Union but the emphasis on the kingdom or, more abstractly, the state.

The emergence of the state as a prime initiator in matters of social policy was associated particularly with England, because the organs of political and financial power were located specifically in England. In Ireland the state was indeed active, at times hyperactive, but it was quickly shadowed by a less tangible entity, a concept more romantic than utilitarian, the Nation. To be sure, none of these terms is new: all of them were current in the reign of Elizabeth. But the manner in which they bore upon the realities of life on the two islands marked the difference between the islands in the period under discussion.

The English and the Irish differed as to the differences between them, nor did they agree on the similarities which exacerbated their dispute. This is not to suggest that relations between the two should be approached in a purely descriptive manner. Were I attempting a political account, I should want to deal with the actual forces at work in English and Irish society – and beyond – which produced the situation I have outlined. That is, I should demonstrate that the comparability and equity I have spoken of is radically distinguishable from any formal or moral notions of justice. But as I am to concentrate on a particular manifestation of Anglo-Irish relations in cultural terms, a further economic and political analysis lies beyond my scope. Nevertheless, we begin with history – and for two reasons. First, the great literary movement towards which our inquiry is directed was deeply concerned with the bonds existing between the past and the present. History was seen as a condition in which the present existed. Yeats's Celtic Revival, Joyce's nightmare. The perspective upon the past varied: it was for Yeats one of longing, for Joyce one of resentment and revolt: for both of them it involved a painful recognition of history as a potent form of reality. And second, even the most fleeting attempt at description carries with it implied historical interpretations: no normative account of how things stand is, in this context at least, without its subterranean assumptions of how things might have been.

Prior to the Norman invasion, Ireland had not been unified in any recognizable form. The Normans who arrived at the end of the twelfth century were never permitted to establish themselves so firmly as to make possible a kingdom rivalling Henry II's England. Over the centuries, the smaller island had never been totally separate from the larger, never totally subdued, nor liberated, nor administered, nor neglected. The Reformation transformed a distinction between Gael and Norman into a schism between Catholic and

Protestant, adding to this a new international dimension to Irish affairs through the possibility of a pan-Catholic alliance between Spain and the unreformed Irish (both Gael and Norman). Sometimes English preoccupations with Europe and (later) America allowed certain Irish factions a measure of free manoeuvre: at other times, quite other arrangements were required. At all times, it was felt that a sense of anomaly affected relations between the two kingdoms. The charges and recriminations generated by this sense of anomaly are familiar enough: it does not seem to have occurred to either party that a dual kingdom incorporating two islands divided by an extensive and treacherous sea constituted an anomaly within their common tradition of social organization inherited from antiquity: that tradition bespoke territorial consolidation and (with some exceptions or delays) centralization. In 1784, C. T. Greville wrote to the Duke of Rutland, Lord-Lieutenant of Ireland under the Rockingham ministry: 'Ireland is too great to be unconnected with us, and too near us to be dependent on a foreign state, and too little to be independent.'[2] The imaginative shape, or shapelessness, of the observation is at least as significant as its content.

In 1784, of course, the American War of Independence was the recent catalyst.[3] Ireland's exclusively Protestant parliament had two years earlier won a measure of legislative independence from Westminster, in the face of Britain's Atlantic preoccupations. Power in Dublin was still divided between the king's representative (with his secretaries), the administration in Dublin Castle, and the factions of the Irish parliament. Since the beginning of the century, when the Williamite wars had intensified the Reformation divisions to an unprecedented level of legislative control, a system had grown up by which the effective running of the king's business was 'undertaken' by a powerful lobby in return for the control of local patronage. The result was that much power rested with a small group who were neither a cabinet nor a civil service: they were the 'undertakers'. And if the system was modified towards the end of the century, it was still the case that both power and authority were vested all but exclusively in the hands of a Protestant élite.

The distressful plight of Irish Catholics under the penal laws has come in for some revisionist analysis in recent years. While a new recognition of the success of many Catholics in business and trade, and the less than absolute application of the law in matters of civil manners and so forth, is timely, it as yet remains undenied that Catholics were excluded from every kind of direct political representation and office. The proportion of the population thus treated is not easily calculated: the question is of course complicated by the exclusion of Protestant dissenters from the establishment.

What is of greater urgency for the modern reader of Anglo-Irish relations is a recognition of the balance of population between Britain and Ireland. In 1796 John Keogh complained to Edmund Burke that 'Government appear to forget that the Inhabitants of Ireland are about One third of all his majesty's Subjects in Europe.'[4] It would be mistaken to interpret this approximate statistic in the light of a twentieth-century definition of democracy as universal suffrage. Nevertheless, Ireland earned the attention, if not always the respect, of British politicians as a substantial part of the king's realm: that the Irish included a large number who were alienated to some degree by reason of their religion and who had a history of collusion with continental foes did not diminish that attention. It may be said in passing that one of the most important of the altered differences between Britain and Ireland as from the late eighteenth to the late nineteenth century was the very substantial shift in demographic proportion caused by industrialization in England and famine and emigration in Ireland. The tensions of the late eighteenth century are perhaps more readily collated to Keogh's statement of proportion than to any head-counting within the denominations in Ireland.

Within Ireland the Catholic majority was politically neutralized, though never to the complete security and satisfaction of the more volatile Protestant representatives. In 1792, Burke sought to explain the constitutional adjustments of 1782 by arguing that internal conditions had altered – not numerically, but yet materially – so as to require an alteration of relations between the two kingdoms. Britain, he maintained,

> saw, that the disposition of the *leading part* of the nation, would not permit them to act any longer the part of a *garrison*. She saw, that true policy did not require that they ever should have appeared in that character; or if it had done so formerly, the reasons had now ceased to operate. She saw that the Irish of her race, were resolved, to build their constitution and their politics, upon another bottom.[5]

Burke did not always advance so positive an account of 1782. He did, however, stress the peculiar difficulties – of language, as much as anything else – caused by the dual alterations of proportionate interest between England and Ireland and between the social groupings within Ireland. 'The Irish of her race' is one of the more analytical versions of a nomenclature which occurs also as 'Anglo-Irish', 'West Briton', and – in the linguistic arena – 'Hiberno-English'. It has the merit of distinguishing between social function (birth, residence, etc. in Ireland) and ancestry (deriving from English planters, etc.), while at the same time conjoining those elements in a more positive manner than the schismatic hyphen of its principal rivals. When the social world of the Anglo-Irish was finally eclipsed (in the

generation of Elizabeth Bowen who has written so beautifully on the subject) it was as if the hyphen, which had always been a signally diminished
equation mark, became a minus sign, a cancellation.

In the same letter of 1792 to Sir Hercules Langrishe, Burke employed
the 'too much and too little' device of C. T. Greville to emphasize his point:
'The Protestants of Ireland are not *alone* sufficiently the people to form a
democracy; and they are *too numerous* to answer the ends and purposes of
an aristocracy.'[6] The internal problem, as Burke presents it, resembles
Greville's in outer form. But 'too great to be unconnected' and 'too little
to be independent' is as near to tautology as paradox. Furthermore, Greville
was speaking of geographical proximity which, while it may be affected by
changes in strategic alliances and in the technology of war and trade, is in
a sense a stable relation. Burke in contrast is dealing with classes, and classes
are not prescribed bodies of men and women. It is true, of course, that men
and women sometimes may behave as if class were just as it is here denied
to be. But as class consists of a series of relations in social, economic, political,
and cultural activity, there will be many individuals involved in more than
one 'class' by dint of the complexity of their social existence. Class conflict,
therefore, does not resemble the warfare of opposing armies, each dressed
in exclusively distinguishing colours. Conflict arises when the requirement
of different sets of relations are brought antagonistically to bear on an area
of social activity where each claims validity.

It will be clear that the operations of language may be crucial in deciding
how such conflicts develop. *Antithesis* (offered by Greville in terms of distance
and proximity, by Burke in terms of class roles and forms of government)
is a frequently employed expression of Anglo-Irish relations at the end of
the eighteenth century. Without comment on or commitment to the substantive arguments embodied in these pronouncements, we note their characteristic balance of similarity and dissimilarity, their neo-classical formalism.
However, the substantive arguments are not absolutely distinguishable from
their formalism. Eighteenth-century rhetoric encouraged the definition of
issues in the shape of resolvable antitheses, by the value it found in such
formulations of moral choice and aesthetic effect. To see the problem as
coherent was to go some way towards its solution. Of course, this last view
of Augustan optimism sometimes disguises the deflection of attention away
from the crucial (but problematic) issues towards others which have the attraction of being resolvable, even if they are to an extent marginal to the
urgent inquiry. Thomas Gray's Christianity in the 'Elegy' is not so much
a matter of personal belief as of an acknowledged and conventional system
of deflected despair: the irresolvable may be lulled to sleep if rocked

on the balanced knees of Antithesis. So volatile a fiction as Godwin's *Caleb Williams* (1794) demonstrates how profoundly difficult it was to narrate politically informed connections across the Irish sea, even in the revolutionary decade. The differences between England and Ireland, however, complicated any attempt to apply the antithetical trope to Anglo-Irish relations. By suppressing or neglecting important areas of concurrence, the hostile commentator (from whichever side of the argument) could present the grounds of comparison as too ill-defined to support any resolution – John Keogh's complaint to Burke focuses precisely on this tactic.

In Burke's writings we find a different reaction. Increasingly as the revolutionary decade advances, recurringly whenever he writes of Ireland, Burke is searching for other, additional rhetorical devices by which to convey a deeper sense of the crisis he dreaded. If solutions are necessarily determined by the range and limitation of the language in which the crisis is explored, then for Burke the revolutionary decade called for something more strictly radical in the political language of those who opposed revolution. The values of Augustanism might be conserved but only by a drastic departure from the norms of Augustan optimism. The gathering darkness of Burke's utterances on Ireland in his last years is well known: it should not be held apart from the stylistic experiments of the *Reflections on the Revolution in France*. Burke was rarely guilty of neglecting the concurrences in order to exaggerate the differences: England and Ireland were bound together in the imperial system, this was as firmly held by Burke as his eloquent denunciation of the Irish undertakers of English policy in Ireland. The underlying unity which he saw at the bottom of Anglo-Irish relations was informed by his acute perception of the internal divisions of Ireland. His formulation of those divisions allows no happy neglect of external realities. Reading the letters of his last seven years we become aware that he all but makes explicit an imminent *tragic* conflict between elements in Irish society which are simultaneously irreconcilable and inseparable. Such a perception of things is no olympian detachment: to it Burke contributes the shape of his own complex origins, the experience of an Irish-born English statesman, of Catholic descent, confronted with the violent purism of revolution. It is convenient to summarize the French Revolution as a contest between Jacobinism and the *ancien régime*: in any such scheme of things, Burke is on the side of the ancients. But he spoke against France as an English Whig, one of the party who consolidated the bourgeois liberties of the constitution: in this he has some affinity, however estranged, with the underlying logic of Jacobinism. If this nexus were not sufficiently complicated, we add also that as a child of Irish Catholicism who increasingly responded to appeals from that quarter, he also spoke and wrote as the victim of triumphant English whiggery. That tragic note sounds the end of Burke's Augustanism, and heralds Yeats's distinctive assimilation of Burkean politics to a tragic aesthetic.

It was Oscar Wilde who observed that we have everything in common with the Americans – except language. And if late twentieth-century tourists are still discovering that words do not mean quite the same in Boston (Mass.) and Boston (Lincs.), it is no less true that the language of politics employed in the late eighteenth century by British and Irish alike had its hidden discrepancies. Where this condition bred new terms, or terms peculiar to one side of the debate, the problem was merely one of familiarity. Where the same word acquired diverging meanings, or developed a new meaning disguised as venerable usage, the results were less easy to control. Of course, to speak of words having meanings on some one-to-one basis is undoubtedly to invoke a concept of language now regarded as naive: this altered perspective on the relationship of language to reality is a further area in which the treachery of an ahistorical, timeless, and universal acceptance of words as fixed should be exposed. Moreover, in time the language of the Anglo-Irish debate is taken up into a growing literature: the relations between so-called ordinary language and literary discourse complicate our approach by positing formal synchronic patterns for analysis and admiration. When Yeats interrogates himself in 'The Man and the Echo'

> Did that play of mine send out
> Certain men the English shot?[7]

he is not inquiring as to his guilt in the matter of James Connolly's death in that he is not attending exclusively to the diachronic patterns of causation and responsibility. He is posing the question – in characteristically dialectical terms – as to how the language of literature relates to life, life here summoned up in the forceful image of death. His theoretical focus, that is, is upon the synthetic nature of literature. If, for a moment, we anticipate the entire extent and conclusion of this present argument, we can note a significant transition: we move from the antithesis of Augustanism to the synthesis of modernism. Neither antithesis nor synthesis is without its contradictions – or rather, Burke abandoned antithesis precisely because it no longer conveyed the full contradiction of the crisis he foresaw. And in Yeats such theoretical inquiries as those of 'The Man and the Echo' usually impinge upon politics with a special and urgent intimacy: it is as if the synthesis were anxious to demonstrate its appetite for 'the real' by publicly displaying the elements it thought to subsume. In due course we shall look

closely at major texts by Burke and Yeats with these general features in mind.
'l'he intervening years are vital to an understanding of the bonds which draw
Yeats and Burke together: divergences of meaning between Yeats's century
and Burke's are at least as treacherous as those between Boston (Mass.) and
Boston (Lincs.).

Ireland was strategically important in the king's realm: its inhabitants
formed a substantial proportion of his European subjects. Its governmental
structure resembled that of Britain: with a monarch (always the reigning
British king or queen), and a parliament consisting of Lords and Commons.
The manner in which the Irish parliament was subordinate to Westminster
and the English privy council need not detain us here, nor the means by
which in the eighteenth century it became the forum of an exclusively
Protestant élite. It is not the Protestantism of the Irish parliament which
distinguished that body from its English counterpart, but rather the differing
denominational allegiances of the parliament and the population *en masse*.
Nevertheless, that lack of concurrence in belief had its effect on the tone
of Irish Protestantism, which was on the whole theologically lower than the
English Established Church. Pluralism, absenteeism, and the use of
ecclesiastical office as a valued token in the system were perhaps no less
evident in Ireland than in England. Laxity, at least a marked lack of
enthusiasm for enthusiasm, was certainly to be detected in the Irish Church.
Transition to nineteenth-century conditions altered many aspects of this image
of Irish Protestantism. Extension of the franchise in the nineteenth century
in effect extended the areas of denominational conflict; and with the Oxford
Movement giving a higher tone to the English Church, and evangelicalism
penetrating the Irish, the isolation of Irish Protestantism grew on several
fronts. Protestant enthusiasm, fired by a new electoral battle with the Catholic
majority in Ireland and by a renewal of 'Reformation' zeal, became a means
towards political ends, and the legacy of that politicizing of the Irish
Protestant churches remains a volatile element in the politics of our own
period.

The very word 'Protestant' had diverging meanings in the two islands,
soon to be joined in the United Kingdom of Great Britain and Ireland.[8] For
the English, the Reformation produced two parties – the Anglican
(Established) Church and Protestant dissenters from the Church: for the
Irish, the distinction was more often between the Protestant (Established)
Church and various dissenting sects, Presbyterian for the most part. In the
twentieth century, the Irish usage has become blurred, but the present
writer's uncle, living in south Ulster in the 1950s, used to distinguish
(jocularly but with a recent propriety) between Protestants and Presbyterians.

Such instances in which Boston (Lincs.) and Boston (Cork) diverge in their use of a word may not seem important. But words combine to form potent and emotive phrases. It is true that in England and Ireland Protestant had its broad and inclusive meaning, and that the concurrence is of broader significance than the divergence. With the arrival of the Hanoverians anxiety about the Protestant Succession was greatly diminished by that dynasty's monotonous reliability in producing male heirs. But towards the end of the century, there emerged a new phrase in Ireland, Protestant Ascendancy, in which the reactions of a revolutionary age were quickly gathered. That now familiar phrase, transparent in its descent to the age of Yeats, is indeed treacherous with altered meanings.

Ascendancy is the central political idea under discussion, Edmund Burke the principal commentator on its emergence in the 1790s. As to the Protestantism of Protestant Ascendancy, two perspectives should be noted at this point. The first is the inclination of some elements in Irish dissent towards deism and to related political notions. These dissenting radicals were distinctively connected with trade, and regarded politics as a matter of commerce rather than theology. The Revd Edward Hudson, writing to the Earl of Charlemont on 5 July 1799 from Ballymena, County Antrim, described these emerging values as they were affected by the abortive rebellion of the previous year: his letter catches the shifting terminology of these new alignments and reactions:

> Things here wear a very different aspect from what they had done for some years past, and indeed, if ever people had reason to be thankful, they of this country have. It is literally a land flowing with gold and silver, which whoever has need not fear the want of milk and honey. Our northerns are not like Dublin tradesmen, who, when trade is good, work one day and drink two. On the contrary, they are working double tides to improve the favourable opportunity . . . The word 'Protestant', which was becoming obsolete in the north, has regained its influence, and all of that description seem drawing closer together. I only wish their affections may not be so entirely to each other as to exclude all others from a share of them. The Orange system has principally contributed to this. I was no friend to the introduction of it into this country, and it has in fact produced the evil I apprehended from it, but, I must confess, it has also produced good which I did not foresee, and which in the then state of the country I did not think could have been produced . . . Why, in the name of God, will they not leave us alone at such a time as this? Why interrupt that tide of prosperity which is flowing in upon us? What a stupid question! That very prosperity induces the attempt.[9]

Hudson is a shrewd witness to Protestant attitudes – his promised land of milk and honey is the profit earned by gold and silver. It is unlikely that

'Protestant' was in danger of becoming obsolete in Ulster prior to 1798, though the elements existing within the broader sense of the term were tending towards divergent political objectives. Certainly the aftermath of the abortive rebellion, together with a wartime economic boom, saw a gradual coming together of the reformed denominations, established and dissenting. The imminent Union with Britain, to which Hudson hesitantly refers in concluding his letter, involved promises of emancipation for Catholics to which the dominant Protestant interest objected. The bankers of Dublin, with the Orangemen, constituted a formidable opposition to Union, which only the appropriate arguments of reward and conjured-up papist aggression could overcome.

The second perspective in which the ascendancy of Protestantism should be considered refers to relations with Catholics rather than with fellow-Protestants. Hudson notes the feeling that Catholics are to be excluded from the affections of the converging Protestants 'and all of that description'. This growing antagonism is hardly new in itself – remember 1690, or 1641 for that matter – but there is a distinctive quality contributed to it by the revolutionary state of Europe. Edmund Burke had expressed the situation more trenchantly than Hudson, in a letter to his son:

> A very great part of the mischiefs that vex the world, arises from words. People soon forget the meaning, but the impression and the passion remain. The word Protestant is the charm that locks up in the dungeon of servitude three millions of your people. It is not amiss to consider this spell of potency, this abracadabra that is hung about the necks of the unhappy, not to heal, but to communicate disease. We sometimes hear of a Protestant *Religion*, frequently of a Protestant *interest*. We hear of the latter the most frequently, because it has a positive meaning. The other has none.[10]

Our two perspectives on the Protestantism of Protestant Ascendancy – a convergence of the reformed denominations, and a growing antagonism towards the Catholics – may of course be conflated. Hudson neatly translates the biblical land of milk and honey into the prosperity of his 'northerns': Burke insists that Protestantism is *interest*, not religion. Both are concerned to acknowledge the talismanic quality of such a word as Protestant: what lies between them in simple chronological terms is the rebellion in which Protestant-becoming-radical is defeated, and Catholic-becoming-rebel is exposed and exhibited. Burke did not live to see the rebellion he all but prophesied, and his was a darkly coloured testimony to sectarian feeling in the 1790s. An authenticating mark – and a limitation – of his account of Protestantism as interest is its ferocity; his account of the birth of Protestant Ascendancy is similarly compromised by the multitude of his own engagements in the image he strives to convey. A fuller investigation into the origins of Protestant Ascendancy will follow; for the moment we have noted its readiness on the margins of our argument, readiness to assume to a grander degree the hypnotic powers attributed by Burke to the phrase. From the literature of Yeats's age we know that those powers were exercised and remarkably transformed. It remains to be seen what particular vacuum will be appropriated by the new talisman.

Ireland, like Britain, was monarchy, aristocracy, and democracy; that is, it was ruled by 'kings, lords, and commons'. The theory was clear enough. In January 1792, it was summarized in the Irish parliament: 'Aristocracy . . . reflects lustre on the crown and lends support and effect to democracy while democracy gives vigour and energy to both, and the sovereignty crowns the constitution with dignity and authority . . .'.[11] This has a suitably Whiggish turn to it, for it is the work of Henry Grattan, doyen of Irish parliamentarians between the constitutional adjustment of 1782 and the Union of 1800. Though he is paraphrasing an English minister's definition, Grattan is also adhering to familiar and traditional explanations. Aristocracy is that element under the constitution which descends from the feudal order of nobles whose military service to the crown was rewarded with hereditary distinction. Of, course the British nobility included many who could not trace their titled line further back than a few generations, and the creation of new peerages was by no means restricted to military men. There was nevertheless a consensus of feeling that the British nobility, no matter how it had developed in post-medieval society, still perpetuated the spirit of its origins. The trouble in Ireland was that the prehistory, so to speak, of aristocracy, was entirely different.

The dislocated sense of an aristocracy in eighteenth-century Ireland has several sources. One of these was the disturbed and divisive history of the medieval period, and its survival in modern consciousness. Another, even more immediate in its impact, was the existence on the Continent (and to some extent at home) of a Catholic aristocracy bearing distinctly Irish titles but excluded from Irish political life. Some of these exiles were descendants of Elizabeth I's defeated Irish earls, others were Jacobite relics, the scions of 'Wild Geese' migrants. The twelfth baron Trimleston, petitioning for Catholic rights in 1759, had returned from exile in France, and had inherited his title and estates. This residual Catholic element among the bearers of Irish titles underlined the influx of newly created beneficiaries of recent confiscation and plantation. For those who had access to the Gaelic poetry of Dáibhí Ó Bruadair (1650-1694) and Aodhagáin O Rathaille (1670-1728) the superiority of the old aristocracy over the new was a familiar theme. In short, the history of the smaller island had seen the development of an Irish peerage with relations to society as a whole quite distinct from those which had given the English aristocracy its lustre.

There was a crucial extension to the evidence of the Irish aristocracy's dislocation from the ideal – the extensive use of the peerage as a form of political patronage. Within a hundred years its ranks almost doubled. R. B. McDowell neatly encapsulates the British attitude to Irish nobility by recording that

> on one occasion George I was said to have professed himself more ready to grant an Irish peerage than a K.B., adding for good measure that he could make a lord but not a gentleman; and George III, it was rumoured, when he would not permit a Welsh baronet to make an avenue from his house to Saint James's Park, softened the refusal by the offer of an Irish peerage.[12]

Thus, in addition to embodying in hereditary form the divisions of Irish history, the peerage also demonstrated Ireland's accessibility to the English administration in matters of rewards for services rendered. After 1782, the Irish opposition became especially interested in this debasement, as they saw it, of the Irish peerage. In his speech of 19 January 1792 from which we have already quoted, Grattan finally apostrophized the English minister he had paraphrased as

> He who sold the aristocracy and bought the democracy – he who best understands in practice what is this infusion of nobility – He who has infused poison into this aristocratic and this democratic division of power, and has crowned the whole with corruption. He well knows all this as far as Ireland is concerned, to be theatric representation, and that the constitution of the country is exactly the reverse of those scenes and farces which are acted on the public stages, of imposture and hypocrisy.[13]

It has been customary to regard this critique by Grattan and his associates of the Irish peerage in terms of Whig liberty. Certainly, the view of Grattan advanced by Yeats in the third section of 'The Tower' owes much to W. E. H. Lecky's consolidation of Grattan's reputation in his *Leaders of Public Opinion in Ireland*:

> I declare
> They shall inherit my pride,
> The pride of people that were
> Bound neither to Cause nor to State,
> Neither to slaves that were spat on,
> Nor to the tyrants that spat,
> The people of Burke and of Grattan
> That gave, though free to refuse –[14]

This is a further instance of Yeats's identification of the peasant and the nobleman, for those who shall inherit his pride are 'upstanding men That climb the streams until The fountain leap'. These lines intimately associate the Connemara fisherman and 'a rich man's flowering lawns' where

> Life overflows without ambitious pains;
> And rains down life until the basin spills.[15]

The evocation of Grattan's magnanimity, and the assumed empathy with Burke, are part of Yeats's transformation of history into symbol. In this the poet exploits the long-standing convention that the Irish parliament in its last two decades is referred to as Grattan's Parliament. If the poem is read as presenting in this third section a eulogy of Grattan, then what is suppressed is the impotence of Grattan's style, the isolation of those 'Bound neither to Cause nor to State', the purely oppositional nature of Grattan's condemnation of Irish aristocracy, 'tyrants that spat'. Many commentators evidently wish to read Yeats in this manner, and have no objection to the suppression in that the eulogy satisfies their sentiments. We may do the poet a greater service if we observe the aptness of his choosing as his spiritual forebear one whose style was only painfully related to his active life. Recently, the biographer of 'Speaker' Foster has declared sententious the explanation of Henry Grattan Junior that his father was 'too high to be sold to any Government', and has seen Grattan's refusal to serve in office as 'flamboyant coyness'.[16] There is certainly a discontinuity between the world of rhetorical trope and that of effective power; in Grattan's experience 'unity of being' was remote. John Fitzgibbon, essentially a pragmatist, felt that 'the recollection of Mr. Grattan's splendid periods is but a slender compensation for poverty and the most absolute dependence on Great Britain.'[17] That was in 1785: Burke's tribute in February 1792 effects a neat balance of Grattan's qualities, though the final clause is revealing:

> Grattans speech is a noble performance. He is a great man, eloquent in conception and in Language, and when that is the Case, being on the Right side is of some importance to the perfection of what is done. It is of great consequence to a Country to have men of Talents and Courage in it, though they have no power.[18]

The connection between Grattan's assault on the Irish peerage and his witholding himself from office should not be drawn too definitively in terms of magnanimity. There can be doubt that a public figure, who declines effective power in office, may yet exercise a beneficial influence on the manner in which the state's business is conducted. However, by the purely oppositional nature of Grattan's critique of Irish aristocracy, I do not simply mean that he was thoroughly opposed to its debasement: I mean that his attitude was shaped and informed purely by that which he opposed. He did not so much propose an alternative view of society, simply a selection of better individuals and better motives. According to Grattan's powerful ally, George Ponsonby, it was a favourite theme in 1792 'to accuse this side of the House as an aristocracy', and Anthony Malcomson has recently argued that the Ponsonby/Grattan notions of reform were aimed at increasing the representation of landed property rather than at a noble-minded giving though free to refuse.[19] What Grattan certainly feared and resented was the tendency towards 'the monarchy of clerks' by which all Irish interests were subordinated to a civil service directed from London.

Historians are familiar with the low reputation of the Irish peerage in the late eighteenth century. The *cause celèbre* in this regard is of course the Act of Union: to ensure its passage, the Crown promised sixteen new baronies and fifteen promotions of existing peers to higher ranks of the nobility.[20] In this way, the Union-title so neatly exemplified in Maria Edgeworth's Lord Clonbrony in *The Absentee* came into existence. It can be argued that twentieth-century notions of political morality should not be read back into a context where very different forms of pension and reward were employed – accordingly the Union-titles merely extend the pattern condemned by Grattan in 1792. But there was one crucial distinction between the creation of – say – eighteen new titles for the 1776 elections and the 1800 exercise. It is this, in the eighteenth century patronage was a reward for services rendered and still renderable: in 1800 the Irish parliamentarians rendered themselves incapable of service. This, at least, is an accepted view with much to recommend it: as Oliver MacDonagh has persuasively argued, the fecklessness displayed by Maria Edgeworth's Rackrents in her novel of 1800 is prophetic of nineteenth-century developments in Irish land-ownership.[21] However, the voluntary liquidation of the Irish parliament and the transfer of Irish representation to Westminster should also be seen in the broader context of European romantic nationalism, a creed which supplied new criteria for the embarrassment of the Irish aristocracy. For many reasons, therefore, we hear little of a positive nature about Irish aristocracy, as such, in the nineteenth century. The term had imploded into a functionless vacuum or was otherwise deprived of any power to impress. The eclipse of one term, however, may make possible the emergence and transformation of another. 'Ascendancy' gradually came to act in Hiberno-English debate many of the roles attributed to aristocracy in England. The means whereby this substitution occurred are not without irony, not without the treachery of altered meaning and forgotten history.

THE BIRTH OF ASCENDANCY

> Ascendancy – shows belief in astrology
> (J. M. Synge)[22]

In the matter of Anglo-Irish culture of the late eighteenth century Edmund Burke is an expert witness. That is, he knows too much. An impartial committee of inquiry is readily confused and irritated by the kind of familiarity and intimacy which Burke lends to his testimony. He is unwilling (and, at times, unable) to reduce his experience to the categories of objectivity. His thought runs ahead to the consequences of an argument, or runs back to the origins of a complaint. It is not that he lacks sagacity or a sense of occasion: on the contrary, his public utterances on Ireland roll with the same music as the *Reflections on the Revolution in France*. There is, however, another side to Burke to which the modern reader has access, the private side of the orator as revealed in his voluminous correspondence. From a consideration of both sides of the witness, we can now see that Burke is not only expert witness, but also prosecutor, plaintiff, and accused.

He had been born in 1729, the second son of Richard Burke, a Dublin attorney. The elder Burke had been a Catholic, and his wife (a Miss Nagle) continued to practise her religion privately. Edmund was educated as a Protestant, entered Trinity College, Dublin, and subsequently the Middle Temple in London. He married Jane Nugent in 1756, whose father Christopher remained a Catholic and a friend of Samuel Johnson's. Burke's career lay almost entirely in England, first as journalist, writer, and secretary, and – after 1765 – as an MP in the Whig interest. He visited Ireland on a number of occasions, but there is no historical foundation for Yeats's line in 'The Seven Sages':

> THE FIRST My great-grandfather spoke to Edmund Burke
> In Grattan's house.[23]

Despite his career in Westminster, Burke remained attached to the country of his birth, championing Irish trade and Catholic emancipation. It is particularly worth noting the coinciding of his campaign against France (commencing in 1790 with the *Reflections*) with his growing commitment to emancipation for Catholics and with his anxiety concerning conditions in Ireland. The ill-fated experiment of appointing Burke's patron, the Earl Fitzwilliam, as Lord-Lieutenant in Ireland marked a key moment in his relationship with his homeland. From the recall of Fitzwilliam in February 1795 to his own death in July 1797, Burke's letters are dominated by the imminence of death and inescapable conflict in Ireland. In December 1796, he wrote to the Revd Thomas Hussey, later Catholic bishop of Waterford:

> You state, what has long been but too obvious, that it seems the unfortunate policy of the Hour, to put to the far largest portion of the Kings Subjects in Ireland, the desperate alternative, between a thankless acquiescence under grievous Oppression, or a refuge in Jacobinism with all its horrors and all its crimes. You prefer the former dismal part of the choice. There is no doubt but that you would have reasons if the election of one of these Evils was at all a security against the other. But they are things very alliable and as closely connected as cause and effect. That Jacobinism, which is Speculative in its Origin, and which arises from Wantonness and fullness of bread, may possibly be kept under by firmness and prudence. The very levity of character which produces it may extinguish it; but the Jacobinism which arises from Penury and irritation, from scorned loyalty, and rejected Allegiance, has much deeper roots. They take their nourishment from the bottom of human Nature and the unalterable constitution of things, and not from humour and caprice or the opinions of the Day about privileges and Liberties.[24]

Burke's sense of the inadequacies of antithesis is evident here. 'If the election of one of these Evils was at all a security against the other' is a conditional clause from which Irish Catholics might derive no security whatever. The letter to Hussey is valuable in that it reveals the vigour – not to say, violence – of Burke's feelings, vigour which was more harmoniously arranged in some of his published comments. It also reveals the identification of opposites which gives to his thought a dialectical compaction and concreteness. It is part of his withering irony to dramatize this tragic pact between the upholders of the Protestant Succession in Ireland and the Jacobins of Paris by means of transferring epithets: thus, the Dublin administration becomes 'the Irish Directory' and Napoleon is 'the Zealous Protestant Buonaparté' whose successes are greeted as 'Protestant Victories on the plains of Lombardy'.[25] There is more to this tactic than a juggling of words, a rearrangement of the terms of a trope: the central implication of Burke's account is that the Catholics of Ireland cannot succeed in their legitimate demands against such a combination of hostile foes.

But Burke's scathing use of Protestant as a synonym for Jacobin or Bonapartist should not lead us to assume him a zealous Catholic partisan. In his early writing on the Penal Laws, he was at pains to speak of 'our common Christianity',[26] and in his letter of 1795 to William Smith he commends particular attention to 'the great points in which the leading divisions are agreed'.[27] He was often accused of secret devotion to the sacraments of the Catholic Church, but the motive was generally malicious.

Undoubtedly Burke's imagination had a decidedly Christian shape – fortitude and charity are characteristic forms which his advice takes in moments of crisis. But even the distressed letters written after the death of his beloved son, Richard, reveal a philosophical temper within his religious belief. In a public pamphlet he described his grief and his consolation:

> The storm has gone over me; and I lie like one of those old oaks which the late hurricane has scattered about me. I am stripped of all my honours; I am torn up by the roots, and lie prostrate on the earth! There, and prostrate there, I most unfeignedly recognize the divine justice, and in some degree submit to it.[28]

The gradually emerging repetitions, and the modulated qualification of the last phrase, reveal Burke as peculiarly sensitive to the manner in which language acts upon feeling. If he employs terms like Protestant provocatively, it is not simply because of his Catholic ancestry: the roots of his late assault upon the Irish Directory lie in his lifelong interest in the language of history. When we look to his account of Protestant Ascendancy, we should recall not only his vigour but also his philosophical temper, his long meditation on Irish affairs and his more immediate anxiety.

Burke's view of history was not so much Irish or English but Anglican. He was profoundly appreciative of the *via media* which the Church of England had established, and had no sympathy with papal medievalism or unitarian anarchy. His more extended writings on Irish history reflect this latitudinarian position while striving simultaneously to respond to deteriorating conditions among the religious factions in Ireland. The *Tracts on the Popery Laws* date from 1765 and arise directly from the recent outbreak of sectarian violence which had touched on his own family. The various letters of the 1790s – to Hercules Langrishe, William Smith, and to his son Richard – are no less implicated in the atmosphere of increasing communal tension. One constant principle of his argument is that, whatever Irish Catholics may or may not have done in the reign of Charles I or Elizabeth, the perpetuation of punishment upon succeeding generations is foolishly divisive. Nor is it legislation alone which perpetuates division; the writing of history is itself an intervention into events which might otherwise be more harmoniously shaped. Referring to the works of Clarendon and Temple, he deplores

> those miserable performances which go about under the names of Histories of Ireland [and which] do indeed represent those events after this manner; and they would persuade us, contrary to the known order of Nature, that indulgence and moderation in Governors is the natural incitement in subjects to rebel.[29]

It is Burke's repeated belief that a relaxation of the laws restricting the rights of Catholics would produce a greater integration of the king's Irish subjects into his realms. In the 1765 *Tracts*, however, he juxtaposes to Clarendon and Temple an alternative record:

> But there is an interior History of Ireland, the genuine voice of its records and monuments, which speaks a very different language from these histories, from Temple and from Clarendon, these restore Nature to its just rights, and policy to its proper order.[30]

We detect here the pre-romantic philosopher of the sublime and the beautiful rather than the author of the *Reflections*; monuments and inner histories are the stuff of mid-century antiquarianism. Though the *Tracts* remained unpublished in Burke's lifetime one can see him entering a crucial and timely qualification to this view in the *Letter to Richard Burke* (1792):

> The miserable Natives of Ireland, who ninety-nine in an hundred are tormented with quite other cares, and are bowed down to labour for the bread of the hour, are not, as gentlemen pretend, plodding with antiquaries for titles of centuries ago to the estates of the great Lords and 'Squires, for whom they labour.[31]

Gentlemen's suspicions of antiquarian research as the latest form of Catholic conspiracy should be considered in the context of a new romantic interest in the past. Sylvester O'Halloran's *General History of Ireland* (1774), Joseph Cooper Walker's *Historical Memoirs of the Irish Bards* (1786), and Charlotte Brooke's *Reliques of Irish Poetry* (1789) are the better-known examples of a movement in historiography to which Burke had made his slight contribution in 1765.[32] The *General History* was to have an influence on Standish O'Grady in the 1870s akin to religious conversion, and in the 1830s the Ordnance Survey discovered that inquiries into local tradition and genealogy produced embarrassing evidence of an 'interior history'.[33] Such consequences did not attend the early antiquarians to any notable extent, though it is noteworthy that the antiquarian O'Halloran in Maria Edgeworth's *The Absentee* plays a central role in reconciling past and present, Jacobite and Williamite. What is significant in the 1790s is not so much the achievement of the researchers as the trepidation of the 'gentlemen'. And Burke's timely qualification is in part designed to placate their anxieties.

These anxieties had European as well as local causes. The French Revolution, though welcomed by the Whigs in general, was soon interpreted as having radical implications for British society. Raymond Williams has discussed the manner in which Jane Austen's fiction relates, not to a *settled* landed society, but to a society in which land is either held or sought as a palpable form of security in a time of great social change.[34] Back in 1765 Burke had already recognized the conserving inertia of property, and found the exclusion of Catholics from long leases positively a threat to social stability:

> This confinement of landed property to one set of hands, and preventing its free circulation through the community, is a most leading article of ill policy; because it is one of the most capital discouragements to all that industry which may be employed on the lasting improvement of the soil . . .[35]

By the 1790s the rights of Catholics to hold land had been modified, but the apprehension of Protestants that their monopoly was thereby threatened increased in proportion to the European crisis rather than the local one. Burke is remarkable for the manner in which he sees economic policy, religious bias, and historiography as forming a coherent social and cultural pattern. Those upon whom he was soon to turn his scorn were remarkable for the manner in which they substituted the single concept or slogan of Protestant Ascendancy for the complexity of a society in crisis.

The progress of the French Revolution required of the British government some further reconciliation with the king's Catholic subjects in Ireland. An unsettled Ireland was a dangerous breach in Britain's defences, and since 1782 (and earlier) Ireland had displayed a plethora of discontents. Political radicalism among Presbyterians and traditional petitions for restored civil rights from Catholics were further complicated by the spread of violence in the countryside. Protestant Peep O' Day Boys and Catholic Defenders were active from the late 1780s onwards, and the Orange Order was born in 1795 as the consequence of accelerating sectarian strife. If the Defenders had some ancestry in the Whiteboy movement of mid-century, and if their name truly reflects some initial emphasis on defensive tactics, the Protestant 'grass roots' organizations represented a new element in Irish unrest. Explicitly sectarian in composition, they approached social and economic matters on the assumption of a supremacy as much mythological as historical. Burke was quite capable of seeing incidents of sectarian prejudice in exaggerated terms, and he may never have fully grasped the implications of the new movement among the Protestant tenantry. In 1792, however, he concentrated most effectively and ironically on the slogan of the hour, Protestant Ascendancy.

It would be foolish to attempt to establish the exact moment at which the phrase was conceived. The elements of the term are, after all, common enough in themselves – even if we make allowances for the slippery meaning of Protestant in Anglo-Irish affairs. Thomas Leland, whose *History of Ireland* escaped Burke's comment in the *Times* by appearing in 1773, is said to have been fully aware of the false colouring of his work and to have justified himself by claiming a need to support 'the English ascendancy in Ireland since the reformation'.[36] By this token, ascendancy is the condition enjoyed by those principles or forces which predominate or are in the ascendant in the sense that a planet may be said to be so. Dr Johnson, in his dictionary, illustrates the word by a quotation from Watts which has, for us, an ironical application – 'Custom has some ascendancy over understanding, and what at one time seemed decent, appears disagreeable afterwards.'[37] As a potent collocation, Protestant Ascendancy may be dated with some certainty to the early weeks of 1792, when Hercules Langrishe and others were active in reviving proposals for a generous restoration of civil rights to Irish Catholics. Given the subsequent currency of the phrase, in particular given the manner in which Yeats will deploy it while invoking Edmund Burke as his mentor, a close history of its evolution in 1792 is called for.

By the end of 1791 the British government were resolved on a relaxation of the penal laws in Ireland. The relative independence of the Dublin parliament together with the complexity of any negotiation with the Irish establishment presented a considerable obstacle to their intentions. On 26 December, Henry Dundas, the Home Secretary, wrote both an official and a private letter to the Earl of Westmorland, the Lord-Lieutenant in Dublin Castle. Emphasizing the importance of conceding this reform to achieve harmony between the two kingdoms, Dundas made it plain that Irish Protestant resistance to the king's advisers and their plans would serve only to isolate them from the traditional support they enjoyed in their relations with Westminster. Westmorland replied in some consternation on 11 January 1792, and while he stressed the strength of the 'Protestant gentry', of the 'Protestant interest', and, bluntly, 'Protestant power', there is no sign of the phrase 'Protestant Ascendancy'.[38] More precisely, the word 'ascendancy' is cited only in such a way as to indicate that its imminent collocation with 'Protestant' has as yet no currency. Proposals to enfranchise Catholics, even if limited to elections for county seats, would mean that 'they would gradually gain an ascendancy, and would so on be enabled to make a successful attack on the tithes and established clergy, so odious to themselves and the Presbyterians . . .'.[39] Between 11 and 14 January, Westmorland communicated the gist of Dundas's dispatch to 'the principal persons called the Irish cabinet', to John Fitzgibbon (the Lord Chancellor), John Beresford, Charles Agar (the Archbishop of Cashel), Sir John Parnell, the Attorney-General, and the Prime Sergeant:

They all agree in the impracticability of carrying in Parliament either the Point
of Arms or Franchise & in the impolicy of attempting it, & they foresee the
Ruin of the Protestant Ascendancy of the Peace & Quiet of the Country in
success of such a proposal.[40]

This less than articulate letter is the earliest (quasi-) official context in which
'the Protestant Ascendancy' has been found. Westmorland's earlier letter,
by not using it, suggests that the phrase may have been introduced at his
meeting with Fitzgibbon, Beresford, and the others. (Indeed it is tempting
to consider the Lord Chancellor as its possible sponsor, bearing in mind
his immediate Catholic forebears.) Within a few days, Major Robert Hobart,
the Chief Secretary, in writing to Dundas repeatedly used the phrase to emphasize the strength of resistance to reform: more particularly he insisted that

the connection between England and Ireland rests absolutely upon the Protestant ascendancy. Abolish distinctions, and you create a Catholic superiority.
If you are to maintain a Protestant Ascendancy, it must be by substituting influence for numbers.[41]

These contexts, whether in Westmorland's correspondence or Hobart's, are,
however, private, and do not amount to more than a couple of letters written within less than a week of each other. The day after Hobart wrote to
Dundas, Westmorland wrote to the Prime Minister, Pitt, detailing the constitution and social structure of Ireland so frankly as to accept Edmund
Burke's term for the situation prior to 1782 as appropriate to conditions
ten years later:

That frame is a Protestant garrison (in the words of Mr. Burke), in possession
of the land, magistracy, and power of the country; holding that property under
the tenure of British power and supremacy, and ready at every instant to crush
the rising of the conquered. If under various circumstances their generals should
go a little refractory, do you lessen your difficulties or facilitate the means of
governing, by dissolving their authority and trusting to your popularity and
good opinion with the common soldiers of the conquered? Allegory apart,
do you conceive England can govern Ireland by the popularity of the
government?[42]

And to drive home the point about estates held under British tenure, and
as the result of conquest, there was the rising murmur among Protestant
landowners, as Westmorland acknowledged, 'the lower Catholics already
talk of their ancient family estates.'[43] These confidential exchanges between
Dublin and London, in which the phrase Protestant Ascendancy emerges
alongside talk of renaissant Catholic claims to land and title, were due to
receive a resounding endorsement in the public forum of the Irish parliament

meeting on 19 January 1792. And yet it was not parliament, but a lesser assembly, which seized upon the new coinage.

The debate on Langrishe's proposals has already been cited in support of Grattan's position at this time. In reply to Langrishe's notion for a relief bill, the member for County Wexford, George Ogle, declared

> for my part, Sir, I ever have maintained, and with my last breath I will maintain the protestant ascendancy; – nor can I think it within the power of human wisdom to do any thing effectual for the Roman Catholics, without endangering that ascendancy in church and state.[44]

It is clear from this, as from Hobart's letter, that the phrase is used as the equivalent to Protestant interest (or to the ascendancy of Protestantism) and not to any specific social 'class' or party. As yet there is no sense of the phrase meaning the Protestant gentry, or indeed the Protestant aristocracy. That such a collective noun should be discerned is quickly evident – the same morphosis is occurring to aristocracy in the 1790s. Wolfe Tone, of all people, on 23 July 1792 confides in his journal that 'the Catholics and the Protestant ascendancy are left to fight it out'.[45] At the same time he records that 'wherever there was a meeting of the Protestant ascendancy, which was the title assumed by that party (and a very impudent one it was), we took care it should be followed by a meeting of the Catholics . . .'.[46] But before the collective noun emerged, some definition had to be imposed as much on the public mind as on the words of the new slogan.

Ogle's phrase and sentiment was to recur throughout the debate in parliament, but elsewhere in Dublin a more extended definition of its meaning was imminent. On Friday 20 January 1792, the Christmas Assembly of the city Corporation met in the Exhibition House, William Street. The ninth item of business resulted in a committee's being established 'to prepare an address to his majesty expressive of our attachment to his majesty's person, family, and government, and our determination to support the present constitution both in church and state'. As the committee's efforts have enshrined one of Anglo-Ireland's most evocative phrases in our rhetoric, it is only proper to record the participants: they were the Recorder (Denis George), with six Aldermen (William Alexander, John Carleton, John Exshaw, Henry Howison, William James, and Nathaniel Warren), and six members of the common council (John Giffard, Ambrose Leet, and Messrs Manders, Powell, Sall, and Twaites.) The address they prepared reads in full:

> To the king's most excellent majesty.
> The humble address of the Lord Mayor, Sheriffs, commons, and citizens of the city of Dublin.

May it please your majesty.
We, your majesty's most dutiful and loyal subjects, the Lord Mayor, Sheriffs, commons, and citizens of the city of Dublin in common council assembled, beg leave to approach the throne with the most unshaken sentiments of loyalty and affectionate regards for your majesty's person, family, and government.

Sensibly impressed with the value of our excellent constitution both in church and state, as established at the glorious revolution, we feel ourselves peculiarly called upon to stand forward at the present crisis to pray your majesty to preserve the Protestant ascendancy in Ireland inviolate and to assure your majesty that we are firmly resolved to support it free from innovation and are determined most zealously to oppose any attempt to overturn the same, having a firm reliance on the attachment of your majesty and that of your royal progeny to that constitution, which the house of Brunswick was called forth to defend.

In testimony whereof, we have caused the common seal of the said city to be hereonto affixed this 20th day of January, in the year of our Lord, 1792.[47]

This is the first stage of the definition of Protestant Ascendancy, which the Corporation will carry a stage further in September of the same year. The crucial development is the identification of ascendancy with the constitution itself, with the principles of the glorious revolution, rather than simply with 'the Protestant interest' or 'Protestant power'. In due course the Corporation transmitted its address to the king through the offices of the Lord-Lieutenant, and proceeded to convey the same sentiments to the two members sitting for the city constituency. These were Henry Grattan and Lord Henry Fitzgerald, brother to Lord Edward Fitzgerald who was to die six years later while resisting arrest as leader of the United Irishmen rebellion. Grattan and Lord Henry were entreated to 'oppose with all your influence and great abilities any alteration that may tend to shake the security of property in this kingdom or subvert the Protestant ascendancy in our happy constitution'.[48] In addition, the Corporation ordered the publication of its address in the *Dublin Journal* and the *Dublin Evening Post*, and the dispatch of copies to the chief magistrates of the cities and corporate towns in the country.[49]

With the English government keen to accommodate the discontented Catholics, the Irish opposition in full cry for reform, and the Catholics themselves organized and articulate, the Corporation may well have feared that parliament might have been carried over in the heat of the moment into an extension of Catholic rights damaging to Protestant interests. And whereas parliament was representative principally of land and patronage, the Corporation had a real interest in maintaining the privileges of Irish Protestants as they bore upon commerce and the professions. Langrishe

wished to see Catholics free to participate equally in trade and the learned
professions, free to bear arms, to intermarry with Protestants, and to vote.
'The Point of Arms' and the franchise were rights which none of
Westmorland's advisers could recommend, for the first would have effectively eliminated the convenient state of affairs whereby only government
supporters among the lower orders had legal access to firearms, while the
second would have soon threatened the permanence of the government itself.
'Mr. Beresford expresses the strongest attachment', Westmorland had
reported, '& desires to do whatever his opinion could justify, but could not
declare even to support any concession without Ld Waterford's approba-
tion, whose opinions at their last conversation were averse.' As for the Archbishop of Cashel, he 'was unwilling to relax at all, tho he saw no mischief
in allowing them admission to Trades & liberty of education, he was averse
to admission to the Law & even intermarriage . . .'[50]

The Corporation of Dublin spoke clearly of 'the security of property',
and in the eyes of a hostile newspaper its motives were basely monopolist:

> We cannot but admire the *modesty* of the Board of Aldermen, in pretending
> to address the worthy representatives of the city of Dublin, to support their
> *alert combination*, in favour of their own authority and consequence: and to
> keep away any possibility of being brought to share the good things of the
> city, with any of their fellow subjects of a certain description – city leases,
> city Maces, city monopolies, and contracts are eligible *douceurs*, which the
> good and loving master G— , with all his tender regards, cannot possibly allow
> his Catholic friends to be troubled with any share of.[51]

The sly association of the Aldermen with the subversive combinations of
working men is part of a deflating metaphor which runs through the *Morning
Post*'s commentary. In its view what is at stake is not the constitution but
material rewards of a municipal monopoly. The *Dublin Chronicle*, reporting
the Corporation proceedings, records that 'Messrs Howison, Saul, Powell,
Cope, Giffard and some other Members spoke in terms of warm condemnation' of Catholic aspirations.[52] Cope it was who moved that an address
be presented, with Bond and Binns objecting. The participation of the common members in the debate underlines its essentially merchant priorities.
Giffard, whom the *Morning Post* singled out for ridicule, was an apothecary
by trade, who advanced himself by an appointment as surveyor and gauger
to the Custom House site when that development was floated under John
Beresford's auspices. In 1792, he represented the Apothecary's Guild on
the Corporation, and was an intermediary linking the Castle and a spy among
the United Irishmen: in 1795 he was dismissed from a post on the *Dublin
Journal* and in need of cash from the Lord-Lieutenant if he were to avoid

ruin.[53] John Giffard, apothecary, gauger, middleman spy, and journalist, is significant not because his fellow members of the Corporation may with facility be symbolized in his career, but because his advancement and insecurity together summarize the conditions which called forth 'Protestant Ascendancy'. The phrase is traceable from Dublin Castle to the parliament in College Green, and thence to the Corporation where the involvement of the guild members was prominent. The January initiative did not in itself succeed, and the Chief Secretary wrote to Westmorland that 'all idea of a Catholic game (if ever such was entertained) is at an end, and that the British Government will decidedly support the Protestant Ascendency.'[54] When Burke came to discuss the emergence of the new phrase he dwelt with a sardonic emphasis on the to-and-fro trading between Corporation and Castle, and on the mentality which characterized Catholic aspirations as a game.

Edmund Burke's involvement in the struggle for Catholic rights was maintained primarily through his son, Richard, who was employed by the Catholic Committee as its agent. Young Burke had come to Dublin on 13 January, and participated in the discussions leading to the parliamentary debate. The House of Commons returned to the issue in February, and in the renewed debate greater attention was given to the meaning of the concept of Protestant Ascendancy. Keen to insist that Irish Protestants should themselves decide the fate of the Catholic question, Richard Sheridan (not the dramatist) advised that

> the Roman Catholics of Ireland may now learn, that it is to the wisdom and liberality of the Protestants of Ireland they ought to look, and that foreign or ministerial negociation [sic] must be ever suspicious and never successful; every man must agree, that they are entitled to every benefit and advantage compatible with the preservation of the Protestant ascendancy . . .[55]

Grattan's parliament is renowned for its achievement of a limited independence from Westminster, and its critics deplored the unreformed basis of its representation in so far as it placed this independence potentially under the control of the intransigents. Sheridan's speech is not untypical of the prickly Irish Protestant insistence on rights surpassing those of the British parliament. Fear of Catholic alliances with French or other external radicals was entirely understandable; fear of negotiations with government ministers is symptomatic of that inwardly directed strategy which was to characterize the culture of the 'Protestant Ascendancy' in the nineteenth century. Sheridan's attitude to Langrishe's renewed proposal was far from dismissive, he thought three of its four proposals 'innocent, perhaps desirable', but he proceeded to elaborate his notion of ascendancy in such a way as to transform his reservation into a veto: as he knew that

'Protestant ascendancy,' might be used perhaps by some in a very narrow, and by others in a too enlarged sense, he begged leave to submit his idea of Protestant ascendancy to the House: by Protestant ascendancy he meant, a Protestant king, to whom only being Protestant we owed allegiance; a Protestant house of peers, composed of Protestant lords spiritual in Protestant succession, of Protestant lords temporal, with Protestant inheritance, and a Protestant house of commons, elected and deputed by Protestant constitutents; in short a Protestant legislative, a Protestant judicial, and a Protestant executive, in all and each of their varieties, degrees, and gradations.[56]

If we recall, however, that broadly similar disabilities were maintained in Britain and that the centrality of religious conformism was a self-evident truth in the late eighteenth century, then the resistance of Irish Protestants can be seen as something more than the defence of commercial and social advantage. The real contrast in the argument is not so much between Catholic and Protestant; but between those like Sheridan and Ogle and, shortly, the Corporation of Dublin who expressed loyalty to Protestant*ism* rather than to king or parliament on the one hand, and those on the other hand like Grattan and Burke who acknowledged the primacy of social relations in discussing matters of individual religious belief. If we are here witnessing the public baptism of what W. B. Yeats will later call 'the Protestant Ascendency with its sense of responsibility',[57] we are also witnessing the early exertions of a new force, described by Grattan as Protestant bigotry without religion. This ideology, descending from the intransigents of Grattan's parliament to the generation of Ian Paisley, is necessarily contradictory: asserting the absolute value of Protestantism above all calculations of social amelioration, it nevertheless founds itself upon ascendancy within society, ascendancy in matters of education, trade, property, political participation. To the eighteenth-century mind, even to the ecclesiastical mind of that period, 'Protestant' connoted certain principles in relation to Christian belief. Protestant*ism* was likely to substitute the protest for the belief. It is this which Burke alludes to in the *Letter to Richard Burke* when he observes sardonically, 'we sometimes hear of a Protestant *Religion*, frequently of a Protestant *interest*. We hear of the latter the most frequently, because it has a positive meaning. The other has none.'[58]

Richard Burke's letters to his father in January and February 1792 form one of the most important accounts of the emergence of Protestant Ascendancy. The phrase, as we have seen, occurred in Ogle's speech of 19 January and is expanded in the Corporation's address to the king the following evening. Young Burke, however, does not use the phrase until about 1 March when he dismisses 'the foolish partizans of the protestant ascendancy' and

'the ascendancy gentlemen'.[59] As late as 6 October he is referring to the
Protestant Ascendancy as 'a new name which the enemies of the Catholics
have adopted'.[60] But before that date his father turned his formidable
rhetorical skills to an analysis of what may be very properly called the new
coinage. Given the concentrated analysis of our phrase, it seems likely that
Richard's letter of *c.* 1 March stimulated his father's endeavours.

The *Letter to Richard Burke* remains unfinished, and it lacks perhaps the
polish of those productions which Burke was able to revise at leisure.[61] Yet
leisure was not always the most conducive state in which he worked, and
the nervous energy of Burke's focus is complementary to the solemn archi-
tectonics of his reflectionary style. Here the object under scrutiny is neither
the idealized past nor the conjured distortions of a Jacobin future; it is a
distinctively shifting and treacherous present:

A word has been lately struck in the mint of the Castle of Dublin; thence
it was conveyed to the Tholsel, or City-hall, where having passed the touch
of the Corporation, – so respectably stamped and vouched, it soon became
current in Parliament, and was carried back by the Speaker of the House of
Commons in great pomp, as an offering of homage from whence it came. The
word is *ascendancy*. It is not absolutely new. But the sense in which I have
hitherto seen it used, was to signify an influence obtained over the minds of
some other person by love and reverence, or by superior management and
dexterity. It had, therefore, to this its promotion, no more than a moral, not
a civil or political use. But I admit it is capable of being so applied; and if
the Lord Mayor of Dublin, and the Speaker of the Irish Parliament, who
recommend the preservation of the Protestant ascendancy, mean to employ
the word in that sense, that is, if they understand by it the preservation of
the influence of that description of gentlemen over the Catholicks, by means
of an authority derived from their wisdom and virtue, and from an opinion
they raise in that people of a pious regard and affection for their freedom and
happiness, it is impossible not to commend their adoption of so apt a term
into the family of politicks. It may be truly said to enrich the language. Even
if the Lord Mayor and Speaker mean to insinuate that this influence is to be
obtained and held by flattering their people, by managing them by skilfully
adapting themselves to the humours and passions of those whom they would
govern, he must be a very untoward critick who would cavil even at this use
of the word, though such cajoleries would perhaps be more prudently practised than professed. These are all meanings laudable, or at least tolerable.
But when we look a little more narrowly, and compare it with the plan to which
it owes its present technical application, I find it has strayed far from its original
sense. It goes much further than the privilege allowed by Horace. It is more
than *parce detorsum*. This Protestant ascendancy means nothing less than an
influence obtained by virtue, by love, or even by artifice and seduction; full

no little an influence derived from the means by which Ministers have obtained an influence, which might be called, without straining, an *ascendancy* in publick Assemblies in England, that is, by a liberal distribution of places and pensions and other graces of Government. This last is wide indeed of the signification of the word. New *ascendancy* is the old mastership. It is neither more nor less than the resolution of one set of people in Ireland, to consider themselves as the sole citizens in the commonwealth; and to keep a dominion over the rest by reducing them to absolute slavery, under a military power; and thus fortified in their power, to divide the publick estate, which is the result of general contribution, as a military booty, solely amongst themselves.[62]

So far Burke has concentrated solely upon the application of the word ascendancy to the new local policy, directed against proposals to grant Catholics civil rights, and he has found disturbing innovations in the usage. His manner is as much hesitant as strategically devious, and his sentences run ahead of the rhythm of his argument. The initial conceit of the phrase as a coinage minted by the public authorities, and then stamped and approved for circulation, is not maintained; instead there follows an involuted recourse to the previous history of ascendancy as a moral term untouched by political or civil usage. This attention to the word as such is then followed by a comparison between ascendancy as it might be achieved by a statesman in the public assemblies of England and the latest Irish usage. 'A *liberal* distribution' [emphasis now added] of patronage evidently distinguishes the English practice from the Irish. With this indirect critique of Irish nepotism, he finally defines new ascendancy as the old mastership.

This is only half of Burke's meditation on the term; he now turns his attention to the Protestant element in Protestant Ascendancy and once again stresses the potency of language as such:

The poor word ascendancy, so soft and melodious in its sound, so lenitive and emollient in its first usage, is now employed to cover to the world, the most rigid and perhaps not the most wise of all plans of policy. The word is large enough in its comprehension. I cannot conceive what mode of oppression in civil life, or what mode of religious persecution, may not come within the methods of preserving an *ascendancy*. In plain old English, as they apply it, it signifies *pride and dominion* on the one part of the relation, and on the other *subserviency and contempt* – and it signifies nothing else. The old words are as fit to be set to musick as the new; but use has long since affixed to them their true signification, and they sound, as the other will, harshly and odiously to the moral and intelligent ears of mankind.

This ascendancy, by being a *Protestant* ascendancy, does not better it from the combination of a note or two more in this anti-harmonick scale. If Protestant

ascendancy means the proscription from citizenship of by far the major part
of the people of any Country, then Protestant ascendancy is a bad thing; and
it ought to have no existence. But there is a deeper evil. By the use that is
so frequently made of the term, and the policy which is engrafted on it, the
name Protestant becomes nothing more or better than the name of a persecuting
faction, with a relation of some sort of theological hostility to others, but without
any sort of ascertained tenets of its own, upon the ground of which it persecutes
other men; for the patrons of this Protestant ascendancy neither do nor can,
by any thing positive, define or describe what they mean by the word Protestant. It is defined, as Cowley defines wit, not by what it is, but by what it
is not.[63]

Once again we can see Burke wrestling with a novel concept. The direction
of his analysis is by now familiar enough. A significant assumption, however,
is that the penal laws did not so much *restrict* the rights of Irish Catholics
as *exclude* them from citizenship. This emphasis becomes important when
Burke develops it in relation to the way in which Protestant Ascendancy
will exacerbate 'that worst of all oppressions, the persecutions of private
Society, and private manners'.[64] The sub-title of Maria Edgeworth's *Castle
Rackrent*, 'an Hibernian tale taken from the facts, and from the manners
of the Irish squires before the year 1782', indicates the extent to which the
novelist approaches society through the microcosm of manners.

Burke's analysis of the new slogan was written in England, in the form
of a letter to his son intended from the outset for publication; although it
may have been commenced before May 1792, when the first portion of a
collected *Works* appeared, the text was unfinished. From this circumstance
we can identify a certain urgent irresolution in Burke's thought on the subject. His letters written later in the year substantiate this conclusion by revealing further evidence of his exploratory and yet vigorous interrogation of the
phrase. One reason for his difficulty was simply distance from the centre
of debate; another was the involuted nature of the debate, generating greater
psychic tension in the participants than observers might at first have found
reasonable. In the Irish House of Commons, the most extensive and accessible account of Ascendancy came – not surprisingly – from Grattan himself.
Richard Burke provided his father with an amusing account of the February
debate, juxtaposing the intransigents and Grattan very effectively:

> Then all the fiery protestants got up and unbottelled their nonsense; when
> they had exhaust'd themselves they began to be a little ashamed of themselves,
> and after two or three just and grave lectures from the other side, they intirely
> changed their tone; It was at last 'our catholic brethren' and the idea of *perpetual*
> exclusion from the franchise, was generally exploded; tho' when ever any of

them argued the point it was upon principles which go to perpetuity and with
increasing strength. If the Ponsonbys had not bitch'd the question and played
the fool, we should have made a great figure even on the division. Grattan
reserved himself to the last and did admirably. Tho' we divided but 25. I know
from the best authority, that there were 50 in the majority who were with us
in their hearts.[65]

Richard did not possess his father's penetrating knowledge of Irish politics
and the deviousness of great factions like that of the Ponsonby brothers.
The elder Burke, however, fully agreed with his son's estimate of Grattan's
performance, and it was on this occasion that he recorded his tribute to Grattan's eloquence and nobility, ending with the telling clause about men of
talents and courage who lack power.[66] Though Grattan's reputation has inevitably suffered since the panegyrics of his son were transposed into art
by W. B. Yeats, his speech on Protestant Ascendancy shows considerable
sensitivity to broader movements in European thought than those of Dublin
Corporation or the Catholic Committee.

Grattan's speech begins by summarizing very succinctly the existing laws
restricting the rights of Catholics, and proceeds immediately to detail three
recent controversies on the subject of political freedom – America, Ireland
in 1782, France in 1789 – which underline the urgency and rationality of
Catholic appeals. The utter evaporation of the Stuart cause, and the distrac-
tion of the papacy in its conflict with France, remove all objects and resources
of Catholic disaffection. The Catholic approaches the Protestant applying
simply for participation in a society which he fully acknowledges as lawful
and without any Jacobite and chimerical rival, 'he desires you to name your
own conditions and terms of abjuration, touching any imputed claim on this
subject.'[67] After this broadly conceived prologue, Grattan then proceeds
less predictably into a theological argument augmenting the general
philosophical case:

> I am well aware in questions of this sort how little religion affects their deter-
> mination: however, we must not, like ardent disputants, in the fury of the
> controversy forget the subject, nor [with] the zeal of the sectarist, lose all
> recollection of the Godhead; it is necessary to remind you, that the Catholics
> acknowledge the same God, and the same Redeemer, and differ from you only
> in the forms of his worship and ceremonies of his commemoration; and that
> however that difference may be erroneous, it is not sufficiently heinous to war-
> rant you in dispensing with the express and prime ordinances of your own
> religion, which enjoin certain fraternal affection towards all men, and par-
> ticularly towards fellow christians, whom you must allow to be saved, and are
> commanded to love . . .[68]

This brief homily may have struck the House as platitudinous: certainly none of the Protestant intransigents saw fit to quote theology in defence of their ascendancy. Yet Grattan's assumptions are significant in two respects. First, they are the ground upon which he erects the rhetorical paradox of the intransigents' position according to which Catholics are 'objects to their brethren of perpetual proscription, and objects to our God . . . of perpetual salvation'.[69] The hypothesis is directed into a contradiction in terms, so to speak, illustrating to the Augustan mind of the Irish parliament the moral logic inherent in Catholic relief. The second respect in which Grattan's theological premises are significant is simply that his assumptions will rapidly disappear in the nineteenth century when anti-Catholic evangelicalism will effectively deny the possibility of salvation to the devout and practising papist.

In this regard, Grattan makes explicit assumptions which are shortly to be challenged, thus pointing once again to the transitional nature of the Protestant Ascendancy debate in the 1790s. No doubt, the hardening of attitude among Irish Protestants in the 1820s and after has its parallel on the Catholic side: in the nineteenth century the Irish priesthood was less tied by bonds of family or class to the dominant Protestant élite, and was by its training more inclined to speak its mind in terms of *ex ecclesia non salus est*. The exclusivism of nineteenth-century sectarian claims has its secular form also, in the emergence of a romantic nationalism which veered in some instances towards theories of racial purity. Grattan's conclusion to his theological discourse touches upon this emergent interest in racial history, while yet reserving for himself a strictly eighteenth-century perspective: if Christianity does not sanction the proscription of fellow Christians, and if the political climate has dissolved the threat of disaffection, 'we must therefore have recourse to some other law':

> we imagine we have found it in our own peculiar situation; that situation we state to be as follows: the Protestants are the few, and have the power; the Catholics have not the power, and are the numbers: but this is not peculiar to us, but common to all nations; the Asiatics and the Greeks, the Greeks and the Italians, the English and the Saxons, the Saxon, English and Normans, the vanquished and the vanquisher, they all at last intermingled; the original tribe was in number superior; and yet that superiority never prevented the incorporation, so that this state of our settlement is not peculiar to Ireland, but the ordinary progress of the population and the circulation of the human species, and as it was the trick of nature, to preserve by intermixture, from dwindling and degeneracy, the animal proportions.[70]

This aspect of Grattan's argument is directed against those provisions of the penal laws which levied penalties in terms of property and personal estate

on those who intermarried between the denominations. It implicitly identifies the urge towards marital introversion which was to become such a concern of Irish Protestants later, and sets up a case which Yeats dismisses in
his drama of *mésalliance, Purgatory* (1938). Indeed Grattan's concluding
words on the subject have – ironically – a Yeatsian ring to them:

> In some tribes it might have been otherwise, but they must have died, before
> they could reach history, a prey to their disputes, or swept off, by the tide
> of other nations washing them away in their little divisions, and leaving
> something better on their shore – solitude or a wiser people.[71]

It is only after these impressive preliminaries that Grattan turns to the
question of Protestant ascendancy. Unlike Burke, who fixes upon the newness
of the coinage, or at least, of the collocation of words, Grattan acknowledges
the existence of the condition now loudly proclaimed as Protestant Ascendancy. In keeping with their very different origins in eighteenth-century
Ireland, he does not share Burke's contempt: 'here another principle is advanced, connected indeed with the argument of [peculiar] situation, the
Protestant ascendancy, I revere it, I wish for ever to preserve it, but in order
to preserve I beg to understand it.'[72] His difficulties here are not those of
Burke who is confronted with a novelty in political phraseology. Grattan
is sincerely attached to the constitution under which Church and State are
Protestant; he merely urges the inclusion of Catholics to the security of this
constitution. His difficulty centres on the problems raised when the condition of Protestant Ascendancy is transformed into the touchstone by which
all issues are to be resolved. In short, he interrogates the new slogan on three
grounds – its ability to attract the Catholic majority to the defence of Ireland
in the event of foreign attack; its ability to resist a Union with England,
and finally and most directly:

> can it defend itself against a corrupt Minister? Is the Protestant ascendancy
> able to prevent oppressive taxes, controul the misapplication of public money,
> obtain any of the constitutional bills we have repeatedly proposed, or repeal
> any of the obnoxious regulations the country had repeatedly lamented?[73]

Answering his own inquiries in the negative, Grattan finds the notion of
Protestant Ascendancy – if it is to be taken as an active force in political
and social life – to be spurious:

> There is in this House one man who has more power in parliament than all
> the Protestant ascendancy; I need not tell you, for you know already, as the
> Protestant parliament is now composed, that which you call the Protestant
> ascendancy is a name. We are governed by the ascendancy of the treasury.[74]

Later, in 1795 when the country was already sliding towards the widespread violence of '98, he summarized the system in Ireland as 'the monarchy of clerks – a government to be carried on by post'.[75] But for the moment, it was a 'ministerial and an aristocrate ascendancy'.[76] 'From all this what do I conclude? That the Protestant ascendancy in Ireland requires a new strength, and that you must find that strength in adopting a people, in a progressive adoption of the Catholic body . . .'[77]

The outcome of the February debates was a limited but significant concession to Catholics who were to be admitted now to the professions, to higher education, and who were no longer to suffer penalties on marriage to Protestants. A proposal to admit them to the franchise was, however, defeated, and in a sense the Protestant Ascendancy declined to adopt the Catholic body politically. In Britain, much of the existing penal legislation had been repealed the previous year, and the reconciliation with Catholics which Pitt sought appeared to be well under way. By the end of the year 1792, deteriorating Anglo-French relations brought the issue once again to the foreground of discussion, and once again the notion of Protestant Ascendancy was both flourished and ridiculed by opposing factions.

Once again the Corporation of Dublin was in the vanguard, though the stimulus to their fervour lies close to Richard Burke. In January, prior to the debate on Langrishe's motion, a sub-committee of the Catholic pressure group had drawn up a paper addressed to the people of Ireland; according to the northern radical William Drennan, the paper, though signed by Edward Byrne (a leading Catholic merchant), was 'said to be drawn up by young Burke'.[78] In April a 'Circular letter proposing a Roman Catholic Convention' was issued (and apparently printed) under Byrne's name, though it too had been devised by Richard.[79] At a post-assembly of the Corporation held on 11 September, a further publication of Byrne's was considered; it was resolved to publish a letter to 'the protestants of Ireland' affirming the aldermen's loyalty to ascendancy. Having rehearsed the circumstances which led to the Glorious Revolution and which called forth 'severe but necessary restrictive laws' the letter turned to 'the protestant ascendancy, which we have resolved *with our lives and fortunes to maintain*':

> And, that no doubt may remain of what we understand by the words 'Protestant Ascendancy,' we have further resolved, that we consider the protestant ascendancy to consist in *A Protestant King of Ireland, A Protestant Parliament, A Protestant Hierarchy, Protestant Electors and Government, The Benches of Justice, The Army and the Revenue. Through all their Branches and Details, Protestant: And this System Supported by a Connection with the Protestant Realm of Britain.*[80]

The final claim of loyalty to Britain passes over in silence the British reforms
of 1791, and instead insists that 'the protestants of Ireland would not be
compelled by any authority whatever to abandon that political situation which
their forefathers won with their swords, and which is therefore their birth-
right; or to surrender their religion at the footstool of popery.'

Much of this was relayed by Richard Burke to his father in London in
his letters of 6 and 10 October. Burke had already expressed his views on
the nature of Protestant Ascendancy – it was the old mastership – but he
was now provoked into more fragmentary (though no less telling) definitions in his reply to his son. He refers contemptuously to 'the Jobbing ascendancy' and their policy 'of representing the Country to be disposed to
rebellion in order to add to their Jobbs for the merit of keeping it under'.[81]
Grattan visited him in England and reported that 'they who think Like them
are in a manner obliged to decline all society' because 'the ascendants are
as hot as fire'.[82] The Ascendancy is, ultimately, 'that Junto of Jobbers'.[83]
There can be no doubt that it was the intervention of the Dublin Corporation, with its interests in commerce, which prompted Burke's image of
Protestant Ascendancy as a word lately struck in the mint. The junto of jobbers embraces more than the Corporation – it touches upon the whole system
of patronage by which the Dublin administration governed the country.
Burke's later comments on the Protestant Ascendancy have that anguished
impatience and abruptness which is characteristic of his last years. Indeed
the last paragraph of the *Letter to Richard Burke* in its incompleteness catches
his central response to the revolutionary decade in Ireland: 'All titles terminate in prescription; in which (differently from Time in the fabulous instances) the son devours the father, and the last prescription eats up all the
former.'[84]

Prejudiced though Burke undoubtedly was on the question, and distraught
though he was in his final years, his assessment of ascendancy carries more
conviction than any other. This is partly due to the purely assertive character
of the ascendants' own definition and justification, who offer nothing to
compare with Grattan's political and theological analysis. William Drennan,
in many ways diametrically opposed to Burke politically, concurs with him
in seeing the Ascendancy as 'only a few men actuated by the most monopoliz-
ing spirit'.[85] Writing from Dublin about April or May of 1793, Drennan
records a temporary commercial consequence of the post-assembly resolutions which the ascendants cannot have anticipated:

> The city appears as quiet as usual, but you meet hosts of manufacturers on
> the quays begging for relief, and probably there will be parochial meetings
> for this purpose, who may take this opportunity of expressing their detestation

of a war that has been the cause of such national calamity but many think
that the war has rather accelerated or ripened the evil than been the sole cause
of it. They date the origin of the calamity from the period of the Protestant
Ascendancy resolutions, in which the Corporation of Dublin was so
distinguished . . .[86]

Drennan's economic analysis can be faulted, but he confirms the importance of the Corporation in giving currency to the new slogan, and thus confirms the date of its adoption. If George Ogle and Richard Sheridan vie
with the Corporation for the distinction of announcing the birth of Protestant Ascendancy, it is to Edmund Burke that we must look for the most
penetrating account of its social origins. By his conceit of the Tholsel and
the mint, and by his repeated accusation of jobbery, Burke emphasized the
close association of Ascendancy and commercial advantages as enjoyed by
a Protestant élite challenged by an emergent Catholic bourgeoisie.

Given the manner by which Protestant Ascendancy became the rallying
cry primarily of the landed classes adhering to the Church of Ireland, the
Burkean imagery is noteworthy, indeed crucial, in revealing the concrete
bourgeois motivation of Ascendancy. In time the phrase will enter Yeats's
political aesthetics, and in the course of that development its identification
with landed property is intensified, despite its origins among the merchant-
aldermen and the farmers of patronage. Lord Abercorn in 1792 dismissed
'the silly . . . phrases of Protestant interest and Protestant Ascendancy',
though in the commonly accepted definitions of later years he was typical
of the Ascendancy position.[87] This transference of the phrase from its
commercial-bourgeois origins to a provenance of landed estate should be
interpreted specifically in relation to the gradual erosion of landed estate
as a political reality during the nineteenth century in Ireland; that is, it should
be seen as the propagation of a false sociology. Such a process can be traced
equally clearly in relation to the alleged historical moment of Ascendancy:
for Yeats and those who follow him, the flowering of the Protestant Ascendancy was a period (rather imprecisely defined) in the eighteenth century
associated broadly with the names of Swift, Berkeley, Goldsmith, Grattan,
and Burke. Recovering the evidence of the Dublin Corporation resolutions,
we can begin to appreciate the extent to which this historical identification
reads back into the reigns of Queen Anne and the first two Georges a condition anxiously asserted in the last revolutionary decade of the century.

There is a third dimension to this transformation of the jobbing ascendants into a cultural tradition, and it is specifically linguistic. The years of
the French Revolution saw a significant change in the language of social relations in England – new words were borrowed from France or were imposed

by the energy of events in Europe and at home. Aristocracy, meaning government by the best (noblest) citizens, has a long pedigree, but *aristocrat* as
meaning an individual who favours such government or is a member of such
a governing 'class' is a popular formation of the French Revolution dated
by the *Oxford Dictionary* simply to the year 1789. An almost identical process can be observed in the case of democracy and democrat. At the general
level, it is obvious that this development is part of the tendency to define
class as the aggregate of numbers of individuals on the basis of birth, status,
function or whatever: accordingly, it is impossible to belong to more than
one class, and this view can be contrasted with the classic Marxist notion
that class is constituted by relations and not by biological individuals. In
more local terms, we can see the same process which affected aristocracy
and democracy at work within the 1790s' notion of ascendancy. George Ogle
and Richard Sheridan essentially meant by Protestant Ascendancy a state
of society in which all executive, legislative, and judicial office was vested
in members of the Established Church. In its September 1792 resolution
the Corporation of Dublin follows suit. But it is entirely in keeping with
the evolution of aristocracy and aristocrat that the personnel should supersede
the principle, and that almost simultaneously ascendancy should be used
to identify a social group. Burke defines new ascendancy as the old mastership but, cautious of neologisms, he hesitates to adopt the group terminology:
'the ascendents' is his usual term which, in its absence of sonority, assists
him to recognize a 'Junto of Jobbers'.[88]

Throughout the summer Catholic meetings and petitions had been
vigorously challenged by Protestant declarations and resolutions. The appearance of this opposition at first gave a check to the plan of the reformers,
until the latter obtained a legal opinion in their favour to the effect that their
procedure, so long as it was peaceably conducted for the purpose of petitioning, was in no way a violation of the law. It was in this autumn mood
of Protestant intransigence that one newspaper sought to typify the ascendancy spirit:

A *Protestant ascendancy* BREWER at Castle Bellingham has unfortunately turned
all his ale to vapid by the warmth of his religious zeal, that all his Roman
Catholic customers have left off drinking it. In vain does he declare he had
no *guile* in signing the manifesto of the *county Louth inquisition* against the
devoted Catholics. They have resolved to drink no man's ale, who would
swallow all their rights, and have come to a resolution of letting his *tub* stand
upon its own bottom. If every little ignorant demogogue was thus spiritedly
bereft of support by the people, on whose characters, principles and national
rights he presumed to trample, we should have less of vapouring for the

ignorance and bigotry of those ascendancy Bashaws who infest society, and bring their little *firkins* of religion to market.[89]

The mocking spirit of this, allied to Burke's more formidable invective, may be difficult to reconcile with the subsequent dignities of the Anglo-Irish Protestant Ascendancy. The Dublin resolutions, personified perhaps a shade unfairly in the wretched figure of John Giffard, *do* relate logically to the sarcasm of the reformers. But the logic is that of a widespread social neurosis, a British and Irish *grande peur*. Ascendancy, by its upward movement from being the synonym of mere interest to being the principle of the constitution itself, facilitated the stimulation of anxiety among Protestants. Yet it took over thirty years to create an electoral context in which the numerical superiority of Catholic voters was fully effective. Approaching the Catholic Emancipation crisis, Baron Rossmore wrote in August 1827 to Daniel O'Connell reporting the contents of a letter he had sent to George Canning, the Prime Minister, 'pointing at the necessity of tearing up the Ascendancy faction by the roots'.[90] Ascendancy was for some, as late as 1827, the badge of faction, but the manner of its evolution and dissemination was covert. Consideration of O'Connell's voluminous correspondence, and of records surviving from one of the conservative groups opposed to him, will illuminate some negative features of Protestant Ascendancy's progress. But for the moment, and in so far as Hobart reports it to London, it appears to be handed down from above – the aldermen encouraging the guild representatives to resolve with their lives and fortunes, emphasize this direction. Yet its effect depended on the reception accorded by middle-class Protestants rather than by London or the Irish nobility. Catholics, reformers, and radicals decried the over-heated rhetoric of Giffard and the Castle Bellingham brewer, but their attitude only tends to confirm the ideological nature of the Ascendancy appeal. Intending to subvert neither Church nor State, Catholics found it difficult to take the plethora of slogans and accusations as the substance of the debate, whereas it was precisely the substitution of ideology for reality which characterized the 1792 crisis. Only Burke, and Burke only to a limited extent, recognized the importance of acknowledging the reality which this substitution ultimately conferred upon a false sociology. This blend of anxiety, assertion, and deluded rationalism leads naturally into the United Irishman rebellion of 1798, and colours the relations between landlord and tenant in the first third of the nineteenth century. Those two areas constitute the ground upon which Anglo-Irish fiction will grow: the events of 1792 provide a vocabulary and not a theme.

That phrases were at the time flying thick and fast may be judged by a letter which Abercorn received from his supporter George Knox in

December 1792, distinguishing finely between Protestant Supremacy and
Protestant Ascendancy.[91] We may conclude from these 'hard and soft' options that in the very late eighteenth century there were two notions of Protestant Ascendancy. One simply was the state of affairs as it stood: of this Burke
wryly suggested that it 'would be more prudently practiced than professed'; and Grattan added that though he revered it he found it difficult to
justify as a political *ne plus ultra*. According to this reading, Protestant Ascendancy did exist prior to 1792 but had not been so named: the naming of
it constituted more than the mere identification of a familiar condition, it
marked a need to go beyond the experience to establish a doctrine. Furthermore, this implicit condition was neither unalterable nor to any high degree
admirable – it was the *status quo* diluted with a hint of compromise and
a tincture of self-interest. The second notion was, in local terms, an aggressive
call to resist the admission of Catholics to citizenship, or it was the doctrine
in the name of which such a call was made. The second notion required
no extensive proto-history, either implicit or explicit, for it was specifically
a response to the pressures of the revolutionary age. In broader terms than
the local, this second interpretation exemplifies the emergence of an ideology,
that is, a false sociology according to which real changes in society are
presented in unreal formulations so as to facilitate these changes by deflec-
ting attention towards the chimeras of abstraction. The larger political implications of this development lie beyond a study of specifically literary forms
of consciousness, though in the Anglo-Irish instance the two are rarely
separable for very long. We have seen how the notion of an aristocracy in
Ireland was bedevilled by an acute consciousness of lapses from the ideal.
(The acute consciousness is at least as important as any deficiency or delin-
quency of morals.) Already, in Regency England, there is soon discernible
tat *embourgeoisement* of the aristocracy which is often thought to be
characteristically Victorian. In Ireland, the pattern differs significantly. A
Protestant élite, administering a largely rural society, assumes the identity
of the Ascendancy, thereby gradually arrogating to itself the status of a raf-
fish aristocracy and the security of a restricted bourgeoisie from which
Catholics will be rebuffed by a flamboyant sectarianism devoid of Christianity. The evangelical fervour of the 1820s and after is an essential part
of this process of exclusion and introversion. As for the culture of this stratum
of Irish society, so memorably incorporated into poetry by W. B. Yeats,
MacNeice saw in it 'nothing but an obsolete bravado, an insidious bonhomie
and a way with horses'.[92] The critic who approaches Yeats by way of his
attitude to the Protestant Ascendancy of late Victorian and Edwardian times
should bear in mind that Yeats, even at his most thoroughly elegiac or

celebratory, is always a dramatic intelligence assuming, assisting or creating dramatic tensions and transformation within the material he chooses to employ. That he should find culture where MacNeice finds bravado is not blindness on Yeats's part, but part of a comprehensive poetic strategy: one is more likely to identify imperception in Yeats if one insists on interpreting the poetry simply as celebration or elegy to the neglect of ironic and dramatic tonalities.

The contradictions inherent in this emergent identity, upon which Yeats was later to meditate so actively, were quickly manifested. It was Edmund Burke's view that for many months rebellion in Ireland was deliberately provoked; and when it came in 1798 it proved a terrible demonstration of the passions represented by the new factionalism and the new phraseology of the decade. An anonymous pamphleteer, writing in the wake of the rebellion, traced the sequence of events from the constitutional revision of 1782 down to the massacres at Wexford Bridge. But, by way of preface, he observed that

> The rebellion was confined to the three counties of Kildare, Wicklow, and Wexford, and more particularly to the two latter, where Protestant Ascendancy and religious distinction have been carried to the greatest lengths but these three counties are not a tenth of the kingdom, nor the Roman Catholics resident in them a fifteenth part of that persuasion.[93]

Rebellion in Ireland, at a time of European war, led directly to the Union of Ireland with Great Britain in 1801. But the sequence of events stemming from the 1792 debates, through provocation and rebellion to Union, provided a traumatic incentive to various parties for the adoption of the term, Protestant Ascendancy. For the Protestants, it was the central object of the Glorious Revolution itself, identified increasingly with a pre-Union golden age, but sedulously maintained in a contemporary mythology of castles and cabins. The final selection of 'the Ascendancy', as distinct from some term comparable in its structure to aristocrats/democrats, is a preference not only for personnel over principle, but it is a preference for an abstraction of class within which the sociology of Ireland may be conjured anew. Burke himself warned his son of the dangers involved in the Catholics adopting the new terminology as a means of demonstrating the moderation of their claims, 'what is it that they got by adopting at all this new Idea of *Protestant* ascendency?'[94] For the Catholics to take up such terms was to render themselves passive before 'this spell of potency, this abracadabra, that is hung about the necks of the unhappy, not to heal but to communicate disease'.[95] Despite these warnings of the insidiously reciprocal effect of an ideological imposition in the language, Protestant Ascendancy is indeed taken up by Irish Catholics as describing at once a degenerate oligarchy and a principle of exclusion from prestige. This manifestly bilateral scheme provided compensation for the renunciations implicit in the Union and in the subsequent modernization of the economy, together with the concomitant cultural trauma.

That Burke recognized the nature of Protestant Ascendancy in its emergence can hardly be doubted. In two observations, more reflective than those of November 1792, he later related the phenomenon to broader perspectives. Indicating a shrewd appreciation of the way in which 'in all ideology men and their circumstances appear upside-down',[96] he proffered a bitterly sardonic tribute: 'I think it very possible, that to a degree the Ascendents were sincere. The understanding is soon debauched over to the passions; and our opinions very easily follow our wishes.'[97] It would be mistaken to summarize this dictum as meaning simply that people usually manage to think to their own advantage. Here indeed is a text fit to be borne in mind as we approach Yeats's ultimate drama of passionate ascendancy, *Purgatory*, for Burke's central meaning is the symbolic identity of our faculties, intellectual and sensual. In another observation he provides a further means of relating the particularities of local politics in Ireland to the broader pattern of those expansionist doctrines he opposed in his major campaigns:

> I think I can hardly overrate the malignity of the principles of the Protestant ascendency, as they affect Ireland; or of Indianism, as they affect these countries, and as they effect Asia; or of Jacobinism, as they affect all Europe, and the state of human Society itself.[98]

The profligate exploitation which Warren Hastings personifies for Burke, the bourgeois monarchy which the Jacobins ultimately bequeath to Honoré Balzac, and the Protestant Ascendancy which the Dublin Aldermen will contribute to Yeats's problematic aesthetics – all these form part of the social fabric in which the romantic movement traced its devices. It has been customary to see many of these as retrospective – the occasional medievalism of Keats, the Hellenism of Shelley, and the pervasive recursus of Wordsworthian memory. And Anglo-Irish literature particularly is accepted as obsessed by the past, dominated by its 'backward look'.[99] Yet no one would question the intensity with which the English romantics were engaged with contemporary experience, were indeed engaged with forming and articulating contemporary experience. It has been the peculiar fate of the Anglo-Irish skelli in the romantic tapestry that its concern with the past should be taken as literal, local, and exclusive. The *Dublin University Magazine*'s attempt to diagnose the condition of literature in Ireland in the 1830s reveals the proper balance of this concern with the past (seen as abbreviated and vestigial) and a complementary apprehension of the future as bodied forth in England's more advanced condition. The process by which Yeats ultimately renders that past literature traditional is necessarily linked to the notional separation of Ireland from England; and the tragic price paid for this transformation of the inchoate into the sublime is the extinction or elimination of that Ascendancy through which the process was sustained. Burke's testimony on the subject of Protestant Ascendancy serves to remind us that our method is literary history, a practical consciousness of the past as produced (in our material) in literature, and not the stratigraphy of events heaped one upon the other in some unchanging diagram. So too his insistence on the affinities of Dublin, Paris, and Bombay should teach us that the childish assumption of Ireland's uniqueness and separateness – Elizabeth Bowen's confusion of Ireland and Island – substitutes geology where one should attend to the intricacies of a metropolitan-colonial culture.

NOTES AND REFERENCES

1 Elizabeth Bowen, *Pictures and Conversations* (London: Allen Lane, 1975), p. 31.
2 Historical Manuscripts Commission (henceforth HMC) Rutland MSS, vol. iii, p. 155; for a further and more elaborate example of antithesis in formulating Anglo-Irish relations in this period see a draft letter from the Earl of Buckinghamshire to Edward Tighe, HMC, Lothian MSS, pp. 394-6.
3 For an analysis of the presence of arguments deriving from American conditions in Irish pamphlets about titles, church affairs etc., see W. J. Mc Cormack, *The Dublin Paper War of 1786–1788* (Dublin: Irish Academic Press, 1993), pp. 74, 78, 92-3, 101-3 etc.
4 *The Correspondence of Edmund Burke*, Thomas W. Copeland et al., ed., vol. ix, May 1796–July 1797, R. B. McDowell and John A. Woods, eds. (Cambridge: Cambridge University Press, 1970), p. 59. On the general issue see K. H. Connell, *The Population of Ireland 1750–1845* (Oxford: Clarendon Press, 1950).
5 'Letter to Sir Hercules Langrishe', *The Writings and Speeches of Edmund Burke*, vol. 9, R. B. McDowell ed. (Oxford: Clarendon Press, 1991), p. 618.
6 Ibid., p. 600.
7 W. B. Yeats, *The Poems*, Daniel Albright ed. (London: Dent, 1990), p. 392.
8 See W. E. H. Lecky, *History of Ireland in the Eighteenth Century* (London, 1898), vol. iv, p. 4 n.
9 HMC Charlemont MSS, vol. ii, pp. 354-5.

10   'Letter to Richard Burke', *Writings and Speeches,* vol. 9, p. 647.
11   *Irish Parliamentary Debates* (Dublin, 1792), vol. xii, p. 7.
12   R. B. McDowell, *Ireland in the Age of Imperialism and Revolution 1760 – 1801* (Oxford: Clarendon Press, 1979), p. 121.
13   *Irish Parliamentary Debates,* vol. xii, p. 7.
14   W. B. Yeats, *The Poems,* p. 244.
15   Ibid., pp. 197-8, 246.
16   A. P. W. Malcomson, *John Foster: The Politics of the Anglo-Irish Ascendancy* (Oxford: Oxford University Press for the Institute of Irish Studies, 1978), pp. 397-8.
17   Quoted ibid., p. 364.
18   Burke, *Correspondence,* vol. vii, pp. 83-4.
19   Malcomson, *John Foster,* op. cit., pp. 355-7.
20   See G. C. Bolton, *The Passing of the Irish Act of Union* (London: Oxford University Press, 1966), pp. 205-7.
21   Oliver MacDonagh, *The Nineteenth Century Novel and Irish Social History* (Dublin: National University of Ireland, 1971), p. 5.
22   Trinity College Dublin (Synge MSS), MS 4373, fo. 22. John Millington Synge's summary of R. G Trench's brief discussion of the word in *On the Study of Words* (1851); see Trench, *On the Study of Words* [and] *English Past and Present* (London: Dent, 1927), p. 63.
23   W. B. Yeats, *The Poems,* p. 291.
24   Burke, *Correspondence,* vol. ix, p. 162.
25   Ibid., pp. 162-3. There are many other instances in the correspondence of this period.
26   'Tracts relating to Popery Laws', *Writings and Speeches,* vol. 9, p. 464.
27   'Letter to William Smith', ibid., p. 660.
28   'A Letter to a Noble Lord', ibid., p. 171.
29   'Tracts', ibid., p. 478-9.
30   Ibid., p. 479.
31   'Letter to Richard Burke', ibid., p. 657.
32   For a general discussion of the antiquarian background to Anglo-Irish literature compare Maurice Harmon and Roger McHugh *Short History of Anglo-Irish Literature* (Dublin: Wolfhound Press, 1982), pp. 65-71, and Margaret McCurtain's essay in Robert O'Driscoll ed., *The Celtic Consciousness* (Dublin: Dolmen Press, 1982), pp. 371-82.
33   For recent comment on this episode see Robert Welch, *Irish Poetry from Moore to Yeats* (Gerrards Cross: Smythe, 1980), pp. 96-103.
34   Raymond Williams, *The City and the Country* (London: Paladin, 1975), pp. 140-5.
35   'Tracts', *Writings and Speeches,* vol. 9, p. 476.
36   See Burke, *Correspondence,* vol. vii, p. 104, n9; the phrase quoted, however, derives from Francis Plowden and dates from the early nineteenth century. For Burke's early encouragement of Leland, and his subsequent disappointment in his *History,* see Walter D. Love, 'Charles O'Conor of Belenagare, and Thomas Leland's "philosophical" history of Ireland', *Irish Historical Studies,* vol. 13 (1962), p. 23.
37   Samuel Johnson, *A Dictionary of the English Language* (London, 1755), vol. i (2G).

38 Westmorland to Henry Dundas, 11 January 1792, quoted in Lecky, op. cit., vol. iii, p. 45. The two letters of 26 December 1791 are preserved in the State Paper Office, Dublin Castle (Westmorland Corresp., Nos. 27 and 29).
39 Westmorland to Dundas, 11 January 1792: Lecky, op. cit., vol. iii, p. 43.
40 Westmorland to Dundas, 14 January 1792 (Westmorland Corresp., No. 42). Lecky (op. cit., vol. iii, p. 41) refers to a meeting of the Irish Privy Council rather than of the Cabinet; for the status and function of the latter at this period, and of the involvement of the Archbishop of Cashel, see Malcomson, *John Foster: The Politics of the Anglo-Irish Ascendancy*, pp. 415-18. For the pre-1792 career of Protestant Ascendancy, and its conceptualization in 1792, see Mc Cormack, *The Dublin Paper War*, pp. 88-91, and esp. pp. 109-35.
41 Robert Hobart to Dundas, 17 January 1792, quoted in Lecky, op. cit., vol. iii, p. 51. Hobart is generally acknowledged as being closer to the Protestant party than Westmorland, his superior; during the Union debates he acted with other lesser members of the Cabinet to stimulate Orange reactions. His taking up of the phrase, Protestant Ascendancy, in January 1792 is characteristic.
42 Westmorland to William Pitt, 18 January 1792, quoted in Lecky, op. cit., vol. iii, pp. 48-9.
43 Ibid., p. 48.
44 *Irish Parliamentary Debates*, vol. xii, p. 24 (19 January 1792).
45 *The Autobiography of Theobald Wolfe Tone 1763–1798*, R. Barry O'Brien, ed., (Dublin: Maunsel, 1910), vol. i, p. 108. It is worth noting that, prior to the excitements generated by the 1792 resolutions, Tone was on very friendly terms with George Knox, MP, a supporter of Lord Abercorn; from his association with the Catholic Committee, Tone went on to become the intellectual leader of the United Irishmen and the founder of the Irish republican tradition, dying by suicide in 1798.
46 Ibid., p. 69.
47 *Calendar of Ancient Records of Dublin*, ed. Lady Gilbert (Dublin: Dollard, 1909), vol. xiv, pp. 241-2. The *Calendar* only provides the surnames of the committee members, and where possible these have been augmented with Christian names by reference to almanacs etc.
48 Ibid., p. 243.
49 Ibid., pp. 243-4.
50 Westmorland to Dundas, 14 January 1792.
51 *The Morning Post; or Dublin Courant*, 24 January 1792.
52 *Dublin Chronicle*, 21 January 1792; for the dissent of Bond and Binns see *Dublin Chronicle*, loc. cit., and *Morning Post*, 21 January 1792.
53 For information etc. on Giffard see Appendix B of *Ascendancy and Tradition*, pp. 402-4.
54 Hobart to Westmorland, 25 January 1792, quoted in Lecky, op. cit., vol. iii, p. 54.
55 *Irish Parliamentary Debates*, vol. xii, p. 134 (18 February 1792).
56 Ibid., pp. 134-5. Sheridan's speech is printed at pp. 133-5.
57 'Commentary on A Parnellite at Parnell's Funeral', W. B. Yeats, *Variorum Edition of the Poems*, Peter Allt and Russell K. Alspach, eds. (New York: Macmillan, 1977; 7th printing), p. 833.
58 'Letter to Richard Burke', *Writings and Speeches*, vol. 9, p. 642-4.

59 Burke, *Correspondence*, vol. vii, pp. 86-9, the letter is addressed to Richard Burke
    Senior, but is endorsed by Edmund Burke's wife, Jane.
60 Ibid., pp. 241-2: the letter (pp. 235-46) is to the Earl Fitzwilliam.
61 See W. B. Todd, *A Bibliography of Edmund Burke* (Godalming: St Paul's
    Bibliographies, 1982), 2nd edn, p. 257, for details of its publication in vol. 5
    (1812) of the *Works*.
62 'Letter to Richard Burke', *Writings and Speeches*, vol. 9, pp. 642-4.
63 Ibid., p. 66.
64 'Letter to Lord Kenmare', ibid., p. 570.
65 Burke, *Correspondence*, vol. vii, pp. 70-1.
66 Ibid., p. 84.
67 *Irish Parliamentary Debates*, vol. xii, p. 165.
68 Idem.
69 Ibid., p. 166.
70 Idem.
71 Idem.
72 Ibid., p. 167.
73 Idem.
74 Idem.
75 *The Parliamentary Register* (Dublin, 1795), vol. xv, p. 189. Quoted in Edmund
    Curtis and R. B. Mc Dowell, *Irish Historical Documents*, 2nd. edn (London:
    Methuen, 1977), p. 226.
76 *Irish Parliamentary Debates*, vol. xii, p. 167.
77 Ibid., p. 169.
78 *The Drennan Letters 1776 – 1819*, D. A. Chart, ed. (Belfast: HMSO, 1931), p.
    73. See Todd, *A Bibliography of Edmund Burke*, p. 278.
79 Todd, *A Bibliography of Edmund Burke*, p. 280.
80 *Calendar of Ancient Records of Dublin*, vol. xiv, pp. 284-7; and see also Richard
    Musgrave, *Memoirs of the Different Rebellions in Ireland* (Dublin, 1802), 3rd edn,
    vol. ii, pp. 222-5.
81 Burke, *Correspondence*, vol. vii, pp. 282, 287.
82 Ibid, p. 289.
83 Ibid., p. 290.
84 'Letter to Richard Burke', *Writings and Speeches*, vol. 9, p. 658.
85 *Drennan Letters*, p. 91.
86 Ibid., p. 158. 'Manufacturers' are of course factory employees.
87 Quoted in Malcomson, *John Foster*, p. 355. Malcomson's is the first biography
    of John Foster, the Speaker of the Irish House of Commons so scorned by Burke
    in the 'Letter to Richard Burke'; it provides a useful account of the Irish political
    and parliamentary context in which ascendancy emerged, though it passes over
    the origins of the slogan with little comment; see pp. 352-3.
88 Burke, *Correspondence*, vol. vii, p. 290.
89 *Morning Post*.
90 *The Correspondence of Daniel O'Connell*, Maurice R. O'Connell, ed., vol. iii,
    1824 – 8 (Dublin: Irish Manuscripts Commission, 1974), p. 343.
91 Quoted in Malcomson, *John Foster*, p. 352.
92 Louis MacNeice, *The Poetry of W. B. Yeats* (London: Faber, 1967), 2nd. edn,
    p. 97.

93 *Protestant Ascendancy and Catholic Emancipation Reconciled by a Legislative Union*
    (London: Wright, 1800), p. 102.
94 Burke, *Correspondence*, vol. vii, p. 292.
95 'Letter to Richard Burke', *Writings and Speeches*, vol. 9, p. 647.
96 Karl Marx and Frederick Engels, *The German Ideology* (London: Lawrence
    and Wishart, 1974), p. 47.
97 Burke, *Correspondence*, vol. viii, p. 138.
98 Ibid., vol. x, p. 32.
99 e.g. Frank O'Connor's history *The Backward Look: A Survey of Irish Literature*
    (London: Macmillan, 1967).

3

Things as They Are

Did the Warwickshire militia, who were chiefly artisans, teach the Irish to drink beer? or did they learn from the Irish to drink whiskey?

(Maria Edgeworth)[1]

THE CASE OF WILLIAM GODWIN

The business of literary historians involves them in negotiations between discourses for which there is rarely an agreed rate or mode of exchange. Among these, the confrontational relationship of the literary and the non-literary is naturally fundamental. The study of Irish literature has, on the whole, been tolerant of (so-called) non-literary texts such as prison-journals, autobiographies, political treatises, and the like. 'A Modest Proposal' is unlikely to disappear from the literary curriculum, though it is protected more by its own unimpeachably Irish credentials rather than by any vocational interest in economics among teachers of literature. It is difficult to imagine the circumstances in which *The Conduct of the Allies* or 'The Widow and Her Cat' will attract the same degree of fond attention.

This reliance on what can only be termed (crudely) subject matter is hardly the basis for critical scholarship. In more strictly literary connections one finds an even less reflective acceptance of geographic setting as the litmus paper by which Irish fiction is detected. The elaboration of some new analytical tools has been a necessary preliminary to the urgent task of considering together those fictions by Maria Edgeworth which are set in Ireland

94

Castle Rackrent (1800), *The Absentee* (1812), *Ormond* (1817) etc. and those intervening fictions by the same author which are set elsewhere – for example *Belinda* (1801), *Patronage* (1814), and *Helen* (1832). One of these new critical terms seeks to refine some of the crudities embedded in notions of geographical setting as generally employed in the discussion of prose fiction, a genre still retaining some affiliations with other forms of writing – memoir, pamphlet-debate, treatise, travelogue – while also claiming its own autonomy. 'Place of interpretation' is at once a textual construct or hermeneutic device, implicit yet repressed in the work shortly to be examined, and it is also an ideological desire articulated and never achieved. The excavation of an ideological concept such as Protestant Ascendancy is no more restricted to the quaking sod or narrow ground of Irish territoriality than is the fiction which transcends latter-day national identities. It has been distinctly noticeable that recent theoretical pronouncements on the topic of Irish literature do not replace cultural nationalism with something (allegedly) more sophisticated; while declaring that intention they effectively retain the theme of nationalism for future purposes.

In the context of the 1790s also, ideology loomed large. Much has been written and said in recent years about the development of Protestant Ascendancy within the lexicon of Irish anti-revolutionary politics from 1792 onwards. In the course of these – sometimes excited – exchanges, attention has been drawn to earlier contexts in which the noun 'ascendancy' appeared, or (more usually) its cognates. Less has been done to examine the great body of evidence unconnected with parliamentary, municipal, and pamphlet discussion occurring in Dublin. Thus, having traced the appropriation of 'ascendancy' from a prior usage notable for its astrological connotations, inquiry has neglected to examine what was happening in, say, literary texts contemporary with the political mobilization of ascendancy ideology in Ireland.

Of course, any notion of evidence 'unconnected' with the Dublin excitements of 1792–3 is vulnerable to correction. For example, Edmund Burke took no part in the debates though his son, Richard, was present in the city and even in the House of Commons during some of the most important of these public discussions. In due course, Burke Senior will become a pervasive influence on novelists, poets, playwrights and essayists. Coleridge became peculiarly attentive to the progress of the campaign for Catholic Emancipation, and so had a retrospective, if scarcely conscious, interest in the College Green antics of January – February 1792. An initial contradiction in this process is centred on the paradox of Burke's opposition to the new concept and Coleridge's later defence of it. In the terminology of more recent politics, Burke's liberalism is a source for Coleridge's toryism. And *Biographia Literaria* (1817) is not wholly unconnected with the resolutions of Dublin Corporation.

Something more than the personal complexities of Burke's position, as the descendant of Irish Catholics and the major prophet of British opposition to the Revolution, is at work here. Even if the familiar argument is accepted, according to which Burke's sympathy with Catholic grievances put him in two minds in relation to the Whig oligarchy, it is impossible to conclude that the revolutionary turbulence of the 1790s simply represented, and in turn was represented by, the inversion of known components within a binary system of power relations. Revolution, it should be recalled, was itself a concept adapted from earlier usage and radicalized so as to serve anew. Neither 'the wheel of fortune' nor 'the world turned upside down' suffices as an image of revolutionary change, for neither conveys the sense of volatility implicit in the pronouncements of the chief actors and repeatedly demonstrated in course of the Revolution itself. Power relations are not simply reversed in this new experience, or programme, of revolution. Power itself is radicalized in ways which the actors themselves could not realize.

It has been claimed on behalf of literature that it can transcend this barrier between actuality and realization. More particularly two novelists, who are in different ways provoked to write by the Revolution and its aftermath, are generally cited as exemplifying this achievement. Walter Scott and Honoré Balzac, though conservative in their personal attitudes towards social and political questions, were in their fiction deeply and brilliantly ironic in their attitude towards the past and towards contemporary values. It may be that the paradox of critical realism – the term is György Lukács', speaking of Thomas Mann and Balzac rather than of Scott – should be sought not only in the work itself but also in the critical perspective and its political moment. One should note with care Lukács' own two-mindedness, first as mystic and then as Bolshevik. Moreover, the notion of critical realism requires closer attention than it has generally received in Anglophone circles where he has been too often vilified or venerated with equal inattention. For the present, however, the question should focus on the exclusion from the debate about Protestant Ascendancy in the 1790s of evidence drawn from expressly radical literature, from, say, that body of fiction in which no transcendental dialectic of authorial preference and textual affiliation is required.

The objection can be raised that, in 1792, no such body of fiction existed. That is, no Irish school of novel-writing had come into being because – as we all know – Maria Edgeworth will not inaugurate that tradition until she publishes *Castle Rackrent* anonymously in 1800. Ironically, the prehistory of that text suggests it was exactly in the year of the Protestant Ascendancy debates that she commenced work on a tale of the manners of Hibernian squires which was later laid aside and then completed at the end of the decade.[2] It is not easy – perhaps it is not advisable – to decide categorically whether *Castle Rackrent* is a radical work or not a radical work. But it is not difficult to observe that Edgeworth's next novel, *Belinda* (appearing as soon as 1801), is set in England, and that unilateral classification of Edgeworth as either an Irish or an English writer would be equally arbitrary.

If we are to search for a body of literature through which the dissemination of a Protestant Ascendancy ideology may be discerned, then presumptive equations of fictional setting with authorial nationality should be dismissed out of hand. And to do so is to concede the possibility of a writer, wholly – say – English by birth and upbringing, who may have been the author of work in which the distinctively Irish political concept of ascendancy was registered. Doubtless some people will protest that, surely, no such equation has ever been declared. One's first response to this objection must be to emphasize the insidious power of undeclared relations of this kind. And yet, to an extent, the protesters are right. The relationship between realistic setting and cultural nationalism cannot be expressed by means of equations, but their absence does not rule out other forms of mediation. On the contrary, the tweedle-dee-dum of these terms should be taken as adequate testimony of their inability to generate anything more than mutual admiration. Attempts to describe Edgeworth's achievement as a whole have shown that a new critical term was required, to augment geographic setting. The term was 'place of interpretation': the work under discussion was *Patronage* (1814), her longest and arguably her best novel.

Unlike geographic setting as it became increasingly prominent in the structure and texture of novelistic fiction, 'place of interpretation' is primarily textual. In the case of Edgeworth's *Patronage*, the setting is at all times English though some highly suggestive incidents occur on the shoreline and even in the tidal-waters of England. A number of these marginally amphibious novels appear round this time – Fanny Burney's *The Wanderer* also dates from 1814, and William Godwin's *Mandeville* from 1817. The crucial role of sea-power in Britain's survival of the revolutionary and Napoleonic wars is an obvious factor here, one registered more discretely and conservatively in Austen's *Mansfield Park*, another of the great novels of 1814. But in connection with Edgeworth's *Patronage*, place of interpretation implicates Ireland which functions as a kind of political unconscious in the novel, a stratum only revealed late in the unfolding of the plot. This might be called the more comprehensive *discourse* of the novel's text.[3] In so naming it, we may also implicate the process of composition as a further unconscious related to the published text, in which case *Patronage* can be placed, not only among the great fictional publications of 1814 – including Walter Scott's *Waverley*, for example – but also among the contending Jacobin and anti-Jacobin novels of the 1790s.

Though consideration of Edgeworth's fiction usually provides an opportunity to refine some of the equipment we conventionally bring to bear on the Anglo-Irish novel, it does little to assist us in examining the immediate and public context of the Protestant Ascendancy debates of 1792. Beyond Dublin, the first notable response came with Edmund Burke's *Letter to Richard Burke*, an intense and ostentatiously unfinished meditation on contemporary affairs intended for public circulation. (See above pp. 75 – 7 etc.) Apart from private correspondence, which remained unpublished for many years, this letter to his son constituted Burke's considered and yet contemptuous analysis of the new concept and the 'junto' (as he termed them) who were propagating ascendancy in Ireland.

Until William Godwin's extensive diaries are fully available, we cannot state uncontrovertible facts about the time and place of his encounter with Burke's 'Letter'. It may seem unlikely that one often regarded as the founder of modern anarchism should positively respond to the prophet of modern toryism. As early as 1783, *The Monthly Review* had carried young Godwin's anonymous endorsement of the Rockingham party among the Whigs, and within three years *The Political Herald and Review* published a lengthy public letter addressed to Burke and written by Godwin under the named Mucius. These early acknowledgements of Burke's place in Godwin's developing views of society and government are firmly lodged in a period when Burke was closely identified with the liberal Rockingham faction, and when the French Revolution was scarcely discernible on the distant horizon. On a broader front, Mucius published a letter 'To the People of Ireland' which also appeared in 1786 in *The Political Herald and Review*.

With the rapid transformation of political values and attitudes in 1789 and the years following, one would expect the differences between Burke and Godwin to be greatly increased and the evidence of their common interests to be diminished. Certainly, the intellectual excitement of the new decade generated more dispute than concord: Burke's *Reflections on the French Revolution* (1790), Tom Paine's *The Rights of Man* (1791-2), and Godwin's *Essay Concerning Political Justice* (1793) are just three of the longer and more enduring contributions to a massive paper war fought at every level, from philosophical treatise to street ballad. Each proved to be highly controversial, and a polarization of opinion began to form round memorable phrases employed by their authors – 'a swinish multitude', 'liberty', and so forth. Yet despite the obvious differences between Burke and Godwin, differences exacerbated by the rapid movement of events and opinions, a later edition of *Political Justice* incorporated warm tributes to the importance of the late Edmund Burke for its author.[4]

We are then brought to the point where Godwin's fiction can be considered. Though he was to publish a further five novels before he died in 1836, *Caleb Williams* remains the one title with which he is immediately identified. Published on 26 May 1794, it had been begun in February of the previous year. Virtually from the outset, it divided opinion as to its merits and its nature. Many early reviewers lined up on the basis of their own political convictions or needs. A more recent view of the novel as a religious allegory or fable would have struck them as far-fetched; after all, for good or ill, its author was also the author of *Political Justice* with which it is closely connected, and *Political Justice* is subversive of both Church and State. Nevertheless, Mary Shelley, in some unpublished notes for a biography of her father, shrewdly attributed the novel's early popularity to its political ambivalence:

> those in the lower classes saw their cause espoused, and their oppressors forcibly and eloquently delineated – while those of higher rank acknowledged and felt the nobleness, sensibility and errors of Falkland with deepest sympathy.[5]

This is a highly suggestive analysis, not so much for any particular accuracy which it may possess in relation to *Caleb Williams*, but rather for its recognition of the stratified readership by which fiction was greeted in the revolutionary era. And yet, it should be emphasized that the novel generates its readership and does not simply address it; in other words, *Caleb Williams* contributes to the peculiar structure of reception to which Mary Shelley alluded. Of more local interest, however, is the reproduction of this structure within the character of Caleb Williams himself, and the concentration of it even more particularly in Williams's highly volatile relations with Mr Falkland.

It is finally impossible to avoid some brief summary of the novel's action. Prior to young Williams's entering Ferdinando Falkland's service, Falkland had travelled in Italy where he overcame a jealous count by an act of generous submission. At home in a 'remote county' of England, this melancholic yet mercurial country squire became locked in dispute with a neighbour called

Tyrrel, a man of respectable birth and no breeding. Tyrrel's bullying is oddly terminated in a crime of which Falkland is suspected. Caleb Williams, employed as Falkland's secretary, and being both loyal and incurably inquisitive, penetrates into remote corners of his master's house and conscience. Falkland reacts guiltily and fearfully; a cat and mouse war begins between employer and secretary, with Falkland threatening Williams as once Tyrrel had bullied his tenants. Even at this early stage, it is clear that nothing stabilizes in *Caleb Williams*. It is as if the word 'fight' veered towards 'flight', and yet Caleb's flight also becomes a form of assault upon his persecutor. In the end, Godwin had to write two conclusions for the novel.

Godwin's masterpiece has remained popular since 1794 for its extraordinary rendering of psychological detail. Less attention has been paid to its very occasional and yet striking use of mythological allusion. Though Godwin was a learned writer, even a pedantic one, his favoured resources were biblical and historical, the two often conjoined in his fascination with the seventeenth-century English revolution. However, in the third chapter of *Caleb Williams*, there occurs a doubled employment of Greek mythology which is more puzzling than its familiar component parts initially suggest.

Describing the manner in which Tyrrel had established himself as undisputed master of the district, the narrator refers to the possibility that some opposition must have been maintained. But no. As the narrator, i.e. Williams himself, expresses the situation – 'all opposition had been quelled with a high hand by this rural Antaeus.'[6] In 1794 Godwin's readers would have no need of the footnote in the splendid *Collected Novels and Memoirs* which explains that the figure mentioned was the son of Poseidon (god of the sea) and of Earth, who received new strength from his mother every time he fell in wrestling. Antaeus may be familiar again in Ireland through W. B. Yeats's observation that the deep-rooted affections of Anglo-Irish writers flourished despite social adversity because, through their fidelity to place, they 'Antaeus-like grew strong'. And the same mythic source has served Seamus Heaney well in providing him with names by which he can figure a contest between England and Ireland.[7]

Back in Volume I of *Caleb Williams*, we are surprised and not surprised to find that Tyrrel is soon bedecked in another Greek allusion, this time of an even more accessible kind. In the paragraph immediately succeeding the one just quoted, the narrator comments on Tyrrel's popularity with women – 'his boisterous wit had peculiar charms for them; and there was no spectacle more flattering to their vanity than the seeing this Hercules exchange his club for a distaff.'[7] We are confronted with a double contradiction here, one which is not dissolved according to the dubious rule that two negatives cancel each other. The first of these is located entirely within the narrator's allusion to Antaeus: for to refer to the *high* hand of Antaeus is to employ a casual modern idiom − high-handedness etc. − with the effect of obliterating the ancient source of the giant's strength, the low earth from which he gained renewal. So, even in the first of his Greek heroic outfits, Tyrrel is presented in contradictory terms, a high-handed Antaeus and so likely to take a fall. His presentation a moment later as a Hercules indicates that he is, in some sense, the agent of his own downfall, though ironically the original Hercules defeated Antaeus by holding him aloft.

In *Political Justice*, Godwin has recourse to some of the same mythological tropes, though with a more conventional effect. The fourth chapter of Book I is devoted to proving that 'The Characters of Men Originate in their External Circumstances'. Part of the argument derives from a consideration of changelings and siblings, whose condition at birth might be thought identical in all cases.[9] 'Hercules and his brother, the robust infant whom scarcely any neglect can destroy, and the infant that is with difficulty reared are undoubtedly from the moment of parturition very different beings.'[10] But this illustration appears only in the revised (1798) edition of *Political Justice* − published after *Caleb Williams* − and not in the first edition of 1793, which had appeared a year before the novel. In other words, the treatise borrows from the fiction and not the other way round, though it must be noted that the version of Hercules' story which appears in *Political Justice* lacks the complex doubleness or irony represented in a 'high-handed' Antaeus.

In what looks like a conventional employment of Greek mythological figures, Godwin indicates the paradoxical operations of power in *Caleb Williams*. It might be argued that the convergence of Hercules and Antaeus in the one character arises from the narrator's emotional state or from his inadequate learning. The latter objection can be readily met by reference to Caleb's early detailing of his education, unusual in one of his class and sufficient to lead to his appointment as Falkland's secretary. And in answer to the other objection one has only to note that the same exchange, or permanent revolution, of power which identifies Hercules with his victim Antaeus also energizes relations between Caleb and his employer. The case of Tyrrel, in which the narrator is scarcely involved personally, is typical in the novel rather than exceptional.

Having noted the peculiar role of Hercules and Antaeus in the characterization of Tyrrel, we might inquire if Godwin assigns any other distinguishing feature to him. The dominance which he exercised in the district where he lived stimulated conflicting responses even within an individual neighbour or acquaintance, and it is sufficient to quote more extensively from the paragraph already cited to discover the term which the narrator found necessary to describe this condition:

> The pleasure that resulted to others from the exuberant sallies of his imagination was therefore not unalloyed with sudden qualms of apprehension and terror. It may be believed that this despotism did not gain its final ascendancy without being contested in the outset. But all opposition had been quelled with a high hand by this rural Antaeus. By the ascendancy of his fortune, and his character among his neighbours, he always reduced his adversary to the necessity of encountering him at his own weapons, and did not dismiss him without making him feel his presumption through every joint in his frame. The tyranny of Mr Tyrrel would not have been patiently endured, had not his colloquial accomplishments perpetually come in aid of that authority which his rank and prowess originally obtained.[11]

These few sentences are replete with words which signify power – despotism, tyranny, authority, rank, etc. But only one of them is employed twice, and that is 'ascendancy'. Moreover, ascendancy functions in this passage in two ways – to signify a power already signified plainly enough in 'despotism' and a more indirect power mediated through 'fortune'. This distinction would be of little significance were it not for the recurrence of the term within the novel.

A little later in Williams's narrative of the conflict between Tyrrel and Falkland, he has recourse once more to the same term. On some social occasion in the district, the latter had recited a poem which was admired by all except Tyrrel who sought to belittle the performance. Though the audience sided with Falkland, it submitted to Tyrrel's vehemence. Yet this success brought little gratification, for

> He found the appearance of his old ascendancy; but he felt its deceitfulness and uncertainty, and was gloomily dissatisfied.[12]

Following the death of a local and celebrated poet – rather confusingly called Mr Clare, though wholly unconnected with the actual poet, John Clare – relations between Tyrrel and Falkland deteriorate even further. The narrative explains the benign influence of literature in this remote district, and the set-back represented in the poet's death:

> This rustic tyrant had been held in involuntary restraint by the intellectual ascendancy of his celebrated neighbour; and notwithstanding the general ferocity of his temper, did not appear till lately to have entertained a hatred against him. In the short time that had elapsed from the period in which Mr Clare had fixed his residence in the neighbourhood to that of the arrival of

Mr Falkland from the continent, the conduct of Mr Tyrrel had even shown
certain tokens of improvement.[13]

Immediately before the death of Tyrrel himself, an incident occurred when
the leaders of society prohibited him from attending a local assembly. In
the absence of Falkland, the rustic tyrant determined to confront his opponents and to force an entry. Despite the opposition of gentlemen in the
room who tried either to jostle him or to dissuade him, Tyrrel

> found the secret effectually to silence the one set, and to shake off the other.
> His muscular form, the well-known eminence of his intellectual powers, the
> long habits to which every man was formed of acknowledging his ascendan-
> cy, were all in his favour.[14]

Here again is the coincidence of physical and psychological power, these
however being both distinguished and combined in the term, ascendancy.
But the sudden return of Falkland, followed rapidly by Tyrrel's unexplain-
ed murder, brings to an end the narrative's elaboration of rustic tyranny
in an uneducated gentleman. And yet, ascendancy does not disappear. On
the contrary, the term is transferred to Falkland who is suspected by Williams
of having murdered Tyrrel. The benign, if absolute, authority of the master
is now directed against his secretary who records his conviction that
Falkland's threats were no empty words – 'I knew his ability, I felt his
ascendancy.'[15]

There is no stability in these relations of power, and Falkland is as prone
to alarm and frenzy as is the persecuted servant. In a very late chapter,
Williams acknowledges that the highly active and reciprocating power of
ascendancy operates even within his own being. Secluded in 'an obscure
market town in Wales', he discovers that scandalous accounts of his own
past were in circulation even there. No direct intervention could account
for this state of affairs, because – the narrator reasons – Falkland cannot
'ride in the whirlwind, shroud himself in clouds and impenetrable darkness,
and scatter destruction upon the earth from his secret habitation.' This echo
of the Book of Psalms serves to remind the reader of Godwin's personal
origins in English dissent, and indicates the possibility of a religious interpretation of *Caleb Williams* as an allegory of the wilful soul which dramatizes
God's benevolence as persecution.[16] But, interiorizing the biblical imagery
of his former description of a Falkland Absconditus, the narrator opts for
a more recent terminology:

> As soon as this hurricane of the mind subsided, and the winds that impelled
> me this way and that were still, one stiff and master gale took its turn of ascen-
> dancy, and drove me to an instant desertion of this once cherished retreat.[17]

In this final occurrence of ascendancy in *Caleb Williams*, the narrator does
not merely employ the term to signify power relations between characters,
relations which are in other ways seen to alternate rapidly so that now Tyrrel,
now Falkland, is local master; now Falkland, now Williams is master/slave.
He articulates this process in himself, acknowledging his subordination to
a 'turn of ascendancy'. Yet, for its acuteness in conceding a merely temporary domination in ascendancy, the statement hardly amounts to self-
knowledge, being closer to self-abasement. The ideological function of ascendancy, propagated through the Dublin Corporation and the Irish parliament
early in 1792, and excoriated in Edmund Burke's as yet unpublished letter
to his son, could hardly be more fully exemplified in fiction.

Even if it be allowed that Godwin had read the *Letter to Richard Burke*,
the connection between his novel and recent political developments in Ireland
remains unclear. The author's visit to Dublin did not occur until several years
after its composition. It is true that he had met Mary Wollstonecraft, his future
wife, as early as November 1791, and true also that Wollstonecraft was partly
Irish.[18] But their intimacy did not commence until much later, and they did
not marry until 1797. These details, even if they were more grossly positive,
could not in any case explain the presence of ascendancy in *Caleb Williams*.
By contrast, the novel itself presents an immanent explanation which serves
also to act as a critique of realist notions of fictional setting. In the fifth chapter
of the final volume, the narrator determined to escape from his persecutor
and so made up his mind 'to bend my course to the nearest sea-port on the
west side of the island, and transport myself to Ireland.'[19] The sea-port remains strictly anonymous, as indeed do most locations in the novel, but the
particular instance is remarkable in that it is the site of Williams' best endeavour to transcend the imminent closure of his narrative. In this resolve,
and in its non-implementation, we touch on the place of interpretation which
may at once make sense of Williams' narrative generally and of its unexpected
and repeated recourse to ascendancy as an account of new relations in power.
For ascendancy cannot be treated as if it were some hermetically localized
product of Dublin rhetoric; it took its place in broader contexts of loyalism
in the British Isles and of European counter-revolutionary politics.[20]

To achieve his ends, the narrator Williams adopted an Irish accent – learned from fellow-prisoners in a gaol! – only to find himself frustrated in the
ambition to quit his native England. Naturally, there are adequate explanations for this, and he is arrested under suspicion of a crime quite unconnected with Mr Falkland's affairs. But prior to the report of this set-back,
Williams had already recorded the peculiarly inadequate reasoning behind
his decision to ship for Ireland:

Ireland had to me the disadvantage of being a dependency of the British government, and therefore a place of less security than most other countries which
are divided from it by the ocean.[21]

In the event, or rather in the text, Ireland names both a desired locus and
an assumed identification which leads to incarceration. It is therefore hardly surprising to discover that Williams, disguising himself as an Irishman,
is taken as such and duly arrested for complicity in a crime of which he
has no knowledge whatsoever. Desire is rewarded with incarceration in a
place-and-time where revolution is frustrated through the ideological operations of new modes of power for which ascendancy acts as a *resumé*. In this
manner, the novel can be shown to seek a place of interpretation which embraces Ireland as a politically articulate component but which is repeatedly
driven back into the anonymity of 'a remote county' of England.

That this should occur in a fiction written during the efflorescence of
romantic particularism in the *Lyrical Ballads* of Wordsworth and Coleridge,
when local habitations were energetically named, underlines the extent to
which *Caleb Williams* declines to accept any identification of geographic
setting with its proper place of interpretation. Beyond the instance of this
one novel, there is a large body of fiction in which the same challenge to
predictable closure, a challenge which proposes social and political rather
than geographic distinctions as its topography, is essayed. One symbolic
representation of this contest between the social and the geographic in
delineations of fictional setting may be found in incidents occurring when
land and ocean meet, incidents (that is) where the definition of the
geographical is still unfinished.

Maria Edgeworth once described the encounter of readers with a climactic incident in one of her novels as 'that dangerous rock upon which poor
authors even after a prosperous voyage are often wrecked sometimes while
their friends were actually hailing them from the shore.'[22] The novel in
question was *The Absentee*, which revolves round crucial re-negotiations of
the hero's social identity as divided between the islands of Britain and
Ireland. Two years later, *Patronage* (1814) opens with a shipwreck scene on
the English coast and concludes only after the ramifications of contemporary
politics have been illuminated through the discovery of an Irish dimension
in a great minister's past and private career. The place of interpretation includes an Ireland which is textual rather than actual in the fiction. Such
amphibious elements in novels of this period by authors as different as
Brockden Brown, Burney, Edgeworth, Godwin, and Maturin suggest that
fictional setting is an arena where highly charged ideological issues are
sublimated.[23] In Jane Austen's *Mansfield Park* a triumphantly conservative

re writing of the West Indian slave trade, the war at sea, and the expansive aggression of empire generally is effected in manor-house, land-locked (near) seclusion.

Caleb Williams could scarcely be more different. The narrator is unable to stabilize his memories, his experiences, his determination to compose a history of himself. In dramatic terms, his insatiable curiosity about Falkland is to blame. But in lexical terms, the intervention of ascendancy signifies the destabilization of power together with its simultaneous redeployment and intensification in rapidly alternating patterns. Marxists would say that, in this respect, the novel treats the succession of order by class. To be sure, that development had commenced centuries earlier, and yet it may be compacted into a fiction of contemporary life as a registration of its significance in the revolutionary age. In anti-revolutionary Britain, the plebeian secretary, Williams, tries to escape from Falkland, his godlike and savage employer, by fleeing to Ireland. But his failure is – so to speak – *a priori*. For escape to Ireland would bring him face to the face with the origins of ascendancy as an ideological concept. Potentially, Ireland is a place of interpretation for *Caleb Williams*. The events of the succeeding few years, and the fate of Godwin's Irish friends, demonstrated how circumscribed that potential would prove to be.

We will find that the ideology of Protestant Ascendancy hibernates in the years after the heady debates of 1792 and, a few contemptuous pamphlets nothwithstanding, it disappears from the general idiom of Irish political debate in the first half of the nineteenth century. In England and among English political activists, it never achieved any established currency, even at the time of the Dublin debates and the attempt to reform Irish legislation in the mid-1790s. Indeed, even in its earliest Irish usage the application of ascendancy to church-state relations elsewhere (in Scotland, Hungary, Denmark etc.) did not survive the paper war of 1786 – 88.

The evidence of William Godwin's writings confirms this pattern. Back in 1785, his public letter to Edmund Burke had dwelled on the temporary eclipse of genius which a few vaporous rivals may effect: his illustration alluded to clouds which can only blot out the sun for a short time. More particularly, he insisted that

> the fervor of the sun and the brightness of his beams cannot fail speedily to regain the ascendancy, and to resume the world with unwonted serenity and lustre.[24]

This is a distinctly pre-revolutionary usage. Broadly speaking, it retains the celestial-cum-planetary association which also characterized the astrological usage. What is in the ascendant is an object and, though the application of the trope has moral implications, the relationship is one-directional, mechanical even, and involves no direct human element. By contrast, ascendancy in *Caleb Williams* is in all its instances infused with complex exchanges between persons exercising power or being exercised by power. What's more, the shift in Godwin's use of the term complies with Burke's scornful analysis of the new slogan of 1792.

The *Letter to Richard Burke* had quickly focused on political machinations among Dublin's leading political figures, while noting that a new word had been minted and circulated in Dublin Castle, in the parliament, and in the city's council. Unimpressed by this verbal innovation, he insisted that 'New *ascendancy* is the old mastership,' and proceeded:

> The poor word ascendancy, so soft and melodious in its sound, so lenitive and emollient in its first usage, is now employed to cover to the world, the most rigid and perhaps not the most wise of all plans of policy. The word is large enough in its comprehension. I cannot conceive what mode of oppression in civil life, or what mode of religious persecution, may not come within the methods of preserving an *ascendancy*. In plain old English, as they apply it, it signifies *pride and dominion* on the one part of the relation, and on the other *subserviency and contempt* – and it signifies nothing else.[25]

Yet while Burke ironically provides a precedent for Godwin's altered use of the term in question, the novelist (or the novel) has gone further. Resisting the innovation because he detests the policy it covered, Burke was inclined to regard the former merely as an impudent deception, or counterfeit term, through which it was possible to discern 'plain old English'. In keeping with this he analysed ascendancy in terms of a simple relation of two parts, in which one element is constantly subordinated to the other. Later on, the *Letter to Richard Burke* acknowledged that fixed signification was scarcely conceivable in practice. 'A very great part of the mischiefs that vex the world, arises from words. People soon forget the meaning, but the impression and the passion remain.'[26] It remained for the work of fiction, however, to demonstrate the extent to which language and power are mutually enabling, to demonstrate indeed their inextricably conjoined functions.

It would be a thankless task to scan the five novels which followed *Caleb Williams* in search of absolute confirmation of the view that, between 1785 and 1794, Godwin's understanding of the noun ascendancy radically changed, and did so in a manner consistent with the possibility – it is no more – that he read Burke's *Letter* of 1792 in manuscript. Nor is there much to be gained by any triumphant proof that he had indeed studied

Burke's ironic analysis of the noun's promotion to conceptual status. And
yet the immediacy of the *Letter* and *Caleb Williams* deserves attention. It
should be recalled that, strictly understood, the title of Godwin's novel is
Things as They Are, with the narrator's name only featuring in the sub-title.
This emphasis on contemporary society, and its inadequacies, should not
be mistaken for an understanding of the British *ancien régime* as unaltered
since its foundation. On the contrary, the decade after 1789 was characterized
by new laws directed against individual radicals and against working-mens'
combinations. The success of this programme of repression is well known,
and can be traced in Godwin's subsequent preference for historical fiction
over the contemporary engagement with 'things as they are'. The defeat of
revolution is signalled by a reversion to the past, an imaginative retrenchment through historical research. The historical novel, it might be noted,
existed in its radical form prior to Walter Scott's launching of the romantic-
conservative version.

Among the novels which Godwin published after *Caleb Williams* one
deserves attention in the present context. Published in 1817, and dedicated
to the recently dead John Philpot Curran, *Mandeville* was subtitled a 'tale
of the seventeenth century in England'. Just as *Caleb Williams* sought to
conclude in Ireland so, by a neat contrast, *Mandeville* opened in Ireland.
More precisely, its narrator commences the account of his dismal life with
a retrospect thrown back onto his birth in Ireland and his escape as an or-
phan from the massacres of October 1641 in the Irish north midlands. Ascendancy occurs in *Mandeville*, but with nothing like the frequency and the
consistency of context which distinguishes its role in *Caleb Williams*. And
yet in tracing his anti-hero back to the bloody insurrection of 1641, Godwin
drew on one of the myths which came to justify and sustain the ideology
of Protestant Ascendancy.[27]

The year 1817 also saw Maria Edgeworth experiment with the historical
novel; while *Ormond* excavates the political and social world of eighteenth-
century Ireland, it has no need of the slogan upon which Yeats was to found
his 1930s' myth of Augustan Ireland. *Ormond* has its alternative place of
interpretation. Indeed it has two, and these are tentatively negotiated overseas,
just as Caleb's desire to escape is mediated through a frustrated passage by
boat to Ireland. To the west of *Ormond*'s corrupt Irish mainland lie the Black
Islands, primitive, colourful, ingenious and outmoded; to the east is Paris,
the home of pre-revolutionary Enlightenment.[28] Enlightenment was to
prove as redundant to the political appetites of the Irish administration so
brilliantly mocked in *Ormond* as the 'native' extravagances of King Corny
in his Islands.

Moving from the literary to the non-literary area, from novel to political tract, we should remind ourselves how readily the categorical boundary can be negotiated. In part, the relative ease of this transference stems from changes which have occurred in the general practice of literary history during the past two or three decades.[29] More locally, however, one had already noted active interchange between the two areas in the romantic period: Burke's *Reflections* have revealed certain structural resemblances to the historical novel, while fiction such as Godwin's (and even Edgeworth's) bear a freight of authorial annotation later novelists would scarcely think decent. The respectability of the Victorian novelists cannot be imputed to their forebears, nor is the inconsequentiality of modern pamphleteers anticipated in writers of the Jacobin and anti-Jacobin camps.

In the wake of the 1792 excitement there followed eight years of growing crisis. Disturbances in south Ulster led to the formation of the Orange Order in 1795. The United Irishmen's campaigns for political reform were succeeded by bloody insurrection and even bloodier repression in 1798. Thereafter, debate of a Union with Great Britain reached its apotheosis in 1801. In the course of a decade political pamphleteering had expanded exponentially, and the Union debates in particular provided a field day for Dublin's printers and booksellers. In all of this material, the concept of Protestant Ascendancy can doubtless be traced in a medley of publications and speeches. Much rarer, however, is any consciously analytical discussion of the concept in this stage of its evolution. In the latter connection, three pamphlets have been chosen for close examination, the third of these being the work of Edward Sheridan, a veteran of the 1786–88 paper war.

Before leaving 1792, we may note in passing an exceedingly long and retrospective production signed by 'Candidus Redintegratus' and printed by James Moore, one of the publishers of the *Parliamentary Register*. Running – or at best, plodding – to more than one hundred pages, *Free Thoughts on the Measures of Opposition, Civil and Religious, from the Commencement of the Last Parliament to the Present Period: with a Modest Plea for the Rights and Ascendancy of Episcopal Protestantism* devotes more than a quarter of its length to a fine denunciation of William Campbell's reply to Richard Woodward's *Present State of the Church of Ireland*, the last named having been the detonating item of the paper war. The oddness of this proportion, and its isolated position in the larger context, underline how infrequently the disputes of 1786–88 were invoked in 1792. Booksellers advertising the work found it economical to shorten the title to *Free Thoughts on Protestant*

Ascendancy, and this compaction is remarkable because Candidus Redintegratus preferred the more pedantic, restricted (and longer) phrase 'the
Episcopal Protestant Church'.[30] In opposing Campbell, in lacerating Whigs
generally, and in stressing episcopalianism, he maintained a tone discernible in the behaviour of Thomas Elrington and other anonymous pamphleteers of the established church. But his *Free Thoughts* did not require
any clearly enunciated notion of Protestant Ascendancy.

The paper war had revolved round Richard Woodward's *Present State*,
published in December 1786. In approaching the republication of this pamphlet in 1808, we can pick our way through the mass of printed material
generated by the crises of the 1790s, the Union, and its aftermath, by isolating
a few items which discuss Protestant Ascendancy in some analytical detail.
Little is known with certainty of *Observations on the Meaning of the Words,
Protestant, Ascendancy, and Orangeman . . .* issued in anonymous response
to one of Patrick Duigenan's attacks upon Henry Grattan. The pamphlet
reads like the work of a young man, and the copy preserved in the Royal
Irish Academy bears on its title-page the inscription 'Doctr. Orpen'. Whether
the text can be firmly ascribed to a particular member of the Orpen family
need not be decided now: what is of interest is the author's disquisition on
language, only a small proportion of which is devoted to the concept here
under examination.

Dublin Corporation strictures on Grattan were 'the essay of a faction,
founded in absurd tenets, and conveyed in unmeaning terms.'[31] From this
confident base, the author advanced to indict Duigenan himself:

> could it however have escaped a person of your philological acumen, that the
> phrase, Protestant ascendancy, in support of which your publication is a most
> elaborate commentary, has no proper meaning affixed to it? Mr Locke,
> somewhere I think asserts, that disputes often continue from ignorance of terms
> . . . Now, let us see how your phrase will bear this touchstone. The substan-
> tive term, ascendancy, there can be no disagreement in the meaning of: it im-
> plies superiority, and without a particular application, may be either political
> or religious, (for the word, ascendancy, no where appears in philosophical
> language) and may be applied by the inhabitants of Russia or Turkey, with
> more propriety to the politics or religion of their country, because the majori-
> ty are all of one profession, than to Ireland, where on your own principles,
> the established religion is professed by not a sixth part of the people.[32]

Burke's remarks in the *Letter to Richard Burke* (1792?) are echoed here,
even as the author virtually insists that Protestant Ascendancy as 'your phrase'
can be assigned to the odious Duigenan. Though Orpen – if that was his
name – paraded Protestant Ascendancy on the title-page, the *Observations*

did not have much more to say on the topic. It is true that there was an explicit endeavour 'to put down the phraseology of Protestantism and Protestant ascendancy,' because the author wanted to see in their place 'the ascendancy of reason, of common sense, and of christianity.'[33] If there are multiple echoes of William Paley, Tom Paine, and Edmund Burke in this triad, the dissonance may have arisen from the writer's youth and relative distance from the heights of power within the political system of Ireland before the Union. There are, after all, few things less resistant to synthesis than the irreconcilable elements of a conflict which occurred safely in the past.

William Ogilvie, tutor and step-father of Lord Edward Fitzgerald, is now known to have written a pro-Union pamphlet published separately in Dublin and London in 1800. The early part of *Protestant Ascendancy and Catholic Emancipation Reconciled* was devoted to an analysis of flaws (as the author thought them) in those decisions of 1782 generally regarded as the achievement of Irish legislative independence. In Ogilvie's opinion, this independence was partly illusory and partly pernicious. The second part of his pamphlet discussed the arrangements pertaining between Britain and Ireland during the years of Grattan's parliament, while the third examined 'The Internal State of Ireland'. It is in this last part that the notion of Protestant Ascendancy emerges.

The discussion commenced with an observation – echoing Paley of close on twenty years earlier – that anomalies inevitably featured in a state where the religious establishment endorsed the allegiance of a minority rather than majority of the population. This emphasis on minority/majority concedes the impact of the French Revolution on liberal 'conservatives' even while revolution is roundly condemned. Moreover, Ogilvie recognized in Protestant Ascendancy something akin to party in the sense that Burke opposed the emergence of party in the British political system. 'Such is the jealousy of the two parties, and such the opposition of *Protestant Ascendancy* and *Catholic Emancipation*, that whatever measure has the appearance of being approved by the one, creates distrust in the other . . .'[34] One might observe in passing that the adoption of the term emancipation, in preference to earlier talk of relief, not only emphasized the moral dimension of the Catholic claims but also indicated their potential to convert into a formidable political movement of party. Certainly Ogilvie was quick to note a conflict of philosophical priorities in the Irish dispute: Protestants under pressure invoked the legality of their position while Catholics stressed a newer, romantic belief – '*statute law* and *natural rights* knock their heads together . . .'[35]

Ogilvie's title proposed a reconciliation between parties and, beyond that, a broader harmonization of relations between Ireland's sectarian divisions within an enlarged kingdom. As with so many early commentators on Protestant Ascendancy, he indulged in an inspection of the future in the hope of finding a lesson for the present:

> If in the year 1798 Ireland had been left to the exercise of her boasted in-
> dependence, or if Great Britain were either now, or at any future period, to
> leave her to settle her contending interests and religious divisions, and to decline
> interfering in her domestic differences, the contest would, indeed, be of short
> duration, and must infallibly be terminated by the overthrow of the present
> establishment in church and state. Protestant Ascendancy, which can only be
> supported by British connexion, must expect to be thrown aside as an insolent
> usurpation; and Catholic Emancipation might be expected, by the law of retalia-
> tion, founded on the vindictive passions of the human heart, to be transform-
> ed into Catholic tyranny, instead of stopping short at Catholic ascendancy . . .
> If, in the recent stuggles, the weight of Great Britain had not been thrown
> into the scale, Protestant Ascendancy and Irish Independence must have kicked
> the beam.[36]

For Ogilvie, the location of Protestant Ascendancy was neither Dublin's common council in 1792 nor its paper war of 1787: he looked to more immediate events. On several occasions, he commented on specific areas which rose in 1798, writing on the first that 'the counties of Wicklow and Wexford, the seat of the rebellion, may be considered Protestant; the provinces of Munster and Connaught, where the Roman Catholics prevail, were never engaged in the rebellion.'[37] Yet Connacht *had* participated, by hosting a French army under General Humbert, and by providing the setting for the Races of Castlebar which led catastrophically (for the rebels) to the Battle of Ballinamuck early in September 1798. Here perhaps Ogilvie made notable distinctions between the behaviour of invader and native, while also remaining oddly silent on the Ulster theatre of rebellion. But his point was more fully worked out on a second appearance:

> If an agreement had been made at the Revolution [i.e. in 1691] to select one
> county in Ireland for trying an experiment of the effect of Protestant Ascen-
> dancy, I defy any man to point out a circumstance that had been wanting to
> make that experiment in the county of Wexford. Who that knew the county
> of Wexford, or had heard of the Protestant boys of Wexford, could have con-
> ceived that the Roman Catholics should have risen there? And yet such is the
> fact: the rebellion not only broke out there, but was marked with atrocities
> that disgrace human nature. Does this example encourage us to extend Protest-
> ant Ascendancy over the rest of the kingdom?[38]

Ogilvie, in effect if not in so many words, identified Protestant Ascendancy with a middleman and yeoman stratum which, in the Wexford of the 1790s, had overreached itself financially and socially. The upstart John Hunter Gowan may have been exceptionally targetted in the *Memoirs* of his Catholic neighbour, Miles Byrne, but the parvenu element in Protestant society was in Ogilvie's analysis once again associated with notions of ascendancy. Characterizing Patrick Duigenan as 'the Fugal man of Protestant Ascendancy', in whose 1790s' writings 'the asperity which religious distinction infuses into party' is strongly portrayed, he further attends to the insecurity of such spokesmen. Duigenan, John Giffard, and Dominic Trant were all born into Irish Catholicism, and in conforming to the establishment they had not always smothered anxieties concerning origin, *per se*, which Protestant Ascendancy ideology was ultimately to assuage. The English-born Richard Woodward, lavishly advertised and industriously circulated in 1786–7, was silent in 1792: by 1800 he was dead.[39] When Ogilvie did come to consider the options before Catholics in 1800 – will they trust British promises of relief accompanying Union? – he was obliged to consider the origins of ideological thinking itself. As against royal approval in the past, and Pitt's promises now,

> will they trust the men who, in 1792, pledged their lives and fortunes, at their county meetings, to support Protestant Ascendancy; and who, in 1793, endeavoured to defeat, when they could not prevent, His Majesty's gracious recommendation of their cause to the Irish parliament, by introducing the exclusion of which they now complain?[40]

By concentrating on the county meetings of late 1792, Ogilvie acknowledged what he elsewhere called 'the present establishment of property'.[41] He was also constantly attentive to the broader implications of Irish ideological debate. France was the cabinet of moral and political examples to be ransacked at a time of crisis. The peculation and jobbery of late-eighteenth-century Ireland resembled all too closely the longer history of arrogant exclusion under the *ancien régime*. In France, the nobility and clergy had enjoyed, just like 'the Protestants of Ireland, exclusive privileges to all the great offices of honour, distinction, and consideration in the state.'[42] The moral was clear, even if Irish difference revolved round religion as well as class: encouragement of the Protestant Ascendancy mentality would provoke a repetition of Wexford in '98 on such a scale that it would more closely resemble France under the Terror. It will remain for Yeats, more than a century and a quarter later, to take up the theme of Protestant Ascendancy and the 'ruin to come' (as Yeats's Swift will be thought to regard the events of 1789 in Paris).

The two pamphlets considered above as beacons lighting our way from 1792 to 1808 were both the work of Protestant authors, however distant or close their positions on the social scale. The Catholic loyalties of James Edward Devereux, author of *Observations on the Factions Which Have Ruled Ireland*, constitute only one reason why his work is discussed here, though his standing was such that he had served as one of the five delegates who in 1793 had presented the Catholic petition to George III at St James's Palace, London. Towards the end of his long life he described his own pamphlet as 'the Father and Mother of [Thomas] Moore's Captain Rock', a remark which neatly connects literary, political, and paramilitary campaigns in the 1820s back into the ideological disputes of two or three decades earlier. *Observations on the Factions* evidently ran to several 'editions', and while a large proportion of its pages were given over to historical questions, room was found for a terse commentary on more recent developments:

> A curious non-descript, unknown to the genuine spirit of the constitution as established at the revolution, the Protestant ascendancy, was now [post-1792] pompously brought forward: the hacks of the FACTION were despatched in every direction, and to every corner of Ireland, to make converts to the worship of their brain; to whose support lives and fortunes were to be devoted, and on whose altars were to be immolated the rights and liberties of born and unborn millions of Irishmen . . .[43]

Devereux, a native of Carrigmenan, remained active in Wexford politics for twenty years and more; his testimony is more valuable as evidence of a regionally concentrated preoccupation with ascendancy than as yet another statement of its latter-day origins.

The third stepping stone which provides the historian of ideas with a textual path from the 1790s to the republished *Present State of the Church of Ireland* in 1808 is yet another anonymous pamphlet, though its place of publication was London rather than Dublin. James Mason (1779 – 1827), the author of *Thoughts on the Protestant Ascendancy in Ireland* (1805) wrote generally in favour of a political reform in Ireland and particularly in sympathetic support of Catholics (including English Catholics) as a social group. He early identified his opponents as

> those who, in an enlightened age, continue narrow-minded and selfish; who bring back to our indignant recollection the dark and gloomy prejudices of the twelfth century; who are learned in the lumbering trash of metaphysical theology; in a word, those whom laws only restrain from the pleasures of persecution, who love government only in its severity, and who worship religion only in its abuses.[44]

From this it is easy to establish the author's general bearings, and also possible (I believe) to detect specific attitudes similar to those expressed by John Philpot Curran in parliament in 1792 and in a published *Letter . . . on the Present State of Ireland*, addressed to Edmund Burke in 1795.[45] Ireland, for Mason, was not essentially different from other European nations. Characterizing it as 'a commercial country' and emphasizing that 'many of its greatest merchants are of the Romish persuasion', he saw its interest lying in 'the preservation of tranquility'. Despite the familiarity of this condition and this aspiration:

> the bad system of morals and manners so universal in that country, might probably be shewn to proceed from the want of a *public opinion*, which can only be found in that state of society, where perfect equality of rights, and a community of interest extend without interruption, from the highest to the lowest orders of the people – where there is neither oppression on the one hand, nor abject submission on the other.[46]

It is within this context of Burkean sentiment and commercial calculation that Mason's isolated thoughts on the Protestant Ascendancy may be considered for, notwithstanding his pamphlet's title, the term occurs on very few occasions. In the first instance, 'the free undisturbed exercise of our reasons' was associated with the Reformation as a right conferred by God on all mankind. 'It is then no longer in the power of the supporter of the Protestant Ascendancy in Ireland, to justify the principles and practice of religious persecution, by the terrible decrees of the Council of Lateran.'[47] Emphasizing the extent to which property in Ireland remained in Protestant hands, and deferring for a moment the comment on great merchants of the Romish persuasion, Mason argued that 'wealth will gain followers, and property secure respect', and proceeded to ask the (for him) rhetorical question 'In what way then is the Protestant Ascendancy, as it is called, to be overturned?'[48] Finally, taking a longer historical view, he concluded that

> there appears to be no doubt that the Protestant Ascendancy has not been beneficial to Ireland: it neither has diminished the number of the Catholics, nor added to the wealth, nor increased the security of the kingdom. On the contrary, by forming two parties in the state, it generated a factious spirit, which has broken out in numerous rebellions, and which still shews itself in the general discontent of the larger proportion of the people.[49]

Mason's presuppositions and reservations here are curiously contradictory. On the one hand, his 'as it is called' indicates that the term to which it refers is incompletely assimilated into the idiom of his subject (Irish politics) or of his readers (who may be predominantly English, given the place of publication). Indeed, the question of a discrepancy between the idioms of these two elements usefully draws attention to the complexity inherent in published writing, whether factual or fictional, discursive or lyric. Thus we find that, on the other hand, Mason seems willing to ascribe to Protestant Ascendancy responsibility for 'numerous rebellions' which (if one allows the Whiteboy risings under that description) take us back to the 1760s. The vapidity of the term, Protestant Ascendancy, is indulged even as its lexical status is queried. His title-page gives centrality to a concept which never reaches centre-stage in the pamphlet proper.

Echoing Burke on the topic of Irish manners, and anticipating in a minor way W. E. H. Lecky on public opinion, James Mason's *Thoughts* of 1805 demonstrates how an ephemeral publication can prompt a critical review of major cultural forces – the relations, for example, between public opinion and Protestant Ascendancy as general and specific formulations of power. Lecky will of course argue that it was Jonathan Swift's great achievement to create a public opinion in Ireland where nothing of that kind had previously operated. However flawed that argument may now seem, it usefully draws attention to an instance where local pamphleteering ('The Drapier's Letters' of 1724) and metropolitan publication of a complex fiction (*Gulliver's Travels* of 1726) mutually inform each other in critical retrospection. The paper war of 1786 – 88 threw up nothing as incisive as the 'Letters' and none of its participants later demonstrated a talent for deliberate fiction; the cultural implications of Protestant Ascendancy still lay buried in the future. In 1985, *Ascendancy and Tradition* advanced a notion of public opinion which took too simplistic a view of the restricted operation of public opinion in eighteenth-century Ireland. In one highly localized instance (the fiction of Sheridan Le Fanu), *Dissolute Characters* in 1993 sought to remedy this defect by introducing Jürgen Habermas's notion of the bourgeois social sphere: but much remains to be done in this area.[50]

One particular phenomenon may be looked at as an example of cultural transmission – systematic republication of ideologically charged texts. The most notable instance in the Irish context is undoubtedly Sir John Temple's history of the 1641 rebellion, first issued in 1646 and periodically re-inserted into public circulation whenever the Catholic issue appeared to be making progress. Here one is witnessing the maintenance of a prejudicial argument throughout a century-long debate. The industrious promotion of no less than four so-called editions of Richard Woodward's *Present State of the Church of Ireland* between 18 December 1786 and the end of the year exemplifies a different mode of ideological intimidation, one in which saturation is achieved by repetitive concentration rather than prolonged availability of a text. This latter strategy is highly appropriate in a period when the notion of ideology itself is in the making. After 1787, however, *The Present State* appears to have lost its appeal, perhaps for the very reason that unsold copies were readily available. Twenty-one years elapsed before it was republished.

The issue of tithes which had so exercised Woodward and his contemporaries in 1786–8 had not been resolved by any provision of the Act of Union (1800). The larger issue of Catholic Emancipation – a term increasingly common – was fuelled by considerations external to the landscape of rural Ireland. As we know, the nineteenth century was close on thirty years old before the matter was confronted. The irony of the situation during the intervening period lay primarily in the fact that resistance to emancipation no longer was concentrated in the ranks of die-hard Irish or Anglo-Irish MPs; English anti-Catholicism flourished after the Union, and even such intellectuals as Wordsworth and Coleridge expressed their antagonism towards concession. If historians of nineteenth-century Ireland have gone a long way towards recognizing that their subject is not an island but a complex vector of the United Kingdom, then there must be hope that historians of England may follow suit. The republication of Woodward's pamphlet in 1808 cannot be considered solely in its local context. Yet if one looks at the broader canvas, it is immediately obvious that the republication was a very minor episode in the long conflict which led to Daniel O'Connell's success in 1829.

The flurry of controversy which occurred in Ireland in 1808 naturally had multiple causes and – to change the metaphor of cause and effect – flowed through divergent channels. In 1807 an imperial government had fallen, principally because of confusion over its policy towards Catholics. Its successor was elected in a campaign in which 'no popery' slogans played a prominent role. The lord-lieutenant in Ireland promoted several figures who had taken part in earlier paper wars. Patrick Duigenan, now secretary of the Orange Order, became a privy councillor, and John Giffard (dismissed under a previous *régime*) was once again rewarded with a lucrative post. But the historian of this aspect of the Catholic question also notes that, in 1809, the lord lieutenant objected on at least one occasion to the toasting of 'Protestant Ascendancy'.[51]

One prompt to controversy took the form of published letters describing a tour of Ireland by John Milner, the Catholic vicar apostolic for the English midlands. At the heart of the argument was the matter of a possible veto, an arrangement whereby the church would accept the monarch's right to approve appointments to the hierarchy in return for substantial concessions. These negotiations implicated the long and bitter history of British relations with the Vatican, and Milner both noted on an international diplomatic stage and strode the boards of Dublin's provincial press. Replies to his *Letters* were profuse, and in addition the theological controversies of the day had acquired a degree of virulence (on the anti-Catholic side certainly) quite unknown in 1787 or 1792. A Catholic called Ward, having published *Errata of the Protestant Bible*, was answered in Dublin by Edward Ryan, one of the lesser controversial supporters of Woodward in 1787. Thomas Elrington also entered the lists, now putting his name to some at least of his publications and concentrating less on directly political matters. The publisher of his *Clergy of the Church of England Truly Ordained* (1808) was John Brook, who was responsible also for the re-appearance in the same year of Woodward's *Present State*. One might be entitled to see Elrington's influence in the resurrection of Woodward.[52]

The new edition was wholly unaltered from that which had served through several so-called editions twenty-one years earlier. Apart from the heading 'A New Edition', the title page took over Woodward's long invocation of the Protestant interest and the insurrection in Munster, though a far more fiercesome insurrection had occurred in the interval. Even the printer William Sleater's idiosyncratic use of the apostrophe – it's precarious situation – was duly preserved, as if responsibility for getting Woodward back into circulation had been given to a simple-minded but scrupulous copyist. The Latin appendices were left without translation, though such had been provided in the later stages of the original edition. No index appeared, nor was any use made of the London preface. An accidental blank in a footnote (on p. 15) remained piously unaltered.

The details may seem – indeed *are*! – highly inconsequential. Yet the failure of Brook's edition of a text which repeatedly (if inconsistently) invoked Protestant Ascendancy is itself significant. A concept, which had been thoroughly established in the political idiom of 1792, has been sidelined thereafter. Given its subsequent cultural ennoblement, the pattern of casual employment in 1786–7, intensive conceptualization in 1792, and later 're-casualization' suggests a complex genealogy. In 1808 the only notable response to republication of Woodward's *Present State* (with its little cargo of ascendancies) came from a veteran of the earlier paper war. Indeed Edward Sheridan sprang into print even before the rumoured re-issue had been accomplished. He brought together the texts of his 1787–8 pamphlets in further answer to the bishop of Cloyne's (now posthumous) arguments. The principal feature of interest in Sheridan's new publication lay in the Introduction which began by reminding readers of the 'very fierce literary war' of two decades earlier.[53] Though he had little of substance to add, the manner in which he related the events of the intervening years revealed a good deal concerning the impact of Protestant Ascendancy ideology. For a start, he nowhere connected the notion, or even the phrase, with Woodward's pamphlet. The current of events flowed too rapidly in his recollection for such minutiae – 'three years had scarce elapsed, from the close of our literary war, when the French revolution began to flatter the subjects, and to alarm the rulers of almost every state in the world.'[54] Here spoke one who had carefully imbibed Burke's interpretation of the Revolution, and the rapid transition to an account of the 1790s disturbances in Armagh maintained an essentially Burkean view of the revolutionary decade, the decade of Caleb Williams's frustrated escape to Ireland. It was precisely at this moment that Sheridan alluded to the new ideological concept with which we have been concerned:

> Ministry and Ascendancy seemed to understand each other perfectly well: Ministry were gratified by these banditti being suffered to harass the country with impunity; and the Ascendancy in its turn was complimented with permission to run down the respectable Catholics by plots, surpassing if possible, in atrocity, that to which the infamous Titus Oates had given his name.[55]

In keeping with Burke's analysis of the Armagh incidents, and his apparent anticipation of a provoked rebellion which duly followed after his death in 1797, Sheridan's account of 1798 concentrated on 'the unparalleled inadequacies of ascendancy calumniators' generally and on the particular inadequacies of an unnamed historian of '98 whose virtual every page betrayed 'a malignity peculiar to an ascendancy bigot'.[56] In this mode, Sheridan revealed himself curiously dependent on a notion which elsewhere he eschewed amid fastidious observations on Woodward's linguistic and stylistic failings. Thus he inveighed against the accumulated wealth of 'three ascendancy families' and against what he termed broadly 'the Irish ascendancy'.[57] Clearly some kind of social élite is implicated here, yet of Protestant Ascendancy in its full canonical form we find nothing.

Though the Unbiassed Irishman's 1808 introduction was in most respects less concentrated than his earlier writings, there is one passage which essays an interpretation of a new kind of history-making then in evidence among opponents of the Catholic cause. To counter this, Sheridan's account of this subliminal reshaping of the past drew on, or contributed to, the numerous allusions to cabalistic or magical procedures offered in mocking explanation of Protestant Ascendancy's pretensions – or power. For, by 1808, the reforms sought by Catholics in 1787, in 1792, and at the time of the Union, were *as a general programme* defeated. Piecemeal concessions had been granted, but the rebellion and its interpretation by contemporary historians (such as Richard Musgrave) ensured that a superior and seemingly indefinable force distorted even the Catholic plea to have the agreed terms of 1800 honoured:

> Every advantage, either natural or acquired, that Ireland could boast of, was kept out of view: her incapacity, her weakness, her ignorance, her vices, were the constant themes of ascendancy patriots, and Ireland, in all her great lineaments, was reduced by the magic of ascendancy to a pigmy form.[58]

Here indeed is ascendancy – if not exactly, Protestant Ascendancy – involuntarily adopted by one resolutely opposed to it. The triumph of Protestant Ascendancy as an ideological concept could hardly have been demonstrated in a more suitably ironical fashion, and that on the eve of its 're-casualisation'. Yet if Sheridan strikes one as bordering on pathos in some passages of his introduction, he also anticipated certain crucial developments in the configuration of the concept. Exonerating Trinity College to some degree, he less deliberately linked Protestant Ascendancy to landed families, and so marked one small step in the transfer of the concept away from the urban area so highly articulated in 1792 and into the fabulously doomed world of the great Irish estates. Much of the nineteenth century would pass before that transformation lent itself as elegaic material to the unlanded magician, W. B. Yeats.

NOTES AND REFERENCES

1   Maria Edgeworth, *Castle Rackrent, Tales and Novels* (London: 1832) vol. 1, p. 94.
2   See Marilyn Butler, *Maria Edgeworth: a Literary Biography* (Oxford: Clarendon Press, 1972); see also W. J. Mc Cormack, *Ascendancy and Tradition in Anglo-Irish Literary History from 1789 to 1939* (Oxford: Clarendon Press, 1985), pp. 99-100.
3   On 'place of interpretation' etc. see some preliminary remarks in W. J. Mc Cormack 'The Tedium of History: An Approach to Maria Edgeworth's *Patronage* (1814)', in Ciaran Brady, ed., *Ideology and the Historians* (Dublin: Lilliput Press), pp. 77-98, esp. pp. 90-96.
4   These are usefully included in Godwin, *Enquiry Concerning Political Justice*, Isaak Kramnick, ed. (London: Penguin, 1985), p. 788. Kramnick reprints the 1798 expanded and revised text. For the original 1793 text see William Godwin, *Political and Philosophical Writings*, Mark Philp, ed. (London: Pickering, 1993), vol. 3 (text) and vol. 4 (variants).
5   Quoted in the introductory note [p. vii] to Pamela Clemit's edition of *Caleb Williams*, in William Godwin, *Collected Novels and Memoirs* (London: Pickering, 1992), vol. 3.
6   Ibid., p. 19.
7   For Yeats see 'The Municipal Gallery Re-visited' in *New Poems* (1938); for

Heaney see *North* (1975).

8 *Caleb Williams*, p. 19.

9 The basic plot of Maria Edgeworth's 'Ennui' (*Tales of Fashionable Life*, 1st series, 1809) might be identified here, though the motif of swapped infants has a folkloric provenance also.

10 See *Enquiry Concerning Political Justice*, Kramnick, (ed.), p. 106, and Philp (ed.), *Political and Philosophical Writings*, vol. 4, p. 21. Philp notes that Hercules did indeed have a twin brother, Iphicles by name. Seamus Heaney's employment of the myth requires studied neglect of Iphicles in order to allegorize difference along a binary pattern of antagonism.

11 *Caleb Williams*, pp. 18-19.

12 Ibid., p. 26.

13 Ibid., p. 34.

14 Ibid., p. 82.

15 Ibid., p. 130.

16 Ibid., pp. 254, 256; cf. *Psalms* 18: 11, 'He made darkness his secret place; his pavilion round about him were dark waters and thick clouds of the skies.'

17 Ibid., p. 258.

18 William St Clair *The Godwins and the Shelleys* (London: Faber, 1989), p. 158.

19 *Caleb Williams*, pp. 212-13.

20 On British loyalism see W. J. Mc Cormack, *The Dublin Paper War of 1786 – 1788* (Dublin: Irish Academic Press, 1993), pp. 106-08, and refs.

21 *Caleb Williams*, p. 213.

22 See Edgeworth to Margaret Ruxton, 20 August 1812: Nat. Lib. Ire. MS 10, 166/865.

23 Apart from novels already mentioned, I have in mind Brockden Brown's *Curwen* and Maturin's *Melmoth the Wanderer*.

24 Godwin, *Political and Philosophical Writings*, (Philip ed.), vol. 1, p. 265.

25 'Letter to Richard Burke' in *The Writings and Speeches of Edmund Burke*, R. B. McDowell ed. (Oxford: Clarendon Press, 1991), p. 644.

26 Ibid., p. 647.

27 In this connection, note Arthur Brown's isolated invocation of Protestant Ascendancy in the parliamentary debates of 1787 (*The Dublin Paper War*, pp. 57, 94) and his rhetorical deployment of the 1641 theme.

28 The comparison of novels by Edgeworth and Godwin will be extended in my forthcoming study of Maria Edgeworth's fiction (Dublin: Gill and Macmillan).

29 For some cogent remarks on these changes, see Ian Small, *Oscar Wilde Revalued: An Essay on New Materials and Methods of Research* (Greensboro (N.C.): ELT Press, 1993), pp. 8, 155-72.

30 Candidus Redintegratus, *Free Thoughts* . . . (Dublin: Moore, 1792), p. 109.

31 *Observations on the Words, Protestant, Ascendancy, and Orangeman* . . . (Dublin: Smyth, 1798), p. 2.

32 Ibid., pp. 3-4.

33 Ibid., p. 14.

34 [W. Ogilvie] *Protestant Ascendancy and Catholic Emancipation Reconciled by a Legislative Union* (Dublin: Milliken, 1800), p. 59.

35 Ibid., p. 60. For William Paley's role in the background to the pamphlet exchanges of 1786–1788, see McCormack, *The Dublin Paper War*, pp. 100-06.

36 Ibid., pp. 54-55.

37 Ibid., p. 35.

38 Ibid., p. 85.

39 On Giffard, see *Ascendancy and Tradition*, Appendix B (pp. 402-04); for the others see *The Dublin Paper War*, pp. 63, 65, 75 etc.

40 [Ogilvie], *Protestant Ascendancy and Catholic Emancipation* . . ., p. 78.

41 Ibid., p. 63. The county meetings of 1792 were not exclusively supportive of Protestant Ascendancy; see *The Dublin Paper War*, pp. 131-33.

42 [Ogilvie], *Protestant Ascendancy and Catholic Emancipation* . . ., p. 89.

43 James Edward Devereux, *Observations on the Factions which have Ruled Ireland* (London: Debrett, 1801), pp. 99-100. The comments about Thomas Moore's *Captain Rock* are embodied in a MS letter from Devereux to James Hardiman preserved in a copy of the *Observations* in the Royal Irish Academy. (On Moore and Ascendancy, see below p. 166.) I am grateful to Kevin Whelan for his comments on Devereux's significance.

44 [James Mason], *Thoughts on the Protestant Ascendancy in Ireland* (London: Harding, 1805), pp. 4-5.

45 See *The Dublin Paper War*, pp. 121, 134-5.

46 [Mason], *Thoughts on the Protestant Ascendancy in Ireland*, p. 95.

47 Ibid., pp. 49-50.

48 Ibid., p. 58.

49 Ibid., p. 78.

50 See *Ascendancy and Tradition*, pp. 298-309; W. J. Mc Cormack, *Dissolute Characters: Irish Literary History Through Balzac, Le Fanu, Yeats and Bowen* (Manchester: Manchester University Press, 1993), pp. 96-97, 103-104; Jürgen Habermas, *The Structural Transformation of the Public Sphere: An Inquiry into a Category of Bourgeois Society*, trans. Thomas Burger (Oxford: Polity Press, 1989), *passim*.

51 S. J. Connolly 'The Catholic Question, 1801 – 1812' in W. E. Vaughan, ed., *Ireland Under the Union: 1, 1801 – 1870* (Oxford: Clarendon Press, 1989), pp. 35-6.

52 On Ryan and Elrington in 1786 – 1788, see *The Dublin Paper War*, pp. 73, 76-7.

53 *The Third Edition of the Unbiassed Irishman* . . . (Dublin: Fitzpatrick, 1808), p. [1]. For an account of Sheridan's role in the earlier exchanges, see *The Dublin Paper War*, pp. 94-95. Another 1808 pamphlet anticipated Woodward's republication, H. B. Dudley's *A Short Address to* . . . *William* [*Stuart*] *Lord Primate of All Ireland* (London: Cadell and Davies, 1809). The author was an Englishman by birth, by profession chancellor of the diocese of Ferns, and also a comic dramatist.

54 *The Third Edition of the Unbiassed Irishman*, p. 5. Influenced no doubt by Irish Catholic disappointment at William Pitt's failure to deliver emancipation after the Union, Sheridan accuses him of having fomented the paper war of 1786 – 1788; indeed 'the literary warfare now under consideration was not his first essay' in undermining Irish self-esteem. No evidence in support of this claim is adduced.

55 Ibid., p. 6.

56 Ibid., pp. 8, 10.

57 Ibid., pp. 13, 17.

58 Ibid., p. 11.

4

Ascendancy and
Cabal, 1800–1840

There is a secret agreement between past generations and the present one. Our coming was expected on earth. Like every generation that preceeded us, we have been endowed with a *weak*
Messianic power, a power to which the past has a claim.
(Walter Benjamin) [1]

YEATS, POETRY AND HISTORY

Attention to the minutiae of pamphlet wars undoubtedly serves to sharpen
one's awareness of the historicity actually behind such grand names as those
of Wordsworth, Coleridge or even Godwin. But while research into these
neglected publications is valuable, it should not degenerate into a concern
with ancient deposits, lost evidence, and venerable distinctions. Literary
history properly commences in that dialectic of present and past without
which one either capitulates to an antiquarianist 'reception theory', or into
the bubble memory currently passing under the name, post-modernism.

It is therefore salutary to be reminded that the term 'Protestant Ascendancy' (usually with capital initials) has had an established usage which has
proved enduring, at least until the present debate. It refers to the social élite
predominant in Ireland after the Battle of the Boyne (1690) and throughout
the eighteenth century. The theory of representationalism, according to which
words (especially nouns) refer without difficult (or indeed any) mediation
to things, could scarcely find more confident devotees than those who speak
of 'the Anglo-Irish Protestant Ascendancy'. Yet for all the seeming precision of this formulation, the continuing need for some interpretation is almost

immediately evident: its striking generalities imply 'Anglican' (as we might now say) for Protestant, 'landed estate' for ascendancy. Thus the established usage of the term is that it should refer to the establishment, ecclesiastical and social. Requiring interpretation, we cannot simply throw ourselves on some impressively long chronological chart and pretend that it provides anything other than an opportunity for dozing over unexamined presuppositions. If one assumes Swift as the inaugurator of Protestant Ascendancy thinking, it is as well to look closely at those forgotten pamphlets of 1800. But if one is tempted to elevate these to the dignity of a founding charter, then later perspectives are required additionally.

The most recent and highly successful survey of Irish history, Robert Fitzroy Foster's *Modern Ireland 1600 – 1972*, confirms for the next twenty years the accepted application even while conceding that the term has yet to be traced in any kind of systematic citation earlier than the 1790s. Custom undoubtedly has its place in stabilizing the terminology of historians and commentators, but it is possible that custom itself deserves examination. Foster regards W. B. Yeats and Elizabeth Bowen as 'quintessential commentators on the Ascendancy psychology', without pausing to ask exactly when and how either came to the topic. Indeed here we might cite once again the quotation from Watts's *Logic* with which Samuel Johnson illustrated 'ascendancy' in his dictionary – '*Custom* or *Fashion*, even in all its Changes, has been ready to have some Degree of Ascendency over our Understanding, and what at one time seem'd decent, appears *obsolete* and *disagreeable* afterward, when the Fashion changes.' Recent custom, however, has rendered agreeable in 'Protestant Ascendancy' what was eloquently thought indecent in the eyes of John Philpot Curran and others at the end of the eighteenth century.[2]

With Yeats, there is at least an obvious place to begin our inquiries. In the Cuala Press (1934) edition of *The King of the Great Clock Tower*, Yeats first published what he called 'Commentary on A Parnellite at Parnell's Funeral'. The poem commented on was at this stage entitled 'A Parnellite on Parnell's Funeral' (later, simply 'Parnell's Funeral'). The sense of personal implication embodied in the longer title is sustained through the prose; indeed what is now the second part of the poem appeared in 1934 as conclusion to this, with the line

The rest I pass, one sentence I unsay.[3]

continuing the commentary by way of dismissing commentary. But this is not the moment to analyse the poem.

Divided into five sections of unequal length, the prose piece provides two fundamentally contrasting statements of Yeats's view of the Protestant Ascendancy. The second section opens:

> When Huguenot artists designed the tapestries for the Irish House of Lords, depicting the battle of the Boyne and the siege of Derry, they celebrated the defeat of their old enemy Louis XIV, and the establishment of a Protestant Ascendency which was to impose upon Catholic Ireland, an oppression copied in all details from that imposed upon the French Protestants. Did my own great-great-grandmother, the Huguenot Marie Voisin feel a vindictive triumph, or did she remember that her friend Archbishop King had been a loyal servant of James II . . .[4]

This is more than a simple historical assertion, and the element of personal implication (through Marie Voisin) should not be neglected. But, beyond these aspects, the passage unambiguously characterizes the Protestant Ascendancy in terms of oppression. And, lest this should be thought of as some temporary lapse into earlier patterns of behaviour, Yeats proceeds to write of the ascendancy's prospectus:

> Armed with this new power, they were to modernise the social structure, with great cruelty but effectively, and to establish our political nationality by quarrelling with England over the wool trade, a protestant monopoly.[5]

Modernization here – and this is virtually unique in Yeats – is tacitly accepted, with the inevitable 'cruelty' of the transformation deflected into the term 'ascendancy' by means of the adverb 'effectively'. It is not easy to think of any other occasion where the poet endorses the 'fast forward' drive of history; where his hopes for Irish nationalism are concerned, a distinctly atavistic account of the culture to be longed for cancels any futuristic aspect of the political programme. One takes note, and with particular care, of this exceptional acceptance of modernization as implemented by (we are told) the early eighteenth-century Protestant Ascendancy. Then, in due course, the third section of the commentary also opens with reference to the crucial term, but in markedly different tones:

> The influence of the French revolution woke the peasantry from the medieval sleep, gave them ideas of social justice and equality, but prepared for a century disastrous to the national intellect. Instead of the Protestant Ascendancy with its sense of responsibility, we had the Garrison, a political party of Protestant and Catholic landowners, merchants and officials. They loved the soil of Ireland; the returned Colonial Governor crossed the Channel to see the May flowers in his park; the merchant loved with an ardour, I have not met elsewhere, some sea-board town where he had made his money, or spent his youth, but they could give to a people they thought unfit for self-government, nothing but a condescending affection.[6]

Again the passage has its own complexity, in which a disguised autobiographical reference (through the merchant's love of a port, i.e. William Middleton's love of Sligo) plays its part. Again, the tone (of the passage in isolation as if the previous section of the commentary were lost in time past) is unambiguous; this time the Protestant Ascendancy is characterized in terms of responsibility. Oppression and responsibility line up neatly, yet without acknowledgement in the commentary, to become yet another of Yeats's antinomies, while the commentary as a whole aspires to be another statement of his philosophy of history. Grammar sometimes appears victimized in Yeats's formulations, as when he summarizes this philosophy:

> The historical dialectic trampled upon their minds in that brutal Ireland, product of two generations of civil war, described by Swift in a well-known sermon; they were the trodden grapes and became wine.[7]

But the message is clear enough. The eighteenth century, coming between the Battle of the Boyne and the French Revolution, is accepted as the era of the Protestant Ascendancy. And that usage is of course generally accepted now, to a degree where its refinement is unthinkable. Yet if the period of the ascendancy's *floruit* is well known, attention should also be paid to the moment in which Yeats finally articulates his double vision of responsibility and oppression.

The writing of 'Parnell's Funeral' gave Yeats unusual trouble. He worked on the poem (and then the commentary) from early 1932 up to April 1933. Lines 16–23 appeared without title in the *Dublin Magazine* of April/June 1932 as part of the introduction to the play *Fighting the Waves*.[8] Death preoccupied Yeats at the time, especially the death of Lady Gregory (22 May 1932) which he feared might mark the close of his own imaginative life. From October 1932 to the following January, he was on tour in the United States and, returning to the poem, he 'rhymed passages from a lecture . . . given in America'.[9] In the preface to the Cuala Press volume he tells us that he consulted a poet not of his own school about his fears; this involved 'a considerable journey', but he oddly declines to name Ezra Pound as his confidant and Italy as his destination. Pound, we are led to believe, talked about nothing but politics:

> All the other modern statesmen were more or less scoundrels except 'Mussolini and that hysterical imitator of his Hitler'. When I objected to his violence he declared that Dante considered all sins intellectual . . .[10]

Back home, death was continuing its work: George Moore, who is named in the commentary but not in the poem, died on 21 January 1933. General Eoin O'Duffy, who is named in the poem but not in the commentary, was dismissed as chief commissioner of the Irish police force on 22 February 1933. The political organization with which O'Duffy was to be identified adopted the blue-shirt and black beret as its uniform in March 1933. In Germany Adolf Hitler, mentioned in neither poem nor commentary, had become Reichskanzler on 30 January 1933.

This coincidence of political events and poetic composition should not be exaggerated into a prompt-book, for all that O'Duffy mediates between the two. Hitler, even in Pound's eyes, was a 'hysterical imitator', and Yeats's attitude to Nazism was always circumspect – or nearly always. What is required is not a determined effort to mobilize evidence in one direction or the other, to prove Yeats's politics fascist or Burkean. Our present concern is simply to give notice of an inquiry – as yet to be fully addressed – into the links between Yeats's view of the eighteenth century and his view of fascism. Certainly, he himself associated 'Parnell's Funeral' with his philosophy of history and his politics, even to the extent of publishing a commentary before the canonical text had reached its final form. That commentary implicates autobiographical and genealogical material and, moreover, provides Yeats with a forum in which to display his several model statements of Protestant Ascendancy. Against the all-but-exclusively Irish material of the 'Commentary on A Parnellite at Parnell's Funeral', one can also set the meta-commentary available through the preface to *The King of the Great Clock Tower*, with its stark revelation of a poet uncertain as to the very survival of his imagination and of a poet arguing whether Hitler was a scoundrel or not.

What one has to hand, therefore, is not a poem to be exposed or fêted; as if its being a poem were merely a code for Secret Agent or Double Agent. A coherent tabulation of texts has been established, or at least commenced, with poem and commentary in their several states of emerging publication, and with meta-commentary also, each occupying its place. The present study attends to one of the larger historical contexts in which Yeats locates Charles Stewart Parnell – and himself. No unmediated collision of the European political crisis in 1933 with Irish history can be contemplated, for the notion (stated thus) is meaningless. What has meaning is language, and it is only through a discriminating and stabilized terminology that interpretation can be attempted. In the commentary, Yeats's terms for Protestant Ascendancy – oppression and responsibility – are both milder than (yet cognate with) those aspects of fascism which most appealed to the poet, force and order. The eighteenth century, he suggests, had seen the gradual adjustment of oppression to become responsibility, only to have that 'sense of responsibility' dissipated in the nineteenth century. The final section of

the commentary charts another succession – O'Connell is followed by
Parnell who is in turn to be destroyed. Such a notion of cyclical displacement and fall is familiar to any reader of Yeats, but now the imagery employed
– again with a disjunctive grammar – is finally amenable to the fascist lik-
ing for *Blut und Boten*:

> When we talked of his pride; of his apparent impassivity when his hands were
> full of blood because he had torn them with his nails, the preceeding epoch
> with its democratic bonhomie, seemed to grin through a horse collar.[11]

Poem and commentary, the two texts are a duel of privilege, with art and
history contending for dominance, and each also illustrating the tem-
porariness of any such dominance. Officially, Yeats would give the laurels
to poetry over and above history, to the poem rather than the commentary.
But the poem – as we shall see – remains so suffused with the naming
of history that the issue remains in a kind of perpetual, sublime doubt. If
I pursue the theme through very different texts which are less than Yeatsian, and by means which do not always eschew historical pedantry, my
justification lies in the contrasting high confidence with which pioneer critics
of Yeats have used the term 'the Protestant Ascendancy'. There is no shortage
of evidence showing how biographers, critics, scholars, Marxists, Americans,
mystics, and autobiographers have accepted the Protestant Ascendancy as
an unchallengeable and transparent fact of Irish social history. Moreover,
'the ascendancy' becomes a familiar short-hand version of this, as if the
noun had never had any other application, as if indeed the ascendancy had
been named in the manner Adam named the animals in the Garden of Eden.
According to this intimate, unanimous usage, the Protestant Ascendancy is
an élite, dating (it seems) back at least to the days of Jonathan Swift and
closely associated with the possession of heritable property in great masses
of accumulation.

FROM WILLIAM PARNELL TO THE REVD JOHN MITCHEL

Among the changes which had occurred between the late eighteenth and
the fourth decade of the nineteenth century was a new apprehension of
language. The famous Victorian passion for passionless speech, for verbal
propriety, bowdlerized Shakespeare, and sexual euphemism is but one aspect
of a larger transformation. In the context of Irish politics, a drastic shift
in theological priorities was at least as important. The religious agenda in
Ireland was alternately written in terms of expectations of Catholic Emancipation or, on the other side of the house, in even more prophetic timetables

of doom and salvation. The evangelical emphasis on the Bible, as the infallible word of God, encouraged the strictest attention to the reading of scripture, and the application of it to practical affairs. O'Connell could rely on a long tradition of Jacobite expectation to sustain his followers, while the more theologically acute among his opponents scrutinized the Book of Revelations for coded messages about Ireland. The extent to which this coloured political debate, indeed more than coloured it, affected its form and texture, should not be underestimated, even if one ultimately regards the theological debate itself as conditioned by social and economic realities. In 1827, a sermon was preached in Kilkenny and published under the title *The Danger of Adding to, or Detracting from, the Written Word of God*: when the author rejected church tradition as a source of doctrine, saying 'we consider it dangerous to admit an unwritten Word as a Rule of Faith', he was by implicit parallel answering O'Connellism also. Not all of this theological pedantry was conservative in implication. An American pamphlet imported to Ireland the same year, entitled *The Doctrine of Pronouns*, argued for a kind of unitarian liberalism. Yet fussy attention to words, and to the exact rendering of scripture, generally characterized a conservative stance in both politics and theology: the two neatly converge in a later pamphlet dedicated to proving the aptness of the word 'beastly' to describe an education gained in Maynooth. In 1839, prize money of £75 was made available to the provost of Trinity College, Dublin, to be awarded to the author of the best essay on 'The Impediments to Knowledge Created by Logomachy, or the Abuse of Words'. The winner, William Fitzgerald, wisely steered away from contemporary political disputes.[12]

William Parnell, who died in 1821, bore a name already made familiar to readers of literature through the poems of his kinsman, Thomas Parnell (1679 – 1718), a friend of Pope's. Though the family name was destined to become unrivalled in its political and literary impact, through the career and death of William Parnell's grandson, William himself changed his style to be known as Parnell-Hayes. He is remembered now as one of the controversialists who kept the Catholic question in the public eye throughout the difficult years after the Union. *An Historical Apology for the Irish Catholics* appeared in 1807: its summary of Irish history was designed to distinguish between Catholicism as such and disloyalty, and in the concluding pages, an effective sentimental emphasis is deliberately employed in the juxtaposition of brief maxims and extended conceits:

> The Catholics can feel; and do suffer.
> The very peasantry acutely feel the stigma cast by government upon their sect and their religion. The lowest order even suffer most. The wealthy

Catholics acquire a degree of consideration and legal security from their property, but the peasantry are left naked to the pelting of the storm, to all the
jibes and jobs of Protestant Ascendancy. . .

    Can we find words to express our astonishment, that the English cabinet
should become an echo, not to the ravings of Bedlam but to a cento of every
thing that is gross, vulgar, and perverse; Dublin guilds, common council-men,
aldermen, corporations; fat fools, that have been hitherto non-descripts in
the classes of science, literature, and good sense. . .

    The Protestants, in their terror of persecution, have become persecutors;
their alarm at Catholic atrocities, has made them atrocious; to hear them speak,
one would imagine that they had been the patient and uncomplaining suf-
ferers from the reign of William till George the Third . . . No, it is not suffering, but it is power, it is the pride of artificial ascendancy, it is the jealousy
of exclusive privilege, that corrupts the understanding, and hardens the
heart.[13]

Parnell's recollection of the 1792 debates informs his interpretation of more
recent manoeuvres at Westminster, just as his association of jobbery with
Protestant Ascendancy echoes Edmund Burke. His view of Protestant
Ascendancy is confined to its municipal origins, extending only to sympathize
with the peasantry on whom the pressure of the new ideology is now exerted. Though he rounded off his little book with a fable about the wolf
who ate the lamb because all that race before him had been implacable
enemies to the wolves, Parnell's impact on a tougher mind – that of Denys
Scully – gives his *Apology* a significance which is difficult to detect within
its limpid pages.

    Compared to Daniel O'Connell or even William Parnell, Denys Scully
is an unfamiliar figure. Born in 1773 to a prosperous Irish Catholic family,
he studied at Cambridge and London before being called to the Irish bar.
Having married an Englishwoman of a good but impoverished old Catholic
family, he was content to operate behind the scenes on behalf of the cause
of Catholic Emancipation. It was this obscure figure who in effect named
the school later given literary immortality in the early pages of *A Portrait
of the Artist as a Young Man*. Writing to the founder on the merits of various
suggested names, Scully commented indirectly on the deception practised
in the business of naming:

As to 'Clongowes Castle', my only repugnance is to the word 'Castle' – and
it seems to me a bad part of the present name. It is becoming vulgar in Ireland,
and almost ludicrous, by the indiscriminate assumption of it – and even where
no Castle, or trace of Castle appears.

    What would you think of *Clongos Vale*, if the locality of the ground cor-
responds to the name of Vale? – or, if not, *Clongos wood*, your own original

intent, if there be sufficient wood to justify the name or, perhaps best of all, *Clongos College*.[14]

Scully's cautious insistence that name and named should comply with some law of verification extends Edmund Burke's advice to the Catholics of Ireland that they should not claim a formal or nominal independence (from legal penalty) before they possess an actual independence of resources. Shrewd observers, including the inevitable spies and informers, regarded him as the real power behind O'Connell's flashier performances. Though he did not die untill 1830 (and so experienced the success of his life-long commitment to the Catholic cause), Scully's physical appearance and awkward personality, aggravated by a riding accident, was to lead to a rift between Liberator and Sponsor.

In 1812, the Catholic cause was once again on the move in Dublin. On 19 December 1811 its principal bookseller-champion, Hugh Fitzpatrick, published an anonymous but lengthy pamphlet, announced as *A Statement of the Penal laws which Aggrieve the Catholics of Ireland*. That evening a demonstration in the form of a lavish dinner party was organized by the leading Catholics, thereby protesting the legal restrictions they laboured under and the prosperity they had nonetheless achieved. The young Percy Bysshe Shelley arrived in Dublin to address a public meeting on 28 February. And in June the second part of Scully's *Statement* was published, still anonymous. So great was its success that, by October, a spurious *Third Part* was issued in the hope of inflaming government against the Catholics. The author of this imposition, Edmund Swift, claimed that 'according to their own stile and own arrangements,' he had endeavoured 'to say for them what they do not yet dare say for themselves.' Though Swift's intervention damaged the Catholic cause, it also acknowledged Scully's importance as a propagandist skilled in the law.[15]

In a number of respects, Scully follows Parnell: indeed he quotes verbatim the passage quoted above together with several surrounding pages. Like Parnell, he traces a history, but he is more concerned to lay bare the vast range of legal restrictions under which Catholics have endured rather than exonerate them for any offences in the remote past. He begins by observing the need for care, even caution, in his choice of words:

> An unguarded phrase may be transplanted into the defamatory pages of some hireling or expectant Pamphleteer: an accidental ambiguity of expression may be wrested or misquoted, so as to make the 'better Sense appear the worse'.[16]

Attentive to the possible misuse of his own words, he also chose to present certain features of the society he lived in by means of an observation on words:

the very name of 'Protestant' secures a competence, and commands Patrician
pre-eminence in Ireland.

   Hence, the peculiar misery of Irish Corporate towns; the general ignorance
and unskilfulness of their tradesmen . . .[17]

This attention to the Protestant lower orders led Scully to one of his rare
admissions of the term under examination here:

> Many of the lower Protestant tradespeople and artisans (sanctioned by the Irish
> Administration) have formed confederacies hostile to their Catholic fellow-
> subjects. Their avowed object is the maintenance of the present enormous
> monopoly of power and profit – termed Protestant Ascendancy – the real
> object (of many at least) are private interest, personal emolument, facility of
> peculation, public discord etc. These people feel, however, that their sway
> is not secure or permanent: and their fears are constantly awake.[18]

Despite this instability of ascendancy, Scully detected a further psychological
aspect which he translated as ideological advantage:

> every Protestant feels himself, and really is, more powerful in society, more
> free in his energies, more elevated in life, than his Catholic neighbour of equal
> merit, property, talents, and education. He alone feels and possesses the right
> and the legal capacity to be a Legislator, and *this consciousness is actual power.*
> [original emphasis] [19]

Here, Scully has recorded that augmentation of mere legitimacy which the
notion of ascendancy provided, and does so of course while writing with
the intention of challenging exclusive legitimacy. The combination of instability and power is well reflected in a brief passage which is repeated in
the *Second Part*; the topic is the entire system of penal laws:

> *It moves in a circle.* It compels Catholic petitions. – Petitions produce resistance.
> – Resistance re-produces this evil spirit, and so the mischief revolves.[20]

Francis Plowden, writing from Cork in 1812, congratulated Scully on his
pamphlet in two parts – together amounting to 370 pages. He singled out
Scully's 'luminous manly patriotic & resistless exposure of the Protestant
Ascendancy . . . You have completely unveiled the idol.'[21] Plowden's compliment is in keeping with the imagery of sorcery and pretence which writers
from Burke onwards had applied to the new coinage. In fact, Scully employed
the magic formula only twice – once (as we have seen) in connection with
the confederacies of Protestant artisans, and once in a brief historical *resumé:*

> In 1782, upon the solemn renunciation of this assumed power on the part
> of the English Parliament, and the restoration of legislative independence to
> Ireland, the friends of the Protestant Ascendancy became alarmed, lest, in

the national enthusiasm for freedom, the chains of the suffering Catholics might be loosened.[22]

In the celebration of Grattan's achievement in 1782 as a national event, Scully undoubtedly contributes to a re-writing of the Irish eighteenth century, a re-writing which ultimately finds its highest expression in Yeats's poetry. Nevertheless, the author of *A Statement of the Penal Laws* firmly ties Protestant Ascendancy to oppression rather than responsibility.

Perhaps because of his preference of private over public activity, Scully's correspondence provides a remarkable insight into the language of emancipation, the role of anonymous pamphleteers, the various gradings of aristocratic, middle-class, and popular activists, the interaction of family and politics. In the six hundred letters from and to Scully, available since 1988, there are only two citations of 'the Protestant Ascendancy'. In the midst of the veto controversy, the Wexford 'general' of 1798 fame, Thomas Cloney, gloomily predicted 'the unnatural union of a nominal Catholic Church with Protestant Ascendancy. What an Anomaly in Religion & Politicks . . .' and went on to resurrect John Keogh's oxymoron of 1804 – 'Orange Catholics'.[23] Cloney's use of the term recalls the arguments of William Ogilvie that the sectarian conflicts of County Wexford after 1782 had paradoxically given rise to the new and destabilized notion of 'ascendancy'. Such regional concentrations, sparse though they are, further undermine any case for regarding 'the Protestant Ascendancy' as having a comprehensive presence throughout Ireland. Scully himself appears not to have used the phrase on his side of the correspondence, despite (or because of) his interest in the tonalities of names and phrases. Yet what is finally striking in these passages from Parnell and Scully is not the occurrence of Protestant Ascendancy, whether in conformity with the notion of its origins in 1792 or otherwise, but the massive testimony to its virtual absence in their work generally.

In connection with Protestant Ascendancy there remains, therefore, a suggestive gap to be filled in. On the one hand we had the highly political and public records of municipal and parliamentary debates in the late eighteenth century.[24] And on the other, there was a late Victorian, Edwardian or even more recent invocation of the Protestant Ascendancy as a sort of Irish sub-aristocracy enduring through the rigours of the nineteenth century when democratic reforms of the franchise (1829, 1832, 1858, 1867, 1872, and 1884) and successive assaults on landed estates progressively transformed the social map of Ireland. This invocation, which is by no means exclusively or specifically Yeatsian, might itself be dated more precisely, but the search for a single, absolute date is probably pointless. It may be far more revealing

to consider what lies in the suggestive gap. A number of specific instances
have been chosen for their broadly representative character – the correspondence of Daniel O'Connell up to 1834 is the first – and in order
to play fair both with the evidence and with those who wish to resent the
argument, numerous brief quotations are given in the succeeding paragraphs.

During the 1820s, O'Connell's campaign for Catholic Emancipation introduced mass politics to the United Kingdom. The increasingly mechanized
press had played a significant part in propagating political ideas in the years
from 1790 to 1829, but O'Connell's partly illiterate following was attuned
more to the spoken than the written word. The ultra-Protestant slogan of
1792, 'Protestant Ascendancy', was not greatly in evidence during the
tumultuous 1820s, though it was occasionally used to stigmatize particularly 'hard-line' members of the Dublin Castle administration. It was in this
sense that Warner William Westenra, 2nd Baron Rossmore, used the phrase
on 19 August 1827, when reporting to O'Connell how he had 'written a
letter to Mr. George Canning of a very strong nature, pointing at the necessity
of tearing up the Ascendancy faction by the roots in this country.'[25]

His lordship might be thought representative of the ascendancy in its now
established usage. No such suspicion hangs over the nine signatories – mostly Catholic clergy – who, in a letter of the following January listed (among
others) their intention 'to convince the Ascendancy men that we are determined to stop at no sacrifice in order to keep the people together . . .'[26]
Rossmore found himself threatened with a libel action in the dying days
of 1828, and in seeking O'Connell's private advice he alluded to 'the Ascendancy B[enc]h'.[27]

It is possible, perhaps, to detect an altered implication in those letters (commencing more or less with the winning of Emancipation) where O'Connell
himself takes up the phrase. On 11 April 1829, the Liberator wrote home
to his wife:

> My darling Love,
>   The bill has passed the Lords last night. It will receive the Royal assent
> on Monday and thus the ascendancy and proud superiority which your
> neighbours had over you will be at an end the day you receive this letter . . .[28]

Years later in August 1832, O'Connell, in correspondence with P. V. Fitz-
Patrick, would return in a more strictly political sense, to the notion of ascendancy as a condition abolished or destroyed at some point in the past –
'A Conservative has but one fault, which is indeed a *thumper*: he wants ascendancy – a thing impossible to be revived.'[29]

These instances are hardly sublime, and indeed the scarcity of reference to the Protestant Ascendancy in O'Connell's correspondence has its discreet eloquence. C. A. Walker, recently elected an MP for the borough of Wexford, wrote in November 1832 of political realignments in terms which require rather more comment:

> There is a very strong (I'll not call it Protestant) but ultra bigotted high church and ascendancy party in this County. They form the majority of the aristocracy of the County but there is also a very formidable Protestant tenantry, strongly tinctured and linked to this aristocracy.[30]

Wexford of course had been the seat of insurrection in 1798. North Wexford had been the home of John Hunter Gowan who, among the new gentry (or even lease-dependent middlemen), distinguished himself in violent service to the Orange cause during the troubles there. The county had been singled out by Lady Louisa Conolly as having had an extreme Protestant faction for decades stretching back well into the eighteenth century. While the significance of regional difference will be attended to in some detail, Wexford should not be regarded as a unique case, unrelatable to political and cultural developments further afield.

Nor should C. A. Walker's association of the terms 'high church and ascendancy' persuade us that the anti-papists of 1798 were flirting with ritualism in 1832. 'High church' should be read as meaning an attitude stressing the exclusive prerogatives of the established church, together with (in the case in question) a jealous antagonism towards evangelical presumption within the church. Post-Napoleonic France witnessed a resurgence of clericalist politics, serving to legitimize the restored but unstable monarchy. Such views found more than a casual echo in the romantic writings of Chateaubriand, the dizzyingly predominant chimaera of the age. 'High church and ascendancy' views in Wexford constituted a highly local variant on the theme, where anti-Catholicism was *de rigeur* and the need for part of the local gentry to legitimize itself perhaps more pressing than in any other Irish county. Walker identified the Protestant bishop of Leighlin and Ferns as the chief director of the ascendancy party: Thomas Elrington (1760–1835) had been a prolific though always anonymous pamphleteer back in the paper war of 1787, one of the very few to take Woodward's Protestant Ascendancy phraseology into that of some of his contributions to the debate on tithes and Catholic claims. His devotion to an exclusivist position was longstanding. The post-war longing for authoritarian rule, the veneration of medieval example, and the re-convergence of church and state was manifest in Ireland as elsewhere in Europe. However, the local situation required an ideological banner from which all of the Church of Rome's devices had been excised. Much reference to 'liberty' among Irish Protestants in the decades after Waterloo – and again after Emancipation – has to be decoded as indicating a rejection of the Catholicism which infused European reaction, rather than an endorsement of any kind of liberalism.

To read Wexford electoral conflicts in terms of French romanticism is neither exaggerated nor irrelevant. French revolutionary thinking had made its decisive impact on the thinking (and even hair-style) of the Wexford 'croppies' in 1798; that reaction should also be susceptible to Parisian influence is only fair. And there was a high degree of reciprocity in this Irish-continental link. At the great Vienna congress of European powers in the autumn of 1814 Great Britain was represented in succession by two Irish Protestants. The first was the foreign secretary, Robert Stewart (1769 – 1822, Viscount Castlereagh), and he was followed by field marshall Arthur Wellesley (1769 – 1852, Duke of Wellington). The latter's epochal defeat of the returned Napoleon at Waterloo in June 1815 brought him the kind of unrivalled authority which ultimately allowed him (as prime minister) to concede Catholic Emancipation in 1829. The political prominence of Irish Protestants in the Tory administrations of the early nineteenth century is a phenomenon deserving more attention. Conversely, the parochial obscurity of phrases used by the likes of Walker or Rossmore should not be wantonly intensified. Mrs O'Connell's release from 'the ascendancy and proud superiority' of her neighbours had its larger European context, even if the canonical formulation of that from which she was liberated (the hauteur of neighbours belonging to 'the Protestant Ascendancy') had not yet been articulated.

In looking at O'Connell's use of the term 'ascendancy' in his correspondence, we can draw on no more than twenty-five letters out of a total of close to three and a half thousand – twelve prior to 1834 are quoted below. Nevertheless, some distinct patterns emerge. In the early 1830s, there are a cluster of references and these generally carry the implication of ascendancy as an attitude no longer available to those who might wish to practise it. Writing again to FitzPatrick in February 1833, O'Connell linked 'the last but powerful remnant of Protestant Ascendancy' with the need to reform the borough corporations.[31] In May of the same year he confided to the same correspondent that

> England can never again *face* danger without being compelled to do justice to Ireland, and the moment the Protestants forget ascendancy and consent to endure equality with cordial good temper, we will be too strong for our enemies.[32]

There were of course those who suggested that O'Connell might come to head up an ascendancy of his own: in September he declared himself ready 'to do everything the most suspicious . . . could desire to obviate the possibility of a Catholic ascendancy'. Indeed he thought 'such an ascendancy is impossible . . .' The same letter welcomes news that the Marquis Wellesley (Wellington's brother) was to become lord lieutenant of Ireland because he 'will be, of course, every day more odious to the survivors of the Ascendancy Party.'[33] Four days later, he is confident that 'nothing prevents the irresistible force of the cry for Repeal [of the Union] but the remaining strength and hopes of several of the Ascendancy Party.'[34] Prospects in the following year included such major alterations to the finances of the Church of Ireland that, in May 1834, O'Connell announced to FitzPatrick that 'at all events, the ascendancy party in Ireland has received a warning such as precedes inevitable dissolution.'[35] If this implies that ascendancy is not yet a thing of the past, O'Connell is even more emphatic when writing on 16 July 1834:

> No, the Orangeists have been too long masters to expect that for the present generation they should submit willingly to an equality of rights; and yet they must submit perforce, for the Government of this country is now too democratic to allow the Irish ascendancy to remain in power any longer.[36]

Here, certainly, O'Connell virtually names a ruling élite, a stratum in Irish society which manages to retain local power even in the face of a reformist government. The élite, however, is never named 'the Protestant Ascendancy', and the improvised nature of the naming can be gauged from the close proximity in the same letter of 'the Orangeists' and 'the Orange party'. In this last instance, and in those referring to the 'ascendancy party' etc., no formal political organisation is alluded to: the party system had evolved mightily since the days of Fox and Burke, but O'Connell still uses 'party' with some of the pejorative implications of eighteenth-century usage – 'faction' might serve him equally well.

We can say of O'Connell's correspondence that, on the rare occasions when it uses the noun 'ascendancy', the implication is generally of a social attitude, or privilege, or perhaps legal right, which has been eclipsed. In 1833–4, there is a cluster of references and these do point to a surviving political element or even social constituency. O'Connell's subsequent political behaviour was to some extent dictated by the need to outmanoeuvre this element and so to bring the Whig government's reformist pressure to bear on the Irish local bastions of the ascendancy mentality, notably in the corporations. It is absolutely the case that O'Connell nowhere associates 'ascendancy' or 'the Protestant Ascendancy' with Jonathan Swift, or even Henry Grattan. Given a choice between 'oppression' and 'responsibility' (Yeats's

terms again'), O'Connell would undoubtedly have found the first apt as a
synonym, the second incomprehensible. Yet the stricter philosophical analyst
would require here that the implication in ascendancy of something already
eclipsed be noted, not as a secondary feature of ascendancy but as its
characteristic.

With access to parliament secured, O'Connell was able in 1835 to enter into
an informal agreement with the English Whig party; this agreement, known
to historians as 'the Lichfield House compact', included an undertaking by
an incoming Whig government to open the borough corporations to Catholics.
Municipal politics had been the first hot-house of Protestant Ascendancy rhetoric
in the 1790s, and the threat to Protestant monopoly in Dublin Corporation
once again called for resistance. But other drastic, even violent alterations of
opinion were occurring in less publicly reported arenas. In Ulster Presbyter-
ianism, a bitter campaign had been waged by the 'orthodox' party against the
remnants of eighteenth-century Arianism. Whether this theological war can
be equated generally with a victory of political conservatism over radicalism
is a question much debated and probably irresolvable.[37] But in the manse at
Newry, County Down, the two issues virtually coincided in the thought of the
minister, John Mitchel, and his soon to be notorious son and namesake.

In October 1835, the Revd John Mitchel preached two sermons and arranged for their publication through the local newspaper office. *The Sect
'Everywhere Spoken Against'* constitutes a proud last-ditch defence of
unitarian liberalism against the triumphant forces of trinitarian Calvinism,
strict doctrinal conformism, and a growing tendency to align Protestant
evangelicalism with aggressive anti-Catholicism. Though the preacher expressed amazement at the allegations laid at the door of his fellow-unitarians,
he can hardly have failed to notice that his cause was already lost:

> Known, as we are, to entertain these views [on the Trinity], we feel equal sur-
> prise and indignation at the hypocritical baseness and malignity of the charge
> – that Unitarians are friendly to Popery, or that they would countenance or
> abet a Popish ascendancy in this country. Unitarians, fairly enough, regard
> themselves as the most consistently Protestant Christians in the land: – but
> their Protestantism does not consist in hatred and abuse of Papists . . .[38]

The old fashioned requirement to love one's neighbour may have stung
some among the orthodox, but few will have subscribed to the political implications of Mitchel's creed. Mankind, in his tenacious view, was inclined
'almost as with one consent, – not to set up – but rather to pull down
ascendancies', and this was an attitude he approved so long as it was guided
by 'moderation and justice'.[39] Certainly, in this besieged corner of Irish
Protestantism, ascendancy found not one supporter.

OLD EMINENCE AMONG THE HOMES OF LEARNING

It would be a mistake to conclude that the formation of a key concept such as the Protestant Ascendancy proceeded solely in political quarters. Indeed, the interaction of political misfortunes with cultural avocations has already been suggested as a powerful dynamic in such formations. Moreover, what is ultimately unfolding is an unusual but far from unique process in which a concept (quite strictly understood in a particular juncture) is progressively loosened so that its terms circulate casually once again, even to the point of their becoming nonce-words. It is in this sense that the 're-phrasing of a concept' is proposed as a short-hand account of the fate of Protestant Ascendancy in the five decades after the Union.

While the narrative of O'Connell's struggle against 'the ascendancy party' can shortly be taken up from the records of the opposite camp, it is worth pausing to consider a remarkable series of review-articles in the *Dublin University Magazine* of 1834, which provides one of the most resounding (if misunderstood) instances of the term 'ascendancy' in use. The *Dublin University Magazine* had been launched in January 1833 in direct response to the Reform Act of 1832 and in less immediate reaction to the success of O'Connell in 1829. Its principal early contributors on ideological matters included the brothers Mortimer and Samuel O'Sullivan, William Archer Butler, and Isaac Butt. In Samuel Ferguson (1810 – 1886), the magazine recruited one destined to make a major contribution to the prehistory of the Anglo-Irish Literary Renaissance, and to earn a place for his name (with those of Thomas Davis and James Clarence Mangan) in a grateful poem by W. B. Yeats:

> Nor may I less be counted one
> With Davis, Mangan, Ferguson,
> Because, to him who ponders well
> My rhymes more than their rhyming tell
> Of things discovered in the deep,
> Where only body's laid asleep.[40]

Ferguson may have been a lesser poet than Yeats, but it is equally certain that his greater achievement came through his research into the early history and culture of Ireland, research lavishly published in lengthy reviews and articles.

Though he had contributed to the *Dublin University Magazine* as early as August 1833, Ferguson in April 1834 commenced what was to be a four-part review of James Hardiman's *Irish Minstrelsy*. This extended review-article, together with translations the author felt obliged to provide in augmentation of Hardiman's efforts, has become a charter document in the history of Anglo-Irish literature. Its influence on subsequent translators and poets is immeasurable, and it has doubtless been read by scholars and artists who spare not a glance for the political articles which surround it, and whose attention to Hardiman is dictated by their attitude towards his more renowned respondent. *Irish Minstrelsy* doubtless has its faults, but, in addition to its substantive worth, it remains a strategically placed record of social attitudes to Gaelic poetry and the world from which that poetry proceeded. Some of Hardiman's comments proved embarrassing, and not solely on scholarly or aesthetic grounds. Defending the plain people of Ireland against a charge of general drunkenness, Hardiman did not so much deny the fact as preserve a few additional facts less frequently broadcast by commentators such as Ferguson. Annotating a poem in Gaelic addressed to hard liquor, the translator recalled an incident occurring during the 1820 Irish visit of the newly crowned George IV:

> One of our 'staunch' Protestant Ascendancy aldermen, thought he could not evince his zeal in a stronger manner than by presenting his sovereign with a few hogsheads, as a sample of Irish loyalty.[41]

Not only does the remark link Protestant Ascendancy with the politics of corporations, it also slyly prompts the reader to recall the 'Aldermen of Skinner's Alley', a heavy-drinking fraternal gathering of 'staunch' Protestant Dublin worthies much addicted to Orange toasts. John Giffard, often credited with coining the term, was a member of the Skinner's Alley club, and in him an aldermanic passion for violence and Protestantism had been epitomized.

We thus have to read the response to Hardiman at a more verbally local level than that splendidly preserved in Ferguson's own splendid translations. In the second instalment of his critique, Ferguson advanced his argument concerning the dichotomy between heart and head, feeling and judgement, which had earlier given shape to his meditation on the role of the Protestant in modern Irish society. That had been entitled 'Dialogue Between the Head and Heart of an Irish Protestant' and it had appeared in the November 1833 issue. In August 1834, he laid down an analysis of Gaelic poetry which smuggled the dichotomy into a quasi-historical account of two cultures. Of the Gaelic love-poets, he wrote:

> Leading such a life, it is strange that they have not exhibited more of the imaginative faculty in songs composed among scenes so well calculated to excite its highest attributes. The cause must have been that paramount supremacy of feeling so conspicuous in every line of their passionate love songs; that ascendency of the heart; that rush of hot blood to the head which smothered the apoplectic intellect. . .[42]

The poets of Connacht, then, lack (in Ferguson's view) the supreme artistic faculty – imagination – recently celebrated in S. T. Coleridge's exposition of romanticism in *Biographia Literaria* (1817). Gaelic culture, for good and ill, lies outside the modern consciousness.

But the *Dublin University Magazine* had more urgent concerns than the lop-sided virtues of a declining primitive culture, and Ferguson's long review of Hardiman did not escape from the passions of the hour. In the third instalment he commented on the growing power of the Catholic clergy in Ireland – 'however reason and free intellect may have been prostrated by the hoofs of a more brutal spiritual ascendancy, virtue . . . has arisen. . .'[43] This last usage of ascendancy – to indict the growing influence of Catholicism in politics – is consistent with the first stage of Yeats's double vision of the eighteenth century, with the difference that now Catholicism and not Protestantism is to be in the ascendant. A resentful diagnosis of something threatening to become 'Catholic ascendancy' will occur spasmodically in the political debates of the 1820s and '30s. While 'an ascendancy of the heart' must bide its time, the anonymous 'Dialogue on the Popular Objections Against the Established Church', preceding Ferguson's review of Hardiman by two months in the *Dublin University Magazine*, catches the mood:

> If religion be not thus protected, especially when a revolutionary spirit is abroad, she will become an instrument or an obstacle to one party in the state. Thus, being the means of ascendancy, she will be polluted, or, if an impediment to ascendancy, she will be overthrown.[44]

Threat to the established church was threat to the Union. And the Union between Great Britain and Ireland in itself constituted a linguistic crux and a political division. A decade later, Ferguson asked of London newspapers in particular

> whether it would not be wiser to adopt a phraseology which would not excite invidious comparisons, and which would be consistent with the theory of the Union which they support. In that theory England and Ireland are alike portions of one United Kingdom, neither ruled by the other, but each by the whole.[45]

Ferguson's concern was for the welfare of 'Irish Unionists, that while becoming every day more sensible of the advantages of connection with Britain . . . are also *pari passu* becoming more attached to their own country'. This latter attachment, Ferguson implies, is cultural rather than political, and in this way it avoids any conflict with the former attachment. His problem, however, lies not so much in reconciling political Unionism with cultural

nationalism as in finding a suitable term to encompass those elements in
society which hold to the double attachment and which are irked by the
intemperate language of the London newspapers:

> Habitual contempts of a country where the nobility and chief gentry, as well
> as a large proportion of the professional and commercial classes, are animated
> by sentiments such as these, cannot be indulged in without the excitement
> of irritation and the creation of danger.
>
> The deportment of the Irish Unionists at the present moment commands
> respect. An agricultural community, they have cheerfully submitted to a change
> in the laws affecting agriculture, detrimental to their own immediate interests,
> but necessary for the commercial advancement of their English fellow-subjects.
> With strong temptations to the gratification of selfish ambition by assuming
> their natural place as leaders of the Irish masses, they adhere devotedly to
> that connection on which they feel the general welfare of the empire to de-
> pend; and – which is perhaps as creditable to them as anything else – they
> have, with little or no Government aid, and without even the encouragement
> of one generous notice from the capital, laid the foundations in their own coun-
> try for schools of science, of letters, and of arts, which bid fair to replace Ireland
> in her old eminence among the homes of learning in the West of Europe.[46]

The substance of this is familiar enough – the final emphasis resting on
the cultural campaign of individuals and bodies as diverse as Ferguson
himself and Eugene O'Curry, the Royal Irish Academy and Young Ireland,
the *Dublin University Magazine* and *The Nation*, Charles Gavan Duffy and
Sheridan Le Fanu. This minor renaissance of the 1830s and 1840s – beginning perhaps even in the mid-1820s with the work of Gerald Griffin, Caesar
Otway, the Banims, and William Carleton – has not been in itself over-
looked. But what Ferguson reveals in his retrospect is the interconnection
between injury to economic interest and commitment to cultural endeavour.
In time, we may diagnose (in the manner of Dr Freud) a case of compensation in the cultural sphere for a loss of access to, and action in, the sphere
of economic reality. 'Old eminence among the homes of learning' is a phrase
sighing with anxious nostalgia; and the process of social modernization –
through industry, through secular and scientific thought, religious excita-
tion and abandonment, population mobility, socialism and class consciousness etc. – was proceeding in Ireland despite and (to a degree) because
of the traditionalist image of Ireland as 'an agricultural community'. Key
aspects of the process were under way long before Ferguson's death in 1886,
though the ideological structures of political discourse disguised the fact by
their operation then and subsequently. Emigration, which drastically altered
demographic patterns throughout the nineteenth century, was absorbed

into a simplified history of Anglo-Irish conflict and Irish-American irreden-
tism. And, to look at things in a different perspective of recognition and
concealment, partition, which was institutionalized in 1920 in terms which
were largely sectarian, had been effectively commenced at least fifty years
earlier in the changing forms of Ulster industry.

For Ferguson, the interconnection was located principally in those
awkwardly listed but partially conveyed social constituents – 'the nobility
. . . gentry . . . professional and commercial classes . . .' Here is virtually
every element in society except the rising urban proletariat and the declining peasantry. Ferguson required some collective noun by which to indicate
a seemingly comprehensive alliance excluding these last two named elements.
But this also was required to be an alliance actually limited so that it will
merge promptly with 'Irish Unionists' and their 'agricultural community'
to rescue the reassuring presuppositions of community at a time when interest has been sacrificed. He is, in a strict sense, at a loss for words. His
difficulty lies in the unavailability then of the now-familiar notion of 'Protestant Ascendancy', consigned to memories of hogshead loyalism, for it is
under such a banner that amalgamation of certain class interests and the
transvaluation of these into cultural pursuits will take place. Nor is it simply a matter of the unavailability of the phrase (as Common Sense might have
argued) for Ferguson's argument is itself the absence of ascendancy, the
evidence of that unease which underpins his sustained campaign for the
resolution of all difference (ethnic, linguistic, social, denominational) in
culture.

It would be useful to examine the transformation in the 1830s and early
1840s of one district in Ferguson's native Ulster, a district in County Down
closely (even covertly) associated with the Yeats family. But the intention
of what follows next is to take such difficulties as Ferguson encountered as
a plummet line to be lowered into the depths of historical and cultural presupposition which surround Yeats's Victorian origins, especially those depths
inhabited by Daniel O'Connell's fiercest critics.

THE IRISH METROPOLITAN CONSERVATIVE SOCIETY

In the 1830s, Irish Tories began to use the term 'conservative/s' with a
distinctive and local pride because, after all, it had been virtually coined
by an Irishman, John Wilson Croker. Despite this new accommodation in
the language, they were institutionally homeless, having no parliament of
their own in which to conduct their internal debates. The Union, which
had brought about this state of affairs, was of course sacrosanct in their eyes,

and all the more so since the emancipation of Catholics in 1829. In the united parliament at Westminster, O'Connell and his followers frequently out-manoeuvred them, and the prospect of a domestic parliament in Dublin where the O'Connellites would constitute (in the tory view) an even greater phalanx of anti-tory, anti-Protestant power was viewed with horror. Neverthe-less, their relations with British governments were nervous, to say the least.

Apart from the official tory party, Irish conservative opinion expressed itself through a number of organizations, some short-lived, some quasi-secret, some limited (in theory at least) to activities such as voter registration. The Orange Order had been suppressed in 1836 – not for the first time – but there existed several 'ginger groups' through which Protestant conservatives sought to clarify their political position and to plan a strategy of resistance to English Whiggery and Irish Catholicism. The most significant of these groups was the Irish Metropolitan Conservative Society which was established on 26 April 1836. Meeting in Dawson Street, Dublin, in the building now occupied by the Royal Irish Academy, the Society had as its leading light the young Isaac Butt, then in his bright Orange phase. Mountifort Longfield, who held a chair in political economy at Trinity College, and the Revd Mortimer O'Sullivan, a vigorous contributor to the *Dublin University Magazine* added the weight of their years, though the latter may not have been formally a member. Records of the debates in the Metropolitan Con-servative Society in the autumn of 1838 amply illustrate an important stage in the development of Protestant Ascendancy before the Famine and the 1848 rebellion.[47]

According to Butt, who was joint secretary, the membership included 'up-wards of seven hundred' registered electors for the city of Dublin, and 'up-wards of one hundred and sixty' electors for the university constituency. These figures suggest that the Society was essentially an urban organiza-tion, though there were 'upwards of one hundred and fifty-eight landed pro-prietors – men not below the rank of Magistrates and Grand Jurors in their respective counties.' Though 'he could attempt no classification of the great mass of mercantile and trading respectability' represented in the member-ship, Butt specified that the Society in September 1838 included thirty-nine physicians, forty-nine clergymen, seventy-five members of the bar, and one hundred and eight solicitors.[48] We can roughly estimate that the Metropolitan Conservative Society had a membership of about one thou-sand, the bulk of whom lived in Dublin and were connected with the pro-fessions or with commerce. From the point of view of the cultural historian, especially concerned with the use of language, the value of the Society's records lies in the fact that this body was not made up of career politicians, and that the speakers (thirty-four in the period referred to) were mostly figures of no great consequence in the world. Such men chose their words without reference to posterity. After all, as Sir Boyle Roche is said to have observed on another occasion, 'Why should I think of posterity, what has posterity ever done for me?'

We shall see in a moment how the loosening notion of ascendancy was treated in these debates. But first of all let us note with care the social composition of the Society. This was a matter not infrequently discussed in Conservative House, and the emphasis repeatedly was laid upon its middle-class base. By November of 1836 it numbered five holders of aristocratic title among its vice-presidents. The officers, however, were mainly professional men – barristers like Butt, university professors like Francis Hodgkinson, or medical doctors like Robert J. Graves and Anthony Meyler. While this social base may strike us as unremarkable, it called for comment at the time. In giving his statistics on membership, Butt defensively concluded that 'he had said enough to silence the slander . . . as to want of respectability.'[49] If outsiders had pointed to a lack of aristocratic support, there was no unanimity within the Society as to whether such support was desirable. A Mr Baker expressed the view that 'it is blinking the question to pretend that we have within the ranks of this society men of station and rank' – he was interrupted with cries of 'we have' – but he continued: 'If we have, what have they given us? They have given us their names – when have they given us their presence?'[50]

Butt astutely realized that a middle course was the Society's only hope of survival. Without aristocratic patronage it could be marginalized as a mere lobby, while the energies of its middle-class activists (including Butt himself) simultaneously demanded and deserved full recognition. The report of his own views indicates the delicate feelings, not to say trepidation, involved in such an examination of class:

> It was not an Association of the aristocracy, nor yet of the gentry, though they had several of the noblest and best of the aristocracy as their members, and many, very many, of the gentry; but their Society was a union of the middling classes of that city . . . the professional, the mercantile, the respectable middling classes were fairly represented . . . He felt this a very embarrassing subject to allude to there; but it was better that this statement should be made there than not made at all.[51]

Later in the year John Thompson – referring to himself as a tradesman though he was more likely a man in trade, a merchant – spoke at length to the Society on the causes of the crisis in which Irish conservative Protestants found themselves. For him 'the evil rests, and the whole blame is to be charged, on the Protestants of Ireland, from the great landed proprietor, down to what is called the Protestant people generally.'[52] The note of self-accusation has been heard on other, more recent occasions of course, but Thompson revealed the extent of class tension in the Society when he singled out the 'cold-hearted Protestant lords of the soil' for especial condemnation. Absenteeism by these landlords had let to mass emigration of 'the old and respectable tenantry' whom he also characterized as 'the respectable, industrious, and high-minded yeomanry of Ireland'. Thompson, unlike Baker, was heckled for these views; and in this difference of response one can judge the sensitivity of the society to the good opinion of landowners and the nobility.[53]

Through this material, quoted at some length, we register the actual existence and the insecurity of the Irish middle-class Protestant in the years before the Famine. Though Protestant Ascendancy had found a temporary spokesman in the Dublin House of Commons in the 1790s, it had been disdained by the city's MPs, Henry Grattan and Lord Henry Fitzgerald. The phrase never became the rallying cry of any particular section of society, though by some accounts it entered the oath of the Orange Order. John Thompson reminded his fellow conservatives that in the period immediately prior to Catholic Emancipation

> The corporation of Dublin received repeated information from our friends in Parliament, from the very highest among them, that unless the Protestants of Ireland would be up and stirring that they must give way . . . At that time, 'tis true, we got up a great Protestant meeting at Morrison's [Hotel]. We had our Protestant representatives and all our leaders posting to Dublin for this all-important dinner. We had 'The Protestant Ascendancy', 'the Glorious Revolution,' with nine times nine.[54]

But, as Thompson made painfully clear in his speech to the metropolitan conservatives, such dinners were really preludes to defeat – the hors d'oeuvre merely introducing a *hors de combat*, if you forgive the conceit. 'The next day arrived; our leaders went on as usual, thinking if their rack-rents came in, and that they were quietly permitted to enjoy the creature comforts of life, it was no great matter what became of their tradesmen or tenantry.' Drinking toasts to 'the Protestant Ascendancy' merely suggested the inoperancy of that notion.

Thompson apart, what do the thirty or so articulate members of the Society have to say on the topic in the course of their autumn debates? If Protestant Ascendancy is the term by which a crucial element in Irish society will shortly be nominated, then the conservatives of 1838 are unconscious of the fact. I find two occasions where the phrase 'Protestant Ascendancy' is used –

one of those has just been cited. In the second case, the speaker was Currell Smyth, who plied a colourful line in anti-Catholic diatribe. Smyth indeed became eloquent if not always coherent as he warmed to the theme: he could, he declared:

> understand Protestant Ascendency – a principle which Englishmen once thought it indispensable should pervade every department of their Government, from its most obscure machinery to the council-chamber and the throne – a principle in which alone I can recognise the palladium of our civil and religious liberties – a principle which had rendered Britain – aye, and will maintain her so, if she adheres to it – confessedly the queen of the nations; so that not a wave of the ocean but is pressed by argosies fraught with her merchandise – not a wind of heaven but wafts wealth to her shores from the uttermost parts of the earth, and oh, nobler and more enduring praise has taught her and enabled her to make the most favored climes a return ten thousand fold more than equivalent for their choicest productions, by imparting to them the humanising arts – the blessings of civilisation, and the light of the glorious Gospel.[55]

This is rousing stuff. But before embarking for uncharted wastes of English grammar, the speaker admits that Protestant Ascendancy was a principle, not a social group, and that it was 'once thought . . . indispensable' in the English constitution. The nostalgic note is sounded here again, as indeed it will be sounded yet again in the commentary on 'Parnell's Funeral'.

Isaac Butt's contributions to the debates were particularly concerned with issues of class, yet nowhere in this material do we find him endorsing Protestant Ascendancy. On the contrary, he spoke repeatedly of 'a Popish ascendancy' or 'an ascendancy of Roman Catholics', and similar phrases were used by Currell Smyth. What is remarkable about the debates, considered as evidence of lexical use, is the frequency in a number of speakers with which the noun 'ascendancy' appears outside the now familiar phrase. Butt talks about 'the just ascendancy of rank' but also worries about 'the downfall of British ascendancy'; Smyth, for his part, fears 'nothing short of ascendancy – rampant, intolerant, Popish ascendancy'.[56] This frequency indicates an uncertainty of terminology, and a consequent reliance on terms which have broad, virtually undefined implications. In due course we can consider why it was the word 'ascendancy' which took on this role in conservative debate. For Butt, at least, there was an assumed association between the two new terms. In November 1838 he warned that 'the Protestants of Ireland must inevitably be finally extinguished as a church in Ireland . . . unless . . . they enjoy some conservative, or ascendant protection by which, as a minority, they may be defended.'[57]

GREAT PROTESTANT MEETINGS, AND MUNICIPAL REFORM (1840)

Theological controversy, and the increasing convergence of religious and political fervour on the Protestant side, forms one important backdrop to the development of ascendancy ideology in the pre-Famine period. Whether as cause or consequence of this state of affairs, a dearth of serious political thought was also characteristic of the period. The conservative camp experienced a serious lack of able leaders. Castlereagh, Croker, Wellington, and Canning were all distinguished Irish leaders of the Tory cause, but their field of activity had been Britain and not Ireland. As architects and exponents of the Union, they regarded London as the centre of their political world, while Dublin became a provincial backwater. Temporarily, but to a significant degree, local leadership fell to churchmen, perhaps because the Church of Ireland retained a distinctive character even after its merger under the terms of the Union. In consequence, the quest for an Irish, Protestant, conservative 'world-view' was conducted in broader terms than the strictly political. The *Dublin University Magazine*, founded in 1833 and surviving for the best part of half a century, has already been noted. It provided a forum for literary, historical, archaeological, and controversial inquiries into the state of Irish culture and the relation of Protestantism to this culture. Though the term conservative has been admitted, in the pages above, as a description of Thomas Elrington and company in 1787, it is really as an aspect of reactions in the 1830s that it earns attention and acceptance.

Among the many conservative ginger groups active in Dublin during the 1830s the Protestant Conservative Society of Ireland was a direct forerunner to the Metropolitan Conservatives. In August and September 1834, several large meetings were organized either openly by the Society or as virtual hostings of 'the Protestants of Ireland'. The Authentic Report of such a meeting, held in the Dublin mansion house on 14 August 1834, is especially valuable for the twenty-page list of those who attended (and a few who sent apologies for their absence). The overlap of names also noted in the proceedings of the Metropolitan Conservatives three years later – Isaac Butt and Currell Smyth are listed – is unremarkable. One is struck perhaps by the presence of publishers and booksellers (Edward Tims, James M'Glashan, William Curry Jnr,) and of the secret service agent H. B. Code. County magnates and clergy too numerous to mention appear also; but among the latter one finds the newly ordained William Butler Yeats, and 'the revd. Dr. Bell, Cuba House, Banagher'. (In 1854, Charlotte Brontë married Arthur Bell Nicholls, her father's curate, and the couple honeymooned in Cuba House.) The Revd William Hamilton Maxwell, novelist and historian, does not appear to have attended, being perhaps more concerned to put up a pheasant rather than put down popery. No members of the Le Fanu family – clerical or lay – are listed, nor is there any sign of the other emerging fiction writers of the day – William Carleton, Charles Lever, and Samuel Lover. But the Revd W. B. Yeats's presence in the lists is perhaps the earliest evidence of his involvement (however passive) in the activities which absorbed his friend Isaac Butt.[58]

Mortimer O'Sullivan was a prominent speaker at the August 1834 meeting, and the September issue of the *Dublin University Magazine* carried a fifteen-page anonymous report written by his brother Samuel O'Sullivan. When a 'protestant delegation to England' sailed from Dublin, their progress was recorded by the same author in the issue of February 1835. Samuel O'Sullivan allowed anonymity to foster brotherly love, reporting that in Liverpool:

> Mr. Mortimer O'Sullivan then entered upon his case; and for nearly three hours delighted and astonished his auditory, by a display of eloquence such as had never been heard by any present, except some old men who remembered Burke, and who were strongly reminded of that great orator, by the rev. speaker.[59]

One absence is particularly striking. In these passionate and public defences of Irish Protestantism and its socio-political privileges, occurring only three years prior to the iterative cabal discussions in the Irish Metropolitan Conservative Society, the Protestant Ascendancy is never mentioned.

In January 1837, another 'Great Protestant Meeting' was held in the mansion house, and the principal speeches were later distributed in pamphlet form by the Metropolitan Conservative Society next door. The Earl of Glengall opened the proceedings by mixing homely metaphor and the security of real estate in a way which must now seem indeed prophetic: 'If you all do not put your shoulders to the wheel, and drag the machine from out the quicksand, in which it is almost engulphed, the days which you will be allowed to hold your Protestant estates are numbered.'[60] A year later, his colleagues in the Society were asking if Glengall contributed anything more than his name to their efforts. Closer to political reality was John Beattie West, an MP for Dublin who had unseated O'Connell in a suspect election contest in 1835. West admitted that 'it is charged against us that this meeting, under a pretense of claiming protection, is assembled to secure an ascendancy of corruption. We repel that accusation, and assert that we are here to oppose an ascendancy of corruption.' Like Glengall, West insisted on a preview of the future in which his enemies would constitute . . . whatever it was that ascendancy would constitute! He declared that

those who, like ourselves, are not blind to the light of history, or insensible
to the lessons of their own experience, will have no difficulty in seeing where
the ascendancy is sought, and for what purpose it is required.[61]

If the Revd Mortimer O'Sullivan appeared as an intellectual giant by comparison, his speech in the mansion house on 24 January 1837 concentrated
on the most pygmy points of language. Still smarting under the blow to
Protestant conservative pride which O'Connell's Lichfield House compact
represented, O'Sullivan painstakingly spelled out the insult heaped on Irish
objections to the agreement at Westminster. He recorded the dispute with
the most pedantic attention to detail:

> A rare defence was set up for this iniquitous compact – set up even in the
> British senate. It was said to those who spoke with merited scorn of the foul
> coalition – 'You have committed a barbarism . . . You have made a false quan-
> tity. The word you have pronounced compact is compact.' I presume we may
> term this defence even with technical propriety, a rhetorical artifice – but
> the grammarian also was called in to have his share. Compact is an adjective
> – compact is a substantive. The conclusion is evident – men who, in com-
> plaining against a breach of faith committed a breach of Syntax and Prosody,
> did not deserve to have their statements respected.[62]

Disparaging comment on the ability of the Irish conservatives to comprehend the exact linguistic formulation of the agreement only underlined
the refusal of the British government to listen to the substance of their objections. But, in more immediate terms, we should note the extraordinary
behaviour of O'Sullivan himself. Standing in front of several hundred people, denouncing what he regarded as a major betrayal of principle, he not
only alluded to the pronunciation of adjectives and nouns but repeated the
parliamentary exchange of views on this philological quibble. Were his audience entranced by this? Were they perhaps amused? Or even bored, be-
mused? The printed record does not allow us to draw many conclusions,
but it is nonetheless safe to say that the audience's attitude to these finicky
discriminations was largely conditioned by their familiarity with theological
dispute, with the precision required in scriptural reading, and with the
literalism encouraged in scriptural interpretation.

Deprived of charismatic leadership, of a secular intelligentsia (no Cobbett, no Mill), of a local parliament, and even of a tradition of debate on
purely political matters, Irish conservatism venerated certain institutions in
addition to the Church with a reverence to which one might have thought
the Church alone due. Dublin Corporation headed the list of these idols,
and for reasons which stretched well beyond the city limits.

An appreciation of the fervour of this comes easier than an understanding of its motive causes. *The Address of the Metropolitan Conservative Society of Ireland to the Protestants of Great Britain, Along with the Speech Delivered by Doctor Anthony Meyler on Submitting it for their Adoption* was published in 1840, prior to the passage of the legislation abolishing Protestant monopolies. Again 'the ascendancy of Popery' was detected or fearfully predicted, both in the address itself and in Meyler's speech. Meyler, however, adds a counterbalancing influence when he acknowledges a desire 'to maintain the ascendancy of the Sacred Volume as the sole standard of our social and religious duties' and 'the ascendancy of gospel truth'.[63] If we decode these Victorian circumlocutions and identify the Bible as his guide, we also should recognize how indiscriminately the term 'ascendancy' is being used in these circles – there is a popish ascendancy, a British ascendancy, Protestant Ascendancy in vague retrospect, an ascendancy of rank, and now an ascendancy of the Sacred Volume. What does not emerge is any acknowledgement of a social group regularly called the Protestant Ascendancy.

Though Meyler delivered the address of Irish Protestants to their British co-religionists, it was the Whately Professor of Political Economy, Isaac Butt, who was chosen to represent the city of Dublin at the bar of the House of Lords. We can scan three of Butt's speeches on the topic of municipal reform in 1840. In the earliest of the three, delivered on 13 February, Butt recites a solemn resolution which spoke of measures 'establishing a Popish ascendancy of the worst kind in the Corporate towns of Ireland', and proceeds on his own behalf to condemn these measures 'giving the Roman Catholic party the ascendancy':

> I will make it clear as the sun at noon-day to your knowledge and judgment, that such ascendancy will be established by the ministerial measure.[64]

Popish ascendancy is repeatedly condemned, at least on one occasion because it is detected as the objective of O'Connell's argument, 'that the Roman Catholic religion is advancing every day – that, after being trodden down and trampled on, it has almost miraculously revived, and is gaining the power and ascendancy it had lost.'[65] Turning to the Duke of Wellington as a possible ally at this late date – a doubtful point in view of his grace's having pushed Catholic Emancipation through – Butt first of all hails him as the man who 'preserved the throne of England from the ascendancy of wild and reckless revolution' before advancing rapidly to insist that Wellington was also 'the statesman who had saved them from Popish ascendancy'.[66] The dexterous placing of Wellington as a foe of Popish ascendancy was a rhetorical, hardly a logical, triumph; for the only papists whom the duke had notably overcome were one and the same as the wild and reckless revolutionists of France. Nevertheless, for Butt and others like him Irish political Catholicism represented a particularly dangerous combination of hierarchical structures and democratic forces. The nervous middle-class basis of this dual fear can be read, not so much in the repeated denunciations of ascendancy as in the equally numerous allusions to Trades Unions.[67]

That was at a Conservative Association dinner. On 15 May 1840, Butt followed Sir Charles Wetherall to the bar of the House of Lords to plead the case of the unreformed corporations. In this capacity he was markedly less prolific of ascendancies, less eagle-eyed in detecting Trade Unionism at work. Dealing with the imminent humiliation of sheriffs' peers under the proposed legislation, Butt came close to identifying the notion of ascendancy with municipal office-holding of a not very elevated kind: 'ascending through various civic gradations, they were at last selected by their fellow-citizens to fill the high and responsible office of sheriff of the City.'[68] It is really in historical retrospect only that he can locate 'designs . . . to establish a Roman catholic ascendancy in Ireland'. This had been in 1798. By comparison his fellow-advocate Wetherall, speaking on the previous day, had been fulsome in condemning the bill: 'It crushes protestantism, gives popery a complete ascendant, and this, amid the silence and waste of an ascendant and unresisted despotism, cries "peace and good government". . .'[69] The term ascendancy was not, it seems, one which a respectful advocate frequently used in addressing the house of peers. It had served manfully at a conservative dinner before the climactic address to the Lords, but when Butt delivered a speech at an official dinner for High Sheriff Tomlinson two months after his appearance at the bar of the House the phrase had disappeared altogether: on that third occasion, he concentrated on legal aspects of an iniquitous 'water-pipe suit'.[70]

Butt's career was to reveal his enormous capacity for adaptation. Anthony Meyler was more doggedly consistent. In the year following municipal reform, he published an eighty-six page pamphlet addressed to the colonial secretary, Lord Stanley, in which he used the word 'ascendancy' at least twenty times. The majority of these instances relate to matters the author deplores – an 'intolerant ascendancy' or a 'priestly ascendancy' – but there is one lengthier passage in which Meyler emphasizes his own liberal credentials: 'The domination of high ascendancy and exclusive Toryism in Ireland has passed away, I trust never to return . . . a new element . . . has already become the lord of the ascendant . . . liberty.'[71]

REGIONAL TENSION, MYTHICAL ROMANCE

In connection with the rebellion of 1798, the importance of Wexford as a regional (and anomalous) theatre of Irish sectarian conflict has been noted. Thirty to forty years later, at the core of the movement involving both the *Dublin University Magazine* and the Metropolitan Conservatives were Mortimer O'Sullivan, his brother Samuel O'Sullivan, and William Archer Butler, all three of them natives of Tipperary and ordained clergymen of the Church of Ireland. To these we might add the name of one other figure, the Revd William Phelan (1789–1830), also from Tipperary, and also – like the others listed – a convert from Catholicism. Phelan's early death has deprived him of the little fame conferred on the others through their involvement with the *Dublin University Magazine*, and he is principally remembered as the co-editor (with Mortimer O'Sullivan) of the 1826 *Digest of Evidence on the State of Ireland*. In terms of sectarian bitterness Phelan tops the poll, followed by his co-editor, then by the more philosophical Samuel O'Sullivan, with Butler trailing a poor fourth on account of his interest in Platonism and poetry. Some of these gentlemen (Currell Smyth springs to mind) are of the company with which William Parnell associated 'Protestant Ascendancy' in 1807 – 'fat fools . . . non-descripts in the classes of science, literature, and good sense . . .'[72] This judgement is harsh, and it ignores the transvaluating dynamic at work throughout all these citations of Protestant Ascendancy, the tawdry as well the sublime. But if Mortimer or Samuel O'Sullivan is categorically a more complex figure than John 'Dog-in-Office' Giffard, neither is yet a Robert Gregory. It is necessary, and numinously so, to run through several generations of fat drunkards and bigotted preachers – caricatures yet representative – in order to reach Gregory and Synge, Plunkett and Parnell, strikingly non-generative exemplars. Romance can only obliterate such origins, it can never change them: such change or transvaluation occurs in an ahistorical present.

Religious conversion, in the individual, enacts a comparable change. The later consequences must wait their turn, for something remains to be said of the mentality displayed and disguised in the utterances of the Metropolitan Conservatives and in the mute evidence of the social constituency they came from. Converts to Protestantism played a prominent part in these politico-theological debates, and something like a post-Newtonian shudder runs through their discourse, as if to indicate the unexhausted energy lurking in even an apparently completed movement, the imminence of some further movement. But even the bed-rock fundamentalism which many converts adopted on entering the Protestant churches might prove to be a stepping-stone to indifference. Kierkegaard demonstrated, in relation to the

story of Abraham's willingness to sacrifice Isaac, that a literalist interpretation of the Bible as history can make genuine religious knowledge impossible. Thus, in addition to the brassy oscillations of inter-denominational
conflict, Irish Victorian polemic constitutes a substantial Old Testament to
which the literary revival of Yeats, Synge, and Lady Gregory stands in the
same (though ironized) relation as the New Testament. The analogy is not
unduly forced: after all both Synge and Lady Gregory were raised in
households regulated by the strictest evangelical principles, while Standish
James O'Grady's account of his first encounter with Irish historical writing
is plainly modelled on the literature of evangelical conversion.[73] In the
earlier period, the good news was less accessible. The O'Sullivans were prophets, prophets of doom for the most part, labouring among a backsliding,
ignorant people given to the worship of false gods.

In 1869, one Irish Whig churchman will even argue that deserters from
the Church of Ireland after disestablishment to the church of Rome are more
likely to come from the ranks of those advocating ascendancy rather than
those who can settle for equality.[74] For ascendancy connotes not dominance
but temporary dominance requiring perpetual adjustment, transference or
reversion. Only the transformation of the concept 'Protestant Ascendancy'
into the seeming-class 'the Protestant Ascendancy' will stabilize that potentially random process. Resentment towards the British authorities has been
explicit, also fear of the more local power of the newly emancipated majority in Ireland. But an arrogant assertion of the intrinsic worth of the Irish
Protestant conservative lobby is also fundamental. This attitude cannot properly be called pride, because it is predicated on the gradual replacement
of power by prestige, or status. Or to be precise, a middle class of a kind
which had not wielded power under the old Irish parliament feels itself
deprived of power and compensates by the self-enhancement of their position in a society which now lacks a local parliament. Something analogical
to the concept of 'the elect' in popular Calvinism is implicit in their self-
valuation, but this election is compensatory for past loss (real or otherwise)
rather than promissory of future bliss. The term 'minority' is entering the
vocabulary of Irish politics with a new application; minority will now denote
not numerical weakness but especial worth. If one cannot (any longer?) be
sure of being elected, it is comforting to regard oneself as *the elect* in some
impermeable social constituency the very security of which is enhanced by
not being named too precisely.

But the common origin of all four zealots named at the onset of the previous
paragraph in a single county is almost as striking as their original birth into
the Catholic Church. The school at Clonmel, attended by all four of these

later zealots for Protestantism, must appear at first sight to be the cause of this remarkable concentration.[75] Doubtless, the proselytizing of the school master can be cited as the agency through which they were converted. But the larger context of County Tipperary requires consideration also. The northern portion of the county (including some frontier areas of Queen's County and Galway, with a few districts of Limerick also) supported a substantial number of Protestant settlers. In the 1820s, emigration to Canada provided an escape for many of these yeoman-type farmers and artisans, while agrarian outrages of the kind associated with 'Captain Rock' were seemingly endemic. Bruce Eliott, an historical geographer, has been able to trace no less than 775 Protestant families emigrating from an area of about thirty-by-forty miles in northern Tipperary between the years 1818 and 1855.[76] This figure may seem small, but the impact of emigration from within a minority cannot be measured simply by arithmetic. Protestant emigration was a strong theme in the speeches of local Tory politicians in the 1830s, as we have seen in the case of John Thompson at the Irish Metropolitan Conservative Association. The presence of Tipperary-born converts did little to mitigate the anxiety felt by such speakers for the future of their rural Protestant communities. But, by the same token, the distinctive conditions prevailing in Tipperary should not be read as generally true for the country as a whole.

In addition to Tipperary as the place of origin of several prominent activists, one has noted the recurrence of County Wexford in discussions of the period. Wexford was notorious for 1798, but its distinctive demographic balance predated the Insurrection, and indeed contributed something to the outbreak of violence. If both of these counties feature in the debates which hover around the not-yet-fully-emergent concept of Protestant Ascendancy, one should note the relatively few references in the debates – a) to the far west where Catholicism was virtually universal; and b) to the north-east where Protestantism was unshakeably established. The Whiteboy disturbances in the mid-1780s were concentrated in Munster, including the very large counties of Tipperary and Cork. Yet in 1798 Cork remained relatively undisturbed, and in the long discussion of Protestant destinies which we have been tracing the names of Cork residents have achived no prominence. It is precisely where the Protestant settlement is insecure, or undergoing various forms of alteration, that observers as different as the Scotsman William Ogilvie and the convert Mortimer O'Sullivan found evidence of the kind which lead them towards the detection of, or longing for, Protestant Ascendancy.

Disillusion with the higher social orders is sounded by one or two figures

among the group whom we find debating ascendancy in its various manifestations, but the centrality of the middle class is accepted by all. Ascendancy
has its astrological context, and what is particularly carried over to the
political domain is an acute sense of temporal duration. The popish ascendancy is anxiously foreseen as the coming threat, its duration is necessarily
of unknown length but its effect must prove fatal to the previous state of
affairs. If there has been an ascendancy of Protestantism, its duration has
been either brief or, at best, strictly limited. One may look back upon it,
just as one may look forward to its more frequently cited counterpart, the
'ascendancy of Roman Catholics'. This emphasis on the past and future requires an ever-increasing mobility of attention. The historical undertaking
is not a measured, contemplative view of the past; on the contrary it is a
veritable oscillation, a rapid shift of the gaze by the Janus-head now facing
one way, now facing the other. To be sure, measured contemplation is desired,
indeed it is the primary objective of the quest, but the quest proceeds in
a far more frenetic, or febrile, manner.

In due course, the generalized notion of 'the Protestant Ascendancy' would
smooth over these regional discrepancies and substitute a unique 'super-
class' at the apex of the Irish social system. But that process could not get
under way while a more prominent local element – the exclusively Protestant borough corporations – still existed. Dublin had ceased to be a capital
city, but for all Irish Protestants it remained the last bastion of monopoly
and privilege, a last defence against democratic head-counting. Other
boroughs – in Cork and Waterford the proportions of Catholic and Protestant made the issue particularly tense – had their own local significance.[77]
All of these lesser boroughs looked to Dublin as the symbolic redoubt of
a beleaguered establishment. And in addition to the municipal reform of
1840, more standardized electoral arrangements in the wake of the various
extensions of the franchise were further homogenizing the practices of administration. But the drastic reduction of local distinctions resulted from
a wider variety of developments throughout the nineteenth century. Some
of these were in themselves traumatic, notably the Famine of 1845 – 47 which
accelerated the movement of people from the impoverished and blight-
stricken districts into the cities, especially the ports, and eastward generally. Some were planned operations of technology and investment, as with
the expansion of the railway network, and the increased centralization of
the linen industry in Belfast.[78]

Beyond all of these, two larger and less palpable forces were at work. The
enormous pressure of the English language was exerted on an alternative
culture (Gaelic-speaking) which had little or no access to stream-driven print

technology, or to the medium of popular journalism. Though the decline of Gaelic had commenced before the Famine, the operation of relief agencies through English transformed the relationship between the languages, stigmatizing Gaelic as the badge of poverty, dependence, and immobility.[79] Emigration (the second force in question) was exclusively available as emigration to the Anglo-phone world – Great Britain, the United States, Canada, Australia. Unlike emigrants from Tzarist Russia, rural Italy, or central Europe – who were also pouring into the American cities at different moments in the nineteenth century – the Irish emigrant experienced a universalizing, undifferentiated phenomenon in the English language. Even when allowances are made for the remarkable preservation of Gaelic culture (notably music, but also poetry and story) in cities such as Boston, New York, and Chicago, Irish emigration passed slowly and agonizingly through the fine sieve of Anglo-phone bureaucracy, in the Irish ports, on board the ships (including coffin-ships), and in the sheds of the US immigration service. And the impact on non-emigrants was scarcely less traumatic in the recognition that their survival was only legible in English.

The origins of Protestant Ascendancy lie on the far side of these most deeply rumpled lines of demarcation. These lines divide and relate Daniel O'Connell's 'Old Ireland' and the modernized metropolitan colony in which W. B. Yeats will commence his literary career. It is important to emphasize the division because so many areas of social control – education, church finance, the franchise, industrialization etc. will differ markedly in 1890. But it is important also to stress the kind of relation – continuity, even – which this difference sustains. Ascendancy ideology, indeed, provides one level of transmission between the two cultural zones. Ulster Protestantism generally undergoes a seismic upheaval in 1859, with profound implications for the patterns in which community and culture, power and status are operative. The Established Church is drastically reformed in 1869, and a programme for Home Rule follows directly in the wake of this. The post-Famine status of Irish landed estate facilitated both shrewd commercial investment and the popular notion of a virtually medieval anachronism. The concept of Protestant Ascendancy, back-dated to the early eighteenth century and distributed throughout the regions, provinces and counties, will provide a seamless web supportive of all that has been marginalized, violated, dismembered, expelled in the course of the nineteenth century. The middle-class Protestant professional man, or the daughter of impoverished gentle folk, will find there a protective colouring unmistakeable from the very similar economic and social circumstances of a Catholic bourgeoisie, at last in command of the municipal corporations. The Church of Ireland, no longer an arm of the state, will supply the very term – 'Revival' – upon which literary production will compensate for the uneven distribution of industrial production. And, finally, the reduction of regional differences will result in a turbulent partition; with the nervous sectarian aspects of Protestant Ascendancy preserved in the northern sector and its compensatory literary prospects patronized in the southern.

If, as Daniel Harris and others have argued, the coterie is a central self-image of literary modernism, then Irish modernism in the late nineteenth century had a ready-made model available for appropriation and cultural aggrandizement. Concern at the emigration of Irish Protestants is expressed in relation to both social and theological objectives which are to a degree jeopardized by such a further reduction of the minority. Emigration – an obsession with some of the metropolitan conservatives, especially those with Tipperary connections – threatens to result in a reversal of the Hegelian dialectic, in the reduction of quality to quantity, worth to mere and diminishing numbers. The kernel of my argument is that, thought of as a social group, 'the Protestant Ascendancy' travels on false papers in that its antiquity cannot be traced before the Famine. To be sure, O'Connell's correspondence indicates a sense of a once-powerful ascendancy faction but, when one looks back to the period invoked, the notion of Protestant Ascendancy is (at best) intermittently discernible. As for the monumentality or sublimity implicit in the term as more recently employed, nothing is more at odds with what we know of John Giffard, Isaac Butt, and Anthony Meyler. Between the squalor of mind and body in Giffard's case and the proto-history informing C. R. Maturin's *Women* – a squalor adequately accommodated in Yeats's *Purgatory* (1938) – and the passionate restraint of a Parnell or Synge, there occurred a transformation in which pretence and aggression are dubiously refined by being largely repressed.

In more recent times, memoirs of Edwardian (or George-the-Fifthian) Ireland such as Beatrice Glenavy's *Today We will Only Gossip* (1964) or Brian Inglis's successive autobiographies, *West Briton* (1962) and *Downstart* (1990) were popularly received as narratives of ascendancy exclusivity, written by former inmates of a doomed world. In so far as they were interpreted as confessions (or at least apologies), they contributed to the notion of ascendancy wickedness in the past and so lent credence to the notion of such a past. Yet, as Inglis makes clear, the social realities behind his family's eminence were founded on the recent profits of a Belfast bakery and a Dublin coal-importing company. Pedigree had little to do with it. Indeed, the Inglises were initially suspect among neighbours who were superior only in having endured *parvenu* status for a somewhat longer trial period.

Inglis's father might be compared to the initially wretched William Dobbin in Thackeray's *Vanity Fair* (1848). Son of a retail grocer at a public school of no distinction, honest and loyal Dobbin finally thrashes the odious Reginald Cuffe. The latter is able to resume his 'ascendency over the boys which his defeat had nearly cost him' only with a timely gesture of magnanimity. The bogus magnanimity certainly helps to decode the nature of Cuffe's regime. Thackeray's casual and isolated employment of the noun (ascendancy) to indicate an influence obtained by brute force is all the more eloquent in that the fuller conceptual term (Protestant Ascendancy) is nowhere required in his account of 'A Country House in Kildare' or of the social existence of Colonel Henry Bruen, sometime MP for County Carlow in the Tory interest.[80]

For the English traveller in 1842, no such concept existed. In addition to poverty, prejudice and whiskey, Thackeray's Ireland (like Cobbett's or Trollope's) was stocked with middle-class evidences eloquent enough in themselves, appalling, amusing, instructive by turn. Thackeray was no profound observer, and therein perhaps lies the value of his writing for an inquiry like the present one. Some later commentators have chosen to ignore testimony of this kind in favour of the contrasting and yet mutually supportive romances which associate Inglis with Lady Gregory while wholly suppressing Anthony Meyler and John Giffard. The process can be described in various ways – as a manifestation of class politics, as ethnogenesis, as mythmaking. The species of authentification employed on ascendancy's behalf is not inappropriate to those 'fighters against history' of whom Nietzsche said:

> Not to drag their generation to the grave, but to found a new one – that is the motive that ever drives them onward; and even if they are born late, there is still a way of living by which they can forget it – and future generations will know them only as the first-comers.[81]

NOTES AND REFERENCES

1   Walter Benjamin, *Illuminations*, trans. Harry Zohn (London: Cape, 1970), p. 256.
2   R. F. Foster, *Modern Ireland 1600–1972* (London: Allen Lane, 1988), p. 168. Samuel Johnson's heavily annotated copy of Isaac Watts's *Logick* . . . (London: Longman, 1745, 8th edn corrected) is preserved in the British Library (see p. 221 for ascendancy; the passage was in place in the first edition of 1725). Here I have quoted from Watts direct rather than use the *Dictionary*'s somewhat abbreviated version; cf. this volume, pp. 67-8.
3   W. B. Yeats, *The King of the Great Clock Tower, Commentaries and Poems* (Dublin: Cuala Press, 1934), p. 29. I quote from this interim collection because it makes evident the interweaving of poetry and prose, and its title even gives precedence

to commentary. The political bearing of Yeats's writing at this time is also more clearly evident here than in the post-war collected editions.

4   Ibid., p. 23.
5   Ibid., pp. 23-4.
6   Ibid., p. 25.
7   Ibid., p. 24.
8   See Allan Wade, *A Bibliography of the Writings of W. B. Yeats* (London: Hart-Davis, 1951), pp. 180-1.
9   See Peter Allt and Russell K. Alspach, *The Variorum Edition of the Poems of W. B. Yeats* (New York: Macmillan, 1966, 3rd printing), p. 855.
10 *The King of the Great Clock Tower*, pp. [iii-iv].
11 Ibid., p. 29.
12 William Fitzgerald, *An Essay on the Impediments to Knowledge Created by Logomachy, or the Abuse of Words* (Dublin: Curry, 1840).
13 William Parnell, *An Historical Apology for the Irish Catholics* (Dublin: H. Fitzpatrick, 1807), p. 144.
14 Brian MacDermot ed., *The Catholic Question in Ireland & England 1798-1822; the Papers of Denys Scully* (Dublin: Irish Academic Press, 1988), p. 496. (Henceforth cited as *Scully Papers.*)
15 Ibid., p. 418, n18.
16 Denys Scully, *A Statement of the Penal Laws which Aggrieve the Catholics of Ireland: With Commentaries. In Two Parts* (Dublin: H. Fitzpatrick, 1812), Part 1, p. v.
17 Ibid., p. 95.
18 Ibid., Part 2, p. 337. (The second part of *A Statement* was published in June 1812, paginated in continuation of the first.)
19 Ibid., Part 1, p. 77.
20 Ibid., Part 1, p. 140; see also Part 2, p. 358. The spurious Part 3 works this device to a significantly different end:

> It moves in a circle. Power begets privation. – Privation compels complaint. – Complaint induces indulgence. – Indulgence generates liberty. – Liberty rises into power. – And so the mischief revolves.

This passage (p. 390 of 'Part 3') appears with the marginal comment, 'The consequences of Ascendancy'.

21 *Scully Papers*, p. 318.
22 Ibid., p. 528.
23 Ibid., pp. 528-9 & n3.
24 The municipal record can be studied through the *Calendar of Ancient Records of Dublin*; see above pp. 70-3.
25 Maurice R. O'Connell ed., *The Correspondence of Daniel O'Connell* (Dublin: Irish Manuscripts Commission, 1974), vol. 3, p. 343 (Letter 1409).
26 Ibid., vol. 3, p. 375 (Letter 1451).
27 Ibid., vol. 4, (pub. 1977), p. 43 (Letter 1550).
28 Ibid., vol. 4, p. 442 (Letter 1915).
29 Ibid., vol. 4, p. 467 (Letter 1934).
30 Ibid., vol. 4, p. 467 (Letter 1934).
31 Ibid., vol. 5, (no pub. date), p. 11 (Letter 1957).
32 Ibid., vol. 5, p. 33 (Letter 1976).

33 Ibid., vol. 5, pp. 69 and 68-9 (Letter 2008).
34 Ibid., vol. 5, p. 72 (Letter 2010).
35 Ibid., vol. 5, p. 138 (Letter 2073).
36 Ibid., vol. 5, p. 153 (Letter 2087).
37 See S. J. Connolly, 'Mass Politics and Sectarian Conflict 1823 – 1830' in W. E. Vaughan ed., *A New History of Ireland: vol. 5, Ireland Under the Union, (1) 1801 – 1870* (Oxford: Clarendon Press, 1989), pp. 74 – 107, esp. 76 – 7.
38 John Mitchel, *The Sect 'Everywhere Spoken Against': Two Sermons Preached at Newry, in October 1835* (Newry: printed at the Telegraph Office by Alexander Peacock, 1835), p. 29.
39 Ibid., p. 30.
40 Peter Allt and Russell K. Alspach, op. cit., p. 138 ('To Ireland in the Coming Times').
41 James Hardiman, *Irish Minstrelsy* (London: Robins, 1831).
42 *Dublin University Magazine*, vol. 4 (August 1834), p. 161.
43 Ibid., vol. 4 (October 1834), p. 447.
44 Ibid., vol. 3 (February 1834), p. 225.
45 Mary Ferguson, *Sir Samuel Ferguson in the Ireland of his Day* (Edinburgh, London: Blackwood, 1896), vol. 1, pp. 238-9.
46 Ibid., vol. 1, p. 239.
47 Material quoted in this section derives from a scrapbook compiled by William Patrickson Pike, sometime an officer of the Society. Preserved in the Royal Irish Academy (RR Gall 20 A 16), this is entitled *Debates of the Irish Metropolitan Conservative Society*, and contains material in addition to the newspaper cuttings from which the quoted matter comes.
48 Ibid., p. 36.
49 Idem.
50 Ibid., p. 70.
51 Ibid., p. 32.
52 Ibid., p. 79. This was almost certainly, the John Thompson of Upper Dorset Street, Dublin, who styled himself 'victualler to the Lord Lieutenant'. By 1844, his address had changed to Victoria Park, County Dublin.
53 Idem.
54 Idem.
55 Ibid., p. 45.
56 Idem.
57 See *Dublin University Magazine*, vol. 10 (Nov. 1838).
58 See *An Authentic Report of the Proceedings at the Meeting of the Protestants of Ireland, held on . . . 14th of August, 1834, in the . . . Mansion-house Dublin* (Dublin: Tims, 1834). The list of attendance appears on pp. 97-116, and opens with an acknowledgement that error undoubtedly will have crept into so lengthy a list compiled in crowded circumstances. Yeats's name is given as 'Rev. W.B. Geats, Dromore'. There is no reason to doubt that the poet's grandfather is indicated; he had been ordained for the diocese of Dromore in 1834 but had not yet been assigned to a parish, and no clergyman of the name Geats can be traced.
59 'The Protestant Deputation to England', *Dublin University Magazine*, vol. 5, (February 1835) pp. 215-35; see p. 216. Evidence for the attribution to Samuel

O'Sullivan is given in the fourth volume of *The Wellesley Index to Victorian Periodicals*.

60 See scrapbook referred to in n46 above; the report-sheet (circulated by the Irish Metropolitan Conservative Society and printed from the type set up for the *Dublin Evening Mail* by John Franklin) has not been paged or foliated; see column 7 as it is pasted down in the scrapbook.

61 Ibid., column 9.

62 Ibid., column 20.

63 *The Address of the Metropolitan Conservative Society of Ireland to the Protestants of Great Britain, Along with the Speech delivered by Doctor Meyler on Submitting it for their Adoption* (Dublin: Warren, 1840), pp. 23, 26.

64 Isaac Butt, *Irish Municipal Reform: the Substance of a Speech . . . 13 February 1840 . . .* (Dublin: Curry, 1840), pp. [5], 6. See Jacqueline Hill, *Ireland After the Union* (Oxford: Oxford University Press, 1989), pp. 1-22.

65 Butt, *Irish Municipal Reform*, p. 16.

66 Ibid. p. 27.

67 Ibid. pp. 8, 11, 12 (twice), 15 etc.

68 Sir Charles Wetherall and Isaac Butt, *The Case of the City of Dublin, The Speeches . . . at the Bar of the House of Lords [14–15 May, 1840]*, p. 78.

69 Ibid. p. 51.

70 Isaac Butt, *A Speech Delivered at the Official Dinner of High Sheriff Tomlinson, in . . . Dublin . . . 14 July 1840* (London: Fraser, 1840), p. 15 etc.

71 Anthony Meyler, *Six Letters Addressed to Lord Stanley on the Political and Religious Condition of Ireland* (Dublin: Carson, 1841), p. 13. (See also pp. 6, 7, 11, 18, 20, 22, 24, 29, 32, 33, 40, 59, 60, 75, 76, 77 etc.)

72 See n12 above.

73 For Standish O'Grady see Vivian Mercier 'Don Quixote as Scholar: the Sources of Standish James O'Grady's *History of Ireland*', *Long Room*, no. 22/3 (1981), pp. 19-24.

74 Edward Stopford, Archdeacon of Meath.

75 The school at Clonmel, an endowed institution, was run by the Revd Richard Carey.

76 Bruce S. Elliott, *Irish Migrants in the Canadas: a New Approach* (Kingstown, Montreal: McGill-Queen's University Press; Belfast: Institute of Irish Studies, 1988), pp. 9–115. It was the pattern of what Elliott calls 'chain migration' which so alarmed Butt and his conservative associates; liberals (in domestic politics) like William Smith O'Brien could approve planned migration from Ireland on imperialist grounds – i.e. developing markets in Australia for British goods etc.

77 'I refer you to Dublin, not because I believe this question to be a metropolitan one. Its evils will be felt throughout Ireland, in the south where our great towns principally are – in Cork, in Limerick, and Waterford – even more than in Dublin.' Butt, *Irish Municipal Reform*, p. 7. The reform affected eleven major corporations, and thirty-seven lesser ones including such assorted Protestant fortresses as Callan in County Kilkenny, Strabane in County Tyrone, and Wicklow.

78 For a general account of the period, attending to this emphasis, see Joseph Lee, *The Modernisation of Irish Society 1848–1918* (Dublin: Gill and Macmillan, 1973).

79   For comment on the traumatic nature of the linguistic shift as it surfaces in James Joyce's short story 'Eveline' see below, pp. 257-63.

80   For Inglis, see in particular *Downstart* (London: Chatto & Windus, 1990), esp. pp. 3-5. The Dobbin/Cuffe fight occurs in the fifth chapter of *Vanity Fair*, the accounts of Kildare and Carlow in the second and third of *The Irish Sketch Book*.

81   Friedrich Nietzsche, *The Use and Abuse of History*, trans. Adrian Collins (Indianapolis: Bobbs-Merrill, 1957), p. 54.

5

Mid-Century
Perspectives

FROM EMANCIPATION TO REBELLION

> Gabriel pointed to the statue, on which lay patches of snow. Then
> he nodded familiarly to it and waved his hand. – Good-night,
> Dan, he said gaily.
>
> (James Joyce)[1]

The Act of Union achieved two principal and perhaps contradictory ends
– it removed Irish parliamentary representation from a separate institution
in Dublin to Westminster where all Members of Parliament for the British
Isles were now united together; it placed the discussion of distinctively Irish
issues in the context of an assembly where Irish representatives were
necessarily a permanent minority. The first consequence is usually com-
memorated with some comment on the disappearance of resident dignitaries
from Dublin which declined to the status of a provincial town. It is important to qualify this implied condemnation of the Irish MPs' remoteness from
their constituents by emphasizing that, on the crucial issue of Catholic Emancipation, a majority of the Irish members had been in favour of relief long
before Westminster conceded the issue in 1829. Majorities at Westminster
had priorities other than Irish ones, and British governments had to consult the complex politics of an industrialized nation before adjusting some
anomaly in Irish local affairs. Behind the intricacies of party politics, and
the deeply reactionary mood inherited from the Napoleonic period, the

question of Catholic Emancipation challenged a newly aggressive evangelical element in British Protestantism.

Apart from Emancipation, the history of Ireland in the 1820s and after has been primarily written with specific reference to land occupation and agrarian problems, with the tithes paid largely by a Catholic tenantry to Protestant rectors, forming a contentious link between the two agitations. The literature of the period is best remembered in the fiction of the brothers John and Michael Banim and of Gerald Griffin. Their cautious attention to the values of a depressed Catholic middle class is characteristic of one skein in the pattern of Daniel O'Connell's long campaign for emancipation. A need to trim the material so as to soothe the excited temper of the times is often visible in their work. The result is often at once tendentious and evasive; one has little sense of a distinctive and coherent *literature* in the 1820s, merely a dossier of workmanlike illustrations. This is not to say that the disturbed decade leading up to emancipation was without influence. Indeed the immediate cause and seat of the agitation associated with 'Captain Rock' – gross mismanagement and violence on the Courtenay estate in County Limerick – will reappear in a subversive and vestigial form in Sheridan Le Fanu's 1864 novel, *Uncle Silas*. A comparison of John Banim and Le Fanu might suggest that the historical influence is most creatively absorbed when it is tensely drawn across a long span of years and when it links conditions which are acknowledged as altering. Immediacy, a consciousness of living in important times, can produce a literature which is totally non-reflexive.

Though the reforms of the 1790s had given Catholics the right to vote, and the 1829 Act gave them the right to sit in parliament, local government remained essentially closed. A conservative historian has described the hundred-odd Irish municipal corporations as 'exclusively and arrogantly protestant . . . with petty peculation and jobbery, bigotry and incompetence as their outstanding characteristics'.[2] It was of course the Corporation of Dublin who had given the lead in 1792 with its resolutions on the theme of Protestant Ascendancy. The larger context of the post-assembly debates in William Street was European revolution, and at the beginning of the revolutionary 1840s the Corporation of Dublin was once again the focus for a discussion of Protestant Ascendancy. History occurs twice, we are told, first as tragedy and then as farce: in 1840 our witness to the Ascendancy debates is not Edmund Burke with his scrupulously ironic analysis of language, but the Revd Tresham Dames Gregg.[3]

Prior to the Irish Municipal Act of 1840, the peculiar character of the corporations created a distinctive area in Irish society where Catholics experienced the weight of the old mastership. Responding to the 'Captain Rock' agitations in the early 1820s, Thomas Moore distinguished carefully between the anxieties of Catholics living in the Ulster countryside 'surrounded by armed Orangemen' and the anxieties of 'the Catholic inhabitants of towns and cities, whom the spirit of Corporation Ascendancy haunts through all the details of life'.[4] Back in the 1790s Moore had been within an inch of involvement in radical, even revolutionary, politics, and he remained no friend of the Irish Establishment. His student days were 'the glorious days of Protestant jobbing . . . the Golden Age of the Ascendancy when jobs and abuses flourished in unchecked luxuriance.'[5] Moore effectively retains a perspective on Protestant Ascendancy which acknowledges its recent, urban, and bourgeois origins. In contrast, we may look at *The Rockite*, an evangelical and fictionalized tract by Charlotte Elizabeth: here the object of Catholicism allegedly is:

> To overthrow the abhorred ascendancy of Protestantism, and once more to reign unrivalled and unchecked, became the sole object of that aspiring apostacy, which would, as God, ever sit in the temple of God, shewing itself to be a god.[6]

What is evidenced here is not so much the valorization of the phrase, Protestant Ascendancy, as the logic by which Henry Grattan's assumption of possible universal salvation for Catholics and Protestants alike is reduced to an exclusivist evangelicalism. The comparison between Moore and Charlotte Elizabeth is revealing, not of some innate sectarian distinction, but of Moore's resistance to Protestant Ascendancy as ideology and the novelist's indulgence of it.

The Famine of 1845 – 7, and the rebellion of 1848, are the dominant events of the decade in Irish history. Yet both can only be understood in the context of political assumptions which permitted them: Whig *laissez-faire* economics contributed as much (or rather, as little) to the fate of the Irish population as the potato blight, and revulsion against Daniel O'Connell's collaboration with English Whiggery played its part in creating the Young Ireland group and William Smith O'Brien's rebellion. Naturally, the political context cannot be appreciated solely in Irish terms: the 1840s are also the decade of Chartism in Britain and revolution in Europe. The restlessness of working people in England and France was not without parallel in Ireland, and though there was little prospect of a coherent working-class movement emerging in Dublin or Belfast, other political elements were keen to bind the working population to them. Industry in Dublin had suffered a decline, and the Reform Act of 1832 (while it fell far short of universal franchise) had the effect of bringing parliamentary electioneering within the experience of a substantial proportion of the citizenry. O'Connell's movement to repeal the Act of Union, launched in July 1840, provided a grand cause requiring a heightened rhetoric of all the protagonists.

Jacqueline Hill has written of the manner in which Protestants among the working class declined to accept the Repealers' arguments that the Union had caused the city's reduced prosperity.[7] Though conservative newspapers were primarily directed towards a middle-class readership, *The Warder* took pains to report the activities of Protestant working-class groups. Of these the most important was the Dublin Protestant Operatives Association, founded by Tresham Dames Gregg. Since September 1840, Sheridan Le Fanu had had a share in the direction both of *The Warder* and of *The Statesman*. *The Warder* was a solid, respectable weekly paper in which Le Fanu retained an interest until 1870, whereas *The Statesman* – in part owned by T. D. Gregg – was flamboyant and aggressive. It ceased publication in 1846, though Le Fanu had not written for it in its last twelve months.[8]

As the creation of Gregg, *The Statesman* became the principal voice of the Dublin Protestant Operatives Association. In 1840, Gregg proudly reported the differences between his paper and the conservative press generally:

> When *The Statesman* commenced its career, it avowed Protestant Ascendancy as its guiding principle. Some of the *soi disant* Protestant newspapers laughed us to scorn – told us that we were behind the spirit of the age. We should be glad to see which of them would venture to murmur against us now – which of them would presume to say that we are unreasonable in looking for all that is demanded by high principle. The question has, in truth, made way. If a proof of this be required, we need only refer to the complaint of Mr. O'Connell – no inferior testimony on such a subject – that gentleman alleges as the most effectual barrier to his anti-union projects, the existence of a strong 'Protestant Ascendancy' party. He is right.[9]

The strong Protestant Ascendancy party was not, of course, orthodox Toryism but the network of fringe groups which had sprung up in the 1830s. The causes of this recrudescence of Protestant Ascendancy as a crusading political force are many – Catholic Emancipation, Tithe War, the suppression of the Orange Order, Melbourne's reforming government, and Thomas Drummond's scrupulous regime as Under-Secretary (1835–40). O'Connell's success in bargaining within the conventions of the united parliament added to the Irish Tories' sense of remoteness from Westminster. For the middle class, the Dublin Metropolitan Conservative Association provided one outlet for their disillusion and ardour, with Gregg's Dublin Protestant

Operatives Association directing itself to the lower classes. Tension between
these bodies was noted by others, apart from Gregg. The difference was
one of manners as much as theory: Le Fanu writing home to his father complained of the embarrassment he felt in being involved with Gregg's paper:

> My vote is overruled by the other two [proprietors] . . . I proposed conver-
> ting the paper into a merely political one, but was overruled. I proposed chang-
> ing it into a staunch Church paper but was overruled. I have no power over
> the Statesman and wash my hands of all responsibility for its tone in point
> of style & of feeling.[10]

Manners and theory are not absolutely distinct of course. Gregg's harangues
to the faithful masses may have offended the son of the Dean of Emly, but
the real grounds of their dispute *were* political. Le Fanu believed that a paper
should either devote itself to politics or to Church affairs: the combination
necessarily veered towards the vulgarly enthusiastic – as with Gregg's accusations of fornication brought against a Catholic priest and his attempt
to 'rescue' a convert-novice from a convent.[11] This is not to suggest that Le
Fanu accepted any separation of Church and State, far from it: but he expected a certain decorum of public discussion.

Gregg's notion of Protestant Ascendancy, if it offended Le Fanu, would
have mortified Edmund Burke. Burke's opponents in the Corporation of
Dublin openly acknowledged the conjunction of 'the security of property
in this kingdom' and 'the Protestant ascendancy in our happy constitution'.[12] The Ascendancy was defined by reference to specific political and
administrative priorities and privileges. Gregg's definitions, however, ac-
centuated the Protestantism of Protestant Ascendancy in a series of published
letters addressed to the Corporation of his day:

> My Lord Mayor and Brethren – 'PROTESTANT ASCENDANCY!' – A sore
> point this with the popular Conservative politicians of the day; they don't know
> what to make of it. The age is so imbued with mock philosophy – this has
> become so much the standard that regulates every thing, and the thought of
> God and of religion is so much driven from us, that the man who confesses
> himself an advocate for Protestant Ascendancy is looked upon as infatuate,
> and laughed at as behind the intelligence of the times.
>
> Still the principle of Protestant Ascendancy is a sound principle which must
> and will be acted on. How? – it is impossible! 'All things are possible to them
> that believe' – 'By the help of my God I will leap over the wall.' Why, what
> can poor abandoned Protestants do? Revolutionise the age – make the cur-
> rent of popular opinion run in the right channel, and pour out large blessings
> on the world, 'not by might nor by power, but by my Spirit, saith the Lord.'
>
> It is absolutely essential that there should be sound views on this subject.

So long as the nonsense which exists on it at present has place, so long as we find Protestants mealy-mouthed about it, so long as we find such worthies as Sir George Murray and Alderman Warren, in the plentitude of their good nature coming forward, and saying, 'we don't require any ascendancy over others' – so long nothing good will be effected. No! no! Let these excellent personages be well assured that the old Protestants who made ascendancy their rallying cry in the time of William the Third, were neither fools nor blind – that we may suspect our philosophy when it compels us to the adoption of a language so very different from theirs.

I can, however, justify these gentlemen. I know that in their own sense of the words they mean a right thing. What they mean to express is this, 'we seek not to act the part of tyrants; we renounce the idea of any unreasonable domination over our Roman Catholic countrymen.' They conceive that such is meant by 'Protestant Ascendancy.' Such an ascendancy they abjure, and so do I, and so does every Christian Protestant. The most strenuous advocates of the principle would abhor such an application of it. No; this were its abuse. In the renunciation of this, we agree with the worthy Alderman and the gallant General, and we only find fault with their language because it is capable of being mistaken.

Still our cry is *'Protestant Ascendancy!'* [13]

Thus on the eve of their eclipse, the city fathers are exhorted to hold tenaciously to ascendancy, in the name of a Williamite rallying cry. 'Unreasonable domination' is abjured but the military triumph of Protestantism is strategically recalled. Gregg opposes any democratic reform of the Corporation, and offers instead an amalgam of evangelical fervour and pseudo-historical allusion. The 'Golden Age' to which Moore mockingly alluded as the period of Protestant jobbing is pressed back in time: on this occasion not only to include the eighteenth century *in toto* but also to associate itself with the origins of the Whig Revolution. Hand-in-hand with this sweeping historical revision, Gregg presents his own definition of a contemporary Protestant Ascendancy, by which he means 'the making of the Word of God, as it ought to be, supreme in the councils of the state', with the effect of overturning O'Connell's 'Apostate Church'. [14] It is hardly necessary to add that the Corporation was reformed, and indeed O'Connell became the first Catholic lord mayor of the city since 1688.

In terms of party politics Gregg's influence may have been negligible, but his significance cannot be measured solely in terms of immediate impact. The messianism so often attributed to Catholic nationalism in later years is latent in his Protestant war-cry. Basically, it utilizes that rare sense of nationalism, meaning the doctrine 'that certain nations (as contrasted with individuals) are the object of divine election'. [15] If a charge of this kind may be levelled at Patrick Pearse with his ideas of blood sacrifice, and at some latter-day saints, it is entirely explicit in Gregg's *Protestant Ascendancy Vindicated and National Regeneration Through the Instrumentation of National Religion Urged*. For a nineteenth-century Irish Protestant Unionist to invoke national regeneration he had need of a considerably long perspective on history. The 'Protestant Nation' of Grattan's phrase had surrendered its identity in 1800, and increasingly the pace of Irish politics had been determined by Catholic problems if not always Catholic energies. By referring to the Catholic Church as apostate, Charlotte Elizabeth and the Revd Mr Gregg sought to emphasize that the original church of Saint Patrick could be identified theologically with the Established Church of Ireland. In this sense the Church of Ireland was, so to speak, aboriginal and national, and Catholicism a series of aberrations provoking the sixteenth-century Reformation. In the context of the 1840s, the essence of the argument was its anti-democratic assumptions, hence Gregg's assiduous attention to the emotions of Protestant operatives. Indeed, Gregg was not so much anti-democratic as anti-political: the ideology he proffered repeatedly substitutes Biblical quotation for social analysis or documentation. In *Protestant Ascendancy*, for example, having defined that term as the word of God supreme in the councils of the state, he proceeds:

> I call the attention, especially, of the humbler classes to the promises made by God himself to the nation which thus exalts and honours his Word. 'It shall come to pass if thou shalt (i.e. as a nation) hearken diligently unto the voice of the Lord thy God. . . .'[16]

The quotation is taken from Deuteronomy 28: 1, and Gregg proceeds to quote *in extenso* all of God's promises to Israel of material prosperity:

> Blessed shalt thou be in the city, and blessed shalt thou be in the field. Blessed shall be the fruit of thy body, and the fruit of thy ground, and the fruit of thy cattle . . .[17]

Irish Protestants, then, are identified with the children of Israel: the Williamite settlement is their promised land, 'and he shall bless thee in the land which the Lord thy God giveth thee. The Lord shall establish thee an holy people unto himself. . . .'[18] Apocalyptic language of this kind has many precedents. The distinctive feature of Gregg's rhetoric is his presentation of social reward in return for an abjuration of social action. And the underlying strategy is to promulgate a false consciousness of history in which Saint Patrick, the Old Testament prophets, William of Orange, and Gregg himself (speaking God's lines) are conjoined. To join this alliance, other Protestants rather than other operatives were cordially invited.

Gregg's exhortation to the doomed exclusivist Corporation may be unmemorable in the university seminar, though it will sound familiar enough to many in Ulster gospel-halls. Sociologists and partisans have striven to describe the emergence of a reactionary Protestant working class, and the task is best left to them.[19] But the process of assimilating the Whig Revolution to the rhetoric of nineteenth-century Protestant Ascendancy has specifically literary consequences. Writing in 1934, W. B. Yeats spoke of four bells, 'four deep tragic notes, equally divided in time, so symbolising the war that ended in the Flight of the Earls; the Battle of the Boyne; the coming of French influence among our peasants; the beginning of our own age. . . .'[20] Here, Yeats may have taken his cue direct from Grattan himself: addressing the Irish parliament in February 1793, he noted three policies towards Catholics – 'the first was that of Cromwell – extermination by operation of the sword; the second was that of Ann – extermination by operation of the laws; and the third was your's – which allowed them a qualified existence!'[21] The process by which Protestant Ascendancy is extended backwards from 1792 to embrace the age of Swift is particularly ironic if we take Swift's excoriating dictum on Queen Anne's Irish viceroy as evidence, 'He is a Presbyterian in politics, and an atheist in religion, but he chuses at present to whore with a Papist.'[22] The multiple innuendo, a mixture one might say of Augustan paradox and hydrochlorate, reaches its most extended form in Swift when he characterizes the Duke of Marlborough, hero supreme of triumphant Whiggery, in his *History of the Four Last Years of the Queen*.

When Tresham Gregg eulogizes the victor of Blenheim he runs the risk of a thunderbolt from Swift's ghost in Saint Patrick's Cathedral. When he associates Protestant Ascendancy indiscriminately with King William, the Corporation, the eighteenth century, he creates a shapeless synthesis in which other imaginations may yet discern irony and order. Gregg's uneasy partner on *The Statesman*, Sheridan Le Fanu, was already composing his early stories and novels at the time of the Irish Municipal Act: indeed, as a member of the Irish Metropolitan Conservative Association he was doubly active as radical conservative and as secret novelist. His first novel, *The Cock and Anchor* (1845), is set in Dublin in the last year of Thomas Wharton's viceroyalty: Swift and Joseph Addison make brief appearances as foils to the genial, venial Wharton. If this is not Swift's first appearance as fictional character, it is certainly an important early contribution to the mythic figure of Yeats's pantheon. But perhaps the most striking aspect of Le Fanu's treatment of the early eighteenth century is his deployment of 'ascendancy' for a complex and ironic effect: conspiring Catholic Jacobites declare that over-ridden, and despised, and scattered as we are, mercenaries and beggars abroad, and landless at home – still something whispers in my ear that there will come at last a retribution, and such a one as will make this perjured, corrupt, and robbing ascendancy a warning and a wonder to all after times.[23]

Le Fanu has chosen to exploit the anachronism of ascendancy's signifying, in 1710, the governing élite in Ireland, and the motivation may well be connected with his apprehension that in 1845 his own class was on the point of eclipse. For one of the symbolic implications of accepting ascendancy to do the work of aristocracy (albeit on behalf of a disguised bourgeoisie) is the attendant notion of a rising and falling pattern: the star which in the ascendant must fade or fall, the Protestant Ascendancy must be succeeded by some other social order. By Yeats's day, the usage of ascendancy as élite was well established, but it is characteristic of his sensitivity to the inner dynamics of a word that he should ally his pride in ascendancy to a cyclical notion of history in which one order is succeeded by another in a perpetual pattern of rising and falling civilizations. Etymologically, as J. M. Synge noted in his reading of Trench's *On the Study of Words*, ascendancy is derived from the language of astrology, and sardonically he summarized the discovery by noting that ascendancy involved a *belief* in astrology. Yeats, less satirical in his attitude to his ancestry, composed his own astrology in *A Vision*. That arcane philosophy speaks principally of world history, of the renaissance, and the loss of 'unity of being'. Yet to a considerable extent it is facilitated by Yeats's experience of the Anglo-Irish Protestant Ascendancy in the nineteenth century, the social experience of that uncertain élite, and the evolution of that linguistic term.

The Cock and Anchor is best approached as a late Irish contribution to the historical novel as founded and developed by Sir Walter Scott. The two-team structure of Jacobites and Williamites, with a hero and heroine drawn from opposing sides, the blending of violent incident and romance, preserve the outward appearance of the Scottish novel. But Le Fanu's first exercise in fiction has also to be read in relation to his politics: accordingly, we find a species of ventriloquism in which the privations of eighteenth-century Catholics may be decoded as symbolizing the indignation of nineteenth-century middle-class Protestants. And this in keeping with the altered association of words, as between 1688 and 1840: Whiggery for the generation of Le Fanu's fictional heroes was the Protestant Succession, the Penal Laws, Ascendancy: Whiggery for Le Fanu's political associates was now closely allied with Catholicism, with the *hoi polloi* and detestable Dan O'Connell at their head. *The Cock and Anchor*, with its neglect of that supernaturalism which had characterized Le Fanu's earlier short stories, with its posited union of Protestant and Catholic, accorded well with the attitudes of Young Ireland. Indeed Le Fanu's second novel, *Torlogh O'Brien*, concludes with two inter-denominational weddings, while simultaneously the author was carried over into some collaboration with Young Irelanders such as Charles Gavan Duffy, Thomas Francis Meagher, and John Mitchel.[24] The motion towards Young Ireland and nationalism was prompted by dread of further reform imposed by an English government, combined with outrage at British reactions to the Irish Famine. But there were necessarily reservations, and when Meagher and Mitchel, with William Smith O'Brien, became implicated in conspiracy, treason, and rebellion in 1848, Le Fanu's sense of self-betrayal was over-whelming. Instead of the harmonies and reconciliations of *The Cock and Anchor*, Le Fanu's fiction of 1848, the long three-part tale 'Richard Marston', is riddled with solitude and division.[25] With this, we note also the re-emergence of the nervous supernaturalism which Le Fanu had purged from his first two novels. In Ireland 1848 brought to an end the minor renaissance of literature associated with Thomas Davis, James Clarence Mangan, and *The Nation*, a company with whom Yeats claimed a touching affinity. More significant, ultimately, was the foundation of the Encumbered Estates Court to begin the dismemberment of a landed estate system fatally shaken by the Famine and its consequences. The development of the Ascendancy as a cultural entity is closely related to the decline of landed estate.

UBI LAPSUS? QUID FECI? SHERIDAN LE FANU AS SUBVERSIVE

> the house, in its silence, seems to be contemplating the swell or
> fall of its own lawns.
>
> (Elizabeth Bowen)[26]

Between *Castle Rackrent* and *Ulysses* only one Irish novel approximates to a total apprehension of social reality, and given that its setting is Derbyshire its totality is necessarily problematic. *Uncle Silas* is in many ways flawed, but it nevertheless represents a bold inquiry into the nature of literary form and its bearing upon reality. Regarded as delinquent in the lists of respec-table novels about castles and cabins set in a cloth of green, and consequently accommodated among the sensationalist productions of Wilkie Collins, Charles Reade, and Le Fanu himself at his more common second-best, *Uncle Silas* calls for analysis in less easily predictable terms. Its thorough-going symmetry, and hermetic completeness, has been established primarily by means of detailing Le Fanu's structural use of Swedenborgian doctrine.[27]

Swedenborgianism, with its elaborate system of correspondences, aligns itself with allegory, and the present inquiry will concentrate on an account of how and why Le Fanu should choose to write in the allegorical mode in his finest fiction. However, allegory is itself in need of some restitution and a preliminary digression is in order.

In his magisterial study of German baroque tragedy, Walter Benjamin initiated a reassessment of the aesthetic status of allegory, which has not been sufficiently assimilated into other areas of European literature. Patrick Healy has suggested that Benjamin's analysis of melancholia can shed light on the Gaelic literature produced during the Baroque period, that is (to use familiar Irish markers) during the period roughly from the Battle of Kinsale to the Williamite/Augustan triumph a century later. However, the turn towards nineteenth-century problems, especially in his writings on Paris and on Baudelaire, may have had the effect of obscuring Benjamin's earlier work. In approaching Le Fanu as Victorian novelist, one is not isolated from narratives of Elizabethan and Jacobean conflict: 'Ultor de Lacy' (1861) finally discloses events of 1601.[28]

It would be perverse, however, to recruit Benjamin to some new module of 'period studies'. His value in the hands of the literary historian relates more tellingly to the problem of the ancient modes and genres as they are maimed and maintained in his own time. Allegory had been relegated to the level of mere ciphering and deciphering by the romantic insistence on transcendence in the symbol: 'even great artists and exceptional theoreticians, such as Yeats, still assume that allegory is a conventional relationship between an illustrative image and its abstract meaning.'[29] The priority, for Benjamin, was not simply the restoration of allegory to respectability as a technique, rather it was the elaboration of a comprehensive typology in which tragedy is distinguished from *Trauerspiel*, myth from history, transcendence from immanence. Insisting on the dialectical nature of allegory in this typology, he speaks of its 'worldly, historical breadth':

> Whereas in the symbol destruction is idealised and the transfigured face of nature is fleetingly revealed in the light of redemption, in allegory the observer is confronted with the *facies hippocratica* of history as a petrified, primordial landscape.[30]

Such speculations may appear to be remote from the birth pangs of Anglo-Irish literature. Yet, if we look forward to Yeats's *Purgatory* or *The Words Upon the Window-Pane*, we will find the distinction between tragedy and *Trauerspiel* may help to relate those plays to earlier Yeatsian drama. Furthermore, Patrick Diskin has pointed out resemblances between J. C. Mangan's

translation of Zacharias Werner's 'Der Vierundzwansigste Februar' in the
Dublin University Magazine and Yeats's *Purgatory* – Werner's play is part
of Benjamin's argument.[31] The culmination of this present inquiry will be
an examination of the way in which *Purgatory* succeeds in revealing the inauthenticity of the history its characters proclaim. One Irish antecedent to
Purgatory, in its association of the Big House and Swedenborgian patterns,
is *Uncle Silas*. And if we look back over the earlier history of Anglo-Irish
literature, *The Absentee* stands out as an example of allegory rendered too
palpable by the historical failure of the programme to which it referred.
(One might offer the embarrassing comparison of Spenser's *Faery Queen*
in which the allegory of Elizabethan *Realpolitik* is transformed by the success of that *Realpolitik*.)

Our principal focus on Le Fanu's allegory will be to examine the manner
in which it assimilates and transforms the materials of history, and relates
that history to other forms of order. It is significant that the sources are exceedingly diverse – Chateaubriand and 'Captain Rock' – for there is a formal logic to the manner in which allegory deliberately seeks to incorporate
such disparate elements. Benjamin speaks of 'the violence of the dialectical
movement'[32] in allegory; and, though he has in mind the plots of his
baroque *Trauerspiel*, it is proper to consider this violence as a structural principle in allegorical forms. Dickens's novels, violent enough in their details,
met much opposition from a neoclassicism which arrogated to itself an exclusive access to the Sublime. In being fully accepted as consummate art,
they revealed a central and controlling dualism. It is often argued that the
causes of Dickensian dualism were biographical, but the Anglo-Irish instance
may be explored in less subjective terms. Client cultures tend to employ imitative forms, and do so for two reasons. First, by modelling their art upon
that of the dominant 'mother' culture, they acknowledge the source of their
identity and definition. In the heightened consciousness of a colonial society imitation tends to veer at times towards pastiche or even parody: thus,
the second motive for the imitative nature of colonial literature is a need
or ability to resist the imposition of identity. Irony binds the positive and
negative elements of this stance: irony distinguishes the work of Swift,
Sheridan, and Burke in the eighteenth century. In moving from *Castle
Rackrent* to *The Absentee* we would note the displacement of irony by a different mode of dual focus, which closely resembles allegory. And the impetus behind this altered literary practice of Maria Edgeworth's is her
realization that Union had not achieved its object of dissolving Irish identity: that double-edged identity survived in ever more complex and overt forms
of social practice. In this problematic manner, the uneasy alliance of allegory

and didactic is revealed. If *Uncle Silas* is unique among Irish novels appearing between *Castle Rackrent* and *Ulysses* in approaching what György Lukács would term totality, it is because in Le Fanu's novel allegory flourishes untrammelled by fond didactic ambitions. Instead of such harmony in unity we have violent dialectic.

To test these speculations, let us begin with a single passage from *Uncle Silas* in which the narrator Maud is speaking of her father, Austin Ruthyn:

> It was his wont to walk up and down thus, without speaking – an exercise which used to remind me of Chateaubriand's father in the great chamber of the Chateau de Combourg. At the far end he nearly disappeared in the gloom, and then returning emerged for a few minutes, like a portrait with a background of shadow, and then again in silence faded nearly out of view.[33]

What Maud has been reminded of is the following passage (translated) from Chateaubriand's *Mémoires d'outre tombe*:

> My father would then set off on his walk, which would end only when it was time to go to bed. He was dressed in a white Petersham gown, or rather a sort of coat that I have seen only him wearing. His half-bald head was covered with a large white cap, held straight in position. As he walked about he would take himself away from the hearth, the vast room being so dimly lit by a single candle that he could no longer be seen: he was only heard still walking about in the shadows: then he would come back slowly towards the light, emerging little by little from the darkness like a ghost, with his white gown, his white cap, and his long pallid face.[34]

Here too the narrator's father walks in a room so as to appear and disappear from and into the darkness. There is, however, a prominent element in Chateaubriand's account which is absent from Maud Ruthyn's. Indeed it is an integral part of the picturesque effect of the *Mémoires* – the reiterated whiteness of the father's appearance. Readers of *Uncle Silas* will know that this element, though absent from the account of Austin Ruthyn, is insinuated repeatedly elsewhere in the novel – not in the description of the narrator's father but in that of her uncle. When she gives us her first impression of Silas, he is an 'apparition, drawn as it seemed in black and white'. Trying to sleep in Bartram-Haugh on that first night under her uncle's roof, she visualizes his face as 'ashy with a pallor on which I looked with fear and pain.' In a crucial scene he is 'dressed in a long white morning gown . . . with the white bandage pinned across his forehead. . . .'[35] Such cameos of Silas's whiteness and paleness could be multiplied by other citations. What is already evident is that Chateaubriand's pallid and perambulating father is reflected in *two* characters in *Uncle Silas*, Austin Ruthyn complying with the manner of walking in and out of the narrator's vision, his brother Silas carrying very many images of bloodless, pallid, white, and ghostly appearance.

We may conclude, therefore, that Le Fanu's allusion to *Mémoires d'outre tombe* is not just simply the kind of casual name-dropping which flatters the reader's vanity. It is, however, less clear-cut than the acknowledgement of a debt or a source. The curious, vestigial presence of this borrowed image has its relevance for Chateaubriand also, for there were really two personalities in the author of the *Mémoires*: on the one hand the astute politician who reverted to Christianity just at the right moment, and on the other, the poet and libertine.[36] These polarities are reflected in the pious austerity of Austin Ruthyn, and the suspected criminality and licence of Silas. The structure of the novel as a whole is a vast series of symmetrical details, often dislocated from their immediate context but corresponding with details secreted elsewhere in the text. It is a two-part symmetry with Austin at Knowl 'corresponding' with Silas at Bartram-Haugh, with life continuing in death, rectitude revealed as guilt, truth replaced by betrayal. Benjamin has summarized the conventional notion of allegory as a relation between an illustrative image (in the work of art) and its abstract meaning (lying outside the work of art). In *Uncle Silas*, this pattern is raised to the second power, so to speak, in that a Swedenborgian reading establishes the novel as a self-referring allegory: assumptions of virtue *are* vices, the soul's experience in death is indistinguishable from the events of life. Thus, one part of *Uncle Silas* provides an allegorical reading of the other, ensuring that an extended allegorical reading – by which the novel as a whole is allegorically related to 'external' reality – is reflexive. By an internal analysis of character disposition, we may say that Silas is the posthumous revelation of the real guilt which lies behind Austin's pious rectitude: if we are to read Austin as allegoric of the Big House philosophy, then that philosophy is also reflected in Silas's homicide, fraud, corruption, and suicide. This identity of opposites in the fiction is ultimately deducible from an analysis of the novel as a whole, but it is offered in the first chapter in that cryptic allusion to Chateaubriand's father both ghostly and pedestrian.

One allusion does not make a novel. For most readers Maud Ruthyn's comparison of her father to Chateaubriand's father remains a decoration sustaining their confidence in the narrative as articulate and well-informed. It is crucial to Le Fanu's curious achievement in *Uncle Silas* that further investigation should undermine this confidence, should reveal a bifurcated response to the source of the allusion which threatens the separate identities of separately named characters. If this were the only instance of its kind in the novel, we might conclude that Le Fanu intended it perhaps as a sardonic joke, perhaps did not intend it at all. Other literary allusions – to Swift's Struldbruggs in *Gulliver's Travels* and to the wizard Michael Scott in Walter Scott's 'Lay of the Last Minstrel', for example – do suggest a consistency of intention: these references to figures who 'survive' death so as to teach a lesson to the living contribute metaphorically to the sense of Silas as a revelation of Austin's real moral condition. Often such references are integrated smoothly to a character's particular circumstances – Silas, for example, reels off verses from French poets with a fluency which we are meant to see as beguiling. Austin, on the other hand, is highly economical in his recourse to such devices, and this is in keeping with his withdrawn personality. In the important scene where he confides in his daughter on the matter of Silas's bad reputation, he allows himself a few Latin tags. Having won her agreement that she should assist in some future recovery of the family's honour – sullied by Silas's suspected crimes – he moves from an unyielding painterly pose into veritable eloquence:

> He turned on me [i.e. Maud] such an approving smile as you might fancy lighting up the rugged features of a pale old Rembrandt.
> 'I can tell you, Maud; if my life could have done it, it should not have been undone – *ubi lapsus, quid feci*. But I had almost made up my mind to change my plan, and leave all to time – *edax rerum* – to illuminate or to *consume*.'[37]

Austin's notion of doing nothing, of leaving all to Time, calls forth a Latin tag of no great obscurity: 'Tempus edax rerum' (Time, the destroyer of all things) comes from Ovid's *Metamorphoses*.[38] But 'ubi lapsus, quid feci' seems, at first glance, inscrutable.

Burke's Peerage and similar works of reference tell us that the motto of the Courtenays of Powderham is 'Ubi lapsus? Quid feci?' translatable as 'Where is my fault? What have I done?' These words which express astonishment at a sudden and undeserved fall are said to have been adopted by the family when they lost the earldom of Devon.[39] More immediately relevant to our problem is an additional note in *Burke's* to the effect that, in 1585, Sir William Courtenay (thirteenth *de jure* Earl of Devon) 'was one of the undertakers to send over settlers for the better planting of Ireland, and thus laid the foundation of the prodigious estates in that kingdom enjoyed by his posterity'.[40] Here, more discretely than in 'Ultor de Lacy', Le Fanu has re-presented the offensive past and unveiled a Baroque sculpture which, so to speak, commemorates a literary villain then unborn, unconceived, unconceivable, Silas with his 'monumental' look. We have then some thematic relevance in Austin Ruthyn's citing the Courtenay motto: the actual

Courtenays and the fictional Ruthyns have suffered a reversal of fortune through no fault – they feel – of their own. And we have a rudimentary link between the Courtenays as Irish planter landlords and Le Fanu as an Irish novelist. The latter link can be immediately confirmed in that the principal Courtenay seat in Ireland was The Castle, Newcastle, Limerick, while Le Fanu was raised at Abington Glebe in the same county.

In critical terms we have reached a stage similar to that when the passage from *Mémoires d'outre tombe* was seen to resemble Maud's account of her father, and before its resemblance to her account of Silas was noticed. In other words, the Courtenay motto has a sort of broad relevance to the context in which it appears – like the Courtenays, Austin wonders where he has made his mistake that he should feel his family's honour tarnished. Its critical contribution to a more diffused and subversive reading of the novel has yet to emerge. If 1585 seems remote from 1864 (when *Uncle Silas* appeared) we should recall that the novel evolved from a short story written in 1838 while Le Fanu was still living in County Limerick. Furthermore in 1838 the Courtenays were variously in the news, and their motto had an ironic propriety.

Le Fanu's father had been appointed to the parish of Abington in 1823, but he postponed his removal thence for some years due to the disturbed state of the county. These disturbances were soon widespread in Munster, and formed part of the background to the Catholic Emancipation crisis. Their origins in Limerick were quite specific and notorious. In late 1821 the county was 'in a very desperate state', according to Matthew Barrington, the Crown Solicitor for Munster.[41] In evidence to a House of Commons committee he said that 'murder, burnings, breaking houses, outrages of every description were committed there'.[42] Asked whether the disturbances had originated on the estate of any particular proprietor, he answered 'It was on the Courtenay estate, and in that neighbourhood.'[43] Numerous other witnesses confirmed this identification of the Courtenays' estate at Newcastle as the starting-point of the widespread violence of 1821–3. The central outrage had been the murder of Thomas Hoskins, son of Alexander Hoskins, the agent on the Courtenay property. This agent, a new appointment and an Englishman unfamiliar with Irish conditions and Irish customs, had established a rigorous and (for him) lucrative regime on the estate, and his determination to profiteer through his office was affirmed by witnesses ranging from the parish priest of Michelstown to the Earl of Kingston.[44] In the expanding wave of violence which followed the murder of Thomas Hoskins, 'Captain Rock' emerged as the eponymous leader of the agitation and the conspiracy – the 'system' as it was called. Thomas Moore's *Memoirs of*

Captain Rock, Mortimer O'Sullivan's *Captain Rock Detected*, and Charlotte Elizabeth's *Rockite* are only three ephemeral monuments to the nationwide consequences of the Courtenay estate disturbances. Blue Books from 1824 to 1832 repeat, with much affecting detail, the role of Hoskins in stimulating the violence.

If we look at the vestigial reference in *Uncle Silas* to this episode in Irish history, we may feel that it is curiously exact and remote; it has about it an abstract air which is potentially hostile to fiction. At the theoretical level one might counter by arguing that allegory is concerned to relate precisely such intractable evidences of abstract consciousness, and that this kind of consciousness is typical of colonial cultures. Yet the remoteness we speak of in *Uncle Silas* is not simply formal, it is thematically central to the depiction of the Ruthyn brothers who are cut off from county politics, Church affairs, even neighbourhood activities. This is voluntary in the case of Austin, and the result of ostracism in the case of Silas – here again are those binary oppositions which so intimately connect the brothers while seeming to distinguish between them. In terms of society as depicted in the novel, we see a landowning class at once wealthy and endangered, remote from other strata of the community. There are servants of course in the Big Houses, but these are either stage-hands as far as the action is concerned or they are extensions of the conspiring, endangered aspect of the master. Tenants on the estate do ultimately play a part in the heroine's escape but their contribution is entirely mechanical and unrelated to any depiction of their lives and values. In other words, *Uncle Silas* could be interpreted as presenting an intensified version of the isolated Anglo-Irish ascendancy for whom local affairs and the religious life of the community were closed. And looking back to the origins of *Ubi lapsus?* in the murder of young Hoskins there would seem to be confirmation of this sense of a conflict of extremes, resulting in Le Fanu's novel in a depiction of one of those extremes – the ascendancy – against a darkened and empty background. To interpret this incident as a fatal conflict between castle and cabin, landlord and peasant would be to accept uncritically the blurred sociology implicit in such terms as 'ascendancy'. That Hoskins Senior was agent for an absentee landlord – William Courtenay being obliged to live abroad at the time – contributes a further element to a stereotyped response.

The facts are more various in their implications. After the Napoleonic War, agriculture was greatly depressed; provincial banking collapsed, and the economy entered a deep recession.[45] The Revd John Kiely, parish priest of Mitchelstown, County Cork, described to the Commons committee the social effects in Munster of the post-war depression:

The times were very bad for the farmers, and there was a peculiar kind of gentry, a kind of middle order between the rich gentry of the country and the peasantry; persons who were generated by the excessive rise of the agricultural produce during the war, and got the education of persons above their rank; by the fall of the times these were reduced to their original level. Without the habit of labour, they associated with the lowest description, and in order to keep themselves in the possession of their lands, and so forth, they deferred to the system [i.e. of agrarian conspiracy], and hence, I believe arose the organisation in the system itself, that could not have been devised by the lowest order of the peasantry.[46]

It is worth confirming this diagnosis by reference to an article appearing in the *Quarterly Journal of Agriculture* in which the earlier notoriety and present quiet prosperity of the Courtenay estates in Ireland are noted.

The discontents were fomented by persons of a much higher class [than the actual assailants], who, being themselves in arrear, perhaps from bad management and extravagant housekeeping, were apprehensive of being called on peremptorily to discharge them.[47]

'Captain Rock', therefore, may be characterized as a middling farmer, short of money and in danger of losing his leases, at the head of a peasant band. Questioned on the murder of young Hoskins, Matthew Barrington told the committee that 'some of the under-tenants on the Courtenay estate did encourage the lower orders' and hired an assassin to kill the agent's son.[48] These middle-men, far from being the simian figures later invented by Punch, may also be found in the novels and tales of Gerald Griffin. No feudal lord nor noble savage is at the heart of the Hoskins affair: it would be more accurately seen as an incident in the annals of an insecure middle class.

Ubi lapsus? Quid feci? The insensitive management of viscount Courtenay's estate in Limerick in the 1820s can hardly in itself explain the motto in *Uncle Silas*. The short story version of the novel, 'Passage in the Secret History of an Irish Countess' had appeared in 1838, and Courtenay had died just three years earlier. William Courtenay, the third viscount, was the only son of William Courtenay and Frances Clack, a Wallingford tavern-owner's daughter. Young Courtenay had been seduced and corrupted by William Beckford of Fonthill: later in life the third viscount was obliged to reside outside England to avoid prosecution. Despite this, in 1831 at the prompting of his third cousin (regrettably another William Courtenay), Beckford's 'Kitty' was declared to be the twenty-ninth *de jure* earl of Devon by a questionable decision of the House of Lords.[49] Thus, the exiled 'Kitty' Courtenay succeeded in reversing the loss of honour which had led his ancestors to adopt their distinctive motto. The irony of this was not lost on contemporaries: Lord Chancellor Brougham was advised that Courtenay was one 'who ought to think himself happy that his titles and estates have not been forfeited or himself paid the debt to the law like the Lord Hungerford of Heytesbury' [beheaded in 1540].[50] When a bill was found against him, he remained abroad, afraid to take his seat in Parliament, his motto raising 'a question which its owner avoids to leave to a tribunal of his country to answer'.[51]

Austin's complacent ejaculation, *Ubi lapsus? Quid feci?*, thus contributes to the structural identification of pious Austin and depraved Silas, for the motto is borrowed from one who was least fitted to bear it. 'Kitty' Courtenay, the twenty-ninth Earl of Devon, died in the Place Vendôme, Paris, in May 1835, and was succeeded by his namesake and third cousin. In the history of this remarkable family – three ancestors had been attainted by the six-teenth century – reversal's reversed at a stroke, and the thirtieth Earl proved to be a model landlord. Indeed between 1843 and 1845 he was chairman of a government commission investigating land tenure in Ireland, its evidence the most revealing indictment of landlordism in the nineteenth century. Naturally, despite the improvements at Newcastle, Sheridan Le Fanu and the Irish Metropolitan Conservative Association deplored the Devon Com-mission's findings. Like Smith O'Brien's rebellion of three years later, it could be drastically interpreted as a betrayal, a blow struck from within at the 'security of property in this kingdom' and 'the Protestant ascendancy in our happy constitution'.[52]

But how can we relate the irony of *Ubi lapsus?*, now decoded, to the opacity of 'Chateaubriand's father in the great chamber of the Chateau de Com-bourg'? If Le Fanu's allegory is to be anything more than occasional exter-nal parallels lodged in the density of inner symmetries, some dynamic organization of the allusions is required to integrate the plot and texture of the fiction as a whole. Of the plot Elizabeth Bowen has observed that it is really a fairy-tale – the Endangered Heiress, the Wicked Uncle, and so forth.[53] But if it is fairy-tale, it is fairy-tale wrought in Victorian embroid-ery, at once garish and restrained. Miss Bowen has also remarked the sex-lessness of the heroine, indeed 'no force from any one of the main characters runs into the channel of sexual feeling.'[54] This is true, provided that we allow its opposite also to be true – that the novel is deeply concerned with the force of sexual feeling, and employs much of its energies ensuring that evidence of this concern is deeply buried in its structure. For these forces are disguised or inhibited on the surface of the action: when Maud's loutish cousin Dudley makes a pass at her, his technique is a rugby-player's and not a roué's. Miss Bowen's contemporary among Anglo-Irish novelists, Francis Stuart, remarked in conversation that, if *Uncle Silas* were written now, Silas and his niece would be locked in sexual *mésalliance*, incestuous intrigue.

Certainly, on the level of sexual implication the novel produces remarkably ingenious responses in readers: the Knight of Glin has recently suggested that the story of the brothers Ruthyn is based on that of the Rochfort family in Westmeath. Robert Rochfort, Lord Bellfield, married for love as his second wife Mary, the daughter of Richard, Viscount Molesworth. They had four children, the last a boy born in 1743. Shortly after this date, his lordship was

> privately informed that she co-habited unlawfully with his younger brother. Upon which he put the question to her, and she with consummate impudence owned the fact, adding that her last child was by him, and that she had no pleasure with any man like that she had with him.[55]

Arthur Rochfort fled to England, but eventually languished in a debtors' prison until death separated him from his brother. The incestuous wife was locked up in Gaulstown, a house just six miles from her husband's seat at Belvedere. Another brother, George, lived in another neighbouring house, and when Lord Bellfield quarrelled with him, he built the largest Gothic sham ruin in Ireland – the 'Jealous Wall' – to blot out the view of the offending brother's residence.

The Knight of Glin admits that the similarity is not very great, and that Le Fanu's novel is 'roughly based' on the Rochfort saga. In seeing a resemblance, he implicitly makes certain assumptions. First, two houses in the neighbourhood of Belvedere, that which imprisons the woman and that which is the offending brother's home, are conflated in order that they resemble Bartram-Haugh, Silas's home and Maud's prison. Second, the relationship between Arthur Rochfort and his sister-in-law is comparable to that between Silas Ruthyn and his niece: both are of course forms of incest – if one admits that sexual bond which Francis Stuart prescribed and which Elizabeth Bowen denied. The violation of sexual taboo had a place in the Courtenay saga also, and even Chateaubriand contributes to the undercurrent of sexual offence in that, at the time his father perambulated in the shadows, the future author of the *Mémoires* was passionately in love with his sister. (Michel Butor traces this passion in the incestuous patterns of Chateaubriand's fiction.[56]) These offences against custom and the law may be said to have one common factor, they were *overvaluations* of blood-relationship (brother/sister) or sexual similarity (male/male).

In *Uncle Silas* nothing so explicitly sexual is admitted. Nevertheless, Silas does attempt to marry off Maud to his own son, her first cousin. While such marriages were not within the tables of forbidden affinity, they were generally disapproved of as genetically short-sighted. The motive behind Silas's scheme is as economically self-centred as it is maritally introverted – the preservation, to his own heir, of Maud's wealth. Moreover, the patterns of overvaluation of blood etc. are counterbalanced by other patterns of under-valuation. Silas's dead wife had been the daughter of a Denbigh innkeeper, and the proposed marriage between Maud and his son Dudley is frustrated by the discovery that Dudley is secretly married to Sarah Mangles of Wigan.[57] 'Kitty' Courtenay's mother had been the daughter of a Walling-ford innkeeper, while the unfortunate Lady Bellfield, on appeal to her father was ignored 'because she was only his bastard by his wife before he mar-ried her'.[58] Of course these are more offences against class and custom than against taboo or even law: yet they illustrate an urge to sexual alliance out-side certain prescribed limits, thus they undervalue these limits. Overvalua-tion in sexual introversion, undervaluation in social *mésalliance* – *Uncle Silas*'s sources reveal a complex network of sexual forces unconfessed upon the surface of the novel.

All of this is entirely in keeping with our findings in other areas. A literary allusion attaching to Austin describes Silas also. A claim of innocent bemuse-ment, an invitation of public scrutiny, is itself revealed to be an accusation. The dual level at which these allusions to Chateaubriand and Courtenay operate, parallels the nineteenth-century Anglo-Irish myth of an Augustan Golden Age. *Uncle Silas*, we should remember, grew from 'Passage in the Secret History of an Irish Countess', a story solidly lodged in the Irish eigh-teenth century. Le Fanu's method is to contribute to this myth by means of expansive evocations of neo-classical architecture which, in the latter half of the novel, is revealed to be echoing, decayed, ruinous. The contribution to myth is simultaneously a subversive critique of assumed rectitude and validity. The suggestion that the story of Knowl and Bartram-Haugh is based on the Rochfort family houses is substantiated further if one notes the ex-emplary extinction of their honours and titles with the Act of Union. Lord Bellfield having been created Earl of Belvedere died in 1774 and was suc-ceeded by his son George. The second Earl was said in 1775 to have been 'left very embarrass'd in his Circumstances, & from his Distress must con-sequently be dependent on the Crown, likely to quarrel with his Brother Robert, a respectable amiable man'.[59] Here we have two elements familiar from *Uncle Silas* – security and property is succeeded by dependence and discord, and (for the second time in two generations) brother quarrels with brother. The second Earl died in 1814 and, by the terms of the Act of Union, all his titles became extinct.[60] The history of the earldom of Belvedere is exemplary in that it is explicitly terminated by the last decision of the Anglo-Irish Protestant parliament: more specifically, it is characterized by the over-valuation of blood in incestuous adultery, and by the undervaluation of blood in the repeated conflict of brothers.

Le Fanu's fiction shows the present as a repetition or indeed a higher confirmation of the past: the past, by producing the degenerate and self-extinguishing present, is condemned as the fount of corruption. In terms of character and action, suicide is the dominant pattern – self-regarding and violent, character destroys itself. Ostensibly, the fault (*lapsus*) lies in a noble propensity to mate with innkeepers' daughters, and this should be read not so much as an echo of eighteenth-century habits but as a nineteenth-century sensitivity among the Anglo-Irish ascendancy on the topic of disagreeable exogamy. Behind this lies a largely unacknowledged code of inbreeding, intensified in the various forms of sexual introversion discernible in the material we have considered. It is the function of Le Fanu's remarkable use of allegory that the decoration of French literary reference and secreted evidences of Irish local and family history may be integrated to the over-all contours of the novel. There is much in *Uncle Silas* to distress the fastidious reader, yet the novel preserves a negative totality in its reflection of social reality. The absence of any middling order of characters, the apparent monopoly of master and servant, is not only a reflection of the false sociology which went into the making of 'ascendancy', it is also a critique in lurid terms of that opting for ideology over an imaginative rationality.

CHARLES LEVER: FROM *HARRY LORREQUER* (1839) TO *LUTTRELL OF ARRAN* (1865)

> I stood in Luttrell's Glen. Ash saplings tossed
> And Zephyr sullenly came, churning the dust.
> A path let in, out of the clash of the light,
> Ferns shivering towards a stream. Broken, as slight
> As flesh, weak with leaves,
> Stone arches bedded in the slope; disused
> Forges withered, half in sight,
> Their cold lids clumsily slammed; moss on smashed eaves.
> (Thomas Kinsella)[61]

Le Fanu's trilogy of the 1860s is the most concentrated Victorian examination of the eighteen century, the Irish eighteenth century as distinct from the Augustan compromise of Pope, Fielding, and Johnson. Yet the morbid psychology of his fiction has – until recently – attracted less attention than the comic extravagances of his friend, Charles Lever. Yeats acknowledged that Lever had 'historical significance' because he so vividly 'expressed a social phase' of 'frieze-coated humanists, dare-devils upon horseback'.[62] The extent to which the eighteenth century has been interpreted by readers of fiction all but exclusively in terms of Jonah Barrington's *Recollections* and Buck Whaley's *Memoirs* would serve as a reliable measure of our need for a genuine literary history and *Kulturgeschichte*. Le Fanu's sensationalist plots and Lever's picaresque comedies are merely the twin strategies of evasion and confession which characterize the Victorian attitude to the Irish past. This is not to say that Lever's comedy constitutes evasion and Le Fanu's sensation enacts confession: each novelist combines in different proportions both attitudes. If Le Fanu has been hitherto neglected because his dominant tone has been interpreted as pathological, Lever may have been the victim of a grosser misinterpretation in being presented as a thoughtless jester. It is true that recent commentators have pointed to a deepening of Lever's involvement with his material in the later novels: what requires emphasis is that both the picaro-heroics of *Harry Lorrequer* (1839) and the sombre depiction of society in Lord Kilgobbin (1872) proceed from Lever's response to altering conventional views of the eighteenth century.[63]

The plot of his early novels revolves round the adventures of a young soldier whose relationship to the society he encounters is both privileged and ignorant. Any possibility of a more intense involvement in social reality, of the kind posited for Colambre in *The Absentee*, is turned aside by excursions to the Peninsular War, to Brussels or the German spas. Half a dozen of Lever's novels of the 1830s and 1840s fit this description, with only the minimum adjustments required to differentiate one novel from another. The base of these novels is Victorian picaresque – an apparently shapeless quest by the hero through unfamiliar and yet entertaining landscapes and through incidents which never threaten real violence or any real offence to moral decorum. Irish readers, influenced by Daniel Corkery, have taken umbrage at the English hero whose ignorance of Irish ways they deem to be a mark of patronizing *ascendancy* attitudes in the author. This is mistaken, for the comic irony of Lever's early novels is that the hero is officially travelling *at home* within the United Kingdom and his bewilderment is an index of the Union's failure. Moreover, the Victorian picaresque hero's ultimate destiny – success in the world apart – is honourable marriage, and Lever's choice of brides for his heroes has a symptomatic interest. In *Harry Lorrequer* (1839), the young English officer ends up married to Lady Jane Callonby just as her father is appointed Viceroy of Ireland. *Jack Hinton* (1843), Lever's third novel, follows the formula closely though it has the added attraction of including Mrs Paul Rooney, the author's version of Maria Edgeworth's Mrs Anastasia Rafferty – indeed one illuminating way to read Lever's picaresque is to interpret it as *The Absentee* drained of social function as to plot, with military pranks provided as a substitute. Jack Hinton, however, finally marries Louisa Bellew whose name encapsulates more than a hint of Catholic nobility.[64]

By the time we reach *Luttrell of Arran* (1865) this pattern has for us a further dimension to its meaning. For Lever's early fiction offers a clear-cut demonstration of the difference – crucial to the practice of literary history – between past significance and present meaning. To say that the comic irony of *Harry Lorrequer* or *Jack Hinton* lies in its *exposé* of the Union is to emphasize the present meaning of the novel read within our latter-day literary history; to speak of the conclusive marriages is to emphasize the significance of the fiction in its day as part of the ideological reinforcement of Union. But, as we have seen already in the case of Lever, these functions of the work – significance and meaning – necessarily interact through the contradictions inherent in each. In the case of both Le Fanu and Lever these contradictions are manifested in formal terms. *Harry Lorrequer* was intended by its author as a series of monthly sketches, but the pressures of serialization in the conservative *Dublin University Magazine* combining with the renewed vitality of the novel-form in the London markets drew the material into the shape of moralized picaresque. In both Le Fanu's and Lever's novels, there is a generic pressure within the fiction towards an acknowledgement of a shorter, interpolated fiction, a tale within a tale. And here again, *Harry Lorrequer* provides a typical example.

In the thirty-ninth chapter the irrepressible O'Leary tells the story of 'the Knight of Kerry and Billy M'Cabe'. A synopsis can be reconstructed from O'Leary's words:

Well, it seems that one day the Knight of Kerry was walking along the Strand in London, killing an hour's time till the House was done prayers . . . his eye was caught by an enormous picture displayed upon the wall of a house, representing a human figure covered with long dark hair, with huge nails upon his hands, and a most dreadful expression of face . . . he heard a man . . . call out 'Walk in, ladies and gentlemen. The most wonderful curiosity ever exhibited – only one shilling – the vild man from Chippoowango, in Africay – eats raw wittles without being cooked, and many other pleasing performances.' The knight paid his money, and was admitted . . . to his very great horror, he beheld . . . a man nearly naked, covered with long, shaggy hair, that grew even over his nose and cheekbones. He sprang about, sometimes on his feet, sometimes all fours, but always uttering the most fearful yells, and glaring upon the crowd in a manner that was really dangerous. The knight did not feel exactly happy . . . and began to wish himself back in the House, even upon a Committee of Privileges, when suddenly the savage gave a more frantic scream than before, and seized upon a morsel of raw beef which a keeper extended to him upon a long fork like a tandem whip . . . Just at this instant some sounds struck upon his ear that surprised him not a little . . . conceive, if you can, his amazement to find that, amid his most fearful cries and wild yells, the savage was talking Irish . . . There he was, jumping four feet high in the air, eating his raw meat, pulling out his hair by handfuls; and amid all this, cursing the whole company to his heart's content, in as good Irish as ever was heard in Tralee. . . . At length something he heard left no further doubt upon his mind, and turning to the savage, he addressed him in Irish, at the same time fixing a look of most scrutinizing import upon him.

'Who are you, you scoundrel?' said the knight.

'Bill M'Cabe, your honour.'

'And what do you mean by playing off these tricks here, instead of earning your bread like an honest man?'

'Whisht,' said Billy, 'and keep the secret. I'm earning the rent for your honour. One must do many a queer thing that pays two pound ten an acre for bad land.'

This was enough: the knight wished Billy every success, and left him . . . This adventure, it seems, had made the worthy knight a great friend to the introduction of poor-laws; for, he remarks very truly, 'more of Billy's countrymen might take a fancy to the savage life, if the secret was found out.'[65]

No doubt there are echoes of Don Quixote in this tale of 'the worthy knight' of Kerry; but Billy M'Cabe's pretence, the fiction of an African within the fiction O'Leary relates to Lorrequer in Lever's novel links literary convention to economic *exposé*. Most of the elements are immediately evident – the rent, the malingering knight ticking off his hard-working tenant, the Irish speaker as savage on the Strand. The interpolated tale whimsically displays an image of social relations which the enfolding tale generically rejects. And yet, if O'Leary's story reveals an aspect of truth, the invitation is there for the reader to see some further measure of truth in Lorrequer's conquest of the future Viceroy's daughter. To read *Harry Lorrequer* requires decisions by the reader as to proportions of revelation and concealment enacted in the fictions of the novel.[66]

But every novel is composed from the language which remains outside that novel, and the tale-within-the-tale is often structurally a return to that larger social dimension by means of an appearance of microcosm. Certainly in 1839 there was a Knight of Kerry alive and well; what is more, he had been a Member of Parliament for over thirty years, though he was finally unseated in the aftermath of the 1832 Reform Act. Maurice Fitzgerald (1774–1849, eighteenth Knight of Kerry) had represented Kerry in the Irish and later the Westminster parliament, and had held various offices in Tory governments. Though he had ceased to be an MP by 1838, the Knight of Kerry was a vigorous opponent of the government's attempt to extend the Poor Law system to Ireland, holding (as an Irish landlord) that the estates could not afford the charge on the rates. Thus, when Lever was writing his chapter in August 1839, his comments on the salutary effect of the Billy M'Cabe encounter upon the Knight's friendship towards the introduction of the Poor Laws are ironical. Moreover, Lever's official setting of the novel in the second decade of the century is simultaneously undermined, and the contemporary function of historical fiction laid bare.[67]

The example of the Knight of Kerry's indirect appearance in *Harry Lorrequer* encourages a similar approach to *Luttrell of Arran*, where historical allusion is even more devious. Before passing to the later novel, one further aspect of the thirty-ninth chapter is unavoidable. The Knight and his tenant are able to converse confidentially, as it were, in the middle of London by virtue of their sharing the Irish language. Triumphantly, the wretched M'Cabe can silence his landlord while simultaneously cursing the ignorant audience whom he entertains. Yet the Irish language cannot be admitted into the discourse of Lever's fiction; it stands beyond the bar of tolerance for such a novel, just as if it were a wild man from Chippoowango. The exchange – here, not an entirely Yeatsian one – between beggar and nobleman successfully leaps over any intervening social element by a combination of shared intimacy (language) and shared displacement (the Strand). When we return to the larger fiction of Harry and Lady Jane etc., the action moves through France, Canada, Strasburg, and eventually Munich where Lorrequer is married to the new viceroy's daughter. The unreality of such a consummate Union is not mute. Whether through residual Irish, or the exotica of a German *mis en scène*, such intimacies of beggar and nobleman, picaro and viceroy, require specific ideological mediations. By the end of the 1840s, Lever's fiction had grown more sombre in tone, partly as a result of criticism directed at the capers of Harry and Jack, and partly as a consequence of the demographic/political disaster of the Famine. The contrast therefore between *Harry Lorrequer* and so late a novel as *Luttrell of Arran* is only startling if one passes over the intervening development. Nevertheless, the novel of 1865 does possess characteristics which demand our attention by way of a comparison with *Lorrequer*. Lever's dedication-page in *Luttrell of Arran* provides a neat initial point of reference through which we can begin a broader analysis.

The novel is dedicated 'To Joseph Sheridan Le Fanu Esq., – He who can write such stories as "Wylder's Hand" or "Uncle Silas" . . .' It is true that the two men had been friendly in the 1840s, and that in 1863 Le Fanu had resumed novel-writing after a sixteen-year interval – here are grounds for a dedication, surely. Yet in 1865 the two had drifted apart, the one to Italy, the other to a reclusive life in Dublin. What prompts the examination of this gesture towards Le Fanu is Lever's choice of name for one group of characters in his novel – the Courtenay sisters, Laura and Georgina. To find, in a novel dedicated explicitly to the author of *Uncle Silas* – which had appeared the year before – characters called Courtenay goes some way towards confirming the analysis of 'Ubi lapsus? Quid Feci?' which assimilated it to Le Fanu's complex allusive system. Yet the Courtenays play a relatively minor part in *Luttrell of Arran*, and that unconnected with the aspects of Courtenay family history drawn upon by Le Fanu. Though very specific details of the novel detonate its meaning, a summary by synopsis and quotation is unavoidable. John Hamilton Luttrell was engaged to marry Georgina Courtenay, having initially fallen for her sister Laura. Prompted to inquire about his rapid exit from 'the Irish university' Georgina discovered that he has been a United Irishman. Pressing him for details to reassure her family she learned from him that many eminent men in public life had been Luttrell's fellow revolutionaries. Mr Courtenay, a friend of Castlereagh in his time, went to the Government: there were investigations, resignations and, in Ireland, demands for the traitor's name:

> 'Why not Luttrell?' said one writer in a famous print. 'His father betrayed us before.' This was an allusion to his having voted for the Union. 'Why not Luttrell?' They entered thereupon into some curious family details, to show how these Luttrells had never been 'true blue' to any cause.[68]

The wedding was cancelled, Luttrell wounded in a duel:

> He would seem to have mixed himself up with the lowest political party in Ireland – men who represent, in a certain shape, the revolutionary section in France – and though the very haughtiest aristocrat I think I ever knew, and at one time the most fastidious 'fine gentleman', there were stories of his having uttered the most violent denunciations of rank, and inveighed in all the set terms of the old French Convention against the distinctions of class. Last of all, I heard that he had married a peasant girl, the daughter of one of his cottier tenants . . .[69]

Mrs Luttrell was never publicly acknowledged as his wife by Luttrell; her family had its own long record of subversion, albeit of a more agrarian than aristocratic kind. Her sister's daughter, Kate, is taken up by Laura

Courtenay's husband who educates her alongside his own daughter, Ada. The 'romantic' element in the novel concerns Kate's social advancement, her seduction by Adolphus Ladarelle, and her ultimate marriage to Harry Luttrell, her aunt's son, by now an honest sailor. Kate has been adopted by old John Luttrell as his daughter and his heir, in the belief that his son is dead, and Ladarelle's object in the fraudulent marriage is her inherited estate. The final marriage, however, brings together the son and the adopted daughter of the ostracized aristocrat-rebel.

Summarized thus, the novel does not amount to much. Yet there are intriguing patterns even in the summary. The husband of the woman Luttrell originally loved 'adopts' Kate, who is subsequently adopted by Luttrell himself – she has thus been the surrogate child of the original couple. Kate is falsely married to Ladarelle – an inadequate bonding – and will be truly married to her cousin/'brother' – a double bonding. Ladarelle has virtually appeared from nowhere, conveniently during Harry's absence (presumed death) at sea. As the similarity of the names suggests 'Ladarelle' is a false Luttrell, attracting into his function that hereditary falseness to all causes which the name symbolized to John Luttrell's comrades. From the drastic social *mésalliance* of the fine gentleman John Hamilton Luttrell and Sally O'Hara of Arran, the novel moves to the introverted marriage of Kate Luttrell and Harry Luttrell: ' "The Luttrell spirit is low enough, I take it, now," said she, blushing. "If their pride can survive this, no peasant blood can be their remedy." '[70] In contrast to the central hero's marriage to Lady Jane or Lady Louisa, his marriage into Viceregal or quasi-recusant circles, the absent hero of *Luttrell of Arran* marries into the peasantry, albeit a peasantry represented by a society-trained heroine. And whereas the picaresque novels had flitted through Paris in 1814 and Bavaria in no time at all, *Luttrell of Arran* finally focuses on an *ur*-Gaelic Ireland, a western isle located rather uncertainly somewhere near the coasts of Galway, Mayo, and/or Donegal. We thus have several kinds of inward motion in a plot which decisively commences with the eclipse of the hero in suddenly exposed (and yet hereditary) guilt. As in *Uncle Silas* this guilt is associated with exclusion from politics; and whereas Le Fanu presents the marriage of first cousins as one threat which hangs over his heroine, Lever employs an intensified form of this inward movement within a family as the climax to his plot. Luttrell, like Silas Ruthyn, has married 'beneath' him; whereas this disgraced Le Fanu's hero/villain, Luttrell's marriage into the O'Hara family is doubly the means of grace – at least as far as the narrative endorses the conclusive marriage of Kate and Harry. Narrative form, or forms, constitutes an important aspect of these mid-century novels. Le Fanu's sustained use of a female narrator

in *Uncle Silas* in part reflects the eclipse of traditionally male heroics in its
Anglo-Irish provenance, and in part also contributes actively to that eclipse.
In Lever's novel of the following year, the anecdotal method of *Harry
Lorrequer* is replaced by a more comprehensive multi-vocal narrative. Lever
liked writing dialogue, and though *Luttrell* is officially an impersonal narrative a great deal of it indeed reaches the reader through the words of specific
characters. The retrospective account of Luttrell's exposure of his political
activities and the results of that exposure appears at times to have the tone
of impersonal narrative, but the first-person pronoun strategically bursts
this appearance towards the end – 'the very haughtiest aristocrat I think
I ever knew . . .'. The reader commences to read aware of the particular
speaker, is then drawn towards an interpretation of what he reads as narrative rather than speech, and is again redirected towards the speaker's
perspective. The technique is far from original in Lever – consider the
drastic application of such a working on and against the reader in *Wuther-
ing Heights* – but it derives its significance by its bearing upon the altering
views of history advanced in the altering narrative.

Arran is not precisely located for the reader where a map-reader would
expect it. It is unlikely that many readers will have paused to worry over
such imprecision, finding the reflection of ecclesiastical ruins, the Irish
language, and occasional references to County Galway an adequate guarantee
that they do not err drastically if they call Inis Mór to mind. Yet such excursions to the topographical world vitiate the strategies of fiction and its reading.
Less easily accommodated to this kind of reading are references to the site
of Luttrell's alleged treason as 'the Irish university'. True, such locutions
may represent a speaker's unfamiliarity with Ireland and its institutions –
thus he avoids the idiomatic 'Trinity College' or 'Dublin University' because
he is unaware that there is only one university in Ireland at the time of the
alleged events. Yet this explanation only shifts the significance of the phrase
from the author to the character or narrator. Furthermore, there was a
notorious inquiry into subversion in Trinity College, conducted by John Fitzgibbon and Patrick Duigenan on the eve of the United Irishmen's
rebellion.[71] Among those examined by the inquisitors were Thomas Moore,
the future melodist, and an obscure friend called Dacre Hamilton.[72] No
Luttrell can be found implicated in these proceedings, while in the novel
the imposition of an oath on the young John Luttrell evidently was attempted after the rebellion. The fictional hero is subsequently denounced as an
informer on his former comrades, and there had indeed been many informers
placed in the ranks of the United Irishmen – the most famous being Francis
Higgins ('the Sham Squire') and Leonard MacNally. As for the associations

of the name Luttrell in 1798, one figure of note bearing that name was Lord Carhampton (Henry Lawes Luttrell, 1743 – 1821), Commander-in-Chief of the forces in Ireland from 1796. (His illegitimate son sat in the Irish parliament from 1798 to 1800, and subsequently became a wit and man of fashion in London.)

Neither of these Luttrells of the period invoked at the opening of Lever's novel seems a likely candidate for the reclusive, embittered aristocrat-rebel. Cautiously, one might notice that there is a blurred resemblance in the circumstances of the novel to some discrete aspects of the Rebellion – the presence of informers, the presence of Luttrells, the inquisition at Trinity – but circumstances and aspects fail to line up in any neat pattern. Pressing such searches for pattern, one might desperately seize on Lord Carhampton's seduction of a gardener's daughter near Woodstock, Oxfordshire, as an original to the *mésalliance* (in Society's terms) with a Catholic peasant girl from Arran. It is true that Carhampton at first vehemently opposed Union, and then supported it, but such a change of heart is not unique or even remarkable in one of his military background.[73]

Two developments are in progress in this 'blurring'. The first is simply a new adjustment between folklore and history, the second a rewriting of the United Irishmen's rebellion in the decade of Fenian rebellion. For the Luttrell family had a larger and more defined place in the folklore of the eighteenth century than in the history of 1798. Two brothers Luttrell were prominent in the ranks of King James's forces prior to the Battle of Aughrim. Simon Luttrell (d. 1698) sat in the Jacobite parliament of 1689 representing the county of Dublin together with Patrick Sarsfield, James's premier Irish general. After the Jacobite defeat, he was attainted for treason and died in exile – his treason was therefore the result of a change of regime and not a change of loyalty. His brother, Henry (1655? – 1717), however, defected to the Williamites immediately prior to the Battle of Aughrim, and took advantage of the terms of the Treaty to secure his position with the new regime. He was shot dead in his sedan-chair on 3 November 1717 in Stafford Street, Dublin; and his grave was violated some eighty years later during the period of the United Irishmen rebellion when his grandson's high-handed methods in putting down discontent had excited popular feeling. According to Macaulay (no friend of Jacobitism), the perpetrators were 'descendents of those whom he had betrayed'.[74] Of the grandson, Lord-Lieutenant Camden wrote that he 'did not confine himself to the strict rules of law'. From a position of unimpeachable, twentieth-century impartiality, *The Complete Peerage* comments of the Luttrells 'they seem to have been an unlovely race.'[75]

Popular opinion of the eighteenth century, therefore, is radically modified
and yet exploited in the pre-history of *Luttrell of Arran*, Luttrell treachery
as Jacobites or to Jacobitism being subliminally drawn upon to justify the
third-hand observation that the family had never been true blue to any cause,
the cause on this occasion being *Jacobin* rather than Jacobite in its leanings.
The third Earl of Carhampton (John Luttrell-Olmius, died 1829, aged about
84) was the last of his line, with whom all his titles became extinct. Like
the shadow of the Rochfort family which may shine behind the dark patterns of *Uncle Silas*, we encounter here a noble ancestry now extinct. Like
the fictional Ruthyns and the historical Rochforts, Luttrell notoriety involves
sibling conflict, the self-division of a family to whom pride and depravity
jointly adhere. It may seem that Lever's novel misses this sibling rivalry,
for we hear nothing of disputatious brothers as such; instead, however, there
is the otherwise inexplicable villain Ladarelle who substitutes for honest
Harry during the latter's presumed death. The *Doppelganger* of Ladarelle/
Luttrell resembles the Ruthyn brothers' relationship in that villainy and virtue are never presented at once, though their presence (separately) in the
novel requires a patterned symmetry to be at all explicable. But the significance of Lever's treatment of Luttrell notoriety is its contribution to the notion of identity consolidated in hereditary guilt. Whereas the discrete material
lying behind Le Fanu's allegory points to guilt in the binary offence of over-
valuation and undervaluation of sexual and blood bonds, Lever's historical
traces serve to point to the coexistence of antagonist political loyalties –
Jacobite and Williamite, originally.

   That synthesis had been anticipated in Irish historical fiction through the
influence of Walter Scott upon – amongst others – John Banim and
Sheridan Le Fanu. The ventriloquism of Le Fanu's *Cock and Anchor* (1845)
had presented the anxieties of the author's caste through the humiliation
and suffering of Jacobite heroes of a bygone age. Lever's implied synthesis
of the Jacobite and Williamite past is merely a further stage upon the same
progression. That progression is, of course, the alignment of history in
resistance to the threats of a reformist government in Britain (for Le Fanu
in the 1830s and 1840s) or to the threat of Fenian and Mazzinian outrage
in the 1860s. The renowned shift in Lever's sympathies (from a mockery
of the native Irish in early novels to a near-nationalist position in *Lord
Kilgobbin* etc.) is simply another statement of that rewriting of history;
rebellions of the past may be rehabilitated, indeed 'romanticized', so as to
be a bulwark against contemporary unrest; the phenomenon is familiar even
today in circles to whom the Provisional IRA are an embarrassment. The
United Irishmen are presented at the opening of *Luttrell of Arran* as an

honourable conspiracy, or at least one which it would be dishonourable for a gentleman to betray. The novel's narrative holds at a distance the confirmation of Luttrell's membership, and also fails quite to confirm that he betrayed anyone. Lever was living in Florence at the time of writing, and he conceded a curious unease about the novel:

> I do not believe 'Luttrell' will do, and my conviction is that the despair that attaches to Ireland, from Parliament down to 'Punch', acts injuriously on all who would try to invest her scenes with interest or endow her people with other qualities than are mentioned in police courts.[76]

The police court exactly identifies the change between the context of pre- and post-Famine. The administration of order had by the 1860s reached a point of public organization in which the pervasive informer system of the 1790s was less effective. In *Luttrell of Arran* the change is acknowledged in the contrasting styles of subversion associated with John Luttrell and his adopted daughter's grandfather, Peter Malone. Luttrell is to be seen, it is hoped, as an aristocratic United Irishman, a testy Philippe Egalité: Malone and his associates are presented as vindictive or misled malefactors, in a mode ostensibly of the eighteenth-century Whiteboys but more recognizably a product of contemporary fears of Fenian secrecy. The police court is the administrative counter to a political conspiracy which cannot be penetrated by noble democrats or sensitively ambiguous informers. In the face of a new republican conspiracy, now *petit bourgeois* and predominantly Catholic in composition, *Luttrell of Arran* offers an image of the United Irishman in aristocratic embrace of a refined peasantry. The Celtic Revival will press home this holy alliance of guilt-ridden ascendancy and marginalized Gaelic peasantry as a bulwark against the politics of class and the sociology of an industrialized metropolitan colony. Its subscribers shall include some unlikely partners.

W. E. GLADSTONE

> How little reaped where they had sown —
> The generous Ascendancy.
>
> (Leslie Daiken)[77]

The significant element, culturally speaking, in the fiction of Sheridan Le Fanu and Charles Lever which we have examined is the technique of subterfuge. Feelings of personal guilt or compromise do not satisfactorily account for the means by which allegories of culpability are unveiled and veiled again. If guilt is repeatedly a hallmark of this soon-to-be-venerable ascendancy there is nevertheless some uncertainty as to the precise location of any identifying guarantee. A guilty past satisfies on two levels – it establishes the reality of one's identity and at the same time sanctions a latter-day dereliction. To the old-style nationalist, convinced of the moral depravity of 'the Anglo-Irish Protestant Ascendancy', we must break the unwelcome news that the ascendancy to a large degree invented its depravity as a small price to be paid for its continued viability as a social entity.

The abashed nationalist has powerful allies, however, and they emerge precisely in the wake of that fiction we have been examining. The 1860s were years of Fenian anxiety, and traditionally the conversion of William Ewart Gladstone to the reformist solution of the Irish question is attributed (grudgingly) to the impact of Fenianism and attendant discontents. The long-awaited extinction of Palmerstonian Whiggery finally came in the election of 1868, and within a few years the Irish established church and the Irish landlord system were in the crucible, and Home Rule poised on the rim. The October 1868 election campaign saw Gladstone touring in Lancashire, delivering a series of immensely long speeches on the priorities of new-style liberalism. The resulting collection of election addresses is impressive not so much for its material – which is naturally somewhat repetitive – as for the ultimate identification of a symbolic focus for a new Irish policy. On 23 October, Gladstone spoke at Hengler's Circus, Wigan; his main themes were already familiar but the climactic paragraph of this final Lancashire rally broke new ground:

> It is clear the Church of Ireland offers to us indeed a great question, but even that question is but one of a group of questions. There is the Church of Ireland, there is the land of Ireland, there is the education of Ireland: there are many subjects, all of which depend upon one greater than them all; they are all so many branches from one trunk, and that trunk is the tree of what is called Protestant ascendency. Gentlemen, I look, for one, to this Protestant people to put down Protestant ascendency which pretends to seek its objects by doing homage to religious truth, and instead of consecrating politics desecrates religion . . . We therefore aim at the destruction of that system of ascendency which, though it has been crippled and curtailed by former measures, yet still must be allowed by all to exist. It is still there, like a tall tree of noxious growth, lifting its head to heaven and darkening and poisoning the land as far as its shadow can extend; it is still there, gentlemen, and now at length the day has come when, as we hope, the axe has been laid to the root of that tree, and it nods and quivers from its top to its base. It wants, gentlemen, one stroke more – the stroke of these elections.[78]

This is Gladstone's most trenchant attack upon the causes, as he sees them, of the Irish Question. In earlier speeches of the campaign he has condemned the trailing of political insignia in Protestant churches and ceremonies, but at Wigan, Orange practices are virtually conflated with the dignities of Protestant Ascendancy. Though the future prime minister is unlikely to have had the Revd T. D. Gregg in mind as he spoke, he too assumes ascendancy to have an ancient pedigree, an outmoded history. Gladstone's central image of course is the tall tree of noxious growth which, though he does not specify it, is the Javanese upas. Ironically, it would appear that the tree attracted more attention than the ascendancy, in the wake of Gladstone's onslaught.

Certainly a number of pamphlets can be cited in support of this contention. In the advertisement pages of *The Fruit of 'The Upas Tree'* (1870) the London-based National Protestant Union mentioned another of its publications, *The Progress of the Church of Rome towards Ascendancy in England*, written by a veteran of earlier sectarian conflicts, J. C. Colquhoun. Thus two years after Gladstone had seemingly conceded the unique (and culpable) association of ascendancy with Irish Protestantism, anti-Catholic evangelicals were persisting in denunciations of a threatened Roman ascendancy. We may feel these fears to have been fabulously unfounded, yet the fabulous element is perhaps in need of attention as such. Three years later still, Gerald Fitzgibbon condemned 'the dissenters of England, who are now leagued with the Irish priests and English republicans, and have formed the Ministry whose boast it has been, that they were "banded together" for the extirpation of the upas tree. . . .' Here too, we may demur at the suggestion that English republicans were included in Gladstone's cabinet, and fail to examine the manner in which the Church of Ireland could derive comfort (or the strength of compensation) from this sinister image of its foes. Speaking on an Irish education bill in the same year, Lord Edmond Fitzmaurice declared that

> It was perfectly certain that a man who possessed a great deal of imagination might, if he stayed out sufficiently long at night, staring at a small star, persuade himself next morning that he had seen a great comet; and it was equally certain that such a man, if he stared long enough at a bush, might persuade himself that he had seen a branch of the upas tree.[79]

There is great aptness in Gladstone's image, for the upas is both a tree which exudes a poisonous juice (*Antiaris toxicaria*) and a legendary or fabulous tree which is so poisonous as to destroy all life around it for many miles. Like the vampire (bat), it connotes a real and specific thing, and a fantasy of the human mind woven from that thing. There is no doubt that upas trees were saved from the axeman on the strength of their legendary powers, and the Protestant Ascendancy is likewise girded round with magical protection. And yet the tree-image has other kinds of ambiguity attaching to it also; just as Burke's notion of the State as an organism indivisible as a tree coexists with the fashion of planting liberty trees symbolic of man's freedom to initiate as well as to perpetuate, so Gladstone's upas comes to mimic Burke's great-rooted blossomer. The assault upon Protestant Ascendancy at Wigan in 1868 absolved Lever from the need subliminally to insinuate a guilty past into his fiction – Lever's late novels are far more explicit in their condemnation of the past than *Luttrell of Arran* – and it lent the dignity of a prime minister's outrage to what had been previously nervous and ill-defined. It is fair to say that, without the consensus encapsulated in Gladstone's denunciation – or without some comparable traumatic specification – the process by which Yeats takes Protestant Ascendancy and renders it as cultural tradition would not have been possible. Gladstonian reform of the Irish Church and the system of land tenure provided the evidence of political renunciation and denial by the Protestant Ascendancy, upon which cultural compensation by way of tradition would eventually build.

The image of Protestant Ascendancy reflected in the Wigan speech had reached the status of public opinion, with all the elusive ramifications this involved. Gladstone's ability to enunciate a statement of Protestant Ascendancy lay largely in his unfamiliarity with the society in which this transformed ideology operated. In Ireland, testimony of a similar scale and intensity is less available. To the Protestant Ascendancy, Protestant Ascendancy required no elaboration or definition; while to the Catholic population – whom Burke had warned so many years earlier – the currency of the *acceptance* of this distinctive sociology was its own validity. Nevertheless, there were of course denunciations of the monopoly Protestants enjoyed in public offices and the professions, and complaints as to the limited extent of Catholic emancipation in a society where an élite regulated the distribution of reward within its own ranks. By 1868, such complaints, allied to a recognition of the Church Establishment and (more remotely) land tenure as political issues embittering the Union, were common enough. What makes *Protestant Ascendency in Ireland: Its Cause and Cure* worthy of attention is the manner in which ascendancy is related to the development of a sectarian sociology.

Its author, Mulhallen Marum, was a Queen's County justice of the peace, a barrister by profession. His recurring concern in the pamphlet was to recommend the concept of *copyhold* as a reform of Irish land tenure, and the commentary on Protestant Ascendancy is partly incidental to that concern. The history of Ireland's woes is extended back to the Reformation and before, with Protestant Ascendancy granted at least a Cromwellian provenance.[80] The resolutions of the Corporation of Dublin in 1792 are quoted *in extenso*, but they are accepted simply as a confirmation of an acknowledged and venerable concept. Marum's notion of Protestant Ascendancy in 1868, then, was simply the dominance of wealth, office, and dignities by Protestants, a state of affairs requiring no differentiation by historical period as to degree, intensity or any other factor. While his title speaks of causes, these are so remote in history as to be virtually a *primum mobile*; as for cures these degenerate into atomized proposals, the product of a campaigner's enthusiasm, mere schemes. Thus, Protestant Ascendancy came to symbolize not simply the permanence of a state of affairs (say, like the monarchy), but its apparent *necessity* whether enjoyed or resented. Burke's metaphor had been 'abracadabra', and indeed the mid-nineteenth-century invocations of Protestant Ascendancy had the tone of magical spells. The crucial stage leading to this experience of Protestant Ascendancy as some inevitable dimension of existence in Ireland was the loss of its history, the process of back-dating the phrase to encompass first of all the eighteenth century generally, then the Williamite wars and the Settlement, and ultimately Cromwell and post-Reformation society *in toto*. That latter position may never have been held or expressed by serious historians – history can be falsified but it cannot actually be annulled – but the tactics were sufficiently widespread to produce what amounted to an eternal image, an iconic representation of history.

Marum's pamphlet links this significantly with the antagonism not only of creeds but of races also. Like the *Dublin University Magazine* of 1837, he compared the interaction of peoples and cultures in England and Ireland, but came to different conclusions. Catholicism, he insisted, was the element in pre-Reformation England which facilitated the amalgamation of Saxon and Norman etc; Protestant Ascendancy in post-Reformation Ireland effected a racial schism: 'The fell spirit of Ascendency stalked through the land, establishing religion as the criterion of race, and smiting the Roman Catholic as of inferior caste – even as the black man on the new continent.'[81] This rather ambiguous period piece of prejudice is a timely reminder that the corollary of Protestant Ascendancy became in due course the revival of Celticism as an exclusive, identifying theory by which the repression of class enacted in Protestant Ascendancy was unwittingly complied with. Marum can refer in passing to 'the Celtic race and creed', unconcerned by the linguistic area of reference involved in 'Celtic'.[82] The sociology of Ireland was to be propagated thereafter in a binary scheme which implied both mutual exclusion among a categorized population and a de-historicized model of dominance/subservience. The ruins of Le Fanu's and Lever's fiction are not simply remnants of English romanticism preserved in a provincial

literature too undeveloped to throw off such anachronisms: they are the static
and shattered, the exclusive and radically divided image of colonial Ireland.

Facies hippocratica is no longer remote from the petrified, primordial landscape encountered in the ruined houses of Le Fanu or the shanty-abbeys
of Lever. In a culture which fossilizes history as unchanging condition,
historical allegory becomes a means of subversion by which anachronism
and dislocated identity draw attention to the reader's task of reading relations between various levels of allusion. Chateaubriand *and* Courtenay, Luttrell as United Irishman – these are not to be taken as fictional exotica
uncertainly controlled by a wayward writer. In the business of reading, within
a coherent literary history, *Uncle Silas* and *Luttrell* present a challenge not
categorically different from *Finnegans Wake* or *Ulysses* where multiple allusion and so-called 'mis-information' also proliferate. The mid-nineteenth
century is not a degeneration of romanticism so much as it is the early
manifestation of modernist anxieties. And Ireland is less a backward and
marginal culture than it is a central if repressed area of British modernism.
This requires careful and discriminating emphasis. Ireland constitutes an
area of *British* modernism by virtue of its place in the British colonial system,
of British *modernism* by virtue of its intimate place in the United Kingdom,
the flagship of high capitalism in the nineteenth century. It is significant
that no adjective derives from the compound noun, United Kingdom, the
language in this detail revealing how no part of the Kingdom could enjoy
the entirety as an attribute of its incorporation, least of all Ireland.

Yeats's view of the Irish nineteenth century was otherwise. It is well known,
and in due course will be subject to scrutiny. In declaring the century void
he demonstrates the romantic priorities of symbolic unity, of which cultural
nationalism was but one expression. No equally extensive Joycean diagnosis
is available though arguably 'The Dead' is an anatomy of Victorian Ireland
in which the (im)balance of the sects is more accurately adjudged than in
complaints such as Mulhallen Marum's. By the time Joyce wrote *Dubliners*,
of course, many of the issues raised by Marum had been resolved. Thomas
Kinsella's summary of an alternative to the Yeatsian view inevitably employs
Joyce:

> Joyce, with a greatness like Yeats's, was able to reject (that is, accept) the whole
> tradition as he found it – as it lay in stunned silence, still recovering from
> the death of its old language. Joyce's isolation is a mask. His relationship with
> the modern world is direct and intimate. He knows the filthy modern tide,
> and he immerses himself in it to do his work. His relationship with Ireland
> is also direct and intimate. In rejecting Ireland he does so on its own terms
> . . . He is the first major Irish voice to speak for Irish reality since the death
> of the Irish language . . . The filthy modern tide does not only run in Ireland,

of course, and Joyce's act of continuity is done with a difference: he simultaneously revives the Irish tradition and admits the modern world . . . So, the Irish writer, if he cares who he is and where he comes from, finds that Joyce and Yeats are the two main objects in view; and I think he finds that Joyce is the true father. I will risk putting it diagrammatically, and say that Yeats stands for the Irish tradition as broken; Joyce stands for it as continuous, or healed – or healing – from its mutilation.[83]

Even in a diagnosis which so signally declines to prescribe Yeats, the tendency to write criticism and literary history as a paraphrase of Yeatsian history is not absent.

NOTES AND REFERENCES

1 James Joyce, *Dubliners*, corrected text ed. Robert Scholes (London: Cape, 1967), p. 245.
2 R. B. Mc Dowell, *Public Opinion and Government Policy in Ireland 1801 – 1846* (London: Faber, 1952), pp. 180-1.
3 Karl Marx, 'The Eighteenth Brumaire of Louis Bonaparte', *Surveys from Exile; Political Writings*, vol. ii, ed. and introd. David Fernbach (London: Allen Lane and New Left Review, 1973), p. 146.
4 [Thomas Moore], *Memoirs of Captain Rock . . . Written by Himself* (London: Longman, 1824), 5th edn, pp. 348-9.
5 Ibid., p. 290.
6 Charlotte Elizabeth, *The Rockite: An Irish Story* (London: Nisbet, 1829), p. 254. An Englishwoman by birth, she married as her second husband Lewis H. Tonna: she lived for many years in County Kilkenny, and wrote voluminously for the evangelical movement.
7 Jacqueline Hill, 'The Protestant Response to Repeal: the Case of the Dublin Working Class', in F. S. L. Lyons and R. A. J. Hawkins, eds., *Ireland Under the Union: Varieties of Tension. Essays in Honour of T. W. Moody* (Oxford: Clarendon Press, 1980), pp. 35-68; in addition to Dr Hill's discussion of Tresham Dames Gregg's influence on the Dublin Protestant working class, an ecclesiastical and theological perspective may be obtained from Desmond Bowen's, *The Protestant Crusade in Ireland 1800 – 1870* (Dublin: Gill and Macmillan, 1978), esp. pp. 108-13.
8 W. J. Mc Cormack, *Sheridan Le Fanu and Victorian Ireland* (2nd rev. ed. Dublin: Lilliput Press, 1991), p. 87.
9 T. D. Gregg, *Protestant Ascendancy Vindicated and National Regeneration Through the Instrumentality of National Religion Urged in a Series of Letters to the Corporation of Dublin* (Dublin: Bleakley, 1840), p. 86.
10 Sheridan Le Fanu to T. P. Le Fanu, undated; quoted in Mc Cormack, *Sheridan Le Fanu and Victorian Ireland*, p. 87.
11 See Bowen, *The Protestant Crusade in Ireland 1800 – 1870*, pp. 108-9.
12 'Address of the Corporation of Dublin to Lord Henry Fitzgerald and Henry Grattan', *Calendar of Ancient Records of Dublin*, Lady Gilbert, ed. (Dublin: Dollard, 1909), vol. xiv, p. 243.

13 Gregg, *Protestant Ascendancy Vindicated*, pp. 62-3.
14 Ibid., p. 87.
15 See the *Oxford English Dictionary*, which cites as its example of the sense
    G. S. Faber on the primitive doctrine of election published in 1842, two years
    after Gregg's pamphlet. For comment on the general topic, published since
    Ascendancy and Tradition (1985), see Conor Cruise O'Brien, *God Land: Reflections
    on Religion and Nationalism* (Cambridge Mass.: Harvard University Press, 1988).
16 Gregg, *Protestant Ascendancy Vindicated*, p. 87. Original parenthesis.
17 Idem.
18 Idem.
19 The bibliography of the Irish question, or the Ulster question, is vast and still
    growing. Liam de Paor's *Divided Ulster* (Penguin Special, 1970) is perhaps the
    best introduction to a contentious subject.
20 Peter Allt and Russell K. Alspach, eds., *The Variorum Edition of the Poems of
    W. B. Yeats* (New York: Macmillan, 1977, 7th printing), p. 832.
21 Daniel Owen Madden, ed., *The Speeches of the Right Hon. Henry Grattan*
    (Dublin: Duffy, 1865), 2nd edn, p. 203.
22 Jonathan Swift, 'Short Character of His Ex___ T___ E___ of W___', *The
    Examiner and Other Pieces 1710–11* (Oxford: Blackwell, 1940), p. 179.
23 [Sheridan Le Fanu], *The Cock and Anchor* (Dublin: Curry, 1845), vol. i, p.
    20. For a discussion of this novel, and its relation to the author's politics,
    see Mc Cormack, *Sheridan Le Fanu and Victorian Ireland*, op. cit., pp. 97-
    100.
24 Details of this episode are provided in Mc Cormack, *Sheridan Le Fanu and Vic-
    torian Ireland*, op. cit., pp. 100-6.
25 'Richard Marston' is extensively analysed in W. J. Mc Cormack, 'J. Sheridan
    Le Fanu's Richard Marston (1848): the History of an Anglo-Irish Text' in *1848:
    The Sociology of Literature*, Francis Barker and Others, eds. (Colchester: Univer-
    sity of Essex, 1978), pp. 107-25; see also Mc Cormack, *Sheridan Le Fanu and
    Victorian Ireland*, pp. 106-10.
26 Elizabeth Bowen, 'The Big House', *Collected Impressions* (London: Longman,
    1950), p. 196.
27 See ch. 5 of Mc Cormack, *Sheridan Le Fanu and Victorian Ireland*.
28 See discussion in W. J. Mc Cormack, *Dissolute Characters: Irish Literary History
    through Balzac, Le Fanu, Yeats and Bowen* (Manchester: Manchester Universi-
    ty Press, 1993), pp. 45-50.
29 Walter Benjamin, *The Origins of German Tragic Drama*, trans. John Osborne
    (London: New Left Books, 1977), p. 162.
30 Ibid., p. 166.
31 Patrick Diskin, 'Yeats's "Purgatory" and Werner's "Der Vierundzwanzigste
    Februar", *Notes and Queries* (August 1979), pp. 340-2. See below, pp. 342-3.
32 Benjamin, *The Origins of German Tragic Drama*, p. 166.
33 J. S. Le Fanu, *Uncle Silas* (Oxford: World's Classics, 1981), p. 2.
34 Trans. Julia Marshall; for the original see René Chateaubriand, *Mémoires d'Outre-
    tombe* (Paris: Flammarion, 1948), vol. i, p. 110.
35 *Uncle Silas*, pp. 190, 194, 279.
36 Michel Butor, *Inventory* (London: Cape, 1970), p. 59.

37 J. S. Le Fanu, *Uncle Silas*, p. 102.
38 Ovid, *Metamorphoses*, xv. 234; see notes to the World's Classics edition for the range of allusion drawn upon by the author.
39 *Handbook of Mottoes*, C. N. Elvin, ed. (London: Heraldry Today, 1963), p. 205.
40 *Burke's Peerage* (London, 1959), 102nd edn, p. 670.
41 House of Commons, '4th Report on the State of Ireland' (1825), p. 121.
42 Ibid.
43 Ibid.
44 House of Lords, '4th Report on the State of Ireland' (1825), pp. 513 and 696. See also Appendix D in *Ascendancy and Tradition*, pp. 405-06.
45 See ch. 5 of L. M. Cullen, *An Economic History of Ireland since 1660* (London: Batsford, 1972).
46 House of Commons, '4th Report on the State of Ireland' (1825).
47 *Quarterly Journal of Agriculture* (1838), p. 394.
48 House of Commons '4th Report on the State of Ireland' (1825), p. 121.
49 See *The Complete Peerage*, George Edward Cokayne, ed.; rev. Vicary Gibbs (London: St Catherine's Press, 1916), vol. iv, p. 336.
50 Ibid.
51 Ibid.
52 See pp. 70 ff. above for the Corporation of Dublin's use of the catchphrase in 1792.
53 Elizabeth Bowen, 'Introduction' to Sheridan Le Fanu, *Uncle Silas* (London: Cresset Press, 1947), p. 7 *et passim*.
54 Ibid., p. 9.
55 Letter of Lord Egmont, 2 May 1743; quoted by the Knight of Glin in 'Foreword' to a sale catalogue published by Messrs Christie's on the occasion of the sale of Belvedere, County Westmeath on 9 July 1980 (p. 1). I am grateful to William O'Sullivan, sometime Keeper of the Manuscripts, Trinity College, Dublin, for drawing my attention to this source. In addition to the general resemblance between the houses and brothers of the Rochfort saga and those of Le Fanu's Ruthyn family in *Uncle Silas*, there is a further area in which the possibility of Le Fanu's debt to the saga is enhanced. Jonathan Swift was a frequent visitor at Gaulstown, the premier Rochfort house, and composed several poems describing the household. Le Fanu, by way of his Sheridan family connections, had inherited some of Swift's papers, wrote about Swift, and generally regarded himself as an indirect literary descendant of the Dean's. Moreover, the title of his first 1860s' novel, *The House by the Church-yard*, echoes in its title a poem by Swift 'On the Little House by the Churchyard of Castlenock' — Castleknock, being on the northern side of the Phoenix Park in Dublin, and the setting of the novel (Chapelizod) being on the south-west. For the Swift poems see *The Poetical Works* (London, 1866, in 3 vols.), vol. iii, pp. 96-8, 167-72. The Castleknock poem is discussed by John P. Harrington in 'Swift Through Le Fanu and Joyce', in *The Irish Tradition in Literature*, Daniel S. Lenoski, ed. (Winnipeg: University of Manitoba Press, 1979), pp. 49-58.
56 See Michel Butor, *Inventory, passim*.
57 Le Fanu, *Uncle Silas*, p. 328.
58 Letter of Lord Egmont, quoted by the Knight of Glin (p. 1). See note 55 above.
59 *The Irish Parliament 1775 from an Official and Contemporary Manuscript*, William

Hunt, ed. (London: Longman; Dublin: Hodges Figgis, 1907), p. 66.

60   For the text of the Act of Union see Edmund Curtis and R. B. McDowell, eds., *Irish Historical Documents 1172-1922* (London: Methuen, 1977), 2nd edn, pp. 208-13. Between 1761 and 1800 a member of the Rochfort family had represented Westmeath continuously in the Irish House of Commons; thus, the Union and the death of Lord Belvedere combined to extinguish the family's political role.

61   Thomas Kinsella, 'Lead', *Another September* (Dublin: Dolmen Press, 1962), p. 44. The poem is one of several — 'Phoenix Park', 'Nightwalker', and the several poems of *Notes from the Land of the Dead* among them — in which Kinsella utilizes the historical landscape of the area lying between the western purlieus of Dublin city and the Phoenix Park. Luttrelstown, once the seat of Colonel Simon Luttrell and acquired by his apostate brother under the penal laws, is an estate near Lucan in County Dublin. In 1983 it was, aptly the centre of controversy with regard to corruption in the planning of land for housing development.

62   W. B. Yeats, 'A Parnellite at Parnell's Funeral', printed with notes to the *Variorum Edition of the Poems*, Allt and Alspach, eds., p. 834.

63   See A. N. Jeffares, *Anglo-Irish Literature* (London: Macmillan; Dublin: Gill and Macmillan, 1982), pp. 121-5. Though it only deals with a few novels, the best recent treatment of Lever is to be found in George O'Brien's doctoral thesis, 'Life on the Land: The Interrelationship between Identity and Community in the Irish Fiction of Maria Edgeworth, William Carleton, and Charles Lever' (unpub. Ph.D. thesis, University of Warwick, 1979).

64   Several members of the Bellew family were active in movements for Catholic relief between 1790 and 1820. During the period of the novel's setting, Sir Edward Bellew represented a moderate wing of the movement: see R. B. McDowell, *Public Opinion and Government Policy in Ireland 1800 – 1846* (London: Faber, 1952), pp. 90, 95, 100, 105; also McDowell, *Ireland in the Age of Imperialism and Revolution 1760 – 1801* (Oxford: Clarendon Press, 1979), pp. 410, 412, 559.

65   [Charles Lever], *Harry Lorrequer* (Dublin, 1839), pp. 262-63.

66   In *Our Mess*, vol. i, *Jack Hinton the Guardsman* (Dublin, 1843), the 6th chapter, 'The Sham Battle' (pp. 37-47), provides another illustration of pretence within the fiction veering towards symbolic reportage.

67   For Maurice Fitzgerald see *DNB* and John S. Crone, *A Concise Dictionary of Irish Biography* (London: Longman, 1928). His attitude to the question of a poor law for Ireland is discussed in Angus Macintyre, *The Liberator: Daniel O'Connell and the Irish Party 1830 – 1847* (London: Hamish Hamilton, 1965).

68   Charles Lever, *Luttrell of Arran* (London, 1865), p. 20.

69   Ibid., p. 22.

70   Ibid., p. 503.

71   For an account of this episode see J. W. Stubbs, *The History of the University of Dublin* (Dublin, 1889), pp. 297-301.

72   See L. A. G. Strong, *The Minstrel Boy: A Portrait of Tom Moore* (London: Hodder and Stoughton, 1937), p. 52. Dacre Hamilton was among the nineteen students expelled as a consequence of the inquisition.

73   Jonathan Swift wrote to Charles Ford on 2 February 1718 – 19: 'We have found out the Fellow that killed Harry Lutterel, but cannot hang him. No doubt you know the Story, but it is very odd that he who hired the murderer should confess

in hope of the Reward . . .'. *Correspondence*, Harold Williams, ed. (Oxford: Clarendon Press, 1963), vol. ii, p. 313.

74 Thomas Babington Macaulay, *The History of England*, C. H. Firth, ed. (London: Macmillan, 1914), vol. iv, p. 2073.

75 For Camden's letter see W. E. H. Lecky, *A History of Ireland in the Eighteenth Century* (London, 1898), vol. iii, p. 419; also *The Complete Peerage*, vol. iii, p. 24.

76 Lever to Dr Burbidge, 26 December 1863, from Cara Capponi, Florence; *Charles Lever: His Life in his Letters*, Edmund Downey, ed. (Edinburgh: Blackwood, 1906), vol. i, p. 393.

77 Leslie Daiken 'Lines Written in a Country Parson's Orchard'; see Kathleen Hoagland, *1000 Years of Irish Poetry* (New York: Grosset and Dunlap, 1962), pp. 759-60.

78 'Speech Delivered in Hengler's Circus, Wigan October 23rd. 1868', *Speeches of the Right Hon. W. E. Gladstone Delivered at Warrington, Ormskirk, Liverpool, Southport, Newtown, Leigh, and Wigan in October 1868* (London, [c. 1868]), pp. 97-8.

79 See [Anon.] *The Fruit of 'The Upas Tree': the Answer to 'The Message of Peace' Exhibited in the Charge of the Judges at the Spring Assizes (Ireland) 1870; With Preface and Appendix* (London: Macintosh (for the National Protestant Union), 1870); Gerald Fitzgibbon, *A Banded Ministry and the Upas Tree* (Dublin: Hodges Figgis, 1873), pp. 25-6, see also pp. 54-5. For Fitzmaurice, see Henry Yule and A. C. Burnell (new ed. by W. Crooke), *Hobson-Jobson: A Glossary of Colloquial Anglo-Indian Words and Phrases* (London: Routledge, 1968), p. 959.

80 E. Mulhallen Marum, *Protestant Ascendency in Ireland: Its Cause and Cure, and the Right of Irish Tenants, under the British Constitution, to Fixity of Tenure, Vindicated* (Dublin, 1868), p. 12.

81 Ibid., p. 42.

82 Ibid., p. 33.

83 Thomas Kinsella, 'The Irish Writer', in *Davis, Mangan, Ferguson? Tradition and the Irish Writer. Writings by W.B. Yeats and by Thomas Kinsella* (Dublin: Dolmen Press, 1970), pp. 64-5.

6

Tribulations
of the
Intelligentsia

We are capable of self-oblivion, as well as of sacrifice.
(William Godwin)[1]

THE GRAVES OF ACADEME

The university of Dublin (Trinity College) in which Butt, Davis, Ferguson,
Le Fanu, Lever had been educated was a unique institution in the Ireland
of their day. It could boast – and occasionally did boast – of its importance as the *alma mater* of Jonathan Swift, George Berkeley, Oliver
Goldsmith, and Edmund Burke. In the first half of the nineteenth century
it was more often characterized as 'the silent sister' of the ancient foundations at Oxford and Cambridge than celebrated for its current reputation.
Three factors contributed to this slighting of Trinity. First, the fashion grew
of the gentry and aristocracy sending their heirs to English public schools,
with a consequent tendency of young men to stay in England for their further education. Second, from 1849 onwards there existed a second university system in Ireland, with colleges in Belfast, Cork, and Galway. These
were established to cater for the higher educational needs of Catholics, and
were piously referred to as 'godless colleges'. Five years later, the Catholic
University of Ireland was founded in Dublin, with John Henry Newman
as rector appointed to remedy that deficiency. Though the last-named institution underwent a tortuous development and later was merged into yet
another, the Queen's (godless) colleges evolved into a national system of

206

university education which cast Trinity's narrow social constituency into relief. The establishment of the Royal University of Ireland in 1880 confirmed the success of Belfast, Cork, and Galway, while the 1882 reorganization of the Catholic University as University College Dublin (and its effective handing over to the Society of Jesus a year later) effectively polarized higher education. Trinity was out in the cold, even if it endured this isolation from the patronage of the rising middle classes in some material comfort.

Subsequent events have tended to engrave this binary system too emphatically in the popular history of Irish education. For example, there was a very considerable English presence in what became University College Dublin; if this is recollected in isolation through the scene in James Joyce's *A Portrait of the Artist as a Young Man* (1916) where Stephen Dedalus trades tundish for funnel with an English-born dean of studies, then the role of Thomas Arnold (1823-1900) should also be recalled. The younger brother of Matthew Arnold served as professor of English literature from 1856 to 1862 in the Catholic University, and in the same office in University College Dublin from 1882 until his death. (In the interim he had de-converted from Catholicism, only to lapse back in 1876.) As his *Manual of English Literature* (1862 and subsequent editions) makes plain, the underlying concern of these new institutions was the teaching of undergraduate students rather than pure research. This priority was philosophically buttressed by *The Idea of a University* (1873) which had its origins in lectures delivered in Dublin by Newman in 1852.

Down in College Green, the Elizabethan foundation was not indifferent to these innovations. A chair of English literature, separated from older disciplines with which the subject had hitherto been linked, was established in 1865. Edward Dowden (1843–1913), the first occupant, was an important figure in the establishment of literary study as an academic discipline and whose writings on Shakespeare (1875) and Shelley (1886) were influential in forming late-Victorian sensibilities. A friend of John Butler Yeats (1839–1922), he had the bad luck to be disliked by the younger Yeats; as a consequence, his reputation has not flourished. Yet Dowden was one of a distinguished group of Trinity dons in the latter half of the nineteenth century. These included John Kells Ingram, J. P. Mahaffy, George Salmon, and R. Y. Tyrrell, whose individual virtues can be listed more readily than they can be shown to constitute a coherent and shared intellectual outlook.[2] The achievements of these men in their specialized fields – political economy, ancient history, mathematics, and classics, respectively – deserve further consideration, just as the remarkable contribution of Jesuit teachers in University College awaits contextualization.[3] However, in the case of the older of these rival colleges in Dublin, academic distinction among the Fellows possessed an outer circle dispersed principally through the sacred and profane hierarchies of the Established Church and the imperial service. Two of the younger Fellows (the geologist Samuel Haughton, 1821–1897, and Joseph Allan Galbraith, 1818–1890 started an Indian Civil Service School which was so successful as to prompt complaints from the unsilent sisters that the imperial administration was increasingly filled with 'crammed youths from the Irish universities or commercial schools'.[4]

Reference has been made to the Stokes family – in particular Whitley Stokes and George Thomas Stokes. When a study is made of the Irish Victorian intelligentsia, attention might usefully focus on family *per se*, as well as on institutions, subject areas, and individual achievements. This is not to suggest that a hereditary principle is at work, but rather to pinpoint one of the discernible ways in which the operations of the professional middle class can be related to economic perpetuation. And if such a study were to broaden its horizon from the conventional obsession with literary matters – to include science, and particularly medicine – then the role of the Collis, Graves, Jellett, Joly families etc. would be crucial. The Graveses functioned not only in medicine, but also in Celtic studies and of course in ecclesiastical affairs: one of their number even made a minor contribution to the paper war of 1786-1788. The Jolys intermarried later with the Synges, whose reputation does not rest exclusively in the theatre. John Lighton Synge (born 1897) is a distinguished physicist and, at one remove from the Dublin branch of the family, Richard Lawrence Millington Synge (born 1914) shared a Nobel Prize for chemistry in 1952. When, in the 1920s and '30s, Yeats became intensely concerned with family, with hereditarian eugenics and 'national intelligence', it is difficult to relate these obsessions to his contemporary concern with the eighteenth century (real or imagined): they are, however, quite at one with a pattern of social and cultural networking characteristic of a period (the Irish Victorian) towards which he adopted an attitude of studied indifference. This assymmetry will take its place in a broader spectrum of Yeats's mytho-historiographical activities.

If William Rowan Hamilton (1805–1865) – discoverer of quaternions, youthful correspondent with the elderly Wordsworth, and president of the Royal Irish Academy at the age of thirty-two – seems a splendidly isolated genius, then a neat reversal of names will reveal his kinship with Archibald Hamilton Rowan (1751–1834), the leading United Irishman of County Down. The Victorian Stokeses also had a rebel in the closet, or at least a Fellow of Trinity insufficiently sound in the 1790s to escape the wrath of the authorities in the prelude to the United Irishman insurrection. Through such details one comes further to appreciate the manner in which the background to Lever's proto-Celtic plot in *Luttrell of Arran* reflects on the difficulties of some respectable families in calmly contemplating all of the Irish past.

A closer connection worked to integrate Thomas Dunbar Ingram (1826 – 1901), younger brother of Comte's translator; he followed up a career as professor of Hindu law at Calcutta with a series of publications between 1887 and 1900 devoted to rebutting the historical 'revisionism' of W. E. H. Lecky (1838-1903), the most distinguished Trinity graduate of the age. History was sometimes generated in quarters additional to those where it might have been expected. For example, Alexander George Richey (1830-1883) was deputy regius professor of feudal and English law when he published his *Lectures on the History of Ireland* (first series 1869): the anomaly is partly explained by the preoccupations of the Erasmus Smith Professor of Modern History (J. W. Barlow, 1826-1913) whose liberal views on damnation kept him embroiled in pamphlet disputes with a future provost.[5] When Barlow finally retired in 1893, he was briefly succeeded by J. B. Bury, who departed for Cambridge in 1902.

There were also unattached but talented individuals whose fates were decided less by kinship than by chance. As far as traffic between the two university systems was concerned, the most notable instance was that of Thomas Maguire (1831 – 1889), a sometime member of the faculty in Galway and the first (latter-day) Catholic to be elected a Fellow of Trinity College: he was probably murdered. Hutchinson Macaulay Posnett (grad. BA, 1887) did labour briefly as a tutor in Trinity, and published three short monographs before departing to New Zealand in 1886. A pupil of J. K. Ingram (who can now be seen as the intellectually dominant figure within the college walls), Posnett was not to continue his master's work in statistical method or in the social sciences more broadly: he became a professor of classics. At the personal level, the subjects on which he wrote as a young man – *The Historical Method in Ethics, Jurisprudence and Political Economy* (1882), *The Ricardian Theory of Rent* (1884) and *Comparative Literature* (1886) – mutely indicate a wealth of talent which was not to find expression inside the old academic structures of pre-independence Ireland.[6] Considered structurally, they indicate a lack of focus or concentration which was to prove the undoing of academic intellectualism in its imminent contest for public approval.

The emergence of new areas of intellectual excitement further contributed to Trinity's near imperceptible decline into an inverted provincialism, a

provincialism earnestly devoted to missionary work on behalf of the empire. Medicine, in which Dublin generally excelled was, by its evolving
nature, an international study; and a dispersal of talent inevitably exceeded
the cultivation of local excellence. Celtic studies was well-rooted in Germany
and France, but its development in the context of Irish universities was
resisted on political grounds. Douglas Hyde (1860-1949), master-strategist
of the Gaelic League's success until 1915, was a graduate of Trinity College
who obtained a chair of modern Irish in 1908 with the transformation of
the Royal University into the National University of Ireland. The displacement of Hyde from among the sons of the rectory and vicarage into a pro-
fessorial appointment in University College Dublin signalled in the academic
groves a wider triumph. Despite their differences, Hyde was of the party
of Yeats, Synge and Lady Gregory, rather than that of Provost Salmon and
Professor Mahaffy. The imaginative arts overcame drab professional
methodology – so much for drabness, so much for method. An amateur
movement, concerned with theatre and the colloquial language, with poetry
and little magazines, had outmanoeuvred the educational establishment to
the point where the oldest academic institution in the country was manifestly
at odds with the cultural and recreational interests of a newly confident
population. Hyde's installation as President of Ireland in 1937 ratifed an
epochal change, and trumpeted the victory of Celticism as the ideological
'science' of the new state.[7]

Trinity's recovery from this eclipse was a slow process, with the Great
War featuring as a massive chasm, or burial-pit, between the Victorian past
and the uncertain future. Politically, the tensions between college and state
were eased through the diplomatic leadership of Albert McConnell, provost from 1952 to 1974. But in academic and intellectual terms, a rapprochement had begun in the 1930s, when the Erasmus Smith professor of history,
Theodore Moody, combined with his opposite number in University College (R. D. Edwards) to launch *Irish Historical Studies*. What is of concern
here is an earlier phase of this commitment to history, a phase in which
two Trinity graduates featured prominently.[8]

John Bagnell Bury (1861 – 1927) was primarily an ancient historian and
classicist who also wrote a *Life of Saint Patrick* (1905). His belief that history
could be developed as a science was rudely shattered by the outbreak of
war in 1914, and more specially by the events of Easter 1916. His work on
a seventeen-volume edition (1896 – 1900) of Gibbon's *Decline and Fall of
the Roman Empire*, completed while he was still in Dublin, might have
prepared him for the revelation that a civilization possessed reverse gears
(like the new motor-car) and was no less dependent on violence in Europe

and at home than it was in its high imperialist campaigns abroad.⁹ The disillusion exposed by the Great War was not just its immediate product: discontent with regimented subsistence in the new cities, indifference towards official creeds and moralities, a more active questioning of age-old assumptions about sexuality and individuality had begun to pervade western European culture, at least since the shock of the Franco-Prussian war of 1870. The small scale of Irish society, its diminished reproductive energies after the Famine, and its location as an island lying off an island, isolated it from many (but by no means all) of these semi-conscious stirrings.

Victorian confidence busied itself in reconciling the vestiges of belief to versions of science. Bury still held that history was a science, much as Ranke had suggested in earlier and happier times. His biography of Patrick broke rank from a long line of studies designed to confirm the distinctiveness of the early Irish church: its composure echoed the manner in which revision of the Church of Ireland hymnal absorbed translations from old Gaelic religious texts, but (unlike the revision of liturgy) failed to function as a mediating, enabling diplomacy. Personally, Bury was an atheist and perhaps that helped him to declare, if not actually to decide, that 'the Roman Catholic conception of St Patrick's work is, generally, nearer to historical fact than the views of some anti-Papal divines'.¹⁰ A comparison with Synge's play, *The Well of the Saints*, produced at the Abbey Theatre in the same year, underlines the contrast between imaginative negotiation and scientific demonstration as approaches to a disputed past. In a sense, Bury's *Life* is unaffected by questions of religious belief though it is a work of religious history, whereas Synge's play can be shown to re-interpret the fundamental idea of the miraculous in ways which inspire multiple and yet mutually supportive responses within a radically divided culture.

One finds in the past evidence of developments which did not occur, and these are often more significant (once they are located) than some well-known and much-visited old themes. The non-emergence in nineteenth-century Ireland of anything like the German *Sozialwissenschaften* (social sciences) has much to do with the increasing role of the Catholic church in higher education. But, as a negative phenomenon, it must also be related to the curious role of political economy in early- and mid-Victorian debates about 'the condition of Ireland'.¹¹ The highly charged nature of these ideological exchanges is registered in John Mitchel's writings, where the idiom is almost exclusively political in its Promethean confrontation with a world system embodied in the British Empire. (Not that Mitchel leaned towards Marxism, far from it.) However, it is ultimately more pervasively registered in the carefully controlled success of the Celticist programme. And perhaps the most significant feature of that development has been its non-development. At a level neither could articulate, political economy and Celticism did business.

FROM LECKY TO YEATS VIA MAX WEBER

Of all the members of Trinity's nomenaclatura mentioned above, only Lecky has generated sufficient retrospective interest to inspire a biography.[12] In the short-to-medium term at least, the bold initiative of professors Moody and Edwards in 1938 led to very little renewed work on the period – the eighteenth century – in the study of which Lecky had been a pioneer. T. D. Ingram's objections had been to Lecky's celebratory attitude towards Henry Grattan and to his critical view of the methods employed to legislate the Union in 1800. As a 'revisionist' – if he was a 'revisionist' – Lecky revised Unionist history and this despite the fact that he wrote his account of late eighteenth-century Ireland as he moved closer to active participation in Unionist politics.[13] His reputation now rests on a classic history of Ireland, in its time abstracted from a multiple-volume history of England, all seemingly written in methodical compliance with chronology and an implicit acceptance of history as an empirical science. This judgement of Lecky neglects to appreciate how innovatory was his use of archival material, nor does it acknowledge his pioneering work as a historian of ideas. These two aspects of his work converge in his treatment of the 1790s, a decade which occupies a disproportionately large position in *The History of Ireland in the Eighteenth Century*. But it is not enough to conclude that this extensive treatment simply results from a greater scale of surviving archival material – and equally facile to assume that it reflects some innate interest of the author's in the revolutionary period. Archives are not just discovered and exploited; at a prior point, they were produced, and their production interacted with structures of record-keeping, memorialization, anticipation, and anxiety.

Lecky's influence deserves serious consideration by literary historians because it pervades certain later disputes, informing both sides of them and thus acting as a kind of 'fifth column' within each. In the early 1920s, the editor of *The Catholic Bulletin* drew extensively on *The History of Ireland in the Eighteenth Century*. W. B. Yeats – his principal antagonist among the literati – found in *Leaders of Public Opinion* the notion that Swift dreaded madness, a notion round which his play, *The Words Upon the Window-Pane*, revolves. It might be possible to argue that Fr Tim Corcoran and Senator Yeats relied on different Leckys, a late and an early Lecky respectively. But such an argument would make too much of changes in emphasis in the historian's attitude towards the eighteenth century, and – additionally – ignores the constant republication of *Leaders of Public Opinion* (1st edn 1861) right into the twentieth century – a two-volume edition appeared in 1903.

In contrast to Lecky, we could see T. B. Ingram and Fr Corcoran as the victims of structural or – less grandly – circumstantial irony. The professor of Hindu law (Calcutta) defended the reputation of eighteenth-century parliamentarians while upholding the Union which eliminated their existence. The Roman Catholic excoriator of Yeats was a fervent republican, a last-ditch defender of the political ideal to which the poet had contributed so much through his creation of the Countess Cathleen and his preservation of John Mitchel's memory. Ingram and Corcoran personify the two masters of whom Stephen Dedalus is a reluctant servant – 'the imperial British state' and 'the holy Roman catholic and apostolic church' – while they also adhere each to an Ireland of his own heart's desire.[14] The irony of these multiple loyalties extends beyond the personal circumstances of the professor and editor – as Stephen Dedalus' complex negotiations wonderfully demonstrate. To that degree, irony is structural in their condition, the republican being an ultramontanist, the Unionists being a vindicator of the last independent parliament in Ireland. Lecky was not unaware of a similar irony in his own political position near the end of the nineteenth century, but his work transcends mere circumstances by absorbing irony into its texture and procedure and by re-presenting chronicle as a release from sequentiality.

Quite apart from his 'national sentiment' or his methodical use of archives, Lecky is thus the first modern historian of Ireland, the first modern Irish historian of European ideas. His first (anonymous) publication, *The Religious Tendencies of the Age* (1860) may be marked by a residual undergraduate earnestness, but it also deploys from the outset an attitude towards its subject which alternates regularly from sympathy to studied indifference and back again. Catholicism is warmly regarded while Puritanism is anatomized: then the procedure is reversed. Nor does latitudinarianism benefit from this comparison of theological extremes, for Lecky summarizes its central position as implying 'that, in fact, though correct doctrine is highly desirable, and though every man should seek after it, it is not essential.'[15] Such dry epitomes – 'the Evangelical system of text warfare' – compete with the extensive essays on the great divisions of western Christianity in which they appear. The question of division is itself subjected to the humorous deployment of a learned trope; the proponents of rival creeds are presented as 'breaking up the rock of truth into small stones, and throwing them at their neighbours'. Here, the reader is expected not only to recognize the wordplay in which Saint Peter becomes the rock (Latin, *petrus*) upon which the

Church is founded, but also to follow through the history of persecution (with the stoning of the first martyr, Saint Stephen, ironically re-assigned to his fellow believers) until the modern adage about people who live in glasshouses takes over.

Anonymity gives the author a usefully unspecified location, or even de-location, with respect to the geography of denominational allegiances in the United Kingdom of 1860. Thus he can write that 'the Roman Catholic peasantry are at least as well acquainted with controversial matters as the Protestants in a corresponding social position', without fear that his identity would de-limit this observation to an experience of Irish conditions or, perhaps, conditions in parts of Scotland.[16] Later some observers of Lecky's career were unfavourably impressed by his even-handed treatment of Catholicism, in its doctrinal and social aspects. *Religious Tendencies* certainly went to some length to create a mental climate within its pages so that controversial aspects of Catholic worship could be dispassionately considered. The long-standing tradition concerning the Virgin Mary's immaculate conception was set against the very recent occasion on which the doctrine was promulgated (8 December 1854). And in answer to the standard Protestant argument against the veneration of saints, Lecky wrote:

> Is love indeed so gross, so material a thing as to be weakened by diffusion? Is it impossible to love God with all our hearts, and at the same time to love our neighbours as ourselves? Do men love their country the less in proportion to their attachment to their families?[17]

His reading of *Reflections on the Revolution in France* is evident here in his bringing together the possible rivals for a man's loyalty – 'the little platoon we belong to' and the 'public affections', in Burke's words. But implicit also is a familiarity with the miscellaneous speeches and letters of the 1790s in which Burke's distaste for the contentions within Christianity and the pretensions of those who speak of 'a protestant religion' is repeatedly incised. Donal McCartney has drawn attention to Lecky's early acquisition of the *Reflections* – bought when he was a still a schoolboy – and his faithful retention of this copy throughout his life.[18] It is customary to assign Burke's influence to a later phase of his career, but a close textual analysis of *The Religious Tendencies* reveals its presence from the outset. The distinguishing feature of Lecky's writing in this regard is not his display, but rather his secretion, of specific sources and instances. Not for him the cataloguing of datable and locatable absurdities or intolerances in the history of religious difference, in the manner of an ostentatiously sceptical voyeur or chucking bigot with his/her own private commitments. The assimilated irony of Lecky's method eliminates colourful incident because such would jeopardize the even dealing by which each major division of western Christianity is evaluated on terms which do not exclude its own but which do not reduce to them. It is perhaps only when he comes to refer to Daniel O'Connell that a specific orientation in the anonymous author himself becomes obtrusive.[19]

The impact of his first publication would not seem to have been great. Yet it took its place immediately in the changing context of Irish literature, at a time when two notable Irish writers were re-orienting their perspectives on history and revelation. In the case of Charles Lever, the harum-scarum novels appearing at the time of Lecky's birth had already been replaced by a more sober attention to the Irish past, but in *Barrington* (1863) and (as we have seen) in *Luttrell of Arran* (1865) Lever showed himself willing to investigate discrete areas of experience unaccommodated in the homogenized comic 'Ireland' of *Harry Lorrequer* (1839).

With Sheridan Le Fanu, a return to novel-writing in 1861 with *The House by the Churchyard* evidenced a different kind of discreteness, one in which the past broke in upon the present through incomplete and inarticulate images. It has been noted elsewhere that Lecky's representation of the Irish eighteenth century in *Leaders of Public Opinion* as an era in which participation in public life gave rise to the crystallization of opinion had its counter-argument in Le Fanu's *The House by the Church-yard* (serialized 1861 – 3) where rumour displaces opinion and privacy is invaded by objects from the past.[20] But a more verifiable instance of influence arises in connection with Lecky's treatment of religious images. Anything which aids us 'in realizing religious truths' has, according to him, 'a beneficial effect on our spiritual condition', and proceeds to argue the case in relation to both popular images and high art. Culture pervades religion and cannot be isolated from it. It may happen therefore that the Roman Catholic (his term) 'is worshipping, though he knows it not, by the aid of a Raphael or a Rubens'.[21] His treatment of Catholic practice also includes sympathetic comment on the veneration of saints and prayer addressed to mediators. 'Departed saints are spectators of earth' is Lecky's summary of this belief, and in promptly citing Saint Paul's famous passage about a great cloud of witnesses (Hebrews 12: 1) he virtually dictates a scene in Le Fanu's *Uncle Silas* (1865), a novel in which pictures and mediators between the dead and the living jostle for the narrator's attention even as she recognizes that she is a phantom watched by a 'cloud of cruel witnesses'.[22]

The larger cultural context in which these little literary exchanges were occurring could be summarized as 'The Declining Sense of the Miraculous', the title of the opening chapter in the first publication to which Lecky put his name. *The History of the Rise and Influence of Rationalism in Europe* appeared in 1865, the year of *Uncle Silas*. McCartney, writing as a biographer, sees *The Religious Tendencies of the Age* as effecting Lecky's release from any commitment to holy orders as a profession – 'a theological problem had converted itself into a historical one.'[23] The verb is more aptly chosen than one might think, for secularizing conversion was a paradox upon which much in Irish Victorian culture depended. Lecky's preference of the literary life over the clerical was embraced nonetheless as a *vocation*. The revivalism of the Literary Revival has long been noted, together with the participation of second-generation exiles from the rectory – Yeats, whose grandfather was rector of Tullylish in County Down; Synge, whose grandfather was rector of Schull in County Cork; and others less eminent. To this one might add the growth of Catholic nationalism as a further, less considered, instance of 'secularizing conversion' whereby political democracy is synthesized with the maintenance of ecclesiastical absolutism.

But the larger cultural context, which incorporates both historical and literary endeavour together with other activities and values, also distinguishes between these to an increasing degree. George Sigerson, an Ulsterman by birth and by education a graduate of the Queen's College Cork, translated Gaelic literature and the writings of Jean-Martin Charcot, the neuro-psychologist, lived to be called 'artificial, unscholarly, a typical provincial celebrity' – and to be so described by that natural scholar, Yeats![24] The new specializations warred jealously on each other; in retrospect, we can see that experimental science, in its philosophical aspect, has been eclipsed in the cultural histories by the rebirth of the older science, alchemy, in Yeats's alembic. The broader conflicts are more readily traced. Lecky's opting for the vocation of literature employs the term 'literature' in an encompassing fashion which Yeats and his associates will not tolerate. Fond of Carlyle's dictum that literature was the one modern church, Lecky was to find such latitudinarianism replaced by the puritanism of those for whom only imaginative writing, formally composed within generic orders, was to be true scripture.

The heightened sense of 'literature' in the *fin de siècle* was not without precedent, in the Romantic period, and during the Renaissance. But the distinctive feature of the latter-day valorization of literature was that it accomplished a more thorough appropriation of the religious sense than had earlier been the case, an appropriation preceded or facilitated by the decline in religious belief and practice in western Europe. Thus the cult of art, especially the written arts, as providing access to transcendental truth, to the divine, only possesses coherence as a historical phenomenon when it is re-united in reflection with the decline of religious concerns in the lives of the masses. Contemptuous of industrialized and mechanically democratized society, the symbolist poet (Yeats, Mallarmé, or Rilke) was in some ways a product of, rather than a rejecter, of its processes of ever-increasing specialization. A declining sense of the miraculous generated magicians of the word. And if it is argued that religious practice in many ways was intensified, rather than diminished, in the course of Irish 'modernization' – the devotional revolution experienced by the Catholic Church in the early Victorian period, the evangelical Revival of 1859 etc. – then one would argue that these extensive practices were stages of the bureaucratization of religious communities which had hitherto conducted their affairs less publicly. In the case of revivalism, it took a political crisis in the 1880s to convert temporary phenomena into the colossus we know as Unionism. Literary revivalism, unimpressed by the new politics of the ballot-box and the ship-yard riot, commences at much the same point.

In European terms, Charles Baudelaire is a veteran and early victim in the epochal struggle between these powers. Max Weber is the sociological theoretician of its origins and consequences though, for all his rigour of method, he is also a victim, in his psychic life and in his politics. In the English-speaking world at least, these developments only became evident in a period significantly later than Baudelaire's. Based in England, with Trinity College relegated to the days of his intellectual infancy, Lecky published his *Rise and Influence of Rationalism* without reference to his Irish origins and education and without reference to the notable figures who constituted the *Leaders of Public Opinion in Ireland*. Though there is a brief anticipation of his celebrated and cool analysis of the causes of the Irish rising in 1641, no reference is made to Jonathan Swift, arguably the real hero of the 1863 anonymous study.[25] It is as if the named author of *The Rise and Influence of Rationalism* was (mutely, of course) acknowledging only *The Religious Tendencies* as a prior publication. In this way, the tendencies of the age were tacitly shown to be rationalistic and not religious. The antagonism of Swift towards the new science, 'the moderns', and the tendencies of *his* age generally, is not admitted.

Lecky did apply himself to elucidating the implications of a growing rationalism for the business of interpretation, in the biblical, historical and literary realms. Fetishism is the origin of many sublime religious practices, for example, veneration of the cross. The practice of allegorical interpretation of the scriptures is matched by elaborate identifications of the cross in other objects:

we are reminded by a writer in the beginning of the second century, the sea
could not be traversed without a mast, which is in the form of a cross. The
earth becomes fertile only when it has been dug by a spade, which is a cross.
The body of man is itself in the same holy form. So also is his face, for the
eyes and nose together form a cross.[26]

Absorbed irony constitutes Lecky's interpretation of this material, for the
order in which he places the mast, the spade, the body etc. culminates in
the reader's consenting to recognize the infinite regression into absurdity
of these instances. Interpretation is thus in a process of rationalizing itself,
reducing the options to an efficient minimum while still providing and requiring choice. On the one hand, the modern world was thus confronted
with important questions about the 'comparative authority of the historical
and the spiritual meanings' of – say – biblical narratives, while a compensating excess of possibilities might now be found in the doctrine of correspondences elaborated by Emanuel Swedenborg and exploited by writers
as different as Baudelaire and Emerson and Yeats.[27] Chapters devoted to the
history of persecution bridge the division between the first and second
volumes of *The Rise and Influence of Rationalism*. The elimination of torture and the growth of tolerance (through 'the doctrine of the incapacity
of the magistrate to decide religious questions') have already been sounded
as sub-themes, among which it was possible to present democracy as 'an
aspect of the Christian spirit.'[28] But a sudden change in tempo brings
Lecky's book towards its conclusion. The second (and final) volume is completed in two chapters only – 'On the Secularisation of Politics' and 'The
Industrial History of Rationalism'. His task is virtually concluded in these
titles, for the emerging message of *Rationalism* is the triumph of knowledge
and freedom as these terms were understood in the mid-nineteenth century.
The evolution of this liberal victory is encapsulated in the summary account
of how the Medicis gave 'an Intellectual Ascendancy to Industry' and oversaw the development of an aristocracy 'formed exclusively from the trading
and mercantile classes'.[29] Despite some illuminating paragraphs on the
history of the stage and on the arts generally, the close of the second volume
of *Rationalism* offers little but confirmation of its thesis. Irony is now dis-
armed by the obvious convergence of writer and reader in a publicly endorsed consensus.

At this point, Max Weber's more penetrating account of de-sacralization
(or *Entzauberung*) is called into play. By this term is meant the progressive
rendering secular either the means or the ends of certain major human activities, and with it goes (at least the technical possibility of) a complementary sacralization in which previously profane, secular or just plain

run-of-the-mill activities would be invested with a transcendent value. While Weber was aware of Lecky's earlier work, *The Protestant Ethic and the Spirit of Capitalism* (1904) had no room for the complacency which ultimately informs *The Rise and Influence of Rationalism*. For Weber, the sequence in which industrialization follows monasticism results in no withering away of religious attitudes. On the contrary, there is a transfer and simultaneous intensification of commitment according to which life in the world was to be pursued as an ascetic vocation in itself. Nothing could be further from Lecky's concluding observations on the oddity of a religious practice which withheld the sacraments from actors than Weber's 'dry pages, interlarded with dead theology and the most most unbearable scholarly apparatus'. Yet the author of this discouraging description also recognizes an 'emotional impact' in Weber's monograph which 'has about it something of the dizzying pessimism of Freud's *Civilization and its Discontents* or of the early novels of H. G. Wells.'[30] Jameson's purpose here is two-fold – to uncover a narrative structure within Weber's theoretical formulations, and to perform an unexpected rescue of Weber for latter-day Marxism by introducing Lévi-Straussian formulae into an analysis of these narratives.

These formulae are far from being generally accepted as the paradigm of the deep structure of myths, and the algebra in which they are couched is relegated to the footnotes.[31] As an abstract testing of the interpretation of Irish literary culture advanced in these pages, however, they can usefully augment the narrative account signalled in the title, *From Burke to Beckett*.[32] That is to say, the formulae are unlikely to impress any loyal reader of a literature which repeatedly inveighs against abstraction. And yet, as an interlude in a broadly narrative treatment of that literature, they might offer a striking anticipation of a 'later' phase of the narrative, with the effect of suggesting that the seemingly discrete, autonomous work of Yeats is already (so to speak) structurally present in a prior phase. In one regard, the current argument goes further than Fredric Jameson's account of Max Weber, for it assumes that the work of Lecky and Yeats can be read not only as separate personal achievements but also as a continuum, even as the components of a synchronic whole, distinct – even different – from those separate achievements. In turn, the oppressiveness represented by such a synthesis is answered by acts of betrayal, wilful derogations: the names we might identify in this connection would notably be those of Joyce and Beckett.

A verbal summary of Lévi-Strauss's formula for the structure of myths, as elaborated by Jameson in his analysis of Weber, goes as follows. The rationalization of ends is to the sacralization of means as is the rationalization of means to the non-finalization (non-establishment as an end) of the sacred. Now some of these functions (rationalization and sacralization) and terms (ends and means) are already familiar from a reading of Lecky's early work. The fundamental crux of the myth analysed by Lévi-Strauss is the relationship, or coincidence, of two apparently contradictory cognitive systems (kinship and cosmology), and a similar relationship is emergent both in the rival claims upon Lecky's sense of vocation (theology or history) and in the divergent senses (discursive or poetic) of what literature constituted in the mid- to late-nineteenth century.

One can now go a good deal further than the inductive method which suggested an unconscious relation between political economy and Celticism. In one formulation, Yeats relates to Lecky by re-converting a historical problem into a theological one. But in another, Lecky's secularizing narrative is sustained in Yeats's religion of art. (In the terms of Lévi-Strauss/Jameson, the sacred is no longer a transcendent 'end', but a kind of sacred-for-itself, what neo-Marxists like Adorno might regard as alienated immanence.) In each, the significant absence is God, rationalized out of activity by the former and unrecalled by the latter – at least until the very final years of the poet's life.

The *deus absconditus* is a theme to be encountered in a variety of modernist crises, ranging from that announced in the market-place by Zarathustra in the 1880s to the rather less noisy creature of Lucien Goldmann in his role as commentator on Pascal and Racine more than half a century later.[33] It has sometimes been fashionable to absorb Nietzsche into radical philosophy, but the distinction between a dead God and a hidden God deserves some residual respect. Nevertheless, the general term under which these Nietzschean and neo-Marxist themes might be accommodated is *Entzauberung*, translated here (in keeping with Jameson's usage) as desacralization, but perhaps better rendered as disenchantment.

A notable feature of the English term is its demoralized position, caught between resentment and desacralization, lacking the heroic negativity of the first and the elegaic outrage of the second. Yet it also conveys the dull pleasantries of Lecky's concluding pages in *The Rise and Influence of Rationalism*, the self-exculpating liberalism of his implicit politics. Now, it was a feature of Jameson's adaptation of Lévi-Strauss to the analysis of Max Weber that the material under examination constituted at some level a *myth*, a contradictory narrative in which incompatible explanations were dramatized, and aesthetically reconciled. Incompatibility is not rife; on the contrary, it is contained within a system of binary oppositions. In the ancient instances – Oedipus etc. – no complete statement of the myth is available, for every variant lacks some element which, however, may surface in a different variant. A wholly 'ideal' text may be conceptualized as looking like the totality of parts for a numberless orchestra of players, but logically it is impossible to realise any such total text.[34]

Lecky is a good deal less systematic than Yeats whose antinomies marshall the material of his thought more rigorously than any opposition in *Leaders of Public Opinion, Rationalism* or *The History of Ireland*. Absorptive irony, the technique of assimilating the circumstantial awkwardness of dual allegiances or conflicts of loyalty necessarily creates at least the *impression* of a non-schematic approach. But, reading across the full orchestral score of the Lecky/Yeats composition, one might detect a crucial tension in their attitude towards Protestant Ascendancy. To the historian, this is an historical question, traceable to the very late eighteenth century. To the poet it is (or becomes) a cultural answer, applicable to the conditions of Yeats's own disenchanted existence and stated in terms of a mythic eighteenth century. The theoretical opportunity provided by Lecky's anticipation (*in parvo*) of a theme in Max Weber might be extended, first by noting a dogmatic limitation to tolerance: in the words of B. E. Lippincott in 1938, when Lecky had observed that 'propertied groups of the middle class may be driven to the use of force in order to defend constitutional liberty, he hinted at a fundamental element in fascism'. On the eve of the Second World War, Lippincott chose to present Lecky as a warning voice; had he read Yeats instead, the American social scientist would have found an eager prophet of propertied violence.

NOTES AND REFERENCES

1   William Godwin, *Enquiry Concerning Political Justice* (London: Penguin, 1985), p. 384.
2   I deal with this academic milieu in 'Lecky, Mark Twain and Literary History', the appendix to Donal McCartney, *W. E. H. Lecky: Historian and Politician 1838-1903* (Dublin: Lilliput Press, 1994), pp. 195-206, esp. pp. 201-2. But see also McCartney, op. cit., *passim*.
3   See however Thomas J. Morrisey *Towards a National University: William Delaney SJ (1835-1924)* (Dublin: Wolfhound Press, 1983).
4   See R. B. McDowell and D. A. Webb, *Trinity College Dublin 1592-1952: an Academic History* (Cambridge: Cambridge University Press, 1982), p. 538 n39, and *English Historical Review*, vol. 83 (1968) p. 271.
5   See W. J. Mc Cormack, *Dissolute Characters: Irish Literary History through Balzac, Le Fanu, Yeats, and Bowen* (Manchester: Manchester University Press, 1993), p. 53, 58-59 n11. Barlow's *Eternal Punishment and Eternal Death* (1865) exemplifies an instance of 'the declining sense of the miraculous' within the Trinity establishment, following just a few months after the publication of Lecky's *Rationalism*.

6   I am grateful to Joep Leerssen for discussing with me the significance of Posnett's pioneering work on comparative literature as a discipline, especially his suggestion that it might have provided a counter to the versions of Celticism advanced by Arnold on the one hand and Hyde etc. on the other.

7   For some preliminary comments on 'ideological sciences' as part of the development of Irish nationality, see my 'The Cult of the Contemporary in Ireland' in P. Dávidházi and J. Karafiáth eds., *Literature and its Cults* (Budapest: Argumentum, 1994), pp. 203-11.

8   See the introduction to Ciaran Brady, ed., *Ideology and the Historians* (Dublin: Lilliput Press, 1991).

9   On Bury's reaction to the War etc. see István Berend 'History as a Scholarly Discipline and *Magistra Vitae*' in Ciaran Brady, ed., *Ideology and the Historians*, pp.187-198, esp. 193.

10   J. B. Bury, *The Life of St Patrick and his Place in History* (London: Macmillan, 1905), pp. vii-viii. For a good account of Bury's career, see George Huxley, 'The Historical Scholarship of John Bagnell Bury', *Greek, Roman and Byzantine Studies*, vol. 17, No. 1 (Spring 1976), pp. 81-104.

11   For a recent treatment of this topic see T. B. Boylan and T. P. Foley, *Political Economy and Colonial Ireland: The Propagation and Ideological Function of Economic Discourse in the Nineteenth Century* (London: Routledge, 1992). But see also the work of R. D. Collison Black, especially *The Statistical and Social Inquiry Society of Ireland, 1847-1947, Centenary Volume, with a History of the Society* (Dublin: Eason, 1947) and *Economic Thought and the Irish Question 1817-1870* (Cambridge: University Press, 1960).

12   I refer here to the recent work by Donal McCartney (see n1 above). There had been a memoir by his wife (1909), a hagiography by J. J. Auchmuty (1946) and even a slim volume of letters (ed. H. Montgomery Hyde, 1947).

13   McCartney, op. cit., pp. 148-50.

14   James Joyce, *Ulysses* (London: Penguin, 1969), p. 26.

15   [Anon.], *The Religious Tendencies of the Age* (London: Saunders, Otley, 1860), p. 11.

16   Ibid., p. 29.

17   Ibid., p. 38.

18   McCartney, op. cit., p. 5; for the phrase from Burke see p. 58 above. In connection with the debate about the currency of 'ascendancy' to which Burke contributed, one should note another piece of Lecky's even dealing, this time on the topic of J. J. Rousseau. Though he regarded the latter as a man of 'uncontrollable passions', he also conceded that 'never was there an author whose writings gained a more wonderful ascendancy over the passions of mankind.' (*Religious Tendencies*, pp. 284, 287). That appears to be the sole appearance of the term in Lecky's analysis of the contemporary religious situation in mid-century.

19   *Religious Tendencies*, pp. 296-304; see also p. 280 where his reading of Burke on the anti-popery laws seems to intrude into a list of proper names – 'The burning of Servetus by Calvin, and of Bocher by Cranmer, the numerous religious executions under Elizabeth, the atrocious penal laws in Ireland, the policy of Laud . . .' The Bohn edition of Burke's *Works* had begun to appear in 1854, though other extensive sources were in print earlier.

20 See 'Lecky, Mark Twain and Literary History', pp. 199-200.

21 *Religious Tendencies*, pp. 44, 46.

22 Ibid., pp. 32-33; for Le Fanu and Saint Paul, see *Dissolute Characters*, p. 88.

23 McCartney, op. cit., p. 18.

24 W. B. Yeats, *Autobiographies* (London: Macmillan, 1955), p. 202.

25 W. E. H. Lecky, *History of the Rise and Influence of Rationalism in Europe* [authorized edition] (London: Longman, 1910), vol. 2, p. 6.

26 Ibid., vol. 1, p. 191.

27 Ibid., vol. 1, p. 264.

28 Ibid., vol. 2, pp. vii, x. The phrases quoted come from the table of contents.

29 Ibid., vol. 2, pp. xi, 294.

30 Fredric Jameson, *The Ideologies of Theory: Essays 1971-1986* (London: Routledge, 1988), vol. 2 (The Syntax of History), p. 19. The quotation is from an essay first published in *New German Critique* in 1973, 'The Vanishing Mediator: or, Max Weber as Storyteller'.

31 See Jameson, op. cit., p. 18. The formula reads:
    $Fx(a):Fy(b) = Fx(b):F\text{-}a(y)$
    where x stands for rationalization
    y stands for sacralization, or conversion into a purely religious value or sanction
    a stands for end
    b stands for means.

    I have adapted Jameson's wording slightly in the name of euphony, and now add Lévi-Strauss's description of the formula – 'a relationship of equivalence is affirmed bewteen two situations respectively defined by an inversion of terms and of relations, under two conditions: (i) that one of the terms be replaced by its contrary (in the above formalization a and -a); (ii) that a correlative inversion be made between the function value and the term value of two elements (above y and a).' *Structural Anthropology* (New York: 1967), p. 225. (Translation modified by Jameson.)

32 I have in mind here a review by Kate Flint of *Dissolute Characters* in *Bullán* (Oxford), No. 1 (1994).

33 See Friedrich Nietzsche, *Thus Spoke Zarathustra*, trans. R. J. Hollingdale (Harmondsworth: Penguin, 1969), p. 41; Lucien Goldmann, *The Hidden God: A Study of Tragic Vision in the Penses of Pascal and the Tragedies of Racine*, trans. Philip Thody (London: Routledge, 1964).

34 For a good account of the structure of myth, with suitable reservations, see Edmund Leach, *Lévi Strauss* (Glasgow: Fontana/Collins, 1974, rev. edn, pp. 59-60.

7

Varieties of Celticism

Standish O'Grady supporting himself between the tables
Speaking to a drunken audience high nonsensical words;
(W. B. Yeats)[1]

I THEORY AS ARTIFICE

No account of Anglo-Irish literature can be complete without some attention to the question of its relation to Gaelic culture, the nineteenth-century decline of Gaelic as a vernacular, and the movement to revive it. An inspection of most books in the field will readily establish that such an attention is rarely granted. In so far as Anglo-Irish studies have been dominated by American and British critics, or by specialists whose academic training has steered them away from the necessary competence in the Gaelic language, this state of affairs can only be noted in silence. There is in addition, however, a symptomatic value in the studious neglect of Gaelic: it mutely signals the extent to which Anglo-Irish literature required the eclipse of Gaelic culture, and signals also the conflicting assumption of self-sufficiency on the part of the Gaelic Revival movement.

The movement associated with the foundation of the Gaelic League in 1893 should be seen in a European perspective of at least a century in duration. The underlying assumptions of the Gaelic Revival, in relation to nationality, culture, and language, form a distinctive part of the legacy of German romanticism. Doubtless there are unique and local factors at work in the Irish experience, just as the romantic origins of its philosophical

224

formulation are not exclusively German. Nevertheless, the name of Johann Gottfried von Herder economically focuses the drastically new view of language initiated by his publication in 1772 of *On the Origins of Speech*. The comparative study of philology, which developed from Herder's work, in turn gave rise to the indefatigable industry of Celtic philologists (many of them German). There is no doubt that scholarship in the area of Celticism constitutes perhaps the most refined and intellectually demanding exercise of the academic mind, but this should not blind us to the specific ideological and historic origins and affiliations of the discipline. No more than Practical Criticism, or econometrics, can Celticism boast of an immaculate conception.

Professor Edward Said has written a provocative and persuasive analysis of the ideological investment of European colonial and imperial ambitions in the academic study of *Orientalism*.[2] No comparable account of Celticism exists, nor indeed is there even any extensive history of the study of the Celtic languages written from within the assumptions of the discipline. There are certainly overlapping areas of impact – the poets who wove the Oriental theme into their work included (with Byron, de Nerval, etc.) Thomas Moore whose *Lalla Rookh* was published in 1817. More substantially, Yeats's early use of Indian imagery does have a specific (if concealed) line of communication with the British interest in the Indian Empire. These will seem isolated examples and unconvincing as such, for our criticism has inculcated in us a respect for the luminous integrity of texts, which are merely sullied by attempts to string up lines of communication with the equally atomized world of events. The totality lying behind the romantics' exploitation of the East, or the modernist commitment to the primitive, can only be recovered by the incorporation of every aspect of human production, behaviour, and speculation into a comprehensive history. Such an endeavour is repeatedly jeopardized by the discovery of potent, guilty, silences – questions which cannot be asked, let alone answered. Said enumerates a series of these in relation to 'western' attitudes to Arab culture, and a similar project is long overdue in the area of Celticism and the Gaelic revival which is its populist equivalent.

One Oriental theme which has a long and orthodox history in Europe, a history transformed and rendered problematic in the nineteenth century is, quite simply, Christianity. Three particular aspects of the notorious Victorian crisis of belief deserve attention here, though their provenance lies well beyond that normally implied by the term 'Victorian'. With the undermining of religious faith as a philosophical position, the sense of comprehensibility which religion had provided was in part replaced by an increased valorization of race as the living guarantee of the reality of the past and the cohesion of a secular society. The erudition of Ernest Renan and the violent irrationality of Julius Langbehn were alike assimilable to the nineteenth-century preoccupation with race, and Renan is particularly relevant in that his scholarly interests included Celtic literature.[3] A further area of comparison between France and Ireland might be identified in the doctrines of political messianism optimistically enounced by Edgar Quinet in 1848 and the pervasive symbolism of messianic sacrifice and redemption found in Patrick Pearse's life and works.[4] Finally, and more familiarly, in Matthew Arnold (and others) there is the investment in literature and in culture generally of the sublime Hope which religious belief had previously entertained. All three of these aspects of Christian decline have a bearing on the emergence of Anglo-Irish literature and its relations with Celticism.

ERNEST RENAN AND MATTHEW ARNOLD

Ernest Renan (1823 – 92) is best known in the English-speaking world as the author of the *Vie de Jésus* (1863), a humanist biographico-romance which led one inspired reader to deplore the absence of a climactic marriage at the end of the story. Renan had studied for the priesthood, and his abandonment of the Church resulted from doubts raised by his philological study of the scriptures. Essentially a humanist who perceived definite laws of progress in Nature and Man, he embarked on a vast examination of the evolution of languages, cultures, and religions as manifestations of the development of the human mind. Philosophically he owed much to Hegel, and while he spoke respectfully of science he was no positivist of the Comtean kind. In turning to examine the remains of Celtic civilization within France, he had available to him conventions by which to establish the desolate beauty of Brittany but his treatment of them is distinctive:

> Every one who travels through the Armorican peninsula experiences a change of the most abrupt description . . . A cold wind arises full of a vague sadness, and carries the soul to other thoughts; the tree tops are bare and twisted . . . a sea that is almost always sombre girdles the horizon with eternal moaning. The same contrast is manifest in the people: to Norman vulgarity, to a plump and prosperous population . . . succeeds a timid and reserved race living altogether within itself, heavy in appearance but capable of profound feeling, and of an adorable delicacy in its religious instincts. A like change is apparent, I am told . . . when one buries oneself in the districts of Ireland where the race has remained pure from all admixture of alien blood. It seems like entering on the subterranean strata of another world, and one experiences in some measure the impression given us by Dante, when he leads us from one circle of his Inferno to another.[5]

The essentially linguistic term Celtic is here seen almost fully clothed in its new usage – the Celts are a race, living virtually outside history, materially disadvantaged, but wonderfully spiritual and poetical. Although 'reserved' and 'living altogether within itself', this race is in practice established by a process of comparison – the Celt is different from the Normans or the Britons, he lacks certain attributes of these more mundanely successful races and possesses other characteristics in greater proportion or in an intenser form, *by comparison*. The Celt vicariously maintains a piety and nobility now rendered impossible for Normans and Britons obliged to live in the world of time, happiness, plenty, and vulgarity. He is a godsend.

Renan's evocation of the Celtic other-world is punctuated with comments which acknowledge to some degree the strategies at work. Its religious genius is noteworthy because 'nowhere has the eternal *illusion* clad itself in more seductive hues' [my emphasis]; and, for all its eternality, 'alas! it too is doomed to disappear, this emerald set in the Western seas.'[6] Seductive appearance, spirituality, impermanence – it is not surprising to find that the Celt has a distinctive place in the sexuality of politics:

> If it be permitted us to assign sex to nations as to individuals, we should have to say without hesitance that the Celtic race . . . is an essentially feminine race. No other has conceived with more delicacy the ideal of woman, or been more fully dominated by it. It is a sort of intoxication, a madness, a vertigo.[7]

Sex, nationhood, and race blur in this passage in a manner which is not characteristic of Renan, but still characteristic of the intellectual movement of which he was usually a more cautious proponent. It is at first reassuring to read that race, though 'of capital importance to the student who occupies himself with the history of mankind . . . has no application in politics'.[8] Renan's concern with race, then, is to be seen as part of a historical enterprise without any practical application in contemporary affairs: it is a category of research and not an objective. Yet the difference between this academicism and the followers of Langbehn is less great than first appears: the practical racists simply deny that there is a politics other than that of race, and Renan's research ultimately is no counter to the philosophical application of Zyklon.

Poetry of the Celtic Races indicates one strand of European thought in mid-century already evident in rough narrative form in Lever's *Luttrell of Arran*. Districts of Ireland where the race has remained pure from all admixture of alien blood provide the guilty, harassed gentleman of the world with a bride, and will provide his son with another: the virtue of Arran, sullied by John Luttrell's intervention, will be restored by his son's marriage to his cousin/sister. Through the lectures of Henri d'Arbois de Jubainville which

J. M. Synge attended at the Collège de France in 1898, Renan and Lever
are held in continuity with the more renowned Aran of the Celtic Revival.
More than any figure of his generation Synge was aware of the bearing, not
to say overbearing, of Herder, Renan, the *Revue celtique*, and *Zeitschrift für
Celtische Philologie* on the local endeavours of Douglas Hyde, Tomás O
Criomhthain, and others.[9]

Renan's essays then form a meeting point between the high sophistication
of comparative philology as developed in Germany, France, and Britain from
the initiative of Herder, and the popular perception of a Celtic fringe as an
aesthetic survival in the industrial age. German scholarship has its part in
that transition, but is less immediately documentable in its ideological negotiations. In Britain, where philology was dominated by Max Müller and the
controversies he excited, Celticism became not so much an academic discipline
– though there are important Welsh, Manx, and Scots Gaelic areas of inquiry – as it became the idiom of a new exchange between the elements of
the United Kingdom, notably in the Great Election of 1868.

Matthew Arnold's Oxford lectures *On the Study of Celtic Literature* (published 1867) stand at a junction between the German philology of Zeuss and
Meyer and the 'Celtic Twilight' of Yeats. Though Arnold begins with
memories of a holiday in Llandudno, and alludes to conditions in Ireland,
the real source of his inspiration is Renan's essay on Celtic poetry, at that
time as yet untranslated into English.[10] These lectures, together with the later
Irish Essays (1882) present a fascinating insight into changing British attitudes
towards Ireland. Notoriously, Arnold speaks of the Celt 'always ready to react
against the despotism of fact' but, as he acknowledges, the phrase properly
belongs to Henri Martin.[11] The Gallic debt should not persuade us that
Arnold is here indulging yet another of his preferences for continental authority
so as to show up the paucity of local examples: Arnold's Celticism is British
through and through in its priorities and in its objective function, but his
allusion to Henri Martin neatly indicates that Celticism is a strategy not exclusively British.

Seamus Deane has remarked on the *racial* connotations of Arnold's
vocabulary, and this is only to be expected given its sources and antecedents.
It is however an oversimplification to suggest that 'Celtic Ireland did not in
fact die with Lady Morgan or with Thomas Moore. It simply removed itself
to England, encased in Burke's capacious reputation, then blossomed there
again in Arnold's essays.'[12] The opening of *On the Study of Celtic Literature*
dramatizes the diverse elements in Arnold's strategy: echoes of Renan and
Burke are simultaneously adjusted so as to produce a new synthetic and British
Celticism:

The summer before last I spent some weeks at Llandudno, on the Welsh coast. The best lodging-houses at Llandudno look eastward, towards Liverpool . . . At last one turns round and looks westward. Everything is changed. Over the mouth of the Conway and its sands is the eternal softness and mild light of the west; the low line of the mystic Anglesey, and the precipitous Penmaen-mawr, and the great group of Carnedd Llewelyn and Carnedd David and their brethren fading away, hill behind hill, in an aerial haze, make the horizon; between the foot of Penmaenmawr and the bending coast of Anglesey, the sea, a silver stream, disappears one knows not whither. On this side Wales, – Wales, where the past still lives, where every place has its tradition, every name its poetry, and where the people, the genuine people, still knows this past, this tradition, this poetry, and lives with it, and clings to it; while, alas, the prosperous Saxon on the other side, the invader from Liverpool and Birkenhead, has long ago forgotten his. And the promontory where Llandudno stands is the very centre of this tradition; it is Creuddyn, *the bloody city*, where every stone has its story . . .[13]

The rhetorical exploitation of a topographical stage has rarely been so strenuously attempted. As in Renan's opening paragraph, the scene is divided between a prosperous horizon represented by lodging-houses (temporary dwellings) and an eternal horizon represented by the philology of stones, places, names. Arnold's second paragraph is just as deft in its manoeuvres:

As I walked up and down, last August year, looking at the waves as they washed this Sigeian land which has never had its Homer . . . suddenly I heard, through the stream of unknown Welsh, words, not English, indeed, but still familiar. They came from a French nurserymaid with some children. Profoundly ignorant of her relationship, this Gaulish Celt moved among her British cousins, speaking her polite neo-Latin tongue, and full of compassionate contempt, probably, for the Welsh barbarians and their jargon. What a revolution was here![14]

It is not excessive to see the maid as Arnold's reworking of Burke's Marie Antoinette, and indeed what a revolution there is in such a transformation. The maid is royal Celt compared with her hosts, the incomprehensible Welsh: for Arnold, she speaks a language which can be variously related to that which he speaks and that which he hears around him at the Llandudno eisteddfod. In the strict sense, then, he is not racialist in his thinking in that he stresses the fusion of peoples and the reduction of linguistic frontiers:

The fusion of all the inhabitants of these islands into one homogeneous, English-speaking whole, the breaking down of barriers between us, the swallowing up of separate provincial nationalities, is a consummation to which the natural course of things irresistibly tends; it is a necessity of what is called modern civilisation, and modern civilisation is a real, legitimate force . . .[15]

The function of the Celtic element in this homogeneous United Kingdom is clear – as with Renan, Arnold sees the Celt as poetically unsuccessful, spiritually intense but disorganized, an embellishment without which 'the Philistinism of our Saxon nature' would be intolerable.[16] Celticism is, therefore, part and parcel of the larger campaign mounted in *Culture and Anarchy*, a campaign directed against middle-class philistines in high places. In 1865 when Arnold delivered the lectures – and even more so in 1867 when they were published – the Celtic lands of Wales and Ireland distinguished themselves drastically. Wales, as the holiday interlude demonstrates, is happily non-political: all that can safely be said of contemporary Ireland is hedged in regret:

> I know my brother Saxons, I know their strength, and I know that the Celtic genius will make nothing of trying to set up barriers against them in the world of fact and brute force, of trying to hold its own against them as a political and social counter-power, as the soul of a hostile nationality. To me there is something mournful (and at this moment, when one sees what is going on in Ireland, how well may one say so!) in hearing a Welshman or an Irishman make pretensions, – natural pretensions, I admit, but how hopelessly vain! – to such a rival self-establishment . . .[17]

It is striking how little of contemporary Ireland Arnold allows his readers to see, allows himself in contrast to the panorama of Llandudno. Though he had been private secretary to the Marquis of Lansdowne when that great Irish landowner was Lord President of the Council in Lord Russell's government (1846–52), Arnold knew nothing of Ireland at first hand. The despotism of fact was unlikely to influence his view of the Irish Celts whom he increasingly identified with Irish Catholics. Indeed, the central strategy of Arnold's Celticism is not racial in any sense that Langbehn would have accepted, but a modernized synthesis of imperialist and sectarian tactics. A most revealing passage in *On the Study of Celtic Literature* demonstrates the way in which comparative philology could be turned to such purposes, and in the course of it we see how unconsciously Arnold accepts the government of India as a Saxon responsibility, a matter of 'brute fact':

> when Mr. Whitley Stokes, one of the very ablest scholars formed in Zeuss's school, a born philologist, – he now occupies, alas! a post under the Government of India, instead of a chair of philology at home, and makes one think mournfully of Montesquieu's saying, that had he been an Englishman he should never have produced his great work, but have caught the contagion of practical life, and devoted himself to what is called 'rising in the world', – when Mr. Whitley Stokes, in his edition of *Cormac's Glossary*, holds up the Irish word *tríath*, the sea, and makes us remark that, though the names *Triton*,

Amphitrite, and those of corresponding Indian and Zend divinities, point to the meaning *sea,* yet it is only Irish which actually supplies the vocable, how delightfully that brings Ireland into the Indo-European concert![18]

It is a pity that the proponents of Practical Criticism shunned the examination of such prose passages as this, for the very shape of the sentences is instinct with subliminal meanings – consider how the regret at Stokes's purely useful exile in India, followed by the allusion to French authority, postpones and then sanctions the bringing of Ireland into the concert; and consider how gracefully 'concert' serves to indicate and conceal what modes of incorporation are ultimately invoked.

Though Arnold emphasizes what he regards as the Celtic element in English literature, and reveres the sanctity and poetry of the Celtic genius, it goes without saying that his assumed norm is industrial, nineteenth-century England. This may seem paradoxical in the author of *Culture and Anarchy,* the apostle of European culture to a philistine people, but the comparative study of Celt and Saxon obliges him to take up a distinct position. The 'steady-going habit' of the Saxon leads up at last 'to the comprehension and interpretation of the world', a world fortunately supplied with 'doors that open, windows that shut, locks that turn, razors that shave, coats that wear, watches that go, and a thousand more such good things . . . the invention of the Philistines'.[19] Flippancy cannot be dismissed as irrelevance, and the drift of Arnold's totting-up of the comprehended world is that it is the world of commodities, all that the Celt has been blessedly unable to master. Thus Celticism serves not only to impose a certain identity on the Irish who are seen entirely outside history and outside any rudimentary sociology, it also serves to legitimize the activities of British industrial capitalism in the world. Far from being the soul of national resistance Celticism, as Arnold presents it, is a consolation, anodyne, or opium.

STANDISH O'GRADY

One of the irritating and yet instructive features of Irish cultural life in the nineteenth century is the proliferation of similar or identical names among different individuals. Savants are irritated by the outsider's confusion of George Thomas Stokes (author of *Ireland and the Celtic Church*) and Whitley Stokes (co-editor of *Thesaurus Paleohibernicus*), or the fusion of Standish Hayes O'Grady (1832 – 1915) and Standish James O'Grady (1846 – 1928). Outsiders, on the other hand, are more likely to inquire as to the significance of this repetitious pattern. More closely defined, the area involved was the Protestant gentry and professional middle class, a small and energetic aspect of Irish society. It is easy to accept the elevated and self-referring memoirs of members of this élite at face value, but Victorian Ireland was in practice a more various and complex society than is often admitted. Reiterated names indicated a desire to confirm identity and demonstrate continuity, just as the acquisition of property and a country 'place' enacted the need for security. In the aftermath of the Famine, and the Encumbered Estates Court sales of property, William Wilde built a villa on the shores of Lough Corrib, and named it *Moytura* after the legendary battle of the gods and aboriginal Irish. He and his wife christened their famous son, Oscar Fingall O'Flahertie Wills Wilde.

When Lord Chancellor Fitzgibbon and Dr Patrick Duigenan conducted their visitation in Trinity College early in 1798, the central figure in their investigation was Whitley Stokes (1763 – 1845), then a fellow of the college attached to the medical school. Stokes had been friendly with members of the United Irishmen, including Wolfe Tone, and was suspended from his fellowship for two years. Whether or not Lever had Stokes in mind as he wrote in *Luttrell of Arran* of subversion and discrimination in 'the Irish university' is an unanswerable question, but by the time the novel was published the Stokes family — like the fictional Luttrells — were looking towards the west of Ireland for mental sustenance. William Wilde led a party from the British Association to the Aran Islands in 1857 which included Samuel Ferguson, George Petrie, and William Stokes, son of the suspect United Irishman. While Lever's novel contributes to one transformation of the United Irishmen in the Victorian imagination by inserting an aristocratic participation in his fictionalizing of the movement, the descendants of those essentially middle-class radicals were channelling their disaffection with the Union into antiquarianism. William Stokes of 1857 was by profession a medical man and his antiquarian interests were those of a gifted amateur; his son, Whitley Stokes (1830 – 1909), completed the transformation in classic style by combining a career in the Indian civil service with a brilliant scholarly achievement as Celticist. Practical orientalism and philological rigour come together in a paradigm of 'patriotism without nationalism'.

It would be wrong to dismiss such patterns as simply the haphazard product of a small community. They are neither accidental at the social level nor deliberate at the biographical level. Instead they should be seen as visible features of a largely concealed totality in which the broader activities of the United Kingdom of Great Britain and Ireland take place. One insistent advocate of this latter point of view was Standish James O'Grady who — it must be conceded — was as much victim as author of the politics he espoused. Here again, the duplicity of names is symptomatic — while

Standish O'Grady (as I shall call him exclusively) was a historical explorer, novelist, and political propagandist, his cousin Standish Hayes O'Grady was a meticulous Celticist, editor of *Silva Gadelica* (2 vols., 1892). In the O'Gradys the immaculate non-politics of Celticism sets off its opposite like the distant explosion caused by a serene grenadier.

Standish O'Grady (1846 – 1928) was born in County Cork, at Castletown Berehaven. His father, Viscount Guillamore, was rector there, but the boy's education at the local school and Tipperary Grammar School, followed by Trinity College, Dublin and the Irish bar, was not the usual course for one of his class. In 1899 he recorded a more pertinent educational experience:

> I think I was in my 24th year when something happened which has since then governed the general trend of my life, and through me that of others. In a country house in the west of Ireland, near the sea, I had to stay indoors one rainy day, and though my appetite for literature was slender enough then, in default of other amusements I spent the time in looking over the books in the library. So I chanced upon O'Halloran's History of Ireland, in three volumes — the first History of Ireland into which I had ever looked. He wrote, I think, in the second decade of this century and before the rise of the Vallency School.[20]

Although the material is obscure to most readers, here is a dramatic conflict between the significance of form and that of content. Psychologically, the passage conforms to many of the conventions of the evangelical testimony — the inauspicious occasion, previous ignorance, the chanced-upon all-changing text. Such considerations might prompt some comment as to why the Anglo-Irish Revival was called a 'revival' — is it not in several of its personalities (Yeats, Synge, and O'Grady himself, and in a varied form, Lady Gregory) the achievement of displaced Irish evangelicals? Certainly, on the basis of the passage quoted, O'Grady is likely to fare better in a discussion of formal rhetoric than of intellectual content for his remarks on Sylvester O'Halloran and Charles Vallancy are a tissue of impossible dates.[21]

Fired by his reading of O'Halloran, and later of Eugene O'Curry, O'Grady became a Victorian sage. Carlyle and Marx featured in his reading as diversely as polemic, fiction, history, and journalism featured in his writing. It is easier to classify his work without regard to genre, and then subsequently to consider his drastic demolition of generic distinctions in the light of his outlook. First, O'Grady became preoccupied with early Irish history and epical material: in this area he wrote what purported to be histories as well as ostensibly fictional material set in this historical setting. Second — and this is not a chronological list of O'Grady's works — there are his various writings on Elizabethan Ireland, including his edition of *Pacata Hibernica*, a contemporary account of the war in Munster. Finally, there are his polemical works commencing with *The Crisis in Ireland* (1882) and including the editing of *The Kilkenny Moderator* and the *All Ireland Review*.

O'Grady has been called the father of the Anglo-Irish revival, and in this regard his versions of the Cuchulain epic have a historical importance in their influence upon Lady Gregory and hence on W. B. Yeats.[22] His writings on Elizabethan Ireland are extensively cast in stories and novels of an adventurous kind, principally intended for a juvenile readership. But the distinctions between history and fiction are jeopardized in the telling inscriptions O'Grady regularly added to presentation copies of his books. *Red Hugh's Captivity* (1889) is described in its subtitle as 'A Picture of Ireland, Social and Political in the Reign of Queen Elizabeth', but an inscription added by O'Grady on the copy he gave to John Quinn reads 'This book is history very slightly dramatized and historical fiction', a remark which can hardly have guided the recipient excessively. On the other hand, *The Bog of Stars* (1893) is annotated by the author 'All the tales . . . may be read as History except the first . . .'. Or again, *The Story of Ireland*:

> I wrote this outline of Irish history rapidly in less than a month; looking up no authority during its composition except for the Battle of the Boyne. I wrote it thinking that the things I remembered because I felt an interest in them, might be interesting to the reader.[23]

This is hardly encouraging to those who are in search of a literary history in which some kind of methodological procedure will be maintained. And yet O'Grady, for all his slipshod enthusiasm and missionary heat, is a useful indicator of the interactions of Ascendancy and Celticism in the last quarter of the nineteenth century.

'The things I remembered because I felt an interest in them, might be interesting to the reader . . .'. True it is merely an annotation hastily scribbled perhaps as he posted the book to John Quinn in America. Nevertheless, it implies a greater importance lying in the subjective consideration of material than in the material *per se*: clearly O'Grady as historian has no truck with the von Ranke school of documented fact. In a further annotation on a copy of *In the Gates of the North* (1901), O'Grady comments: 'As to the manner of composition — I read all the old stories of Cuculain that I could find and the tale found here just *emerged* out of the consequent memories and meditations'.[24] (Original emphasis.) No historical writing of any worth descends direct from the facts in a simple and wholly straightforward manner — so much may be agreed. But O'Grady's recurrent emphasis on the emergence of his writing 'out of the consequent memories and meditations' which follow his encounter with the latter-day evidences of history should be distinguished from any dialectical notion of history as mediation. As the passage recording his first discovery of Irish history (or was it literature? he is unsure.) O'Grady's *forte* is a kind of style. He admires the heroic gesture of Cuchulain, and is uninterested in the distinction between myth and chronicle. The validity of words is established by the memories they evoke; time is essentially conceived as the barrier between inner and outer worlds rather than the index of change and process in an objective social existence.

A predictable assessment of Standish O'Grady is that, in attempting many things, he failed in all. As a scholar he is frankly incompetent; as a novelist, he is concerned only with rudimentary aspects of the form; as a political writer, he is intermittently loud and silent. A more telling analysis might suggest that O'Grady symbolized in an uncanny way an incompleteness of social character which is highly relevant to the consequences of the ideology of Protestant Ascendancy. The O'Gradys of Limerick (where the family originated) were emerging in the years from 1820 onwards as a politically powerful and active family.[25] His father having taken holy orders, Standish O'Grady grew up in Castletown Berehaven rectory at a time when the Church, as a profession and a source of income, was staggering away from the disaster of the Tithe War and staggering towards Disestablishment. The family's legal background in the late eighteenth century placed them above the level of corporation politics where Protestant Ascendancy first took root, but landlordism on a small scale combined with dependence on a clerical income in the nineteenth steered the O'Gradys (or at least this branch of them) precisely towards those areas of Irish society in which the metamorphoses of Protestant Ascendancy were to take place. With an irony I fear unconscious, O'Grady's political writings expose the pretensions of Protestant Ascendancy in late Victorian days while his researches into the past demonstrate the allurement of Celticism at its least rigorous. These alternating commitments in his work are as it were the rival identities between which he never ultimately chose, not out of weakness but out of an apprehension of their partial unreality. The Standish O'Grady we meet in Yeats's writings is largely a creation of the poet's, the poet having experienced a similar self-division but having also pressed it to the point of dramatic confrontation.

Absurdity is all too easy to find in O'Grady. Take the episode of his editing *The Kilkenny Moderator*: in 1898, O'Grady took control of this thoroughly obscure and undistinguishedly loyal newspaper at the behest of a local magnate, Otway Cuffe, heir to the earldom of Desart, and within months he had involved his patron and his paper in a tea-cup scandal touching upon two continents. At the height of the Boer War, O'Grady decided to recruit an embryonic army through whom Irish consciousness might assert itself. with the militia training to fight for the British in the Transvaal and an 'Irish Brigade' recruiting support for the Boers, O'Grady was obliged to look elsewhere for his recruits and lighted upon the Church Lads Brigade, the Boys' Brigade, and the local Foxhounds. So far, the business was merely pathetic, but when the Colonel of the Kilkenny Militia was discovered to have appropriated £6,000 from the Desart estate (of which he had been agent) local passions were raised. The Bishop of Ossory then invited the Colonel (in his official capacity) to address a review of the Church Lads Brigade, and O'Grady's newspaper intervened wrathfully:

> We are not at war with the Bishop but with the great and dominant social power in our midst, reaching up to the Throne and down to the smallest Kilkenny huxter, a power which has almost obliterated a sense of honour and public morality in the minds of a few and dulled and paralysed the conscience of the community . . .[26]

The great power was the Marquis of Ormonde who had indeed been recently visited by the future George V and his wife and was shortly to receive Edward VII and his queen. Not surprisingly libel writs were thick in the air. O'Grady had earlier accused the Marquis of neglecting important political interests, and the Church Lads Brigade provided a convenient but ludicrous focus for the quarrel. More coldly considered, however, the episode exposed the largely decorative nature of Irish class terminology and the futility of cultural enterprise within the preserves of what was assumed to be the Protestant Ascendancy. It was O'Grady, however, rather than the Marquis who represented the Ascendancy, and his class rather than any residual aristocracy which led the movement known as the Celtic Revival.

O'Grady's political writings *per se* commenced with *The Crisis in Ireland* (1882) in which he exhorted the landowners — or ex-landowners as they were soon to be — to take real heed of the existence and reality of the Land League and the epochal changes implied for Irish society. This was followed by *Toryism and the Tory Democracy* (1886) in which he took his lead from Randolph Churchill's perception of the conservatives' need to protect landlordism from a combination of capital and labour: this extended pamphlet is classically evangelical in its approach, addressing Irish landlords first as a group and then singling out one nameless representative who is earnestly exhorted to take up his cross. The third political booklet, *All Ireland* (1898), deals with the revelations of the Childers Commission, a governmental body whose report proved the over-taxing of Ireland under the Union by a gross amount. All three works, in common with the novels and the 'histories' are obsessed with the notion of leadership, a quality singularly absent in the Ireland O'Grady sees around him, where no one is willing to forgo simple pleasures in order to assume the role of national Messiah. Two subsidiary elements, however, are in truth of great significance — the first is O'Grady's recurrent attention to the condition of Irish aristocracy, and the second is his recurring metaphor of illusion.

In his introduction to *Pacata Hibernica* (1896) he condemned as doubly false 'Mr Froude's picture of the upright, God-fearing, and civilized Englishman contending against a flood of Celtic barbarism' in the Tudor period.[27] The Celtic element, identified here with the Irish population as a whole, is seen as elevated, civilized, and yet demotic. And when he is seeking to explain the condition of Ireland under the Union, he alludes to 'The Stupefaction of the Ultonians', one of his favourite episodes from primitive literature in which a great enchantment is at work:

> The political understanding of Ireland to-day is under a spell and its will paralysed. If proof be demanded for this startling assertion, how can proof to any good result be supplied? It is the same spellbound understanding which will consider the proof.[28]

The imagery of spells, enchantments, and phantoms pervades the entire work, and the operations of ideology are well described in such terms:

> We worship phantoms, and phantoms powerless *per se* once worshipped — so they tell me — become endowed with a terrible and malignant vitality and activity . . . Heavy as lead, cold as death, the Great Enchantment obsesses the soul of the land, and not one but all classes lie supine under its sway — supine under the fanning of gigantic wings.
>
> It covers the whole land, every class and order of men in this Island are held inescapably in the grip of that dead hand. With such a document in our possession as the Report of the Childers Commission, with such a preponderating political power as ours, and with such hosts of good British friends, why can we do nothing? — strengthless, purposeless and resourceless, as were the Ultonians sunk under the curse of the great mother and queen whom they had outraged, drowned in the avenging tides of that fountain of their life which they had polluted.[29]

Paralysis and pollution are metaphors which will reappear in more familiar contexts in Joyce's *Dubliners* and Yeats's *Purgatory* — here at least their political sense is inescapable. Politics, in such a condition as he sees Ireland, is described by O'Grady in two further metaphors emphasizing the partly apprehended nature of reality — Ireland is confronted by 'the Veiled Player', or her cards are in the hands of 'the Unknown Dealer'. The implication O'Grady obsessively strives to convey is the hidden or but partly known

nature of that which confronts him. The spells and enchantments which
have woven this condition are located, he claims, in the imperial parliament,
'that seemingly august yet really absurd assembly'. Parliament is the forum
of class conflict, says O'Grady anticipating Carl Schmitt, and class conflict
detracts from the national unity which is required in the crisis. Yet, this
contempt for class politics is followed immediately by the most passionate
outburst of the essay in which a specific class is denounced at length:

> Aristocracies come and go like the waves of the sea; and some fall nobly and
> others ignobly. As I write, this Protestant Anglo-Irish aristocracy which, once
> owned all Ireland from the centre to the sea, is rotting from the land in the
> most dismal farce-tragedy of all time, without one brave deed, one brave word.
> Our last Irish aristocracy was Catholic, intensely and fanatically Royalist and
> Cavalier, and compounded of elements which were Norman-Irish and Milesian-
> Irish . . . Who laments the destruction of our present Anglo-Irish aristocracy?
> Perhaps in Ireland not one. They fall from the land while innumerable eyes
> are dry, and their fall will not be bewailed in one piteous dirge or one mourn-
> ful melody.[30]

The meaning of ascendancy implies the inevitability of a fall, just as it had
arisen like a star in the astrological charts. O'Grady's bitter condemnation
of the Protestant Anglo-Irish aristocracy is remarkable in its total avoidance
of the term Protestant Ascendancy, and its sarcastic insistence on the
aristocratic status of the useless class under pressure. It remained to Yeats
in particular to provide a suitable dirge and melody for the fall of the Protestant Ascendancy. Ernest Boyd characterized O'Grady's politics as a
'detestation of triumphant commercialism'.[31] His separatism is based on a
rejection of middle-class hegemony in the Union, and that founded on the
notion that no such hegemony operated in Irish society. Given the evidence
of the rich shopkeeper sailing at Kingstown while his son hunts with a
fashionable pack, 'the brewer and distiller, the successful manufacturer and
contractor, the stock-broker', such a notion is at least unstable.[32] And at this
point, the operations of Celticism once again become evident, not as the
regalia of anti-imperialism but as the milesian source of an unassailable
aristocracy, unassailable because enchantingly unreal. In George Bernard
Shaw's *Man and Superman* (1903) Don Juan observes that 'nothing is real
here. That is the horror of damnation.'[33] It would be rash to interpret Shaw
as intending an *exposé* of colonialism with its elaborate simulacrum of a
metropolitan society, its theatrical representations — in Arnold's term —
its concert. It would be rash so to interpret Shaw, and yet he allows us to
recall that curiously unnecessary image in Renan's essay on Celtic poetry
in which he compares entrance into Brittany or Ireland to 'the impression
given us by Dante, when he leads us from one circle of his Inferno to

another'.[34] Truly it is Yeats's *Purgatory* which alone can rid us of such hellish notions.

Why should a play perform this rescue operation or emancipatory task? Is it not more proper to look to philosophical, political, or critical work for relief? If, as Aijaz Ahmad cogently argues in a sensitive and yet rigorous chapter, the principal popular theoretician of post-colonial discourse is more in debt to Nietzsche than has been admitted, then the assistance available may turn out to be oddly elusive. For, according to this argument, Edward Said's insight into the colonial condition and post-colonial potentiality is itself limited by his implicit denial of historical knowledge and his tacit admission that 'representation is always-already a misrepresentation'.[35] Lukács' notions of art are less handicapped in their ability to prompt critical knowledge of their own genesis and value. Against this, it has been argued often that Lukács emphasis on the unconscious truthfulness of a Balzac or Scott is really a form of idealism, not very different from the romantic notion of transcendent genius.

In Said's defence, it might be said that *Orientalism* continues to be a useful work precisely because it mobilizes a great mass of factual information, and additionally because it is written by one who apprciates the worth of artistic form. Unfortunately, Said's Irish followers do not read enough beyond *Orientalism*, especially neglecting the animadversions on fashion in theory. And his role as an activist in Palestinian politics has all too readily encouraged a return to nationalism among Irish commentators who once scorned such atavism. Meanwhile, if the play's the thing, which play might perform the reflexive role assigned to it in critical modernism? And if there is a transcendent genius in the field we are exploring, what kind of unconscious truth about his or her society might be detected?

II ART AS PRAXIS IN *THE WELL OF THE SAINTS* (1905)

Among the plays of J. M. Synge, *The Playboy of the Western World* occupies an unassailable pre-eminence. Some of the reasons for this are well established – its energy and diversity, its treatment of romantic love, its eloquence. There are other factors less openly at work in promoting *The Playboy* – for example, an undercurrent of concentrated realism operating in harmony with the play's allusive breadth. Its reputation has of course gone through numerous phases, with the riots of 1907 providing the basis for altered perception and response. Yeats's propagandistic conversion of the dead Synge into 'a peasant playwright' constituted only one permutation within the range of possibilities opened up by the riots. Until the Lantern

Theatre productions by Liam Miller in the 1960s, the harsh irony which
informs Synge's masterpiece seems to have been sedulously avoided – lest
the riots break out all over again. Perhaps an unacknowledged motive in
the Irish public's sustained admiration of *The Playboy* is a collective need
to avoid any suggestion of riotous condemnation. In that sense, it is Synge's
most public play, a text embraced by the Irish people lest it escape their
control.

Synge's drama is replete with temptations. The early plays' localized settings faithfully reflect the notion of pastoral Ireland advanced by the
nineteenth-century movement for land reform and home rule, but their plots
threaten to desecrate the holy ground by introducing evidence of deviant
sexuality – near-incest, pre-marital experience, adultery transcending class
boundaries. Nor does Synge conceal the hardship imposed by locale upon
human frailty. The Abbey audiences were lured by the possibility of their
petit bourgeois dreams achieving representation through the highest cultural
medium, and simultaneously repelled by the recognition of their own latent
unconformity.

Even the sublime one-act tragedy of island life – *Riders to the Sea* (1904)
– jeopardizes its promise of stoic dignity when Maurya's great final speech
is interrupted by her neighbours' banal insistence that she has forgotten the
nails. Without these, no coffin can be made, no death can be absorbed
decently into the community of the living. The missing nails raise issues
of acquisition and purchase articulated poignantly earlier in the play. From
the remnants of clothing forwarded to Maurya's household, the absent body
of a drowned seaman could not be identified as her son's. 'It's the same
stuff, Nora; but if it is itself aren't there great rolls of it in the shops of
Galway, and isn't it many another man may have a shirt of it as well as
Michael himself?'[36] The discovery of mass-produced goods and travelling
salesmen in the background of Synge's peasant drama should not surprise
anyone who knows more about peasants than Yeats in this connection
pretended to.

Despite the richness of *The Playboy* and the ironic sublimity of *Riders
to the Sea*, it may yet emerge that neither is properly central to the achievement of J. M. Synge. Such a judgement will turn upon the issue of defining
Synge, of placing him in relation not only to audience and source, literary
context and style of production, but also in relation to matters once larger
and microscopic. Where does Synge himself stand within the hectic political
and social debates of the period in which he worked? Where does he stand
– where does his notion of self appear – in the calculus of privacy/
publicity?

A LINE OF ACTION

Given the brevity of his career as a dramatist, there has been an understandable tendency to treat the plays as a developing sequence from the stark simplicity of the one-acters to the brocaded mythic density of the unfinished *Deirdre of the Sorrows*. In this progression, *The Well of the Saints* (1905) appears to occupy a crucial position, sharing both the rural location of the former and the remote historical setting of the last. Leaving aside *Deirdre* the plays can however be classified along a different axis. *Riders to the Sea* and *The Playboy* constitute a western (or Atlantic) group, to be associated with Synge's prose masterpiece, *The Aran Islands* (1907). A complementary group (beginning with a play never satisfactorily completed, *When the Moon Has Set*) includes *In the Shadow of the Glen* and *The Tinkers' Wedding*: to this eastern (or Wicklow) group it seems natural to assign *The Well of the Saints*.[37]

The opening stage directions surely confirm this analysis, when they refer to 'some lonely mountainous district on the east of Ireland'. But just as the temporal setting – 'one or more centuries ago' – creates more problems than it solves, so the curiously non-idiomatic phrase, 'on the east of Ireland', draws attention to an imprecision. The dramatist who went through seventeen drafts of a single act of *The Playboy* was unlikely to have casually committed a solecism in introducing his most intellectually coherent play. For such *The Well of the Saints* undoubtedly is, with its delicately modulated dramatizing of imaginative vision and its characters' eloquent defence of artistic freedom:

> for if it's a right some of you have to be working and sweating the like of Timmy the smith, and a right some of you have to be fasting and praying and talking holy talk the like of yourself, I'm thinking it's a good right ourselves have to be sitting blind, hearing a soft wind turning round the little leaves of the spring and feeling the sun, and we not tormenting our souls with the sight of the grey days, and the holy men, and the dirty feet is trampling the world.[38]

The characters are road-side beggars. If they had had their sight, or had avoided virtual enslavement to Timmy the smith when they briefly repossessed their sight, they would have been tramps. Martin Doul (*dall* = Gaelic for blind) climactically stigmatizes those who see and sweat with the trampling of nature under foot, and so plays upon his own deprived exemption from two kinds of tramp(l)ing. In a very different idiom, one can read Martin's declaration as an assertion of privacy over engagement in a debased public world which knows labour only as a means of participation.

But Synge's dramatic idiom is less crude, less assertively philosophical. Word-play is pervasive in *The Well of the Saints*, to a degree which encourages no casual assimilation of a location 'on the east of Ireland'.

These words only make sense as one term within a polarity. Within the land mass, the east of Ireland relates in a complementary fashion to the west. It is true that 'the west of Ireland' does possess a high degree of idiomatic familiarity, and may even lend a kind of temporary authority to the other term. But the preposition 'on' has displaced the more likely 'in', and in do-ing so introduces a second polarity – that of location inside/outside the land mass. 'On the east of Ireland' implies a coastline, and with it a move-ment towards Ireland from some external point of perspective or reference. The setting of the play can be imaginatively described therefore as marginal, on but not of its location, residually conscious of a seaboard by which it has been reached.

All of this grammatical fuss is only justified because the more specific location officially declared in the play's title is never encountered therein. The saint who comes with miraculous powers to cure the blind beggars of 'a lonely mountainous district on the east of Ireland' is a tramp himself, one who has found his holy water elsewhere on his travels. Characteristically, Synge transmits this intelligence to the beggars through an intermediary:

> TIMMY.   Did ever you hear tell of a place across a bit of the sea, where there is an island, and the grave of the four beautiful saints?
>
> MARY DOUL.   I've heard people have walked round from the west and they speaking of that.
>
> TIMMY.   There's a green ferny well, I'm told behind of that place, and if you put a drop of the water out of it, on the eyes of a blind man, you'll make him see as well as any person is walking the world.[39]

The source of the saint's miraculous power constantly retreats before descrip-tion. It is an island, but one which can somehow be reached by those who 'have walked round' to that place. Yet the location is more specifically a well *behind* an island, or perhaps behind 'that place' where saints are buried. To specify is to acknowledge indefinability, to concede (if not to articulate) the inability of the word to eliminate a realm of alternate possibility. Thus, at a general level, one should note how this piece of dialogue – and indeed, Synge's *oeuvre* in its unfinished entirety – works to destroy any notion of language as a system of synonyms; there is no place which can be signified in different phrases. Or in one phrase either; the well of the saints remains permanently absent from the play it names. This sophisticated apprehen-sion of dramatic language has its theoretical counterpart in the lectures delivered in Paris by Ferdinand de Saussure from 1907 onwards. Published posthumously by students, Saussure's *Cours de linguistique générale* should remind us of the debt Synge owed to the French intellectual tradition.[40]

More particularly, Synge had attended lectures on Celtic philology at the Sorbonne in 1898, and had published occasional reviews and articles on related topics.[41] His philosophical reading was eclectic, and the Yeatsian reduction of Synge to native genius travesties the man's deliberate and conscientious study of Marx, Herbert Spencer, Nietzsche and others. If Synge is anti-philosophical in his drama, this attitude is grounded in a knowledge of and respect for philosophy. *The Well of the Saints* touches on more than the philological aspect of Celticism or the potential of the new linguistics to illuminate the dynamics of literary style. The generalized setting in a 'lonely mountainous district on the east of Ireland, one or more centuries ago' is given further point in the stage directions prefacing the first act; these curtly specify the 'ruined doorway of church with bushes beside it'. The opening of the second act sardonically reworks this setting, for the audience sees. Martin Doul now against the background of a village forge, more precisely 'the door of a forge', with 'a well near centre with board over it'.[42] Through the replication of a door, the ruined church has been displaced by a place of labour loud with Timmy's hammering offstage: the source of miracles which cannot be realized on stage is now doubled by a well where water is drawn for the villagers' day-to-day needs.

The ruined church and its doorway are familiar details from the iconography of nineteenth-century idealizations of the Celtic past. The Romanesque architecture of monasteries such as Glendalough and Clonmacnois provided images of desolation and survival for the cultural manifestos of Young Ireland and its successors. In the Christmas 1879 issue of the *Weekly News*, the distinctively Irish round tower is swaddled in the Stars and Stripes, suggesting a fallen Celtic past redeemed in an Irish-American future. The same national emblem features in contrasting ways in *John Bull's Other Island*, George Bernard Shaw's dramatization of Edwardian Ireland, and in the Cyclops episode of James Joyce's *Ulysses*, retrospectively set in the same period. But Synge's Celtic-Romanesque is ironic in a manner quite different from the inversions of Shavian comedy and the grosser comedy of Joyce's pastiche. And central to the achievement of this personal irony is the uncertainty of 'one or more centuries ago'. Is *The Well of the Saints* set in Celtic Ireland or in Celticist Ireland? If the former, then the saint might be seen as a Christian invader, a bringer of the gospel to the benighted heathen. If the latter, then he may be little more than an itinerant and ignorant preacher, a montebank, or – as the last act strongly suggests – a bully of very limited resources. The play, for obvious dramatic reasons, declines to specify any fixed period for its setting.

Among Synge's sources for the play were a fifteenth-century French farce about Saint Martin and a piece of folklore associated with the Aran Islands.[43] Though the second of these is the more familiar, we should not neglect the force of the other. Saint Martin is replaced by a character who is no saint and a saint who is not Martin. Saint Martin's charity towards the poor was presented as a model of Christian identification, but Synge's characters veer off sharply from any suggestion of consensus or fellow-feeling. So with the doubled sources of the play. The disparity of the two mirrors the refusal of the play to declare itself ancient or modern. This in turn recalls the manner in which the well in question is both distant and close to hand, accessible over water or by walking. In short, Synge retains the western (Aran Islands) source for the play when Timmy the smith reports on the grave of the four beautiful saints while officially locating the action 'on the east of Ireland'. Timmy's direct reference to the province of Leinster is only one of an intricate pattern of place-names occurring in the first act and, while the saint himself gives a brief account of his journey from 'Cashla Bay', earlier drafts had included a more detailed itinerary.[44]

These place-names deserve closer scrutiny. Initially let us list them alphabetically, omitting only two items – Ireland, which occurs several times as the broadest term of reference, and Leinster (one occurrence only) which is just a moderately reduced version of the same broad context. The following statistics emerge:

	OCCURRENCES IN		
PLACE-NAME	Act I	Act II	Act III
Annagolan	1		
Ballinatone	2		
Cahir Iveraghig		2	
Cashla Bay	1		
Clash	3		
Glenassil	1		
Grianan	2	3	1
Laragh	1		
Rathvanna		1	
Reeks of Cork		2	

In formal terms, one notes the progressive disappearance of specified place-names as in the three successive acts. However, this pattern should not be taken simply as resulting from the play's initial need to inform the audience of its setting and a subsequent reliance on their memory of these details. Other patterns emerge, with their few exceptions. Most of these names, with slight modifications of spelling, can be found on a large-scale map of a single district. The exceptions should be cleared up before that map is scrutinized. According to a rough final typescript of the play, however, Cashla Bay is 'Casilagh Bay' from where the saint's journey has taken him 'beyond the Corrib into Athenry'. These references to well-known County Galway place-names unambiguously establishes a western source of the miraculous water, though the saint's incursionary relationship to the land is also maintained. Two other names in the play – Cahir Iveraghig (variously spelled) and the Reeks of Cork – can be loosely associated with Munster, and this is quite in keeping with Martin Doul's citation of them as remote and sunny places, quite different from the locale in which he lives.[45]

The map is now in front of us. The remaining seven names can be divided into two groups. Clash, Ballinatone, and Grianan constitute the first, with Annagolan, Glenassil, Laragh and Rathvanna making up the second. The first three names relate to one back-road in County Wicklow, running from the village of Ballinaclash, past the church at Ballinatone, to the bridge at Greenan – a distance of 2.4 miles. In keeping with local practice, the first name is abbreviated to produce 'Clash', which in the play neatly conveys the antagonism implicit between the blind beggars and the sighted community. The third is consistently spelled in its Gaelic form, which underlines the name's derivation from *griain* (= the sun), a usage which echoes the ecstatic invocations with which Synge's unfinished autobiographical play concludes.[46] Ballinatone is assimilated without any modification. These three constitute what I will call the principal *line of action* in the play.

The four other names lie further off. Annagolan is consistently rendered in the typescripts as Annamoe, actual but quite different places in County Wicklow. The change has the effect of drawing this casual reference closer to the topographical line of action. For, while Annagolan is a townland in the uplands parish of Derrylossary, Annamoe is a village lying in the valley immediately to the east of Greenan. (Greenan to Annamoe is 10.4 miles by road, though a route across the open hills would be shorter.) Laragh is just a short distance away in the same valley – 7.6 miles from Greenan – while Glenassil (not an actual name) might be identified with Glenmacnass (the glen of the waterfall) which is well up-river from Laragh.

That leaves Rathvanna for placement, a name not to be found on the map of Wicklow. It ostentatiously resembles Aghavannagh, a high remote area lying well to the south-west of the line of action, though Conavalla (a mountain to the north at the head of Glenmalure, the latter 7.1 miles from Greenan) might also be noted. A map-name closer to Synge's Rathvanna is Raheenavine (pronounced locally Rannavine) which, according to the great John O'Donovan, is in Gaelic *Raithín na bhfian*, or 'the small fort of the Fianna.'[47] Raheenavine lies south of Ballinaclash, just to the east of the straight road to Aughrim. And Aughrim deserves mention because it appears in drafts of *The Well of the Saints*.

Readers will be more familiar with the place of the same name near Ballinasloe in County Galway; in the Battle of Aughrim in 1691 a Jacobite army was heavily defeated there. To distinguish itself, Eachdhruim uí Bhroinn, in Wicklow, takes its full name from the local family uí Broinn or (in English) Byrne. Thus an unstated link exists between the suppressed place-name Aughrim in Synge's play and the one character who bears a modern surname (Molly Byrne). Mediating between these microscopic nominal details is the Battle of Aughrim (fought in the west, not too far from Athenry) which inaugurated the modern Ireland Yeats celebrates as a product of ascendancy cruelty. Certainly, the transfer of miraculous cures from Galway to Wicklow, and the preservation of the awkward locution 'on the east of Ireland', is central to the absence of a source in the play for its title.

Nicholas Grene, who (like the present writer) acquired part of his early education in Ballinatone, has drawn up an excellent diagram to illustrate what he rightly terms the psychic dynamics of *The Well of the Saints*.[48] The present inquiry might be said to concentrate instead on *statics* if, by that term, something other than a pejorative judgement can be registered. Social scientists have employed the word to indicate informally a theory of consensus (J. S. Mill) or the study of the effects caused by particular small-scale changes rather than by change generally within a system (J. M. Keynes). Here statics is employed in a heuristic fashion, to study the action of forces in the play inducing equilibrium or relative rest. Names, as I will argue, constitute one such static force.

None of this should be taken as denying that the dramatic merits of the play are very substantial. But in contrasting it to the exuberance of *The Playboy* one could have cited the playwright's own account of his determination to reduce variety by emphasizing a monochrome quality – 'all in shades of one colour'.[49] The extensive use made of place-names is not dramatic in any conventional sense, though the alteration to Ballinatone in Mary Doul's first reference to the place avoided the less euphonious Ballynahinch. Saddlemyer notes a progression in Synge's revision of this speech – from 'below in the west', through 'Ballynahinch' etc. to the final Ballinatone. She says of this that 'Synge gradually becomes more specific', though quite how

Ballinatone can be more specific than Ballynahinch is unclear. The significance of the change lies elsewhere and, as with the location of the well of the play's title, that significance is not specified.[50]

A concerted orientation of the play's implied location on a single line of action is effected by the recurrence of (Ballina)clash, Ballinatone, and Grianan (Greenan), which account in all for eleven of the fifteen occasions on which a Wicklow place-name is used. Moreover, the last of the three (Grianan) is the only place-name to survive in the final act where Martin and Mary determine to leave the seeing community and head south, even though the hardship involved is spelled out. Dramatically, the beggars will turn their back on the place of the sun – and yet head south – and this anti-heliotropism is the largest indication of their embraced blindness. On the map, the line of action had lead northwards into an area of considerable settlement by Protestants, culminating in the Kemmis estate, the gates of which are visible from the Ballinatone side of Greenan bridge. William Kemmis (1777-1864), who had been crown solicitor for Leinster, was 'high Orange' in Daniel O'Connell's estimate, and his legacy lived on.[51] Many of these settlers were, in the late nineteenth century, small farmers; some were the descendants of people who had fled from Wexford in 1798. To serve their spiritual needs, the Church of Ireland had erected a new church and primary school at Ballinatone in 1838.

VANISHING MEDIATORS

Among those buried in the graveyard is the 'original' for Timmy the smith: James Smith, who worked the forge at Ballinaclash and thus enacted the name he bore, was born in 1874, just three years Synge's junior. Though the search for 'originals' is fraught with temptation, the case of Jim Smith (as he was known) may be exceptional in several regards. The identity of name and trade facilitates the near-exclusion of surnames from the dramatis personae of *The Well of the Saints*. It also dually may suggest (if only to the author) the play's pre-modern setting, when such trade-names were coming into use, and its composition in an age of divided labour. Moreover, Tim (as he was called in the first draft[52]) plays a central, even controlling role in the action, replicating in the desacralized world the saint's role as a bringer of miraculous cures. Thus, Timmy acts as herald of the good news in Act I, announcing the arrival of the saint in the district, and introducing the blind beggars to him. In the second, he is the unsympathetic employer of Martin Doul, now recovered of his sight and so obliged to work for his living. The final scene has Timmy ready to marry Molly Byrne, a happy

situation from which he is able to offer to intervene with the saint for a repetition of his 'miracle', which had temporarily restored the sight of the beggars. Ultimately, he predicts their near-certain death just after they have
quit the stage on their blind journey southwards. Within the action, Timmy
the smith acts as a kind of stage-director, or surrogate dramatist. He stands
alone between the blind man and the saint, or virtually so, to negotiate the
interactions of bodily and spiritual decrepitude.[53] It would be grossly
reductive to see Timmy as Synge's spokesman in the play, and yet some
attention should be paid to the closeness in age between the dramatist and
Timmy's original and to their sharing a confessional background in the
Church of Ireland. Just as Synge is a vanishing mediator in the play, so James
Smith contributes by the absence of his latter-day affiliation.

In changing Ballynahinch for Ballinatone, then, Synge did more than confirm an eastern location for the play. According to the saint, the miraculous
water comes from the vicinity of a 'bare starving rock' where is 'the grave
of the four beauties of God'. These four are, so to speak through translation
of implied Gaelic, four beautiful people; and indeed in Aran is a place called
Ceathrar Ailinn. In the first book of *The Aran Islands*, Synge recorded how,
he turned off a road 'to look at an old ruined church of the Ceathair Aluinn
(The Four Beautiful Persons), and a holy well near it that is famous for cures
of blindness and epilepsy'.[54] Confirmation of a western source could hardly be more emphatic. Yet, within *The Well of the Saints*, it is Mary Doul
rather than the saint who is most closely associated with such imagery. For,
as she declares (and as her husband confirms), 'it was "the beautiful dark
woman", they did call me in Ballinatone.' (Or, in Martin's words, 'I am
wedded with the beautiful dark woman of Ballinatone.'[55]) On the two occasions when that place-name is invoked, Mary's publicly acknowledged
status as a beautiful person is re-affirmed. Of course, in cosmetic terms,
Mary will be revealed as less than beautiful, but the lexical pattern of the
text insists on re-assigning the idea of personal beauty to Ballinatone, and
with personal beauty spiritual beauty is implied also. Given that the only
church on the line of action was that of the Church of Ireland, we can see
further confirmation of the transformation of Ceathair Aluinn into
Ballinatone.

The action of the play can now be appreciated in larger terms than those
simply of onomastics. The ancient Celtic church is implicitly identified with
the latter-day Church of Ireland, while the actual (and recently constructed)
church at Ballinatone is replaced in the play by a ruined doorway. This two-
way transaction implicates major themes of nineteenth-century historiography
and cultural re-alignment. The claims of the Church of Ireland to be the

direct and legitimate successor to Saint Patrick's mission in the fifth cen-
tury had been extensively made in such Victorian works as Bishop Mant's
History of the Church of Ireland which found it possible to speak of a 'papal
usurpation in the twelfth century' breaking the continuity of the Established
Church with a proto-Protestantism in Glendalough and Ceathair Aluinn.
The Patrician tradition was claimed (by D. A. Beaufort) exclusively for the
Church of Ireland at least as early as 1788, and versions of it can be traced
back to earlier periods.[56] Nevertheless, as a major theme in Irish Protestant church history, Celticism is a Victorian phenomenon, one greatly
magnified by the shock of disestablishment in 1869. George Stokes's *Ireland
and the Celtic Church* (1886) appeared when Synge was fifteen, and he read
it during his last year as an undergraduate at Trinity College. Of the alternatives available to believing post-establishment members of the Church of
Ireland – Celticism and Evangelicalism – the former provided some opportunity for intellectual engagement. Synge's domestic background was
saturated in evangelical fervour, and his revolt against that inheritance played
an important part in his development as a person and as a playwright.[57]

Though he had been brought up from infancy to manhood in the Dublin
suburbs, his domestic background included strong associations with County Wicklow. Until 1890, it was his mother's practice to take her children
– she was a widow – to Greystones every summer, approving this resort
for its predominantly Protestant (and evangelical) ethos. About twelve miles
from the sea-side village stood Glanmore, a gothicized country house with
a small demesne attached, owned by a branch of the family which had taken
evangelicalism so far as to quit the Church of Ireland for the Plymouth
Brethren.[58] The loss of Glanmore from the possession of Synges wounded
the pride of some in the dramatist's immediate family, one of his brothers
regarding it as a personal mission to restore his people to a social eminence
which the progress of the nineteenth century had made utterly impossible.
Finally, other, more modest, Wicklow houses contributed to Synge's growing knowledge of rural Ireland: these were Castle Kevin and Tomriland
House, two solid residences which Mrs Kathleen Synge rented for holidays
in the early 1890s. Within sight of each other, they stood south of Derrylossary and east of Annamoe, on the desolate upland bog of central Wicklow.
These two houses, by their proximity to Annamoe, also stand off-stage of
The Well of the Saints.

The line of action in *The Well of the Saints* can thus be correlated to the
dramatist's own movements in a district where his family's fortunes had
markedly changed for the worse. The Clash-Greenan axis – if so crude a
term may be tolerated for a moment – relates to the several properties or

occasional residences of the Synges (Glanmore, Castle Kevin, Tomriland House) by intermediaries (Annamoe and Laragh) alluded to in the play as lying close to hand. In one sense – the Roman sense – the place-names essential to *The Well of the Saints* are *termini*: that is, markers of a frontier, border 'posts'. This frontier at once separates and correlates possession and non-possession – even property and propriety – on the one side. Dispossession and irregularity stand on the other. The frontier has a historical as well as a topographical position. Synge's nephew analysed the decline of the family from which he distanced himself:

> These people, who had lost much of their money and most of their libraries and learning, increased their class-consciousness in self-defence . . . Their emotions had suffered violence; their beliefs had become restrictive; if anyone among them chanced to inherit the genius of their race, he found himself unhonoured by his kin.[59]

It has not been fashionable to consider Edward Stephens's biographical reading of Synge's plays, and indeed his argument is strongly coloured by his own autobiographical proclivities. As with critics of *Ulysses* – another text with a problematic relation to its author's career in the world of telegrams and anger – those who insist on reading Synge's drama within a self-contained system are not immune to historical criticism.[60] The urge to relate myth and text in such a way as to use one as the confirming alibi of the other, and then to assign to each a self-delighting integrity, is perhaps more thoroughly a political interpretation than anything attempted by György Lukács. From the 1960s onwards, the mobilization of Synge as 'box-office' has required the studied repression, by his interpreters, of a static dimension through which uncomfortable and persistent ideological conflicts are discernible.

One of these can be pinpointed in the centrality of Ballinatone. By transposing terms from a ruined church-site on the Aran Islands to a nineteenth-century revivalist establishment church, Synge mimics a Celticist strategy which can be readily traced in the re-ordering of the Church of Ireland hymnal and the adoption of Romanesque features in a number of late-nineteenth-century Church buildings. The dramatis personae of *The Well of the Saints* signal no denominational affiliations – the setting of 'one or more centuries ago' tacitly allows for such evasion. But the transformation of the four beautiful persons into Mary Doul, 'the beautiful dark woman of Ballinatone', introduces a covert affiliation to the once-established church. The ruined condition of the doorway in Act One doubly signifies the ancient church of the Ceathrar Ailinn and the post-established church of Mrs Kathleen Synge.

Let us now reconstruct the full list of Wicklow place-names occurring in *The Well of the Saints*, in drafts for the play, including some names approximating to non-actual names used by Synge. To each of these is added a date in parentheses:

> Aghavannagh (1668)
> Annagolan (1660)
> Annamoe (1668)
> Aughrim (1569)
> Ballinaclash (1639)
> Ballinatone (1605)
> Ballymoney (1573)
> Conavalla (1617)
> Glenmacnass (1760)
> Greenan (1605)
> Laragh (1601)
> Raheenavine (1760)

These dates derive from Liam Price's directory of Wicklow place-names, and they represent the earliest occurrence of the name (in a form approximating to the present-day version) on a map, deed, survey or other documentation. They are of course English-language names, or rather Englished versions of names originally occurring in Gaelic. The maps, deeds etc. form part of an administration; they lie on one side of a demarcation both political and linguistic. Rather than see this phenomenon simply as damning evidence of colonialism, we should additionally see it as a negotiation between languages, even to some extent a compromise imposed by the defeated upon their aggressors. The place of Wicklow in the history of English rule in Ireland is highly anomalous. Though it lies immediately south of the capital city – Clash is just forty miles from Dublin by road – Wicklow was the last county to be formally established by the English administration, and as late as 1798 it was difficult, even impenetrable territory for government troops. In 1580, Fiach MacHugh O'Byrne defeated Lord Deputy Grey at the Battle of Glenmalure: more than two hundred years later, the Protestant rebel Joseph Holt set up camp in the Devil's Glen, close to Glanmore. In the latter connection, one should note that Synge considered the dramatic possibilities of Wicklow's stormy history, even going to the lengths of composing some dialogue between a 'protestant woman' and a 'papist woman' for a play about the 1798 rebellion.

In terms of language use, Wicklow has long been monoglot and Anglophone, and yet its speech is highly distinctive. Its place-names impose the essential Gaelic elements – Avon- (from *abhann*, a river), Bally- (from *baile*, a townland), Kil- (from *cill*, a church, or *coill*, a wood),

Glen- (from *gleann*, a Gaelic word borrowed into English generally). And so on. When Synge's drama invokes such names it also implicates a process of change and continuity; in these elements, and within so articulate a political consciousness as Wicklow's, history and location may be read as consubstantial. Historical action, of the kind Frank Fay sought from Synge in March 1904, was strictly unnecessary in a play like *The Well of the Saints* for place-name accommodates such grossly dramatic elements, and modulates conflict into formal discord, the 'monochrome' which Synge sought.[61] It is in this sense that one can speak of the play's statics – and intend a compliment or at least a tribute to its intellectual subtlety and play-full strength.

Matthew Arnold had aimed at a different kind of reconciliation in which the Irish were assigned an aesthetic role as distinct from a productive one, but a version of this programmatic Celticism can be detected in Synge's portrayal of the beggars momentarily incorporated as Timmy the smith's little work-force. When considering the initial location of the play, we noted how the setting can be imaginatively described as *marginal*, on but not of its location, *residually* conscious of a seaboard by which it has been reached. These are the attributes of the Celt in a sequence of 'Celticisms' which achieve mobilization in the nineteenth century. By the 1890s, 'Celtic' had become a trade-mark in Irish literary circles. Yet despite this later currency, Yeats's adopting the phrase 'Celtic Twilight' for his 1893 collection of tales had been and remained a strategic decision and not a declaration of identity. Metropolitan cultural values, and exotic themes culled from Indian literatures, theosophy, and Buddhism, were gradually discounted in favour of the west of Ireland, or village Ireland, or vestigial Ireland. That it was a strategic rather than an intrinsic aspect of his aesthetic project may be gauged by the adjective's failure to appear anywhere in his poetry and drama, that extensive and vibrant body of modernist writing in which Cuchulain and the Sidhe, Diarmuid and Gráinne, Deirdre and the Sons of Usneach act out their destinies in the twentieth century.

It is a presupposition of this literary Celticism that value is inherent in the residual and the marginal, and these combine to articulate precisely the kind of setting which Synge employs in *The Well of the Saints*. The residual relates to time and the usually incomplete surviving evidences of past entities – ruined doorway or broken cross. To Celticists of the broad church it will be familiar through the figure of the Dying Gaul; political scientists will recognize a latter-simulacrum in the Whingeing Bully, a notable player in Irish ideological affairs, especially in Ulster. In contrast to the residual, the notions of marginality and peripherality relate in quite specific ways to space. Together they form the axis of dramatic action, and it is no accident that the success of the Celtic Revival was achieved through the theatre.

Thus, *The Well of the Saints* is, at a deep level, a meditation on its own ideological origins and aesthetic credo. Its Celticism is an enabling ideology by means of which the dramatist reflects on the terms of his own survival.[62] The meditative aspect of Synge's imagination was acknowledged by Yeats in 'The Municipal Gallery Revisited', a poem which also invokes Antaeus to figure the paradoxical strength of a fallen ascendancy. In a stanza rare in Yeats's work for its breach of decorum in allowing the previous stanza to complete its sentence by taking up an opening line, he continued:

> John Synge, I and Augusta Gregory, thought
> All that we did, all that we said or sang
> Must come from contact with the soil, from that
> Contact everything Antaeus-like grew strong.
> We three alone in modern times had brought
> Everything down to that sole test again,
> Dream of the noble and the beggar-man.[63]

These seven lines of an eight-line stanza enact in their formal incompleteness the impossibility of equating a source of strength with its application. The elusiveness of the well in *The Well of the Saints* makes the point in a more honest manner, and disencumbers its beggars from any obligation to rub shoulders with a Yeatsian nobility. But it is Synge's use of sensory deprivation – the sightlessness of Martin and Mary – which provides a subtle response to the cultural *impasse* of the dispossessed minor landowners who came together in the Celtic Revival. The intensification of other faculties, resulting or at least following from the loss of one faculty (sight in the Douls' case) acts as a trope for the enlarged cultural claims of the politically marginalized gentry, saving them from mere bohemianism (George Moore and Synge in Paris) and from the puppetry of 'the coloniser who refuses' (Yeats in the IRB, or in his barrel-organ anti-English phase). It is not power in the Herculean or even Antaean sense which concerns Synge but influence. Yeats's preoccupation with strength, in contrast, declares itself in the elimination of precisely that middle-class condition (between the noble and beggar-man) into which minor landowners like his grandfather and Synge's had fallen. The politics of his preference for strength over influence ultimately finds expression in terms of fascism. At that point, Synge's role in opposition is taken up in their different ways by Samuel Beckett and Elizabeth Bowen. Their characterization will exploit sensual deprivation – even infantilism – as a mode of analysing the corrosive effect of an aesthetic based on the bodily integrity of a rubber-ball Antaeus.

NOTES AND REFERENCES

1   W. B. Yeats, 'Beautiful Lofty Things', *Collected Poems* (London: Macmillan, 1963), p. 348.
2   Edward W. Said, *Orientalism* (London: Routledge and Kegan Paul, 1978).
3   For Langbehn and the German strand of racist thought see George L. Mosse, *The Crisis of German Ideology: Intellectual Origins of the Third Reich* (London: Weidenfeld and Nicolson, 1970). Said deals quite extensively with Renan's orientalist preoccupations.
4   See in this connection Ceri Crossley, 'Edgar Quinet and Messianic Nationalism in the Years preceding 1848', in Francis Barker et al., eds., *1848: The Sociology of Literature* (Chelmsford: University of Essex, 1978), pp. 265-76.
5   Ernest Renan, *Poetry of the Celtic Races and Other Essays*, trans. W. G. Hutchinson (London, [1896], pp. 1-2.
6   Ibid., p. 2.
7   Ibid., p. 8.
8   Ibid., p. 74; this quotation comes from the essay 'What is a Nation?'
9   See Declan Kiberd, *Synge and the Irish Language* (London: Macmillan, 1979).
10 Matthew Arnold, *Lectures and Essays in Criticism*, R. H. Super, ed. (Ann Arbor: University of Michigan, 1962).
11 Ibid., p. 344 n.
12 Seamus Deane, 'An Example of Tradition', *Crane Bag*, vol. 3, No. I (1979), p. 46.
13 Matthew Arnold, *Lectures and Essays in Criticism*, p. 291.
14 Ibid., p. 292.
15 Ibid., pp. 296-7.
16 Ibid., p. 295.
17 Ibid., p. 298.
18 Ibid., p. 334.
19 Ibid., p. 348.
20 Standish O'Grady, *Selected Essays and Passages*, Ernest A. Boyd, ed. (Dublin: Talbot Press [n.d.]), p. 3. The quotation comes from a fragmentary autobiography, 'A Wet Day', first published in *The Irish Homestead* in 1899.
21 For O'Grady's carelessness and unreliability as a scholar see V. H. S. Mercier, 'Don Quixote as Scholar: The Sources of Standish James O'Grady's *History of Ireland*', *Long Room*, vols. 22/23 (Spring/Autumn 1981), pp. 19-24. In this particular connection, note that Sylvester O'Halloran's *General History of Ireland* was published in 1774, and Charles Vallancey published what the *DNB* rightly calls 'worthless tracts on Irish philology and history, 1772-1802'.
22 See Ernest A. Boyd's *Ireland's Literary Renaissance* (New York: John Lane, 1916), pp. 26-54; V. H. S. Mercier points to O'Grady's acknowledgement of a debt to Whitley Stokes's edition and translation of one Cuchulain source in the *Revue celtique*; see Mercier, loc. cit., p. 21.
23 These transcripts of O'Grady's annotations are printed in John R. McKenna, 'The Standish O'Grady Collection at Colby College: a Checklist', *Colby Library Quarterly*, series 4, vol. 16 (November 1958), pp. 291-303.
24 Ibid., p. 295.
25 See R. B. McDowell, *Public Opinion and Government Policy in Ireland 1801-1846* (London: Faber, 1952), pp. 43-4.

26 My source for this incident, and quotations from *The Kilkenny Moderator*, is Hubert Butler, 'Anglo-Irish Twilight: the Last Ormonde War', *Journal of the Butler Society*, vol. 1, No. 8 (1978/9), pp. 631-41.

27 Standish O'Grady, *Selected Essays and Passages*, op. cit., p. 163.

28 Ibid., p. 174.

29 Ibid., pp. 178-9.

30 Ibid., pp. 180-1.

31 Ibid., 'Introduction', p. 16.

32 Ibid., p. 203.

33 Bernard Shaw, *Collected Plays with Their Prefaces*, vol. ii (London: Max Reinhardt, The Bodley Head, 1971), p. 637.

34 Ernest Renan, *Poetry of the Celtic Races and Other Essays*, op. cit., p. 2.

35 Aijaz Ahmad, *In Theory: Classes, Nations, Literatures* (London: Verso, 1992), p. 194. The phrase in quotation marks is Ahmad's, not Said's.

36 J.M. Synge, *Collected Works III: Plays, Book 1*, Ann Saddlemyer, ed. (Oxford: Clarendon Press, 1968), p. 15.

37 For an excellent account of Synge see Mary King, *The Drama of J. M. Synge* (London: Fourth Estate, 1985).

38 *Plays 1*, op. cit., p. 149.

39 Ibid., p. 79.

40 For a good introduction to this topic see Jonathan Culler, *Saussure* (London: Fontana, 1976).

41 See David H. Greene and Edward Stephens, *J. M. Synge 1871-1909* (New York: Macmillan, 1959), pp. 71-3. There is no satisfactory biography of Synge, especially with regard to his intellectual development. But, for a specialist treatment, see Declan Kiberd, *Synge and the Irish Language* (Dublin: Gill and Macmillan, 1993, 2nd rev. edn).

42 *Plays 1*, pp. 71, 103.

43 Greene and Stephens, pp. 134-5.

44 *Plays 1*, pp. 77, 89-91.

45 See *Plays 1*, pp. 90-1 where Ann Saddlemyer cites the MS, and the canonical text insists that the saint was 'after bringing [a power of water] in a little curagh into Cashla Bay'.

46 In addition to the text of 'When the Moon Has Set' in *Plays 1*, pp. 155-77; see the edition in two acts, assembled with commentary by Mary King in *Long Room*, No. 24-25 (1982), pp. 9-40.

47 Data derives principally from Liam Price, *The Place-names of Co. Wicklow* (Dublin: Dublin Institute for Advanced Studies, 1945-1967), in seven parts, paginated as one.

48 Nicholas Grene, *Synge: A Critical Study of the Plays* (London: Macmillan, 1975), pp. 110-31, esp. p. 112.

49 See Saddlemyer's 'Introduction' in *Plays 1*, p. xiii, quoting W. G. Fay and C. Carswell, *The Fays of the Abbey Theatre* (London: Rich and Cowan, 1935).

50 See Saddlemyer's 'Introduction' in *Plays 1*, p. 72. There is a Ballynahinch in County Galway, and this evidence contributes to the pattern of an action transferred from the west to the east, a transfer occurring both in the composition/ revision of the play and in the travels of the saint prior to the commencement

of the dramatic action. There is also a Ballynahinch in Wicklow, though the modern English name appears to be a corruption.

51   In the graveyard at Ballinatone are buried William Gilbert Kemmis (died 1881, aged 75), and Col. William Kemmis (died 1900, aged 63), also the latter's son, Captain W. D. O. Kemmis at whose death (and the death of his widow) the estate passed out of the family's possession.

52   See *Plays 1*, p. 74 n10.

53   There are five named male speakers in the play. Apart from the saint, Martin and Timmy, the remaining two (Mat Simon and Patch Ruadh) have between them only thirteen very brief speeches. Most of these function on a 'hiss the villain' level of dramatic significance, and there is evidence that Synge on at least one occasion re-assigned a speech to 'People' generally. (See Saddlemyer, *Plays 1*, p. 142 n6.)

54   J. M. Synge, *Collected Works*, vol. 2, Alan Price, ed., *Prose* (London: Oxford University Press, 1966), p. 56.

55   *Plays 1*, pp. 73, 87.

56   Richard Mant, *History of the Church of Ireland from the Reformation to the Revolution with a Preliminary Survey of the Papal Usurpation in the Twelfth Century . . .* (London: 1840, 2 vols.); [Daniel Augustus Beaufort], *A Short Account of the Doctrines and Practices of the Church of Rome Divested of All Controversy* (Dublin: 1788).

57   See Greene and Stephens, op. cit., p. 28 for Synge's reading; see Edward Stephens, *My Uncle John*, Andrew Carpenter, ed. (London: Oxford University Press, 1974), *passim.*

58   Though this last denomination may seen an exotic among the Wicklow hills, the sect had originated there in the zealous activities of the Revd John Nelson Darby (1800-1882) while holding a curacy under the patronage of Lady Powerscourt: it only acquired its English name on secession from the Church of Ireland and the establishment of a community in Plymouth.

59   Stephens, *My Uncle John*, p. 16.

60   On the Joycean aspect of this problem see Fredric Jameson '*Ulysses* in History' in W. J. Mc Cormack and Alistair Stead, eds., *James Joyce and Modern Literature* (London: Routledge, 1982), pp. 126-41.

61   On Fay's approach to Synge, see Saddlemyer, *Plays 1*, p. 215. The dialogue referred to is transcribed on pp. 215-17.

62   I discuss the question of Celticism as an enabling ideology at greater length in a paper delivered to a seminar organized by the Royal Irish Academy and the European Science Foundation in March 1993, the proceedings of which will be edited by Terence Brown.

63   W. B. Yeats, *The Poems*, Daniel Albright ed. (London: Dent, 1990), pp. 367-8.

8

James Joyce:
Bás nó Beatha

> The Irish language, Mahaffy said
> Is a couple of books written clerkly,
> A dirty word in a song or two –
> 'Matter a damn' says Berkeley.[1]

'EVELINE'

In 1898, writing in the magazine *Outlook*, Joseph Conrad observed drily: 'Life is life, and art is art – and truth is hard to find in either'.[2] His official topic was the sea-fiction of Captain Marryat and Fenimore Cooper, but the real object of this thought was Kipling's notorious line:

> Oh, East is East, and West is West, and never the twain shall meet . . .[3]

Reading Conrad nowadays we find it easy to assimilate his treatment of imperial expansion and exploitation to a comprehensive criticism of his fiction. *Heart of Darkness* is a set text in schools and (as Lionel Trilling remarked of *Ulysses*) it has lost its power to disturb. Comparing Conrad and Joyce, we would want – initially at least – to locate their powers of disturbance in different areas – Conrad's in his moral irony, Joyce's in his stylistic disorientation. Here we should stress the continuity which leads from the novels of Henry James, Joseph Conrad, and Ford Madox Ford to the more distinctly experimental canon of modernist fiction.

In considering the Irish contribution to modernist literature in English, we have available an all-too-prominent political timetable in the events which

led from the demand for Irish Home Rule within the United Kingdom to
the establishment of the Irish Free State. The recent renaissance of interest
in Joyce's politics has not, however, been characterized by any inquiry into
the dominant political, social, and economic relationships in which and of
which he wrote. Among these the role of language as at once the mirror
and lamp of social reality is crucial. In this regard we should stress the essential unity – that is, historical continuity – of all Joyce's fiction from *Dubliners*
to *Finnegans Wake*. A casual glance at pages from each of these books will
apparently jeopardize this claim, but only apparently so – continuity in
a period of revolutionary change and frustration may not be confused with
constancy. From 'Ivy Day in the Committee Room' to the dream of Ear-
wicker, Joyce strove to find forms in which history and technique become
a single problem. No doubt a definition of modernism centred on technique could be conveniently introduced here, but definitions in their exhaustive
length have the effect of excluding as often as they include. Rather than
deal in identifying characteristics, I would approach the process of definition with the problematic relationship between text and world, a feature
which is found in diachronic form in the attenuated relation of past and
present manifest in various mechanical concepts of history. Hugh Kenner,
writing specifically about *Ulysses*, alludes to 'the enchained determinisms
in which Western high thought was immobilizing itself at the century's turn',
but insists on restricting his insight to space and physics.[4] Textual hermeti-
cism and historical discontinuity – these are not so much principles of
modernism as they are underlying anxieties.

In the preface to *The Political Unconscious*, Fredric Jameson emphasizes
the virtually trans-historical imperative of dialectical thought, 'Always
historicize!'[5] It is not enough merely to place the object in its historical
context: the reader, the subject (so to speak) of criticism is also historically
placed. The interaction of these historicized objects and subjects is the proper
concern of criticism. Conrad and Kipling serve to remind us of the larger
perspective in which modernist literature in English has its genesis, crisis
in the Empire, commercial exploitation of Africa and Asia, the arms race
in Europe. Joyce's early reading of socialist thinkers should not be seen solely
as a personal trait, a sensitive rebel's response to the inadequacies of Irish
nationalism. It is intimately part of the emergence of the nexus of political
and aesthetic concerns which distinguish the Irish contribution to English
language modernism. As a metropolitan colony within the United Kingdom,
Irish society was especially susceptible to the contradictory movements of
British domestic and global policy.

Joyce's own account of the society in which he wrote is well known. Of

Dubliners he said: 'My intention was to write a chapter of the moral history of my country and I chose Dublin for the scene because that city seemed to me the centre of paralysis.'[6] Conventionally, this analysis is taken as being somehow literally true; Dublin in 1904 was static, immobile, devoid of the ability to translate intention into action, that is, paralysed. The image was certainly one that appealed to Joyce, for on 7 January 1904 he had concluded the semi-fictional essay 'A Portrait of the Artist' with the declaration:

> To these multitudes, not as yet in the wombs of humanity but surely engenderable there, he would give the word. Man and woman, out of you comes the nation that is to come, the lightning of your masses in travail; the competitive order is employed against itself, the aristocracries [sic] are supplanted; and amid the general paralysis of an insane society, the confederate will issues in action.[7]

What emerges from this curious manifesto is not so much an impressive politics – far from it – but our renewed apprehension of the metaphorical basis of Joyce's idea of society as paralysed. His devotion to Flaubert and the art of nineteenth-century France is more than a search for *le mot juste*, but implicates that French preoccupation with disease, especially socially reprobated disease, as a total metaphor for social reality.[8] The organicist metaphors which constitute Joyce's political longing culminate in 'the general paralysis of an insane society', which resounds with the medical shorthand for the terminal stage of severe syphilitic infection – general paralysis of the insane, GPI.[9] The artist portrayed in the essay, however, will give the word by which sexual generation and the birth of a sane society will issue. If the aetiology of this paralysis be considered, we discover that Joyce's theme is sexual excess as much as it is sexual decay and impotence, that behind the absence of motion implicit in paralysis there lies a history of uncontrolled – because unformulated – motion.

The interaction of sexuality and language in Joyce's fiction is immediately accessible in 'Eveline' which has a good claim to be representative of his short stories. The story is deliberately divided by a single asterisk into two parts. The first is based on a mental present within which Eveline is indirectly reported to meditate on past events in her life:

> Even now, though she was over nineteen, she sometimes felt herself in danger of her father's violence. She knew it was that that had given her the palpitations. When they were growing up he had never gone for her, like he used to go for Harry and Ernest, because she was a girl; but latterly he had begun to threaten her and say what he would do to her only for her dead mother's sake.[10]

The indirect reporting of Eveline's recollection of her father's threat creates a stylistic feature of great opacity. One might have expected him to threaten in terms of what he would not do but for her mother's sake.[11] The particular form which Joyce has chosen both emotively intensifies the threat and formally suppresses it, and this is in keeping with Eveline's ultimate inability actively to quit this bondage in her father's house. Technically, the crucial feature here is the implication for Joyce's narrative of the different conventions governing spoken language and written language. If we say that, with Joyce, technique has thematic ambitions this is not to suggest some internalizing 'fiction-about-fiction' quality; on the contrary, this feature is one by which he draws the reader's attention to the possibilities of revitalized intercourse between language and social reality.

One reason for taking 'Eveline' as typical of *Dubliners* is precisely this feature. From 'The Sisters' to 'The Dead' the characters frequently become engaged in a false consciousness of some crucial moment in their past or conjure deliberately some anticipated moment in the future. Aware of the frailty of their mental present which, paradoxically, binds them with an iron control, they seek to establish their first-person-singular existences more objectively, even if that additional security should take the form of anguish or guilt or pain. In 'Eveline' this development is discernible on two levels: psychologically, the girl hears now in the mental present sounds which remind her of her mother's last night. Stylistically, the reader encounters 'the odour of dusty cretonne', a phrase with which the story has opened. Both levels initiate at this point a process of *recursus:*

> As she mused the pitiful vision of her mother's life laid its spell on the very quick of her being – that life of commonplace sacrifices closing in final craziness. She trembled as she heard again her mother's voice saying constantly with foolish insistence:
> – Derevaun Seraun! Derevaun Seraun!
> She stood up in a sudden impulse of terror. Escape! She must escape . . .[12]

Her ultimate topographical immobility – her inability to join Frank on the boat – is counterbalanced by this fluidity of movement on the temporal plane, 'she heard again her mother's voice.' Paralysis at the barrier is the counterpart of an excess of movement between past and present. And within the story this binary opposition is expressed at a further linguistic level, for Eveline who hears words when they are not spoken never speaks.

Eveline cannot be said to act: instead she *opts*. Her opting for the internally known and structured world of her father's house is consistent with the non-emergence of her ego (grammatically her 'I') in the narrative. At a further level it is consistent with the strategy adopted by Mr Duffy in that most chilling of the *Dubliners* stories, 'A Painful Case':

> He had an odd autobiographical habit which led him to compose in his mind
> from time to time a short sentence about himself containing a subject in the
> third person and a predicate in the past tense.[13]

It would be quite feasible at this point to adopt Freud's distinction between the manifest and latent content of dreams as a means of analysing the
critical and therapeutic function of Joyce's narratives. For, just as Freud takes
over the model of a philological hermeneutic in developing the techniques
of psychoanalysis – and this at the moment when philology was engaged
in its own realignment with 'Celticism' – so Joyce creates within his
characterization dreams of the past ('nightmares of history') of which only
the manifest content is immediately intelligible to the characters. The reader's
function of course involves the elucidation of a latent meaning according
to which the narrative is transformed. By means of a technique introduced
by Joyce at a late stage into 'Aeolus', a newspaper caption provides the title
for the story involving Mr Duffy: 'A Painful Case' is the subtitle of a
newspaper article fulsomely cited in the narrative. The phrase is of course
a journalistic euphemism for suicide, and Duffy's conscious efforts are
directed towards consolidating the euphemistic view, towards repressing the
latent accusation of his own moral responsibility. In 'Eveline', the recollection of the heroine's mother's dying words results in their apparent mean-
inglessness, again involving the repression of a latent meaning.

The site of Eveline's traumatic and contradictory opting for escape is the
inscrutable recollected phrase, 'Derevaun Seraun'. Brendan O Hehir has written that the words are 'probably gibberish but phonetically like Irish', and
proceeds to offer possible original Irish Gaelic words of which these are cor-
ruptions.[14] The range of possibilities becomes teasingly wide, but one particular combination would reconstruct the dying mother's words as (with
English translations):

> dearbhán   seireán
> (small) genuine thing   little sea-anemone

Here perhaps is a thematically relevant allusion to a creature who, like
Eveline, clings to the rocks and will not breast the waves. The distortion
of this *ur*-message might be located at either of two levels, on that of the
older woman's deathbed confusion, or on that of Eveline's recollection. As
with 'he had begun to . . . say what he would do to her' the reader has
no access to the formal alternative of further information from the past. The

narrative method of the stories mimics the dreamer's censorship of his or
her dream, but in doing so by means of meaningless words draws attention
to the act of censorship. The words, as Eveline recollects them, both stimulate
and frustrate her wish to escape.

'Meaningless' is a relative term, and the corruption is more specific than
a mere phonological inexactitude. Words of one language are recalled within
another, a problem which diachronically involves the largest perspective of
nineteenth-century Irish history, the displacement of Gaelic by English as
the vernacular language. Nor can the insistent New Critic protect 'Derevaun Seraun' from a dialectical relation to history: he can neither integrate
the words to a formal analysis nor can he (with any confidence) declare them
absolutely meaningless. Officially committed to denying the significance of
linguistic change, he is confronted by an enactment of linguistic change at
two levels – that of the displacement of one language by another within
the story so as briefly to reverse the historical displacement, and that of the
corruption of certain words into other words as to require the elicitation of
some latent meaning.

The broader historical area in which this feature of Joyce's work should
be read may be illuminated by reference to a hitherto unnoticed metaphor
in the story. The first paragraph of 'Eveline' reads in its entirety:

> She sat at the window watching the evening invade the avenue. Her head was
> leaned against the window curtains, and in her nostrils was the odour of dus-
> ty cretonne. She was tired.[15]

The significant, neglected word is of course 'invade'; the rest of the paragraph
can be seen as muted anticipations of the story's end. The active form of
the first verb ('She sat . . .') alters after 'invade' to a series of passive and
decreasingly concrete forms ('Her head was leaned . . .'). The military
metaphor operates within the paragraph to initiate stages of Eveline's opting for inaction. Within the story as a whole it is taken up only once, in
the second part, when the crowd on the quays is particularized as 'soldiers
with brown baggages'.[16] Rather than conclude that the metaphor has simply been exploited in narrative terms, we should note the dialectical operation of technique and theme in Joyce's fiction, by which means we note also
Joyce to be a critical modernist. For the last end of Eveline is a silence which
transcends narrative method:

> He was shouted at to go on but he still called to her. She set her white face
> to him, passive, like a helpless animal. Her eyes gave him no sign of love or
> farewell or recognition.[17]

The invasion of the first paragraph marks the commencement of the English
language's advance within the narrative of Eveline's reverie, which in turn

centres upon a disruption of that advance. Richard Ellmann comments that Joyce's 'Eveline' is a counterpart to 'The Countess Cathleen': accordingly Yeats's play 'had extolled the virtue of self-sacrifice' and Joyce's story 'evokes the counter virtue of self-realization'.[18] Though this seems simultaneously to go too far in interpretation and not far enough, we can agree that behind both nominal heroines lies the personification of Ireland as Patient Woman, *an tsean bhean bhocht*. Yet Eveline's refusal to travel can only be ambiguously related to the troops with brown baggages, for the events of the narrative cannot be elevated to the level of theme if by such a reading we exclude once again the critical function of the therapeutic fiction. If they are departing invaders does Eveline opt for some domestic form of Home Rule in North Richmond Street; alternatively does she refuse to travel with them and by so refusing acknowledge their continuing power over her – is she an abstentionist?

While resisting such simplified allegories, we still may remind ourselves that in analysing the imagery of Joyce's fiction we attend positively to the concrete social realities both of the text's historical context and of our own historical condition as readers. Joyce was closer than Yeats or Synge to the social realities which made Ireland potentially revolutionary in this period of European crisis. One consequence of this intimacy might be described as Joyce's lack of illusion as to the odds-against chances of revolution in Ireland. A comparison with Yeats in terms of their attitudes to Hitler would be banal; a more profound comparison might focus on the manner in which each responded to the late nineteenth-century legacy of imperialist formalism conveniently represented here by Kipling. 'The Ballad of East and West', with its initial autonomous self-defining easts and wests, rapidly moves to a fourth line assimilable to Yeats's Blue Shirt melodies:

> But there is neither East nor West, Border, nor Breed, nor Birth,
> When two strong men stand face to face, though they come from the ends
> of the earth![19]

Deplorable sentiment apart, one notes conflict and cancellation as resulting from the unmediated valorization of east and west. 'Eveline' poses equally unmediated and mutually excluding alternatives: instead of conflict and cancellation, we find paralysis.

THE DEATH OF THE LANGUAGE

The short stories of *Dubliners* take their place in a field already defined by Flaubert and Maupassant in France, and concurrently by Chekhov in Russia.

Such a generic context, however, fails to place their author in a cultural context or, rather, the irony of the fiction succeeds in undermining the reader's faith in that possibility. The problem with Joyce, therefore, was his apparent disjunction from any tradition which touched upon his material. Certainly he could be accounted for in terms of genre – but 'The Dead' brought *Dubliners* to a climax in which genre was no longer an adequate explanation. It was Joyce's tangential relation to any Irish tradition which gave his early fiction its shock effect for local readers. Nothing was self-evident, nothing was concealed.

Traditionally, this state of affairs is translated into the proposition that Joyce was a Catholic, and that Catholics had little or no place in the Anglo-Irish Renaissance. But Catholicism in Ireland was not (and to a degree, is not) a matter of theology but of the relation between money and culture. In the literary critic's sense, Edward Martyn was not a Catholic, despite his piety and his Palestrina choir. What distinguishes the Protestant from the Catholic in cultural terms is his relation with the past, his possession of a history. Protestant Ascendancy provided the Edwardian Irish middle class with an eighteenth-century pedigree in which material and cultural prosperity were rationally linked. It was left to Yeats to transpose this sociological phenomenon into a literary tradition. To the Edwardian Irish Catholic, the eighteenth century meant little apart from echoes of deprivation: the Nugents and the Barnewalls, through whom Maria Edgeworth had been able to envisage a restored and regenerated social class, were lost to sight.[20] Intervening between those costume figures and the generation of John Joyce, the nineteenth century dominated the scene. Instead of the ratifying sequence which Protestant Ascendancy supplied to the Protestant bourgeoisie as a possession, history possessed the Catholic imagination in a frenzy of simultaneity. Here, money – cash rather than capital in most cases – was a relatively new element connected to the collapse of a pre-Famine economy in which subsistence outweighed trade for the bulk of the populace.[21] Here, culture found some degree of continuity through the Church and its offices, for the linguistic transformation of the nineteenth century inhibited sequential memory. (Joyce's notions of Irish history, at least prior to the artificially engendered inquiries which were involved in composing *Finnegans Wake*, were little more than commonplace.)

One recent commentator on this 'death of the Irish language' has tried to explain it as 'a millenial or utopian movement' characterized by 'panic, hysteria, or utopianism, or by any mixture of these emotions'.[22] High fertility, combined with dependence on an unreliable diet (based on the potato), produced not only famine but the recurring fear of recurring famine.

According to the utopian explanation, the Irish rural population abandoned the Gaelic language because it stigmatized them as potential victims, and because the English language was the key to migration, employment, and security. The argument has many faults if it is taken as a causal explanation of socio-economic events, but it is entirely at one with the view that the nineteenth century provided for the Irish Catholic an experience of history as trauma. And by trauma we mean not simply shock but precisely that form of dream-work which evidently contradicts the wish-fulfilling function of dreams.

One problem of comparative analysis arises here. We want to bring together Joyce and some earlier cultural production in which the post-famine trauma is absent. But mid-eighteenth-century Gaelic-speaking Ireland had not possessed the social or technical opportunities to create a literature. It is true that the poetry of Aodhaghán Ó Rathaille (1670 – 1726) makes it clear that in Augustan Ireland the aristocrats remained parvenus, but Ó Rathaille's poetic conventions are far removed from the theme involved here. Brian Merriman's *Cúirt an Mheán Oíche* (*c*.1780), with its employment of liberating dream as a means of permitting sexual frankness, suggests a possible comparison with the 'Circe' of *Ulysses*. Closer to Joyce, however, is the following passage from an autobiographical work in Gaelic which, for the sake of dramatic effect, I quote initially in the original:

> Is cuimhin liom mé a bheith ar bhrollach mo mháthar. Ceithre bliana a bhíos sular baineadh de dhiúl mé. Is mé dríodar an chrúiscín, deireadh an áil. Sin é an réasún ar fágadh chomh fada ar na cíocha mé.
>
> Bhíos i mo pheata ina theannta sin. Ceathrar deirféar agam agus gach duine acu ag cur a ghoblaigh féin in mo bhéal. Bhíos mar a bhéadh gearrcach éin acu: Máire Dhónaill, Cait Dhónaill, Eibhlín Dhónaill agus Nora Dhónaill, Pádraig Dhónaill agus Tomás Dhónaill.

> I was born on St Thomas's day in the year 1856. I can recall being at my mother's breast, for I was four years old before I was weaned. I am 'the scrapings of the pot', the last of the litter. That's why I was left so long at the breasts. I was a spoilt child, too. Four sisters I had, and every one of them putting her own titbit into my mouth. They treated me like a young bird in the nest. Maura Donel, Kate Donel, Eileen Donel, and Nora Donel — those were their names. My brother was Pats Donel, and I am Tomas Donel.[23]

I intend no disrespect to the translator if I point to certain discrepancies between the original and the English version — there is no fixed rate of exchange between languages. But the most monoglot reader can see that the first sentence of the translation has no equivalent whatever in the original. It may be that Robin Flower was discretely providing his English reader with a necessary historical pointer in providing a date; alternatively, he is shaping the passage by implying a connection between the writer's birth-day and his name. What he has modified, however, is the simplicity with which suckling at the breast is established as primary memory, as memory which depends on no '*can* recall': 'I remember being on the breast of my mother. Four years I was before I was taken from suckling'.[24] Moreover, the list of siblings is by Flower modulated stylistically so as to break it down, reduce it. These are probably inevitable consequences of translation but they underline the immense psychic difficulty of rendering in English the potency of Ó Criomhthain's words. No English-language memoir of this kind was possible within Joyce's lifetime, and yet *An tOileánach* was published in 1929.

The atmosphere in which Ó Criomhthain's book was received was con-ditioned by two powerful and contradictory motifs. One was the familiar (perhaps, tactically exaggerated) puritanism of semi-independent Catholic Ireland, in which official censorship was hyper-active.[25] The other was the establishment of Gaelic as the inert *primum mobile* of the new state. But the embarrassment which this conflict of values generated from time to time had a larger and older source upon which to draw. That earlier reservoir was the propagation in the nineteenth century of a sectarian schematization of the emotions which reinforced the sense of history as trauma:

> All Protestants are not virtuous, nor are Protestant peoples without their share of irregular sexual intercourse, self-stupifaction by alcohol, and so forth; but, bad as their backsliding may be, it is not as character-killing as the sensuality engendered by the Roman system; and whenever Protestantism is in the ascend-ant [*sic*], there also health, energy, integrity, and industry will be found in the ascendant. This is stated as a fact, and not for the purpose of insulting the Catholics. Nothing could be further from the thoughts of one, like myself, whose kith and kin are all Catholics. Roman sensuality debases the mind, because it is more in thought than in action . . .[26]

Thus, although Ó Criomhthain was a native of the most westerly islands and so might be dismissed as culturally marginal or residual, the aftermath of linguistic trauma was turned to provide the complementary ideology to Protestant Ascendancy. If this sounds tiresomely like local broadcasting from darkest Ulster, it is worth noting that, in the year of Joyce's hegira (1904), Max Weber commenced publication of *The Protestant Ethic and the Spirit of Capitalism*. Joyce's greatest fiction, *Ulysses*, demonstrates how symbolically effective marginal Dublin might be in the unmasking of consumer capitalism.

In 1904 'the death of the language' was already a cliché, and attempts to revive Gaelic were already under way. As a student at the Royal Universi-ty, Joyce remained unimpressed by the arguments of the Gaelic League though he briefly attended League meetings. Pressure from this quarter is not prominent among the difficulties young Stephen Dedalus encountered. Though Stephen's diary records that he fears the old man with red-rimmed horny eyes who had spoken Gaelic to John Francis Mulrennan, the entry significantly ends, 'no. I mean him no harm.'[27] The controversies aroused by the Gaelic League's revivalism produced significantly paradoxical reactions. Thus, two professors in Trinity College sought to show that Gaelic was purely a scholarly concern, involving venerable texts rather than contemporary speakers.[28] The Gaelic League and associated revivalist language movement are significant not solely for some mystical '*volk*-ish' quality inherent in the residual vernacular, but as the corollary to the emasculation of English as spoken and written in the metropolitan colony. Of course, related developments affected Victorian England, where genteel speech among the middle classes came increasingly to resemble the conventions of written language. But in Ireland language change took place against the background of that larger transformation — the displacement of Gaelic by English. The historical causes of that larger phenomenon are complex — the penetration of rural Ireland by commerce, the demographic upheaval of the Famine, populist politics, and journalism might be relevantly cited. However, if we look for more than a descriptive analysis we should consider if the underlying characteristic of the Gaelic language central to its eclipse is not sexual. High fertility, illegitimacy, early marriages, and large families were associated with those southern and western areas in which the 1840s Famine had been most devastating. For the most part, these were also Gaelic-speaking areas. To speak Gaelic was to identify oneself with the stricken, dangerously fecund community, to distance oneself from charity and relief. Moreover, the Gaelic language did not distinguish — and English increasingly did — between polite and coarse registers in describing bodily functions, in swearing, and so forth. (To speak Gaelic was to make explicit aspects of human biology which English was tending to disguise.) Within the United Kingdom, where its political role was anomalous and its economy divergent, Ireland experienced an intense cultural trauma through the medium of linguistic change. Other areas of Britain underwent similar if less intense alterations of convention — Thomas Hardy's fiction provides eloquent evidence on this point — but the close bond between moral, economic, and linguistic change is distinctively Irish. Nevertheless, this pattern is not uniquely Irish nor is it the result simply of famine: increased fertility in the nineteenth century was common in Europe, and the abandonment of Gaelic necessitated by migration had already commenced prior to 1845. The Famine, however, provided a traumatic account of social and economic change and rendered it capable of interpretation as cultural change.[29] In turn, the cultural significance of the Irish experience is not its uniqueness but precisely the manner in which it impinges upon the development of British society, both domestic and imperial, at the turn of the century.

The mobility engendered by mid-century famine and its consequences contributed signally to the perception of a Catholic middle class in Ireland as a category rather than as a formation. For the most part such 'perceivers' were of course members of a bourgeoisie which had in 1792 sailed under the colours of a Protestant ascendancy.[30] Yeats's Celtic Twilight sought a 'dream of the noble and the beggarman', and thus sought both to acknowledge the immiseration of the nineteenth century and to leap-frog back across the Famine to an era of Whiggish hegemony.[31] In more specifically linguistic terms, he sought a cultural synthesis under the guise of 'a written speech'.[32] This synthesis longed to exclude the middle classes and urban life, the material which Joyce chose for all his fiction. In *A Portrait of the Artist as a Young Man*, he integrates one potent image of rural life by way of Davin's account to Stephen of his encounter with the young woman in the Ballyhoura mountains. The fertility and guilelessness of the woman, as described to him by Davin, prompts Stephen to see her 'as a type of her race and of his own, a batlike soul waking to the consciousness of itself in darkness and secrecy and loneliness . . .'.[33] The immediately succeeding pages chart important stages of Stephen's development — his response to the slogan *Vive l'Irlande*, his acknowledgement that 'the Ireland of Tone and of Parnell seemed to have receded in space', his discussion with the English dean of studies first about Thomistic aesthetics and then about the notorious discriminations on the English language itself, as spoken in England and Drumcondra.[34]

In the days immediately prior to his 'flight' Stephen returns in his diary to an image of residual Gaelic Ireland, this time in the form of John Francis Mulrennan's interlocutor rather than the bare-breasted revenant of Davin's recollection. By this point Stephen has achieved some solider hold upon the ordinary world, and with it a more relaxed attitude to the rural, recently-Gaelic world reported upon by Mulrennan / Synge. Nevertheless, the aesthete has not been dissolved, though his aestheticism is directed against a specific target, the early poetry of W. B. Yeats:

> *April 6, later.* Michael Robartes remembers forgotten beauty and, when his arms wrap her round, he presses in his arms the loveliness which has long faded from the world. Not this. Not at all. I desire to press in my arms the loveliness which has not yet come into the world.[35]

Together with the parody of Synge and the paraphrasing of Yeats, the recurrent tabulation of dates serves to draw attention to the historical moment of the novel's climax. Furthermore, Joyce's aesthetic (as distinct from Stephen's superficial aestheticism) indicates that the meaning of the work of art lies not only in its historical genesis but also in its future reception.

NIGHTMARES OF HISTORY

Joyce's letters often give the impression of being written by Gerty MacDowell; they hang their little displays of fabric and fabrication on the most tenuous associative line. In this they also reveal their genuine profundity. Writing to his brother Stanislaus in January 1907, he recorded his reaction to Kipling's *Plain Tales from the Hills:*

> If I knew Ireland as well as R. K. seems to know India I fancy I could write something good. But it is becoming a mist in my brain rapidly. I have the idea of three or four little immortal stories in my head but I am too cold to write them. Besides, where's the good. Ibsen, of course, may have liked that kind of sport [i.e. total absorption in his work regardless of his environment]. But then he never broke with his set. I mean, imagine Roberts or Fay, with an allowance from the Irish Republic moving round Europe with correspondence tied at his heels like a goat's tether and you have H[enrik]I[bsen].[36]

Joyce did not live to see an Irish Republic established. The letter to Stanislaus, however, indicates that as early as 1907 he envisaged no very positive relationship between the artist as an old man and any newborn state. In 1922, after the publication of *Ulysses*, he was indeed approached by Desmond Fitzgerald (an Irish Free State minister) who proposed advancing Joyce's name to the Nobel Committee. Of this scheme he was highly sceptical, and in the event Yeats got the government nomination and the prize, Joyce being the first to send a telegram of congratulation.[37] The historical 'gap' between the setting of *Ulysses* (1904) and its eventual publication (1922) is crossed by the electrical charge of these altered relations between Joyce and his native land. The stories of *Dubliners*, like *A Portrait of the Artist as a Young Man*, posit a future by means of the placing of the reader in relation to the therapeutic narrative, a future which is in the simplest sense real. *Ulysses*, on the other hand, looks forward to the present. And (one is tempted to add) *Finnegans Wake* looks forward to what's past, or passing, or to come.

Joyce's fiction after *A Portrait of the Artist as a Young Man* consists of two historical novels. The point, a crude but necessary one, is clarified if juxtaposed with T. S. Eliot's familiar description of the Homeric parallel as a way of ordering 'the immense panorama of futility and anarchy which is contemporary history'.[38] Theodor Adorno's response to György Lukács's dismissal of Joyce as a decadent is worth recalling in the context of a discussion of the historical character of his fiction:

> Even in Joyce's case we do not find the timeless image of man which Lukács would like to foist on him, but man as the product of history. For all his Irish folklore, Joyce does not invoke a mythology beyond the world he depicts, but instead strives to mythologize it, i.e. to create its essence, whether benign or maleficent, by applying the technique of stylization so despised by the Lukács of today. One is almost tempted to measure the achievements of modernist writing by inquiring whether historical moments are given substance as such within their works, or whether they are diluted into some sort of timelessness.[39]

Generally speaking, one welcomes this kind of discrimination, especially Adorno's insistence that 'art exists in the real world and has a function in it, and the two are connected by a large number of mediating links. Nevertheless, as art it remains the antithesis of that which is the case.'[40] However, 'man as the product of history' is one version of the overwhelming question that Stephen Dedalus asks himself on his visit to Dublin from Paris.

In 1908, during his pre-Marxist phase, Lukács defined a condition of emergent modernism which in his subsequent work he strove to dissolve sometimes with subtlety, sometimes with other means. 'Every written work', he observed, 'even if it is no more than a consonance of beautiful words, leads us to a great door — through which there is no passage.'[41] As a general principle this urgently needs to be historicized and particularized, first by emphasizing its reference to emergent modernism rather than 'every written work', and secondly by pointing to its status as a description of a condition implicit in the modernist aesthetic — as Lukács sees it — rather than as an objective account of modernist texts. It is of course cognate with Conrad's dictum on the elusiveness of truth in either 'Life' or 'Art' when these are hermetically isolated and hypostasized. The essential quality which is jeopardized is that mediated access to history which Joyce's critical method in *Dubliners* had sought to re-establish. In seeking to historicize Joyce's contribution to European modernism we cannot afford to neglect the colonial condition of the society upon which he chose to concentrate, and its *potential* transformation in the years between 1882 and 1922. In the case of *Dubliners* and *A Portrait* the temporal discrepancy between historical setting and composition is minimal, though in the later of these it is perceptibly widening through the agency of the biographical narrative. With *Ulysses* the discrepancy achieved structural proportions — '16 June 1904' in *Ulysses* embodies a function far more significant than 'April 6, later' in *A Portrait*. In political terms, the transition encompasses the emergence of the Free State and the modification of Ireland's colonial relationship to Britain.

Hugh Kenner has likened one interpretation of *Ulysses* to Laplace's cosmos — 'all chains of action and reaction are folded in, coupled end to end, determined.' Such a cosmos, he adds in a telling metaphor, 'perpetually trembles in its sleep while undergoing no real events'.[42] When we meet Stephen in the opening episode of *Ulysses* he is 'displeased and sleepy'.[43] His night's rest has been disturbed by moans emitted by the dreaming Haines who shortly summarizes Anglo-Irish relations in the phrase 'It seems history is to blame.'[44] Haines is a Laplacian. Stephen, on the other hand, has a different account to offer though it is mediated only to the reader by means of the famous *monologue intérieure*:

> In a dream, silently, she had come to him, her wasted body within its loose graveclothes giving off an odour of wax and rosewood, her breath bent over him with mute secret words, a faint odour of wetted ashes.
>
> Her glazing eyes, staring out of death, to shake and bend my soul. On me alone. The ghostcandle to light her agony. Ghostly light on the tortured face. Her hoarse loud breath rattling in horror, while all prayed on their knees. Her eyes on me to strike me down. *Liliata rutilantium te confessorum turma circumdet: iubilantium te virginum chorus excipiat.*
>
> Ghoul! Chewer of corpses!
>
> No, mother! Let me be and let me live.[45]

The substance of this passage has reached us just five pages earlier:

> Silently, in a dream she had come to him after her death, her wasted body within its loose brown graveclothes giving off an odour of wax and rosewood, her breath, that had bent upon him, mute, reproachful, a faint odour of wetted ashes.[46]

The repetition certainly constitutes one element of Stephen's developing rhythm in the prose, the curve of his emotion. But rhythm here is not simply a matter of musical approximation in verbal form; it has specific conceptual effects also. In addition to the newly introduced liturgical quotation, we are now given an intensified evocation of the ghostly figure, in phrases devoid of finite verbs and hence seeking temporarily to abolish time. When, in 'Circe', we encounter by way of phantasmagoric stage-direction another variation upon this passage, it is to inaugurate Stephen's apocalyptic reconciliation of Time and Space, the rigid polarities of both his aesthetics and his anxious metaphysics:

(Stephen's mother, emaciated, rises stark through the floor in leper grey with a wreath of faded orange blossoms and a torn bridal veil, her face worn and noseless, green with grave mould. Her hair is scant and lank. She fixes her bluecircled hollow eyesockets on Stephen and opens her toothless mouth uttering a silent word. A choir of virgins and confessors sing voicelessly.)

THE CHOIR:
Liliata rutilantium te confessorum . . .
Iubilantium te virginum . . . .
[. . .]

THE MOTHER: *(With smouldering eyes)* Repent! O, the fire of hell!

STEPHEN: *(Panting)* The corpsechewer! Raw head and bloody bones!
[. . .]

THE MOTHER: *(In the agony of her deathrattle)* Have mercy on Stephen, Lord, for my sake! Inexpressible was my anguish when expiring with love, grief and agony on Mount Calvary.

STEPHEN: *Nothung!*
(He lifts his ashplant high with both hands and smashes the chandelier. Time's livid final flame leaps and, in the following darkness, ruin of all space, shattered glass and toppling masonry.) [47]

Just as the grammatical immediacy of 'Her eyes on me to strike me down' does not mimic a scene in the novel, so the conclusive imagery of 'Circe' records no resolution of Stephen's psychological difficulties – *Ulysses* is no pseudobiographical study in realism. These variations on the rhythm of Stephen's nightmare serve, however, to relate other themes in the fiction, and indeed the focus here is central to Joyce's work as a whole: just as 'Let me be and let me live' recalls Stephen's ultimate ability to face the horny-eyed Old Man of the *Portrait* diary, so the deathbed recalls Eveline's mother and her 'secret words'. Joyce had begun to orchestrate a sentence on the theme of the revenant mother as early as 1904; its passage to 1922 is also its passage through the styles of *Ulysses*. [48]

These themes are in essence history and aesthetics which, at the outset, are for Stephen the imposed starting-point and longed-for destination of his search for authenticity. But, as problematic hero, Stephen's most potent characteristic is his recognition of the polar interaction of these values in his particular situation. Dream, the involuntary experience in a subjective present of events which ostensibly occurred in the past, is the dominant metaphor employed in *Ulysses* to represent this crucial condition. The novel opens with a disagreement between the wakened dreamers, reaches its climax in a stylistic transformation of matter into manner, quantity into quality when the 'Circe' episode adopts the literary equivalent of dream and its analysis.[49] Finally, Molly's soliloquy transforms the *monologue intérieure* (which has earlier detained Stephen within his search) into a renewed balance of past and present and future. Yet it is as early as 'Nestor' that Stephen makes explicit, with a grammatical precision we neglect at our peril, the importance of this pervasive metaphor:

— History, Stephen said, is a nightmare from which I am trying to awake.[50]

Commentators have been casual in referring to Joyce and 'the nightmare of history'. That misquoted phrase contains an ambiguity Stephen is anxious to avoid, though he explores its grammatical base in another context. Meditating on the words *amor matris* he notes and implies the coexistence of a subjective genitive (the love of a mother for X) and an objective genitive (the love of X for a mother) in the Latin construction. 'The nightmare of history' offers a parallel at least within the different conventions of another language: it may point to a nightmare which history endures (say, the Reign of Terror, Senator McCarthy's ascendancy, or the plagues of Egypt, according to your taste); or it may point to the enduring of history by X in the manner of a nightmare. The distinction is less than absolute, just as history and the life of an individual may not be absolutely distinguished – and here the parallel between Latin and English genitives reveals its limitations. But the form of words which Joyce has Stephen adopt, together with Joyce's obsessional elimination of perverted commas, makes it clear that Stephen refers to the second category. If we recall Stephen's recollected dream, we know that the revenant mother is his dominant image of history, and thus in speaking to Mr Deasy he identifies himself with a particular reading of Irish culture.

It is no accident that the Latin phrase on which Stephen effects his distinction of objective and subjective genitives invokes the maternal relationship, and the correlation greatly advances our attempts to historicize Joyce's fiction. Stephen's dream-revenant is implicitly cannibalistic, the vengeance wrought on the author of that aphorism which defined Ireland as 'an old sow that eats her farrow'.[51] Immediately before the recollection of his dying mother's secret words, Stephen recalls playing the piano for her: the song he has played is Joyce's setting of a poem by Yeats:

A cloud began to cover the sun slowly, shadowing the bay in deeper green. It lay behind him, a bowl of bitter waters. Fergus' song: I sang it alone in the house, holding down the long dark chords. Her door was open: she wanted to hear my music.[52]

The relationship between the poem in 'The Countess Cathleen' and the decisive action of the titular heroine is contrapuntal: Fergus has been king of Ireland but chose the vocation of poet so as to find peace in the woods; the countess sacrifices her serenity and risks her soul in order to save a starving and plundered tenantry – she acts symbolically as mother to her people. Throughout *Ulysses* Stephen is preoccupied with the larger implications of his mother's death, for his 'nightmare' is located at the scene of her death and his (non-)involvement in it. Stephen, to be sure, is faced with less drastic alternatives than those personified in Yeats's play by Cathleen and Fergus; but, just as he all but concluded his diary in *A Portrait of the Artist as a Young Man* with an allusion to Yeatsian nostalgia, so here at the beginning of *Ulysses* we find his dilemma dramatized by reference to a Yeatsian brooding on 'love's bitter mystery'. At the end of the fourth chapter of *A Portrait* Stephen had resolved that the artist's mission was 'to recreate life out of life'.[53] At the beginning of the first chapter of *Ulysses* he is tempted to the re-creation of second-hand art out of art.

Fergus's song is significant for Stephen because it may be a point of departure from the world of history, process, and consumption. Yet what it offers is not so much a retreat from life as a conveniently arty terminology for nature – 'the deep wood's *woven* shade'. Yeats's poem exemplifies in a thoroughly unconscious way Lukács' diagnosis of art as a great door through which there is no passage. Stephen's introspection, intensified as the revision of the early episode was effected, is a structurally introspective representative of the novel's latent hermetic closure. Traditional accounts of *Ulysses* have interpreted Stephen's meeting with Bloom as providing, for both men, a renewed access to reality and release from their interior preoccupations. But as Stephen has painstakingly revealed to Deasy, the material of his introspection is history itself: his experience within the novel will involve a comprehensive adjustment of relation both to text and world. These preoccupations are given their head in the third episode when Stephen walks on Sandymount Strand. Characteristically, his meditations on his family, his trip to Paris, his fellow lodgers in the tower, are introduced by a meditation on the nature of art:

> Stephen closed his eyes to hear his boots crush crackling wrack and shells. You are walking through it howsomever. I am, a stride at a time. A very short space of time through very short times of space. Five, six: the *nacheinander.* Exactly: and that is the ineluctable modality of the audible. Open your eyes. No. Jesus! If I fell over a cliff that beetles o'er his base, fell through the *nebeneinander* ineluctably! I am getting on nicely in the dark. My ash sword hangs at my side. Tap with it: they do. My two feet in his boots are at the end of his legs, *nebeneinander.*[54]

The art of this episode, according to Stuart Gilbert's schema, is philology, and the second sentence is 'Signatures of all things I am here to read . . .'[55] The allusion to Jacob Boehme offers a possibility of dynamically rendering nature intelligible to a degree only approximated and mocked by nineteenth-century philology. Stephen in *A Portrait* had listened silently to Donovan's glib citation of Lessing's aesthetics: now he is led to recall his differentiation of the verbal arts which deal with objects one after another ('nacheinander') in time, and the visual arts which deal with objects next to one another ('nebeneinander') in space.[56] By alluding to *Hamlet*, Stephen translates this distinction into an analogy of movement on two axes – if you walk over a cliff you cease to move on the horizontal axis though you move with increasing rapidity through it, on the vertical axis. *Nacheinander*, we might say, characterizes that mechanical order which Kenner calls Laplace's cosmos; *nebeneinander* the simultaneity of all events in the 'nightmare of history'. In colonial Ireland sequence and simultaneity are rival experiences of history.

Stephen's aesthetic meditation has its complement in Bloom's recurring puzzlement by the phenomenon of parallax, by reference to which we explain the apparent displacement or difference in the apparent position of an object caused by an actual change or difference of the position of the observer.[57] In a sense, what Time is to Stephen, Space is to Bloom. One is tempted to see the novel as requiring a resolution based on a time/space concept similar to that proposed initially by Einstein in 1905, were it not for the fact that 'resolution' is precisely what such a continuum jeopardizes. As a consequence, many approaches to *Ulysses* are actually directed at a non-existent, or recently extinct, target. The reconciliation of father and son, which critics of the archetype-and-myth school fondly celebrate, is more properly considered as the effort of Joyce's critical modernism to overcome the urge towards autonomy that characterizes so many modernist texts. Strictly speaking, Stephen without Bloom is unthinkable, Bloom without Stephen unthinking; thus the structuralist may read *Ulysses* as Joyce's effort to bring together the problematic author (Stephen) and the problematic reader (Bloom). But in what sense is such fiction historical? None that Walter Scott would immediately recognize. If the composition of *Finnegans Wake* outlasts Scott's entire career as prolific novelist, that of *Ulysses* more clearly reveals the historical nature of the fiction. To Carlo Linati in September 1920 Joyce declared his attitude to the Greek myth in terms which make the point effectively, 'My intention is to transpose the myth *sub specie temporis nostri*.'[58] The contrast here is not between then and now but between Eternity and time, between the metaphysical beyond into which Stephen fears he may walk on Sandymount Strand and the world of historical time to which the movement of the novel restores him. Fifteen years earlier Joyce had conceived his Odyssey as a short story for *Dubliners*, and its evolution as a long novel had necessarily brought alterations of conception and execution. Kenner has written of the ironic mood which the novel would have had if it had ended with 'The Wandering Rocks', and written also of the increasing uncertainty and unreliability of the narrators' methods, as 'The Sirens', 'Cyclops', 'Nausicaa', 'The Oxen of the Sun', and 'Circe' progressively illustrate.[59] To demonstrate his point Kenner cites the cheating reference to 'Mr Bloom's dental windows'[60] which is only cleared up eighty-five pages later with a denial that Leopold is any relative whatever of Bloom the dentist. Such red herrings certainly multiply – how can C. B. O'C. F. T. Farrell frown at the Metropolitan Hall when he halts at Wilde's corner, for the Hall is three-quarters of a mile away on the other side of the river?[61] What has happened is not just that Joyce is extending a naturalist novel (episodes 1 – 10) in a different mode; the novel comes to acknowledge the historical nature of its attention to 16 June 1904. With reference to Bloom the dentist Kenner observes:

> True, we can imagine a reader from whom 'Mr Bloom's dental windows' would have instantly invoked the actual Marcus Bloom, dentist, who practised in 1904 at 2 Clare Street: a reader who would have known that vanished, pre-rebellion Dublin as intimately as do Joyce's Dubliners. But not even in 1922 can there have been many left alive who both commanded such lore and were capable of reading 250 pages into the difficult *Ulysses*.[62]

Professor Kenner's fundamental anti-historicism here takes the form of historical exaggeration: after all, the six years between the Easter Rebellion and the publication of *Ulysses* had not seen the death of so many Dubliners and potential readers, nor had the Rebellion and its suppression caused the city to 'vanish'. Such sentiment distracts us from a more thoughtful consideration of events occurring between the conception and publication of the novel – among them, massive labour unrest in Dublin, the Rebellion, the murder of Joyce's friend Sheehy-Skeffington, the Great War, the internment of Stanislaus Joyce in Austria, Revolution in Russia and Germany. Across Europe and within Ireland, historical change had rendered 16 June 1904 no longer contemporary. Seen in this light the changing styles of *Ulysses* do not so much chronicle the events of one specific day as they seek to come to terms with the changing perspectives upon a 'fixed' day which a revolutionary period generated. *Ulysses* is thus historical in two senses, first in that it takes as its setting a date which is progressively seen as historical; and second, as a stylistic consequence, the process of composition itself is historicized.

Both *Dubliners* and *A Portrait* posited a future reader whom the texts awaited: Joycean irony and the conventions of *Bildungsroman* contributed to that perspective. *Ulysses*, on the other hand, is in danger of containing its author and reader. Or to put it in different terms, *Ulysses* appears all but 'posthumously': in 1922 old Troy of the D.M.P. is virtually an anachronism and the Citizen is on the point of assuming his functions. Joyce's youthful notions (of 7 January 1904) concerning the masses in travail and the end of a competitive social order find no fulfilment in the Irish Free State. This local timetable has its European tabulation also in the irresolution of 1918 and the failure of revolution in Germany and the west. To relate modernist literature to the crisis of western society is hardly original: nevertheless we await some dialectically satisfactory account of the disproportionate Irish contribution. Yeats's Anglo-Irish tradition is a classic instance of wisdom after the event, and the Parnellite trauma the symbol (manifest content) rather than the source of cultural energy. A dialectically thorough analysis of the Anglo-Irish Renaissance would take into account the contradictions implicit in the incorporation of a colonial and metropolitan system within the United Kingdom, and relate this feature to the function of sectarian ideologies in Ireland. The Great Famine, with the broader socio-economic pattern of which it is part, assisted in translating these contradictions into cultural terms, indeed gave occasion to that linguistic disjunction we have noted in homeopathic form in 'Eveline'. At the aesthetic level such an account of the Anglo-Irish phenomenon would have many tasks, but in the present context we may specify one element. Yeatsian and Joycean paradigms are conveniently summarized in two slogans – the Celtic Twilight, the nightmare of history. These are of course problems to Yeats and Joyce as much as they are programmes, but they illustrate the centrality of the sectarian conflict to the elaboration of Anglo-Irish literature. For Yeats, typical of that self-conceived and self-deceived bourgeois element known as the Protestant Ascendancy, history passively awaited formulation, invention, faith. For Joyce, urban inheritor of an abandoned language, history excelled itself, being prolific, obsessive, intolerable. To see these rival experiences of history in terms of *colon* and *colonisé* is tempting but grossly so; a more profoundly historical inquiry will reveal their mutual interaction within a larger political strategy.

Hence the significance of academic criticism's reluctance to consider Joyce and Yeats together in a fully comparative analysis. The uncritical acceptance of Yeats's rewriting of literary history, like the refusal to acknowledge the metaphorical nature of Joycean 'paralysis', perpetuates convenient myths. The role imposed on Joyce at least as far as his reception is concerned resembles that of the academic portrayal of Gaelic revivalism – he is at once pedant and pornographer, who gave us 'a couple of books written clerkly' and restored a dirty word or two. Similarly, we should note that *Ulysses*'s renowned openness to life is not without its problematic aspect, its contextual limitations, though here too we may take the opportunity to establish a Yeatsian comparison. It is specifically in 'Hades' that Bloom provides us with thoughts that at once qualify any naïve acceptance of the novel as celebration and reveal a positive disposition in any comparison with Yeats:

> Plenty to see and hear and feel yet. Feel live warm beings near you. Let them sleep in their maggoty beds. They are not going to get me this innings. Warm beds: warm fullblooded life.[63]

The parallel is obvious, the Old Man in *Purgatory*:

> I saw it fifty years ago
> Before the thunderbolt had riven it,
> Green leaves, ripe leaves, leaves thick as butter,
> Fat greasy life.[64]

The enclosure dreaded and desired by modernist literature is perhaps never so fully and awe-fully enacted as in Yeats's play where the speakers know not their own death. *Purgatory* as a meditation on Irish history, the Big House, and sectarian *mésalliance* subversively and persuasively reveals the manner in which those who formulate their history and consciously invest their faith in it are ultimately enclosed in all that they unconsciously exclude and repress. Yeats's *Purgatory* is Hell, and by a pleasing corollary Joyce's 'Hades' is processive, purgatorial. Bloom, by winding the adage 'The Irishman's house is his coffin' out of his funereal mood, puts both Englishmen and castles in their place; furthermore we note that Bloom returns to his house and to his warm bed. Yet the distinguishing, Joycean *mot juste* is Bloom's 'yet', a possible continuity of that critical modernism which history called forth and frustrated between 1904 and 1922.

FINNEGANS WAKE   13.04–13.19

Where is this continuity to be traced – in latter-day Irish literature written in English or Gaelic, in the *nouveau roman* of Robbe-Grillet and Beckett, in Joyce's own *Finnegans Wake*? Beyond these literary texts there lies a vast tract of critical discourse whose existence is scarcely conceivable without the *Wake* and the earlier Joycean preludes to the *Wake*. No adequate treatment of even one of these Joycean legacies can be attempted here: instead we may be content with emphasizing the continuity which links *Finnegans*

Wake to the earlier work in which Joyce's critical modernism first bravely
manifested itself. In discussing the *Wake* one necessarily discusses its critics
for Joyce's compositional method guarantees that every reading of his novel
is a critical response and not a passive acceptance. Of course some commentators have striven to reduce their response to the level of a naturalist
appreciation: J. B. Lyons, for example, labours sedulously to prove that Irish
priests were immune to venereal disease and crowns his argument by citing
as evidence of Joyce's modified and softened attitudes to his early environ-
ment the following passage from *Finnegans Wake*:

> Since the bouts of Hebear and Hairyman the cornflowers have been staying
> at Ballymun, the duskrose has choosed out Goatstown's hedges, twolips have
> pressed togatherthem by sweet Rush, townland of twinedlights, the whitethorn
> and the redthorn have fairygeyed the mayvalleys of Knockmaroon . . .[65]

To fear and yet practise a literal reading of 'The Sisters' leads Lyons to see
this passage as 'vivid with life', a rebuke to those who cling to the stultify-
ing idea of paralysis, and not to see that his example is Joyce's parody of
Edgar Quinet's rhapsody on botanical survival and human mortality.[66]

Generally speaking, we may regard literalism as the least bothersome of
the approaches adopted towards *Finnegans Wake*. The static application of
the very philology Joyce strove to defeat is more characteristic. Adeline
Glasheen, in the preface to *A Census of Finnegans Wake*, insists that 'Joyce
did not forsake received religion in order to enslave himself, as most rationalists
have done, to received history.'[67] Hence, in her interpretation of *Finnegans
Wake* 'Waterloo and the Resurrection are events of the same order.'[68] From
this dubious if seemingly harmless observation Miss Glasheen advances
towards the dehistoricizing of all Joyce's work. Let us take a sample passage:

> So This Is Dyoublong?
> Hush! Caution! Echoland!
> How charmingly exquisite! It reminds you of the outwashed engravure that
> we used to be blurring on the blotchwall of his innkempt house. Used they?
> (I am sure that tiring chabelshoveller with the mujikal chocolat box, Miry
> Mitchel, is listening) I say, the remains of the outworn gravemure where used
> to be blurried the Ptollmens of the Incabus. Used we? (He is only pretendant
> to be stugging at the jubalee harp from a second existed lishener, Fiery Farrelly.)
> It is well known.[69]

In fairness, it should be noted that Miss Glasheen's annotation relies on information from another source, Mrs Christiani's *Scandinavian Elements of
'Finnegans Wake'*. Nevertheless, as the form in which the *Census* presents
its case is itself significant I quote Miss Glasheen verbatim:

*FARRELLY, Fiery, and Miry Mitchel – Mrs Christiani says: 'Fiery' = French *fier*, 'proud'; 'Farrelly' = Danish *farlig*, 'dangerous'; she, therefore, identifies FF with Nicholas Proud (q.v.), and Miry (Russian *mir* = 'peace') Mitchel (q.v.) with St Michael (q.v.). I am sure there is a lot of truth in this explanation.[70]

As Nicholas Proud is identified with the Devil (Nicholas = Old Nick = Lucifer = Pride), this reveals Fiery Farrelly and Miry Mitchel to be an eternal opposition of Devil and Archangel, as in Milton (q.v.). Not only does the lexicographical arrangement of information mimic the metaphysical interpretation it implies, it also suppresses the indicative shapes and tones of Joyce's prose. Rhyme (cf. 'miry') tells us to pronounce 'Fiery' as adjectival of English 'fire', and Fiery Farrelly thus begins to sound and look like a plausible Irish name. In the *Annotations*, Roland McHugh glosses it as 'Feardorcha O'Farrelly (fl. 1736), Ir. poet' and offers no suggestion for Miry Mitchel.[71] He does however interpret 'So This is Dyoublong?' as an allusion to M. J. MacManus's *So This is Dublin* (1927) which derides Joyce. However, 'Hush! Caution! Echoland!' echoes a passage in George Moore's *A Drama in Muslin* (1886) which, significantly, is set in Dublin in the year of Joyce's birth, 1882; the paragraph parodies characteristic stylistic flourishes of Moore's.[72] If this echo is recognized, it becomes feasible to see in Miry Mitchel a reflection of Susan Langstaff Mitchell (1866–1926) who satirized Moore in verse and who wrote a mock biography of him.[73] As rhyme links Miry and Fiery, Fiery Farrelly might then be treated as an allusion to Agnes O'Farrelly, a Gaelic League enthusiast and sometime professor at University College, Dublin. Both women are gently mocked in Moore's *Hail and Farewell*, thus forming a perfect circle of literary allusion.[74]

The result of this exegesis is not some claim that *Finnegans Wake* is about Irish literary skirmishes rather than the war in Heaven. It is however salutary if we recognize that the crucial element in reading *Finnegans Wake* is not the identification of referents but the elucidation and advancement of relationship between various levels of allusion. That Joyce should refer to a novel dealing with 'the moral idea of Dublin in 1882' indicates the degree to which his last great novel conforms to the programme announced to Grant Richards in 1906 – 'to write a chapter of the moral history of my country'. Superficially, the *Wake* looks unlike *Dubliners*, and yet the technique of forcing the reader to change roles (and become momentarily, a speaker) so as to perceive the relationship between Fiery Farrelly and Miry Mitchel was employed by Joyce as early as 1904 in writing 'Eveline'. Moreover, between 1904 and 1939, Joyce's country had undergone drastic historical adjustments. It had, to be sure, failed to realize the liberation of the 'masses in travail' and it still laboured within the competitive order of western capitalism:

nevertheless it had formally inaugurated the revolt against the imperial and colonial system of the great powers – Joyce's interest in African colonialism is manifest in *Finnegans Wake*, and rubs shoulders with deft allusions to the fratricidal violence of post-1921 Ireland.[75] *Finnegans Wake* is necessarily cryptic, obscure, and baffling, because its underlying concern is subversive and its tactics those of retrenchment and renewed silence, exile and cunning. *Finnegans Wake* extends Joyce's critical modernism not in its alleged 'experimentalism' but in its self-conscious examination of the processes of history and language, history in language. Once again one might emphasize that Joyce's method may employ the rituals of philology but his ends are far removed from such scholasticism; so too his theme in *Finnegans Wake* is guilt and failure for the very reason that such a rendering articulate is a stage within the process of liberation. The naïve programme of release from 'the general paralysis of an insane society' announced in 1904 is itself subjected to a scrutiny of its sexuality in the festive comedy to which *Finnegans Wake* looks forward.

Speaking at the third Conference on Irish Politics and Culture at the University of Halle-Wittenberg, Professor Joachim Krehayn charted the turning tide of Marxist attitudes towards Joyce. He had been unfairly neglected in the past, and new editions of his works were in progress: Joyce had been reconsidered, and reissued, but in the long run he remained distinctively an Irish author whose relevance in the German Democratic Republic must be limited. As editor of the new edition of *Dubliners*, Krehayn was clearly not speaking from a position of hostility or reluctant approval.[76] His relegation of Joyce as distinctively an Irish writer has a symptomatic value which extends far beyond the frontiers of Germany. And this must stimulate a confession of deep unease on the part of the present writer. For, if Joyce is rescued from the New Critics, the mythologists, and the philologists, and is instead regarded as an exemplary subject of literary history, should not one concede the marginality of the history which he in turn works upon? Certainly, English critics have been notoriously reluctant to commit themselves at length, as if their commentary might constitute some form of trespass in the affairs of a friendly and neighbouring state. Dr Leavis on Joyce scarcely amounts to a slim pamphlet, and much of it repetitious as if the bother of considering a second example were excessive.[77] The same might be said of Raymond Williams, who transfers the *aperçus* of *The English Novel* (1970) to *The Country and the City* (1973) almost verbatim.[78] Such embarrassment in confronting Joyce might in itself form the material for an analysis of cultural relations between Britain and Ireland, but for the moment we should concentrate on the immediate issue of Joyce's obsessive exploitation of the

minutiae of Irish topography, the arcana of local affairs in Dublin, the sounds
and smells of Chapelizod, all that an outsider might justifiably complain
he cannot master.

In what sense – or, perhaps one should say, to what ends – can Susan
L. Mitchell, the Metropolitan Hall, and 'Derevaun Seraun' concern the contemporary reader and writer? An answer could be provided at length, in
which the culture of 'secondary' nations is shown to have been crucial in
shaping twentieth-century cosmopolitan art – Strindberg's Sweden,
Sibelius's Finland, and Picasso's Spain are not the 'great powers' of August
1914. But this indiscriminate listing of small nations and irredentist provinces is really little more than sentimentality. More precisely, one should
point to Ireland's early experience of independence and neo-colonialism and
the prior history of that status, and to Ireland's late experience of linguistic
trauma in the colonial period. This, together with the contradictions of the
disunited kingdom,[79] provides the crude framework for an analysis in terms
of Althusserian 'overdetermination'. Of course, all this is true of Yeats as
well as Joyce; as we have seen, the two Irish authors adopted drastically different attitudes towards history, genre, and language. Approaching Joyce's
texts more closely, one might specify a particular feature of Irish colonial
experience which is taken up in *Ulysses* and which is given structural status
there. In the prolonged and bitter 'lock-out' of 1913, the leader of the Employ-
ers' Federation was William Martin Murphy, a newspaper magnate: in 1916,
the same Murphy used his press to insist upon the execution of the socialist
James Connolly who was consequently shot in his wheel-chair. Ireland's underdeveloped industrial sector was well known, and the absence of genuine
workers in *Ulysses* cause for complaint by primitive Marxists. But the centrality of the press in the organization of Irish capitalism in the revolutionary
period is at once a sign of industry's undeveloped state and its advanced consciousness, for control of communications takes the place of the steel-mills
or the manufactories. Joyce's Citizen knows Murphy as 'the Bantry jobber',
and Murphy's hostility to Parnell is the cause of his animus. The 'Aeolus'
episode, however, transcends the simple attention to the press as topic, and
its language achieves the 'ruination of the referential powers of language'.[80]
Moreover, 'Aeolus' perfectly demonstrates the historical quality of Joyce's composition for, having published the episode in *The Little Review* in October
1918, Joyce further expanded it and its catalogue of rhetorical devices and
broke it up with sixty-three journalistic captions or headlines. 'Aeolus' opens
with tram-men's cries, Guinness barrels, and advertisements: communications and consumerism dominate with all their unreal promises of fulfilment. Far from missing the essential features of industrial society, *Ulysses*

concentrates upon the most potent features of life in such a society.

The development of language implicit in Joyce's radical revision of 'Aeolus' totally undermines the classic notion of the work of art as an end in itself, the sort of creation the Stephen of *A Portrait* aspires to. In terms of character, we have seen that the Stephen of *Ulysses* does not simply achieve a renewed access to reality via Bloom's kitchen. But Joyce's revolutionary practice here distinguishes him drastically from Yeats, and the distinction embraces concepts of history as well as art. In Yeats one finds repeatedly that, within a poem or play, a figure is presented as achieving form by assimilation to some further level of art; thus, in 'Easter 1916', the concluding lines of the poem ritualize names which, by being written out in verse, are changed utterly.[81] This metaformalism does indeed undergo a sea-change in the later work (where its effects are more ironic), but in 'Cathleen ní Houlihan' its compensatory function is clear. The Old Woman, having prophesied that 'many that are redcheeked now will be pale-cheeked', proceeds to move from prose to verse and with this shift to offer an aesthetic immortality in legend for those who support her cause:

> They shall be remembered for ever,
> They shall be alive for ever,
> They shall be speaking for ever,
> The people shall hear them for ever.[82]

Considered in terms of plot, this curtain line of the disguised Countess anticipates the imminent defeat of the rebels – the setting is Killala, 1798. If Yeats's late plays reveal the manner in which those who formulate their history and consciously invest their faith in it are ultimately enclosed in all that they unconsciously exclude and repress, then 'Cathleen ní Houlihan' (written before Yeats's explicit adoption of the Ascendancy view of Irish history) lays the ground for this ultimate irony. The play attempts to advance two unrelated and unrelatable perspectives upon history; for the family in the cottage there is all the freedom and unpredictability of the future, the sense of potential and participation; for the lyrical Countess, there is the metadramatic knowledge of history and its closures, the certainty, indeed predetermination of an illusory future. And here we find in Yeats the counter-truth to Stephen's experience of history; for, having observed that *colon* and *colonisé* are too exclusivist in their implications to describe the formulator and the recipient of history respectively – and Stephen is recipient by virtue of his nightmares – we find in Yeats an antithetical statement of the polarity. The Old Woman's song is a significant point of reference and comparison because it too lies behind the passage from *Finnegans Wake* we have taken as our focus; the paragraph continues:

Lokk for himself and see the old butte new. Dbln. W.K.O.O. Hear? By the
mausolime wall. Fimfim fimfim. With a grand funferall. Fumfum fumfum.
'Tis optophone which ontophanes. List! Wheatstone's magic lyer. *They will
be tuggling foriver. They will be lichening for allof. They will be pretumbling forover.
The harpsdischord shall be theirs for ollaves.*[83] [Emphasis added]

McHugh's *Annotations* offer real aid here, for he tells us that Wheatstone
invented a box 'shaped like a lyre, into which piano's vibrations passed,
which then appeared to play itself'.[84] In other words, the Aeolian Harp in
mass-production. The art of Moore and the early Yeats offers illusory com-
pensations for the disappointments which its history imposes. Joyce's critical
modernism fully acknowledges the defeat of his idealistic 1904 programme
of cultural liberation, yet it proceeds through *Ulysses* and *Finnegans Wake*
to interrogate the terms of that defeat and to assume (and so render possible) a future readership.

I have spoken of Joyce as offering a possible continuity of that critical
modernism which was called forth and frustrated in the years between 1904
and 1922. Continuity, of course, is not simply a matter of futurist extension, and it may be equally valid to look to an earlier moment of literary
history for an effective placing of Joyce's achievement. 'Wise passiveness
in time' is in part a definition of Wordsworth's Christian stoicism, but it
also catches the frustrations of a young man whose faith in revolution was
(in his view) betrayed. That the great revolution of Joyce's time was Bolshevik
rather than bourgeois must be noted, together with the confusedly bourgeois-
and-more promptings of the Irish rebellion. Yet while it was never Bolshevik,
Joyce's attitude to revolution, as to history, was not permitted to be one of
privileged faith. The dialectical transformation of quantity into quality, function into symbol, is seen in essentially romantic terms in lines from 'Michael'
which may none the less be quoted in this Joycean context:

> The length of full seven years from time to time
> He at the building of this Sheep-fold wrought,
> And left the work unfinished when he died.[85]

In the more exposed position of Irish modernist in the age of Russian revolution, Joyce's image of literary conscience, literary conservation cannot be
the sheep-fold. In *Ulysses* we have seen that even in Hell, Bloom can assert
the dignity of the common man, though in a style which we should progressively read for its limitations. Wordsworthian pastoral, which might be
called the formalism of Nature, similarly claims to be the language of men
speaking to men. At the conclusion of the second chapter of Book III in

Finnegans Wake, the narrator provides a superficially similar and attractive vision of natural rhythms re-emerging:

> Brave footsore Haun! Work your progress! Hold to! Now! Win out, ye divil ye! The silent cock shall crow at last. The west shall shake the east awake. Walk while ye have the night for morn, lightbreakfastbringer, morroweth whereon every past shall full fost sleep. Amain.[86]

It is true that west and east are here restored to some mutually defining rhythm, and true too that the 'lightbreakfastbringer' lightly knocks on the head that domesticating myth of *Ulysses* interpretation whereby Leopold's patriarchal stature is restored in his ordering of breakfast from Molly. But Book III is described by Campbell and Morton as 'the book of the desired future; not the future really germinating in the nursery upstairs . . . but the mirage-future of the idealizing daydreams of the half-broken father'.[87] Once again, Joyce obliges the reader of *Finnegans Wake* to change roles, this time in order to recognize the specific speaker of the words on the page. It is true that the passage is comic, but with this higher recognition its comedy approaches that critical revelation of a festive conclusion which is the end of history. In the first version of the passage Shaun is hailed 'heart & soul you are of Shamrogueshire'[88] and the entire rhetoric here is a parody of *biedermeier* Free State self-sufficiency, a hermetic and deluded protectionism. Joyce's mimicry, in *Dubliners* as much as in *Finnegans Wake*, mocks a mockery. Thus it draws the reader towards his creation of an order which is not competitive and in which life and art positively define each other.

CLICHÉ REVIVIDUS!

In 1975, Philippe Sollers declared that 'since *Finnegans Wake* was written English no longer exists. It no longer exists as self-sufficient language, no more indeed than does any other language, Joyce introduces a permanent carrying-over of sense from language to languages, statement to statements, punctuality of enunciation-subject to series.'[89] A little later in the same paper, Sollers takes issue with the objection that Joyce had failed in that he retained a base-language, English. The problem, as Sollers saw it, was 'not that of a base-language but rather of a filter language.'[90] With much of this we can agree, but I am concerned here to raise two issues which may relocate Sollers's radical reading of Joyce's fiction, both historically and linguistically.

The first issue revolves around the point in Joyce's career where this *Aufhebung* of English occurs. For Sollers, and the Tel Quel group general-ly, *Finnegans Wake* is the crucial textual moment. Yet the *Wake* appeared

serially, its title withheld behind a serial surrogate title, *Work in Progress.*
The distance, historically, between the completion of *Ulysses* and the commencement of *Finnegans Wake* is less than we may imagine. And the progressive radicalizing of styles in *Ulysses* indicates (as clearly as anything we
find in the *Wake*) that it, too, is veritably a work in progress. All of Joyce's
work, from the earliest of the *Dubliners* to the 'last word' of the *Wake*, contributes to a potential unity — by unity meaning that process of continuity
and arrest of which Benjamin speaks in the 'Theses on History.'[91]

The second issue focuses on Sollers's assumption that the language at the
heart of the Joyce problem is English. Doubtless Joyce wrote in English
in something like the sense that Faulkner wrote in English. That is, a command of English is a necessary but far from sufficient linguistic requirement in the reader. On the other hand, Joyce is an Irish writer; and if this
is conventionally accepted as a socio-geographical placing, we should
remember that Mairtín Ó Cadhain is an Irish writer also, that the Gaelic
language exists in both vernacular and literary forms. Here, my concern
will be to indicate (however briefly) the relation between that language and
Joyce's achievement, specifically with reference to the broad view of modern
literature implicit in my citing of Walter Benjamin and Philippe Sollers. More
bluntly, my concern to relate the author of *Dubliners* to the Gaelic language
is not a local one.

Of course, a more conservative view of Joyce's relation to English is that,
far from transcending it, he destroyed it. In this view, the contortions and
meanderings of the late episodes of *Ulysses* are already the death throes of
the language, as far as Joyce was concerned. Even so fine a critic as A. Walton
Litz nods in this direction when he writes of the 'Eumaeus' episode in terms
of its 'relinquishment to fatigue,' and other commentators have been less
cautious than Litz.[92] Certainly, we can distinguish stylistically between this
episode and those of 'Nausicaa' and 'Cyclops', where ordinary life is also
treated to linguistic exhaustion. In 'Cyclops', the vulgar and transparent
simplicity of the Nameless One is contrapuntally arranged with the gigan-
tism of Gaelic-Myth-Translationese, with all the latter's attendant exhaustive
lists. In 'Nausicaa', mass-circulation sentimental fiction — and not 'school-
girl language', as Litz would have it[93] — imposes its style on Gerty and her
companions. Related to, yet distinct from these discourses, 'Eumaeus' is
thoroughgoing in the journalistic clichés of its style:

> The vicinity of the young man he certainly relished, educated, *distingué,* and
> impulsive into the bargain, far and away the pick of the bunch, though you
> wouldn't think he had it in him . . . yet you would. Besides he said the pic-
> ture was handsome which, say what you like, it was, though at the moment

she was distinctly stouter. And why not? An awful lot of makebelieve went on about that sort of thing involving a lifelong slur with the usual splash page of letterpress about the same old matrimonial tangle alleging misconduct with professional golfer or the newest stage favourite instead of being honest and aboveboard about the whole business.[94]

Of course, the newspaper has been prominent in *Ulysses* virtually from the start, but here we see it insinuating its tired phrases into Bloom's exhaustion. In Aeolus it had official status as setting, and the intrusive headlines achieve an important effect in contributing to that breakdown of the referential limitations within which the novel's language has been largely content up to that point. The exhaustion of language in 'Eumaeus', the omnipresence of the press — these are important contexts in which Joyce's relation to cliché and the Gaelic language may be considered.

Captions apart, the narrative of 'Aeolus' stays pretty clear of that particular characteristic of journalistic language which pervades 'Eumaeus' — the cliché. It is in 'Cyclops', and then more decisively in 'Nausicaa', that exhaustion displays itself in the language. Of course, the entire metaphor of exhaustion as applied to language requires exegesis as to its romantic ideology. Some crucial questions we might therefore ask about cliché are these: Who or what exhausted the language? What reward or result did the exhausters get for their efforts? What has been exhausted from the language? In what service did it become exhausted? These questions raise issues which, if answered fully (as they cannot be here), would relate the entire sphere of language and its description historically to the dominant modes of production generally. For the moment we must choose strategic and detonating, if isolated, issues. 'Into the bargain', 'the pick of the bunch', 'honest and aboveboard' may be English clichés, but why is there no English word for cliché? How does cliché, as a socio-linguistic phenomenon, relate to languages other than English?

It will come as no great surprise to learn that the term cliché derives from the French, specifically from the verb to click. The particular socio-economic area from which the borrowing is made is important, however: the specialized language of the printing trade and later of the processes of reproducing plate-illustrations and photographs. *Grand Larousse* encapsulates the French history of the term vividly:

CLICHÉ . . . n.m. (part. passé substantivé de *clicher* . . . 1809, Wailly, au sens 1; sens 2 – 3, 1866, Larousse).

1. Planche métallique plane ou cintrée, portant en relief la reproduction d'une composition typographique et des illustrations qui l'accompagnent, en vue de l'impression.

2. Négatif d'une photographie, servant à tirer les épreuves positives . . .

3. *Fig.* et *péjor.* Idée, expression trop souvent répétée: *Ajoutez à cela un style tout neuf roulant l'imprévu, un style d'où tout cliché* est banni, et qui, par l'originalité voulue de la phrase et de l'image, interdit toute banalité à la pensée (Daudet).[95]

English initially takes up the noun in something like its technical sense, and we find a writer in 1832 virtually recording the transaction: 'a process for copying, called in France *clichée.*'[96] Charles Darwin in 1868 was offered 'clichés of some woodcuts,' and it is only in 1892 in *Longman's Magazine* that the word emerges with its meaning of 'a stereotyped expression, a common place phrase.'[97] Even here, a certain bewitchment appears to be at work, for in defining *cliché* as we now know it, the supplement to the Oxford English Dictionary employs as adjective a term (stereotype) which itself derives from the original printing trade context of *cliché* in French. One explanation of the ultimate derivation of the word within printing parlance in France is that the clicking involved was 'le bruit que faisait la matrice en s'abbattant sur le metal en fusion,'[98] and Larousse proceeds to date this to *c.* 1803. The history of *cliché* is therefore clear; it emerges within the increasing sophistication and industrialization of printing during the romantic period. And looking at the full range of contexts in which *cliché* is thereafter employed, we find that the common denominator is the mechanical reproduction of languages or of signs or of the constitutive elements of languages and signs. A piece of print, reusable in countless words, or a plate which may be reproduced in different books and with different captions, a photographical negative which can be 'developed' into a realistic sign for the visible world — these are the *clichés* which led to the English linguistic phenomenon of the 'worn-out expression,' the *cliché.*

It is tempting to argue that, as a socio-linguistic phenomenon in English, the cliché emerges in the late nineteenth century, for by doing so one could relate it directly to the crisis in literary culture which accompanied High Capitalism, a crisis in which Joyce (and the Irish Modernists generally) played a leading role. Though the English language resists assimilating a term for the phenomenon until the 1890s, the cliché had been evident earlier. Indeed, one interpretive perspective on it might relate it to the processes of reification and animation of which Marx speaks in the early chapters of *Das Kapital*, processes which are everywhere evident in the styles of Charles Dickens and Alfred Tennyson. Cliché, accordingly, is the reification of a phrase within a language increasingly thought of in terms of organic virtues (such as animation). Yet something like the cliché had been in evidence even earlier than the mid-Victorian period. Christopher Ricks points to Jonathan

Swift's *Polite Conversation* as a precursor to his own witty discourse on the topic.[99] Ricks, however, is in part deceived by his own brio: Swift's material is essentially *spoken*, and the banalities he records carry with them the inflections of social encounter, social error, social embarrassment, and insensitivity. Clichés, on the other hand are essentially *printed*, and insofar as modern speakers employ clichés, they are simply indicators of the domination exercised by mass-produced printed language over their seemingly independent expression. As far as the idea of the cliché as a stylistic fault is concerned, we are nearer to a full statement of the ideology behind the notion if we read *Biographia Literaria*, where Coleridge, deploring mechanical fancy and the proliferation of writing, illustrates 'the present state of our language, in its relation to literature, by a pressroom of larger and smaller stereotype pieces.'[100] Clichés, then, are indicators of a more complex historical moment than that summarized in a phrase like 'High Capitalism'. They stand on the frontier between language which is produced through known human agencies (whether individual or social, speaking or writing) and language which is produced by machinery in an economy which fully permits the infinite reproduction of any one element in any possible context.

Machine printing, as introduced throughout the nineteenth century, already held within it the possibility of self-generating, de-socialized, and unexperienced language. The newspaper is only one area in which this possibility was early achieved. Mr Bloom in *Ulysses* recognizes the serial nature of this industrial development and its human concomitants: 'The machines clanked in threefour time. Thump, thump, thump. Now if he got paralysed there and no one knew how to stop them they'd clank on and on the same, print it over and over and up and back. Monkeydoodle the whole thing.'[101] The condition which, befalling Mr Nannetti, would result in this endless reproduction of 'news' is Joycean paralysis. The extreme instances of the human concomitant of endless language reproduction linked to linguistic reification are presented elsewhere in the novel. Across the city, seen discontinuously and repeatedly are the men perceived both in the city and in the typography of the novel as H.E.L.Y.'S., the sandwich-boards who are the true clichés of *Ulysses*, worn-out human beings metempsychosed into placards, pieces of print. The English language masks this process by employing a foreign term to negotiate the transfer between technology and humanity. The hidden dimensions of cliché organize the repression of the process by naming it exotically, and thus frustrating its exposure at home.

That the concept of cliché is at once modern and interlingual, existing on the frontiers of spoken and printed language, leads us on to consider the kinds of frontier upon which Joyce's work is located, both historically and linguistically. Another way of expressing the matter would be to speak of the necessary *interfaces* constituting Joyce's English — though I am not convinced that the elegance of structuralist dialect is preferable to literary history. Daniel Corkery, writing in 1931, identified to his own satisfaction 'three great forces which, working for long in the Irish national being, have made it so different from the English national being. These are (1) the religious consciousness of the people; (2) Irish nationalism; and (3) the land.'[102] Leaving aside the tautology of his second point, we proceed to note that Corkery passes silently over *A Portrait of the Artist as a Young Man* when he asks rhetorically, 'who can name a novel dealing adequately with Irish religious consciousness? And as for nationalism, in practice he recommends poetry in the Gaelic language — 'prose is no medium to express it in.' Given that the land was not an issue in Joyce's urban society, it is clear that the author of *A Portrait* and *Ulysses* fails Corkery's tests of Irishness on all three counts — plus his failure to write at all in Gaelic!

Yet, historically, Joyce stands precisely at a juncture where Catholic nationalism disregards its rural and Gaelic culture in favour of an engagement with British democracy and its very different codes and discourses. The roots of the process lie deep in the history of the century, but it is with the Parnellite movement that they manifest themselves above ground in vigorous though short-lived growth. That Joyce reflects this transition (*trahison?*) dialectically rather than affirmatively or satirically is of course lost on Professor Corkery. Yet in considering the interfaces which 'English cliché' presents, we may be able to catch Joycean dialectics at work (as work in progress).

A central stylistic element in the Gaelic language is known as *na cura cainte*, literally translatable as 'the runs (or throws) of speech.' One should emphasize the definite article — here are *the* runs of speech — which indicates their normative status within the language as conventionally conceived. Fluent Gaelic requires the proper incorporation of sometimes quite lengthy phrases which have an established and recognized existence *as units*. Thus, someone enjoying good fortune or otherwise in high spirits is said to be *ar muin na muiche* (on the back of the pig). However, the significant feature of *na cura cainte* is not their metaphoric base, but their relative length as units and their status as lexical elements. A throw of speech may run to six or eight words, employed with the weight and density of a single element.

Of course *na cura cainte* might be equated with English idioms. But in the nineteenth century when cliché is establishing itself, the social experience symbolized in the two languages differed dramatically. cliché is a new fault of style, and the notion of style relates to the individual speaker or writer rather than to the language considered systemically with its characteristic idioms. Cliché comes from a production of language which is increasingly removed from the individual's control, and its locus — the printing house, the newspaper office — is one only marginally associated with the Gaelic language. Gaelic, though it possessed a fine and ancient literature, survived orally. And in the nineteenth century, when efforts were being made to advance its use, its characteristic virtues were identified in oral terms — the runs of *speech*. Fredric Jameson has argued that the growing preoccupation with style in English, and the need for a discipline of stylistics, is a consequence of the abandonment of that classical system of education which was built around Latin and Greek texts: 'Style is essentially that which in modern middle-class culture replaces the *rhetoric* of the classical period. The two categories may be most usefully distinguished through the value and role they assign to the individual personality.'[103] And while English literature was progressively liberating itself from classical pedagogy in the nineteenth century, Irish culture still cited Greek and Roman tropes as models for the hedge scholar's emulation.[104] The particular feature known as *na cura cainte* is therefore to be recognized as proceeding from the overlap of linguistic economies: in the Irish vector, the bourgeois individual remained still a potential figure, while in the English, he trembles in anticipation of the mechanical eclipse of his idiom by cliché.

There is, of course, an explicitly political level at which this history may be read, though the topic is too great for inclusion here. One might add, however, that such formulaic elements in Gaelic point to the language's survival orally during the prolonged period of suppression which Gaelic culture endured. In the absence of printing houses, newspapers, and entrepreneurial publishers operating through that language, what would have been literature in less politically suppressed and economically underdeveloped societies became oral in Gaelic. The attendant transformation of literary forms into oral art (folk poetry, recitation, story-telling, etc.) encouraged the preservation of formulaic elements reminiscent of ancient epic rather than contemporaneous literary culture. That *na cura cainte* should be regarded as a desideratum in written Gaelic is, of course, a reflection of that absence of a sophisticated printed literature in the past, and also a reflection of the nationalist ideology under which the revival of the language was attempted at the end of the nineteenth century.

Both these considerations were active in Joyce's youth, as we can observe quite simply by recalling Stephen Dedalus's disagreements with the Gaelic League. It has long been recognized, however, that Joyce was far from ignorant of the language, even if he never took seriously such a theory of national culture as Daniel Corkery's. Brendan O Hehir has tabulated thousands

of Gaelic elements in the canon, from *Dubliners* to *Finnegans Wake*, and while
these hardly constitute a base language to rival English, they may go some
way toward unsettling the notion of English as somehow the natural and
pure base language which Joyce might be assumed to employ. English is
notorious for the number of influences it has absorbed — Germanic,
Romance, and Celtic. But the difference between the mongrel language of
George Eliot — now that we acknowledge the 'impurity' of all forms of
English — and that of Joyce is that Joyce's English is affected by the death
or disappearance of another language (Gaelic) and not simply by its life.
Without taking upon ourselves an examination of these thousands of words
and phrases, we may yet find that the distinction between so-called English
cliché and Gaelic *na cura cainte* can illuminate the kinds of ideological investment in language which *Ulysses* makes. The very term cliché hides its
mechanical and industrial provenance through its exoticism, just as in Joyce's
Dublin industry is said to have been marginal or even non-existent. Yet it
is precisely the industrialization of communications (of language) which is
central to *Ulysses* and the society it treats, the free-lance advertisement
salesman, the industrialized press with its enthymemic editor, the newspaper
offices which repeatedly provide markers for the characters' movements,
the techniques of reporting and misprinting that generate characters for Circe.
In 'Aeolus', Joyce gives us a reader's digest of rhetorical tropes, devoting
the third paragraph (under its newspaper headline) to chiasmus, a device
in which the terms of the second of two parallel phrases reverse the order
of the first: 'Grossbooted draymen rolled barrels dullthudding out of Prince's
stores and bumped them up on the brewery float. On the brewery float
bumped dullthudding barrels rolled by grossbooted draymen out of Prince's
stores.'[105] The topic, suitably enough, is consumption (of Guinness) and we
might note at this point that the cliché encapsulates not so much the exhaustion of language but its consumption, its consumption on a scale and
in a system deserving to be termed consumerism. The passage exploits
phrases which have the external contours of cliché (the fossilized phrase,
etc.) but compound adjectives 'render strange' this commonplace feature
of the language. The substitution grammatically of barrels for draymen, and
vice versa, does not mimic the processes of animation and reification at work
in an alienated economy. On the contrary, it is the inability of the grammar
to absorb fully such a total exchange — it seems in the second sentence as
if the draymen are from Prince's stores — that points to a resistance to this
process as something which is neither inevitable or natural. In Professor
McHugh's hedge-school, the pupils Bloom and Dedalus are more aware
of the lessons learned by a study of language than are the instructors. Joyce's

phrases here are not clichés; the element of 'making strange' in his compound adjectives hives off such phrases from the romantic-organic assumptions which lie behind the idea of cliché as dead, or exhausted, or fossilized language.

Dead language does figure in Joyce's fiction, and at a remarkably early stage. Eveline exists upon the inner side of a language frontier, within the pale of 'living English,' yet the recall of a dead language affects her to the extent that she follows her mother into deathlike silence and immobility. In the final story of *Dubliners*, Gabriel Conroy is crucially unsettled by Miss Ivors, who departs on the taunting Gaelic phrase 'Beannacht libh.' These words not only conjure for Gabriel the western rural world in which his wife grew up (and to which he has just refused to contemplate a holiday return), they also enact a significant grammatical error. As the person leaving those whom she is addressing Miss Ivors should rightly have said 'Beannacht agaibh.' The particular form attributed to Miss Ivors suggests early in the story that it is really Gabriel (with another, or others) who is setting out on his journey westward, who is leaving his aunts' party. Before this anticipation is symbolically rewarded in the final paragraphs of the story, Gabriel ruminates on the cliché-laden speech he inevitably will deliver. Cut off from the runs of speech, has he merely cliché to cling to, Gabriel who has denied that Gaelic is his language and who writes for the newspapers? In 'Eveline' and 'The Dead,' the Gaelic phrase intervenes to prompt a resolution favouring individual expression and independence. For Eveline, the prompt is inadequate; for Gabriel it is transformed into something far more significant than mere individuality.

Joyce's engagement with this dead language is suitably ambiguous. In *A Portrait of the Artist*, the Gaelic League is disregarded by Stephen; but when his friend Davin reports his sexually charged encounter with the bare-breasted woman in the Ballyhoura Mountains (a Gaelic-speaking area at the time), the language of the novel swings toward a form of English in which Gaelic influence is perceptible: 'Well, I started to walk and on I went and it was coming on night when I got into the Ballyhoura hills; that's better than ten miles from Kilmallock and there's a long lonely road after that. You wouldn't see the sign of a christian house along the road or hear a sound. It was pitch dark almost. Once or twice I stopped by the way under a bush to redden my pipe and only for the dew was thick I'd have stretched out there and slept.'[106] Davin's narrative indicates quite satisfactorily that Joyce was quite capable of writing the sort of fiction that ultimately came from the pens of Sean O Faolain and Frank O'Connor. Yet Davin's adventure in this Gaelic-speaking district — it is, is it not, a novel experience to discuss

A Portrait as containing such an incident? — reaches a conclusion seemingly at odds with the resurgent Gaelic words of 'Eveline.' Davin speaks to a
woman at a cottage door: 'I thought by her figure and by something in the
look of her eyes that she must be carrying a child. She kept me in talk a
long while at the door and I thought it strange because her breast and her
shoulders were bare. She asked was I tired and would I like to stop the night
there. She said she was all alone in the house and that her husband had
gone that morning to Queenstown'.[107]

What are these moments when the dead language asserts itself in Joyce's
English? The death-bed . . . the abandoned pregnant woman . . . On the
one hand they can be described as primary scenes — death, fertility, possible copulation — on the other, they are essentially translinguistic. Eveline
recalls in English words that her mother spoke in Gaelic; Davin tells Stephen
in English of an invitation he received (implicitly) in Gaelic. Both women
are abandoned by men at or heading towards ports, places of emigration.
Even Gabriel and Miss Ivors's exchange on the dance-floor, for all its apparent triviality, leads on to Gabriel's discovery of his dead rival in the west
of Ireland. Sexual crisis, migration, death, and 'language difficulty' come
together. Just as the Joycean narrative consistently seeks to break down the
rigid categories of life and death to reveal a larger and more positive interaction than those formulated in the bourgeois world as life-in-death and death-
in-life, so too the categorization of languages (English, not Gaelic: Gaelic,
not English) is progressively undermined. Joyce should be seen not simply
as part of an English-language tradition which includes Sterne, Conrad,
Beckett, and Nabokov, but seen also as the first modern Irish novelist, the
novelist who writes not only in English but also out of Gaelic. William
Carleton is perhaps his only predecessor in this regard.

The world through which Stephen Dedalus walks at the opening of *Ulysses*
is neither English nor Irish: it is colonial. One measure of that is evident in
the concentration of Dublin industry in the areas of consumption, areas more
than adequately treated in the alcohol-and-ink suffused pages of the novel.
Stephen, at once rebelling against religion and quoting the mystics, thinks
that 'signatures of all things I am here to read . . . coloured signs'.[108] Yet this
world is also one of systematic repetition: Mulligan's parodic quotations, the
schoolboy's answers, Stephen's own mulling on Lessing. Everything is threatened with over-use, with being rendered worn out, exhausted. Stephen's difficulty in pinning down Proteus in such a world is a distinctly modern and
colonial one: nothing is real, everything is simulacrum or denial. The reproduction of languages and images is the reality of *Ulysses*. It is Bloom rather than
Stephen who is aware that the cliché can be made to swell a scene or two.

Bloom, in a sense we neglect to our disadvantage, is a master of cliché. Against the ambitious idealism of Stephen's surname, Bloom advances not creativity or invention, but endlessly reproducible and translatable pseudo-names. For Bloom, like the much-benigned Gaels of the past, is constantly under pressure. He requires for survival a language which is not so much remarkable for its vivacity and idiom as reliable and resourceful. Against the multiplicity of images and signs of Edwardian Dublin he offers no heroic, singleminded resistance of style. Instead he presents a polyvalent language characterized in various senses by containment. One reading of 'Cyclops', therefore, would stress the Citizen's ironic dependence on English cliché in his loud advocacy of things Irish and Gaelic, and Bloom's parallel exploitation of a run of speech when the subject turns to anti-Semitic matters: 'That can be explained by science, says Bloom. It's only a natural phenomenon, don't you see, because on account of the . . .'[109] And in the midst of this conflict of languages, the nameless narrator reminds us of another of the novel's true clichés, Denis Breen, whose waking hours are tormented by a postcard bearing the letters UP, and whose sleep has been destroyed by a nightmare in which the ace of spades chases him up the stair-case. Breen's mental instability is the converse of H.E.L.Y.'S. physical rigidity as clichés. And the cause of Breen's condition is, by day and by night, a single card, a sign magically possessing a power over him to the extent of endangering his sanity. Bloom, who had briefly courted Mrs Breen before either of them married, must see in Breen a projection of his own potential fate at the hands of an infinitely mobile sign-system.

This leads us to consider a more central and difficult question, already raised under its own pseudonym. What modes of production are we dealing with when we read Joyce's fiction? For Philippe Sollers, the answer lies conveniently in the very date of publication of *Finnegans Wake*, 1939; for it is 'the most formidably anti-fascist book produced between the two wars.'[110] Here, the emphasis is both local and global. But the earlier fiction also engages with those social and economic modes which led to fascism, especially the mechanization of language and the growth of a passive, depoliticized consumerism. Nevertheless, our question remains to be answered, and in transfering the focus from modes of production in general to the specific area of communications I am simply acknowledging the colonial nexus in which the larger issue exists.

If we take the issue of what is exhausted from the language in the process of *clichant*, we confront difficult and yet familiar problems. 'Aeolus' is founded on the metaphor of expelled breath or wind (from whatever quarter); and the schema of *Ulysses*, with its attributive bodily organ for episodes, barring the first three, endorses this ideology of the natural body, of nature as an adequate symbol. If we see the late episodes of the novel working against this ideology (in that they work against the affability of word and object), it must be yet conceded that 'Penelope' reasserts this ideology emphatically — this is the problematic conclusion of *Ulysses* which calls forth *Finnegans Wake*. The supreme instance of exhaustion, whether of language or of human beings, is death; it is also the supreme commonplace. Consider Rudolph Virag's letter to his son, recollected poignantly in broken phrases which are and are not clichés: 'Tomorrow will be a week that I received . . . it is no use Leopold to be . . . with your dear mother . . . that is not more to stand . . . to her . . . all for me is out . . . be kind to Athos, Leopold . . . my dear son . . . always. . . of me . . . *das Herz* . . . *Gott* . . . *dein* . . .'.[111]

Once again the border of life and death is translingual: English, broken English, German/Yiddish. 'Be kind to Athos' cannot be a cliché in the mouth of a dying man, and the coming together of this interlingual feature and the moment of recollected death is Joyce's supreme deconstructive effort against the pressures which turn human beings into clichés. The profound ideological investment in language which *Ulysses* represents can be traced in many such exchanges. And for all the naturalism of Penelope, it is worth noting that the 'monologue' is not spoken, but both thought and written (though by no one agency). Progressively, the reader is obliged to see the affability of word and object as phony and violent, is obliged to engage in elaborate exercises in translation to liberate from the domination of mass-produced language what Dante described as both an action and a passion.

NOTES AND REFERENCES

1 Anonymous ballad quoted in Ruth Dudley Edwards, *Patrick Pearse: The Triumph of Failure* (London: Gollancz, 1977), p. 38. Its date is *c.* 1899.
2 Joseph Conrad, 'Tales of the Sea', *Notes on Life and Letters* (London: Grant, 1925), p. 57.
3 Rudyard Kipling 'The Ballad of East and West', *A Choice of Kipling's Verse*, T. S. Eliot, ed. (London: Faber, 1967), p. 111.
4 Hugh Kenner, *Ulysses* (London: Allen and Unwin, 1980), p. 149.
5 Fredric Jameson, *The Political Unconscious: Narrative as a Socially Symbolic Act* (London: Methuen; Ithaca: Cornell University Press, 1981), p. 9.
6 Joyce to Grant Richards, 5 May 1906, *Letters of James Joyce*, vol. ii, Richard Ellmann, ed. (London: Faber, 1966), p. 134.
7 *The James Joyce Archive*, 'A Portrait of the Artist as a Young Man', *A Facsimile of Epiphanies, Notes, Manuscripts, & Typescripts*, Hans Walter Gabler, ed. (New York, London: Garland, 1978), pp. 84-5.
8 For an account of this dimension to nineteenth-century French culture see Roger L. Williams, *The Horror of Life* (London: Weidenfeld and Nicolson, 1980).

9   In *James Joyce: A Student's Guide* (London: Routledge and Kegan Paul, 1978),
    Matthew Hodgart cites (p. 45) an article by Burton A. Waisbren and Florence
    L. Walzl, 'Paresis and the Priest: James Joyce's Symbolic Use of Syphilis in
    "The Sisters"', *Annals of Internal Medicine*, vol. 80 (1974), pp. 758-62, in which
    symptoms are discussed and a diagnosis of tertiary syphilis advanced for Father
    Flynn. Hodgart makes the casual and yet positive remark that paralysis is a
    condition 'in which the majority of the human race has always found itself'
    (p. 46), which, if it is too easily universalist, nevertheless acknowledges the sym-
    bolic nature of Joyce's fiction. J. B. Lyons in 'Animadversions on Paralysis as
    a Symbol in "The Sisters"', *James Joyce Quarterly*, vol. 11, No. 3 (1974), pp.
    257-65, engages in much special pleading on the question of priestly purity,
    and ignores the question of symbolism. John Garvin, in *James Joyce's Disunited
    Kingdom and the Irish Dimension* (Dublin: Gill and Macmillan, 1976), has far
    more sensible things to say on the topic (pp. 37-42).
10 James Joyce, *Dubliners*, corrected text, Robert Scholes, ed. (London: Cape, 1967),
    pp. 38-9.
11 I have in mind the idiomatic 'What I wouldn't do but . . .!', where 'but' serves
    as a pseudo-negative negating 'not'. The point is discussed further in my paper,
    'James Joyce's "Eveline" and a Problem of Modernism', in *Irland: Gesellschaft
    und Kultur*, vol. iii, Dorothea Siegmund-Schultze, ed. (Halle: Martin-Luther
    Universität, 1982), pp. 252-64.
12 Joyce, *Dubliners*, p. 41.
13 Ibid., p. 120.
14 Brendan O Hehir, *A Gaelic Lexicon of Finnegans Wake* (Berkeley, Los Angeles:
    University of California Press, 1967), pp. 333-4. See also Johannes Hedberg
    'Derevaun Seraun – A Joycean Puzzle', *Moderna Sprach*, vol. 60 (1966), pp.
    109-10; also, James MacKillop, 'Beurla on It; Yeats, Joyce, and the Irish
    Language', *Eire/Ireland*, vol. 15, No. 1(1980), pp. 138-48, esp. p. 139.
15 Joyce, *Dubliners*, p. 37.
16 Ibid., p. 42.
17 Ibid., p. 43.
18 Richard Ellmann, *James Joyce* (New York: Oxford University Press, 1959), p.
    170. I refer above to critical silence on the metaphoric 'invade' of the opening
    paragraph of 'Eveline': it may be useful to note one critic who has ventured
    an opinion on its tone. Warren Beek, in *Joyce's Dubliners: Substance, Vision and
    Art* (Durham, NC: Duke University Press, 1969), suggests that 'The word 'in-
    vade', especially connoting the dusk, suggests a suspended mood without stress-
    ing it' (pp. 112-13). Given the American presence in Vietnam at the time Beek
    was writing it is only fair to point out that since those days academic criticism
    has provided a less myopic perspective on modernist fiction and global politics
    – cf. Conrad's Kurtz in full US army regalia in *Apocalypse Now*.
19 Kipling, loc. cit.
20 See Mc Cormack, *Ascendancy and Tradition*, pp. 135-44.
21 See, however, Peter Costello's *James Joyce: the Years of Growth 1882-1915* (Lon-
    don: Rheinhart, 1992), pp. 25-46, for a reconsideration of Catholic prosperity.
22 Seán de Fréine, 'The Dominance of the English Language in the Nineteenth
    Century', in Diarmaid Ó Muirithe, ed., *The English Language in Ireland* (Dublin,
    Cork: Mercier Press/Radio Telefis Éireann, 1977), pp. 82-3.

23   Tomás Ó Criomhthain, *An t-Oileánach* (Baile Atha Cliath: Cló Talbot, 1973), p. 13; *The Islandman*, trans. Robin Flower (Oxford: Oxford University Press, 1978), 3rd edn, p. 1.

24   Translated by the present writer.

25   For evidence of unofficial censoring, occurring as late as the 1950s, of material linking breast-feeding and the Famine, see Cormac Ó Gráda, 'Making History in Ireland in the 1940s and 1950s: the Saga of the Great Famine', *The Irish Review*, no. 12 (1992), p. 104, n22.

26   Michael J. F. McCarthy, *Irish Land and Irish Liberty: A Study of the New Lords of the Soil* (London: Robert Scott, 1911), p. 196.

27   *A Portrait of the Artist as a Young Man* (London: Cape, 1968), corrected edn, p. 256.

28   Ruth Dudley Edwards, *Patrick Pearse: The Triumph of Failure*, pp. 38-41.

29   The principal works on the famine are R. D. Edwards and T. D. Williams, eds., *The Great Famine* (Dublin: Brown and Nolan, 1956), and Cecil Woodham-Smith, *The Great Hunger* (London: Hamish Hamilton, 1962). Two important books by Louis Cullen provide valuably broader contexts for the crisis – *An Economic History of Ireland Since 1660* (London: Batsford, 1972), and *The Emergence of Modern Ireland 1600-1900* (London: Batsford, 1981), the latter providing far more commentary and analysis on cultural matters than its title might initially suggest. In relation to the interaction of language and sexuality, such commentaries as McCarthy's are highly revealing. In Irish, Peadar Ó Laoghaire's *Mo Sgéal Féin* (1915) and the diary of Amhlaigh Ó Suilleabháin provide excellent primary material.

30   The preface to E. P. Thompson's *The Making of the English Working Class* (Harmondsworth: Penguin, 1968) is a brief, and suitably challenging, introduction to the theory of class in which the notion that groups of people *as* groups constitute classes is countered by the Marxist view of class as based on relations. Below the argument about literature which is the present book's principal concern, there is a further argument according to which Protestant Ascendancy enters crucially into Irish class conflict, apparently to differentiate between unique Irish conditions and the norms of nineteenth-century social experience elsewhere. In this way, sectarianism provided a means of enforcing, or attempting to enforce, rigid categorization of classes on social process. There is nothing very new in this, but the discussion of literature and history may serve to show how central was the role of culture in this enforcement and in resistance to it.

31   W. B. Yeats, 'The Municipal Gallery Revisited', *The Poems*, Daniel Albright ed. (London: Dent, 1990), p. 368.

32   'Upon a House Shaken by the Land Agitation', ibid., p. 145

33   Joyce, *A Portrait of the Artist*, pp. 186-7.

34   Ibid., pp. 187-94.

35   Ibid., p. 255.

36   James Joyce, *Letters*, vol. ii, p. 205.

37   Ellmann, *James Joyce*, p. 546.

38   T. S. Eliot, '*Ulysses*, Order, and Myth', *Selected Prose*, ed. Frank Kermode (London: Faber, 1975), p. 177.

39   *Aesthetics and Politics: Ernst Bloch, Georg Lukács, Bertolt Brecht, Walter Benjamin,*

Theodor Adorno (London: New Left Books, 1977), pp. 158-9.
40 Ibid., p. 159.
41 György Lukács, *Soul and Form*, trans. Anna Bostock (London: Merlin Press, 1974), p. 113.
42 Kenner, *Ulysses*, pp. 149-50.
43 James Joyce, *Ulysses* (Harmondsworth: Penguin, 1969), p. 9.
44 Ibid., p. 27.
45 Ibid., p. 16.
46 Ibid., p. 11.
47 Ibid., pp. 515-17. Bracketed ellipses mark omissions; the others are Joyce's.
48 For the 1904 origins see *The James Joyce Archive:* 'A Portrait . . .', etc., pp. 33, 47, 49, 53, 141.
49 Colin MacCabe, *James Joyce and the Revolution of the Word* (London: Macmillan, 1978), p. 128; see also Hugh Kenner, 'Circe', in *James Joyce's Ulysses: Critical Essays*, Clive Hart and David Hayman, eds. (Berkeley: University of California Press, 1974), p. 360.
50 Joyce, *Ulysses*, p. 40.
51 Joyce, *Portrait*, p. 208.
52 Joyce, *Ulysses*, pp. 15-16.
53 Joyce, *Portrait*, p. 176.
54 Joyce, *Ulysses*, pp. 42-3.
55 Ibid., p. 42.
56 See Fritz Senn, 'Esthetic Theories', *James Joyce Quarterly*, vol. 2, No. 2 (1965), pp. 134-6.
57 *Oxford English Dictionary;* Kenner in *Ulysses* traces the parallax allusions, p.5 n11 etc.
58 *Letters of James Joyce*, Stuart Gilbert, ed. (London: Faber, 1957), pp. 146-7.
59 Kenner, *Ulysses*, p. 151.
60 Kenner, *Ulysses*, p. 249.
61 See Appendix E of *Ascendancy and Tradition*, p. 406.
62 Kenner, *Ulysses*, p. 65.
63 Joyce, *Ulysses*, pp. 116-17.
64 W. B. Yeats, 'Purgatory', *Collected Plays* (London: Macmillan, 1963), pp. 681-2.
65 James Joyce, *Finnegans Wake* (London: Faber, 1964), pp. 14-15. This view of the passage as parody is reinforced if we note a similarity to the moment in *Ulysses* (p. 79) reporting Bloom's murmured version of Martha Clifford's love-letter, 'Angry tulips with you darling manflower punish your cactus if you don't please poor forgetmenot . . .', etc.
66 J. B. Lyons, 'Animadversions on Paralysis as a Symbol in "The Sisters", *James Joyce Quarterly*, vol. 11, No. 3 (1974), p. 265.
67 Adeline Glasheen, *A Census of Finnegans Wake* (Evanston: Northwestern University Press, 1956), p. vii.
68 Idem.
69 Joyce, *Finnegans Wake*, p. 13.
70 Adeline Glasheen, *Third Census of Finnegans Wake* (Berkeley, Los Angeles, London: University of California Press, 1977), p. 90; see also Dounia Bunis Christiani, *Scandinavian Elements of Finnegans Wake* (Evanston: Northwestern University Press, 1965), p. 92. (Miss Christiani is a mite more tentative in her

interpretation than Miss Glasheen acknowledges.)
71 Roland McHugh, *Annotations to Finnegans Wake* (London: Routledge and Kegan Paul, 1980), p. 13.
72 See Appendix F of *Ascendancy and Tradition* (pp. 406-07), for 'the moral idea of Dublin' etc.
73 See S. L. Mitchell, *Aids to the Immortality of Certain Persons in Ireland* (Dublin; London: Maunsell, 1913), and *George Moore* (Dublin; London: Maunsell, 1916; also reissued by Talbot Press, 1929). If purists argue that *Finnegans Wake* refers to Miry Mitchel (not Mitchell), it might be pointed out that Miss Mitchell misspells John Mitchel as Mitchell, thus endorsing Joycean error – see Mitchell's *George Moore*, p. 60.
74 George Moore, *Hail and Farewell: Ave, Salve, Vale*, Richard Cave, ed. (Gerrards Cross: Smythe, 1976), pp. 587, 644, 748, 751.
75 I am grateful to Dr Pieter Bekker for his comments in conversation on African elements in *Finnegans Wake* and on Joyce's interest in the history of colonialism. Some time around 1909–10 Joyce ironically noted in an address book:
England
She is successful with savages, her mind being akin to theirs (*James Joyce Archive* 'A Portrait . . .', etc., p. 123).
As in so many other areas, Joyce's relation with the primitivist side of modernism is deeply critical.
76 Joachim Krehayn, 'James Joyce, Nationalautor und Weltliteratur', *Irland: Gesellschaft und Kultur*, vol. iii, pp. 265-71. See also Wolfgang Wicht's provoking and impressive paper, 'Yeats and Joyce: Some General Remarks' (pp. 204-12 in the same collection) which relates Joyce to the international nature of the transition to monopoly capitalism rather than to the cosmopolitan decadence of modernism as denounced by Lukács. For a more recent assessment, see Ferenc Takács, 'The Idol Diabolized: James Joyce in East-European Marxist Criticism', in P. Dávidházi and J. Karafiáth, eds., *Literature and its Cults* (Budapest: Argumentum, 1994), pp. 249-57.
77 See, e.g., *The Great Tradition* (1948) (London: Chatto, 1973), pp. 25-6, and *The Common Pursuit* (1952) (London: Chatto, 1965), p. 284. Leavis's most extensive commentary on the topic was 'James Joyce and the Revolution of the Word', *Scrutiny*, vol. ii, No. 2 (1933), pp. 193-201.
78 Raymond Williams, *The English Novel from Dickens to Lawrence* (London: Chatto, 1970), pp. 164-8; and *The Country and the City* (Frogmore: Paladin, n.d.), pp. 291-5.
79 Joyce, *Finnegans Wake*, p. 188. For a stimulating essay on some aspects of the colonial/national timetable see L. M. Cullen, 'The Cultural Basis of Modern Irish Nationalism', in Rosalind Mitcheson, ed., *The Roots of Nationalism: Studies in Northern Europe* (Edinburgh: Donald, 1980), pp. 91-106.
80 Colin MacCabe, *James Joyce and the Revolution of the Word*, p. 115.
81 W. B. Yeats, 'Easter 1916', *The Poems*, p. 230.
82 W. B. Yeats, 'Cathleen ní Houlihan', *Collected Plays*, p. 86.
83 Joyce, *Finnegans Wake*, p. 13; emphasis added to parallel the four lines of Yeats's play.
84 Roland McHugh, *Annotations to Finnegan's Wake*, p. 13.
85 William Wordsworth, 'Michael, a Pastoral Poem', *Poetry and Prose*, W. M.

Merchant, ed. (London: Rupert Hart-Davis, 1969), p. 205.
86 Joyce, *Finnegans Wake*, p. 473.
87 Joseph Campbell and Henry Morton Robinson, *A Skeleton Key to Finnegans Wake* (London: Faber, 1947), pp. 211-12.
88 *A First Draft Version of Finnegans Wake*, David Hayman, ed. (London: Faber, 1963), p. 227.
89 Phillippe Sollers, 'Joyce and Co', *Tri Quarterly*, No. 38 (Winter 1977), p. 107.
90 Ibid., p. 116.
91 For the 'Theses on History', see the selection of Benjamin's writings translated under the title *Illuminations* (New York: Schocken Books, 1986).
92 A. Walton Litz, *The Art of James Joyce* (London: Oxford University Press, 1961), p. 45.
93 Ibid.
94 Joyce, *Ulysses*, p. 94.
95 *Grand Larousse de la langue française* (Paris: Larousse, 1972), vol. 2, p. 763.
96 *Oxford English Dictionary*, ed., S. V. 'cliché,' citing Charles Babbage, *The Economy of Manufactures*, 3rd edn, 1832.
97 Ibid., citing Charles Darwin's *Life*, 1887, which refers to 1868; see *Supplement to the Oxford English Dictionary* for the 1892 reference.
98 *Grand Larousse de la langue française* (Paris: Larousse, 1972).
99 *The State of the Language*, Leonard Michaels and Christopher Ricks, eds. (Los Angeles and London: University of California Press, 1980), pp. 54-63.
100 S. T. Coleridge, *Biographia Literaria*, James Engell and W. Jackson Bate, eds. (Princeton: Princeton University Press, 1983), vol. 1, p. 39.
101 Joyce, *Ulysses*, p. 121.
102 Daniel Corkery, *Synge and Anglo-Irish Literature* (New York: Russell and Russell, 1965), p. 19.
103 Fredric Jameson, *Marxism and Form* (Princeton: Princeton University Press, 1971), pp. 333-4.
104 See Fiona Macintosh, *Dying Acts* (Cork: Cork University Press, 1994).
105 Joyce, *Ulysses*, p. 118.
106 Joyce, *A Portrait*, pp. 186-7.
107 Ibid., p. 187.
108 Joyce, *Ulysses*, p. 42.
109 Ibid., p. 303.
110 Sollers, 'Joyce and Co', p. 109.
111 Joyce, *Ulysses*, p. 644.

9

Yeats and the Invention
of Tradition

The crime of Tradition was a new one . . .
(J. H. Blunt)[1]

ANXIOUS CERTITUDE

The term tradition has had an honoured place in literary criticism, thanks
largely to its deployment by T. S. Eliot and F. R. Leavis. Its status has been
enhanced by the manner in which some critics have discerned behind the
great tradition of modern English literature a neo-Platonic tradition. In the
figure of W. B. Yeats these two senses of tradition converge, together with
the added vibrancy of that traditional lore which the poet absorbed from
his study of Irish folk culture. 'Traditional sanctity',[2] consequently, carries
with it a rich synthesis of implications. Yeatsian critics have been assiduous
in assimilating these qualities to their own work, and one recent commentator on Anglo-Irish literature manages in the course of just sixteen pages
to invoke tradition twenty-three times, a frequency only rivalled by the first-
person singular pronoun. This nervous insistence is perhaps timely in that
the values which tradition is often thought to ratify are undoubtedly under
pressure in Ireland. But beyond this local anxiety there is the wider concern for the future of literary criticism itself, besieged as it is by such new
disciplines as the sociology of culture, structuralism of various kinds, and
a radical philosophy of literary history. In that wider struggle for the hearts
and minds of Arts Faculties, tradition is a highly contentious term in which

302

the indebtedness to continental (especially German) thought of the various challengers provides them with a drastically different perspective on tradition than that available through Eliot's essay on 'Tradition and the Individual Talent' or Leavis's *Great Tradition*. If tradition is frequently identified with a conservative literary history we should remind ourselves that traditional societies are those which have no sense of their own historicity.

In short, behind the literary critics' valorization of tradition, the word and the social practices surrounding it carry the most varied implications. If for a moment we follow the example of Eamon de Valera and consult the *Oxford Dictionary*, tradition is revealed to have a series of usages we should not neglect.[3] The first meaning is a legal one – 'handing over'. *Traditio* 'was a mode of transferring the ownership of private property in Roman law.'[4] Here, it is worth noting the distinction between the handing over of an object or a property, and the handing over of ownership or rights to such an object or property. For while the latter possesses a normative element, in that it was thus ownership was handed over, the physical handing over of an object might well be in conflict with legal requirements. In this way tradition came to mean 'a giving up, surrender, betrayal' in which rights or responsibilities are subordinate to other considerations or motivations. Judas's betrayal of his leader was 'cryste ys tradicion and passion', while tradition was also used to mean the 'surrender of sacred books in times of persecution' – as for example in the reign of Diocletian. This non-normative sense of tradition (a sense generally connoting moral offence) may be secondary now to the valorized sense of tradition as legitimate 'handing down', but we should be alert to the precise historical conditions in which the matter is given its prominence in British literary criticism.

Etymologically entailing a 'handing down', tradition is too often taken as synonymous with what is handed down rather than with the social and cultural dynamics of the process of handing down, the place of this in the modes of production of the period and the historical character of that period. This tendency to identify tradition with its objects can be traced in Eliot's subsequent reflection on his own essay. But its reassessment as a concept close to the heart of the Yeatsian aesthetic is in keeping with a scrutiny of the intensification of class as group or category (rather than as social formation) in the term ascendancy. Yeats's encounter with it comes first by way of folk tradition, and it is fitting that our subsequent inquiry into his most (idiosyncratically) neo-Platonic play, *Purgatory*, will involve a demonstration of the element of historical process in the timeless material he collected as amateur folklorist.

That late nineteenth-century emergence of Anglo-Irish literature requires sychronization with continental developments as well as with the changing perceptions of class inside the United Kingdom. Perhaps the most telling divergence between British and European intellectual developments was the growth of sociology in Germany, Italy, and France as the intellectual meeting-ground of urgent political, cultural, and philosophical concerns.[5] British sociology remained indebted to the positivism of Comte and J. S. Mill, and on the islands grand schematization was reserved for the development of a British school of anthropology. It is significant that the study of primitive society became prominent in the intellectual superstructure of the greatest imperial economy the world had known, and that at a time when High Capitalism was entering its crisis. Sir James Frazer's *Golden Bough* (1890 – 1914) and Max Weber's *The Protestant Ethic and the Spirit of Capitalism* (1904 – 5) are emblems of these contrasting preoccupations.

Weber is important not solely for his attempt to correlate changes in Christian theology with economic development, but for the broader differentiation between such rationalization in industrial and developed societies and the organization of traditional societies.[6] Traditional here signified a mode of continuity and cohesion drastically different from the pattern of climaxes and changes which progressively revolutionized post-medieval western Europe. Within the larger sense of Europe, traditional societies existed though for the most part as residual elements within political units already well advanced in their industrialization – southern Italy, for example. Given Weber's highly ambiguous attitude to the most recent rationalization to be reached in Europe – that of imminent proletarian revolution – traditional societies had for him something of that double sense present in the Latin usages of the term. Tradition was the means of transmission and succession in societies which were economically outmoded and politically subordinate: tradition also was the alternative to crisis and revolution. The first of these senses of tradition relates to a diachronic order in society, albeit a vestigial and threatened one: the second relates to an internalized apprehension of order conceived in synchronic resistance to history and its changes.

The publication of Weber's work in 1904 – 5 is a marker in that European nexus of which Anglo-Irish literature forms a sizeable and influential aspect. The 'Protestantism' of its title serves also as a reminder of the disjunction occurring between the acquisitive ethic and reformed theology in the Irish circumstances of Protestant Ascendancy. One further area linking this marginality and the centre of European politics in the twentieth century is marked by G. B. Shaw's interest in the 'New Protestantism' of Houston Stewart Chamberlain, British apologist for Hitler and politicized racism.[7] Yet for all that Shaw's family embody the bourgeois element in

Dublin's Protestant Ascendancy, and for all his interest in the strong man
theory of politics, he remains tangential to the real line of action uniting
nineteenth-century Irish culture and the trauma of twentieth-century politics
on the continent. Shavian politics was by no means hostile to theory, but
its preference was for practice. Notoriously, Shaw regarded traditional reputations as the material for modern satire, his treatment of Shakespeare being
only the most blatant. Yet, through his exploitation of Caesar, Shakespeare,
and Napoleon, Shaw held his version of left-wing naturalism and positivism
in touch with a historical dynamic. In Germany, Nietzsche represented one
particular form of historical scepticism, strongly laced as always with Nietzschean irony. It is however with the work of Martin Heidegger that anti-
historicism, combined with a thoroughgoing metaphysical abstraction, that
German thought made its most penetrating analysis of tradition. Yeats's lack
of interest in German culture was fairly comprehensive. Apart from Goethe
and Nietzsche (whose theories of the *daemonic* appealed to him) no German figure earned more than his passing acknowledgement. Yet, in his last
essays, *On the Boiler* (1939), he went out of his way to praise Edmund Husserl
whose *Ideas* he considered a modern restatement of Berkeleyan immaterialism.[8] That brief gesture towards the domestication of German
phenomenology is characteristic of Yeatsian procedures in the construction
of Irish Augustan tradition: analogy permits Husserl to be accommodated
in a schema whose coherence is determined by the intensity of such gestures:
analogically, Parnell becomes Cuchulain, or Swift is resurrected to repri-
mand the epigones of the Irish Free State. In 1909 he wrote,

> Every day I notice some new analogy between [the] long-established life of
> the well-born and the artist's life. We come from the permanent things and
> create them, and instead of old blood we have old emotions and we carry in
> our head that form of society which aristocracies create now and then for some
> brief moment at Urbino or Versailles.[9]

The very term 'Anglo-Irish literature' is valid solely by virtue of the intensity of need which underwrites the analogies upon which it is constructed.
In calling it a tradition, however, we do more to highlight those needs than
to confirm those analogies. Yeatsian landscape, for example, or the construction of Yeats's Goldsmith, are intellectual endeavours *at interpretation*, interpretation shot through with specific anxieties and ambitions. Through
such details as these – landscape, Goldsmith's biography, etc. – I hope
to unmask the Yeatsian tradition; in the words of Heidegger 'this hardened
tradition must be loosened up, and the concealments which it has brought
about must be dissolved.'[10]

Tradition, for Heidegger, is the entire tradition of ontology which has dominated philosophy since the days of the Greeks. It is, therefore, the most general and comprehensive sense of the term, under which the particularities of recent literary criticism may be considered separately:

> When tradition thus becomes master, it does so in such a way that what it 'transmits' is made so inaccessible, proximally and for the most part, that it rather becomes concealed. Tradition takes what has come down to us and delivers it over to self-evidence; it blocks our access to those primordial 'sources' from which the categories and concepts handed down to us have been in part quite genuinely drawn. Indeed it makes us forget that they have had such an origin, and makes us suppose that the necessity of going back to these sources is something which we need not even understand . . .[11]

But for all his insistence that Being possesses 'historiological interests' and his zeal for an interpretation which is philologically objective, Heidegger's inquiry into the operations of tradition does not lead in the direction of history. While the political implications of Heideggerian ontology became clear after the accession of Hitler, the unmasking of tradition as cousin-german to ideology can contribute to the reorientation of Anglo-Irish literature within the broader context of twentieth-century European culture.

Since the opening paragraphs of this chapter were published in 1985, the evidence proving Heidegger's energetic participation in Nazism has been mightily augmented, especially by Victor Farias and Hugo Ott. The implications of their research for literary theorists are further intensified by revelations of Paul de Man's wartime anti-Semitic activities.[12] It is for these reasons, rather than any inadequacy in his argument, that Conor Cruise O'Brien's essay of 1965, 'Passion and Cunning', has been vigorously ignored. Some topics have become too hot even for their former handlers.

The Yeatsian synthesis of tradition, in which folklore, Platonism, and the Irish Augustans join forces, is badly in need of such an analysis. Yet it must not be thought that Yeats and Heidegger are at loggerheads totally: in their different ways each exemplifies an attitude to human society which is characteristic of the modernist crisis. According to Heidegger, modern man lives in a fallen world of inauthenticity; according to Yeats, man has lost that Unity of Being of which Dante spoke. But whereas Marx sought to analyse that situation with the intention of bringing about its transformation in an active and actual future, Yeats and Heidegger saw no such solution, imminent or remote. Wrenching ontology out of its Platonic timelessness, Heidegger delivered it over to no historical process. His passive acceptance of National Socialist rule in Germany is entirely consistent with his philosophical rejection of history and his search for a primordial 'presence'. Yeats's intermittent and yet reiterated approval of Mussolini and

Hitler may have been punctuated with specific reservations and specific commendations: nevertheless, it saw the past as more authentically real than any mundane political programme. In such attitudes Hitlerian power found a convenient source of authority.

'POETRY AND TRADITION' (1907)

> Someone lacking a tradition who would like to have one is like
> a man unhappily in love.
>
> (Ludwig Wittgenstein)[13]

Discussing the several versions of phenomenology which have affected literary debate, Frank Lentricchia singles out the early Yeats to illustrate the affinity between Husserl's *Ideas* of 1913 and emergent modernism. In 'The Autumn of the Body' (1898) Yeats had declared that writers all over Europe were struggling against 'that "externality" which a time of scientific and political thought has brought into literature'.[14] The essay concludes with an enthusiastic summary of Mallarmé's manifesto in favour of a poetry dedicated to making 'an entire word hitherto unknown to the language'; the arts will deal with 'the essences of things, and not with things'.[15] If the sources of this search for poetic autonomy lie deep in nineteenth-century French culture, with Flaubert as well as Mallarmé, the affinity to German phenomenology can be traced clearly along three crucial lines – a vigorous anti-psychologism, the abstention from any natural standpoint in relation to perception, and the concentration instead upon 'the eidetic reduction'. By this last procedure, the phenomenologist discards those phenomena which are inessential to the idea in question and is left with 'a specification of the essential ones'.[16] Thus, while Yeats was fond of recommending forms and transmissions of knowledge peculiar to folk-culture, or elaborated more systematically in neo-Platonic theory, there was simultaneously available a philosophy propounding a broadly similar doctrine.

Yeats's essay 'Poetry and Tradition' is a curious illustration of his phenomenologist tendencies. Like so much of his prose, it is stuffed with opinions on matters about which he felt poets should not concern themselves. One topic upon which it has remarkably little to say is tradition, and in this the essay demonstrates both the phenomenological procedure and the problematic history of Yeatsian aesthetics. It is divided into four numbered parts, and these might be given headings such as 'Irish History from Henry Grattan to John O'Leary', 'Style', 'Breeding and Freedom', and 'John

O'Leary and Class'. Such headings of course would crudely distort Yeats's
argument which is effective precisely because it is not signposted – in this
way the evasiveness of tradition is itself masked from the reader. Those who
consider the early Yeats indecisive by comparison with the single-minded
rhetoric of *On the Boiler* should note the following passage from the first part:

> New from the influence, mainly the personal influence, of William Morris,
> I dreamed of enlarging Irish hate, till we had come to hate with a passion
> of patriotism what Morris and Ruskin hated.[17]

That commitment to positive hate will be echoed in the 'General Introduction for my Work' but here in the essay of 1907 its role is more puzzling.
Why should patriotism provide a model for the passion of Morris and Ruskin
or their Irish disciples? One answer lies in the fact that Yeats originally
published his essay under the title 'Poetry and Patriotism', and that the
amended title fails to reflect upon what had previously been an echo of the
title. Yet the essay found the poetry of the Young Ireland school inadequate
in that it was merely patriotic, and praised John O'Leary precisely because
he never accepted patriotism as an end in itself.

The second part of the essay is briefer and less discursive. In it, Yeats
defines style 'which is but high breeding in words and in argument'.[18] This
association of literary style with pedigree and manners is expanded into a
more explicit sociological prejudice: the writer 'has at all times the freedom
of the wellbred, and being bred to the tact of words can take what theme
he pleases, unlike the linen-drapers, who are rightly compelled to be very
strict in their conversation.'[19] 'Breeding' of course is a species of portmanteau word in which two related but distinct ideas converge: breeding
may mean the deliberate genetic planning and selection of – say – pets
or domestic animals; breeding may also mean refined or approved behaviour
fostered by training and education. 'Born and bred' distinguishes between
the two meanings. In his *Journal* Yeats spoke of the *analogy* between the
'long-established life of the well-born and the artist's life', and the analogical
procedure is one step along the way towards abolishing that distinction.
Yeats's commitment to spiritualism and theosophy, doctrines that deny or
minimize the body, is accompanied by his constant recourse to metaphors
drawn from the body and its 'breeding'.

'Poetry and Tradition' succeeds in introducing the topic of tradition by
reference to the 'spiritism' of Irish country people as an element in the final
conflict which will re-establish lost Unity of Being:

> Perhaps, too, it would be possible to find in that new philosophy of spiritism
> coming to a seeming climax in the work of Frederic Myers, and in the

investigations of uncounted obscure persons, what could change the country spiritism into a reasoned belief that would put its might into all the rest . . . We were to forge in Ireland a new sword on our old traditional anvil for that great battle that must in the end re-establish the old, confident, joyous world.[20]

This is as near to a prediction as Yeats allows himself, and significantly he predicts the old world, speaks of re-establishing the past rather than of establishing a future. Lionel Johnson is praised for his ability to relate Irish tradition to a greater tradition and 'he was in all a traditionalist, gathering out of the past phrases, moods, attitudes . . .'.[21] Yet these constitute virtually all the references to tradition in the course of the entire essay, the opening and closing sections of which might be more properly published under the original title, 'Poetry and Patriotism'.

Nevertheless, the order of the four sections, like the alteration of the title, has its particular significance. Having muffled William Morris's socialism, and shifted from a discussion of O'Leary's approval of artistic integrity to the definition of style as breeding, Yeats returns in the final section to deliver a more extended judgement on O'Leary and his times:

I could not foresee that a new class, which had begun to rise into power under the shadow of Parnell, would change the nature of the Irish movement, which, needing no longer great sacrifices, nor bringing any great risk to individuals could do without exceptional men, and those activities of the mind that are founded on the exceptional moment. John O'Leary had spent much of his thought in an unavailing war with the agrarian party, believing it the root of change, but the fox that crept into the badger's hole did not come from there. Power passed to small shopkeepers, to clerks, to that very class who had seemed to John O'Leary so ready to bend to the power of others, to men who had risen above the traditions of the countryman, without learning those of cultivated life or even educating themselves, and who because of their poverty, their ignorance, their superstitious piety, are much subject to all kinds of fear.[22]

If this sounds like 'épater les bourgeois' one should remember the difference between French and Irish social life – Ireland, despite well-publicized rake-hellish elements, had no bohemianism on which to base an assault on public opinion. Yeats's analysis is a mixture of unconscious Protestant Ascendancy views on history and class, and a conscious but unconfessed anti-Catholicism. What is more important, of course, is the manifest unoriginality of the complaint – which is rather more amusingly presented in Maria Edgeworth's *Absentee*.

The strategies of 'Poetry and Tradition' are now more evident. A historical statement about the nature of change in Irish society between the time of Grattan and the death of Parnell is interrupted by two briefer, more intense statements on style and artistic freedom. Style is breeding, the artist is an aristocrat by vocation. The blatancy of historical interpretation is modified by the positioning of the two sections dealing with style: indeed, the insertion of these suggests a breakdown of historical continuity which is reproduced in the alienation of the poet from a new bourgeois and philistine public. That this new element is not so new is disguised by the sectional divisions of the essay, and the result is to emphasize that qualitative break which characterizes all readings of Anglo-Irish modernism. Style is breeding – this is Yeats's own highly distinctive way of dealing with the embarrassment of literary inheritance. Officially, the argument might have been more aptly titled 'Poetry or Patriotism' but unofficially Yeats is unwilling to relinquish all rights to the impurities of politics. 'Poetry and Tradition', however, is an apparent misnomer also, for there is little on the subject of tradition *per se*. 'Poetry from Tradition' would be more accurate both in the implication that poetry derives much of its power from that source, and for the more important suggestion that poetry results from an experience of separation from that source, that apparent unity of belief and action which Yeats refers to as 'the traditions of the countryman'. By positing a historical continuity from the late eighteenth century to the era of O'Leary and Parnell, and by then intruding into that continuity with the claims of style and aristocratic freedom, Yeats at once takes the first steps towards the enunciation of his Irish Augustan tradition and concedes the less than unproblematic nature of this identification of history with that tradition. Yet his final choice of title, and the preceding decisions and eliminations, enact that process of eidetic reduction which confers upon tradition that hypnotic intensity which it has long possessed for literary critics.

There is no one canonical statement of Yeats's Anglo-Irish tradition. It may be clearly traced in a variety of texts, poems such as 'The Seven Sages', the play *The Words Upon the Window-Pane*, and the introduction to that play, 'Pages from a Diary in 1930', etc., etc. The sources I have named are all relatively late, and there is a certain logic in seeing Yeats's Augustanism as part of his reaction to developments in the Irish Free State – that is, his eighteenth century was conceived as a counter-truth to a new semi-independent Ireland. As we have seen, however, elements of the theory may be found certainly as early as 1907, and the basic 'aristocratic' assumptions on which it depends stem from his campaigns in favour of Lady Gregory and John M. Synge as inheritors of Parnell's tragic mantle. The poem 'Upon a House Shaken by the Land Agitation' (1910) is a turning-point, a recognition of altered economic relations and modes of production, and of impending modifications of relation between the elements of the United Kingdom.

Given this diffused statement of Yeats's tradition, it may be useful precisely to indicate my own approach to the problem here. In the first section of this chapter, I have stressed the problematic nature of the concept of tradition in the modernist generation. In the second I have dealt with Yeats's own attempt to relate poetry to tradition in his essay of 1907. The next section but one will deal briefly with the Victorian treatment of Swift, Berkeley, and Burke, and this introduced by a consideration of Yeatsian landscape as a form of urgent memory. The fifth section will follow on this by demonstrating in more detail how Goldsmith's biography was constructed in the nineteenth century, and how the figure of that name in Yeats's poems is part of a dramatic strategy based on a repressed sectarian psychology. Finally, we come to a broader discussion of that much-postponed topic, the nature of Anglo-Irish literature itself. Only by such preparation can we hope to do justice to the complex issues raised by the play *Purgatory* which I take to be Yeats's ultimate interrogation of tradition. But first we should consider looking at evidence suggesting that the poet had no monopoly on the major terms of the rhetoric he ultimately commanded.

REBIRTH OF A NEW ASCENDANCY

It may seem unlikely that any connection could be established between the sonorous and disciplined verse of W. B. Yeats and the kind of ephemeral, shapeless productions in pamphlet form which were treated in earlier pages. It may seem – the appearance is again deceptive – that a progressive development has been traced in which literary sublimity emerges out of inchoate party feeling and disputation, just as Michelangelo's David is said to have emerged from a mass of stone. For disputation and composition lie closely together in Yeats's activities, and not simply as source and product. The extent of his political writing in prose is only now recognizable when it is collected and formally organized between two covers. Prior to such republication, it had seemed as if the poet transcended the quarrels of his day or – at worst – commented upon them from an olympian detachment.

Such detachment owed not a little to the dignity implicit in his affiliation to the Protestant Ascendancy, even if there were those who questioned whether this affiliation had been a birth-right or an act of personal appropriation. The right or, at least, the power to link his name with those of Jonathan Swift, George Berkeley, Oliver Goldsmith, Edmund Burke, and Henry

Grattan, underpinned his re-creation of an eighteenth century to which he provided a splendid, elegiac last flourish. But the eighteenth century served a variety of rhetorical and propagandistic purposes at the beginning of the twentieth: through Wolfe Tone links were forged between latter-day separatism and Irish Jacobinism, and even so distinctly non-Protestant a journal as *The Catholic Bulletin* mobilized eighteenth-century allusions to bolster its own politics. What's more, Yeats was repeatedly a victim of this strategy, to the point where his subsequent elaboration of a Protestant Ascendancy rhetoric might be suspected of being a defensive reaction rather than an initiative launched on its own terms.

Through 1921, the *Bulletin*'s editorials were naturally preoccupied with the course of the Anglo-Irish war and the negotiation of a treaty. In the issue of January 1922, they dwelt on ambiguities emerging in the London talks, especially those relating to the status which Ireland might possess after a successful treaty. 'Dominion' was not readily definable, and the *Bulletin* was impatient with the failure to establish exactly what was conceded by the British government in the course of negotiations: 'Apparently this "mystery" status, which Ireland has received, is not the same status which Molyneux, Swift, and Lucas interpreted as being hers, and which they had not the slightest difficulty in lucidly defining in their time.'[23] This litany of names was repeated, with the addition of others, as if the eighteenth-century contexts in which these figures had worked constituted a single, unified political occasion comparable to that in which de Valera, Michael Colllins, and Lloyd George now found themselves. The same conglomeration of discrete moments and highly different figures will characterize Yeats's Ascendancy tradition when he comes to invent it ten or more years later.

For the moment, however, the *Bulletin* displayed no interest in Yeats or any of his colleagues in the cultural revival which had done so much to make these negotiations towards independence possible. Even a piece on 'Anarchy in Literature' (March 1922) passed him over without comment. The April editorial took the form of an extended historical survey in which the privations of Irish Catholics in the eighteenth century were rehearsed. The failure of the Volunteers in 1783 to support relief for Catholics was blamed on 'the old Protestant ascendancy spirit' and the derisive name, Back Lane Parliament (under which a Catholic Convention met in Dublin), was said to have been the work of 'the Ascendancy people'.[24] Tone continues to be the hero of the historical parallel, the Protestant supporter of Catholic emancipation. The significance of this extended editorial meditation at a time of incipient civil war can hardly be ignored. A series of articles headed 'Events of Easter Week' commenced in the same issue with an account of 'Ireland's trinity of martyr priests', two of whom (Canon Magnier and Fr M. J. Griffin) were murdered more than four years after the rebellion of Easter 1916.[25] Discrete events of the recent past were as amenable to compaction as those of the eighteenth century. The synthetic history produced by such processes, in which 1916 and 1922 are constituted as a single event, was precisely the target unwittingly struck by Seán O'Casey in *The Plough and the Stars* with consequent rioting in the Abbey Theatre.

The *Catholic Bulletin* was an intelligently directed organ of opinion, combining dedication to the church in all spiritual matters and to the cause of republicanism in the context of local politics. If Yeats lay beyond its remit, its writers nevertheless included some of his associates. To the issue of June 1922, Constance Markievicz contributed a poem written while she was a prisoner in Mountjoy Jail the previous year.[26] And the *Bulletin* was always attentive to a culture in which Yeats increasingly interested himself – that of Italy. 'Notes from Rome' featured in virtually every issue, principally to provide news of ecclesiastical affairs, and in December 1922 to announce triumphantly the triumph of Benito Mussolini.

At the beginning of 1923, the magazine introduced a new feature designed to assist school pupils among its readers to tackle public examinations. This emphasis on education, mechanical and doctrinaire though the model answers provided undoubtedly were, coincides with Yeats's own growing interest not only in education – he was now a father – but specifically in the theories of the philosopher Giovanni Gentile (1875-1944) who was Mussolini's minister of education from October 1922 to July 1924. Yeats was not averse to posing as a Catholic intellectual on occasion – he adopted that mask when he wrote an anonymous editorial for *To-Morrow* in August 1924[27] – and, as part of his performance as 'smiling public man' he undertook an official visit to a convent school in Waterford. Later, in the 1930s, he certainly read Catholic propagandist literature though the occasion was usually one in which he had been explicitly condemned as a pernicious influence. It would be rash to conclude that he noted, in the *Bulletin* of February 1923, quotations from Mussolini's newspaper *Popolo d'Italia*, which anticipated his own brand of anti-English feeling and posed a question for an ideal future – 'what phantoms would then populate the British solitude?' – which parallels his late meditation on 'our Irish solitude'.[28]

Be that as it may, the treatment of education in the columns of the *Catholic Bulletin* resurrected the politics of the 1790s and simultaneously brought the discussion closer to Yeats. According to an editorial in early 1923, the place of Trinity College Dublin in the new political order of things would be determined by that institution's anti-national and anti-Catholic record,

for – contrary to the claims of its spokesmen – the college's admission
of Catholics in 1793 was achieved against its will. Having once again linked
the events of the 1790s to those of the 1920s, the editorial then proceeded
to endorse the activities of 'vigilance committees' dedicated to the policing
of the new nation's reading matter, because 'there is ample reason to believe
that the Post Office service is being availed of for the purveying of utterly
debased books and circulars throughout Ireland.'[29] Evidently referring to
a rare public appearance by James Joyce's *Ulysses*, the anonymous writer
continued:

> in a prominent shop in a prominent street in Dublin, the central position in
> the display window has been occupied for several weeks in the winter now
> just closing, by a large volume which can only be described as a vast, shapeless,
> and hideous heap of the most utterly depraved and beastly filth. The writer,
> who lays his scene in Dublin, and the book itself are not to be named here.
> Even in Paris it was not found easy to procure for the work a publisher: for
> Paris and her government are at last waking up to the evils of such publica-
> tions. Quite recently a notable French novelist has had his name struck, by
> Presidential decree, from the roll of the Legion of Honour, for an unworthy
> publication of this character.[30]

In its continuing treatment of education, the same editorial demonstrates
the effect of partition in Ireland, especially the manner in which Catholic
experience in the new (sub-) state of Northern Ireland – represented as one
of resisting a hostile establishment – was directly applied to problems arising between the Catholic majority in the Free State and the tiny non-Catholic
minority. The *Bulletin*'s construction of a coherent general policy included
not only this presentation of Irish Catholicism as still oppressed by alien
forces, but it deployed the 'Students' Bureau' to link disparate academic
questions into an implied programme. A specimen examination paper in
history consisting of thirteen questions opened with the following suggestive
sequence:

> What were the chief causes which led to the Insurrection of 1798?
> Give an account of the composition of the ancient Roman City-State.
> When was a dictator appointed? What part did the people play in the
> government?
> Write a note on land tenure in ancient Ireland.
> What was the nature of the Reformation struggle in England in its first stage?
> Trace its further development.[31]

It is hard to avoid the conclusion that editorial interest in the 1790s as a time
of 'persecution' is transferred to the happier topic of a recently established

Roman dictator, whose corporativist principles might even have been anticipated in ancient Irish land-holding practices, in a golden era destroyed by a series of intrusions of which the English Reformation was the most spiritually reprehensible. The argument was not always conducted in so indirect a manner, as the incorporation of 1920 into 'the events of Easter week' has shown.

Yeats's cultural assumptions inevitably featured in this programmatic rewriting. A feature on the 'country houses' of Ireland indiscriminately ascribed their building to Cromwellian and puritan settlers, though the authority of W. E. H. Lecky was also judiciously invoked.[32] A sequel on 'The "Town Houses" of the Colonial Ascendancy in Dublin', by the same author, managed to assign these to the work of a 'Cromwellian ascendancy' though now it is Swift and Berkeley who are cited as models of fair comment.[33] J.J. Murphy's articles form an unintended prelude to the *Bulletin*'s later campaign against Yeats. They are based on an extensive reading of eighteenth-century memoirs and histories, and combine some veneration of Swift and others as 'patriots' with a less predictable deployment of Lecky's history of the same period. Of Yeats there is no discernible trace. The following year, however, brought a sudden change of tactics.

The editorial for January 1924 referred to 'the newly enriched New Ascendancy' of whom (it seems) the trustees of the National Library were representative. The campaign against 'the most utterly depraved, beastly filth' now merged with the excoriation of the (allegedly) eighteenth-century Ascendancy, and this done by targetting the neologistic New Ascendancy. The prompt to this alteration of the *Bulletin*'s aproach was undoubtedly the appointment of several writers – not including Joyce of course, for government had its reservations also! – to the Senate. On 28 November 1923 the editorial noted with precision

> Senator Oliver St John Gogarty, writer of odes in ordinary and extraordinary to Trinity College as well as to the Tailteann Games Committee, and sole author of much else that is curious and perhaps facetious, moved congratulations to Senator William Butler Pollexfen Yeats, on the award of the Nobel Prize for Literature.[34]

The writer's grasp of irony was unable to handle even so palpably ironic a poem as 'September 1913', quoting the line 'Romantic Ireland's dead and gone' as a literal statement, though adding 'which, being interpreted, means a notice to quit issued to all who adhere to Irish ideals, as affecting the education and the spirit of the country'. This foolishness might be ascribed to the writer's unfamiliarity with the techniques of poetic discourse – he had invariably quoted prose literature – but the description of Alfred Nobel as 'a deceased anti-Christian manufacturer of dynamite', and the characterization of the Prize as 'the Stockholm dole', reveal incipient monomania. Yeats was challenged to defend both his art and the superlatives which Gogarty had used in congratulating the poet. 'What music, what perfection, what ideal? Let Senator Yeats answer.'[35]

No answer was the firm reply. But the New Ascendancy continued to feature in the *Bulletin*, notably in a series of articles by Conor Malone.[36] The April 1924 editorial identified the Royal Irish Academy as an 'Ascendancy Institution' and this despite its long record of devotion to Gaelic scholarship. Discussion as to where the parliament of the Free State should establish its permanent seat – a topic on which Yeats spoke in the Senate – led the editor into a prolonged denunciation of 'The Old House' in College Green, where the eighteenth-century parliament had met until the Union of 1800. 'Some of the New Ascendancy, Senator Pollexfen Yeats and his satillites' were mocked for their alleged longing to re-occupy the old house. 'But none of the Pollexfen propagandists, none of the pullulating penmen of the daily press' had equalled Agnes O'Farrelly's enthusiasm in this cause – and she is mockingly quoted to prove the point. Two prominent lexical extravagances are mobilized to support this onslaught – Yeats is repeatedly named Pollexfen, and the generality of eighteenth-century grandees branded as 'Ascendancy bashaws'.[37]

Is this just the further derangement of a propagandist keen to associate ascendancy with exotic names? On the contrary, the bashaw – a corrupt version of *pasha*, used in English as a synonym for grandee or any imperious figure – had been frequently used in the late eighteenth century (cf. Godwin's *Caleb Williams*) in conjunction with the kind of *soi-disant* dignity also associated with the term Protestant Ascendancy. The *Bulletin*'s line of supply was Lecky, drawing on Burke or on contemporaries of Burke. If bashaw had a broad provenance as a term of abuse, Pollexfen in contrast was highly specific. Yeats's mother, Susan Pollexfen, was the daughter of a Sligo family notable for its freemasonic activities, and for these reasons the surname was a useful synopsis of much that ultra-Catholic propagandists loathed in 1924. In deriding the modest efforts of Agnes O'Farrelly in the same breath as dismissing the Pollexfen propagandists, the *Bulletin* reiterated what was virtually a challenge to Yeats, for it dubbed her poem a 'poetic plea for the preservation of the Ascendancy'.[38]

When Yeats served on a Senate committee charged to inquire into the state of learning in Celtic Studies, he was again presented as Senator W. B. Pollexfen Yeats in an article which quoted derisively from the report he and Alice

Stopford Green had written, and which damned the Academy as 'the notorious mismanaging stronghold of the Ascendancy'. Later in the same issue, a meditation on Dublin Corporation's ethical standards permitted allusion to 'ascendancy business methods': as in its references to the 1790s, the *Bulletin* retained a shrewd sense of the term's mercantile origins.[39]

Nevertheless, at the end of 1924 the New Ascendancy rhetoric was still loudly audible. Alongside this latter-day political campaign against the assimilation of non-Catholic intellectuals to the Free State went a retrospective associating not only the generation of Swift but even that of Queen Elizabeth with the hated Old Ascendancy.[40] But Yeats had been tempted into retaliation, and consequently his contributions in *To-Morrow* were roundly condemned in successive editorials. That Yeats, Lennox Robinson, Francis Stuart and other writers in the short-lived paper loudly declared that they founded their art on the immortality of the soul mattered little. 'Leda and the Swan' served only to remind the editor of *Ulysses* – 'the recent Augustan Ascendancy and the Associated Aesthetes shows that when they exalt one and other they only expose one another. Their Swan Song has been penned, printed, and produced: the putrescence of their output has now to stink in public.'[41]

The *Kulturkampf* continued. Catholics were warned against any collaborating with a public library system sponsored by the Andrew Carnegie Trust, and a certain pride was taken in the collapse of 'a rather pretentious Catholic charitable enterprise' which had acknowledged the help of 'Catholic "rats" who frequent Trinity College'.[42] Of course, this is deplorable, but it would be a mistake to ignore how skilfully the argument is deployed, not only to a relatively unsophisticated readership but simultaneously against the most sophisticated readership in the country. Ascendancy was a central element in linking the persecution of Catholics in the past with the frustration of their self-appointed literary advisers in the Free State. Ascendancy paved the way for the incrimination of Yeats in the columns of the *Bulletin*, and Yeats's chosen medium of response (*To-Morrow*) ignominiously ceased publication after two issues.

When the government decided to introduce legislation prohibiting divorce, Yeats was a government nominee in the Senate; he was also vehemently opposed to the curtailment of civil rights in this area. His speech is well known: in practice, he prepared two speeches, one which he sent to *The Irish Statesman* from his holidays in Mussolinian Italy (where divorce was prohibited) in March 1925, and one which he contributed to the actual Senate debate in June of the same year. Though he deliberately referred to meetings of the Catholic Truth Society, cited the legal position in several predominantly

Catholic countries, and generally displayed an awareness of variety in Catholic attitudes towards sexuality and marriage, and though he also delivered himself of a splendid rhetorical performance – 'we are the people of Grattan; we are the people of Swift, the people of Emmet, the people of Parnell . . .' – nothing in either speech was heard of the Protestant Ascendancy.[43] That concept was evidently not yet required, even if Yeats's defeat in 1925 contributed to the build-up of political tensions which saw the exploitation of Ascendancy in the 1930s. By then, the European context in which Yeats was increasingly engrossed gave an added flavour to the vocabulary of élitist politics, while the passage of time had further confirmed the associations with Ascendancy which the *Catholic Bulletin* had striven over several years to inculcate in the public mind.

Yeats's later celebration of Protestant Ascendancy in 1934 can thus be seen as a reactive development in which the initiative had been seized by a significant sector of the Catholic intelligentsia. It may be argued that the *Bulletin* was scarcely representative of public opinion in the Free State, being ardently republican as well as relentlessly clericalist. In its promotion of a comprehensive off-the-peg ideology, it reproduced some items from Yeats's bespoke philosophy, at least as the latter developed in the next decade – approval of Mussolini, concern for education, anxiety over the electoral success of the left in France, untrammeled hatred of England. The poet's thought was subtle where the *Bulletin* was blunt, and yet in noting the growth of antagonism between them we should also acknowledge common interests. Thus, while it is usual to reserve the term 'intelligentsia' for an alienated corps of advanced opinion, at odds with authority and generally sympathetic to the claim of the arts, the unusual circumstances of the Free State in the 1920s allowed a magazine almost craven in its several orthodoxies to become a beacon of *la petite intelligentsia*, a thoroughly philistine paper which published poems.

The skill of the *Bulletin*'s campaign is nowhere better reflected than in its coinage of 'the New Ascendancy'. The phrase simultaneously identified Yeats and his associates with the corruption and exploitation of eighteenth-century Ireland *and* suggested they were not that old ascendancy but some latter-day, presumptive simulacrum thereof. Perhaps Fr Corcoran was unaware that, in a profound sense, Ascendancy always was a simulacrum. And, though historians may regard Yeats's Ascendancy rhetoric as just that and little more, it may have contributed to the frustration of clericalist ambitions to control every aspect of Irish public life – and many aspects of Irish private lives also. Despite the prohibition of divorce and the implementation of a strict state censorship of books, the grand schemata of the *Catholic*

Bulletin did not find universal support even among pious Irish Catholics. The totalizing project failed, and for that reason its ideological basis can be readily excavated. By a complementary logic, *From Burke to Beckett* aspires to be no comprehensive account of the culture it investigates, in the hope that partisan completeness may be outwitted.

CONSTRUCTING THE EIGHTEENTH CENTURY

> I wish someone would one day attempt a *tragic history of literature*
> showing how the various nations, which now take their highest
> pride in the great writers and artists they can show, treated them
> while they were alive.
>
> (Arthur Schopenhauer) [44]

As literary hero, Jonathan Swift possesses two complementary but contrasting qualities. He is himself immovably a man of integrity though one frequently moved in his emotional response to human folly. He acts as catalyst upon those whom he meets, changing their lives and accelerating their proper advance, yet he remains sequestered in his own obscurity, a darkness not of his own making though it mirrors the Christian humility his public mask too often fails to express. Among Irish authors, Sheridan Le Fanu, Thomas Caulfield Irwin, W. B. Yeats, Denis Johnston, Austin Clarke, and Sybil Le Brocquy have responded to the mystique of Swift as fictional hero. In essence, Swift is a shorthand term for crucial romantic themes, and the historical reasons why a writer born in the seventeenth century should take on this romantic role from the 1840s to the 1960s undoubtedly involve Swift's tangential relation to Augustanism, a relation which is itself an aspect of the entire political nexus of Anglo-Irish relations to which Swift devoted so much of his energies after his fall from grace in London. [45] In *The Sense of an Ending*, Frank Kermode has provided a cautionary account of how 'fictions can degenerate into myths whenever they are not consciously held to be fictive' – and the case of Swift (not to mention the notoriously elusive and omnipresent Goldsmith) illustrates the extent to which Anglo-Irish culture is haunted by ghostly fictions who still pack considerable mythic punch. [46] That such revenants do not always take the form of the individual human figure is evident if we consider the fond attention lavished on so-called eighteenth-century architecture. The deeper exchanges between architecture and human society lie, however, beyond the horizons of this present study.

Nevertheless landscape mediates between these terms, and in a way which can be rendered historically vital once more. Between the abolition of the Irish parliament in 1800 and the Treaty of 1921, Ireland had become an anomaly in which a heightened consciousness of distinguishing features flourished. Allegedly, at one end of the social scale (or rather, somewhere just below the middle), insurgent claims to social and political authority emphasized certain interpretations of the past as the facts of an argument; near the other, a superannuated élite stressed their perceptions of time and landscape as evidence of their survival. (The analysis of class implied in these observations is far from adequate, yet it serves to underline a common attachment to 'fact'.) Joyce's *Ulysses* is not only a celebration, by way of parody, of the encyclopaedic method: it is the initiation rite accorded to certain social 'facts' – the arrival of the urban *petit bourgeoisie*, the impact of consumerism, etc., etc. The landscape of Yeats's early poetry – and of much that he wrote later also – is a synthesis of geographical, linguistic, historical, and mythological reference to 'facts'. All such facts, whether Joycean or Yeatsian, exist in a state of perpetual challenge or permanent change, for they are part of an undefined culture, subject to the (seemingly) arbitrary manipulations which the colonial system requires. This effect is not restricted to the physical territory of Ireland, it pervades the social fabric of the United Kingdom as a whole. In *Reveries Over Childhood & Youth*, the young Yeats's experience of London topography is recorded:

> No matter how charming the place (and there is a little stream in a hollow where Wimbledon Common flows into Coombe Wood that is pleasant to the memory), I knew that those other boys saw something I did not see. I was a stranger there. There was something in their way of saying the names of places that made me feel this.[47]

To contrast this simply to the landscape of home is to miss all the subtleties of Yeats's implication of class and history in such passages. There is a passage in Yeats's introduction to Lady Gregory's *Cuchulain of Muirthemne* which reveals the sense of urgent mediation in such readings of the landscape:

> We Irish should keep these personages much in our hearts, they lived in the places where we ride and go marketing, and sometimes they have met one another on the hills that cast their shadow upon our doors at evening. If we will but tell these stories to our children the Land will begin again to be a Holy Land, as it was before men gave their hearts to Greece and Rome and Judea. When I was a child I had only to climb the hill behind the house to see long, blue, ragged hills flowing along the southern horizon. What beauty was lost to me, what depth of emotion is still perhaps lacking in me, because

nobody told me, not even the merchant captains who knew everything, that Cruachan of the Enchantments lay behind those long, blue, ragged hills.[48]

It is not difficult to see that the true significance of these words is all but the precise opposite of their literal meaning. For those for whom the hills automatically had mythological references, those who needed no dictionary to decode place-names, there was little sense of any creative discovery in the landscape. The obvious requires no statement. But to Yeats it was precisely the barrier, which he came to recognize between his childhood experience and those obvious meanings, which generated a poetic significance. To accomplish this transformation by which a knowledge of ignorance becomes art Yeats performs certain adjustments to the facts of his own life – 'the house', posing as the family (perhaps, ancestral) home, was in reality a place of holiday resort owned by relatives: 'the merchant captains', demythologized, were those relatives. Any reassessment of Yeats must acknowledge the primal authority for him of his belief that such facts are subject to the transformation of art. In acknowledging this, we go no further than the orthodoxies of romanticism. But the adjustments to Yeats's place in Irish society, to what is conveniently if inadequately called class, should advise us that the specifically Anglo-Irish manifestation of romanticism-becoming-modernism will involve political matters of the greatest weight. For the argument rests precisely on that fatal line distinguishing between Kermode's fictions and his myths. It is one thing for Yeats to fudge his history for artistic purposes: it is another for critics, tourists, and other politicians to accept those fictions as effective myths.

Central to any such re-assessment is Yeats's own historical position *vis-à-vis* the eighteenth century. The impression that the tradition of Swift and Burke was his discovery is of course part of a dramatic technique pervasive in Yeats's mythologizing. Neither Swift, Berkeley, Goldsmith nor Burke required resuscitation as individual reputations, though undoubtedly Yeats's association of the four added a new dimension to each. As a corollary, his lack of interest in Henry Brooke, Edmond Malone, and R. B. Sheridan is a further conditioning factor in the isolation of those who will come to exemplify the traditional role. Even more drastically, Yeats was prone to identify his own comparative ignorance of Gaelic culture with objective judgement, and his lack of curiosity on this question left him open to an uncritical inheritance of Victorian views of the Irish past, especially in the case of Goldsmith. Finally, while we should recall that Yeats's attitude between 1890 and 1930 swung from a rejection of the Irish Augustans as irrelevant to the Celtic Revival to a veritable establishment of Swift and Burke as the unofficial opposition in the politics of the Irish Free State, it is also true that association, lack of interest, rejection, and veneration proceed in a historical continuum.

Although Swift disturbed the Victorians, a decidedly sympathetic account of his life appeared in Lecky's *Leaders of Public Opinion in Ireland*.[49] Lecky saw his subjects as mediators between the imposed order of colonial government and the impotent politics of Jacobite resentment. Yeats in the course of time came to accept Swift and with him a neo-Jacobitism of his own. In the 1890s, however, he had no use for a mediator with the people of Ireland; they were accessible, he felt sure, through folklore and a literature based on folk tradition. Yeats's respect for Swift is not without precedent in Lecky's early work, and indeed the same author's monumental study of the Irish eighteenth century is an integral part of the historical readjustment which Yeats dramatizes in his work.

Turning to Burke we are of course returning to the origins of this inquiry into Anglo-Irish literature and its political connotations. Burke's Victorian reputation is too well known to need repetition here; half a dozen biographies testify to his position in British thought, and Disraeli's choice of title (earl of Beaconsfield) was a visible appropriation of Burke's place in political history. By 1882, however, a new reading is emerging: in *Irish Essays and Others* Matthew Arnold had taken as his chief witness to Irish conditions and the Irish psyche the author of the *Reflections*. We have seen that there is little paradox in the principal ideologue of the new imperialism – for it was thus the Victorians read Burke – becoming a key figure in Arnold's investment in Celtic culture. Was it not Burke himself who taught us to love the little platoon we belong to as our first duty towards humanity? The particularism of *Lyrical Ballads* was not absent from the *Reflections*, it was simply stated in universal terms. With Arnold, it is stated more explicitly in global terms.

With Berkeley the altering terms of debate are less publicly accessible. In 1824 Maria Edgeworth had corresponded with an American lady on literary matters, and recommended 'that most amiable man and bishop' whose *Querist* inquiries 'are all or almost all applicable at the present day to the state of Ireland'.[50] Two points should be noted, the less important being that the American had read nothing of Berkeley. More importantly, Maria Edgeworth considered Berkeley's contribution to be a fundamentally utilitarian one, an analysis of economic and social questions affecting the well-being of Ireland. Later, in 1865, we find Isaac Butt – who was shortly to initiate the Home Government Association which affected the development of cultural tradition in a far wider sphere than the strictly economic – choosing Berkeley as the subject of a prestigious afternoon lecture in

Dublin.[51] There is perhaps nothing entirely original in Butt's assessment of the Bishop of Cloyne, yet in contrast to Maria Edgeworth he sees Berkeley's work as a unified view of reality in which economics, optics, and metaphysics are aspects of one central argument. Furthermore, he links this idealism to Wordsworth's 'Immortality Ode'. Butt is echoing on the one hand certain contemporary philosophers who had resurrected some of Berkeley's views on sense-perception and, on the other, a distinctly Victorian and pious interpretation of romanticism. Nevertheless, the projected solipsism of Berkeley's philosophy and the protectionism which Butt read into his economics are welded into a kind of comprehensive account of Berkeley. A more determinedly objective view of the philosopher resulted in the publication in 1871 of an edition of his works, including for the first time the *Commentaries* from which Yeats culled the anti-Lockean tag. 'We Irish do not hold with this.'[52]

Discussing Berkeley then, we can trace a specifically Irish prologue to Yeats's enthusiasm; stages of which are Maria Edgeworth's strictly practical reading, Butt's more comprehensive account marked by strictly *period* emphases on piety and poetry, and finally Yeats's own early discounting of Berkeley (with Swift) as a significant exemplar for the Celtic Revival. Closely following this last declaration, there is the second Fraser edition of 1901. However, a broader background immediately presents itself. The polar extremes of Berkeley's reputation as either ultra-empiricist or supreme idealist were observed by Coleridge even within the pages of one work, *Siris*, which is 'announced as an Essay on Tarwater, which beginning with Tar ends with the Trinity'.[53] Donald Davie, writing in 1955, claimed that Berkeley 'until twenty or thirty years ago, was regarded as a proto-Romantic philosopher, one of the fathers of subjective idealism; and Yeats became interested in him at just about the time when Berkeleyans began to challenge this reading of him . . .'[54] But the challenge to Berkeley as subjective idealist was part of a larger revision of British intellectual history, the reassertion by Bertrand Russell, G. E. Moore, and others of the empiricist tradition eclipsed in the latter half of the nineteenth century by neo-Hegelian idealism. Fraser's editions of Berkeley in 1871 and 1901 virtually delimit the period of idealist dominance in Cambridge. That later date of course takes us close to a further change in the history of philosophy to which we have already alluded, the origins of phenomenology and the general crisis of European culture known as modernism. One is tempted to seize on A. D. Nuttall's advice to the reader approaching Berkeley – 'do not allow yourself to be elevated by the dexterous, liberating thought you are about to watch; only remember that you will end exactly where you began.'[55]

OLIVER GOLDSMITH: TRADITIONAL BIOGRAPHY

> And yet when I arrived at page two of the narrative I saw the
> extreme putridity of the social system out of which Goldsmith
> had reared his flower.
>
> (James Joyce)[56]

In dealing with Goldsmith's biography there are two crucial historical
moments. The first of these is the collection of documents preserved in
Trinity College Dublin, and known as the 1641 Depositions. In due course,
we shall exhume material from the Revd John Goldsmith's account of his
sufferings during the Irish rebellion of that year, and relate the suppression
of such genealogical traces to the question of the construction of a Goldsmith
biography. The other historical moment is likewise textual, the following
lines of Yeats's:

> Oliver Goldsmith sang what he had seen,
> Roads full of beggars, cattle in the fields,
> But never saw the trefoil stained with blood,
> The avenging leaf those fields raised up against it.[57]

The historical Goldsmith stands midway between these two moments, but
the ideological nature of the biographical enterprise is not best revealed by
strict adherence to chronology. Instead let us turn to John Forster's Victorian life of the poet.

Forster published *The Life and Times of Oliver Goldsmith* in 1871. When
he had earlier ventured into the field, he had been attacked by a rival
biographer, James Prior, essentially on a charge of plagiarism. Returning
to the question in 1871, Forster declared that the attack had been on Prior's
part 'nothing less than the claim to an absolute property in facts'.[58] As to
his own work, he continued: 'Not only are very numerous corrections to
every former publication relating to Goldsmith here made, and a great many
new facts brought forward, but each fact, whether old or new, is given from
its first authority.'[59] This talismanic addiction to facts (and to the word
'fact') permits Forster to ignore entirely the question of Goldsmith's origins
and the larger perspective of his place in the formation of Anglo-Irish society.
Given the date at which he is writing, Forster does not have to concern
himself with the issue of Anglo-Irish literature or the Irish Augustan tradition. And yet the Victorian Goldsmith (like the Victorian Swift) is one source
for the Yeatsian model of the same name.

The lines I have quoted from 'The Seven Sages', in common with Yeats's usual placing of Goldsmith, are explicitly dramatic. Goldsmith is seen or accounted for in dramatic relation to Swift or Burke. He represents the happy imperception of imminent revolution which is counterbalanced by Swift's involuntary witnessing of 'the ruin to come' in *The Words Upon the Window-Pane.* Each figure acts in complementary relation to others, and Goldsmith is consistently seen 'sipping at the honey-pot of his mind'.[60] The Yeatsian universe is always a matter of antinomies, and Goldsmith's permanent, partial function is to embody a transitory unity between antinomies. Thus he unites expression and perception, sings what he sees, and his vision specifies the beggars as well as the noblemen. Goldsmith, in Yeats's system, contributes permanence with inadequate acknowledgement of that process inherent in permanence; Swift, one might say, stands for the reverse – an excessive awareness of the process of imminent 'ruin' unchecked by the actual. Unable to see the bloodstained trefoil (shamrock and gibbet?), Goldsmith embodies a state of pre-lapsarian harmony, pristine innocence, the perfect conjunction of word and object, signifier and signified. As against this, we see Swift as fallen, knowing, self-divided, ironic, savage.

It is worth emphasizing at this point the degree to which this Yeatsian view of the Irish eighteenth century is a romantic construct, in which a Victorian positivism and a Nietzschean opposition of knowledge to power are all but explicit. That Yeats celebrates the age as 'that one Irish century that escaped from darkness and confusion' is no abdication from such a dualism.[61] Swift and Berkeley, Goldsmith and Burke may be recruited as dramatis personae in an enactment of this play, yet it is admitted (tacitly) that they too were a reversal of the age, that Swift was evicted from court circles, Berkeley sequestered in remote Cork, Goldsmith jeered into eccentricity, and Burke held in continued opposition. Thus, while the eighteenth century shows up the 'darkness' of the nineteenth, Swift and Goldsmith by their knowledge and innocence show up the tawdry mechanical achievements of the Augustan hegemony. As Swift rarely ceased from saying, pre-eminent among these mechanical achievements was the administration of Ireland whose land was largely owned by those Berkeley characterized as 'vultures with iron bowels'.[62] Properly indifferent to questions of localized setting and the preoccupation with naturalism, Joyce could read a few pages of *The Vicar of Wakefield* and diagnose the kind of culture in which Goldsmith worked – but in 1905 Joyce was also unaffected by the imminent Yeatsian myth of the Anglo-Irish Augustans. Looking at the symmetry of Swiftian knowledge and Goldsmithian innocence, we come finally to recognize the intensity of ideological investment in this myth.

The Protestant tradition which Yeats thus creates is to be seen in the historical moment of its articulation and not of its alleged setting alone. That is to say, it follows upon the dead Parnell, and the exertions of Augusta Gregory and Horace Plunkett after the turn of the century. By extending these values as exemplary to the new Free State, it contributes a family tree to that version of Victorian philanthropy which Yeats disguises as aristocratic service. This 'non-political' service may be elevated into a tradition by the invocation of a sequence of such figures – from Swift to Burke. The contradiction at the centre of this formulation is precisely this, that its sequence is not historical but mythic, and its order dramatic rather than diachronic. Add to this, the by now self-evidently oppositional nature of this service and Yeats's tragic aesthetic is seen as the vehicle by which a specifically *fin de siècle* social dichotomy is provided with a resonant history, an Edenic past from which it is a falling-away nobly transformed.

Here we may resume contact with the issue of Goldsmith's biography and its metamorphosis. Yeats's categorization of Irish society, like his periodization of its history, required polar terms, and these he found in the Catholic/Protestant antagonism. From the 1790s onwards, these terms had gradually shifted from a relationship of mutual hostility (i.e. rival versions of the same creed) to one of mutual exclusivity. In this the deployment of sectarian feeling contributed to the perception of a rigidly stratified class system in Ireland, in which class is intensively perceived as a group rather than as the complex relations of a social formation. Goldsmith, within the Yeatsian schema, while embodying an innocent harmony of the 'seen' and the 'sung', is required to remain within a back-dated eighteenth-century reflection of this essentially post-revolutionary sociology.

It is at this point that the first of our historical moments should be considered, the 1641 Depositions:

> John Goldsmith, parson of Burrishoole, in the county of Mayo, sworn and examined, says that between three and four years before the last rebellion in Ireland began, Francis Goldsmith, the deponents brother, who is a Romish priest of good account, living at and being Captain Major of the castle of Antwerp in Brabant, wrote and sent a letter to this deponent . . . which was delivered to him, this deponent, by one Father Richard Barret, a Jesuit and Spanish preacher . . . This letter, as this deponent has heard, was first delivered at Antwerp aforesaid to Malone, the arch-Jesuit that dwelt in Dublin . . . he is hereby persuaded that the said Malone had forewardly revealed the intended plot of rebellion to this deponents said brother which induced him so earnestly to write for this deponent, his wife and children to leave the kingdom and so escape the danger thereof which this deponent did not suspect, nor in any way understand, until the latter end of July next . . .[63]

Even as historical evidence of the rebellion, this document contains serious defects – as legal testimony it is and was less than worthless. Nevertheless, together with the subsequent confession of 'having been formerly a romish priest and converted to the protestant religion by the light of God', it establishes our poet's family's origins as including active Catholics. More surprisingly, the resemblance of the Revd John Goldsmith's experiences in 1641 to the conventional view of poor Nol has not been noted. (To have had three-and-a-half years' notice – on good authority! – of a rebellion universally execrated for its precipitative treachery, and yet to have been pathetically embroiled as victim, this indeed is worthy of Oliver Goldsmith's reputation for thriftless vulnerability.) One reason for this failure to note Goldsmith's Catholic pedigree may be identified in Sir John Temple's omission of such associations in reporting the case of the Revd John Goldsmith – though he was not averse to using them in other instances.[64] That the document was known to biographers almost from the outset cannot be denied: James Prior cited it at some length in the opening pages of his 1837 *Life*.[65] Prior, however, was also the biographer of Burke (1824) and was well aware of Burke's contemptuous dismissal of the Depositions as propaganda.[66]

Prior uncritically cites the Depositions in 1837, but John Forster has entirely eliminated them by the time his *Life* first appeared in 1848. Forster's laundering of Goldsmith's ancestry, while it superficially appears to remove crude innuendo and self-contradictory evidence of a bygone controversy, is a far more damaging blow to genuine historical veracity than Prior's unanalytical citations of the Depositions. However, the onward march of a sectarian sociology of Ireland (together with a romanticizing of the eighteenth century in retrospect) required the elimination of the admission that Goldsmith's ancestor had been a Catholic priest, and that in the 1630s there had been affable correspondence between the Goldsmith brothers, one Catholic, one Protestant. It is true of course that the poet and his brother told Thomas Percy about a forebear called Juan Romeiro, a Spanish tutor who settled and married a good Protestant Miss Goldsmith.[67] That 'tradition' of course is a conveniently narrative explanation (John the Swordfish) of a more significant social transformation occurring between the early seventeenth and late eighteenth century. The late Gerald Simms observed in this connection that 'Oliver Goldsmith's Irish background was very different from that of Jonathan Swift . . .'.[68] and we might add that these differences amount to a demolition of the ironically nationalistic model which Yeats imposed on Goldsmith and Swift as a rebuke to de Valera and Cosgrave. However, such exercises as these are meaningless if they do not also establish the historical continuity which led to the Yeatsian model. Instead of Yeats's Goldsmith, we substitute no seemingly pristine Goldsmith's Goldsmith, but instead seek to recover every stage of the process by which Johnson, Percy, Prior, Forster, and others contribute to the neo-romantic Goldsmith of 'The Seven Sages'. Our reading of the poet does not itself recover that figure, rather it contributes a further element to the object of its own attention. In this way, tradition successively ratifies and condemns itself.

THE ANGLO-IRISH LITERARY TRADITION

> The tradition of the dead generations weighs like a nightmare
> on the minds of the living. And, just when they appear to be
> engaged in the revolutionary transformation of themselves and
> their material surroundings, in the creation of something which
> does not yet exist, precisely in such epochs of revolutionary crisis
> they timidly conjure up the spirits of the past to help them . . .
> (Karl Marx)[69]

Can we therefore come at last to a conclusion, lay the ghost of Yeats's tradition, define the limits of Anglo-Irish literature within newly ratified frontiers, and . . . so to bed? It is not so easy. For one thing, we have yet to confront the ultimate Yeatsian working out of tradition (in *Purgatory*), the moment at which the local politics of Catholic Nationalism and Protestant Ascendancy throw vast shadows lit by the ghastly presence of Europe. For another, deconstruction which unmasks one system in the pretence of establishing none leads at best either to densely annotated scepticism or simply to a rearranged curriculum of events. Literary history requires more, because more is required of it in the peculiar circumstances of Irish culture.

A literature which includes Yeats and Joyce is in no imminent danger of neglect; they, together with Synge, Shaw, O'Casey, Wilde, and Moore, ensure the viability of Anglo-Irish literature as an academic industry. And, though there are difficulties attaching to the term 'Anglo-Irish literature' it is too late to purge it from our critical vocabulary. There is of course a general linguistic ambiguity lying behind the specifically Anglo-Irish problems – there are the multiple ways in which the word 'literature' is used. Though the sense of 'imaginatively composed and formally organized written works' predominates, there is also the looser (or larger) sense of 'written works about, or commentaries upon, a subject or topic' – thus there is the literature of industrial disputes, of parapsychology, and so forth. This ambiguity is a radical one for it brings together in the one term the rival claims of form and content, manner and matter, style and theme. But there is another dimension: by English literature we mean at times the literature produced by the English people or the English nation, and the moment of English literature's emergence can be related to specific developments in English politics and social institutions; at other times, however, English literature is the sum of texts (wherever written) in the English language. Anglo-Irish literature, therefore, is not so much a description or a definition, but an eclectic convenience. We must take care that we do not attempt false analogies on the basis of the term's outward resemblance to 'English literature'. For to do so would be to disclose a curious instability in the noun 'Anglo-Ireland' and its adjectival derivative, an instability which might suggest a route to discovering contradictions in our implicit notions of Ireland, England, Britain, etc.

One previous attempt at a theory of Anglo-Irish literature deserves notice here. For Daniel Corkery, literature was national in so far as it dealt with the experience of the Irish people. His concept of the Irish people, their experience, and the way that literature 'deals with' experience, was fundamentally crude – exile, non-Catholicism, a neglect of local setting were sufficient to disqualify a Shaw or a Moore. But to see that Corkery was not without distinguished predecessors in this approach, one has only to consider Yeats's early quarrel with Edward Dowden and his rejection of Swift and Berkeley (in the 1880s) as irrelevant to the new rural consciousness, the new nationalism. And yet there is something curiously abstract about the notion of an Augustan tradition in Ireland. Even if we leave aside the question of Yeats's debt to the Victorians in his construction of the Goldsmith of 'The Seven Sages', it remains true that the common identity which the Irish Augustans possess is the paradoxical sharing of isolation. (This becomes evident at a further level if one considers the relationship of Gaelic literature to Berkeley, say, or Grattan.) We should be careful that we do not replace nationalist or Yeatsian myths with a museum curator's display model of history. The idea that research can reconstruct a miraculously untarnished and unchanging work of art, the 'ding-an-sich', is ludicrous. Every act of criticism and interpretation is an attempt to bring together past and present, and we should be cheated if we were to accept literature simply as the graph of history. Robert Weimann has suggested that 'it is surely no idealism to assume that the work of art is not merely a product, but a 'producer' of its age; not merely a mirror of the past, but a lamp to the future', and he associates this approach with Marx's 'special forms of production – as in the sense that the work of art can produce its audience, and influence their attitudes and values'.[70] This is sensible as far as it goes; it is perhaps advisable to emphasize that literature is not only a form of knowledge which might be translated into others – into statistical data, social analysis, or political history. Literature is a special form of knowledge in that it not only knows but *informs*; it both longs for and imposes order. It is simultaneously a form of knowledge and a knowledge of form. The idea of Corkery and Marx in cahoots is perhaps fanciful, and yet neither gave sufficient attention to the special forms of production which might operate in an advanced colonial society in which the manufacture of literary ideology in the modernist period became pre-eminent.

T. S. Eliot's famous essay 'Tradition and the Individual Talent' appeared in 1919 and leads directly into the post-war phase of English-language modernism. At work on 'The Waste Land', Eliot is concerned in the essay to relate the modernism and traditionalism of his values:

> What happens when a new work of art is created is something that happens simultaneously to all the works of art which preceded it. The existing monuments form an ideal order among themselves, which is modified by the introduction of the new (the really new) work of art among them. The existing order is complete before the new work arrives, for order to persist after the supervention of novelty, the *whole* existing order must be, if ever so slightly, altered; and so the relations, proportions, values of each work of art toward the whole are readjusted; and this is conformity between the old and the new.[71]

Here we have the declarative heart of an essay which began tentatively enough, 'In English writing we seldom speak of tradition, though we occasionally apply its name in deploring its absence.' From this cautious opening Eliot proceeds in a way which has been inadequately noted to deal with literature through the metaphor of *works*, that is mental objects rather than the relations or processes conveniently summarized and concentrated in the metaphor of their being separate things. Wishing to establish relations between contemporary literature and that of the past, he is prepared to minimize the relational existence of literature *per se*. Here, the valorization of the past as more real than the present and the increased autonomy of the modernist work of art are shown to be hand in hand. In a later essay, Eliot reformulates his fundamental point but significantly conceives a series of great artists whose genius is apparently quantifiable: 'Whenever a Virgil, a Dante, a Shakespeare, a Goethe is born, the whole future of European poetry is altered.'[72] By 1948, the modernist emphasis on the ability of the present to affect the past has dwindled to this less exciting announcement. The truth is that every event in literary history is potentially a present event, and the past cannot simply be inherited; as Eliot rightly observed in 1919, 'if you want it you must obtain it by great labour.'[73]

I he continuing process of representing the past, of achieving a re-vision
of it, is indeed asserted by Yeats himself, thus sanctioning the eclipse of
his own assertion:

> Civilisation is hooped together, brought
> Under a rule, under the semblance of peace
> By manifold illusion; but man's life is thought,
> And he, despite his terror, cannot cease
> Ravening through century after century,
> Ravening, raging, and uprooting that he may come
> Into the desolation of reality.[74]

To refer these lines to Nietzsche, to a modernist aesthetic, to Yeats's interest
in a secret or symbolist history, is in each case possible. Possible also is it
to demonstrate that, with these lines available to us, we can now re-read
that splendid, nervous passage from Burke's *Reflections on the Revolution
in France* opening with the assertion that 'society is indeed a contract', proceeding to elevate that contract into a universal, moral imperative, and concluding with a staccato evocation of the 'antagonistic world of madness,
discord, vice, confusion and unavailing sorrow' which must follow any violation of the contract.[75] In other words, we could now come at last to the
conclusion that the Anglo-Irish tradition begins with Burke rather than Swift,
Burke rather even than Maria Edgeworth. Yet to do so would be to abdicate
from the business of identifying the operative historical points of focus
through which literary history becomes effective, in favour of yet another
chronology.

Leaving aside, then the question of Burke and Yeats, we can concentrate
more profitably on the method rather than the material. Three historical
points of focus are involved, the first revolving round the reader's specific
responsibilities. In *Truth and Method* Hans-Georg Gadamer has provided
guidance in this connection:

> The reader does not exist before whose eyes the great book of world history
> lies open. But nor does the reader exist who, when he has his text before him,
> simply reads what is there. Rather, all reading involves application, so that
> a person reading a text is himself part of the meaning he apprehends. He
> belongs to the text that he is reading.[76]

The term which Gadamer provocatively uses for the characteristic which
the reader brings to his text is prejudice: there can be no view of past literature
which is not positively affected by the prejudices of the reader. Because,
for Gadamer, all experience is experience of human finitude it follows that
the reader is obliged to be aware of his own position in the historical process: by prejudice he means a consciousness of all those attitudes, needs,

abilities, and inadequacies which characterize the reader as he confirms his relationship with the past by the act of reading. And the term which Gadamer uses for this relationship is properly dialectic, that is, question and answer, dramatic conversation. 'Tradition is not simply a process that we learn to know and be in command of through experience; it is language, i.e. it expresses itself like a "Thou". A "Thou" is not an object, but stands in relationship with us.'[77] Only through such a revised concept of reading itself can we begin to discover a new tradition, a tradition in which the future is acknowledged as real. Through the work of Samuel Beckett and Elizabeth Bowen it may emerge that the better sense of tradition is betrayal, that is, betrayal of the past in the name of a possibly continuing present.

The second historical point of focus through which literary history can become effective centres on the question of the nature of the literary text. One can see that the tacit assumption of Eliot's modernist aesthetic was that literature consists of artefacts, objects or works which possess a degree of autonomy criticism has no need to challenge. Now that the moment of the New Critics has passed this concept of the work of literature probably has few serious advocates. With the renovation of psychoanalysis in France and elsewhere, and with other related practices emphasizing other forms of repression as active within and around the official contours of an artwork, it is more profitable now to consider if significant absences do not constitute a meaning of literature and art. The genesis of a text is a function of the text's meaning, just as the reader too contributes his application in the act of reading. It is not enough, however, simply to regard all texts from the canon as equally susceptible to these altered procedures: in order to identify the text which forms an operative historical point of focus one needs to draw upon a historical materialism which reads history as possessing more than a determined past. In other words, the entire political unconscious which underlies the extensive cultural production we have called Anglo-Irish literature must be articulatable through the reading of this text, if the text is effectively an operative focus. In the following chapter I take Yeats's play *Purgatory* to be such a text, and in analysing it I hope to show that its significant absences also throw light on the repressed history of Yeats's tradition, the history which has been betrayed by the ideological operations of Protestant Ascendancy. Using Edmund Burke and W. B. Yeats as the poles of an argument, and concluding with an examination of *Purgatory* seen as the ablation of this tradition, I read the play as the supreme statement of Yeats's tradition, but I require the term 'ablation' to convey the play's complexity in both defining and destroying the tradition it brings to completion. Far from employing such terminology to divert attention from an inquiry into the social base of Irish culture, and the modes of production therein, I hope to ground my argument very solidly on the evidence of the author's social experience. Perhaps one might say that this experience influenced the play. It is preferable to speak of the text's genesis through this experience and through the broader medium of the language in which it finds itself. There is a *pensée* of Pascal's which can summarize the position for us:

> Since everything then is cause and effect, dependent and supporting, mediate and intermediate, and all is held together by a natural though imperceptible chain, which binds together things most distant and most different, I hold it equally impossible to know the parts without knowing the whole, and to know the whole without knowing the parts in detail.[78]

But there is a third historical point of focus, larger than reader or effective text. It is not simply the epoch, as Hippolyte Taine argued, though *Purgatory's* place in the era of fascism can hardly be passed over without comment. It is rather the suppressed history of such crises, the business of the literary historian being the identification of that suppression as it turns the larger historical sequence towards a particular ideological purpose. In charting the Victorian construction of a Goldsmith biography, we have already observed the obverse of this suppression. In examining *Purgatory* we will encounter a particularly pure form of this suppressed Victorian history. A full account of Yeats's place in the history of Victorian thought remains to be written: here in looking briefly at Lecky, Arnold, Forster, or even Dowden as precursors we are not bound to seek for verbal echoes or to document loans and borrowings. Yeats is the culmination of a mid- and late-Victorian re-reading of the Irish eighteenth century, a re-reading which can be conveniently dated from Arnold's Oxford lectures *On the Study of Celtic Literature* given in the year of the Irish poet's birth.

However, there is silence in Yeats's rhetoric also: hand in hand with the invocation of Swift and Burke there are elisions and lacunae. Take, for example, a passage where he seeks a universal metaphysic which yet retains the appearance of the concrete world, one of those visions of the disembodied and yet muscular world to which his phenomenological tendencies led him:

> It was indeed Swedenborg who . . . discovered a world of spirits where there was a scenery like that of earth, human forms, grotesque or beautiful, senses that knew pleasure and pain, marriage and war, all that could be painted upon canvas, or put into stories to make one's hair stand up.[79]

The probability exists here that Yeats has the fiction of Sheridan Le Fanu in mind, for in *Uncle Silas* and in the short stories of *In a Glass Darkly*

Le Fanu explicitly used Swedenborgian doctrines in his sensational plots. Nevertheless, Yeats's prose remains inscrutable, refusing to divulge a name. Now, Liam Miller has revealed that the earliest draft of *The Words Upon the Window-Pane* connects the theme of the play to Le Fanu's fiction, especially the tales of *In a Glass Darkly*.[80] The point is not simply that Yeats suppressed the nineteenth-century avenue by which he sought to approach Jonathan Swift, the central (and absent) character of the play. Le Fanu had indeed family links with Swift (through the Sheridans) and had inherited a number of relics of the Dean's. More significantly however, the specific function of Swedenborgianism in Le Fanu's fiction was to provide a symbolism through which neurosis was analysed; and while the characters of the stories seem discrete and private when considered individually, the overall structure of *In a Glass Darkly* transforms their personal symptoms into a cultural malaise explicitly related to the French Revolution and 'the ruin to come'. The suppression of the Le Fanu reference and its attendant apparatus is dramatically effective; more specifically, its effect is of a consciously tragic kind. Without the intervention of Le Fanu's bourgeois neurosis, the image of Swift is projected directly on to the audience's imagination with the minimum of historical or narrative mediation. That is, the Dean is caught in the truth of his own prophecy.

The elimination of the Le Fanu reference from the early stages of the play's genesis is not just a negative feature of the play, something we know by virtue of our scholarly prurience. In *The Words Upon the Window-Pane* Swift's tragic vision of civilization's end is prefaced and produced by the vulgarity of table-rapping and a distinctly *petit-bourgeois* cast of spiritualists. As they discuss their contributions to the séance, practise their lines for the longed-for encounter with departed spirits, and criticize their fellows, the figures constitute a play-within-the-play. They may also be regarded as an audience awaiting Swift's performance, though ironically they will have departed before his spirit speaks through Mrs Henderson. Their departure, the elimination of the play-within, the obliteration of Mrs Henderson's voice by that of Swift, enacts the suppression of those historical connections by which Yeats reaches Swift. The discarding of Le Fanu's *In a Glass Darkly* is an integral part of the structure and meaning of the play.

What then is the significance of this suppressed history? What particular value has *The Words Upon the Window-Pane* as a demonstration of this suppression? Despite (or perhaps because of) the immaturity and unevenness of his work, Le Fanu was the literary spokesman of the Irish Victorian middle classes, a formation uniquely affected by the notions of Protestant Ascendancy. In Marx's terms one might see Le Fanu's colleagues timidly conjuring up the spirits of the past to help them. What Yeats's play achieves – and with a vengeance! – is to take that metaphor of spirit-conjuring seriously and to eliminate the timid bourgeois who foolishly have recourse to such theatrical props. The redundancy of the so-called Ascendancy, the prevalence of exile settings, the location of identity solely in guilt – these are the hallmarks of Le Fanu's fiction. Swedenborg's solipsistic cosmology allowed him to reveal the purposelessness of the Great House in *Uncle Silas*, while in *In a Glass Darkly* the same doctrines provided an analysis of individual neurosis. What Le Fanu and his characters find unacceptable, unintelligible, is their merely contingent existence, their bourgeois condition. Yeats's exclusion of all this stems from his recognition of the *validity* of Le Fanu's diagnosis, validity that is within the circumstances (the prejudices as Gadamer would have it) of Yeats's own historical position as reader. In order that Yeats may artistically acknowledge his own origins in the self-destructive world of Le Fanu – and to transform those origins artistically – he must expunge them from his work. They form a negative mould, an antithetical shape from which Yeats's imagination releases itself. To be specific, one can see the sequence of events in *The Words Upon the Window-Pane* as an implied or desired causation: the departure/suppression of the *petit-bourgeois* cast will allow unmediated access to aristocratic tradition in Swift, but that revelation is necessarily tragic in itself, and admonitory to us.

And the notion of tradition is peculiarly relevant here, especially if we note Freud's radical reinterpretation of the artistic urge. Connecting individual neurosis and civilization (*Kultur*) he argues that 'neuroses ultimately reveal themselves as attempts to solve on an individual basis the problems of wish compensation that ought to be solved socially by institutions.'[81] For Freud, *Kultur* only shows the ways men have attempted 'to bind their unsatisfied wishes under the varying conditions of fulfilment and denial by reality . . .'.[82] I have already suggested how reality in Ireland underwent a continuous process of obfuscation, or was atomized into a scintillation of facticity. Thus, it is doubly true that in colonial Ireland tradition offered a publicly sanctioned compensation for necessary cultural renunciations.[83]

Marx . . . Eliot . . . Gadamer all three perspectives cited here are called into being, called into question, by the concentration and purity of *Purgatory*. The sight of conjured spirits dramatizes once again the tragedy of Protestant Ascendancy, but not in the aesthetic self-congratulation of *The Words Upon the Window-Pane* – there is no Swift to bolster the pretence that this drama is remediable history. As Eliot astutely observed, after the supervention of this novelty the whole pre-existing order is modified, however slightly, modified and changed by the apparent dramatization of unchanging process. Finally, we read this text applying ourselves to its meaning, finding our meaning there in murderous consequence of endogamous pride.

NOTES AND REFERENCES

1 John Henry Blunt, *Dictionary of Sects* (London, 1874), p. 128. See Howard Caygill, 'Benjamin, Heidegger and the Destruction of Tradition' in Andrew Benjamin and Peter Osborne (eds.), *Walter Benjamin's Philosophy: Destruction and Experience* (London: Routledge, 1994), pp. 12-13, for a more recent explanation of the same ambiguity.
2 W. B. Yeats, 'Coole Park and Ballylee, 1931', *The Poems*, Daniel Albright, ed. (London: Dent. 1990), p. 294.
3 Except where otherwise stated all citations in this paragraph may be found in the *Oxford English Dictionary*, s.v. 'tradition'.
4 Edward Shils, *Tradition* (London: Faber, 1981), p. 16.
5 See for this background H. Stuart Hughes, *Consciousness and Society: The Reorientation of European Social Thought 1890–1930* (Brighton: Harvester Press, 1979), 2nd edn.
6 See Edward Shils, op. cit., *passim*.
7 'You have only to compare a great Protestant Manifesto like Houston Chamberlain's *Foundations of the Nineteenth Century* with the panics of Sir Edward Carson and Lord Londonderry to realize how completely Ireland has been kept out of the mighty stream of modern Protestantism by her preoccupation with her unnatural political condition.' G. B. Shaw, *The Matter with Ireland* (London: Cape, 1962), pp. 68-9. Chamberlain's book had been published in 1911.
8 See W. B. Yeats, *Explorations* (London: Macmillan, 1962), p. 435 n.
9 W. B. Yeats, 'Journal', *Memoirs*, Denis Donoghue, ed. (London: Macmillan, 1972), p. 156.
10 Martin Heidegger, *Being and Time*, trans. John Macquarrie and Edward Robinson (Oxford: Blackwell, 1980), p. 44.
11 Ibid., p. 43.
12 See Victor Farias, *Heidegger et le nazisme* (Lagnaise, 1987); Hugo Ott, *Martin Heidegger: a Political Life* (London, Harper Collins, 1993); Ortwin de Graef, *Serenity in Crisis: a Preface to Paul de Man, 1939–1960* (Lincoln: Univ. of Nebraska Press, 1993). De Graef's study traces de Man's development up to and including the influential essay, 'Image and Emblem in Yeats' which de Man published in 1960. I was living in Antwerp when in 1987, news broke of de Man's wartime journalism in the Anglophone academic world. A Belgian, to whom this was not news, added glumly 'He also stole books.' My own reference in the next paragraph to Heidegger's 'passive acceptance of National Socialist rule in Germany' is clearly now an understatement.
13 Ludwig Wittgenstein, *Culture and Value*, trans. Peter Winch (Oxford: Blackwell, 1980), p. 76e.
14 W. B. Yeats, 'The Autumn of the Body', *Essays and Introductions* (London: Macmillan, 1961), p. 189; see Frank Lentricchia, *After the New Criticism* (London: Athlone Press, 1980), pp. 67-8.

15 W. B. Yeats, 'The Autumn of the Body', *Essays and Introductions*, p. 193.
16 Roger Waterhouse, *A Heidegger Critique* (Brighton: Harvester Press, 1981), p. 30.
17 W. B. Yeats, 'Poetry and Tradition', *Essays and Introductions*, p. 248.
18 Ibid., p. 253.
19 Ibid.
20 Ibid., p. 249.
21 Ibid., p. 258.
22 Ibid., pp. 259-60. It is worth noting here that the essay appeared first in December 1908 in a Cuala Press limited edition under the title 'Poetry and Patriotism'; by the time it was collected in *The Cutting of an Agate* (1912), its familiar title was well established.
23 *The Catholic Bulletin*, vol. 12, No. 1 (January 1922), p. 5.
24 Ibid., vol. 12, No. 4 (April 1922), pp. 198, 202. The editor pays due attention to the role of J. E. Devereux in describing various petitions for relief (see p. 203).
25 Ibid., vol. 12 No. 4 (April 1922), pp. 256-62. No date is provided for the death of third victim, Fr James O'Callaghan. By the June 1922 issue the series title has become 'Events of Easter Week – and After', but my diagnosis stands.
26 See 'The Volunteers' (dated February 1921) in ibid., vol. 12, No. 6, p. 380.
27 'To All Artists and Writers'; see W. B. Yeats *Writings on Politics and Irish Literature* forthcoming (1995) from Penguin Books.
28 *The Catholic Bulletin*, vol. 13 No. 2 (February 1923), p. 83. (Punctuation supplied.) Cf. Yeats 'Bishop Berkeley' (1931), *Essays and Introductions*, p. 400.
29 Ibid., vol. 13, No. 3 (March 1923), p. 131.
30 Ibid., vol. 13, No. 3 (March 1923), p. 132.
31 Ibid., p. 189.
32 Ibid., vol. 13, No. 6 (June 1923), pp. 369-73. The author was The Revd J. J. Murphy.
33 Ibid., vol. 13, No. 7 (July 1923), pp. 440-44. See also Murphy's 'An "Ascendancy Man" Described by Himself: John Carden (1771 – 1858)', Ibid., vol. 13, No. 8 (August 1923), pp. 531-3; 'Social Life of the Ascendancy as Described by Themselves' vol. 13, No. 9 (September 1923), pp. 625-9; 'The Ascendancy and the Gael,' vol. 13, No. 10 (October 1923), pp. 708-11. Though imaginative writers including Maria Edgeworth, Mary Martin, and Somerville and Ross are repeatedly cited – rarely to their advantage – Yeats does not appear to feature in Murphy's articles.
34 Ibid., vol. 14, No. 1 (January 1924), p. 5.
35 Ibid., pp. 6-7.
36 See 'The Very Newest History of Ireland', vol. 14, No. 1 (January 1924), pp. 48-53, 'Mr. Stephen Gwynn's Historical Propaganda', No. 2 (February 1924), pp. 126-131, 'Shane Leslie Patronises the Irish', vol. 14, No. 3 (March 1924), pp. 211-7.
37 Agnes O'Farrelly was a lecturer in modern Irish at University College Dublin, whose poem 'The Old House' had appeared in *The Irish Independent* of 29 January 1924; for a contrasting assimilation of her name into literature, see the analysis of *Finnegans Wake* on pp. 279-80 above. For the bashaws see, *The Catholic Bulletin*, vol. 14, No. 3 (March 1924), p. 171.
38 Ibid., vol. 14, No. 3 (March 1924), p. 171.
39 Ibid., vol. 14, No. 7 (July 1924), pp. 556 and 565.
40 Ibid., vol. 14, No. 10 (October 1924), p. 861 etc.

41   Ibid., vol. 14, No. 11 (November 1924), p. 937. Something of the condition
      in which the academic teaching of literature existed in Ireland at the time may
      be judged from this editorial. It began by quoting with approval the opinion
      of W. Fitzjohn Trench, professor of English at Trinity College, on the subject
      of *Ulysses* ('rakes hell and the sewers for dirt'). It ended by commending a speech
      at the Annual Conference of the Catholic Truth Society by Robert Donovan:
      'some of the very worst writings came from men who from their names and
      origin, might have been expected to be on the C.T.S. platform.' Robert Donovan
      held the chair of English literature at University College, and later combined
      that honour with chairmanship of the Censorship Board in which connection
      he banned the novels of his former colleague, Austin Clarke. A member of the
      Trinity English department subsequently served on the Censorship Appeals
      Board.

42   Ibid., vol. 14, No. 12 (December 1924), pp. 1021-22. In 1925 the *Bulletin*
      published several further attacks on 'ascendancy outposts in medicine' (January)
      and maintained its interest in history, 'The Ascendancy Church and Popular
      Education (1824–1827)' (April).

43   Donald R. Pearse, ed. *The Senate Speeches of W. B. Yeats* (London: Faber, 1961),
      pp. 89-102, 156-160 (quotation p. 99).

44   Arthur Schopenhauer, *Essays and Aphorisms*, sel. and trans. R. J. Hollingdale
      (Harmondsworth: Penguin, 1970), pp. 210-11.

45   For an authoritative but succinct account of this complex area see J. A. Downie's
      biography of Swift (London: Routledge and Kegan Paul, 1984).

46   Frank Kermode, *The Sense of an Ending* (London: Oxford University Press,
      1968), p. 39.

47   W. B. Yeats, 'Reveries Over Childhood and Youth', *Autobiographies* (London:
      Macmillan, 1955), p. 49.

48   W. B. Yeats, *Explorations* (London: Macmillan, 1962), pp. 12-13.

49   See Donal MacCartney, 'Lecky's *Leaders of Public Opinion in Ireland*', *Irish
      Historical Studies*, vol. 14 (1964–5), pp. 119-41.

50   *The Education of the Heart: The Correspondence of Rachel Mordecai Lazarus and
      Maria Edgeworth*, Edgar E. MacDonald, ed. (Chapel Hill: University of North
      Carolina Press, 1977), p. 58. Maria Edgeworth's copy of the 2-vol. edition of
      Berkeley's *Works* (Dublin, 1784) is in the library of King's College, Cambridge.

51   Isaac Butt, 'Berkeley', *Afternoon Readings in the Museum, St. Stephen's Green,
      Dublin* (London: [1866]), pp. 185-224.

52   W. B. Yeats, *Explorations*, p. 333. Yeats's insistence on the anti-English direc-
      tion of Berkeley's argument is a fine example of analysis by way of predisposed
      need. The four entries (392, 393, 394, 398) in Notebook B where Berkeley refers
      to 'we Irish men' etc. appear in the context of an argument against 'the
      Philosophers', 'the Mathematicians', 'Materialists Nihilarians', etc. His use of
      'we Irish' is simply a recourse to the view of ordinary people, the people of
      the place he lived and worked in. Indeed, entry 406 speaks scathingly of
      'hypothetical Gentlemen' and in the *Three Dialogues* Berkeley prefers butchers
      to professional philosophers, 'I have quitted several of the sublime notions I
      had got in their schools for vulgar opinions.' These latter citations might as
      easily suggest a class bias in Berkeley's deliberately argumentative method:
      A. A. Luce, in the notes to the standard edition of the *Philosophical Commentaries*,

discounts any notion of aggressive nationalism. (*Works of George Berkeley*, vol. i (London: Nelson, 1943), p. 124.) See, for more recent comment, W. J. Mc Cormack, 'Isaac Butt (1813 – 79) and the Inner Failure of Protestant Home Rule' in Ciaran Brady, ed., *Worsted in the Game: Losses in Irish History* (Dublin: Lilliput Press, 1989), pp. 121-31.

53   S. T. Coleridge, *Biographia Literaria*, George Watson, ed. (London: Dent, 1960), p. 166.

54   Donald Davie, 'Yeats, Berkeley, and Romanticism', in S. P. Rosenbaum, ed., *English Literature and British Philosophy* (Chicago, London: University of Chicago Press, 1971), pp. 278-9. This essay was first published in *Irish Writing*, vol. 31 (Summer, 1955), pp. 36-41. A further development of these influences is discussed in A. P. Swarbrick, 'Donald Davie, Berkeley, and "Common Sense"', *Long Room*, Nos. 20/21(1980), pp. 29-35.

55   A. D. Nuttall, *A Common Sky: Philosophy and the Literary Imagination* (London: Chatto and Windus, 1974), p. 30.

56   *Letters of James Joyce*, vol. ii, Richard Ellmann, ed. (London: Faber, 1966), p. 99. (JJ to Stanislaus J, 19 July 1905.)

57   W. B. Yeats, 'The Seven Sages', *The Poems* p. 291

58   John Forster, *Life and Times of Oliver Goldsmith* (London: Chapman and Hall, 1875), 6th edn, p. vii.

59   Ibid., p. ix. Aijaz Ahmad rightly protests in *In Theory: Classes, Nations, Literatures* (London: Verso, 1992) at the habit of 'a wide range of historians around the globe — some of the Indian Subalternists, for example' to encourage the putting of quotation marks round the word 'fact' (p. 194). In the present context I was anxious not to erode confidence in the possibility of historical knowledge, but rather to challenge the value of isolated, discrete, facts or atomic data.

60   W. B. Yeats, 'Blood and the Moon', *The Poems*, p. 287.

61   Yeats, 'Introduction to 'The Words Upon the Window-Pane', *Explorations*, p. 345.

62   'A Word to the Wise' *The Works of George Berkeley*, A. A. Luce and T. E. Jessop, eds. (London: Nelson, 1953), vol. iii, p. 243.

63   Trinity College, Dublin, MS 831, fo. 145 etc. Some of this material was included in Mary Hickson, *Ireland in the Seventeenth Century*, 2 vols. (London, 1884).

64   Sir John Temple, *The Irish Rebellion; or, an History of the beginnings and first progress of the general rebellion raised within the kingdom of Ireland, upon the three and twentieth day of October, in the year 1641. Together with the barbarous cruelties and bloody massacres which ensued thereupon* (London, 1646), pp. 67, 116-18. The most dispassionate analysis of Temple's unreliability, and of the Depositions generally, is still W. E. H. Lecky in his *History of Ireland in the Eighteenth Century* (London, 1896), vol. i, pp. 72-6.

65   James Prior, *The Life of Oliver Goldsmith* (London, 1837), vol. i, pp. 2-3. Prior's source may well have been Temple's highly influential and grossly prejudicial *History* of events in which he personally had lost a great deal of money.

66   See 'the rascally collection in the College relative to the pretended Massacre in 1641', Burke to Richard Burke Jnr, 20 March 1792, *The Correspondence of Edmund Burke*, vol. vii, P. J. Marshall and John A. Woods, eds. (Cambridge: Cambridge University Press, 1968), p. 104.

67   See Katherine C. Balderston, *The History and Sources of Percy's Memoir of*

Goldsmith (Cambridge: Cambridge University Press, 1926), p. 13. Patrick Murray has surveyed the factual problems of the Goldsmith biography, though he is not concerned to draw interpretive conclusions, 'Goldsmith's Ancestry: Fact and Tradition', in Harman Murtagh, ed., *Irish Midland Studies* (Athlone: Old Athlone Society, 1980), pp. 147-58.

68   I am grateful to Dr Hugh Shields who provided me with a copy of an unpublished paper (from which I quote here) delivered by his father-in-law, the late Professor J. G. Simms, at a Goldsmith centenary celebration in 1974.

69   Karl Marx, 'The Eighteenth Brumaire of Louis Bonaparte', *Surveys from Exile*, David Fernbach, ed. (London: Allen Lane, 1973), p. 146.

70   Robert Weimann, *Structure and Society in Literary History: Studies in the History and Theory of Historical Criticism* (London: Lawrence and Wishart, 1977), p. 48.

71   T. S. Eliot, 'Tradition and the Individual Talent', *Selected Prose*, Frank Kermode, ed. (London: Faber, 1975), pp. 38-9.

72   T. S. Eliot, *Notes towards the Definition of Culture* (London: Faber, 1948), p. 114.

73   Eliot, 'Tradition and the Individual Talent', p. 38.

74   W. B. Yeats, 'Meru' (Supernatural Songs), *The Poems*, p. 339.

75   Edmund Burke, *Reflections on the Revolution in France* (Harmondsworth: Penguin, 1969), pp. 194-5. See Patrick J. Keane's 'Revolutions French and Russian: Burke, Wordsworth, and the Genesis of Yeats's "The Second Coming"', *Bulletin of Research in the Humanities*, vol. 82, No. 1 (Spring 1979), pp. 18-52.

76   Hans-Georg Gadamer, *Truth and Method*, trans. and ed. Garrett Barden and John Cumming (London: Sheed and Ward, 1975), p. 304.

77   Ibid., p. 321.

78   Blaise Pascal, *Pensées* (London: Dent, 1931), p. 20.

79   Yeats, *Explorations*, p. 32.

80   Liam Miller, *The Noble Drama of W. B. Yeats* (Dublin: Dolmen Press, 1977), p. 287.

81   Sigmund Freud, 'The Claims of Psychoanalysis to Scientific Interest', quoted by Jürgen Habermas, *Knowledge and Human Interests*, trans. Jeremy J. Shapiro (Boston: Beacon Press, 1971), p. 276.

82   Idem.

83   This sentence is in part a rephrasing of Habermas, on Freud (Habermas, op. cit., p. 276). The later chapters of *Knowledge and Human Interests* suggest the broad application of the method of psychoanalysis as a literary hermeneutic, because 'Freud always patterned the interpretation of dreams after the hermeneutic model of philological research' (p. 214).

10

On *Purgatory*

A second chance — that's the delusion. There never was to be
but one. We work in the dark – we do what we can – we give
what we have. Our doubt is our passion and our passion is our
task. The rest is the madness of art.

(Henry James)[1]

SOURCES AND FORMS

What is *Purgatory?* Its successful stage-career proves that it is effectively
a play. On the other hand, the text itself resembles those dialogue poems
which Yeats wrote at various stages of his life. For a play, it seems limited
in its presentation of setting; for a poem, it seems overloaded with action.
These generic uncertainties should be read positively as evidence of Yeats's
full engagement in *Purgatory*, Yeats the dramatist, Yeats the poet. But the
uncertainties also mark a crisis in modernist aesthetic categories, a railing
against form or the persistent erection of one form as a bulwark against
another.

This unease – the term is too bland, but let it pass – in *Purgatory* has
local and global implications. For, while we can show that the play draws
extensively on Yeats's experience of Irish social history, we can also point
to parallels in, say, German culture. Some of these German parallels may
have their own prior association in Irish literary history; others – those involving Wagner, notably – suddenly open up the entire horizon of twentieth-
century European cultural crisis. With this perspective in mind, the shadowy

341

setting of *Purgatory* may stimulate once again that sense of embarrassment at the confluence of mighty reputations and marginal references which has already been discussed. Of course, followers of Lucien Goldmann's genetic structuralism may find in all these parallels material for an analysis of the homologies between the deep consciousness of a specific period and the structures of certain crucial works of literature. Such works are then seen to possess a 'world-historical view'.[2] In *Le Dieu caché*, Goldmann had elaborated this theory in analysing Pascal's *Pensées* and Racine's tragic drama and relating the structures of these works to the theological and social structures of Jansenism – he was, it should be noted, less successful in applying the method to twentieth-century literature. The relatively marginal position of Jansenism in France, as opposed to official Catholicism, should encourage those who are dismayed by the marginality of Ireland in relation to European affairs: not only did Yeats reproduce the proportions of marginality/centrality which Goldmann encountered in Pascal, but Yeats shared with Racine a specifically *tragic* outlook. It is worth noting these effective horizons within which Goldmann's original research was conducted before accepting the fashionable dismissal of genetic structuralism and its homologies. In the Anglo-Irish field marginality is *de rigueur* and, in that sub-set of the field known as Yeats, tragedy is pervasive. *Purgatory* brings together these characteristics, together with the generic tensions outlined above.

It is crucial to Goldmann's argument, of course, that the correlation of historical period or epoch and specific literary works is based on the form of the latter and not on their contents. It is only in inferior writing that one finds simple relations between content and context, and in such novels or plays one can only encounter an '*unachieved* consciousness of the time'.[3] The resemblance between *Purgatory* and an obscure German romantic play neatly illustrates this distinction. Zacharias Werner's 'Vierundzwanzig Februar' (1809) certainly resembles the plot of Yeats's play in several striking respects – recurrent murder within the family, the tyranny of Fate or a determined destiny, coincidence, etc.[4] The appeal of German romanticism in Ireland, and especially in what has been termed 'Anglo-Ireland', was very great indeed – the notorious weakness of the German middle class and the undeveloped condition of the German state offered parallels to the Protestant Ascendancy. If the landowners of Davitt's day gave the impression of possessing a heritage as venerable as that of pre-Bismarckian Junkers in Prussia, there is plenty of literary evidence as to where this belief originated. *Purgatory* does not derive its world-historical view from its resemblance to degenerate versions of *Sturm und Drang* – indeed, one significant divergence between the two plays is particularly important.

Werner's play makes specific the sectarian divisions of Swiss mountain society in which it is set, whereas Yeats's final version of *Purgatory* is silent on the Protestant/Catholic antagonism. In a manuscript scenario prepared in advance of the text, however, Yeats had specified as a crucial aspect of the *mésalliance* at the heart of the play that the marriage between the Lady and the Groom had taken place in a Catholic church – the lady had demeaned herself not simply by marrying her stablegroom but by marrying outside the sectarian 'tribe'.[5] Bearing this proto-history of the canonical text in mind, we confront the casual but heartfelt condemnation of *Purgatory*'s ritual of aestheticized murder as fascist. But it is not simply the manifest content of the play which relates it to epochal catastrophe; its sources and forms are far more eloquent. Evidence of the play's genesis, in the manuscript scenario and in earlier utterances of Yeats's, specifies its assumption of the Protestant/Catholic antagonism as tribal if not racial, as the operational field of taboo and totem. One crucial structural aspect of the play becomes therefore the suppression of this specified ideology in the canonical text.

Purgatory occupies a special place in the Yeatsian canon, yet its significance depends not on its uniqueness but on its centrality. Written virtually at the close of the poet's life it illuminates a great deal of his drama which, without *Purgatory*, might seem merely experimental. And while achieving a very distinctive language at once poetic and dramatic, it succeeds also in integrating much that had appeared casual in Yeats's prose. It is in such terms that we view the centrality of the play to Yeats's career, and beyond that perspective it is *Purgatory* above all else which reveals the nature of that modernism which Yeats did so much to render possible in English.

From the outset, heroism was at the heart of the Yeatsian aesthetic. As a consequence, dramatic technique (if not always dramatic form) closely engaged the poet's attention. From the Cuchulain of *On Baile's Strand* (1904) to *The Death of Cuchulain* (1939) the encounter which defines Yeatsian heroism is the potentially evasive nature of death itself – the hero fights the ungovernable tide, the Old Man pleads for an end to process and consequence. That death should not be frankly confrontable is the essence of the tragic hero's dilemma: doomed, he is yet uncertain if he can trust to his own doom. Yeats's tragedies revolve around what Fredric Jameson has described in another context as 'heroic cynicism'.[6] In *Purgatory* Yeats finally confronts that cynicism of form which modernism depended upon.

Like *The Words Upon the Window-Pane* and *The Death of Cuchulain*, *Purgatory* deals with the burden of the past. Much of it can be seen as – *inter alia* – Yeats's meditation on his own previous meditation: it is a self-scrutiny, and in this it has its affinities with 'The Dead'. Yet in its historical concern Joyce's short story adopts what may appear to be a naïve transparency in its anatomy of nineteenth-century Ireland while the play is frequently taken to evoke the famous Yeatsian eighteenth century, 'that one Irish century that escaped from darkness and confusion'.[7] Like Burke's *Reflections*, the play adopts as its style and form a dominant metaphor which it reveals as virtually redundant. In *Purgatory* the dominant metaphor is pollution, especially hereditary pollution; the characters on stage appear to suffer the consequences of ancestral offence. The stratagem of bringing pollution to an end by killing the boy is pathetic self-deception. As with Burke's Great House, the dominant metaphor of the play turns sardonically upon itself.

Donald Torchiana concluded *Yeats and Georgian Ireland* with an analysis of *Purgatory* in the context of its appearance in the poet's handbook of violent diatribe, *On the Boiler*. As his title suggests, Torchiana is concerned to see the play as 'the symbolic tragedy of the eighteenth century and its consequence for modern Ireland.'[8] While his documentation of Yeats's current interest in eugenics and Nazi legislation tactfully reminds us of the modern context in which the play was written, the acceptance of Yeats's superficial allusions to the eighteenth century successfully conceals the real logic of Yeats's relationship with fascism. Source and style, in the case of *Purgatory*, combine most effectively to point to the nineteenth-century origins of that historical movement which reached its apotheosis in European fascism.

The most frequently cited source for the play is *The Celtic Twilight* (the expanded edition of 1902). Here Yeats recorded many West of Ireland tales about the Devil, purgatory, the dead, and their ghosts. An informant from County Galway had confided: 'And another time I saw Purgatory. It seemed to be in a level place, and no walls around it, but it all one bright blaze, and the souls standing in it.'[9] Undoubtedly, this is a source for the play – if one wishes to take a fairly simplistic view of the relationship between source and art. The immediately previous paragraph of Yeats's account of the Galway seer offers an observation in which a more reciprocal kind of source is at work:

> I have seen Hell myself. I had a sight of it one time in a vision. It had a very high wall around it – all of metal, and an archway, and a straight walk into it, just like what'ud be leading into a gentleman's orchard, but the edges were not trimmed with box, but with red-hot metal.[10]

That Hell should be described in the terminology of a gentleman's residence would have appealed politically to Yeats in 1902 to a degree inconceivable in 1938. Peasants' accounts of the Devil tend to see him in the garb of their social superiors, which in turn suggests that he looks very much like a folklore collector. In 1902, however, Yeats was determined to exploit folklore as a direct communication with 'Ireland', and to do so he suspended attention to his own social position in Ireland. The period of his activities as a collector of lore is significant in that it coincides with the collapse of the landlord system and the eclipse of the resident gentry. We recognize 'Upon a House Shaken by the Land Agitation' (1910) as a turning-point in Yeats's career, the point after which he resumes attention to his own position in Irish society. It has been customary to identify 'land agitation' as the culminating activity of tenants and propagandists; this is sentimental. Yeats was sufficiently shrewd to know that Wyndham's Act of 1903 did more than merely codify the agitation of half a century. It signalled *government's* abandonment of the Irish Big House. *The Celtic Twilight*, in recording the gentleman's orchard in Hell's fire, records a specifically nineteenth-century folk-imagination.

In the course of this argument I shall be concerned to show how the sources Yeats drew upon in 1938 for *Purgatory* have a concentration in time which is revealing; their period is, roughly speaking, very late Victorian and Edwardian. That is to say they are located in the years when Irish politics was more evidently and palpably concerned with social issues rather than nationalist principles. Writing his *Reveries Over Childhood & Youth* in 1914, Yeats recalled his childhood excursions to Castle Dargan in County Sligo. Again, to capture the reciprocal quality of the poet's involvement with his material, we must look beyond the familiar sentences and quote *in extenso:*

> Sometimes I would ride to Castle Dargan, where lived a brawling squireen, married to one of my Middleton cousins, and once I went thither on a visit with my cousin George Middleton. It was, I dare say, the last household where I could have found the reckless Ireland of a hundred years ago in final degradation. But I liked the place for the romance of its two ruined castles facing one another across a little lake, Castle Dargan and Castle Fury. The squireen lived in a small house whither his family had moved from their castle some time in the eighteenth century, and two old Miss Furys, who let lodgings in Sligo, were the last remnants of the breed of the other ruin. Once in every year he drove to Sligo for the two old women, that they might look upon the ancestral stones and remember their gentility, and he would put his wildest horses into the shafts to enjoy their terror.
>
> He himself, with a reeling imagination, knew not what he could be at to find a spur for the heavy hours. The first day I came there, he gave my cousin a revolver, (we were upon the high road), and to show it off, or his own shooting, he shot a passing chicken; and half an hour later, when he had brought us to the lake's edge under his castle, now but the broken corner of a tower with a winding stair, he fired at or over an old countryman who was walking on

the far edge of the lake. The next day I heard him settling the matter with
the old countryman over a bottle of whiskey, and both were in good humour
. . . At last he quarrelled with my great-uncle William Middleton, and to avenge
himself gathered a rabble of wild country lads and mounted them and himself
upon the most broken-down rascally horses he could lay hands on and mar-
ched them through Sligo under a land-league banner. After that, having now
neither friends nor money, he made off to Australia or to Canada.

I fished for pike at Castle Dargan and shot at birds with a muzzle-loading
pistol until somebody shot a rabbit and I heard it squeal. From that on I would
kill nothing but the dumb fish.

XI

We left Bedford Park for a long thatched house at Howth, Co. Dublin. The
land war was now at its height and our Kildare land, that had been in the
family for many generations, was slipping from us. Rents had fallen more
and more, we had to sell to pay some charge or mortgage . . .[11]

There is much material for drama here. If the practical jokes and extraneous
violence look back to Buck Whaley and the rake-hellish life of regency days,
they also confirm that the Old Man in *Purgatory* in asking 'Where are the
jokes and stories of a house/It's threshold gone to patch a pig-sty?' may
not be referring to any remoter history than that of the 1870s. Here, in
autobiographical form, we have the Big House deserted, the debauched
master, the shameful mediation of whiskey between the classes – all features
of the play of 1938. The passage also implicates Yeats himself, not only in
the damage done by Land League agitation to the Yeats's rents in Kildare,
but also in the surrogate huntin' and shootin', soon rejected for the more
discreet killing of 'dumb fish'. Once again, a source for *Purgatory* is revealed
to contain a dialectical presence of the author himself; it is no mere raw
material for reflection.

In his biography of the poet, J. M. Hone records a ghost story which Yeats
told at a Friday evening gathering in Charles Ricketts's house. Hone's commentary dates the occasion to the years immediately preceding the Great
War, and connects it to the essay 'Swedenborg, Mediums and the Desolate
Places' which subsequently appeared as an epilogue to Lady Gregory's
Visions and Beliefs of the West of Ireland. Though Hone's version, supplied
by Thomas Lowinsky, an artist who had been present for Yeats's performance, retains marks of its transmission, there are clear suggestions of
Purgatory:

Centuries ago there lived in a castle in Ireland a man and wife. To their abound-
ing sorrow they remained childless despite prayers and pilgrimages. At last,

when they had long given up all hope, the woman, to her joy, found herself
pregnant. Her husband, who till then had been tender and trusting, became
sullen and suspicious, often giving himself up to lonely bouts of drinking.
Barely had the child been born when the man, roaring drunk, rushed into
the upper chamber where his wife lay. With cries of 'Bastard, bastard' he
wrested the baby from her breast, and with the screaming infant in his arms
strode raging from the room. Down the winding wooden stairs he ran into
the hall, where, all reason fled, he beat and beat the tiny thing against anything
he could. From her bed the mother rose and followed . . . to arrive too late.
Her son was dead. Picking him up from where had had been flung, she turned
and slowly climbed the spiral stairs that led to the threshold of her room. She
moved as in a trance till, through the open door, the sight of the bed brought
her to earth with a spasm of despair. Vehemently clasping the child, in a flash
she bent beneath the bar which fenced the stairs, and dropped, like a singed
moth, to the stone floor below. The man, his frenzy spent, was overwhelmed
with grief. He sought consolation in taking another wife by whom he had
other sons. Thus a family was founded and generation followed generation,
each living much the same uneventful bucolic lives as those whom they succeeded. Although they cared for their castle and husbanded its land, each
in turn from time to time abandoned himself to the same solitary bouts. The
house as a rule was a happy place but, during those spells, when its master
was saturated with drink, an ashen woman would drift past him, ascending
the curved stairs. Transfixed, he would wait the tragedy that he knew he was
doomed only to see when he was drunk. Always with the same simple gesture
she would reach the topmost step; always in the same way, pause, then bend,
to drop a fluttering mass. Yet when he peered down he could see nothing.
With the years the family vice grew like a cancer until it ate away their entire
fortune and they were reduced to poverty. To crown their misery fire gutted
the castle. The descendant to whom it belonged was without the money or
the desire to re-build. Indolent and inane, he left with few regrets to live in
far-distant Dublin. Thenceforth the family and its fount seemed after countless
years to have severed every bond. But destinies and traditions are hard to break
and one day the grandson of this deserter was drawn to the very spot. His
boon companion, killed by the kick of a horse, was to be buried within sight
of the crumbling towers. Moved partly by affection for his friend, partly by
curiosity to see the place whence his stock had sprung, the survivor of this
long line had journeyed to attend the funeral. He met many friends and tip-
pled with them all and, drunk, he found himself at dusk before the sombre
shell of a stronghold. There being no door, he walked straight into the empty
well up the wall of which had twined the oaken stairs. As he gazed he saw
a fragile dishevelled form glide past him up and round the walls as though
the steps were still there. Almost at the top she stopped, then with a burst
of emotion dived, to disappear. The man knew no surprise. He felt that he
had watched this melancholy scene innumerable times before – and for an

instant he dimly understood that neither his children nor yet his children's children could ever purge themselves of a crime that they had inherited with their blood.[12]

Many of the sparse details of the play can be found here in narrative form – the drunken husband, the woman seen in repetition of her trauma, the returned heir or grandson, the notion of hereditary suffering. Even if we admit that this last source only reaches us at third hand, it shares with *The Celtic Twilight* and *Reveries* the tone and structure of late Victorian and Edwardian recollection. To seize upon 'centuries ago' as sanctioning an eighteenth-century provenance for the tale is to travesty the basic conventions of oral narrative, especially of the supernatural tale. The central and significant feature of the events at Ricketts's house is that, in 1914 or thereabouts, Yeats found a tale of recurring and hereditary suffering a satisfactory narrative; he found it to have *form*. When we come to *Purgatory*, utter dissatisfaction, a railing against form within form, is the dominant tone.

In connection with these sources we have to ask how Yeats transforms the raw material of ghost story and childhood recollection into the tight structure of *Purgatory*. It might be more precise to say that it is Yeats's recollection of this material in 1938 which can be properly regarded as the play's source. And while this refinement would involve a further consideration of Yeats's newspaper interview on the subject of Nazi respect for the ancient sanctities, it may be more critically profitable to concentrate on the texts in hand. A major distinction between the play and its source is that the drama specifically spurns narrative. In relation to the story told at Ricketts's, we can see that this process is achieved by the deliberate elimination of the psychological rationale of the father's drunken fury – his suspicion that the child is not his – in favour of class hatred. The logic of the ghost story identifies violent fury (for which no adequate justification is provided) as the cause of hereditary suffering; that the origin of this fury may be a suspicion of *mésalliance* is secondary. In *Purgatory* of course fury and *mésalliance* are placed in immediate conjunction in a manner approved by (at least) the Old Man. At a structural level we can describe this transformation of the material as the elimination of all notions of linear time in favour of 'other events that lie side by side in space [,] complements one of another',[13] as Yeats puts it in *On the Boiler*. For the agony of the different generations in *Purgatory* has only the appearance of sequence; dramatically, the Old Man and the Boy go through their violent ritual simultaneously with the Bride and Groom. In the idiom of Saussurean linguistics, the play prefers the synchronic to the diachronic axis. That preference, of course, has been pervasive in modernist literature, and even more so in the practical criticism it has begotten, being the basis of an aesthetic justifying the text as autonomous and 'self-delighting'.

Despite Practical Criticism and the New Criticism, that sense of autonomy was of course never absolute. Novelists such as Joyce and Thomas Mann employed an irony which is directed as much at the pretensions of artistic form as at an intractable world. Irony in Yeats, however, enjoys a less official status, and the problem is doubly sensitive in the case of *Purgatory*, requiring some method of responding critically to those explicit avowals of Nazi attitude which are concentrated in the interview printed in the *Irish Independent* after the first performance of the play in August 1938. In advance of that encounter with German legislation some further traces of the play's origin may still prove valuable.

'ASCENDENCY WITH ITS SENSE OF RESPONSIBILITY . . .'

The Celtic Twilight, Reveries, and the story told at Ricketts's offer comparisons which only approximate to something in *Purgatory*. Each in isolation would fail to prove itself the seed from which the play grew. Nevertheless, the collocations of house, ghost, and returning degenerate heir impose themselves as evidence of a prima-facie quality. There is a plausibly insidious process by which *The Tower* and the many allusions to Big Houses in the poems of that period are read as a personal hallmark of Yeats, a process which leads critics to an autobiographical reading of *Purgatory*. Torchiana confidently identifies the lines 'to kill a house / Where great men grew up, married, died, / I here declare a capital offence' as spoken 'in what is certainly Yeats's own voice'.[14] Harold Bloom has reservations about the play, and concludes: 'Yeats is not separate enough from the old man's rage to render the play's conclusion coherent. That hardly makes the play less powerful, but perhaps we ought to resent a work that has so palpable a design upon us.'[15] In effect, Bloom points to features of *Purgatory* in which it aligns itself, not so much with other plays or poems by Yeats, but with those vital commentaries which surround and augment other texts in the 1930s – 'The King of the Great Clock Tower', 'Parnell's Funeral' etc.

Now my position is delicate, and I must try to formulate it with some precision. I am pointing to the immediacy of Yeats's historical experience of nineteenth-century social change in those tales which resemble *Purgatory* – here the squireen relative and his Land League antics are especially relevant. I resist, however, the idea of the Old Man's speech as a statement verbatim from the poet. I wish to show that, prior to the last despairing lines, the play, *read as a dramatic text*, establishes real relations with the world it comes from. Those final lines are seen as a cry of despair from within the self-regulating modernist art-work, an appeal for release from the sovereignty of the text. If the source material for *Purgatory* can be shown to have its roots in the disturbed soil of nineteenth- (and early twentieth-) century social change, we may turn to an examination of style in search of Yeats's transformative method.

A central passage from the Old Man's exposition reads:

> Great people lived and died in this house;
> Magistrates, colonels, members of Parliament,
> Captains and Governors, and long ago
> Men that had fought at Aughrim and the Boyne.
> Some that had gone on Government work
> To London or to India came home to die,
> Or came from London every spring
> To look at the may-blossom in the park.[16]

The Old Man commends these great people and their relationship with the house; the offence he condemns most eloquently in his father is that 'he killed the house . . .' For this passage we can find remarkable parallels in two sources. The first is in Yeats's own voice, his 'Commentary on "A Parnellite at Parnell's Funeral"':

The influence of the French Revolution woke the peasantry from the medieval sleep, gave them ideas of social justice and equality, but prepared for a century disastrous to the national intellect. Instead of the Protestant Ascendency with its sense of responsibility, we had the Garrison, a political party of Protestant and Catholic landowners, merchants and officials. They loved the soil of Ireland; the returned Colonial Governor crossed the Channel to see the May flowers in his park, the merchant loved with an ardour, I have not met elsewhere, some sea-board town where he had made his money, or spent his youth, but they could give to a people they thought unfit for self-government, nothing but a condescending affection. They preferred frieze-coated humanists, dare-devils upon horseback, to ordinary men and women.[17]

Edmund Burke was our starting-point, and let us now briefly return to Burke. No passage from Yeats echoes the author of the *Reflections* more clearly than that quoted above; its rhythm integrates the particular and the abstract in a manner Burke would have approved. And the vocabulary of social distinction derives from Burke's writings on Irish history. Yet here we must scrutinize Yeats closely: the terms are Burkean but their meanings have undergone a process of interchange which acknowledges (at least) the intervening century. Ascendancy and Garrison are, then, terms common to Burke and Yeats. In his letter of 1792 to Sir Hercules Langrishe, Burke employs 'garrison' to describe the role of the Protestant settlers prior to the constitutional reform of 1782; Britain, he claims,

> saw, that the disposition of the *leading part* of the nation would not permit them to act any longer the part of a *garrison*. She saw, that true policy did not require that they ever should have appeared in that character; or if it had done so formerly, the reasons had now ceased to operate. She saw that the Irish of her race, were resolved, to build their constitution and their politics, upon another bottom.[18]

The garrison, for Burke was the means by which Ireland was held to the crown, before the reforms of 1782 granted a measure of equity in trade and liberty in law-making. At another level the garrison was the condition in which Ireland existed within the king's dominions.

Burke's garrison resented their condition: Yeats's, however, clung to theirs as the only means by which they might attach themselves to their lands. For Burke, garrison is Ireland before 1782; for Yeats it is Ireland after 1800. But if garrison is an older term than Yeats admitted, 'ascendancy' has the more exciting history. First circulating in the 1790s, it was for Burke virtually the equivalent of junto or clique, and denominated the arrogant political undertakers of the College Green parliament:

> New *ascendancy* is the old mastership. It is neither more nor less than the resolution of one set of people in Ireland, to consider themselves as the sole citizens in the commonwealth; and to keep a dominion over the rest by reducing them to absolute slavery, under a military power.[19]

For Burke, ascendancy is jobs, for Yeats responsibility.

In the 'Commentary on "A Parnellite at Parnell's Funeral"' Yeats is not writing history; so much is clear. He is perhaps engaged with one more of those antinomies which run through his imagination, wisdom against power, the wisdom of the old 'national intellect' at war with the new power of O'Connellite democracy. But the commentary, ostensibly upon 'Parnell's Funeral', more explicitly is echoed in *Purgatory* – 'the returned Colonial Governor [who] crossed the Channel to see the May flowers in his park' becoming 'Some . . . came from London every spring / To look at the may-blossom in the park', while the Governor retains his place in the play alongside magistrates, colonels, Members of Parliament. The most zealous literary metaphysician, whether sceptic or structuralist, could hardly deny the congruity of the two passages. And the tone of the commentary is as evidently not commending as the Old Man's speech is commending. Here we have congruity and contradiction at once. It seems that, if the speech is 'certainly Yeats's own voice', we must find some higher authority for the prose commentary, or – better still – find some larger notion of the author's relationship with his drama.

If we pass by 'the Protestant Ascendency with its sense of responsibility' we come to Yeats's garrison, the political party of landowners, merchants, and officials. The tone here does not seem to hide any reserve of ambiguity. It is true that there is an element of wistful regret that the Ascendancy should have declined to such a condition; it is appreciated also that, unable to offer more than condescending affection to the population of Ireland, the merchants and governors loved its soil. And yet having taken these subordinate issues into account, we still find that Yeats sees these figures as smaller imaginations, diminished presences.

This transvaluation, occurring between the commentary and the play, is all the more remarkable when considered in the light of their common source. In her journal on 3 June 1922 Lady Gregory had written: 'I have been out till after 9 o'c. Everything is beautiful, one must stand to look at blossoming tree after tree; the thorns in the Park that W. used to come over from London to see at this time of year best of all'.[20] Yeats, who visited Coole two days later, saw and remembered the entry. Donald Torchiana notes that Mrs Yeats felt sure the poet thought such trips of Sir William Gregory's all too typical of garrison irresponsibility and sentiment. The career of Sir William, some time governor of Ceylon and MP for Galway, is also that of the succession of proprietors invoked in *Purgatory*; his father having been permanent head of the Irish civil service in the 1820s, the contribution of officials is accommodated also. Yet the careers of these Gregorys lie exclusively within the nineteenth century, after the Union, after the Ascendancy had given way – in Yeats's scenario – to the garrison. *Purgatory* may well have been written with Coole Park in mind, but Yeats did not entirely transform his notion of garrison irresponsibility into Ascendancy celebration. The text, approached carefully, can reveal its own mordant perspective upon the Big House.

Let us look closely at the play, in particular its recital of previous proprietors in the Big House – 'magistrates, colonels, members of Parliament, / Captains and Governors'. Does Yeats have in mind here the resident magistrate of Somerville and Ross's stories, the well-meaning and vaguely comprehending Major Yeates? Almost certainly not. And yet the R.M. stories can serve to remind us that the magistracy was an institution of less than absolute dignity. Until the Whig reforms of the 1830s, it carried no salary, and its patronage was restricted to the resident gentlemen of a county. Through them, rights of property and a simplified jurisprudence were administered to the tenantry. Magistrates were not necessarily men of great substance, intellect or learning; William Le Fanu recalled a 'stirring' magistrate of the 1820s whose utter devotion to authority and partial grasp of literacy led him to begin all his reports 'Dear Government . . .'. With the introduction of a stipendiary magistracy, the social base of the office was broadened and a less thoroughly Williamite interpretation of law admitted. Needless to say, the garrison resented this development.

And so to the colonels. Defined by the dictionary as the superior officer of a regiment, the colonel was traditionally a man most immediately regarded as a soldier's leader, generals being unconnected to any one regiment. However, in the large number of civilians who retained the rank as an honorific, many were not the retired commanders of regular army regiments, but the headmen of county militias or yeomanry corps. Colonel Henry Bruen, the long serving MP for Carlow in the first half of the nineteenth century, was of this latter kind. Colonels, then, may be either the heroes of foreign battlefields or takers of the salute at local coat-trailing reviews.

This disrespectful analysis should be kept in perspective. It is not to the point to prove that Yeats's pantheon consisted simply of well-dressed rogues or impostors. What is significant, however, is that the magistrates and colonels are not necessarily 'great people' in any open, social sense. Being succeeded by

> Some that had gone on Government work
> To London or to India came home to die
> Or came from London every spring
> To look at the may-blossom in the park . . .[21]

they are not excluded from Yeats's prosaic contempt for garrison sentiment. Loving the land and condescending to the tenantry, nineteenth-century estate owners enacted in their emotions the precarious social relationships underlying property. Latter-day absentees, they were too marginally in possession to risk the open ridicule of Ireland which had characterized Maria Edgeworth's Clonbronys in *The Absentee*. In so far as *Purgatory* is amenable to historical analysis – and we are certainly not restricted to such an approach – it reveals evidence of specifically *nineteenth-century* social patterns. Because Yeats has elsewhere spoken warmly of the eighteenth century, and because the Old Man of the play is taken literally as Yeats's oracle, the lines above are read as an objective (and yet Yeatsian!) eulogy of the 'one Irish century that escaped from darkness and confusion'. Indeed darkness and confusion is the condition of *Purgatory* as understood by the Old Man.

METALANGUAGE, METADRAMA

If we turn for a moment to the structure of the play, some illustration of the nature of its modernist anxiety may emerge. I have said that, formally, the play employs Platonic and Swedenborgian concepts of 'dreaming back' or phantasmagoria to describe the experience of the dead. But *Purgatory*, far from serving to make accessible some 'radical innocence', actually reveals ineradicable guilt; there can be no end to the consequence upon themselves of the Bride and Groom's *mésalliance*. This late admission of Yeats's is central to the problematic nature of modernism with its enthusiasm for the self-delighting integrity of the literary text. However, aspirations to Renaissance completeness – the same enthusiasm in thematic guise – may be the best evidence of its unavailability. *Purgatory* abandons such assumptions of integrity and self-completeness in the final lines where Plato and Swedenborg are cast aside:

> O God,
> Release my mother's soul from its dream!
> Mankind can do no more. Appease
> The misery of the living and the remorse of the dead.[22]

The appeal to God is neither Yeats's acceptance of theism nor the character's surrender to established values. In these last lines *Purgatory* is forced to appeal beyond itself for some order which will bring to an end, to completion, its intolerable self-generation. The modernist aesthetic finally reaches out in supplication from the isolation of the work of art to a world it had thought to apply itself to. The God of *Purgatory* is blatantly not that of the churches, though it may have some affinity to Blake's Nobodaddy. Maybe the appeal is directed to us, the audience to whom Prospero needs appeal at the conclusion of *The Tempest* for release and meaning, the audience to whom Timon bequeathed his own wild and contradictory epitaphs. Such a self-consciously metadramatic device is in keeping with much of the play's structure.

To suggest that the dominant metaphor of a work turns in upon itself may be to do nothing more than point to a pervasive irony. And irony is no exclusive property of modernism. But the particular manner in which *Purgatory* implodes is not simply ironic: it employs devices closely identified with modernist technique – metalinguistic and metadramatic reference. To take metalinguistics first, we can begin by noting how the play draws attention to the verbal nature of its settings, implied and explicit. The Old Man's speech gradually transforms the House into a human metaphor:

> he killed the house; to kill a house
> Where great men grew up, married, died,
> I here declare a capital offence.[23]

This speech is the culminating focus of a movement away from larger perspectives (the theory of phantasmagoria, the social background of Bride and Groom), and the ruined house is directly available to the audience as man's condition. However, within the speech, a further interiorization is already at work. 'All/The intricate passages of the house' refers immediately to the complex architecture of the building *known from within;* it also posits a metaphorical interpretation according to which the house is a difficult text, its intricate passages obscure to our understanding. This metaphor is supported throughout the play not only by the Old Man's initial command 'Study that house,/I think about its jokes and stories . . .' but also by the recurring references to his own incomplete education, his own limited ability to decipher what is before him. As the one who burnt the house he is the 'author' of its ruined condition. We call this delineation of the house metalinguistic because, within the verbal ordering of the play, it is further identified with other verbal constructs – 'what the butler said', and

> old books and books made fine
> By eighteenth-century French binding, books
> Modern and ancient, books by the ton.[24]

This metalinguistic aspect of the play is – most people will agree – unobtrusive. It is part of the deception to which Harold Bloom ascribes the play's success. Certainly *Purgatory*'s concentrated unity is in part due to the manner in which the setting and the text act mutually as tenor and vehicle one for the other. Yet this unity is also a form of radical division, for being so hermetically complete the play distinguishes itself drastically from all that it is not. As the Old Man creates the Big House by his speech, the play presents him as achieving Coriolanus' vain wish that a man be author of himself. If, as I have argued elsewhere, 'the Big House', like Protestant Ascendancy, enters the vocabulary of cultural discussion at the tail-end of a process which it serves (retrospectively) to name', then its complex structure and function as a speech act must also be acknowledged.[25] Thus the Big House is not a unified entity with a single fixed location, but rather a dialogic movement in which the position of the speaker (writer) and auditor (reader) deeply affects the significance of the utterance – the Big House. Experiment will show that the phrase may be used between speakers who exist socially outside the location so designated, or by a speaker coming from within addressing an outsider. In speech-act theory, there is both an illocutionary (intention-related) and perlocutionary (effect-related) aspect to such an utterance, and these constitute no perfectly balanced harmony.

Yet the House and the Tree stand radically apart from him and apart from each other. These, the primary elements of the setting, are at one and the same time static and mutually repelling. This congruence of unity and disunity can be traced in the texture of the play's style. A passage such as

> It's louder now because he rides
> Upon a gravelled avenue
> All grass to-day.[26]

achieves its effect of drawing past and present, event and re-enactment, into a single image by the elision of the connective – 'a gravelled avenue [that is] all grass to-day'. Placing the two nouns together Yeats suggests their identity, and it would seem that style and content are at one. However, the conclusion of the play will reveal that this effect is appearance merely, and so we notice in addition that, though the two nouns are indeed brought together, they are held in tension, held reservedly apart by the line division:

> Upon a gravelled avenue
> All grass to-day.

A refined tense exploitation of line-division indicates the poetic (as distinct from dramatic) text, and the use with it of what amounts to a dual syntax recurs in *Purgatory*; a further striking example is the elision of 'should' from the lines

> And if he [should] touch he must beget
> And you must bear his murderer . . .[27]

to create the *appearance* of a present tense in 'touch'. The corollary applies a few lines later:

> If I should throw
> A stick or a stone they would not hear . . .[28]

where the 'should' draws attention specifically to the subordinate role which the Old Man believes himself to have in the drama he is watching.

If, instead of looking within the Old Man's speeches, we look at the relationship between them and the Boy's contribution to the dialogue a very different aspect of *Purgatory* comes to light. On several occasions early in the play, the Old Man continues his exposition across the interjection of the Boy's lines, as if the Boy did not exist. For example,

OLD MAN	The souls in Purgatory that come back
	To habitations and familiar spots.
BOY	Your wits are out again.
OLD MAN	Re-live
	Their transgressions, and that not once
	But many times . . .[29]

Here, the commencement of the Old Man's second speech with a finite verb draws attention to the first and its grammatical incompleteness as a sentence. And yet the maintenance of a poetic line (rhythmically thus, 'Your wits are out again. Re-live') makes a formal acknowledgement of the Boy's perspective. We find a dichotomy between speech and action which is gradually both exposed and resolved by the murder of the Boy. Yet the killing only achieves a state of affairs which, in one stylistic respect, the Old Man had initially assumed. The circularity of *Purgatory* is evident in its minutest stylistic details.

These features of the play take on a greater significance if we move on to its metadramatic dimensions. Just as the Old Man creates the setting by establishing its verbal nature, so he is involved in establishing the original sin of social *mésalliance* as a drama whose performance he now perforce witnesses:

> He has gone to the other side of the house,
> Gone to the stable, put the horse up.
> She has gone down to open the door.
> This night she is no better than her man
> And does not mind that he is half drunk,
> She is mad about him. They mount the stairs.
> She brings him into her own chamber.
> And that is the marriage-chamber now.
> The window is dimly lit again.

And later

> The window is lit up because my father
> Has come to find a glass for his whiskey.
> He leans there like some tired beast.[30]

For us, the Old Man makes accessible areas we cannot see; or, if we see certain scenes we cannot, without his commentary, interpret them. There are two levels of this original drama, or drama of origins. First, there is the historical marriage and mating of Bride and Groom, which reaches us through the Old Man's exposition. Second, there is the re-enactment in the soul of the Bride of her offence as she 'dreams back' through the events of her life in search of peace or 'radical innocence'; this reaches us by virtue of the Old Man's attendance as audience. By such elision of verbs as we have noted, the play places these two levels side by side: the Old Man watches at once the bridal night, his own conception, and the endless repetition of these offences in the dreaming back. The result is of course that he is more than the audience at the drama, he is an absent character in it:

> Go fetch Tertullian: he and I
> Will ravel all that problem out
> Whilst those two lie upon the mattress
> Begetting me.[31]

To the best of my knowledge, no one has convincingly explained the prominent invocation of Quintus Septimus Floreus Tertullien (*c.* 160 – 220AD). In a quite different context, however, Howard Caygill has emphasized Tertullien's importance in extending the legal term 'traditio', to the religious sphere as part of his wholesale translation of Christian experience into the language of Roman law.[32] Certainly, the negotiation between rival discourses is highly relevant to the play. The Old Man exists in a multiple dramatic relation. He is a character in the play we are watching; he is audience to Bride and Groom in their re-enactment, and he is also a character in the original drama. But further, he is the dramatizer of these *ur*-events; it is he who renders them drama by transmitting them to us in speech synchronized to their performance. He is, on this level, both dramatist and audience. His attendance before the Big House and the Tree is not accidental, but part of the script to which he repeatedly draws our attention, the House as 'intricate passages', as *Purgatory*.

THE FASCIST CHARGE [1985]

> The stage shows the middle of a room. A great ash-tree thrusts
> its branches through the roof. Downstage right is the hearth with,
> behind it, a store room. Back centre the great entrance door . . .

This is not the set for some avant-garde production of *Purgatory* in which the familiar elements of the play's sparse design have been juggled about to achieve exciting notices in the theatrical press. It is the opening scene of *Die Walküre*, the second opera of Richard Wagner's mythological cycle *Der Ring des Nibelungen*. The elements are indeed similar – house and tree are crucial in each scene. But Wagner's tree merges with the roof, and its trunk is in effect the pillar upon which the house rests. Yeats, in stark contrast, separates the two elements, and places his characters between, as it were, the polar antagonism of Nature and Artefact.

I invoke Wagner because the issue of Yeats's compact with fascism should be kept in perspective. As early as 1898 Shaw had elaborated an anti-capitalist interpretation of *The Ring* which, if it does nothing else, demonstrates the common idiom of German romanticism in Marx and Wagner.[33] And it was Nietzsche, arch-romantic and bitter opponent of German militarism, who recognized Wagner as the author of the original myths at the heart of the Second and (later) the Third Reich. These German allusions are not exotic: the movement in European culture which gives meaning to Gaelic revivalism, to the Victorian Irish gentry's interest in philology, is German romanticism. (Synge's predecessors include Zeuss and Windisch as well as O'Grady and O'Donovan.) We are mistaken if we accept nineteenth-century notions of history as biological science, and, as a consequence, literature as unreflective truth: this way lies the *Volk* and the burning of *Ulysses*. If interpretation is truly a critical relation between text and reader, we should acknowledge that, just as the text is a specific form of a social production (language), so the reader is a particular member and expression of a known culture. In the case of *Purgatory* our reappraisal of the play's historical nature is not some positivistic rebuke to Yeats. Far more important than any adjustments of our estimate of the poet as historian is a revitalized consciousness of our own historical predicament. The nadir of the Anglo-Irish élite in the Irish Free State found many expressions, the burnt-out house being the most celebrated. In the immediate aftermath of that period it was appropriate to see *Purgatory* in terms of that élite's eighteenth-century heyday. In critical terms the play was read as a neo-classical elegy for neo-classicism. The philistine Victorian bourgeoisie excoriated by Yeats in his early journalism was, by its own aesthetic, entitled to think of its past as aristocratic, noble, proud. But this should be distinguished from the habit of some present-day commentators of seeing pre-independent Ireland as the playground of belted earls and 'droit de seigneur'. The need of senescent nationalism to conjure up an aristocratic past is rooted in its own bourgeois condition, a condition it shares with its alleged historical foe. *Purgatory* therefore is now the focus of a critique directed at the romantic reading of history. Modernism as the culmination of romantic philosophy is its proper context.

In conclusion, some examination of key structures in *Purgatory* may take place in the arena between philosophy and literary technique. 'Dreaming back', the phantasmagoria of Plato and Swedenborg, is symbolically

integrated in the play because it is Yeats's account of history. While the surface of *Purgatory* emphasizes causality almost to the point of obsession, the
result is not an unambiguous view of history as process: the metadramatic
complexity of the Old Man ensures that the successive events of history are
also accessible simultaneously, as events that lie side by side, complements
one of another. In this view of history we find an idealism fraught with solipsistic anxiety; in this simultaneity we find a preference for synchronic order
at the expense of diachronic logic. The Old Man of the play (not unlike
figures in Tennyson's dramatic monologues) is poised tensely upon a
penultimate moment. The play is eschatological in that it attends to 'the
last things', but its attendance can never quite be transformed into presence,
because in the presence of those last things, speech, especially dramatic
speech, is inconceivable. The Old Man approaches the condition of
Cuchulain, but if tragedy is a joy to the dying hero, there is neither joy nor
death. In so far as he articulates a cynical acceptance of his doom the Old
Man retains a vestigial heroism; however, if we permit ourselves to anticipate
The Death of Cuchulain we are made aware of the drastic distinction between Hero and Old Man which Yeats resorts to; in his last play, the complexities of the Old Man's role, as director of the play he announces, amount
to formal cynicism. The Yeatsian hero is finally permitted to die, but the
price paid is acknowledged in terms of the text's cynical rejection of its own
form.

T. R. Henn has complained, mildly enough, that *Purgatory* suffers perhaps
'from the disadvantage that we must accept Yeats's theory that past actions
are re-created by the dead in time'.[34] But the phantasmagoria is more closely associated with Yeats's idealistic notion of history than this would suggest. Furthermore, the doctrine of purgatory is no theological *donnée* upon
which the playwright may perform strictly limited variations. The soul in
purgatorial fire experiences precisely the same frustration as the hero to
whom death is elusive: both possess consciousness without vision, both must
recoil from that which is longed for. If one were to translate this terminology
into secular or classical allusion, one would see Yeats as concerned essentially with the *daemonic*. Romantic literature, Shelley as much as Goethe,
has seen in the mediate condition of the daemon an image of the artist's
attempt to transform material into method, and method into action.

Yeats's place in that tradition has long been recognized. Yet if we look
more locally at the materials of his work as poet and playwright, we will
find in the history of the Victorian Anglo-Irish élite a daemonic reading of
their experience which is relevant to all those sources of *Purgatory* we have
examined. Before he discovered the method of art to be virtually the nature

of language itself, J. M. Synge struggled to express this history in a play which he called *When the Moon Has Set*. Like the temporal dimension of *Purgatory*, the title of Synge's play acknowledges two potential movements neither of which is endorsed: neither greater darkness nor greater light. In one version of the play, Synge's alter ego comments: 'I suppose it is a good thing that this aristocracy is dying out. They were neither human nor divine.'[35] It is a strictly inartistic line. Nevertheless it concentrates a historical reality with which Yeats had to struggle over many years. Only in *Purgatory* did he exploit the daemonic as a metaphor specifically for the distinctive sociology from which his work rose in an act of self-identification and reflection.

If, then, we distinguish sharply between Yeats's attention to the decline of Ireland's landed gentry and Wagner's role as celebrant of Teutonic assertiveness, may the accusation of fascism brought against the poet be at last dismissed? Certainly, since Conor Cruise O'Brien published his essay 'Passion and Cunning' in 1965, no account of Yeats's ideas has been able to avoid the topic.[36] Unlike his friend Ezra Pound, Yeats's association with fascism was exclusively located in the pre-war period, and no spectacular trial or incarceration concentrates the issues for us. An interest in Yeats's fascism, one might say, has its own historical locus and is not unrelated to the altering politics of Ireland from the mid-sixties onwards. The trouble has been that most accounts rely almost exclusively on Yeats's utterances about Mussolini, 'modern heterogeneity', and so on, without reference to questions of history and form. Yet history and form cannot be ignored as we turn to look at his own reported commentary on *Purgatory*.

The play was first performed at the Abbey Theatre on 10 August 1938 in the course of a festival during which the directors of the theatre, speaking through Lennox Robinson, were anxious to stress the Abbey's *national* status and *national* preoccupations. Yeats participated in a discussion of his new play, and his comments to an interviewer were published in the *Irish Independent* of 13 August. Donald Torchiana has very valuably drawn attention to the importance of these comments for an interpretation of the play, though his re-publishing of the heart of the interview has not led many others to take it into consideration in assessing Yeats's politics. As reported by the paper Yeats declared:

> There is no allegory in *Purgatory*, nor, so far as I can remember, in anything I have written . . . William Blake said that allegory is made, not by inspiration, but by the daughters of memory. I agree, and have avoided it.
>
> Symbolism is another matter. There is symbolism in every work of art. A work of art moves us because it expresses or symbolizes something in ourselves or in the general life of men.

Father Connolly said that my plot is perfectly clear but that he does not understand my meaning. My plot is my meaning. I think the dead suffer remorse and re-create their old lives just as I have described. There are mediaeval Japanese plays about it, and much in the folklore of all countries.

In my play, a spirit suffers because of its share, when alive, in the destruction of an honoured house; that destruction is taking place all over Ireland today. Sometimes it is the result of poverty, but more often because a new individualistic generation has lost interest in the ancient sanctities.

I know of old houses, old pictures, old furniture that have been sold without apparent regret. In some few cases a house has been destroyed by a *mésalliance*. I have founded my play on this exceptional case, partly because of my interest in certain problems of eugenics, partly because it enables me to depict more vividly than would otherwise be possible the tragedy of the house.

In Germany there is special legislation to enable old families to go on living where their fathers lived. The problem is not Irish, but European, though it is perhaps more acute here than elsewhere.[37]

Yeats postulates three means by which houses have been destroyed. The first of these is poverty, upon which he has nothing further to say, not even to the effect that this poverty must inevitably have constituted a reverse of fortune in a family possessing such a house. The second, perhaps incorporating the first, is public sale, or sale at least conducted without apparent regret or reservation. 'Old' is now repeatedly emphasized as if to achieve an antiquity which is otherwise unreliable. When we recall the uncertain scale of the Irish 'Big House', the recent emergence of 'the Protestant Ascendancy', and the essentially Victorian/Edwardian sub-text of allusion in the play, this emphasis is noteworthy. It may be that Yeats had in mind the destruction of Coole Park after Lady Gregory's death: if this was so, then the house's origins in mercantile profits from the East India Company should be noted also. But if sale – whether reluctant or otherwise – unquestionably results in destruction of the house – whether old or not so old – we should note Yeats's assumption that the house and the family are virtually identical, are metaphor one of the other. The transmission of the house by sale, even if it is to another family or another owner, does not count. This assumption is all the more significant when we come to the third means of destruction – *mésalliance* – for the second has already been infused with the notion of house and family as one flesh, as sacramentally a blessed union. It is not enough to say, as Cullingford proposes for a general thesis, that in such matters Yeats follows Burke rather than Mussolini or Hitler – between 1791 and 1938 the whole ideology of a bonding between blood and place (*Lebensraum*) had taken on different overtones.[38] *Mésalliance* is a prejudicial term which fails to announce precisely what it is prejudiced against – class inferiority, 'racial' difference, sectarian difference. To see that the term has ambiguous force even today in Irish affairs one has only to consult Brian Friel's significantly titled play, *Translations:*

> Do you know the Greek word *endogamein*? It means to marry within the tribe. And the word *exogamein* means to marry outside the tribe. And you don't cross those borders casually – both sides get very angry. Now, the problem is this: Is Athene sufficiently mortal or am I sufficiently godlike for the marriage to be acceptable to her people and to my people?[39]

To a degree which he has perhaps not recognized the speaker is an endo-gamist, and the entire cultural tension between Synge's *When the Moon Has Set* and Yeats's *Purgatory* is sprung between an exposition of exogamy within a sectarian culture and a dramatization of the consequences of such exogamy in a setting which has masked its sectarian ideology.

Mésalliance is a prejudicial term then, and no universal equation of *mésalliance* and destruction can stand without the vigorous implementation of that prejudicial element. In the play the *mésalliance* is ostensibly one of class, allied to moral habits (drunkenness etc.) not unknown among all classes. But in a draft of the play, sectarian *mésalliance* had been admitted: vestigially it survives in the Old Man's reference to learning Latin from the Catholic curate. The suppression of that sectarian reference leads in the *Irish Independent* commentary to Yeats's decision to found his play on the excep-tional case, partly because of his interest in eugenics. The biological con-cept of race, of selective breeding, replaces that of sectarianism, while at the same time retaining a strong element of class-hatred. The *mésalliance* of *Purgatory* can never be specified purely in terms of race or class, because the repressed ideology of sectarianism vitiates these alternatives. And if the parentage of the Boy accidentally recalls the parentage attributed to John Giffard, the Dog-in-Office, then we can posit Protestant Ascendancy as an absent meaning of *Purgatory*, and acknowledge too that nothing is acciden-tal in Yeats's philosophy of history. Yeats's own marriage to an Englishwoman provided him with the material for a passionate concentration on his own alienation from the Irish linguistic past.

Elizabeth Cullingford finds Yeats not guilty of fascism, but her neglect of all discussion of what fascism is and was renders the acquittal doubtful. Grattan Freyer disagrees and significantly describes Yeats's political place in 'the anti-democratic tradition'.[40] Both Cullingford and Freyer are silent on *Purgatory* and ignore the *Irish Independent* interview which Torchiana had made available fifteen years earlier. The essays in *On the Boiler* which were excluded from *Explorations* when Mrs Yeats was overseeing the publica-tion of an interim collected works certainly provide additional evidence of

Yeats's strongly authoritarian opinions – and *Purgatory* was first published
in *On the Boiler*.[41] There is, however, a far more accessible statement of
Yeats's political position in the late 1930s, in the final paragraph of 'A General
Introduction for my Work':

> When I stand upon O'Connell Bridge in the half-light and notice that discord-
> ant architecture, all those electric signs, where modern heterogeneity has taken
> physical form, a vague hatred comes upon out of my own dark and I am cer-
> tain that wherever in Europe there are minds strong enough to lead others
> the same vague hatred rises. In four or five or in less generations this hatred
> will have issued in violence and imposed some kind of rule of kindred. I can-
> not know the nature of that rule, for its opposite fills the light; all I can do
> to bring it nearer is to intensify my hatred.[42]

The passage deserves comparison with the interview: in both Yeats shifts
his ground. To the *Irish Independent*, he said that 'the problem is not Irish,
but European, though it is perhaps more acute here than elsewhere.'[43] In
the 'Introduction', he identifies his hatred with that of European strong
minds whose ultimate rule he cannot know because its opposite now fills
the light, or half-light, in Ireland, now. If Yeats approved fascism because
he disliked de Valera, fascism is not thereby abated in its 'vague hatred'.
But it is pointless to seek explicit endorsements of Mussolini or the Nazis
in the manner of Ezra Pound: Yeats's involvement in fascism is a projection
of certain latent developments in his inheritance of Protestant Ascendancy,
a projection which is necessarily distorted and contradictory, but also for
those reasons, valid. That is, his political judgements contain a revelation
of the objective of their subject, even at the expense of consistency. This
is not to say that Protestant Ascendancy was proto-fascist, but rather to identify the manner in which Yeats imaginatively enacts the connections and
disconnections between that Irish ideology within the United Kingdom and
the broader European movement of fascism.

The shifts of ground are therefore symptomatic. We concentrate on style
here for a variety of reasons. (It is 13 August 1938, Germany mobilized for
the invasion of Czechoslovakia on 12 August, Yeats is interested in eugenics
and Nazi legislation.) We have found a revealing intimacy between style and
substance in Yeats, even when that intimacy was violent. The sentence concerning old families in Germany certainly approved the Nazi attitude to inheritance and blood continuity in the sense that it proves its presence in
Yeats's mind. And a great deal of Yeats went further than such strict approving. Yet the style of the sentence is helpful: 'to go on living' is one of
those club-footed phrases we find in Yeats when he is shuffling round uncertain topics. The Yeatsian 'ancient sanctitites' cannot be legislated into the

future, nor can Cuchulain be 'enabled' to survive. This rhythmical betrayal of the cause is not to be taken as the poet's innocence, evidence that he never really knew what he was doing in his fascism. On the contrary it is proof of his perception of the spurious nature of fascist aristocracy, Hitlerian authority. Thus, it is not enough to say that he saw through fascism: there is the permanent suspicion that he would have been prepared to see it through, had he lived. His point of perspective, however, was O'Connell Bridge, rather than the Bridge of Sighs.

The editor of 'A General Introduction' annotates the final paragraph with a quotation from the 1930 'Pages from a Diary' – 'tradition is kindred.'[44] The modernist valorization of tradition is part and parcel of the susceptibility to extreme right-wing politics which affected Yeats, Eliot, and Pound. As a barrier between history and the now, tradition facilitated the rewriting of literature in terms of order and the transmission of power. In 'Pages from a Diary' the guts of the matter are displayed without affectation; that preference of genealogy over historical genesis, of biology and over-determined blood-relationship over social dynamics, is one statement of the fascist longing to resolve all contradictions in a single conflagration. The intellectual sources of Yeats's fascist leanings may be various, but the ideology of Protestant Ascendancy anticipated in certain restricted circumstances several of these preferences. The noble past invoked in *Purgatory* is revealed by the play to be in part bogus. The manner in which sources for the play may be traced in Yeats's prose allows the reader to document the poet's stylistic transformation of an unclear Irish bourgeois history into the permanence of aristocratic value. Yet the play insists on permanence as process, process as permanence, and it sends its audience once more in quest of release to history – the text's dramatic context, its theatrical occasion (together with the internal emphasis on metadrama), is in this respect crucial in liberating *Purgatory* from the charge of aestheticizing ritual murder. That Yeats's prose, drama, and poetry incorporate such evidence is a mark of his artistic greatness, of his integrity. No one who has ignored the authentic dramatization of his inauthentic tradition in *Purgatory* may easily point the finger at Yeats as fascist. Just as Joyce's therapeutic fictions establish him as a critical modernist, in that his work contains a critique of modernist aesthetics, so we may say of Yeats's political dramas that they constitute a critical fascism. Beyond that, of course, it is necessary to add that the active reader's reception contributes to and modifies and (potentially) transforms any such essentialist definition of the work's meaning.

THE FASCIST CHARGE [1994]. THE RELEVANCE OF CARL SCHMITT [15]

Republication of Conor Cruise O'Brien's 1965 essay on Yeats's politics did not result in any upsurge of interest in the topic. By 1989 academic radicalism had discoursed itself into a corner – well-appointed, with promotion prospects – in which historical narrative and a moral concern with documented mass-killing seemed less pressing than professional and procedural matters. If there were exceptions to this pattern – and Noam Chomsky certainly stood out as a courageous critic of US policy in central America and elsewhere – they were often to be found in disciplines further along the corridor than English Literature or Cultural Studies. As for the case of Yeats in particular and the continuing violence in Northern Ireland, the specific neglect of 'Passion and Cunning' in its quietly revised version derived in part from a widespread apprehension that its author had shifted ground also. But to a greater extent, it derived from a general unwillingness among university professors to hold Yeats the poet responsible for whatever it was he might have said on the subjects of fascism and terror.

Even Michel Foucault seemed contaminated by this kind of thing; in an interview which all but concludes the influential *Foucault Reader*, he observed that 'there is a very tenuous "analytic" link between a philosophic conception and the concrete political attitude of someone who is appealing to it.' [46] While this position has struck Germans and Germanists as highly unsatisfactory – for it disregards the argument that Heidegger's political activities were virtually an application of his ontology – Foucault was in fact trying to underline the frailty of human nature (so to speak). In his eyes, the radical theoreticians of political engagement – Sartre, de Beauvoir and Merleau-Ponty – had done nothing for the Resistance during the Nazi occupation of France, while the historian of mathematics Cavaillès had been an activist. If Foucault appears to concentrate on philosophers, while Yeats must be considered primarily as a creative writer, one should recall that two of his inactive/engagé philosophers were also novelists. Since 1987, the case of Paul de Man has further embarrassed the academic avant-garde which has found itself suddenly dependent on the old commercial principle of limited liability. Richard Wolin, who did so much to make Walter Benjamin accessible to the English-speaking world, is thus driven to complain of 'the poststructuralist interest in exposing the limitations of theory in general, which is always suspected of promoting covert, "foundationalist" tendencies.' [47] In a most disturbing fashion, radical theory has depoliticized itself in some uncanny re-enactment of the *Wirtschaftswunder* (or economic miracle) of Konrad Adenauer's Federal Republic of Germany. Historical knowledge, whether in relation to critical practice or political atrocity or the development of mathematics, is put at the mercy (*in parvo*) of free market forces – little demand, less supply.

The illustration of these changes by means of an image based on German conditions is peculiarly apt. If the Weimar Republic nursed both Critical Theory and National Socialism in the years between the Great War and the accession of Hitler, then the recently re-united republic has been host to a revival of neo-fascist violence and neo-conservative propaganda unequalled even in Le Pen's France or Berlusconi's Italy. An understanding of fascism's appeal to intellectuals in the 1920s and '30s can never be adequately founded on investigations which concentrate on Mussolini, and in the case of Yeats just such a concentration was maintained by the principal commentators. The collective publication of his political writings will undoubtedly assist in reviewing the issues involved. The progressive release of further volumes of *The Collected Letters* will illuminate nuances of reservation and calculation which he generally managed to eliminate from his public utterances. Meanwhile, in a period when the zealots of Irish cultural politics have been preoccupied with other issues, the question has been kept alive by a few critics. In America, Michael North continued the business of probing the connections between poetics and politics in classic modernism, though the figures treated in *The Political Aesthetic of Yeats, Eliot, and Pound* are so familiar that no major extension of the argument is achieved by comparing their positions once more.[48] The question of procedure, line of approach, is clearly important, especially at a time when certain varieties of theory have been embarrassed by revelations of the political stances adopted by their patron saints in the days of the Reich. Consequently, John Kelly's 1988 paper, 'The Fifth Bell: Race and Class in Yeats's Political Thought' is significant beyond its content, for it admirably demonstrates the worth of a criticism which respects meticulous scholarship and moral acuity in equal measure.[49] If postmodernist scepticism on the issue of historical knowledge is to be overcome, then a tenacious practice of editorial scholarship, informed by a new awareness of the theoretical aspects of editing, may play as large a part as any re-formulation of grand theory.

Certainly, the prolonged debate among West German historians on the so-called revisionist account of the Holocaust was at a secondary level a debate about methodology, especially with regard to editorial practice. If no documentary evidence of Hitler's ordering the Final Solution could now be found, then (for some of the revisionists) this was sufficient not only to exonerate the Führer but even the Nazi movement in its most strictly defined official existence.[50] Whatever happened, if it happened, was unauthorized. This procedure, acting in concert with the highly developed amnesia of post-war Germans, threatens to rewrite history by obliterating it. The relevance of the *Historikerskreit* to a study of Anglo-Irish literature does not depend, as some genuinely worried critics have suggested, on an illogical or otherwise improper attempt to implicate the poet in unspeakably dreadful events occurring years after his death. We have seen exactly how explicit Yeats was on the topic of Nazi legislation, as late as August 1938. The larger questions remaining must surely relate to the literary, intellectual and political antecedents of such an endorsement, viewed not only in the restricted area of his own utterances but in the broader pattern of cultural discussion occurring between the world wars.

Habermas, looking back over his own upbringing, remarked that 'after 1945 we read Carl Schmitt and Heidegger and Hans Freyer and even Ernst Junger differently'.[51] To readers of Anglo-Irish literature, Heidegger will be the most familiar of these names, while Carl Schmitt has yet to become a name. *Dasein* and Unity of Being deserve a comparative analysis by some one technically qualified in modern philosphy, though even a historian of ideas can see in the lives of Heidegger and Yeats a fateful convergence on the year 1934. The novelist, Ernst Junger, suggests a different kind of comparison, one based on the notion of the artist as occupying some privileged reservation from mundane reality. By contrast, Schmitt, the constitutional lawyer, presses for decisive engagement with the world of action: his interests overlap in numerous details with those of Yeats.

As a writer, Schmitt's decade is the 1920s. Born in 1888, he was shaped by the Great War and Germany's defeat. At the close of the Weimar years, he was a legal adviser to the government, yet by May 1933 he was enrolled in the Nazi Party. One of his English translators has written that 'in spite of his support for the Republic, his criticism of the Nazis, and his ties to prominent Jews . . . Schmitt managed to execute a brilliant and astonishingly smooth transition from Weimar to the Third Reich.'[52] Perhaps instead of 'smooth transition' one needs to invoke a concept dear to Schmitt himself — decisionism. In the closing paragraphs of *The Crisis of Parliamentary Democracy* (Die geistesgeschichtliche Lage des heutigen Parlamentarismus, 1923 & 1926), he had cited the friendship of Patrick Pearse and James Connolly as a (rare) example of the combination of national and class consciousness, and proceeded to invoke Mussolini's speech of October 1922 in Naples as conclusive proof of the superiority of the national myth (his term and Mussolini's) over socialism.[53] What Pearse valuably possessed, in Schmitt's eyes, was the power to decide and to intervene.

If the means of intervention was violent, its target was parliamentarism. In Schmitt's view, the institution of parliament had become corrupted not

just in its practice but in its very nature. It had become a liberal discussion
group and, confronted by the choice between Christ and Barrabas, liberals
(he believed) would have set up a sub-committee. In the days of Edmund
Burke, parliament had been an effective instrument of government, but the
course of the nineteenth century and the upheavals of war and revolution
in the first two decades of the twentieth had rendered it useless, or nearly
so. Burke is a recurring point of reference for Schmitt, especially in *Political
Romanticism* where the desideratum of 'balance' in social arrangements since
the eighteenth century is generally deplored. Already, Schmitt's preoccupations mirror not only Yeats's interest in Burke but also Ezra Pound's obsession with the early history of the United States and its later degeneracy.[54]
In other words, these German political writings of the early '20s quickly
manifest a relationship with the work of at least two major Anglophone
modernist poets. Perhaps one should draw the line at invoking 'the mood
of the times', and let that highly informal explanation stand as sufficient
for the moment. But Schmitt's familiarity with Pearse's death argues in
favour of taking the consideration of his possible links with Yeats at least
one or two stages further.

There is, for example, the role of his sometime patron, the Jewish
economist Moritz Julius Bonn. Little known in the English-speaking world,
apart from a carefully casual autobiography published after the war, Bonn
had written his doctoral thesis on Irish agriculture under colonial rule. He
visited Ireland at the end of the nineteenth century and again in 1912, having made the acquaintance of Lady Gregory, Yeats and others associated
with the Literary Revival. His working relationship with Schmitt lasted at
least until well into the Weimar period, though the author of *Political Romanticism* does not feature in Bonn's published recollections.[55] Through Bonn,
Schmitt would have had first hand accounts of the course of Irish politics
since the death of Parnell up to and including the establishment of the Free
State in 1921.

Though the fate of the Weimar Republic was to divide Bonn and Schmitt
on fundamental grounds, they had shared a common interest in the place
of parliament in modern political structures, a question central to the survival of German liberalism. Schmitt's right-wing politics was not, at least
prior to 1933, simply a matter of anti-democratic authoritarianism. On the
contrary, he argued that the tendency to identify democracy with parliamentary rule was to blame for many of the ills of modern society and for the
insecurity of the state. Democracy, as he envisaged it, might be better off
without representative chambers. Disillusion with parliamentary rule was
hardly based on extensive German experience, but there were plenty of

French and English complaints upon which to draw. Extension of the franchise, and the mobilization of women's movements for further extension, had been cited as evidence of government's falling into the hands of the masses. Corruption, of the kinds found in most human institutions, had been identified as a major feature of the French Republic against which General Boulanger had threatened armed reaction. And in Britain, in the eyes of Yeats and others, the consequences of the fall of Parnell had included the handing over of judgemental authority to a public opinion insufficiently educated for the task. Yet when one finds Yeats sounding this particular trumpet, he is doing so in the 1920s rather than in the immediate aftermath of Parnell's defeat and death in 1891. Addressing the Royal Academy of Sweden on the occasion of his being awarded the Nobel prize in 1923, he began by reminding his audience that the literary movement collectively honoured through his name had begun when 'a disillusioned and embittered Ireland turned from parliamentary politics.' He continued, with a striking emphasis, 'an event was conceived, and the race began, as I think, to be troubled by that event's long gestation.'[56]

Yet if it is possible to correlate the utterances of Schmitt and Yeats on the topic of parliamentarism in the year 1923, it is equally clear that major differences existed between them. For a start, Schmitt attached himself politically to the Catholic Party, whereas Yeats increasingly worked to associate himself with a Protestant tradition. Yeats deplored democracy though he took a seat in a democratic parliament; Schmitt deplored parliament and saw the possibilities of democracy finding its salvation in a dictatorship. Nevertheless, Yeats's membership of the Irish Senate never inhibited him from inveighing against democratic politics, as in the brief but timely article headed 'From Democracy to Authority' which appeared in the *Irish Times* of February 1924. Moreover, there were moments when Yeats could play the part of a Catholic intellectual to advantage, as when he wrote a pseudonymous editorial for *To-morrow*, a very short-lived literary newspaper published in Dublin in August 1924.

Looking ahead to the 1930s, when Schmitt would retain his academic position and even associate with some of the more radical elements within the Nazi movement, one does not find in Yeats the kind of categorical objection to the wholesale suppression of civil rights, to the rule of terror, to racial persecution which one might have expected from the opponent of book-censorship in the Irish Free State. Of course, Yeats cited his exclusively Irish concerns when questioned about European affairs. But the conclusion of his 'Commentary' on the three songs he had written for the Blue Shirts does not specify any statute of territorial limitation in relation to the arena in which he was prepared to act:

If any Government or party undertake this work it will need force, marching men; (the logic of fanaticism, whether in a woman or a mob is drawn from a premise protected by ignorance and therefore irrefutable); it will promise not this or that measure but a discipline, a way of life; that sacred drama must to all native eyes and ears become the greatest of the parables. There is no such government or party today; should either appear I offer it these trivial songs and what remains to me of life.[57]

That was written between the public announcement and the formal notification of Yeats's being awarded the Goethe Plakette by the recently Nazified city council of Frankfurt am Main. And, as we have seen, his second last play owes a debt to a *Sturm und Drang* dramatist of the eighteenth and early nineteenth century, Zacharias Werner, whom Schmitt managed to introduce into his discussion of Burke.[58] Even debts acquired through James Clarence Mangan can bear inflationary interest rates in the 1920s and '30s.

These remarks on the relevance of Carl Schmitt to the question of Yeats's attitudes towards totalitarian politics and fascism are not intended to do more than indicate the extent of the European literary and cultural history in which Yeats should be considered. There are other obvious lines of inquiry – the influence of English Catholicism and the right-wing politics of Hilaire Belloc and G. K. Chesterton in the first decade of the Irish Free State, for example, or the conspiracy theories of Nesta Webster whose views on the French Revolution circulated widely after the Great War. There were also other options in the 1920s and '30s, nor were Irish writers wholly isolated from these.

NOTES AND REFERENCES

1   Henry James, 'The Middle Years', *Novels and Tales* (Clifton, NJ: A. M. Kelley, [c.1974], The New York Edition), vol. xvi, p. 105.
2   Raymond Williams, 'Marxism, Structuralism and Literary Analysis', *New Left Review*, 129 (September-October 1981), pp. 51-66 (p. 58).
3   Ibid., p. 58.
4   See James Clarence Mangan's translation of Werner's play under the title 'The Twenty-fourth of February', in The *Dublin University Magazine*, vol. 10, no. 55 (July 1837), pp. 26-53.
5   Cited by Donald Torchiana in *Yeats and Georgian Ireland* (Evanston: North-western University Press, 1966), pp. 220 and 361.
6   Fredric Jameson, 'The Vanishing Mediator: Narrative Structure in Max Weber', *New German Critique*, vol. 1 (Winter 1973), pp. 52-89.
7   W. B. Yeats, *Explorations* (London: Macmillan, 1962), p. 365.
8   Torchiana, *Yeats and Georgian Ireland*, p. 351.
9   W. B. Yeats, *The Celtic Twilight*, rev. and enlarged edn (London: Bullen, 1902), p. 77.
10 Idem. A further amusing element of folklore's reflection of bourgeois Ireland's

interest occurs in Yeats's account of a Mayo woman whose demon-lover manifested himself in a strange manner; she was waiting by the roadside 'when something came flapping and rolling along the road up to her feet. It had the likeness of a newspaper, and presently it flapped up into her face, and she knew by the size of it that it was the *Irish Times*' (ibid., p. 69). The *Irish Times*, at this time, was a liberal unionist paper closely identified with the Protestant Ascendancy.

11 W. B. Yeats, *Reveries Over Childhood and Youth* (London: Macmillan, 1916), pp. 99-103.

12 J. M. Hone, *W. B. Yeats 1865–1939* (London: Macmillan, 1962), 2nd edn, pp. 283-4.

13 W. B. Yeats, *On the Boiler* (Churchtown: Cuala Press, 1939), p. 36. It is perhaps worth noting that this astringent analysis of Irish life was written 'here in Monte Carlo' (p. 37).

14 Torchiana, *Yeats and Georgian Ireland*, p. 362.

15 Harold Bloom, *Yeats* (New York: Oxford University Press, 1970), p. 429.

16 W. B. Yeats, *Collected Plays* (London: Macmillan, 1963), p. 683.

17 W. B. Yeats, *The Variorum Edition of the Poems*, Peter Allt and Russell Alspach, eds. (New York: Macmillan, 1957), pp. 833-4.

18 'Letter to Sir Hercules Langrishe', *Writings and Speeches of Edmund Burke*, R. B. McDowell ed. (Oxford: Clarendon Press, 1991), vol. 9, p. 618.

19 'Letter to Richard Burke', in *Writings and Speeches*, vol. 9, p. 644. See Chapter 4 above for further discussion of Burke and Yeats.

21 W. B. Yeats, *Collected Plays*, p. 683.

22 Ibid., p. 689.

23 Ibid., p. 683.

24 Ibid, p. 684.

25 See W. J. Mc Cormack, 'Setting and Ideology, with Reference to the Fiction of Maria Edgeworth', in Otto Rauchbauer, ed., *Ancestral Voices: the Big House in Anglo-Irish Literature* (Hildesheim: Olms Verlag, 1992), pp. 33-60, esp. p. 49.

26 Yeats, *Collected Plays*, p. 685.

27 Ibid., p. 686.

28 Ibid., p. 686.

29 Ibid., p. 682.

30 Ibid., pp. 685-7.

31 Ibid., p. 686.

32 See F. A. C. Wilson, *W. B. Yeats and Tradition* (London: Gollancz, 1958), p. 152 etc. for a valuable scholarly discussion of the play; see also Caygill in Andrew Benjamin and Peter Osborne eds., *Walter Benjamin's Philosophy: Destruction and Experience* (London: Routledge, 1994), p. 12. It is worth noting that in *Purgatory*, Tertullien is the only actual human person named, if we except Adam who slips in through the Old Man's misquotation of D. G. Rossetti's 'Eden Bower' (see Wilson, loc. cit.). Yeats had, as a young man, warned Katherine Tynan against any reliance on 'the tapestry-like scenery of Rossetti'.

33 See G. B. Shaw, *The Perfect Wagnerite: A Commentary on the Ring of the Nibelings* (London, 1898).

34 T. R. Henn, *The Harvest of Tragedy* (London: Methuen, 1956), p. 209.

On Purgatory 373

35 J. M. Synge, *Collected Works*, vol. iii, *Plays* (II) (London: Oxford University Press, 1968), p. 162.

36 Conor Cruise O'Brien, 'Passion and Cunning: An Essay on the Politics of W. B. Yeats', *In Excited Reverie*, A. Norman Jeffares and K. G. W. Cross, eds. (London: Macmillan, 1965), p. 278 n.

37 Torchiana, *Yeats and Georgian Ireland*, pp. 357-8, was the first to publish this material, which is also included in A. Norman Jeffares and A. S. Knowland, *A Commentary on the Collected Plays of W. B. Yeats* (London: Macmillan, 1975), p. 275. For the original interview and some related material see *Irish Independent*, 13 August 1938, p. 9.

38 Elizabeth Cullingford, *Yeats, Ireland, and Fascism* (London: Macmillan, 1981), p. 154 *et passim*.

39 Brian Friel, *Translations* (London: Faber & Faber, 1981), p. 68.

40 Grattan Freyer, *W. B. Yeats and the Anti-Democratic Tradition* (Dublin: Gill and Macmillan 1981). The other notable contribution to the debate was Patrick Cosgrove's reply to Conor Cruise O'Brien, 'Yeats, Fascism, and Conor O'Brien', *London Magazine*, July 1967.

41 Torchiana discusses the place of *Purgatory* in the context of *On the Boiler*, in *Yeats and Georgian Ireland*, pp. 844-52.

42 Edward Callan, ed., *Yeats on Yeats: The Last Introductions and the "Dublin" Edition* (Mountrath: Dolmen Press, 1981), pp. 72-3.

43 *Irish Independent*, 13 August 1938, p. 9; see n37, above.

44 Callan, ed., *Yeats on Yeats*, p. 73.

45 In contrast to the procedure generally adopted in modifying sections of *Ascendancy and Tradition* for incorporation into the present book, I have chosen here to maintain (with very minor corrections) the original section called 'The Fascist Charge' and to add a wholly new section with the same title: these are distinguished by dates in square brackets.

46 Paul Rainbow ed., *The Foucault Reader* (New York: Pantheon Books, 1984) p. 374.

47 'Introduction' p. viii, in Jürgen Habermas, *The New Conservatism; Cultural Criticism and the Historians' Debate*, trans. Shierry Weber Nicholsen (Cambridge: Polity Press, 1989).

48 Michael North, *The Political Aesthetic of Yeats, Eliot, and Pound* (Cambridge University Press, 1991).

49 The article is published in Okifumi Komesu and Masaru Sekine, eds., *Irish Writers and Politics* (Gerrards Cross: Smythe, 1989), pp. 109-75.

50 The best introduction to this complicated debate is Richard J. Evans, *In Hitler's Shadow: West German Historians and the Attempt to Escape from the Nazi Past* (London: Tauris, 1989).

51 Habermas, *The New Conservatism*, p. 236. The remark occurs in an article called 'On the Public Use of History' which might be usefully read by disputants in the debate about revisionism in Irish historiography; for the major documents of this dispute see Ciaran Brady (ed.), *Interpreting Irish History: the Debate on Historical Revisionism* (Dublin: Irish Academic Press, 1994); see, for a very different appropriation of the revisionist label, Edna Longley, *The Living Stream: Literature and Revisionism in Ireland* (Newcastle upon Tyne: Bloodaxe, 1994).

52 Guy Oakes, 'Translator's Introduction' in Carl Schmitt, *Political Romanticism* (Cambridge, Mass.: MIT Press, 1986), p. xi.
53 Carl Schmitt, *The Crisis of Parliamentary Democracy*; trans. Eileen Kennedy (Cambridge, Mass.: MIT Press, 1985), pp. 75-6.
54 Schmitt, *Political Romanticism* pp. 28-9, 33, 41, 46-7, 58, 60, 63, 81, 88, 110, 112, 114-16, 122, 125, 128, 130-2, 141, 145. On Schmitt's interest in America and 'The Federalist', see *The Crisis of Parliamentary Democracy*, pp. 40-5.
55 See M. J. Bonn, *Wandering Scholar* (London: Cohen & West, 1949).
56 W. B. Yeats, *Autobiographies* (London: Macmillan, 1955), p 559.
57 W. B. Yeats, *The King of the Great Clock Tower, Commentaries and Poems* (Dublin: Cuala Press, 1934), p. 37. The commentary is dated, April 1934.
58 See Schmitt, *Political Romanticism*, pp. 32, 58.

11

Infancy and History:
Beckett, Bowen and Critical Theory

One must have tradition in oneself, to hate it properly.
(Theodor Adorno)[1]

I AGAINST A BACKGROUND

We have now reached an advanced point in this revision of *Ascendancy and Tradition*, so advanced a point indeed that it is necessary to admit the inadequacy of the undertaking. Too much remains to be done, too much will inevitably remain outside, unfinished, unarticulated, even unrecognized in such an apology as the present sentence. It is tempting to attempt a list of acknowledged failings, sins of omission – nineteenth-century poetry and drama, the fiction of William Carleton, the so-called autobiography of J. C. Mangan, Shaw's autobiographical jottings, the *oeuvre complet* of Oscar Wilde, George Moore's odd combination of naturalism and orientalism, Augusta Gregory, Seán O'Casey and Denis Johnston, the remarkable and lonely career of Thomas Kinsella – and so on *ad finitem*. Instead have we not dwelled too long on the minor attractions – pamphlets, sensational novels, lurid editorials – as well as on the tediously predictable monuments, Yeats, Synge, and Joyce?

Walter Benjamin's Italian editor, Giorgio Agamben, has assembled a series of brief philosophical essays under the title, *The Coming Community* (La Communita cheviene) and subtitled another as 'essays on the destruction of experience'. The distance between these two perspectives could be characterized in a variety of ways, but for the present it is sufficient to note the elegance and difficulty with which his prospect of a revolutionary future is elaborated and the rigour with which he demonstrates the everyday occurrence of non-experience. What links the two exercises is an awareness of the dreadful plenitude which has obliterated authentic experience, a catastrophe which his master identified with the Great War. Of course, to invoke 'authentic' experience is to run the risk of positing some pure moment or locus in the past when the ideal was real, and it is important to note the tactical status of the adjective in Agamben and Benjamin's argument. In more local terms one can recognize this modern condition especially through the phenomenon of a proliferating literary tradition – the endless list of names endlessly re-inscribed with one more citation. Thus imaginary communities are exported into the past, with the loss to the present of any active prospect of community.[2]

Independent Ireland is unique among Anglophone countries in believing that it underwent a political revolution in the twentieth century. This belief is not unconnected with a constitutional insistence that its first language is Gaelic. Despite, or perhaps because of, energetic official sponsorship of Gaelic culture, the international literary image of Ireland is mediated all but exclusively through the English tongue, and this notwithstanding the achievement of Seán Ó Riordáin in lyric poetry, Mairtín Ó Cadhain in prose fiction and, more recently, the work of other younger writers in Gaelic as different as Tomás Mac Síomóin and Nuala Ní Dhomhnaill. While bilingualism of a kind is enjoying some favour among writers today – Pearse Hutchinson, Michael Hartnett etc. – the pioneering efforts of Eoghan Ó Tuairisc (Eugene Waters) and Breandán Ó Beacháin (Brendan Behan) have been largely forgotten. Nor did Pan-Celticism ever make an impression: early independent Ireland's relations with neighbouring Wales appear to have been almost nonexistent, though Anglophone Welsh writers (notably R. S. Thomas in his youth) were in touch with literary Dublin. After 1921 no discernible effort was made by major Irish writers to respond to the new cultural objectives of the state. Yeats never mastered Gaelic, and Joyce persisted in an exile where French, Italian and German served him adequately. Beyond the cultural resonance of these names, one should note the manner in which an academic/social élite was replaced by a cultural/political one. If this seems a bloodless exchange in terms of race and religion, it should not be assumed that subsequent negotiations between the academy and politics abjured the deft exploitation of denominational difference.

The principal figures of the Irish literary revival – not only Yeats and Joyce, but also Shaw, Gregory and even O'Casey – lived through the years of turbulent change, having commenced their careers in what had been un-questionably a different political context to that inaugurated in 1921. The notables who did not live to see that happy day – Wilde who died in 1900 and Synge in 1909 – have been drastically periodized, Wilde as a *fin de siècle* dandy, Synge as an Edwardian ruralist. In part, the disjunction is graphically represented in the separation from Britain with, however, parti-tion of the island of Ireland constituting an alternative representation of the historical rift. The coincidence in the Irish Free State – by no means a col-laboration – of anti-intellectualism and Gaelicism served further to create a linguistic tension with the authority to challenge the ascendancy of English but without the power to install Gaelic as an alternative. *Finnegans Wake* is the only substantial evidence of a revolutionary potential within the cir-cumscribed ideology of Home-Rule-Becoming-The-Free-State. But, to com-plement its reputation as a unique item in the Irish avant-garde, one should note both an atavistic element in the *Wake* itself and the simultaneous presence of stylistic experiment not only in Beckett but also in Elizabeth Bowen.

Cultural resistance to the programme implicit in such organs of opinion as *The Catholic Bulletin* was complicated by the extent to which the grandees of the literary movement shared a common inheritance with Fr Corcoran and his contributors.[3] While auguries for a Free State policy towards the arts should certainly not be sought in the pages of the *Bulletin* exclusively, the impact of new censorship laws in 1929 powerfully suggested that the first decade of independence would be characterized by intensified pressure upon the practitioners of imaginative literature. For younger writers, who had no credit lodged in the bank of national experience, the new régime looked wholly philistine. Bowen was still in England and her early work gave only rare indications of any preoccupation with the cultural life of her native Ireland. Less protected by social and geographic distance, Beckett's early prose works were repeatedly interrupted by snide remarks about aspects of Irish peasant culture – e.g. corduroy trousers and censoriousness – deemed typical. Other negotiations were effected by Joseph O'Neill (1886–1953), a Celticist by training who returned to join the Irish civil ser-vice and wrote a series of prophetic historical novels, and by Francis Hackett (1883–1962), a restless emigré novelist and imaginative historian.[4]

Influence as (so to speak) unmediated pressure, rather than as tradition, is discernible in Beckett's 1930s' fiction. When, in *Murphy* (1938), the demented Neary is mercifully prevented from assaulting a statue of Cuchulain which commemorates the Easter Rising by identifying its leaders with the great mythic hero, the perpetrator's account of his spiritual condition disrespectfully implicates both Yeats and Synge. 'That Red Branch bum was the camel's back' signals that a last straw has broken his endurance while also indelicately echoing the biblical observation about what can and cannot pass through the eye of an needle. Cuchulain, rendered Victorianly as 'the Red Branch knight', is demoted to the status of misfit or bum, while the precise location of Neary's interest in marbled anatomy is also given away. To mitigate this perversion of the heroic past, Neary's rescuer (Wylie) feels the need to assure an investigating policeman of the conventional femaleness of a statue so assaulted – 'not a feather out of her [sic] . . . No blood, no brains, nothing.' Neary's subsequent explanation of how 'the limit of Cork endurance had been reached' draws on the sublime final gesture of *Riders to the Sea* to gloss his expulsion from a distinctly less heroic landscape:

> 'My grove on Grand Parade,' said Neary, 'is wiped as a man wipeth a plate, wiping it and turning it upside down.'
> 'And your whiskers?', said Wylie.
> 'Suppressed without pity,' said Neary, 'in discharge of a vow, never again to ventilate a virility denied discharge into its predestined channel.'
> 'These are dark sayings,' said Wylie.
> Neary turned his cup upside down.[5]

The object of this satire is not so much Synge, the author in 1904 of *Riders to the Sea*, as it is the travestied Synge whom the Abbey Theatre exploited in the 1930s as a peasant dramatist. What is disinterred by the betrayal of Synge's text is precisely the suppressed origin of Synge's own marvellous stage direction. In the Old Testament, the chosen people were occasionally abandoned by their God in punishment for their forsaking his commandments. Such an occasion is recorded in 2 Kings where we read how God condemned Manasseh, saying:

> And I will stretch over Jerusalem the line of Samaria, and the plummet of the house of Ahab: and I will wipe Jerusalem as a man wipeth a dish, wiping it, and turning it upside down.
> And I will forsake the remnant of mine inheritance. . . (2 Kings 21: 13-14)

God's judgement (Hellenized and humanized by Synge in the figure of Maurya/*moira*, Greek for fate) had been in the play of 1904 transformed into a stoic self-making in acceptance of death. Thanks to Matthew Arnold, this conjunction of the Hellenic and Hebraic would have been virtually impossible in an English context: its availability to Synge as a dramatist stems from his intellectual training in a university where the classics, Hebrew, and Gaelic were all taught in a context of missionary training upon which he resolutely turned his back.[6] Skitting *Riders to the Sea, Murphy* restores the sense of an unfaithful remnant of God's people, being unable of course to restore the remnant itself. Yet in suggesting a dynamic, if also ironic, inheritance of Synge by Beckett, one should not too precipitously settle for an adjusted chronology as tradition. A passing reference to Seán O'Casey (1884 – 1964) can serve as a reminder that there were those who held that no revolution, in any socialist sense at least, had occurred in 1916 or in 1921. The survival of O'Casey – as also Yeats's school friend W. K. Magee (the critic 'John Eglinton', 1868 – 1961), and Walter Starkie (1894 – 1976, a director of the Abbey) – into the age of Godot can serve to undercut any simplistic reliance on chronology. For in the early 1960s, Beckett did not feature in the Dublin bookshops as an *Irish* author. *More Pricks than Kicks* (1934) and *Watt* (1953) were banned, and the fringe theatre which attempted to introduce Beckett the dramatist to Dublin audiences was raided by the police – though not in connection with a Beckett production.[7] This was the era in which learned commentaries on Yeats and Joyce began to appear in great quantities, and living authors were recognizable by their own recognition of the green-letter dates (1916, 1921 etc.) as inaugurating moments. The fiction of Liam O'Flaherty (1897 – 1984), Seán O'Faolain (1900 – 1991), and Frank O'Connor (1903 – 1966) may have drawn some of its energy from the post-war disillusion of the 1920s, but it acknowledged the cardinal status of 'the revolutionary years'. It was only later, through the dogged research of J. C. C. Mays and a few others, that a parallel movement in Irish writing has been discovered to orbit round the eccentric figure of Flann O'Brien (1912 – 1966), a movement in which the uneasy truce between romanticism and realism characteristic of the O'Connor/O'Faolain school was ignored in favour of a more experimental and fantastical mode. In addition to Flann O'Brien, one might here cite the prose writings of Jack Yeats (1871 – 1957), and the novels of Joseph O'Neill (1886 – 1953) and Francis Stuart (born 1902).

Thus, when the book trade ignored Beckett in the early 1960s, it did so as part of a wider neglect. An unthinking reliance on realistic setting in fiction led to Beckett's classification as scarcely Irish, despite the testimonials of the Censorship Board. The plays fared somewhat better, perhaps because student productions generated a small demand for scripts. But as the post-war texts, dramatic as well as fictional, were for the most part written in French, Beckett's distance from the canon was safely established. The irony of this alienation was lost on all but a few surviving members of Beckett's circle in Dublin: the author of *Comment C'est* (1961) had experienced the reality of partition in the early 1920s more directly than any of the national caucus. Born in Dublin, he was a pupil at Portora Royal School in Enniskillen when the several partitioning enactments of the period were effected – the Government of Ireland Act (1920) and the legal and constitutional instruments attendant on the Treaty of 1921 and its aftermath. As Enniskillen lies north of the border in Northern Ireland in County Fermanagh, every vacation and half-term break involved Beckett in a species of international travel. He entered Portora in the autumn of 1920, and stayed until the spring of 1923, thus arriving at the point where an 'unilateral' partition was imposed and remaining throughout the worst months of the War of Independence and the Civil War. Before hostilities ended, and while Beckett was still at Portora, the southern provisional government actively promoted violent disturbance in the north; Enniskillen was central in resisting republican incursions. In February 1922, a local newspaper reported the capture of 'desperados' in the town; four months later, two hundred British troops (with artillery) were despatched from Enniskillen to recapture a village further west in County Fermanagh. In the course of the operation, a fortified position in the south was shelled, seized, and then held for two years.[8] The altering relations between territory and power, between division and authority, the violent ambiguity of Black-and-Tan terrorism, the emergence of a uniformed southern army where previously had been an unknown number of 'mufti' volunteers, border warfare and fratricidal civil conflict – these tangible features of Beckett's late childhood and adolescence are not wholly remote from the intimate dislocations of his writing.

It is well known that he became a writer through apprenticeship to James Joyce, acting as his amanuensis in Paris in the late 1920s while *Work in Progress* was in progress. One of his earliest publications was *Our Exagmination Round his Factification for Incamination of Work in Progress*, a collection of essays written in tribute to Joyce, which Beckett edited in 1929. His contribution, 'Dante . . . Bruno. Vico . . . Joyce', doubled as a startling tribute to his own education at Trinity College Dublin from which he had graduated in 1927. After 1921 the College had withdrawn into itself, and the new government believed (with reason) that Trinity was a bastion of pro-British sentiment where the actuality of the Irish state, of independence and partition had not fully registered. This situation was compounded by the distance existing between the vast majority of the southern population (as Catholics) and the Protestant minority (looking towards Trinity as a refuge and strength). Partition had increased the *proportions* of majority to minority within the new state as compared to the island as a whole, though it also was soon found to have reduced open conflictual tension between them. Beckett's affiliation to Joyce, rather than to Yeats, was an early sign of exile from the small community into which he was born, even if it was not operative as a *rapprochement* with the generality of Irish citizens.

That small community should not be identified in Yeatsian terms. Beckett's father had been something in the building trade, a member – at best – of the non-learned professions. Socially, Bill was not so far removed from the Joyces, though denominational difference ensured that no comparison was possible. In the Beckett household, Protestant allegiance was zealously maintained by May (née Roe), a pious low church woman who worried about her son's salvation. This latter element gave the Becketts some affinity with the evangelicalism of the Synge household (thirty years earlier) and even more distinctly with the attitudes of the Mattesons into which family J. M. Synge had early longed to marry. However, the lost inheritance of landed estate, which informed Synge's development, had no counterpart in Beckett's. The Becketts were upwardly mobile – with a house in the new and would-be exclusive Foxrock suburbs of Dublin – and here they also differentiated themselves from the feckless (or luckless) Joyces. Samuel Beckett's upbringing, then, was solidly middle-class, with the qualification that the successful middle class of his youth characterized itself ideologically in such additional terms (Catholic and nationalist) as the Becketts and their like declined. When we find Beckett attaching himself to Joyce's circle in Paris, the implications are not simply those of precocious intellectualism but also of revolt. After the passage of seventy years it is easier to observe the degree to which that group retained links with Catholicism – Roman Catholicism rather than the Irish version doubtless – though the point is quietly made by Beckett's inclusion of Thomas MacGreevy among contributors to the *Exagmination*, and by his friendship with Brian Coffey.

Beckett took a degree in modern languages at Trinity College, graduating BA in the autumn of 1927.[9] His tutor (a member of the academic staff appointed to oversee an undergraduate's general welfare) was A. A. Luce, an exponent of Berkeleyan immaterialism and an expert on Descartes. The instructors who influenced him were Thomas Rudmose-Brown and Walter Starkie, the fomer teaching French, the latter Italian and Spanish. By all accounts, the two heartily detested each other. While this antagonism may have provided excitement for their contemporaries, a more important historical fracture marks them off from their solemn Victorian predecessors, the self-confirming coterie of individually talented dons. Rudmose-Brown, who was Scottish, appears to have taken the establishment of the new state in his stride: he may even have been moderately radical in his political views. Starkie, a native Dubliner and a Catholic, had no trouble with the state. His father was a distinguished educationalist, and he himself served as a director of the Abbey Theatre for many years. He was also a member of the Centre pour les études fascistes in Lausanne and an admirer of Mussolini. It is said that Rudmose-Brown once described Starkie as 'the off-spring of a spoon and a wet dream', a remark sufficiently depraved to deserve incorporation into *Murphy*. Instead, Starkie is briefly summoned up in the third part of *Watt*, in the person of Fitzwein, committeeman.[10]

Beckett's early writings were principally critical: the essay on Joyce (1929) was followed by a brief monograph on Marcel Proust (1931). His poetry, intermittently written throughout his adult life, is attuned to the same pitch as that of McGreevy and Coffey. *Whoroscope*, the best known of the poems, achieved publication in 1930 by winning a prize sponsored by the aristocratic exile, Nancy Cunard. Requiring something on the theme of time, she appears to have set up a competition with the sole intention of rewarding the impoverished Beckett with some cash. Time pervades Beckett's early preoccupations, and does not fail to sustain itself into the later writings. But there is a philosophical currency, tapped in the pre-war work, which undergoes radical scrutiny in the course of the war, to re-emerge in a different mode thereafter.

The impact of Einsteinian physics was first registered conceptually, and in Beckett's case prompted the comic treatment of Cartesianism which constitutes *Whoroscope*'s main achievement. At the end of the thirties, in *Murphy*, one of the hero's fantasies centres on the sensation 'of being a missile without provenance or target, caught up in a tumult of non-Newtonian motion,' a prospect which is simultaneously rendered as repetitive stylistic detail at once idiomatic and relativistic – 'so pleasant that pleasant was not the word.'[11] The intellectualism of Beckett's pre-war writings – a daunting range of allusion, the deployment of obscure words throughout an already vast personal lexicon, the seemingly uninterruptible articulation of the narratives – gives way to a prose no less comic but considerably more humble and halting in its rhythms. The second impact of the twentieth-century scientific revolution on Beckett was existential or (to use an old word in the old ways) *moral*. The notion of Time itself suffered in both phases of the turbulent dialogue between experiment and meditation, with consequences for our views not only of natural time and its specialized physiological sub-divisions human and non-human, but also for the elaboration of historical time as a philosophical subject.[12] That time, in these numerous senses, is implicated in the reflective procedures of literary history hardly needs to be stated. Yet, before proceeding to look closely at some examples of Beckett's pre-war work, we might pause to consider if the Einsteinian notion of 'a missile without provenance' does not provide some insight into the problems of sequentiality which literary history gives rise to.

In *The World, the Text, and the Critic*, Edward Said characterized Jonathan Swift as an intellectual *devant le lettre*; that is, he anticipated the role of the late eighteenth-century man of ideas, or high hack, and did so in circumstances of peculiar difficulty – difficulty for himself. For Swift had no 'reserve capital': he had no means of advancing himself in the world save through the church or through patrons whom he foundly unfailingly ungrateful.[13] This notion of an intellectual, at once historically placed at a time of exceptional danger and lacking inherited position or influence, fits Beckett as well as it does Swift. For what really distinguishes Beckett from Yeats and Synge is his lack of 'background'; and in so far as Joyce bothered to invoke the familial and tribal histories of the Catholic Joyces, it marks him from the author of *Finnegans Wake* also. Posthumously, a background has been claimed for him, notably by Vivian Mercier, who attended Portora some years after Beckett and who could claim a common Huguenot inheritance.[14] Except that, in twentieth-century Ireland, a Huguenot inheritance is a contradiction in terms: as a confessional allegiance, the French Church (as it had been termed) was long ago absorbed into the Church of Ireland; and as a social group of considerable importance in banking and manufacturing, it had been displaced by the growth of the nineteenth-century Catholic middle classes. Eschewing the litany of eminent Irish Huguenot names – Fleury, La Touche, Le Fanu, Maturin etc. – and in this sense denying himself a provenance, Beckett negotiated with an imposed literary inheritance by way of textual betrayal. Synge is the ostensible victim in the instance already cited from *Murphy*. Another, mentioned by Mercier as an instance of Beckett's biblical allusiveness, may now be considered in support of the contention that Beckett lacked 'background'.

The starting point is Mr Tyler's placid admission in *All that Fall* to Mrs Rooney that he had been saying little of importance:

> I was merely cursing, under my breath, God and man, under my breath, and the wet Saturday afternoon of my conception.

For Mercier, a hidden biblical allusion to Job 3:3 is at work, for there we read 'Let the day perish wherein I was born, and the night in which it was said, There is a man child conceived.' While this is unquestionably the case, there is surely also a literary allusion to the last moment of Yeats's play, *The Words upon the Window-pane* (1934), in which a female medium suddenly repossessed by the spirit of Jonathan Swift cries – 'Perish the day on which I was born'. Given the common obsession with childlessness among central characters in the two plays, and given Beckett's habit of skitting Yeats from *Murphy* through at least to 'but the clouds . . .' (written 1976), a debt to the older writer seems proven. This relationship might also be written in terms of influence (that is, of Yeats's power) or of appropriation (that is, of Beckett's power) rather than of debt. I prefer to see such transactions as fundamentally textual, and for that reason propose a different set of related terms – tradition, traduction, translation – according to which *All that Fall* betrays Yeats's eighteenth-century tradition by refusing to name either Yeats or Swift.

The first substantial publication of Beckett's to reach the English-reading public was *More Pricks than Kicks*, issued by the London house of Chatto and Windus in 1934, the year of *The Words upon the Window-pane*. The Pauline allusiveness of the title did not fool the censors who were no more impressed by the pastiche of Joyce's concluding paragraph in *Dubliners*, round which Beckett constructed 'A Wet Night', one of the best stories in the book.[15] But the two collections of short stories do not simply converge on Beckett's comic and fluent re-writing of Joyce's snow-storm. *Dubliners* concludes in the drifting consciousness of Gabriel Conroy who (it has been suggested) is the unnamed narrator of the opening stories: *More Pricks* almost sustains a single linking character throughout all ten stories, though Belacqua Shuah dies in the penultimate story, 'Yellow', where an attempt is made to narrate the fatal process:

> By Christ! he did die!
> They had clean forgotten to auscultate him!

even though Belacqua (dead here) had been the implied (third-person) narrator at the story's opening. Given this ambitious undertaking, the parody of Joyce's 'The Dead' is of more than stylistic interest:

> the rain fell in a uniform untroubled manner. It fell upon the bay, the littoral, the mountains and the plains, and notably upon the Central Bog it fell with a resolute uniformity.[16]

The key term is *uniform*. The unrelenting articulation of Beckett's early narratives threatens to absorb all the diversity of allusion, aside and incident into a single omniscience. Nothing, it seems, can resist his narrative presumption. One is grateful for comic lapses (as when Belacqua's widow realizes that 'she had begun to survive him'), or more formal acknowledgements of unbridgeable distinctions. For example, the opening story, 'Dante and the Lobster', concludes with an education in cookery provided by Belacqua's suburban aunt:

> 'You make a fuss' she said angrily 'and upset me and then lash into it for your dinner.'

> She lifted the lobster clear of the table. It had about thirty seconds to live.
> Well, thought Belacqua, it's a quick death, God help us all.
> It is not.[17]

Quite how the last sentence manages to stand outside the ferocious authority of Beckett's narrative is uncertain, but the admission of death's processive terror (even for lobsters) prefigures the manner in which Belacqua's corpse will divide onlookers at the laying-out, 'like the keys between nations in Velasquez's *Lances*, like the water between Buda and Pest, and so on, hyphen of reality.'[18] It is all a mite artificial, like the purple prose of Gabriel Conroy's swooning absorption into the uniformity of the living and the dead. The reader knows *now* that the same author will later produce *Malone Dies* (1951 in French, 1956 in English) and the other texts, dramatic as well as fictional, in which death is carefully examined. Agamben points to a striking passage in the second book of Montaigne's essays in which the consequences of a violent fall from horseback were sifted in terms of 'the ultimate goal of experience' being 'a nearing to death – that is, man's advance to maturity through an anticipation of death as the extreme limit of experience'.[19] If Beckett had 'background' perhaps it was French and intellectual rather than Anglo-Irish and cultural. But rather than trace his evolution as a creative writer, it may prove more productive first to consider some of the drudgery involved in his career as one lacking reserve capital.

There are several reasons why this should be so. A bilingual author must always be of interest when he is engaged in translation and, additionally, the idea of 'evolution' is not self-evidently appropriate to the dynamics of a literary corpus. The high reputation of the biological sciences in the nineteenth century had been sustained into the era of Einstein and Weber by the brio of popularizing evolutionists whom Yeats accused of destroying his traditional belief. One of these, T. H. Huxley, has been suggested by Hugh Kenner as a possible source for Beckett's favourite metaphor of games in *Murphy* and *Endgame* (1957 in French, 1958 in English).[20] If there is a change in Beckett's work, from pre-war to post-war, it is certainly incompatible with ideas of evolution. As with *Murphy*'s exploitation of Synge and *All that Fall*'s of Yeats, Beckettian texts which play with games may as likely derive from Standish O'Grady's 'veiled player' (see above pp. 237-38). Here again, the betrayal of tradition is enacted in not naming names. To suggest the local mediation in O'Grady is not to discount a better-known source in Huxley, though perhaps the very concept of source is modified in the process just as the status of knowledge is jeopardized in confrontation with death. The tendency to recount Beckett's career, stage by stage, is closely linked with rival campaigns aligning him to French existentialism, the British theatre, an Anglo-Irish tradition. This canonizing of texts and abandoned texts, authorial translations and posthumous early work has more to do with the reconstruction of academic syllabi than with any critical response to the disasters of twentieth-century history. Translation attracts such an intelligence as Beckett's because the name suppressed is that of Beckett himself.

THE NEGRO ANTHOLOGY (1934)

Fabulously rich and politically radical, Nancy Cunard financed the 1934 publication of a large dossier of material dealing with the culture and every-day lives of black peoples from East Africa to Haiti. In well over a hundred articles, with many photographs and line drawings, *The Negro Anthology* covered jazz, slavery, bronze statuary, trade unionism, magic and initiation, brothels, comic-cuts and – *passim* – European colonialism. Most of this was originally written in languages other than English. Nobody contributed more to it than Beckett who translated nineteen pieces in all, a body of prose amounting to well over one hundred thousand words. As with *Whoroscope*, a fiscal link can be discerned, along which Cunard transferred a tiny por-tion of her 'reserve capital' to the hard-up intellectual. (It is sentimental to regard Beckett as ever being impoverished, for he always had access to family support, with the entailed bourgeois embarrassments.) Money can-not wholly explain his commitment to a project which not only sought to highlight European racism but which also was published by Wishart of Lon-don in January 1935 to raise funds for the French Communist Party. Nor did Beckett wash his hands of this exercise in political *belles lettres*; as recently as 1988, he permitted one of the pieces he had translated to be included in a 70th birthday tribute to Nelson Mandela.

'Murderous Humanitarianism' is signed by eleven members of the Sur-realist Group of Paris, including André Breton and Paul Eluard: its uncom-promising (doctrinaire, if you like) support of proletarian revolution is spiced with denunciations of 'christian ignominy' and those 'votaries of corpses and theosophies [who] wash down the warrens of Himalayan monasteries'. It may seem that the content is pure surrealism, though a further reading of 2 Kings 21 would also provide some colourful denunciation of political evil and religious enchantment. The style, however, has acquired something in translation – 'irretentions of nostalgia' is pure Beckett of the *Murphy* vintage.[21] Though most of the material he was commissioned to translate was less challenging, an extract from his version of an historical article by Jacques Boulanger indicates considerable investment in style:

> In 1915 the Republic of Hayti was presided over by one William Sam, who was so little appreciated as an administrator that steps were being taken to have him removed. Now it appears that William Sam, being alive to this, saw fit to execute no fewer than 200 hostages drawn from the most distinguished families throughout the country. He may have counted on the radical nature of this proceeding to reinstate him in the good graces of his fellow citizens, but the contrary was the case, and William Sam referred himself with all speed to the sanctuary of the French Legation. Here in due course there arrived some members of his flock to pay their addresses. Having saluted him with such heartiness as to break his two arms they threw him out of the window to the waiting populace, and William Sam terminated his career as mincemeat.[22]

This seems distinguished, as a masterly handling of grammatical tenses, ironic cliché ('being alive' is especially good), and Conradian delayed decoding. Given the political context in which Beckett will make his transition from English to French – the occasion upon which conscience is activated or, rather, activates itself – the vast array of politicized texts on which he cut his teeth as a translator is surely not without interest. In practice, however, the biographical response has been to discount his involvement with Cunard (who was not only an eccentric and wealthy enthusiast for black culture but a communist to boot) as mere hack-work undertaken for the money it would bring in. Yet the circumstances deserve closer attention. First, *The Negro Anthology* is the only evidence of Beckett's taking on such commissions in the 1930s – apart from a few isolated poems – and surely other less ideologically distinctive opportunities to make a few bob must have presented themselves. Second, Cunard was *very* rich, and had she wished simply to assist the young Irishman she could have done do without requiring a hundred thousand words in return. Third, the commitment is not wholly unique in Beckett's pre-war career, for he responded positively to a questionnaire on writers' attitudes to the Spanish Civil War. True, his biographer Deirdre Bair dismisses the response as 'facetious' – it consisted of the single compound word UPTHEREPUBLIC. Instead of dismissing the answer, one might consider the significance of the question. In 1937, Beckett had few credentials as an author; his inclusion among those to be canvassed represents an interpretation of his likely support for the Spanish government against Franco's insurrection.

Arguing that for more than three years Beckett had talked about going to Spain, a project rendered impossible by the Civil War, Bair exemplifies the way in which her subject has been marketed as a characteristically non-political figure. His visit to Nazi Germany between September 1936 and April 1937 is dominated in her account by a concern – his concern – about his health. While it would be wrong to see in the traveller of 1936 some foreshadowing of the Resistance courier of 1940, the manner in which Beckett's return from Berlin is followed up by his anti-fascist declaration about Spain is noteworthy. In order to maintain her position, Bair is obliged to dismiss the *Negro Anthology* business in a single paragraph, concluding that Beckett's contributions were 'solid, impersonal translations, undistinguished by any individual touch.'[23] It is clear that Bair has as little feeling for style as she has sense of the preoccupations of the 1930s' European intelligentsia – her Beckett is a very Anglo-American product. But a further glance at some statistics should persuade us that his involvement requires attention. No other translator contributed more than five pieces (these from Spanish), and the only other translators from French were Nancy Cunard herself and her cousin Edward, who contributed two each. In effect, Beckett was responsible for virtually all of the originally Francophone material. *The Negro Anthology* constitutes his largest prose work, and hence his largest single publication of any kind.

Neglect of these statistics may stem from the rarity of the book itself, and from its subordination of the translator's name to those of his 'originals'. Yet this aspect of the publication interacts with the problems of omniscient or 'uniform' narrative simultaneously proceeding in *More Pricks than Kicks* and the still-unpublished *Murphy*. Beckett in the anthology becomes nineteen voices, a dissembled dramatic text. Perhaps a biographer may be forgiven for overlooking the political significance of this, in the light of her commencing work just after the 1960s had closed. That decade had generated a notion of politics so potentially comprehensive as to allow only sleep as an alternative engagement. An ideal insomnia permitted no derogation from a political reading of every detail of life, and so the perpetual revolution of Paris in May 1968 was projected by the researcher back into the 1930s. Yet, in Yeats's comprehensive vision of things, a similar drive towards total mobilization of spirit, intellect, and body was evident in the years when Beckett commenced publishing fiction in English. The need to escape from omniscient narrative was also a need to find release from a Yeatsian tradition, encoded in *Murphy* as astrological prediction and a final skitting – in Sighle Kennedy's view at least – of 'The Only Jealousy of Emer', a further exchange with the complete hero, Cuchulain.[24]

It is as well to set a personal context in which this transition is prepared. In the mid-1930s, Beckett was still caught up with psychological ailments which had haunted his youth. Indeed he was registered at the Tavistock Clinic in London, and was undergoing analysis by Wilfrid Bion when *The Negro Anthology* was published. For the son of a provincial bourgeois family, psychoanalysis in 1934, and at the Tavistock Clinic, amounted to putting oneself in the hands of the medicine-man, a rejection of conventional diagnoses and therapies in favour of a politically suspect and alien philosophy. (In Germany, psychoanalysis was branded as a 'Jewish science'.) Beckett's difficulties with his family not only led him to the Tavistock, the Clinic constituted one of the issues over which he disputed with them. Though Beckett's domestic background was unquestionably bourgeois, it was not solely bourgeois, or at least not unrelievably conventional. The uncertainty of his professional debut as academic teacher reflected this option. In September 1928 he made his third trip from Ireland to the continent. But instead of France (where his professional interests lay) he went to Kassel, a hundred-odd miles north of Frankfurt-am-Main. His motive in choosing Germany was personal, his focus a cousin, Peggy Sinclair, whose father (married to Beckett's aunt) was a Jewish art-dealer. As a consequence of these Hiberno-Jewish connections in Europe, he even abandoned his new-found family (the Joyces in Paris) for the last days of 1928 which he spent once more with the Sinclairs. Quite apart from his relationship with Peggy, Beckett greatly enjoyed the bohemian ambiance of a household where paintings and drawings were casually examined and discussed. He passed late summer 1929 in the same company, on holiday at a Baltic resort.

Through his initial preoccupations with Peggy Sinclair, Beckett had established a relationship with Germany of a kind which particularly qualified him to study the political situation. Peggy, who suffered from tuberculosis, died in May 1933. For some time she had been engaged to be married, and the bond between her and Beckett was less sexually charged than it had been formerly (at least for him). Vestigial allusions to their shared interests and places of resort may be identified in the later works as, for example, in *All that Fall* where reference is made to Fontane's novel, *Effi Briest*, which the two had read while holidaying on the Baltic. As the novel is set in the same region of Germany, the personal referentiality deserves note. Even after Hitler's accession and Peggy's death, Beckett maintained his interest in Germany, ostensibly in modern German painting. John Pilling has usefully listed the towns Beckett visited during a six-month period in 1936/7 – including Berlin, Brunswich, Dresden, Halle, Hamburg, Hanover, Leipzig, Lubeck, Luneburg, Munich, Nuremburg, Regensburg, Weimar, and Wurzburg. Art was in the air in Nazi Germany at the time: in December Hitler travelled to Munich to open a new gallery, taking the opportunity to denounce 'degenerate art' with all the zeal of an ex-painter, and specifically blaming Jewish art-dealers. The mock exhibition included work by many artists whom Beckett admired, and even some whom he may have known or at least met. He had an introduction from his aunt Cissie Sinclair and Cecil Salkeld in Dublin which put him in touch with Dr Willi Grohmann, former director of the Zwinger Gallery in Dresden. Grohmann, who was ostracised by many because he was a Jew, took Beckett to see several private collections of contemporary art, including work by Chagall, Kokoschka, Mondrian, Nolde and Picasso.

In international affairs, this was also a time of great tension. Before Beckett left Germany, Austria had been effectively annexed to the Reich in March 1938. (Two months earlier, Freud had flown out of Vienna to London where he died before the end of the year.) Show trials were proceeding apace in the Soviet Union, though at home in Ireland a new constitution was inaugurated and Anglo-Irish relations showed signs of improvement. If Irish affairs seem puny by comparison, the interconnection of local and international, cultural and political matters was well illustrated in a number of controversies about literary and other prizes. In February 1934, Yeats was awarded the Goethe-Plakette by the newly Nazified city council of Frankfurt, a distinction which compromized his position some years later when efforts were made to nominate a concentration-camp prisoner, the pacifist Carl von Ossietszky, for a Nobel Prize. This was the period when Beckett was travelling in Germany, and when Thomas Mann was organizing opposition to the Reich among German *emigrés*. Contemptuous of democracy in 1918, and fastidious in distancing himself from contemporary social affairs, Mann had gradually re-oriented himself in the course of the 1920s, becoming the leader of German opinion first from a Swiss and later an American exile. One can, in effect, characterize Samuel Beckett as a European bourgeois in the style of Mann rather than an Irish bohemian in the manner of Yeats. Such a classification, however oversimplified it must be in certain regards, is all the more urgent in that Irish society scarcely possessed a vocabulary to indicate the stratifications of a class system like the English one or the particular status of German *Burgertum*. It is in this (empty) context that Yeats's concurrent revival and re-assignment of 'ascendancy' ideological elements – sectarian, historical, mytho-poetic, or whatever – has to be assessed. The Becketts neither fitted into the residual dignities of the so-called Protestant Ascendancy nor into the new political order established by the Catholic middle classes. Samuel Beckett's early psychosomatic disorders – boils, cysts etc. – might even be read as symptoms of non-integration displayed on the Irish body politic in its first decade or so of institutional independence. If these had their correlatives in the border incursions, hostage-takings and civil tumult of his late school-days, then the self-effacing translations of *The Negro Anthology* provide analogies in the form of non-originals. In the famous last words of *Watt*, 'no symbols where none intended'.

VESTIGES OR EMBERS

During the prolonged period when friends were attempting to place *Watt* with a publisher in Britain or the United States, the suggestion was made to Beckett that he abandon the experiment and write a 'realistic account' of his war-time experience instead. The implication, that the novel dealt with the events of 1939–45 in some fashion, deserves attention even if the underlying interpretive mode is grossly commercial. On the surface nothing in *Watt* remotely represents war, neither the Wehrmacht nor Maquis varieties. But there is an episode in Part III where narration shifts into the first person to tell of Watt's experience in the grounds of Mr Knott's house. Movement there is restricted by complicated fences so that the narrator and Watt can only make contact through holes in the fences or by means of occasional channels between enfenced areas. While these restrictions are in keeping with the implication that Mr Knott's establishment is a medical or 'mental' home of some sort, they also fit the case of an internment camp or outdoor prison. Here we also read one of the most intriguing accounts of Watt's language:

> Watt spoke also with scant regard for grammar, for syntax, for pronunciation, for enunciation, and very likely, if the truth were known, for spelling too, as these are generally received. Proper names, however, both of places and of persons, such as Knott, Christ, Gomorrha, Cork, he articulated with great deliberation, and from his discourse these emerged, palms, atolls, at long intervals, for he seldom specified, in a most refreshing manner.[25]

'Intervals' is the key word, for it not only indicates the temporal discontinuities of Watt's speech but also the spacial constriction in which he spoke to the narrator. The *intervallum* was the area between ramparts in a Roman fort, and the word's English usage constitutes a transfer from the spacial to the temporal axis. Watt has been 'transferred' into Knott's care, and his preference for proper nouns over all other linguistic elements demonstrates his attachment to reference rather than to relation. Names refer to things, but language is relational. Historically, one might see this scene as having some origin in accounts Beckett would have heard in Dublin of internment in the Curragh camp during the Irish Civil War – Francis Stuart has described to the present writer a conversation through fences and across security zones in 1923 with Peadar O'Donnell, the two men being in adjacent compounds. A post-Soviet exhibition of miniscule art-works, vestiges of the gulag system, was held in Amsterdam in the winter of 1993/4 and served to confirm the interpretation of *Watt* Part III as in part at least based on incarceration. In the jargon of the gulag, Watt had been 'in the zone'.

Watt also contains a hilarious account of Trinity College committees, Irish state prohibitions in the area of personal medicine, the more absurd aspects of Celticism, and the hobby-horses of W. B. Yeats, these disguised topics introduced and peopled by a string of Watt's beloved proper names. Digression introduces the story of Mr Ernest Louit, who had worked on a dissertation called *The Mathematical Intuitions of the Visicelts*. Researched at the College's expense in County Clare, this work depended on the abilities of 'Mr Thomas Nackybal, native of Burren', and with this location the folkloristic enthusiasms of Lady Gregory and Yeats enter the frame, Burren village lying a mile east of Gregory's summer house (Mount Vernon) and close to Finevara, setting of Yeats's 'The Dreaming of the Bones'. A committee of five is convened to hear Louit's defence of his work, but despite the relative fewness of their number they are unable quite to co-ordinate their responses:

> Mr Fitzwein, tired of looking at the back of Mr Magershon's head, cranes forward and looks at Mr O'Meldon, on his right but one at the end of the table. But Mr O'Meldon, tired of craning forward looking at Mr MacStern, is now craning backward looking at Mr de Baker, on his left but two.[26]

Four pages of this constitute an early example of Beckettian permutation, but no more than the five names of the committeemen are required to support the comedy. These names may seem vacant, mere items in the sorry-go-round of academic approval. But if we concede that Magershon is virtually a name concluding in -*son*, then all five of them cease to be referential only and exhibit their relational base. The prefixes Mac and Fitz both signify son-ship, while the O' in O'Meldon (a bastard case) is the Gaelic prefix for a more general descent or affiliation. De Baker (another linguistic mongrel) is structured on a broadly similar French namestyle. Thus, the committee not only fails to assess Louit's research, it fatally undermines Watt's reliance on proper names as reliably referential. Relation is everywhere. Except perhaps in the oddly named Nackybal; his demonstration of mental arithmetic is of course a fraud, despite an upbringing uncomplicated by

> any instruction other than that treating of such agricultural themes, indispensible to the exercise of his profession, as the rock-potato, the clover-thatch, every man his own fertiliser, turf versus combustion and the fly-catching pig,

with the result that he cannot, nor ever could, read or write, or, without the assistance of his fingers, and his toes, add, subtract, multiply or divide the smallest whole number to, from, by or into another.[27]

Beyond the official approval of noble savagery in the Irish state's acceptance of peasant wisdom as the measure of all things, this surely parodies Yeats's far more sinister curriculum in *On the Boiler* (1939). Having a few pages earlier declared that 'forcing reading and writing on those who wanted neither was a worst part of the violence which for two centuries has been creating that hell wherein we suffer', Yeats continued

> I assume that some tragic crisis shall so alter Europe and all opinion that the Irish government will teach the great majority of its school-children nothing but ploughing, harrowing, sowing, curry-combing, bicycle-cleaning, drill-driving . . . trouser-patching, and playing upon the Squiffer, all things that serve human dignity, unless indeed it decide that these things are better taught at home, in which case it can leave the poor children at peace.[28]

The violence of the Yeatsian credo hardly needs emphasis, likewise his lack of any experience in matters of warfare. 'Man has created death', Yeats wrote in a short and moving poem commemorating Kevin O'Higgins who was assassinated in 1927. The idealism of this, in a strict philosophical sense of idealism, may have some generic affinity to the seedy solipsism of *More Pricks than Kicks* and *Murphy*, but by 1939 Beckett was already modifying the omniscient narrative of his fiction so as to acknowledge death rather than overcome it. *Watt* is the first of the major works in which the central figure is not written triumphantly off. In Part III, however, there is a deflection of the earlier suave if accidental killing of the 'hero'. Echoing, unconsciously no doubt, a passage in *Gulliver's Travels* where a medical treatment is fatally applied to a dog, Mr Ernst Louit, in trying to account for the expenditure of fifteen shillings of College money on boots, answered

> that in the late afternoon of November the twenty-first, in the vicinity of Handcross, they had unfortunately been sucked off his feet by a bog, which in the fading light, and the confusion of his senses consequent on prolonged inanition, he had mistaken for a field of late onions. To the hope then politely expressed that O'Connor had enjoyed his brief outing, Louit with grateful acknowledgement replied that he had been reluctantly obliged, on the same occasion, to hold O'Connor head downward in the morass, until his faithful heart had ceased to beat, and then roast him, in his skin, which he could not bring himself to remove, over a fire of flags and cotton-blossoms. He took no credit for this, O'Connor in his place would have done the same for him.[29]

Stylistic analysis of this howling passage will reveal a great deal, but central to the outcome will be the gratuitous killing of a dog narrated as the consequence of lost boots, and the dog's being named in a more recognizably human fashion (O'Connor) than the killer (Louit). The implication of the final sentence, as quoted, underlines the interchangeability of human and non-human, even unto death. If there is a 'tradition' of Irish writing, in which ferocious humanism plays a sustained part from Swift to Beckett, it is only accessible through a disavowal of its Yeatsian transmission.

In keeping with this, death does not come for Watt. Shortly before the narrative gives way to the 'Addenda' quoted above, the hero has passed a portion of the night in a railway station waiting-room unbeknownst to an official who opens up each morning with a violent emphasis:

> Mr Nolan then, having unlocked and hurled, against their jambs, the wicket and the booking-office door, came to the door of the waiting-room. Had his whistle been less piercing, and his entry less resounding, he might have heard, behind the door, a disquieting sound, that of soliloquy, under dictation, and proceeded with care. But no, he turned the key and dealt, with his boot, the door a dunt that sent it flying inwards at a great speed.
>
> The innumerable semicircles thus brilliantly begun did not end, as on all previous mornings, in the bang that Mr Nolan loved, no, but they were all cut short, all without exception, at the same point. And the reason for that was this, that Watt, where he stood swaying, murmuring, was nearer the waiting-room door that the waiting-room door was wide.[30]

There are many grounds on which this passage might be considered. First, it recalls some of the dexterous word-play employed by Beckett in accounting for the death of William Sam as originally told by Jacques Boulanger: the advance from 'resounding' to 'sound' for example, the six occurrences of the impending door, the implied description of a schizoid experience as 'soliloquy, under dictation', or the inner-onomatopoeia of 'the reason for that was this, that Watt . . .' to account for a head violently struck. Second, the incident differs from that recounted by Agamben from Montaigne (p. 385 above), perhaps by being less nearly fatal, and certainly by having no equivalent of the essayist's first-hand if delayed account of recovered senses. Third, the location of this accident at a railway station anticipates a less openly accounted-for railway accident at the close of *All that Fall* where, however, the outcome is to be fatal for a figure hitherto unheard of in the play, a child. And if Alec Reid was right in describing *Watt* as 'a strange, fantastical, comic novel set in the country round Foxrock, County Dublin', then the play and the novel's last pages share a location in Leopardstown railway station. The overlap of texts, both in their sorry referentiality and in their common occupation of the writer's time, is a feature of Beckett's work which only a full scholarly inspection of the remains will make possible. Hugh Kenner has pointed out, not only that *All that Fall* began (in English in 1956) while Beckett was finishing *Fin de partie* (or *Endgame*) in French, but that they share 'a tyrannical blind man' and 'the terminal evocation of a doomed child'.[31] While tyranny hardly needs academic confirmation, the ambiguous centrality of the infant state for Beckett, in its occasional presence and more palpable absence, has been surveyed by Terence Brown.[32]

We know that the composition of the novel was prolonged and complicated. Ann Beer has pointed to the significance of a revised date for Beckett's commencing work on *Watt* – 11 February 1941 in German occupied Paris, rather than late summer of the following year in Vichy France.[33] Bilingualism, therefore, is not so much a matter of a post-war adoption of French as it is a war-time maintenance of English. In conversation, Alec Reid once remarked to the present writer that Beckett had recalled one particular image from the journey from Paris to Rousillon – the sight of a man hanged on top of a dung-hill. It does not require further evidence to suggest that a change between *More Pricks than Kicks* and *Watt* is likely to involve altered attitudes towards death. Not only Belacqua in the 1934 collection of short stories, but also Murphy in *Murphy* (1938) had been narrated into death and posthumous knock-about indignities. Murphy's final disposal satirically avoids another betrayal of the national canon only to become embroiled in a grim anticipation of the ultimate barbarism shortly to unfold in Europe. Instead of being flushed down the lavatory of the Abbey Theatre as he desired, he is kicked from death (so to speak) as a misidentified object of public-house football:

> Some hours later Cooper took the packet of ash from his pocket, where earlier in the evening he had put it for greater security, and threw it angrily at a man who had given him great offence. It bounced, burst, off the wall on to the floor, where at once it became the object of much dribbling, passing, trapping, shooting, punching, heading and even some recognition from the gentleman's code. By closing time the body, mind, and soul of Murphy were freely distributed over the floor of the saloon; and before another dayspring greyed the earth had been swept away with the sand, the beer, the butts, the glass, the matches, the spits, the vomit. [34]

Even as one wants to argue that what will follow is qualitatively finer, there are clearly features of this black comedy which deserve attention. When the packet which had been Murphy becomes 'the object of much dribbling', the exchange between bodily existence and mechanical disposal not only specifies exactly the kind of reification which dare not speak its name but also insinuates a sense of the perversely erotic gratification underlying sadistic indifference to the *disjecta membra*. And to be an object of dribbling is already to have joined 'the spits, the vomit' with which the night will end. Before it ends, there is a pleasantly gratuitous aside at the expense of rugby union football (Beckett was a first class cricketer) and a heavy, ironic betrayal of St Luke's Gospel. In my copy of the King James bible – the same as that which Vivian Mercier assures us was available to Beckett – the point at issue occurs right at the end of the Benedictus:

> And thou, child, shalt be called the prophet of the Highest: for thou shalt go before the face of the Lord to prepare his ways;
> To give knowledge of salvation unto his people by the remission of their sins,
> Through the tender mercy of our God; whereby the dayspring from on high hath visited us,
> To give light to them that sit in darkness and in the shadow of death, to guide our feet into the way of peace.

Beckett's omniscient narrator was right – not light but greyness (to say a minimal least) was to follow this annunciation of a death. Just as the death of Murphy is momentarily pinned on the unmistakably biblical word, 'dayspring' which features in the announcement of John the Baptist's mission, so *Murphy* was published in the last year of peace, and the war was to concentrate in the most unspeakable manner on those who are promised peace in the Benedictus. The presence/absence of John the Baptist at the end of *Murphy* signifies a specific – and specifically anachronistic – form of spiritual quest. This is a search, not for a Messiah or Pandit Suk, but for a mode in which a contemporary annunciation might be articulated, or at least mimed as in *Waiting for Godot*. Instead of salvation, damnation will figure in Beckett's godless theology; yet, in the sharpest contradistinction to Yeats's late encounter with Christian theology (in *Purgatory*), Beckett will strive to mitigate spiritual states by an emphasis on the still small efficacy of words. While there is 'hellish hope', while Winnie in *Happy Days* (1961) can rely on her story when all else fails, then annunciation forestalls eternal punishment.

With reference to *Waiting for Godot*, Beckett allowed that a Christian interpretation was justified – 'Yes, Christianity is a mythology with which I am perfectly familiar, so naturally I use it.' And Stan Gontarski has shown how even so seemingly whimsical a piece as *Happy Days* is infused with allusions to religious literature – Dante and Milton are particularly relevant as poetic narrators of hopeless realms, of defeat.[35] The high generality of religious themes in Beckett does not exclude the co-existence of specific if fragmentary allusions. In Peggy Sinclair, Beckett had already identified and lost a Jewish beloved, and in the plays the far from omniscient Mr Rooney can combine virtually in one breath an allusion to the novel Sinclair and Beckett read together in Germany with an exasperated instancing of indeterminable numbers:

> We shall draw the blinds. You will read to me. I think Effie is going to commit adultery with the Major. [*Brief drag of feet.*] Wait! [*Feet cease. Stick tapping at steps.*] I have been up and down these steps five thousand times and still I do not know how many there are.[36]

The comic exploitation – or even travesty – of radio drama which is delightful here constitutes a wholescale transvaluation of materials. Let us not make heavy weather of the dragging steps and the trains, or even of the Major as military commander: instead, a few proto-textual details and the insight of a pioneer critic of Beckett's drama will clarify, if not lighten, the collocation of whimsy and terror which is finally *All that Fall*.

Among the discrete details transmitted by Deirdre Bair, as a gloss on the radio play, is a seemingly unimportant textual datum – Miss McGlone of the final script had once been Miss Beamish in the early drafts. The discreteness is all. This character does not appear in *All that Fall* – nobody does – but she impinges on the action solely through Mrs Rooney's doubled reference to the old woman alone in a great empty house who plays music. Dan Rooney, who is finally linked in no explicit way to the death of a child in or under the train he arrived on at Leopardstown, identifies the music in question as Schubert's 'Death and the Maiden'. Miss Beamish takes the name of a woman who was part of the odd community of aliens in Rousillon from 1942 to the end of the war. Discreteness still is all. Bair elsewhere oddly suggests that this Miss Beamish 'professed to being a novelist' and 'loudly claimed to everyone that she was a first cousin of Winston Churchill.'[37] Discretion, rather than discreteness, is now the order of the day. For Hermann Goering, more certainly than Churchill, can be established as a (distant) relative of Annie O'Meara de Vic Beamish (born 1883 in Dublin) who undoubtedly was a novelist and playwright, writing under the name Noel de Vic Beamish.[38] The family chronicler provides a summary of her war-time experience which indirectly raises questions as to exactly how Beckett and his future wife ended precisely where they did, following their escape from Paris:

> As she was resident in Cannes at the time of the German occupation and is a British Subject she was ordered in 1942 out of Cannes to a small village by name Roussillon. Here she had contact with the Resistance Movement and had

some of their arms hidden in her garden at a time when she was 'denounced' and visited by a German patrol. Interest in her manuscripts on the table, a Dublin birth certificate and her command of German probably saved her from a firing squad if not more summary death.[39]

The Beamishes make no reference to Churchill. But when the exasperated Moran is checking with his namesake-son about the purchase of a bicycle, there is a sardonic lapse – 'Who is this bicycle for, I said, Goering?'[40]

It is vital to recognize that the (suppressed) allusion to Noel Beamish does not authorize a systematic referential reading of the play, even if recourse elsewhere to Fontane's novel be seen as a self-referentiality on the playwright's part. On the contrary, the significance of the detail lies in its discreteness, its detachment from system. If we consider the conventional, largely nineteenth-century, notion of literary activity as composition – an activity which is organized from the centre by a controlling, autonomous mind, and which arranges (or composes) the components of observation, experience and ratiocination according to a programme of enhancing coherence – then Beckett's procedures might aptly be called *decomposition*. The arrogant narrator of the early fiction is gradually replaced by the still eloquent organizer of *Watt*, for which however, a list of addenda (or distenda?) must be provided. The turning point is nicely described by Molloy himself, when he confides that

> Not to want to say, not to know what you want to say, not to be able to say what you think you want to say, and never to stop saying, or hardly ever, that is the thing to keep in mind, even in the heat of composition.[41]

With *Molloy* (in French, 1951), first-person narration arrives, and a complementary dissolution of anything remotely like omniscience or even confidence. The transfer from one language to another is soon mirrored in an exchange of genres, for *En Attendant Godot* followed in 1952. In all of this it is possible to see the working out of factors and tensions implicit in the translations of *The Negro Anthology*.

In keeping with this chronology of decreasing authority in Beckett's work, a catalogue of Irish references might – but need not – be constructed to illustrate the same theme in terms of topographical precision. Accordingly, one would note – or ignore – the detailed streetscape and suburban hinterland of Dublin in *More Pricks than Kicks*, the abandoned Irish cities in *Murphy*, the retreat to unnamed but (to the incurably initiated) recognizable asylums in Foxrock of *Watt* and *All that Fall*. And so on. In a series of valuable photographic images, Eoin O'Brien has illustrated the theme and brought out its self-defeating character. For if Molloy and Krapp muse on the role of canals in the nameless city they have dwelt in, Dublin offers to confirm the existence of two canals to those already possessed of that information.[42] Nevertheless, one could persevere in excavating place-names from late texts. In *Not I*, for example, which was written in English in 1972 and can claim to have left behind the conventions of drama and fiction alike, there is a suddenly intrusive reference to Croker's Acres, a solitary reference doubled within two lines of the frantic monologue. While this is a purely informal place-name, it can be located on a map of the immediate environs of Beckett's childhood home in south County Dublin.[43]

Against the seemingly autobiographical pressure which results in Croker's Acres, there is an historical impetus palpable in the Sedan (scene of French defeat in 1870) and the Ardennes (site of Hitler's last stand after the Normandy landings) of *Endgame*. If schematics are in order, then there is Luneberg in *The Expelled* mediating between these two forces, for the last-named place is associated with Beckett and Peggy Sinclair's brief sojourn in Germany. Yet danger attends such research, in that any consideration of these place-names results in a systematic implication which is transferred from the considerer to the author or to the texts themselves.

Less prone to subjective reading are the personal names which pepper Beckett's plays and novels. Certain brief dramatic texts sound as if they were musically composed round the sound of such a detail, notably 'Eh Joe' and 'Roughs for Theatre I'. The succession of M-names – 'all these Murphys, Molloys and Malones do not fool me'[44] – indicates from an early point in his career that arbitrariness may invade so sovereign a domain as character, suddenly to empty that notion of all its baroque eccentricities and distinctions, leaving just a verbal husk, or frame, behind. And Beckett's monosyllabic character-names are famous – Hamm and Clov, Krapp, Bim, Vi and Flo and Ru. More striking if less memorable are the fuller names – 'His Grace and Most Reverend Father in God Carolus Hunter' together with 'a Mr Johnson, or Johnston, or perhaps I should say John*stone*' and not forgetting Mr Shower or Cooker, all in or not in *Happy Days*. The progressive break-down of these names in Winnie's recollection of them suggests not her failing powers but rather an alteration in the bearing of individual identity upon language.

What one has to say, finally, is that these are names, not places or persons, not in the last analysis even place-names and personal names. After the war, or thereabouts, Beckett's practice was so far from being referential that the vestiges of a former practice act as a betraying confirmation of a personal survival repeatedly bemoaned. In European lyric poetry, the guilt of the survivor is a post-war theme variously explored and confronted in

Johannes Bobrowski, Paul Celan and Agnes Nemes Nagy. And Theodor
Adorno announced a condition rather than a programme in the phrase 'no
poetry after Auschwitz'. The integrity of the writer requires some agreement
between ethical integrity and structural integrity, between conscience and
personal identity; yet it is only by reliance each on the tattered, insufficient
remains of the other that ethics and structure can survive in the last analysis.
Yet as Molloy's *desidera* for composition indicated, the last analysis is not
easily anticipated; 'not to want to say' can only be accomplished through
the pains of saying, wanting, and so on back towards their negation.

It is in this light that one sees the value of decomposition as a term to
account for some of the peculiarities of Beckett's writing and the changes
which occur within it from the 1930s through to the 1980s. One does not
have to look far to find evidence in the fiction of name-amnesia, of moments
where characters fail to recall the names of places or persons or where they
are forced to provide names (but palpably bogus ones) as if to answer some
pressure requiring specificity. Thus in *Molloy*, we learn about places called
Hole and Turdy, which are sparked off (as it were) by an unguarded reference
to Condom on the Baise. Moran, in the concluding pages of the novel, assures
the reader that, though his son bears exactly the same names, 'this cannot
lead to confusion.'[45] In *Not I*, the relationship between an unnamed adult
and an unnamed infant is central but never quite specified, and the logico-
philosophical nostrum of Moran may be applicable – 'the falsity of the terms
does not necessarily imply that of the relation.'[46] The crucial collocation
in these passages is that between naming and infancy.

These share a relation with death, for death is their cancellation, in the
termination of all which naming and infancy initiated. Giorgio Agamben
argues that an experience of language – in an age where experience itself
has been virtually destroyed – may theoretically exist in infancy, an experience
'which is not merely a silence or a deficiency of names'. Though he is alert
to literary history, he has nothing to say about Beckett in all of this, despite
the congruence in Beckett's later work of regression towards infancy, nominal-
istic amnesia, a longing for written silence instead of narration, and a com-
pulsion to speak. If there is such a thing as mute experience, it is characterized
by an absence of names, and at this point – *pace* Watt's dyslexia – one might
note how the word 'names' is embedded in amnes-ia. If there was no such
infancy, then language would become a game in the (allegedly) Wittgenstein-
ian sense of operating simply in obedience to its own internal rules. But

> from the point where there is experience, where is infancy, whose expropria-
> tion is the subject of language, then language appears as the place where
> experience must become truth.[47]

This is not a phenomenological account of a stage in biological development, of what child psychologists call language acquisition. As the concluding words just quoted may suggest, Agamben is alluding to Walter Benjamin's concept of a 'truth content' which may be revealed historically through the exhibition of the material content of a work of art – Baudelaire's poems about wine were Benjamin's immediate concern.[48] Several opportunities arise from this conjunction of truth and infancy. Benjamin's identification of the Great War as the occasion of a massive destruction of experience is not limited solely to survivors and veterans, neither to those who were shell-shocked for life nor those who (after an interval) were able to compose memoirs and 'war books'.[49]

ELIZABETH BOWEN'S INFANTILISM

The formative gulf in Beckett's development was the Second World War, with the various transpositions of genre, language, narrative tone etc. exemplifying the contradictions in keeping with which one would characterize development as a gulf. The case of Elizabeth Bowen is doubly affected, in that both wars impact within her work, the First as a highly mobile traumatic memory, the Second as fluid occasion, dissolving present. In quite a different manner to Beckett, she too lacked 'background'. In terms of land and pedigree, she was more than a cut above the Yeatses, but as a member of the generation born at the turn of the century she stood apart from the western alliance of Gregorys, Martyns, Moores, and their displaced neighbours in the Dublin suburbs. Her parents' alienation from their County Cork home, her father's illness, her own early removal to the English Home Counties, deprived her of that localized tribalism so characteristic of the Coole Park circle. An (officially) deranged relative's murder in 1916 of the pacifist Francis Sheehy Skeffington (together with other victims conventionally forgotten in the annals) did not ease Bowen's relationship with the new state. Yet on her return to Ireland at the outbreak of the Second World War, she had little difficulty in getting on with Sean O'Faolain, despite their differences of class. Perhaps he had become an internal exile during her absence, just as the reality of her 'background' has come to gratify an insecure biographer.

A notable feature of Bowen's writing during the war was her recourse to the conventions of the Victorian ghost story, deployed with great subtlety in *The Demon Lover and Other Stories*, first published in collective form in October 1945. The following year, she wrote an introduction for a new edition of Sheridan Le Fanu's *Uncle Silas*, a piece which stands at the head of her

Collected Impressions (1950). These backward glances towards nineteenth-century Irish writing hardly constitute a literary history, but they do counter-balance Beckett's distinctly more hostile incursions into the Anglo-Irish canon. Moreover, Bowen's modest critical exercises were augmented by her formidable historical research in *Bowen's Court* (1942). The Second World War unmistakably was an occasion when tradition became activated, either as desire, or as ironic fulfilment, or even as a provocation of drastic change.

The Heat of the Day (1949) is the *locus classicus* within her work, a novel in which the familiar entities which are presumed to be identities – self and nation, notably – are parsed in all their ambiguity.[50] Among her short stories, 'The Demon Lover' brings the two wars together in the experience of a woman (Mrs Drover) who has briefly returned to her London home in 1941 only to discover there a letter from her lover of August 1916, a soldier killed in action later that year. Anxious to avoid anything which might facilitate a re-union of any kind, she hastens away, uncharacteristically taking a taxi: it

> *had* turned before she, surprised by its knowing movement, recollected that she had not 'said where'. She leaned forward to scratch at the glass panel that divided the driver's head from her own.
> The driver braked to what was almost a stop, turned round and slid the glass panel back: the jolt of this flung Mrs Drover forward till her face was almost into the glass. Through the aperture driver and passenger, not six inches betwen them, remained for an eternity eye to eye. Mrs Drover's mouth hung open for some seconds before she could issue her first scream. After that she continued to scream freely and to beat with her gloved hands on the glass all round as the taxi, accelerating without mercy, made off with her into the hinterland of deserted streets.[51]

When two world wars collide, time is seriously jeopardized. Their doing so, or the likelihood of their doing so, had been signalled as early in the story as the provision of the woman's name, which is to say in the first line of type immediately below the story's title. Lover is clearly linked to Drover, and in the final paragraph the nameless driver who had been her lover confirms this. On one level, we should note a romance-like aptness in the name which faciliates the effect: but then the pastoral associations of the woman's name (cf. Pádraig Colum's poem 'The Drover') are modified by the specification of her Christian name – Kathleen – which reaches the reader through the letter somehow left by her dead lover (who signs simply as K) in the blitz-threatened house. Though the two names are never brought together in the story, Kathleen Drover (thus synthetically integrated) strongly suggests an Irish provenance. At another level, we might invoke Roman Jakobson's theories about 'the semantics of rhyme', according to which the intervention of 'driver' between 'lover' and 'drover' can be read as effecting the disruption of conventional rhyme and so signifies the ironic coming together of the two people 'for an eternity eye to eye'. Bowen's prose is post-Yeatsian poetry.

Other stories of the period are more explicit, lacking the opacity of the traditional supernatural tale. In 'Sunday Afternoon', people are gathered at an Italianate villa outside Dublin to hear – with varying degrees of interest – Henry Russel's experiences of the London bombing. He concedes that, yes, it is frightening. 'But as it does not connect with the rest of life, it is difficult, you know, to know what one feels. One's feelings seem to have no language for anything so preposterous. As for thoughts – '[52] Here he is broken off right at the start of what promised to be a veritable prose-verse analysis: the close proximity to each other of the two 'know's and of 'one feels' to 'one's feelings' provides a prose equivalent to rhyme so that Henry is on the edge of formalizing his analysis, and it is no insignificant detail that interruption comes to cut him off from 'thoughts'. Yet Maria, who has intervened, is possessed of her own insight into the nature of the distant experience, for she declares that 'there is really nothing, till one knows it oneself.' Another man, though older than the girl, is less subtle in speaking of the bombs:

> 'Henry is probably right,' said Ronald Cuffe, 'in considering that this – this outrage is *not* important. There is no place for it in human experience; it apparently cannot make a place of its own. It will have no literature.'[53]

Maria is keen to escape to England, and in her adolescent ardour at table shakes a petal from some flowers on to the cucumber sandwiches. 'This little bit of destruction was watched by the older people with fascination, with a kind of appeasement, as though it were a guarantee against something worse.' Anxious to retain her among themselves, the adults seek to turn the conversation away from the war, appeasing her with details of Henry's boring life in a London Ministry – 'You work in an office, then, since the war?' The preposition blurs the moment of the incident for the latter-day reader, because 'since' does not necessarily convey the meaning of 'since the war *began*'. Keen still to deter Maria, someone emphasizes that such tedium would be hers – 'this is not like a war history, you know' – to which Maria responds, 'It is not in history yet.'[54] When she ambushes Henry on his way down the avenue to catch a bus, and successfully obtains his London address, he seeks to ward her off by renaming her:

'Goodbye,' he said, 'Miranda.'

' – Maria –'

'Miranda. This is the end of *you*. Perhaps it is just as well.'

'I'll be seeing you –'

'You'll come round my door in London – with your little new number chained to your wrist.'

'The trouble with you is you're half old.'

Maria ran out through the gates to stop the bus, and Henry got on to it and was quickly carried away.[55]

'Sunday Afternoon' was included in *Look at All Those Roses* in 1941. The ambiguity of 'since' has only arisen since the end of the war, as the story itself enters history. Maria's determination in that direction may be counteracted by Henry's re-baptism of her, for he names her after Prospero's daughter in *The Tempest*. If we read this as Henry's effort to reinforce the domestic pressure on Maria to stay at home on the peaceful island while war rages in the world, to initiate her into the spells her aunt cannot quite weave, then we must recall also that it is through Miranda that the warring kingdoms of Shakespeare's play are to be reconciled, in her marriage to Ferdinand. The disparity in age rules out any such union betwen Henry and her, and the story ends with the girl's curious description of him as 'half-old'.

The uncertain age, uncertain experience, of young women is familiar in Bowen's pre-war fiction, from Lois in *The Last September* (1929) to Portia in *The Death of the Heart* (1938). These predate Bowen's public interest in Le Fanu and the ghost story, but her comments on *Uncle Silas* illuminate the centrality of a figure whom we have been tracing in some of the war-time stories. In this Victorian 'romance of terror' as she terms it:

> the reactions of Maud, the narrator-heroine, throughout are those of a highly intelligent, still more highly sensitive, child of twelve. This may, to a degree, be accounted for by seclusion and a repressive father – but not, I think entirely: I should doubt whether Le Fanu himself realized Maud's abnormality as a heroine. She is an uncertain keyboard, on which some notes sound clearly, deeply, and truly, others not at all. There is no question, here, of Victorian censorship, with its suggestive gaps: Maud, on the subject of anything she does feel, is uninhibited, sometimes disconcerting. And equally, in the feeling of people round her we are to take it that, child-like, she misses nothing. The distribution of power throughout the writing is equal, even: the briefest scene is accorded brimming sensuous content. We must in fact note how Maud's sensuousness (which is un-English) disperses, expends itself through the story in so much small change. She shows, at every turn, the carelessness, or acquiescence, of the predestined person: Maud is, by nature, a bride of

Death. She delays, she equivocates, she looks wildly sideways; she delights in fire and candlelight, bedroom tea-drinking, coy feminine company, but her bias is marked. The wind blowing her way from the family mausoleum troubles our heroine like a mating cry.[56]

As the last sentence clearly shows, this introduction is specific to the novel concerned – there is such a mausoleum and Maud does visit it in suggestive circumstances. But Bowen's analysis is also general in that it is concerned to deal with typical aspects of the book's plotting and characterization, the Babes in the Wood, the Wicked Uncle, Beauty in Distress. These she traces back to the gothic romances, but she is also concerned to argue that *Uncle Silas* is Irish in two specific ways, despite its setting somewhere in the Derbyshire/Yorkshire wilds of northern England – 'it is sexless, and it shows a sublimated infantilism.'[57] Quite whether this amounts to two or just one factor depends on what Bowen may mean by the term, infantilism. A dictionary definition, drawing on a source in 1895 intervening between Le Fanu and Bowen, gives us 'the state of being mentally or physically undeveloped'. But, on closer examination, the source turns out to be a work on *Female Offenders*, in the introduction to which 'sexual peculiarities, such as feminism in men, masculism [sic] in women, and infantilism in both' are considered. Aiming to distinguish *Uncle Silas* as both sexless and exemplary of that condition, Bowen uncovers the interconnections between sexuality and infantilism. These implications only break the surface of her own work in *Eva Trout* (1969) where issues of male and female homosexuality make their first appearance. For the moment, we are to read this image of Maud Ruthyn as of a pre-adolescent adult, a non-nubile Beauty in Distress, a child who knows: she is abnormal *as a fictional heroine*, not in any external pathological sense. Her perspective on the Great House is both privileged and prejudiced, in that a female cannot hope to claim property except by way of exception. Her view of power is at once informed and external. Her sense of propriety and loyalty is undercut by a need to assert what in a male heir would be automatic. Thus her dalliance in prolonged infancy is also an affront to business sense, and can only be admitted in a sublimated form.

Twentieth-century fiction has not always been so discreet. In Bowen's own generation William Faulkner assigned the first part of *The Sound and the Fury* (1931) to Benjy, whose idiot tale is later amplified by his brothers. Bowen's 'Her Table Spread' had been published the previous year and, while it has no personal narrator, the character of Valeria Cuffe presents a figure who is 'abnormal – at twenty-five, of statuesque development, still detained in childhood'. The indirect free style of narration indicates that these words occur to Alban (a visitor from London, like Henry Russel in 'Sunday

Afternoon') to describe his hostess somewhere on the southern Irish coast, though he does not utter them. A naval destroyer is lying offshore, because, 'by a term of the Treaty, English ships were permitted to anchor in these waters.' Miss Cuffe is most anxious that the sailors who had visited earlier in the year will return on this night – ' "*Will they remember?* " Valeria's bust was almost on the table.'[58] The emphasis here conveys something of Valeria's psychic abnormality without clearly indicating whether she has spoken. Repressed speech is a striking feature of the writing in 'Her Table Spread'. While Valeria's aunt cries 'Come *in*!' as the heiress strays out under the rain, what is thought is a good deal more explicit – 'she would die of a chill, childless, in fact unwedded; the Castle would have to be sold and where would they all be?' When Yeats, in 'Meditations in Time of Civil War', contemplates the transmission of property from violent appropriation to cultured possession, he looks apprehensively forward to the possibility of 'the great-grandson of that house' being 'but a mouse'. The mandarin in-humanness of his vocabulary is counterbalanced by the damp, unstable brilliancy of Bowen's story, in which the declension of property *as such* is personified in the confusion of Valeria's mind and the stacatto freedom of her body. Mistaking Alban for one of her unknown naval suitors, she per-sists in this error as in her self-characterization as princess. Her infancy blooms as romance, not in the sense of sexual liaison, but as literary genre. With two attendant women, Valeria is hidden in the dark gardens – 'their unseen faces were all three lovely'. Thus captivated Alban, who 'had failed to love; nobody did anything about this; partners at dinner gave less than half their attention', is finally 'for a moment not exiled'. It is 'as though all three said: "My darling . . ." '[59] The illusion into which he is drawn protects him from the illusion into which they would draw him.

If Valeria Cuffe, Maria of 'Sunday Afternoon', and Mrs Drover are now realigned as a sequence in time, it may seem that a progression away from infantilism towards maturity is evident – only to be rudely cancelled by the return of the past in a demon taxi-driver. *The Heat of the Day* is remarkable in the absence of any such figure, for Stella Rodney emerges as a rock of sense amid the tempests of world war and domestic treachery. Bowen's post-war fiction has generally disappointed even her appreciative critics. But the juncture does not have to be explained in personal terms alone. The death of Yeats in 1939, and of Joyce in 1941, together with the emergence of drama as Beckett's new mode of writing in the post-war years, provides a larger context in which Bowen's declension can be studied. *A World of Love* (1955) re-investigates the Anglo-Irish Big House, implicates the Great War and even (through the dead Guy) has recourse to Le Fanu, nearly a century earlier, as author of *Guy Deverell* (1865). Like the photographs in 'The Happy Autumn Fields', a bunch of old letters brings together past and present. The most oddly sensuous detail – 'all salt from the wrist being now on tongue' – merges with a contorted syntax:

> Ghosts could have no place in this active darkness – more, tonight was a night which had changed hands, going back again to its lordly owners: time again was into the clutch of herself and Guy. Stamped was the hour, as were their others.[60]

This is not to be a sensationalism of persons only, 'as land knows everywhere is a frontier'.[61] But the pressure counterbalancing the fantasia of young Jane's engagement in the life of dead Guy is the *nouveau riche* vulgarity of Lady Latterly whose kind have not so much inherited the earth as bought up options. Fantasia, in the view of at least one critic, has brought Jane to a point where she is 'someone ready for an adult love affair'.[62] But *Eva Trout* will reverse much of this, locating post-war insecurity and vulgarity both in a well-established area of rural England and in an itinerary of breathless action, Worcestershire today, Chicago last week, then Fontainebleau. Child of an international liaison, cast under the protection of a man who had been her father's lover, the titular heroine is – we are pointedly told at the outset – 'not defective in any way'.[63] Nevertheless, 'what caused the girl to express herself like a displaced person?'

> The explanation – that from infancy onward Eva had had as attendants dis-placed persons, those at a price being the most obtainable, to whose society she'd been largely consigned – for some reason never appeared: too simple, perhaps?[64]

The appearance of an explanation which never appeared undermines its ade-quacy, and the intensity of relation between language and infancy is further heightened when Eva decides to adopt a child, Jeremy, who is both deaf and dumb. Sensory deprivation had been treated by Bowen earlier in 'Sum-mer Night', and Jeremy is in some ways only a more extreme version of a theme she had been concerned with for decades – the power innocence draws from its own depletion. Not sublimated infantilism but 'sublimated monotony' provides a basis for the early collaboration of Eva and Jeremy in 'successive American cities'. They enjoy a 'cinematographic existence, with no sound track', so that they are 'near as twins in a womb'. This peripatetic existence is described in the prose narrative as a *fugue*, which may flatter admirers of baroque music but in practice refers to a technical Freudian term, relating to the behaviour of Great War victims of shell-shock induced amnesia, a seemingly unpatterned but ultimately purposeful wandering.

But when they return to England, 'her mistrust of or objection to verbal intercourse – which she had understood to be fundamental – began to be undermined.'[65] The child's parthogenetic origins, if origins he has apart from being putatively his mother's twin, isolate him further from Eva. Her decision to put him in the care of a sculptress sets him up on a predictable identification with the artistic vocation, but for the fact that the sculptress declines to speak of Jeremy's orginality while cleaving to her own (creative) discounting of language – 'words do not connect, for me; I am visual purely.'[66] Among adults, Jeremy's most distinctive characteristics will be denied or appropriated.

Intellectually patronized, he is nevertheless a body among bodies. Older than a child not adopted, Jeremy is involved in post-infantile 'moments of joyful complicity' with his new mother, 'capering naked on Eva's bed like Cupid cavorting over the couch of Venus'. Yet, when the boy is temporarily missing, the sculptress is locked 'in some kind of travail' as if attempting by an effort of conscience to give birth (and so restore) the child Eva never had.[67] Eva's own encounter with bodies has a casual register in her infatuation with a Cambridge undergraduate, but among the pictures in the National Portrait Gallery it acquires a greater precision. 'She went through a doorway into the Stuart area of betrayers and betrayed, of whom the majority, less taut than those in the rooms before, had a free-flowing lavishness and engagingness.' This London tableau sets up various oppositions, verbal and visual, past and present, but it also picks up the manner in which Eva's *ersatz* appropriation of language back in England makes her 'traitorous to the years with Jeremy' in America.[68] A vocabulary of treason traces the wretched search for a loyalty, or point of communion, which is increasingly remote in the world of *Eva Trout*. Many of Bowen's novels had dealt with betrayal in personal relations, especially the betrayal of the young by adults. But in *Eva Trout* betrayal, while remaining morally reprehensible, takes on the character of a necessary evil. Non-affiliation promises to be a more effective prime mover in a society bonded by guilt and gluttony and glitter. When Jeremy is taken to France, and treatment is sought there for his profound infancy, he responds by beginning 'to formulate, or attempt to formulate, French words, and he started to accord to the lips of speakers, other than Eva, a level, exacting, scientific attention denied formerly.'[69] By what must be now almost a foregone concluson, Jeremy shoots Eva to death.

Readers who found it difficult to make sense of *Eva Trout* may have been ill-served by their familiarity with Bowen's previous fiction, for on such a basis it must willy-nilly disappoint expectations. If Jeremy is to be seen as the product of some post-war parthogenesis, in whom natural means and expressions of emotion have been supplanted, then perhaps the novel should be approached with similar notions in mind. This is not say that it, like him, is a disaster. But different rules of interpretation are required, a kind of textual lip-reading. *A World of Love* had experimented with the possibility of a supernatural short story written at novelistic length: *Eva Trout* goes further, attempting a ghost story without ghosts, or at least without ghosts as conventionally presented.

Drawing on Lévi-Strauss's concept of myth, Giorgio Agamben develops his argument about language and infancy in an essay called 'In Playland'. Beyond the adult/child distinction, upon which the logic of initiation rites is based, there is a more fundamental opposition of the living and the dead. But children correspond less to the dead than to ghosts:

> Within the perspective of signifying function, adults and dead belong to the same order, that of stable signifiers and continuity between diachrony and synchrony . . . But children and ghosts, as unstable signifiers, represent the discontinuity between the two worlds. The dead person is not the ancestor: this is the meaning of the ghost. The ancestor is not the living man: this is the meaning of the child.[70]

The Victorian ghost-story, however it may have been integrated into commercial publishing, was not just a passive response to 'the crisis of faith' or the alarms and excitements of nineteenth-century medical advance. So too, in any application of Lévi-Strauss to latter-day literary work, one is close to uncovering ways of living and dying. That is, 'adults submit to becoming ghosts so that the ghosts can become dead, and the dead become children so that the children can become men and women.'[71] The logic of this in the case of *Eva Trout*, preoccupied as it is with the consequences of unprecedented killing in the Second World War, is not hard to discover. Eva stoutly refuses to become the ghost she would be in a short story, and so must be abruptly rendered dead; until she submits to that process Jeremy, the (dead) child she never had, is detained before language in that state of pure infancy in which he experiences everything amid a society immunized, by survival of the wars, to experience less and less. When he begins to acquire the rudiments of speech, the language is not his 'native' English, but another tongue.

It is tempting to return to Yeats's *Purgatory* and attempt an analysis of a similar kind: there the ghosts are unrelievedly adult, and the child is sacrificed in reverse-initiation rites designed to bring consequence to an end. Within the very brief historical perspective Yeats concerned himself with, it would be possible to argue that Lévi-Strauss's distinction between 'cold' societies and 'hot' ones casts light on the poet's energetic campaign in the

1930s, through eugenics and historiography, to re-establish a less-changing society. It may be that there is in Bowen's work as a whole little concrete evidence of 'a coming community' but the value even of a profoundly frustrated desire for such is not negligible. Precedence, rather than consequence, is to be brought to an end, though the price paid is never to be underestimated. The child survives his parent, even if through the violence of liberating her from a society she cannot cope with.[72] The contrast with *Purgatory* could hardly be plainer. Instead of lauding Yeats's dubious anti-colonial record, radical critics might abandon the inverted snobbery of their distaste for Elizabeth Bowen. Of course such an exercise lies beyond the scope of the present study, requiring as it would consideration of his engagement with the Oedipal drama of Sophocles, upon which Lévi-Strauss constructed the most elaborate of his models. Bowen's legacy may be the example her work provides of a sustained search for a means of enabling society to structure itself in the face of dogmas of the past. The armchair hyperbole of Yeats's 'the hell wherein we suffer' is exactly a confusion of eternity and history, and is best countered by a return to Beckett's 'hell of stories'. In *All that Fall* Mr Rooney's sinister inquiry – 'did you ever wish to kill a child?' – may be answered in the play's final moments when the death of a child is announced, but its orientation has been already exposed in his next question but one. 'Shall we go on backwards now a little?' If the radio play seems jolly compared to the dustbins of *Endgame* in which Hamm keeps his parents, we should recall with T. W. Adorno 'the fleeting image of the child, a very weak reminiscence of Fortinbras or the Child King' which is reported by Clov near the play's conclusion.[73]

II INIMITABLE EXEMPLAR: ADORNO ON BECKETT

> He crossed at Nassau street corner and stood before the window of Yeates and Son, pricing the field glasses. Or will I drop into old Harris's and have a chat with young Sinclair? Wellmannered fellow. Probably at his lunch. Must get those old glasses of mine set right. Goerz lenses, six guineas. Germans making their way everywhere.
>
> (James Joyce)[74]

The vestigial representations which may be discovered by the all-too-knowing reader of Beckett's fiction and drama extend a hand towards such literary allusions as Adorno tentatively identifies in the small boy seen by Clov just before *Endgame* ends. The Christ Child is at once archetypical of the miraculously provided infant and wholly anachronistic, but Fortinbras as an explanation can be explained if we take the vestigiality of Beckett's work to its microscopic limits. For it is relatively easy to reconstruct Adorno's logic, and to find in it a verification of interpretations offered above. If Hamm is read as a truncated Hamlet – just as Flo, Vi and Ru are truncated names – then the figure who arrives as the play ends might well be a Fortinbras, albeit an infant one.

Nor is the notion of Beckett's texts sustaining just a few surviving letters of a once canonical name inapplicable elsewhere in his uncanonisable work. In *Embers*, a radio play dating from 1959, young Ada is inexpertly practicing at the piano, her errors prompting the music master to scream the name of the right note six times – 'Eff! Eff! . . . Eff! Eff! . . . Eff! . . . Eff!' Reiterated, and punctuated with exclamation marks, the name is virtually articulated as that of the German heroine (Effi) in Fontane's novel, the novel casually treated in *All that Fall* and memorably read by Beckett and Peggy Sinclair before the war in Germany.[75] In these details the plays do not offer any opportunity to reconstruct a metadrama beyond their truncated codes; on the contrary, the audience is forcibly impressed by the absence of completeness, by the undirected form of allusiveness, by a postdated mode of address. At the same time, the gulf between this and the relative security of bourgeois existence in the early chapters of Joyce's *Ulysses* is mocked in the Dante-esque sufferings of Beckett's suburbans. Nevertheless we now read the 'Lestrygonians' episode (where Mr Bloom considers calling on the young man who will be Peggy Sinclair's father or uncle) in a literary historical perspective which informs it with the incipience of later events: contemplating a shipping disaster in New York, in which many were burned or drowned, Bloom draws on the still unfamiliar term, holocaust.[76] In 1922 Joyce himself wrote and read 'Goerz lenses' through the intervening prism of the Great War.

It has been argued in the preceding pages that the Second World War constituted a gulf of development in Beckett's work. In terms of Irish history, such a point is difficult to name, given southern Ireland's official neutrality and relative isolation during the conflict, and given also the highly problematic nature of Northern Ireland's involvement as part of the United Kingdom. It is argued also that the same point – with similar attendant difficulties – marks the end of a literary epoch. (The deaths of Yeats and Joyce, in 1939 and 1941 respectively, signal the occasion with pomp.) What is less readily discovered is any *critical* recognition, among those who write Irish literary history, of the significance of the War, politically, culturally, morally.

From Burke to Beckett

In part, the difficulties arise from the tendency of historians to preserve
the national frontiers of their specialized research even after they have revi-
sioned nationalism out of sight. Some attention to the experience of
peripheral Europe during the major conflagrations of the twentieth century,
in which Ireland might take its place in a discussion of Finland and Sweden,
Hungary and Yugoslavia, or even Iceland and Norway, would open up the
possibilities of comparative study. In the absence of any such attention, it
has been possible for a well known professor to argue in public that Yeats's
relations with Nazi Germany should be judged in the light of the Church
of Ireland's difficulties with Eamon de Valera. Myopia of this kind leaps
through the needle's eye to proclaim it's own broad perspectives. Popular,
even populist, myths of involvement in wartime Europe proliferate even during the last decade of the century. By myth one means, again but in
degenerate form, those aesthetic resolutions of contradiction as to origin,
identity, and orientation towards the transcendent which Lévi-Strauss
described in his *Structural Anthropology*. One set of these latter-day Irish
myths relates to the IRA's attitudes towards Republican Spain and towards
Nazi Germany; another relates the Ulster experience on the Somme in 1916
and the role of Roger Casement as traitor to his class, his country and his sex.

Even when conscious efforts to overcome populism and to enter a comparative discussion are attempted, the habits of Irish particularism often survive. Thus, when Edna Longley bravely marked the seventy-fifth anniversary
of Easter 1916 by writing an article focused on the contemporary experience
of Ulstermen, her endeavour both mobilized and derailed the argument of
Paul Fussell's well-known study of *The Great War and Modern Memory*. Calling her contribution to a Field Day enterprise, 'The Rising, the Somme,
and Irish Memory', she failed to note the extent to which her title diverges
from Fussell's. For him, memory is examined in the altered and altering
conditions of modernity: a dynamic relationship informs the succession of
adjective by noun. 'Irish memory', in contrast, merely states a limitation,
and no one is surprised to find that, within a paragraph her Irish memory
has sectarianized itself as 'Ulster Protestant memory' versus 'Catholic
memory'. If this observation seems harsh, it is no less so than Longley's
own judgement that talk of 'Irishness' has 'a totalitarian tinge'.[77] Something
a little less obtuse is required in the analysis of the term and its cognates.

In an intellectual climate where such *aperçus* are taken, or at least, offered
seriously, it is difficult to revert to the twentieth-century history of continental
Europe without embarrassment. If the exchanges which have culminated
in public assemblies debating the faults of a three-volume anthology of Irish
writing have had a common, coherent theme, then the *manner* in which

literature relates to politics constitutes a major item of concern. One of the depressing ironies of the current situation in Irish criticism is that those who argue for a separation of poetry and politics seem least likely to disengage from the battle of bad language, to present an account of Swift's rhyme-patterns or the paragraph structure of English blank verse. Eminent protagonists grow great on what they hate. It has been a long time since the critics produced any criticism and, if these terms strike persons as too *désengagés*, a similar complaint about Weetabix theorists is already available in the opening pages of the present work.

Critical theory offers not so much to resolve these local difficulties as to expose the complexity which manipulates their gross simplicities. The merit of Adorno's lengthy analysis of *Endgame* is precisely its insistence on the doubled temporal perspective of the play, its emphasis on a fundamental contradiction of vestigial referentiality. (Is this an echo from the fascist past, *or* an image of the thermo-nuclear future? No to both; it is both.) As the deconstructor of his own canon, Beckett remains our contemporary. And at a time when the discussion of 'culture' has become a spectator sport, consideration of critical theory in its engagement with a forty-year-old text may provide a fitting conclusion to a study of a literature conditioned by intimidating notions of ascendancy, tradition and betrayal.

For some time it has been usual to regard Samuel Beckett as *un pur*, unconcerned with and uncontaminated by anything beyond the realm of artistic creation. Of course, a comprehensive critique of his writings would jeopardize all this, with their acknowledgement that 'to be an artist is to fail, as no other dare fail.'[78] The customary view, however, is bolstered by powerful (if concealed) presuppositions about integrity and the exemplary status of the bourgeois subject. Is this not ironic in an artist who wrote of the artist as one who recognized a 'breakdown of the object', amendable perhaps to a 'breakdown of the subject', concluding 'it comes to the same thing - rupture of the lines of communication'?[79] Despite this, Beckett's artistic integrity has come in for its share of vituperation (meanly, though also passingly, from the pen of György Lukács) as well as approval. It remains to be seen if a finer insight into his art does not proceed from a philosophical stance, Marxist, too readily dismissed as readily hostile. It is this limited objective which is attempted here. It might be argued that Beckett was not always a 'creative' writer in the sense approved by his admirers. 'Having launched himself with a prize poem on the set theme of Time, Joyce's amanuensis went on diligently to publish dialogues on contemporary painting, and to translate a large body of Mexican poetry . . .' the argument might go. Such a perspective has been rejected by Beckett, of course, but in highly questionable terms. To Gabriel d'Aubarède in 1961:

> I'm no intellectual. All I am is feeling. *Molloy* and the others came to me the day I became aware of my own folly.[80]

And twelve years later:

> I realized that I knew nothing. I sat down in my mother's little house in Ireland and began to write *Molloy*.[81]

Leaving aside the re-enactment here of Descartes' inaugurating doubt, we see the juxtaposing of intellectualism and emotion as misleading, however deft. After all *Molloy* begins:

> I am in my mother's room. It's I who live there now. I don't know how I got there. Perhaps in an ambulance, certainly a vehicle of some kind. I was helped. I'd never have got there alone. There's this man who comes every week. Perhaps I got here thanks to him. He says not. He gives me money and takes away the pages. So many pages, so much money.[82]

If the opening sentence appears to identify the fictional moment and the moment of the fiction's composition, the passage proceeds quickly to establish more complex, alternating currents – there/here etc. If, to Beckett, all that he was was feeling, then the narrator of *Molloy* has chosen the specialized feeling of intellection as his initial subject matter. In the novel, Molloy considers that his mother may well be dead – 'I mean enough to bury' – and that he has taken her place. The novelist, on the other hand, left Ireland and his mother to return to France and the writing of the novel. While making allowances for 'perhaps' as the key word in Beckett, we can still say that movement, as regards narrator and novelist (narrator as pseudo-novelist, and novelist as pseudo-narrator) is *antithetical*. If writing is the subject matter of this writing, it is presented more as a matter of commerce and exchange than High Art.

The day upon which Beckett became aware of his own unknowing marks a kind of intersection between historical and personal lines. Deirdre Bair tells us that *Molloy* was begun in September 1947 and completed by the following January, and throughout this period Beckett was in France. His visit home to Ireland had occurred earlier in 1947, and was in fact organized round his birthday which he wished to spend with his mother. Two years earlier, he had promptly left France for Ireland (in April 1945, even before the war was over), repeating the visit in 1946.[83] Thus, either the day of extreme Cartesian doubt may be taken as hypothetical, or a date for the commencement of work on *Molloy* must be pressed back in time. Though it was not his immediate post-war return to Dublin, the occasion – as Beckett himself presents it – links the family reunion and the opening of his career as a novelist writing in French. It marked his survival of World War II, of years spent in hiding and earlier years of active resistance to the German occupation of France: it marked also his absolute realization of his mother's approaching death, of family dissolution.

Antithesis and exchange characterize much in Beckett's prolonged struggle to comprehend the barbarism of his age. *Molloy* was composed in French with the aid of Marie Peron who had been a member with him of the same resistance cell in Paris. The earlier novels were written on different assumptions: *Murphy* is articulate to a fault, in contrast to Murphy; *Watt* possesses a geometrical audacity which leaves Watt cutting a very poor figure. But now, adopting monologue at the same time that its author adopts French, the new novel leaves behind the seedy solipism of omniscient narration. This recourse to monologue is replete with rich paradox, not only in its power to banish solipsism. If, to some degree, Beckett required Madame Peron's linguistic assistance – and Beckett's fluency in French had allowed him pass among natives even in time of war – we should note also that *Molloy* in English is presented as a translation not by the author, but 'by Patrick Bowles in collaboration with the author'.[84] In the preface to *The Playboy of the Western World*, J. M. Synge had written that 'All art is a collaboration'; his successor was uniquely placed in post-war France to savour the bitter ambiguity of the term.[85]

This richly paradoxical, inclusive monologism is accompanied in *Molloy* with Beckett's growing concern with 'the pair' – Molloy and Moran, Malone and Macmann – which becomes central in the plays from *Waiting for Godot* onwards. In the fiction also, the concept of 'the pair' is deeply problematic, intractable and yet irresolute in itself. Molloy reports a singular experience:

> And when I see my hands, on the sheet, which they love to floccillate already, they are not mine, less than ever mine, I have no arms, they are a couple, they play with the sheet, love-play perhaps, trying to get up perhaps, one on top of the other. But it doesn't last, I bring them back, little by little, towards me, it's resting time. And with my feet it's the same, sometimes, when I see them at the foot of the bed, one with toes, the other without. And that is more deserving of mention. For my legs, corresponding here to my arms of a moment ago, are both stiff now and very sore, and I shouldn't be able to forget them as I can my arms, which are more or less sound and well. And yet I do forget them and I watch the couple as they watch each other, a great way off.[86]

The integral privacy of the Beckettian character and his aesthetic insulation from historical process, as rendered fabulous by the critics, may yet be illuminated in a way which interprets the central concern with 'the pair' as part of a post-war literary conflict of the greatest political and philosophical interest.

There is a significant deviation in Michael T. Jones's translation of T. W. Adorno's essay, 'Versuch, das Endspiel zu verstehen'.[87] Insisting that in Beckett's play an important and new historical moment is revealed, Adorno identified it with the experience cited 'im Titel des kulturindustriellen Schundbuchs "Kaputt".'[88] Jones, at once eager to vivify Adorno for English readers and a mite neglectful of his master's talent for lethal allusion at imperceptibly acute angles, renders the passage as follows:

> French existentialism had tackled history. In Beckett, history devours existentialism. In *Endgame*, a historical moment is revealed, the experience of which was cited in the title of the culture industry's rubbish book *Corpsed*. After the Second World War, everything is destroyed, even resurrected culture, without knowing it; humanity vegetates along, crawling, after events which even the survivors cannot really survive, on a pile of ruins which even renders futile self-reflection of one's own battered state. From the marketplace, as the play's pragmatic precondition, that fact is stripped away [quotes playscript, concluding]:
>
>> CLOV: What all is? In a word? Is that what you want to know? Just a moment. (*He turns the telescope on the without, looks, lowers the telescope, turns towards HAMM.*) Corpsed. (*Pause*) Well? Content?[89]

'Corpsed', Clov's verdict/description of 'the without' has been appropriated by the translator to name the culture industry's junkbook. The deviation (from 'Kaputt') is a nice one, especially if we are alert to the verb to corpse as a piece of actor's jargon – 'deliberately to confuse a fellow actor on stage, preventing him from speaking or acting as required'. To the question implicit in Clov's laconic epithet – in the cosmic *Trauerspiel* what fellow-player has corpsed the without? – Adorno implicitly answers by directing attention to 'the within', the inner sanctum privileged once again by the 'jargon of authenticity' he detected in Karl Jaspers' existentialism.[90] But, more particularly, in the detail lost in Jones's translation, Adorno indicts a particular kind of writing – ultra 'verismo' reports of Second World War experiences – summed up and dismissed in the obliquity of that nominal reference to Curzio Malaparte's *Kaputt* (1945). Adorno's 'historical moment' was not simply the Second World War, but the resultant domination of all humanity by nuclear terrorism, and of western society by (in addition) the culture industry.[91] It is in this context that he regards *Endgame* as an exemplary work which refuses assimilation.

Adorno's writings on Beckett, scattered and fragmentary though they are, constitute a unique occasion in which a sophisticated Marxist aesthetician attends to the works of a dramatist and novelist conventionally associated with very different company. Adorno's name is inseparable from that of the Frankfurt *Institut für Sozialforschung* from its early years in the Weimar republic, through exile in the United States of America in war-time, to re-establishment in the federal republic.[92] The Beckett industry, on the other hand, is a concern either French or Irish, with heavy American investment certainly, but hardly German. The German philosopher's familiarity with Beckett appears to have begun after the war, and the essay at present under discussion is dedicated in English (or American!) 'to S. B. in memory of Paris, Fall 1958', the essay itself first appearing in 1961.[93] A prolific and (in a superficial sense) unsystematic writer, Adorno began in May 1961 to draft his *Aesthetische Theorie*. When he died in August 1969, the work was unfinalized but essentially complete; among the author's preparations for publication was a decision or intention to dedicate the *Theory* to Beckett. It is in keeping with the monastic charity of all parties to this intention that it should be recorded rather than displayed in the posthumous publication.[94] The *Aesthetic Theory* is peppered with allusions to Beckett's work, the plays for the most part, but it contains nothing as extended as the 1961 essay on *Endgame*.

Adorno's appreciation of Beckett is part and parcel of his sustained campaign against existentialism. By extension Beckett is embroiled in a larger German philosophical struggle between the phenomenologists (Edmund Husserl and Martin Heidegger) on the one side and the Frankfurt critical theorists on the other.[95] Furthermore, Adorno uses the occasion of *Endgame* to settle a few scores with his old fellow-Marxist sparring partner, György Lukács.[96] The extracts (non-continuous) which follow are intended to summarize the essay as it bears upon our present concerns:

> Anything Beckett offers us by way of philosophy he at the same time reduces to culture-trash, no different from the countless scraps of learning which he employs in the wake of the Anglo-Saxon tradition, particularly that of Joyce and Eliot.

> The interpretation of *Endgame* cannot pretend to proclaim the play's meaning with the aid of philosophical mediation. Understanding it can involve nothing else than understanding its incomprehensibility, or reconstructing its meaning-structure – to the effect, that it has none. Isolated, thought no longer pretends, as the Idea once did, to be itself the meaning of the structure – a transcendence which would be engendered and guaranteed by the work's own immanence. Instead, thought transforms itself into a kind of second-class material, like the philosophemes in Thomas Mann's *The Magic Mountain* and *Doctor Faustus* whose destiny it is to replace that sensate immediacy which is diminished in the self-reflective work of art.

The catastrophes that inspire *Endgame* have exploded the individual whose substantiality and absoluteness was the element common to Kierkegaard, Jaspers, and the Sartrean version of existentialism. Even to victims of the concentration camps existentialism had attributed freedom either inwardly to accept or reject the tortures inflicted on them. *Endgame* destroys such illusions. The individual as a historical category, as the outcome of the capitalist process of alienation and as a defiant protest against it, has become openly a transient thing.

Endgame is exemplary. It yields to the impossibility of dealing with materials, of representation according to nineteenth-century practice. And yields also to the insight that subjective modes of reaction, which mediate the laws of form rather than reflect reality, are themselves no absolute first principle but rather a last principle, objectively posited. All content of subjectivity, which necessarily hypostatizes itself, is trace and shadow of the world, from which it withdraws in order not to serve that semblance and conformity the world demands. Beckett responds to that condition not with unchanging reserves or 'provisions' (*Vorrat*), but rather with what is still permitted, precariously and uncertainly, by the antagonistic tendencies. His dramaturgy resembles the fun that Old Germany used to offer – knocking about between the quaint signposts of Baden and Bavaria, as if they encompassed in some domain of freedom. *Endgame* takes place in a zone of indifference between inner and outer; it remains neutral between – on the one hand – the 'materials' in the absence of which subjectivity could not manifest itself nor even exist, and – on the other – an animating impulse which blurs the materials as if that impulse had breathed on the glass through which they are seen.

Beckett's rubbish-bins are the emblems of a culture restored after Auschwitz.[97]

The twin priorities of Adorno's lengthy analysis thus emerge as the specification of a historical moment to which the play is intimately related, and the elaboration of its formal characteristics. At the polemical level, the first point is directed against the existentialist, the second against Lukács and the socialist realism (rather unfairly) identified with him. But there are other, more important, levels. In the *Aesthetic Theory*, Adorno presents Beckett's plays as exemplifying 'the proper relation betwen . . . two contradictory desiderata, i.e. successful figuration and adequate social content'.[98] Furthermore,

Beckett focuses on the negativity of the subject as being the true form of objectivity – a theme that calls for radically subjective figuration . . . Those childlike but bloody clowns' faces in Beckett are the historical truth about the subject: it has disintegrated. By comparison, socialist realism is really infantile. *Waiting for Godot* revolves round the theme of lordship-and-bondage grown senile and demented in an era when exploitation of human labour persists although it could well be abolished. This motif, truly one of the essential characteristics of present-day society, is taken up again in *Endgame*. In both instances Beckett's technique pushes this Hegelian theme to the periphery: lordship and bondage are reduced to an anecdote in terms of both dramatic function and social criticism.[99]

If, in *Endgame*, Beckett's technique pushes a Hegelian theme to the periphery it may still be true that it pushes that theme to the extreme also. Dialectical *Aufhebung* of the Hegelian kind is both overcoming and fulfilment. And, as we shall see, anecdote in Beckett's drama is more than once an occasion of peculiarly profound implications. The historical moment of Adorno's own *Aesthetic Theory* cannot be omitted from consideration. Writing at the height of the 'economic miracle' in post-war federal Germany, even the ever-sceptical critical theorist tacitly accepted that the conditions existed for the possible abolition of human labour, and it is in the context of these conditions as perceived by Adorno that we should read his diagnosis of Beckett. It is characteristic of Adorno's mandarin, highly allusive style that the Hegelian theme he spots in Beckett is left untreated – or virtually so – just as his initial, contemptuous half-reference to the culture industry's 'rubbish book' hides and releases a post-war critique.

In *The Phenomenology of Mind* (1807), Hegel argued that 'self-consciousness exists . . . in that, and by the fact that, it exists for another self-consciousness.'[100] His treatment of the consequential movements is at once monumentally dull and intrinsically dramatic, coming to concentrate on two 'moments' which:

> stand as two opposed forms or modes of consciousness. The one is independent, and its essential nature is to be itself; the other is dependent, and its essence is life or existence for another. The former is the Master, or Lord, the latter the Bondsman.[101]

In elaborating this parable further, Hegel acknowledges the crucial role of human labour in transforming relations between these moments, and concludes that 'just as lordship showed its essential nature to be the reverse of what it wants to be, so, too, bondage will, when completed, pass into the opposite of what it immediately is . . .'[102] In time, Marx will take up this Hegelian dialectic to show that the *Phenomenology* had reversed the relations between labour and consciousness, and the materialist re-writing of Hegel re-emerges in the twentieth century, notably in certain texts of Lukács.[103] For Adorno, this legacy posed peculiar problems but there can be no doubt that the Hegelian theme in *Endgame* is precisely that of consciousness-as-pair, the complex dramatic monologue of Hamm and Clov which is in turn counterpointed by the pathetically intrusive contributions of Nell and Nagg in their dustbins. For Marxists, of course, Hegel's recourse to parable as a means of approach to the actual social processes of human labour only serves to emphasize his incorrigible idealism. Yet, by the same token, the 'pairs' in Beckett's work articulate equally fundamental human concerns, even if a not-dissimilar remoteness of social reality manifests itself both formally and materially.

A further dimension to Adorno's linking of Hegel and Beckett deserves attention. The *Phenomenology*, for all the ponderous abstraction of its tonalities, was deeply concerned with historical reality. Hegel's famous formulation of 'the unhappy consciousness' (*unglückliches Bewusstein*) derived from his analysis of post-medieval attempts to establish permanent and reliable connections between man's mental insecurity and some Immutable Reality. More immediately topical were the late pages of the *Phenomenology*, the section called in English 'Absolute freedom and terror'.[104] The essay on *Endgame* concerns itself intensively with the unprecedented problem of the writer 'after Auschwitz'.

Working on his *Minima Moralia* (1951) in exile during the Second World War, Adorno turned a distinctly ironic eye upon the author of the *Phenomenology*. The twenty-ninth section of the *Minima*, one of the most thoroughly epigrammatic sections, commences with Proust and concludes with an inversion – 'The whole is the false' – of Hegelian dogma.[105] Two associates of the Frankfurt School wrote less cryptically on related matters. In *Reason and Revolution* Herbert Marcuse insisted that

> the relation of lord to servant is . . . neither an eternal nor a natural one, but is rooted in a definite mode of labour, and in man's relation to the products of his labour.[106]

And whereas Hegel had posited a general model of human existence according to which

> life proceeds to negation and its pain; and only through the resolution of opposition and contradiction will it gain its affirmation. If however, it should remain in contradiction without overcoming it, then it will perish in it . . .[107]

Ernst Bloch reformulated this position in terms appropriate to the political priorities and historical condition which – broadly speaking – he shared with Adorno, Lukács and Marcuse, a reformulation apt to Adorno's reading of Beckett:

> History does not repeat itself; yet wherever something did not become history and did not make history, then history will by all means be repeated.[108]

This central notion of the critical theorists – that historical process and philosophical reflection have a complex conjuncture – is energetically reformulated by Adorno in various writings on the 'culture industry', as he contemptuously termed the restructuring of relations between production and the arts in the era of fascism and post-fascism. *Minima Moralia* nowhere mentions Samuel Beckett, and it is likely that Adorno was not familiar with Beckett's pre-war writings, but the collection of extended aphorisms sub-titled 'Reflections from damaged life' may yet cast a new light on Beckett's unusual combination of bourgeois rectitude and – simply – courage.

It is fitting that so many of the Marxist critics involved in this discussion of Beckett and Adorno should be Jewish – not only Adorno himself, but also Bloch, Lukács, Marcuse, and Walter Benjamin. For Beckett's engagement with the public events of his lifetime has been repeatedly prompted by his loyalty to Jewish friends. This is true both of events locally in Ireland (and so of little political consequence) and of events in France under German occupation when the consequences were of the most unspeakable kind. In Ireland, these friends included Leslie Daiken and A. J. Leventhal; in Paris, Paul Leon (murdered 1942); in Rousillon, Henri Heyden. According to Richard Ellmann, Beckett spoke to Joyce about Nazi persecution of the Jews when the creator of Bloom once praised German precision.

Beckett's renowned entanglement in the Dublin court case arising from Oliver St J. Gogarty's anti-semitism took the form of his giving evidence for his Jewish relatives, the brothers Sinclair.[109] William ('Boss') Sinclair died in May 1937 in Rathdrum, County Wicklow. Before his death he had read Gogarty's *As I Was Going Down Sackville Street*, and obliged his brother Morris Sinclair to seek legal redress for the libel on their family. The case was heard in November. Beckett gave evidence for the plaintiff and was duly humiliated by Gogarty's counsel, J. M. Fitzgerald, K. C., who, in refer-ring to Beckett as the 'bawd and blasphemer from Paris', upheld the best traditions of the Irish bar. But the jury found for the plaintiff. By December Beckett was once more in Paris, set upon the course which led to his involve-ment in the resistance and to the writing of *Watt*.

Beckett's war-time experiences do not require summary here. Suffice it to say that distress at the fate of Jewish friends prompted his involvement. In the oblique light of Adorno's comparison of Beckett's post-war writing and Curzio Malaparte's *Kaputt*, it is worth noting that Beckett's initial at-tempts to get *Watt* published were countered by suggestions that he should not have disguised 'his wartime memories within the framework of fiction' but written a 'realistic account' of them instead. Unknown perhaps in 1946, he was not immune to those pressures which launched the post-war culture industry. But he resisted them. In addition note the unmistakeable Jewish significations which Beckett inscribed in his post-war work – the controlling figure Youdi in (or not-in?) *Molloy*, the name Levi in drafts of *Waiting for Godot*, and the concealed Jewish jokes which (only?) Adorno detected in *Endgame*,[110] these including not only the classic story of the Tailor and the Creator:

> my dear Sir, look – (*disdainful gesture, disgustedly*) – at the world – (*pause*) – and look – (*loving gesture, proudly*) – at my TROUSERS![111]

but also a version of the circus routine in which the Jewish husband, discovering his wife and his best friend making love on the sofa, throws out the sofa, rather than break up either of the bogus pairings upon which his life depends.[112] These anecdotes with which Hamm and Clov pass their death-after-life are thrown-away lines by which the abandoned subjects sustain themselves. In the early essay where he had commented on a decisive rupture in communications, Beckett allowed that 'the artist who is aware of this may state the space that intervenes between him and the world of objects.'[113] The exact delicacy with which his post-war writing acknowledges 'the Jewish question' without capitulating to demands for a 'realistic' account of his wartime experiences and activities testifies to the strength of this initial aesthetic observation, while echoing in an uncanny way Adorno's meditations on the problematic of subject/object. Writing on Proust and Valéry, Adorno later defined the work of art not as 'pure Being' in any sense 'but rather as a "force-field" between subject and object'.[114]

'Wovon man nicht sprechen kann, darüber muss man schweigen.' The final sentence of Ludwig Wittgenstein's *Tractatus Logico-philosophicus* (1921) is given in the original German, partly as a link across the gulf thought to separate central European culture and traditional insular philosophy, partly also to indicate the metaphysical potential of an 'exact delicacy' like Beckett's. It is time to approach Malaparte's *Kaputt* (1945). That book's remarkable licence in turn compels Adorno's attention and his most oblique, his almost silent condemnation. At first peep Malaparte appears to be an odd point of comparison. A captain in the Italian army and sometime war-correspondent for *Corriere della Sera*, Malaparte wrote about his experiences of the eastern front (Lapland to the Ukraine, including Poland), where he was attached to various German and Romanian units. *Kaputt*, however, has a pronounced narrative squint as it attempts to accommodate Prince Eugene of Sweden, as addressee, with – among other topics – Himmler naked in a sauna. For Adorno it was a travesty of writing. Even the prefatory note revealed several priorities from which he can only have retreated (initially) in shock:

The chief character is *Kaputt*, the gay and gruesome monster. Nothing can convey better than this hard, mysterious German word *Kaputt* – which literally means, 'broken, finished, gone to pieces, gone to ruin' – the sense of what we are, of what Europe is – a pile of rubble. But I prefer this *Kaputt* Europe to the Europe of yesterday – and of twenty or thirty years ago.[115]

'The sense of what we are' pinpoints exactly what, in existentialism, Adorno opposed – an unreflective, savouring worship of existence *per se*. The substance of *Kaputt* offended in more intimate and more professional ways also. Its first section gratuitously entitled (after Proust) 'Du Côté de Guermantes', the book systematically yet casually applied the arts to the business of ennobling barbarism even while officially decrying it. Though he implicitly condemned Reichsminister Hans Frank (self-styled 'deutscher König von Polen') for his boast that 'Furtwangler and Karajan will come to Cracow next spring to conduct a series of concerts',[116] Malaparte himself compared lines of corpses in the Warsaw ghetto to art. Far from confirming some anticipatory realism in the painter, he sought to render the dead unreal – 'they were stiff and hard, they looked like wooden statues. Just like the dead Jews in a Chagall canvas.'[117] When he was at Jassy (in Moldavia, June 1941) a pogrom of between 500 and 7,000 Jews took place; he was reading Harold Nicholson's biography of Lord Dufferin at the time – the 1937 printing, to be exact. A Gestapo offficer who accompanied the author through the ghetto 'moved among the Jews like an angel of Jehovah'.[118] Such double blasphemy was even enshrined in the book's epigraph with a parade of philological scruple concerning the Jewish derivation of the word 'kaputt':

(von hebraischen Koppâroth, Opfer, oder französisch Capot, matsch) zugrunde gerichtet, entzwei . . .

the source given as Meyer's *Conversationlexicon* of 1860.[119] And here one encounters the ironic significance of the translator's substitution of 'corpsed' for 'kaputt', for the emendation neglects Adorno's scornful neglect of Malaparte's implication that the Jews, in providing German with a root for their verbal trash, did for themselves. This enlightened blindness, this total inability to recognize the dreadful historical actuality of the present, stood in utter contrast to Beckett's *Endgame*. Malaparte's timely account of his horror at the events he oversaw promptly became a component in post-war Europe's crash-course in amnesia, an amnesia effected by the proliferation of strictly useless *aides mémoires*. This larger phenomenon Adorno recognized as the historic mission of 'the culture industry'. But, more particularly, *Endgame* is singled out for commendation because for Beckett – as for Paul Celan and Agnes Nemes Nagy – even the survivors cannot survive. Nor does their art pretend otherwise. In that there are bodily survivors, such art declines to resume its old reputation for spirituality. The master-and-slave anecdotes of client and tailor, tailor and Creator, possess ironically the dialectic which Hegel intended and Adorno denied in the original philosophical fable. The 'pairs' actually incorporated to Beckett's plays find no comparable resolution; though they elegantly endure. Adorno turns a related kind of irony on Malaparte. He who named the unnameable remains unnamed.

The political context of these developments extends back at least as far as the late 1930s when Adorno began to examine the growth of what he termed the culture industry. Commercialized hedonism under the Weimar republic, the highly fetishized paraphernalia of Nazism, the consumerism of dreams in Hollywood – these were stages of a historical process he observed with fastidious distaste. *Dialectic of Enlightenment* (1944/47), which he wrote with Max Horkheimer, consisted of five substantial essays scrutinizing the concept of enlightenment, its engagement with myth, with morality. Before concluding with 'Elements of anti-semitism: limits of enlightenment', the authors devote their longest essay to 'The culture industry: enlightenment as mass deception'. Undoubtedly linked to his empirical work on authoritarian personality, the film industry and so forth, this analysis is also part and parcel of Adorno's metaphysical interests, subjected of course to the actualities of history. 'Everything derives from consciousness: for Malebranche and Berkeley, from the consciousness of God; in mass art, from the consciousness of the production team.'[120] Intellectual spleen perhaps, Eurocentric misgivings about jazz, and a carefully difficult style inured Adorno to the blandishments of America. Yet, show-biz and Nazism had something in common:

> The enlightened self-control with which the assimilated Jews managed to forget the painful memories of domination by others . . . led them straight from their own long-suffering community into the modern bourgeoisie, which was moving inexorably toward reversion to cold repression and organization as a pure 'race'.[121]

Adorno's preoccupation with the theme of domination in the immediately post-war years led him to see in *Endgame* a suitably damaged anticipation of nuclear catastrophe and a strangely integral after-image of the Jewish holocaust:

> The *dramatis personae* resemble those who dream their own death, in a shelter where 'it's time it ended'. The end of the world is played down as if it were a matter of course. Every drama supposedly set in the atomic age would mock itself, if only because its plot would hopelessly falsify the historical horror

of anonymity by shoving such horror into the characters and actions of men and women . . . The violence of the unspeakable is mimicked by a reluctance to mention it. Beckett keeps it nebulous. One can only speak in euphemisms about what is incommensurate with all experience, just as in Germany one speaks of the murder of the Jews.[122]

As with the progress from Berkeley to mass art, the individual human subject remained even here a central problematic. It was not simply an illusion to be jettisoned, as the advanced structuralists proposed. It was not to be easily collectivized with Lukács and others, and certainly not worshipped after the manner of the existentialists. Of the three options, the Lukácsian was the least unattractive for all that Adorno had come to despair of the working class as the great 'subject' of future history. Central to this pessimism was his appreciation of the power behind what had appeared to many as merely superficial changes in the relations between art and production inside western capitalism. 'The rising collectivist order is a mockery of a classless one.'[123]

The early pages of *Minima Moralia*, where this line of thought is pursued, are given over to rapidly alternating estimates of the bourgeois's place in the new order. The argument runs back to Hegel who 'in hypostasizing both bourgeois society and its fundamental category, the individual, did not truly carry through the dialectic between the two.'[124] But there is an unexpected bonus:

> In the period of his decay, the individual's experience of himself and what he encounters contributes once more to knowledge, which he had merely obscured as long as he continued unshaken to construe himself positively as the dominant category. In face of the totalitarian unison with which the eradication of difference is proclaimed as a purpose in itself, even part of the social force of liberation may have temporarily withdrawn to the individual sphere. If critical theory lingers there, it is not only with a bad conscience.[125]

The succeeding meditations on altering forms of private housing, family manners, modes of address, and other aspects of bourgeois differentiation, are taken up in the essay on *Endgame* where Adorno speculates on the psychic material behind the play:

> There sticks in Beckett's memory something like an apoplectic middleaged man taking his midday nap, a cloth over his eyes to keep out the light or the flies; it makes him unrecognizable. This image . . . becomes a sign only after one has become aware of the face's loss of identity, and aware also of the repulsive nature of that physical concern which reduces the man to his body and places him already among corpses. Beckett focusses on such aspects until that family routine – from which they stem – pales into irrelevance. The

tableau begins with Hamm covered by an old sheet; at the end, he places near his face the hankerchief, his last possession.[126]

In *Molloy*, the first narrator's 'physical' concern with his body produces a comic yet sustained consciousness-as-pair. But the bourgeois routine, emblemized in a *pater familias* dominant in his solitude, is significant here in that Adorno had elsewhere used very similar phrases to describe the victim of fascist torture.[127] Again, *Endgame* has both anticipatory and retrospective powers, just as the bourgeois retains a possible worth in the era of his decay and parodic rejuvenation.

In the *Dialectic of Enlightenment*, the authors had already perceived, with searing irony, the gulf between classical philosophy and this utterly new culture – 'amusement carries out that purgation of the emotions which Aristotle once attributed to tragedy . . . the culture industry reveals the truth about catharsis as it did about style.'[128] In the posthumous *Aesthetic Theory*, Beckett exemplifies the artist who recognizes the equally unacceptable extremes of 'nuanced expression' and a starkly superficial mimesis:

> Between poetic euphemisms and discursive barbarity there is indeed precious little room for true art. It is this small in-between space that is Beckett's terrain.[129]

This metaphor of the in-between requires careful attention lest it be prematurely taken up as an omen of some imminent re-establishment of easy relations between subject and object. Beckett's drama is all too often summarized as dealing with 'the modern break-down in communications' – as if break-down itself were not a highly revealing metaphor of incompetent mechanism. Adorno accepted no such explanation, with its covert nostalgia for a supposed era of unimpeded unanimity between subjects who were never objects to each other. Thus, *Waiting for Godot* and *Endgame* exemplify a dictum of Adorno's according to which 'art maintains its integrity only by refusing to go along with communication.'[130] At one and the same time an unrepentant Hegelian and a diagnostician of aesthetic malaise, he insists that 'what is called "communication" today is the adaptation of spirit to useful aims and, worse, to commodity fetishism'.[131]

Despite this seemingly arcane and advanced philosophizing, one is brought tantalisingly close to the possible source for a sociology of Irish literature in Adorno's treatment of Samuel Beckett's decent bourgeois origins. In the past, literature in Ireland together with its criticism proceeded along amiably agreed paths, conducting any intellectual transactions which arose in a spirit of easygoing relaxation – like friends on a country walk of a Sunday afternoon, sorting out discrepancies in the petty cash. In other words, the bourgeois character of the literature was glossed over by veneerings of local (Parnellism for Joyce, Ascendancy for Yeats) and international (Primitivism for Synge, Decadence for Wilde) manufacture. Meanwhile, a distinctly bourgeois style of criticism, affectionate, anti-intellectual, dismissive, thrived. Gradually, this was augmented by the arrival of foreign scholarship, but the American scholars were happy to pretend that anecdotal inconsequentiality was one of the very things they most admired in their new property. The literature *per se* was not slow to take a hint, of course, and for several years now the Culture Industry has been thriving in Ireland, with the help of a refurbished sectarianism.[132]

NOTES AND REFERENCES

1 T. W. Adorno, *Minima Moralia* (London: New Left Books, 1974), p. 52.
2 See Giorgio Agamben, *The Coming Community*, trans. Michael Hardt (Minneapolis: University of Minnesota Press, 1993); and *Infancy and History: Essays on the Destruction of Experience*, trans. Liz Heron (London: Verso, 1993).
3 For a more positive view of Corcoran's place in Irish education, see R. Dudley Edwards *Agenda for Irish History 1978–2018* in Ciaran Brady ed., *Interpreting Irish History: the Debate on Historical Revisionism* (Dublin: Irish Academic Press, 1994), p. 57n5, also p. 231.
4 O'Neill remains largely unknown, despite the fact that *Wind from the North* (1934) was adopted as a school-approved text and was also translated into Gaelic. For Hackett, see his wife's account of their Irish residence, Lis Pihl ed., *Signe Toksvig's Irish Diaries 1926–1937* (Dublin: Lilliput Press, 1994). Significantly there is no reference in these to Beckett, and Bowen only appears once when she is 'stupidly afffected'.
5 Samuel Beckett, *Murphy* (London: Calder, 1963), pp. 34-36. Cf the stage direction 'Maurya puts the empty cup mouth downwards on the table. . .' in J. M. Synge *Collected Works* (*Plays 1*) (London: Oxford University Press, 1968), p. 25. The association of Neary's explanation with 2 Kings may be strengthened if one notes that Manasseh's offences in God's eyes included the building of a grove (2 Kings 21:3) where pagan deities were worshipped.
6 I am grateful to Fiona Macintosh for her comment on the comparative placing of classics in Victorian Irish and British context; see her *Dying Acts: Death in Ancient Greek and Modern Irish Tragic Drama* (Cork: Cork University Press, 1994), for an acute reading of Yeats, Synge, and O'Casey in this connection.
7 See Alan Simpson, *Beckett and Behan and a Theatre in Dublin* (1962). Tennessee Williams' *The Rose Tattoo* was the play at which the authorities jibbed.
8 Dennis Kennedy, *The Widening Gulf: Northern Attitudes to the Independent Irish State 1919–49* (Belfast: Blackstaff, 1988), pp. 73, 77.
9 For the biographical details see Deirdre Bair, *Samuel Beckett: a Biography*, (London: Cape, 1978).

10　I am grateful to Terence Brown for confirming my suspicion of Fitzwein. In '*Watt*, Knott, and Beckett's Bilingualism', *Journal of Beckett Studies*, 10 (1985), pp. 37-75, Ann Beer provides a great wealth of detail from the manuscript sources of the novel, including references to a proto-character called Quin. The latter name, though it had already surfaced in passing in *More Pricks than Kicks*, probably derives from E. G. Quin (1910-1986), a Celtic scholar and a contemporary of Beckett's in Trinity.

11　*Murphy*, p. 79.

12　See Reinhardt Koselleck, *Futures Past: On the Semantics of Historical Time*, trans. Keith Tribe (Cambridge, Mass: MIT Press, 1985).

13　E. W. Said, *The World, the Text, and the Critic* (Cambridge, Mass: Harvard University Press, 1983), p. 87.

14　On Beckett see Vivian Mercier, *Modern Irish Literature: Sources and Founders* (Oxford: Clarendon Press, 1994), pp. 312-26 ('Samuel Beckett and the Bible') and his earlier *Beckett/Beckett* (New York: Oxford University Press, 1977), esp. p. 30n on Huguenots. The more recent of these books appeared too late for anything but a brief acknowledgment here, but Mercier's discussion of other biblical echoes in Beckett's work helps to confirm my own analysis of Neary's wiped plate in *Murphy*.

15　Cf. Acts 9:5 'And he said, Who art thou, Lord? And the Lord said, I am Jesus whom thou persecutest: it is hard for for thee to kick against the pricks.'

16　Samuel Beckett, *More Pricks than Kicks* (London: Calder, 1970), pp. 186, 87.

17　Ibid., p. 21.

18　Ibid., p. 194.

19　Michel de Montaigne, *The Complete Essays*, trans. M. A. Screech (London: Penguin, 1991), pp. 416-27. For Agamben's comments, see *Infancy and History*, pp. 19, 37-39. Bair's brief account of Beckett's undergraduate reading in French makes no reference to Montaigne.

20　Hugh Kenner, *A Reader's Guide to Samuel Beckett* (London: Thames and Hudson, 1973), p. 127.

21　W. J. Mc Cormack, ed., *In the Prison of his Days* (Dublin: Lilliput Press, 1988), p. 35.

22　*The Negro Anthology* (London: Wishart, 1934), p. 471.

23　Deirdre Bair, op. cit., p. 179. In 1956, Beckett assured Cunard that he still had his copy of the *Anthology* 'unlike most of what I once had.' (ibid., pp. 470-1).

24　See Sighle Kennedy, *Murphy's Bed: a Study of Real Sources and Surreal Associations in Samuel Beckett's First Novel* (Lewisberg: Bucknell University Press, 1971), pp. 297-8 and n23.

25　Samuel Beckett, *Watt* (New York: Grove Press, 1970), p. 156.

26　Ibid., p. 175.

27　Ibid., p. 174.

28　W. B. Yeats, *On the Boiler* (Dublin: Cuala Press, 1939), pp. 11, 27-28. Rather than question Yeats's politics directly on this passage, perhaps one might consider his use of the adjective 'poor' and the noun 'peace' in the tragic context he envisages.

29　*Watt*, pp. 172-3. The flags, it might be pointed out, are bog-irises, though the protean application of the word to flowers, flat rocks and national drapery is worth noting. For consideration of the comparable passage in Swift, see

W. J. Mc Cormack, 'On Gulliver's Travels' in Jeremy Hawthorn ed., *Narrative from Malory to Motion Pictures* (London: Arnold, 1985), pp. 71-84.

30 *Watt*, p. 237.
31 Alec Reid, *All I Can Manage, More that I Could; an Approach to the Plays of Samuel Beckett* (Dublin: Dolmen Press, 1968), p. 14. Hugh Kenner, op. cit., p. 162.
32 Terence Brown, 'Some young doom: Beckett and the Child' *Hermathena*, No. 41 (1986), pp. 56-64.
33 See her detailed article in the *Journal of Beckett Studies*, No. 10 (1985), esp. p. 47. See also n9 above.
34 Beckett, *Murphy*, p. 187.
35 Stan Gontarski, ed., *On Beckett: Essays and Criticism* (New York: Grove Press, 1986), pp. 308-24.
36 Samuel Beckett, *Collected Shorter Plays* (London: Faber, 1987), p. 29
37 Bair, op. cit., pp. 490, 323.
38 Carin von Foch (daughter of Huldine Beamish (1860 – 1931) and her Swedish husband), married Hermann Goering in 1923; his wife and mother-in-law died in the same year. His mother-in-law's Swedish mother died two years later, in 1933, and was buried in Clonmel, County Tipperary.
39 C. T. M. Beamish, *Beamish: a Genealogical Study of a Family in County Cork and Elsewhere* (privately published, 1950), p. 113. The novelist's full name was Anne O'Meara Beamish, her father having been Frank John de Vic Beamish (1852 – 1907) who taught English in the University of Rouen; her mother was the first white woman to travel up the Nile, living for two years in primitive conditions at Assuan.
40 Samuel Beckett, *Molloy* (New York: Grove Press, 1970), p. 196. I am grateful to David Wheatley for this point.
41 Ibid., p. 36.
42 Eoin O'Brien, *The Beckett Country* (Dublin: Black Cat Press, 1986).
43 Samuel Beckett, *Collected Shorter Plays* (London: Faber, 1984), p. 220. Richard Welsted (Boss) Croker (1841 – 1922), was an Irish-born Tammany Hall politician who retired to manorial splendour at a house called Glencairn which he reconstructed at great expense. Shortly before his death, the house was raided for firearms by republican Irregulars. See Noelle Ryan, *Samuel Beckett – Early Days in Foxrock*; and Patrick Cronin, *Boss Croker of New York City and Glencairn* (both Foxrock: Foxrock Local History Club, 1982).
44 Samuel Beckett, *The Unnamable* (New York: Grove Press, 1970), p. 21.
45 *Molloy*, p. 125.
46 Ibid., p. 152.
47 Agamben, *Infancy and History*, p. 51.
48 Ibid., p. 114-15, quoting a letter (9 December, 1938) from Benjamin to T. W. Adorno.
49 Walter Benjamin, 'The Storyteller' in *Illuminations*, trans. Harry Zohn (London: Cape, 1870), p. 84.
50 See W. J. Mc Cormack, *Dissolute Characters* (Manchester: Manchester University Press, 1993), pp. 214-30 etc.
51 Elizabeth Bowen, *The Collected Short Stories* (London: Cape, 1980), p. 666.
52 Ibid., p. 617.

53   Ibid., p. 618.
54   Ibid., p. 620.
55   Ibid., p. 622.
56   Elizabeth Bowen, *Collected Impressions* (London: Longmans, 1950), pp. 4-5.
57   Ibid., p. 4.
58   Bowen, *Collected Short Stories*, pp. 418-19. I am not aware that anyone has ex-
     plained the title of this story. Clearly, Miss Cuffe's table is spread in the sense
     that she is hosting a dinner party. But all we read is that 'dinner was being
     served very slowly'; within one or two sentences the guests have retired to the
     drawing-room. It may be more to the point to notice that Alban 'saw now that
     he was less than half the feast . . .' (p. 420). In her fantasizing, Valeria believes
     that her other guests 'had so fallen in with her plans . . . that the dinner became
     a betrothal feast' (p. 422). In such a union, the man would indeed be half the
     feast, but the grossness of 'Valeria's bust was almost on the table' discourages
     the thought. The story's title may echo two eighteenth-century hymns which
     appear in the Church of Ireland hymnal – 'Author of life divine Who hast a
     table spread . . .' (by the Wesley brothers) and 'My God, and is thy table spread
     . . .' by Philip Doddridge. The Wesleyan emphasis on the sacrament of holy
     communion as a 'love feast' lead to an emotionalism which the movement had
     to check. One might then read 'Her Table Spread' as a pathology of Irish Protest-
     antism, ending in delusion and imminent expropriation.
59   Ibid., pp. 420, 424.
60   Elizabeth Bowen, *A World of Love* (London: Cape, 1955), pp. 112, 114.
61   Ibid., p. 116.
62   Heather Bryant Jordan, *How Will the Heart Endure: Elizabeth Bowen and the
     Landscape of War* (Ann Arbor: University of Michigan Press, 1992), p. 178.
63   Elizabeth Bowen, *Eva Trout; Or, Changing Scenes* (London: Cape, 1969),
     p. 26.
64   Ibid., p. 18.
65   Ibid., p. 221.
66   Ibid., pp. 223, 232.
67   Ibid., pp. 222, 232.
68   Ibid., pp. 228, 221.
69   Ibid., p. 254.
70   Agamben, *Infancy and History*, pp. 83-84.
71   Ibid., p. 85. Agamben resorts to Lévi-Straussian diagrams to indicate the 'quan-
     tum leap' in which the unstable signifiers (ghosts and children) are the ciphers
     which drive the process by which social system as such is made possible. 'Within
     this perspective, ghosts and children, belonging neither to the signifiers of
     diachrony nor to those of synchrony, appear as the signifiers of the same signi-
     fying opposition between the two worlds which constitute the potential for a
     social system. They are, therefore, the signifiers of the signifying function,
     without which there would be neither human time nor history.' (p. 84).
72   The idea that Jeremy 'liberates' Eva is Hermione Lee's: see her *Elizabeth Bowen:
     an Estimation* (London: Vision, 1981), p. 210.
73   Beckett, *Complete Dramatic Works*, p. 191. T. W. Adorno, *Notes to Literature*
     (New York: Columbia University Press, 1991), vol. 1, pp. 270-1.
74   James Joyce, *Ulysses* (Harmondsworth: Penguin, 1969), p. 166.

75   Beckett, *Complete Dramatic Works* (London: Faber, 1986), p. 259.

76   Joyce, *Ulysses*, p. 182.

77   Edna Longley, *The Living Stream: Literature and Revisionism in Ireland* (Newcastle Upon Tyne: Bloodaxe, 1994), pp. 69-85, 179. The essay first appeared in Theo Dorgan and Máirín Ní Dhonnchadha, eds., *Revising the Rising* (Derry: Field Day, 1991). Recent discussion of the contribution of Ulstermen to the casualties of the Great War has been greatly aided by the publication of Philip Orr's *The Road to Somme*. (Belfast, 1987).

78   'Three dialogues: iii, Bram van Velde' [1949], in Samuel Beckett, *Disjecta: Miscellaneous Writings and a Dramatic Fragment* (London: Calder, 1983), p. 145. John Pilling (*Samuel Beckett*, London, Boston: Routledge, 1976, p. 199) compares Hegel's view of romanticism as necessarily an 'art of failure'.

79   'Recent Irish poetry' (1934) in *Disjecta*, p. 70.

80   Quoted in Vivian Mercier, *Beckett/Beckett* (New York: Oxford University Press, 1977), p. 36.

81   Ibid. p. 161.

82   Samuel Beckett, *Molloy: a novel*, translated from the French by Patrick Bowles in collaboration with the author (New York: Grove Press, 1970), (*Collected works*), p. 7.

83   Biographical details extracted from Deirdre Bair, op. cit., pp. 336, 348, 364-6 etc.

84   See n40 above: the citation differs in other editions.

85   J. M. Synge, Preface to *The Playboy of the Western World: Collected works* vol. iv, plays, bk ii (Oxford University Press, 1969), p. 53.

86   *Molloy*, p. 89.

87   T. W. Adorno, 'Trying to understand *Endgame*' trans. Michael T. Jones, *New German Critique*, No. 26 (1982), pp. 119-50.

88   T. W. Adorno, *Noten zur Literatur II* (Frankfurt-am-Main: Suhrkamp, 1961). Subsequent page references to the German text relate to the volume of the same name in the *Surkamp Gesammelte Schriften* (1970 onwards).

89   *New German Critique*, loc. cit., p. 122; Beckett, *Complete Dramatic Works*, p. 106.

90   Adorno's principal account of existentialism – half argument, half satire – is *The Jargon of Authenticity*, trans. Knut Tarnowski and Frederic Will (London: Routledge, 1973).

91   On this topic see Theodor Adorno and Max Horkheimer, *Dialetic of Enlightenment*, trans. John Cumming (London: Verso, 1979); Theodor Adorno, *Minima Moralia; Reflections from Damaged Life*, trans E. F. N. Jephcott, (London: New Left Books, 1974); Theodor W. Adorno 'Culture and administration', *Telos*, No. 37 (Fall 1978), pp. 93-111. A useful bibliography of works in English by and relating to Adorno can be found in Eugene Lunn, *Marxism and Modernism: An Historical Study of Lukács, Brecht, Benjamin and Adorno* (London: Verso, 1985).

92   For Adorno's career during these stages, see Martin Jay, *The Dialectical Imagination: A History of the Frankfurt School and the Institute of Social Research, 1923 – 50* (London: Heinemann, 1973). Jay has also published a short study of Adorno in the Fontana Modern Masters series.

93   See *New German Critique*, loc. cit., p. 119.

94   T. W. Adorno, *Aesthetic Theory*, Gretel Adorno and Rolf Tiedemann eds., trans. C. Lenhardt (London, Boston: Routledge, 1984), p. 498.

95   Adorno's opposition to Husslerian phenomenology is the subject of his *Against Epistemology: A Metacritique*, trans. Willis Domingo (Oxford: Blackwell, 1982).

96   The extended debate about modernism is documented in Ernst Bloch, György Lukács, Bertolt Brecht, Walter Benjamin, Theodor Adorno, *Aesthetics and Politics*, trans. and ed. Ronald Taylor; afterword by Fredric Jameson (London: New Left Books, 1977).

97   These extracts are taken from *Noten zur Literatur II*, pp. 281, 283, 286, 290, 292, 311; the translation is basically that of Michael T. Jones, with modifications; see *New German Critique*, loc. cit., pp. 119, 120-21, 123, 126, 127, 143. See also T. W. Adorno, *Notes to Literature*, Rolf Tiedemann ed., Shierry Weber Nicholsen trans. (New York: Columbia University Press, 1991), vol. 1, pp. 241-75.

98   Adorno, *Aesthetic Theory*, p. 353.

99   Ibid., p. 354.

100   G. W. F. Hegel, *The Phenomenology of Mind*, trans. J. B. Baillie (London: Allen Unwin, 1931, 2nd rev. edn), p. 229. The section from which these quotations come is reprinted in Paul Connerton ed., *Critical Sociology: Selected Readings* (Harmondsworth: Penguin), pp. 41-50, an anthology which contains a useful selection of material by Frankfurt School thinkers.

101   Hegel, *The Phenomenology of Mind*, p. 234.

102   Ibid., p. 237.

103   See in particular Lukács's *Young Hegel* (1966: English, 1975).

104   Hegel, *The Phenomenology of Mind*, pp. 599-610.

105   Adorno, *Minima Moralia*, p. 50; cf. Hegel, *The Phenomenology of Mind*, p. 81.

106   Herbert Marcuse, *Reason and Revolution: Hegel and the Rise of Social Theory* (London: Routledge, 1955, 2nd edn), p. 115.

107   G. W. F. Hegel, *Aesthetik*, F. Bassenge ed. (Frankfurt: 1951), vol. 1, p. 104. Quoted in Hans-Joachim Schulz, *The Hell of Stories: A Hegelian Approach to the Novels of Samuel Beckett* (The Hague, Paris: Mouton, 1973) Schulz's short book is disappointing; for a consideration of Hegel's legacy in this immediate connection see, W. Martin Ludke, *Ammerkungen zu einer 'Logik des Zerfalls': Adorno-Beckett* (Frankfurt-am-Main: Suhrkamp, 1981), pp. 114-131 ('Herr und Knecht in der Geschichte des Verfalls'). For an orthodox Marxist point of view see Thomas Metscher, 'Geschichte und Mythos bei Beckett' in *Das Argument*, vol. 26 (1963).

108   See Oskar Negt, 'Ernst Bloch – the German Philosopher of the October Revolution', *New German Critique*, No. 4 (Winter 1975), pp. 3-16; see also Bloch's own essay 'A Jubilee for Renegades', loc. cit., pp. 17-25.

109   Bair, *A Biography: Samuel Beckett*, pp. 259, 266-9.

110   See Adorno, *Noten zur Literatur 11*, pp. 299, 301; also Jones's translation in *New German Critque*, No. 26 (1982), pp. 133, 135.

111   Beckett, *Complete Dramatic Works*, p. 103.

112   Adorno, *Noten zur Literatur*, p. 301; Jones (trans.), p. 135.

113   *Disjecta*, p. 70.

114   Quoted in Martin Jay, *Dialectical Imagination*, p. 177. The essay appears in an English translation in Andrew Arato and Eike Gebhardt (eds), *The Essential Frankfurt School Reader* (Oxford: Blackwell, 1978), pp. 497-511.

115   Curzio Malaparte, *Kaputt*, trans. Cesare Foligno (London: Redman, 1948), p. 9.

116 Ibid., p. 73.
117 Ibid., p. 94.
118 Idem.
119 I take this detail from the text in Malaparte's *Opere complete* (*Kaputt*, Vallecchi Editore, 1963, p. 7). It appears to have been omitted from English language editions.
120 Adorno and Horkheimer, *Dialectic of Enlightenment*, op. cit., p. 125.
121 Ibid., p. 169.
122 See Adorno, *Noten zur Literatur II*, p. 286; Jones (trans.), p. 123.
123 Adorno, *Minima Moralia*, p. 23.
124 Ibid., p. 17.
125 Ibid., pp. 17-18.
126 See Adorno, *Noten zur Literatur II*, p. 297; Jones (trans.), p. 131.
127 Jones refers the reader to Adorno and Horkheimer, *Dialectic of Enlightenment*, p. 234, without comment on the content of the passage referred to.
128 Adorno and Horkheimer, *Dialectic of Enlightenment*, p. 144.
129 Adorno, *Aesthetic Theory*, p. 47.
130 Ibid., p. 443.
131 Ibid., p. 109.
132 The background to this enterprise is the subject of my *The Battle of the Books* (Gigginstown: Lilliput Press, 1986).

12

From the Banks of the Danube:
A Personal Report on the State of
Literary History

> These few general remarks to begin with. What am I to do, what
> shall I do, what should I do, in my situation, how proceed? By
> aporia pure and simple?
>
> (Samuel Beckett)[1]

On an early visit to Budapest, I called to the Lukács Archivum to establish
whether I might be allowed to do research there at some time in the future.
The young woman who opened the door heard my inquiry in polite silence,
and then waved me in off the quays towards the stairs – 'why not start now?'
Embarrassed by my own success I found it difficult to define exactly what
it was I hoped to accomplish when I returned the following spring. I was
left in no doubt as to the excellence of the facilities and the affability of the
staff. My prior knowledge of György Lukács (1885–1971) had of course
been obtained from books – English translations of those books which
Lukács had written in German, no one abroad having bothered to consider
the Hungarian work. Their author was ten years dead, and his status was
still debatable.[2] Or not debatable. For many Hungarian intellectuals hedged their bets when it came to discussion of the former professor, former
commissar, former mystic, the Bolshevik aesthete. Neither the establishment
nor the dissidents claimed him, and yet his old apartment on Belgrad Rakpart
was not only preserved but staffed and indexed and generally kept in good
running order.

Personal opinions were less ceremonious. The poet Agnes Nemes Nagy

434

dismissed Lukács the literary critic with the words – 'never buy hair restorer from a bald man!' Others had more convoluted ways of dealing with the legend. It was recalled how the novelist Tibor Déry contrived a prolonged encounter over drinks between Lukács and István Vas. At the climax of their critical reflections, Vas suddenly changed tack – 'all very well, György, but how *could* you decimate a regiment?' And Lukács snapped back, 'What would you have done in my position?' The extremes meet in Lukács' career. A young man studying in the Archivum took pity on my plodding efforts to establish precisely what the author of *Soul and Form, Theory of the Novel, The Historical Novel*, and *Studies in European Realism* had read in English. He asked if I had ever come across Lukács' history of the Communist Party. I had never heard of it. We crossed the cluttered living room turned library, and he pointed to a squat volume on a shelf. A history of the Jesuit Order, annotated with a sort of code. In *The Magic Mountain*, Thomas Mann had cast the ultra-intellectual Naphta in the mould of Lukács, and somewhat more than mid-way through that artistic anatomy of Europe on the eve of the Great War Naphta revealed his affinity with the Society of Jesus:

> The idea of the society is rooted in and inseparably bound up with the absolute. By consequence, it is terroristic; that is to say, anti-liberal. It lifts the burden from the individual conscience, and consecrates in the name of the Absolute every means even to bloodshed, even to crime.[3]

The allegorizing of communism as a religion predates Mann's novel, and as an edict of damnation receives an answer in the redemptive Marxism of Walter Benjamin. If Lukács' failure to confront the reality of Stalin's 'absolute' continues to discredit him in the eyes of many Anglophone readers, they might reconsider the attachment of so great a poet as Yeats to the value of terror as a philosophical inspiration. And when Benjamin committed suicide in 1940, the future doyen of Yale Deconstruction was preparing for an interim stint as anti-semite journalist in Belgium. With implication in a politics which turns lethal as their base, the charges laid against Lukács in the Budapest cafés are not unique in the annals of twentieth-century thought. Nevertheless the admission, that no ready and easy way can be found to immunize thought (including 'creative' thought) from the century's unbearable record of slaughter and destruction, should not be treated as cancelling notions of responsibility, of what Naphta mockingly called 'the individual conscience'.

Does the evidence in the Archivum mitigate against the charges preferred against Lukács? My limited purpose in 1983 had been to discover

exactly what books by the major Irish modernist writers Lukács had read
before denouncing the entire modernist project in *The Meaning of Contemporary Realism* (1962; German edition, 1957). An answer may be usefully
prefaced with another of those Budapest anecdotes which have already been
cited. Ferenc Takács, one of Beckett's Hungarian translators, asked me if
I had heard of the film critic Béla Balázs, whom (at the time) I knew only
as Bartók's librettist. Well, he said, Balázs and Lukács fell out in 1918 and
thereafter one finds very few specific references to works of literature in
Lukács' criticism. Balázs, it seemed, read the books, told his friend about
them, and the friend then drew up his responses.[4] In the light of this, what
of merely Irish interest was one to expect in Lukács' library? There was
a large amount of work by Oscar Wilde and G. B. Shaw, quite heavily annotated or marked with marginal lines and the like; but this scarcely exceeded what one would expect of any Central European intellectual active
in the years surrounding the Great War. There was no sign of Synge, and
only the slightest trace of Yeats. Of Joyce, however, it was possible to establish
beyond all doubt that Lukács had read the two-volume German translation
of *Ulysses*, and that most other texts (not, however, including *Finnegans Wake*)
were available to him either in English or in translation. His *Ulysses* bears
two slight markings, one of the passage where it is observed that there is
something of the artist about old Bloom. The copy appears also to have been
inundated with occasional spillage. It is tempting to conclude that Lukács
had little interest in Joyce's work, made only the most banal indications of
having read the text, and oddly mimicked what he regarded as *Ulysses'* excessive attention to sense-data by splashing white wine over its pages. But
Leopold Bloom is a fictional character closely resembling the character
Lukács left behind when, in December 1918, he embraced Bolshevism. Both
were nineteenth-century Hungarian Jews, both were exiles, both had 'a touch
of the artist'. Lukács' early essays, dedicated to Leo Popper, raise commentary on literature to the level of literature just as critical theory later seeks
to subject the procedures of inquiry to a scrutiny similar to that they apply
to their object.

The potential resemblance between the two can hardly have escaped
Lukács who knew the paintings and drawings of Ferenc Martyn (1899–
1986). Born in Hungary, the descendent of a recent (and by no means
wealthy) Irish 'wild goose' nineteenth-century *emigré* from Galway, Martyn
was foremost among those Hungarian painters who opposed fascism through
the medium of art. In a series of graphics based on Joyce's *Ulysses*, Martyn
turned the Dublin-born Virag into a mirror image of Kaposvár-born Martyn,
and did so through the mediation of the cuckold-antlered Shakespeare of

the 'Circe' episode and the Hungarian folk myth of the boy who 'cries out to be changed into a stag'. These empirical details may go some way towards endorsing a charitable interpretation of the few marks which distinguish Lukács' copy of *Ulysses*, but in themselves they do little to ease problems thrown up by his determined adherence to a Marxist-Hegelian notion of *totality*.

Any casting of Lukács as a 'hard-line' theorist relies implicitly on a characterization of Benjamin as an eirenic thinker whose Marxism was tempered by his theological interests.[5] No attentive reader of the 'Theses on the Philosophy of History' could retain for more than a moment the notion of their author as in any way a 'soft' or pacifist exponent of dialectical materialism. Successive crises in Europe between the wars may have driven Benjamin to adopt more than one position which subsequently appears to be inconsistent or even ill thought out, but none of these offers promising material for a thorough-going refiguration of critical theory alternative to that implicit in Lukács' long and complex development.[6] The problem for those intrigued by the possibilities of renewing critical theory in the very late twentieth century is based on those concepts common to, and not disputed by, Lukács and Benjamin.

In the jargon of today, the problem can be posed in terms of 'post-metaphysical thinking'. From the critique of instrumental reason, advanced first by Max Horkheimer and later by T. W. Adorno, there has arisen a plethora of irrationalisms dedicated to very different objectives and pursuits, with post-modernism being only the most recent in a doubtful lineage. In this connection Lukács' late contribution to the history of western philosophy – *The Destruction of Reason* (1980; German edition, 1962) – does form the basis for the differentiation of emphases within *post-war* critical theory. If his sustained hostility to Nietzsche appears naïve by comparison with the readings advanced by others, it nonetheless counteracts the Gadarene enthusiasm of the Derridean school. Yet in Lukács, the persistent problematic remains his concept of totality, derived through Marx from Hegel, and so serving to smuggle a philosophy of the Absolute into what might alternatively be regarded as discrete issues of social policy, literary criticism, etc. His preference for Mann over Joyce, for example, is less predicated on the (ultimate) realization that Mann acknowledged a political and cultural responsibility in the novelist than it is on a suspicion of the free-floating sense-data of *Ulysses* as contrasted with the orchestrated ironic-Platonic dialogues of *The Magic Mountain*. As for Beckett, Lukács in *The Meaning of Contemporary Realism* confines himself to a few brief allusions to *Molloy*, complaining about the 'attentuation of reality' resulting from the use of stream of consciousness narrative and an 'abnormal' narrator. Quite what might characterize normative presuppositions and procedures is not clear, except that the objective representation of a totality of social relations is the *desideratum*.

The author of *The Historical Novel*, who had truly revolutionized twentieth-century responses to Walter Scott and who had rescued Balzac from the metaphysical camp, proves less illuminating as a reader of contemporary fiction. But disillusion with Lukács often fails to take into account the extra-ordinary conditions in which he worked – as a Bolshevik of suspect ortho-doxy, as a Jewish exile in Vienna and Moscow, as a participant in the anti-Soviet government of Imre Nagy in 1956, again an *emigré* albeit princi-pally in his own country, and so forth. *The Meaning of Contemporary Realism* cannot simply be read as a timeless response to certain texts: a series of prefaces and an introduction were required before the reversals of the mid-1950s could even be recorded, let alone analysed. It is worth noting that much of the book's polemic is directed away from modernist work emanating from societies which the author knew at first hand, to concen-trate instead on safely distant offenders. Thus of the nine authors discussed, one is largely endorsed (this is Thomas Mann inevitably); and of the eight called to task generally, four wrote in a language (English) Lukács imperfectly commanded, and two of these (Joyce and Beckett) came from a country of which (frankly) he knew nothing. Finally, one might note that in his last decades Lukács had returned to certain philosophical questions which had preoccupied him early in his career: perhaps literary criticism had never been a central project, even while his friendship with Balázs was alive.

These less than respectful observations should not be taken as definitive. Lukács can take some credit for the continental revival of interest in Laurence Sterne, through the Wildean critical dialogue 'Richness, Chaos and Form' which he published in 1910. (In this context, the low estimate of Swift's importance in Hungarian literary discourse remains puzzling.) The revalua-tion of Scott and Balzac accomplished by Lukács in *The Historical Novel* and elsewhere made possible newly dynamic readings of Maria Edgeworth and Sheridan Le Fanu. The perceptive, if highly 'period', observation of 1908 that 'every written work, even if it is no more than a consonance of beautiful words, leads us to a great door – through which there is no passage' bleakly describes a condition of literature in which neither social process nor the biological reality of death can be mediated.[7] The former problem is allegedly resolved in Saussurean linguistics, while the latter mutely points to a tragic interpretation of the political endeavour as such. These implica-tions are relevant in any attempt to reinvigorate the practice of literary history.

In addition, from Lukács' notion of critical realism it has been possible to evolve a further interpretive term – critical modernism – by means of which certain crucial distinctions between the work of Joyce and Beckett on the one, and Yeats on the other, can be elaborated.

In the essays of Walter Benjamin, further distinctions can be discovered, by means of which the too-familiar category of dramatic tragedy can be at once broken down and historically informed. The *Trauerspiel* anatomized in *The Origins of German Tragic Drama* not only assists, as a concept, in classifying Yeats's plays in a fuller and more revealing manner, it would also make possible the detection of a *Trauerliteratur*, even a *Trauerkultur* in which literary genre would no longer function as a classifying element. Instead, the theme of mourning might bring together hitherto discrete matters – for example, the economic and the existential as they meet in human death. Here too the possibility of overcoming metaphysical thinking could be formulated in non-metaphysical terms. Clearly, the implications of such an undertaking have no restricted Irish remit, though the work of James Clarence Mangan and the non-dramatic work of Synge call out for re-examination.

In the first of the 'Theses on the Philosophy of History', Benjamin sets up an unlikely tableau:

> The story is told of an automaton constructed in such a way that it could play a winning game of chess, answering each move of an opponent with a counter-move. A puppet in Turkish attire and with a hookah in its mouth sat before a chessboard placed on a large table. A system of mirrors created the illusion that this table was transparent from all sides. Actually, a little hunchback who was an expert chess player sat inside and guided the puppet's hand by means of strings. One can imagine a philosophical counterpart to this device. The puppet called 'historical materialism' is to win all the time. It can easily be a match for anyone if it enlists the services of theology, which today, as we know, is wizened and has to keep out of sight.[8]

Nothing could better illustrate the complex nature of Benjamin's irony, his absorption in political and religious speculation, and the merely demonstrative force of arguments by analogy. In a busy article, Rebecca Comay has referred to the 'radical uninterpretability' of the first thesis, as if to set its author up as a prophet of postmodernism.[9] Of more value, however, is her relating of Benjamin's parable to Beckett's play about Hamm and Clov. One of her epigraphs cites the definition of chess in Samuel Johnson's dictionary – 'a nice and abstruse game, in which two sets of puppets are moved in opposition to each other'. In 1937, Beckett commenced work on *Éleuthéria*, a play about Johnson's relationship with Hester Thrale, and while the project has never seen the light of day, it claimed enough of

Beckett's loyalty to oblige him to regard *Waiting for Godot* as his second play. Although its strictly theoretical aspect may be slight, we have identified here a further detail linking Beckett's pre-war concerns with the emergence of his drama in the 1950s. Johnson may replace both T. H. Huxley and Standish O'Grady as a likely 'source' for the chess imagery of *Murphy* and *Endgame*, though the greater achievement may be further to undermine the notion of source as a positivistic datum.

Charles Rosen, in one of the finest essays devoted to the writer, discovers in Benjamin's religious concerns a 'return to early Romantic philosophy and criticism' and in this he associates him with Yeats and André Breton. 'The preservation of mystical forms of thought means for him not their resurrection but their transformation just as, in the seventeenth century, allegorical technique preserved the pagan deities by transforming them into emblematic fragments, presenting them as ruins.'[10] This may be so, but Yeats and Benjamin also differ profoundly in their address to the transcendental. The difference can be best illustrated by consideration of their rival attitudes towards history, Yeats busy transforming fragments of a presumptive national chronicle into a myth of the past, Benjamin scrupulously preserving the fragment as fragment and largely eschewing history, even a history of art. That they should differ in politics hardly needs to be said.

Recent deployments of Benjamin's 'philosophy' have rarely provided grist to the literary historian's mill. Indeed, s/he has undergone a crisis of confidence similar to that afflicting historians generally, having earlier withstood the challenge of the New Criticism and Reception Theory. Currently overshadowed by the more glamorous findings of the New Historicism, literary history scorns capital initials and awaits the collapse of fashion into coherence. Even so genial an advocate of the historical method as David Perkins presents his case under a questioning title – *Is Literary History Possible?* – before invoking the aspiration of A. W. Schlegel at the end of the eighteenth century – 'that history and theory should be one'.[11] Other practitioners have buttressed their work in literary history with substantial publications in seemingly empirical disciplines – Marilyn Butler as biographer of Maria Edgeworth, Jerome McGann as editor of Byron.[12] In a polemical piece called 'Shall These Bones Live?', McGann argued for 'a revisionary policy which would not be a reactionary one' through which he could associate himself with textual and bibliographical work of a fairly traditional kind while maintaining the critical stance he epitomized in a favoured quotation from Max Horkheimer – 'ever since the transition from religious longing to conscious social practice, there continues to exist an illusion which can be exposed but never entirely banished. It is the image of a 'perfect social justice.'[13]

Of course both McGann, speaking to an academic audience in New York in 1981, and Horkheimer, writing much earlier and in quite different circumstances, require to be read historically. It is tempting to summarize the former's position as a feisty defence of scholarly method, but to do so would be to miss an opportunity of considering what it was in McGann's professional and social circumstance which prevented him from simply approving 'dryasdust scholarship'. (His immediate point of reference was an article called 'On the Use of Advertisements in Bibliographical Studies' by William Todd.) If one accepts the term 'affirmative action' as a form of social engineering by means of which certain sectors in the population – women, ethnic or religious minorities, homosexuals, the disabled – may be promoted in the face of ingrained prejudice, then it is worth recalling Benjamin's glum contrasting of life-affirmative literature and issueless satire, a contrast in which the one was shown to be as noisily vacant as the other. The inhibition under which McGann laboured was precisely the illusory (probably self-deceived) belief – not his, but one pervasive in the larger audience he addressed – that some little advance towards 'perfect social justice' could be gained from affirmation in the shape of polemics heavily marked with the yellow-liner (Gender in Free-Indirect Style, Decolonizing the Novel, etc.) whereas a paper on small ads in the 1790s did nothing for nobody. It is in such circumstances that literary history is in danger of being constantly outmoded by seemingly answerable complaints of the day.

Thus a return to literary history calls for a thorough redeployment of archival research, bibliographical analyis, textual criticism, collation and all the other time-consuming practices which we had thought banished by the word-processor. More is involved, of course, notably a renegotiation of terms between the academy and special interest politics. It may be that the academy as we know it – university departments of literary and historical teaching and research – will cease to be the location in which such work can be conducted. That is, the academy may decide to be a special interest itself, and go with the flow. Certainly, the single most important item on any agenda for such redeployments and renegotiations will be the allocation of time. 'Go with the flow' produces results, but they too *go*. The attitudes implicit in postmodernism officially approve the temporary and the amorphous, but in doing so they do more than extend into time respectable notions of physical fragmentariness. Postmodernism legitimizes the pathological condition it diagnoses in post-industrial capitalism.

Critical theory, if it had a single voice, might well reply – 'told you so'. After all, the work of Butler and McGann eloquently demonstrates that even such traditional practices as the editing of poems and the writing of biographies raise, by necessity, fundamental theoretical issues. In a real sense, practitioners of literary study are now catching up with E. P. Thompson whose witty polemic against Althusser in 1978 might have saved us all a lot of time.[14] Even the study of booksellers' advertisements in the Dublin newspapers of a three-month period from December 1786 to February 1787, however dull the resulting summary, has its bearing upon major historiographical issues.[15] Three decades ago historians were content with a figure of about fifty as the number of pamphlets discussing the issue of union between Great Britain and Ireland in the years 1797–1800. Today, by dint of little more than persistence aided by a scepticism born of theoretical parents, that statistic has now increased by a factor of five, to total more than 250 separate publications.[16] Altered perspectives on Protestant Ascendancy have altered attitudes towards Yeats, to twentieth-century Irish poetry, and so to the modernist movement itself. And increased access to the discussion of political union at the end of the eighteenth century implicates a reassessment of romantic imagery (including the term, 'union'). Meanwhile, the figure of Edmund Burke has become yet again the focus of revisionary (and perhaps reactionary) historical writing by Conor Cruise O'Brien.

Critical writing takes time, its dialectical character involves processes of reflection and reflexivity which cannot be truncated or compacted or taken as read. In that it also requires the writer to become aware of the limitations on self which it embraces as part of its material, critical writing involves a history of that self. Intellectual positions are not adopted as a matter of choice, though they may with time become recognitions of necessity rather than of the necessitous self. The coda to *Ascendancy and Tradition* complained angrily about the economic and political condition of Britain in the early 1980s; written while James Callaghan was 'in charge', it appeared in print after its author had left and after Margaret Thatcher had commenced her revolutionizing of public attitudes towards education, towards society ('does not exist'), towards the freebooting individual self. It is possible now to see how unprepared for this wholescale rewriting of cultural relations the marginal constituency of the humanities or human sciences was.

In the years preceding the crisis, the study of literature in English proceeded in university departments of quite disparate kinds. Some were still enthralled by the prestige of T. S. Eliot, the critic as well as the poet, who exercised an influence similar if less pervasive to that effected in Ireland by Yeats through his mytho-historiography. Disciples of F. R. Leavis reinforced Eliot's influence, not only in policing the canon but also in repulsing overtures from other disciplines, notably sociology. There arose departments of literary study in which the sociological perspective came to establish a compensating one-eyed sovereignty. A series of annual conferences in the University of Essex provided a platform for the introduction of Althusserian 'structural marxism' (the lower case initial was creeping in also) to a debate which, in the time-honoured cliché, generated more heat than light. Self-styled 'traditional' departments also survived, though by now everybody was under extreme financial pressure. Overseas post-graduate students were suddenly fee-charged virtually out of existence, a political decision which had severe repercussions on the teaching of Irish literature in the British university where I worked. Indians, Egyptians, Nigerians who had brought an invaluable diversity to the discussion of a problematic national literature were eliminated by what was essentially a racialist policy.

Elsewhere in the university, colleagues were pursuing interests which interacted with mine but which could never be brought into a single academic forum. In the Department of History, John A. Woods was working on the last details of the superb edition of Edmund Burke's *Correspondence* for which he had acted as co-editor with several other scholars. From Sociology, Janet Wolff published *The Social Production of Art* in 1981; her range included Hans-Georg Gadamer and Trevor Griffiths. The discussion of the 'Tonio Kruger problem', with which her 1981 volume opened, restated in the sublime terms of Thomas Mann's fiction precisely the problems of isolation, objectivity, representation, and consolidated purpose which affected the seminar room and the factory floor.

I believe that I *can* recall an actual discussion in which all three of us participated – Wolff, Woods, and myself – but it would be wrong to suggest that we shared even one common purpose, apart from a commitment to intellectual confrontation with aesthetic and historical issues. Officially, the annual conference on Sociology and Literature at Essex sponsored just such confrontations, but in practice other agendas prevailed. At a session dedicated to the year 1789, a speaker seeking to elucidate Wordsworth's 'Lucy' poems announced that 'the avenue to history has been closed'. At another – the last I attended – a vote to choose a topic for a future conference rejected the proposal of 'Culture and Northern Ireland' in favour of 'The Theory of Theory'. Professional solidarity found in Lacan and Althusser adequate arguments to justify introspection.

The Thatcher years decimated the British universities, and did worse damage to the society surrounding them. If Irish institutions have escaped the ideological conflicts between stuffiness and claptrap, moralism and pedantry, which left their English colleagues paralysed in the face of Boadicea, the time-warp responsible has also persistently deprived them of the funds which might have developed the critical study of Irish culture.

Tour operators write the curriculum. The time required, not just for critical
reflection but for any sustained enterprise (say, the biography or collected
letters of a major writer), so transcends the game-plan of winter TV schedules
and summer schools that sustained effort is impossible. Indeed, intermittent
contact is a structural feature of the game-plan, to the exclusion of respons-
ive dialogue between the exhausted researcher and the avid consumer. From
the beginning of inquiries to the writing of the last word in any substantial
undertaking, a biographer or editor will suffer a hundred rapidly changing
inducements, assaults, temptations, dismissals, condescensions, offers of
extreme unction, mindless praise, ditto abuse – all in the name of fashion
trading as this theory or that. *Ars longa, vita brevis. . .*

Yet it would be foolish to conclude that, supported by a contrite university system, generous allocations of research funds, and gadgets of unprecedented virtuosity and speed, literary history can ultimately re-present
the past. David Perkins neatly underlines the folly of any such ambition,
arguing that if 'the only complete literary history would be the past itself
. . . this would not *be* a history, because it would not be interpretive and
explanatory.'[17] In a word, then, it is the selective aspect of such studies as
the present one which establishes them as contributions to literary history.
In the area of Irish culture, the converse of this proposition has recently
been demonstrated in the unhappy reception given to *The Field Day
Anthology of Irish Writing*.

Originally designed by Seamus Deane, a general editor in whom a
sophisticated command of literary theory (especially French theory) combined with local insight and poetic talent, the final three-volume product
all too comprehensively aspired to represent the entirety of writing (in at
least three languages) associated with Ireland. This was literary history conducted by the ostensive method. Consequently, the Introduction found itself
arguing, with discernible embarrassment, that 'there *is* a story here, a meta-
narrative which is, we believe, hospitable to all the micro-narratives that,
from time to time, have achieved prominence as the official version of the
true history, political and literary, of the island's past and present.'[18] It
would be instructive to submit this to analysis in the terms provided for narrative history by Hayden White in *Tropics of Discourse*, especially those terms
involving the transformation of chronicle into story and the subsequent
(paradoxical) impoverishment of the narrative as the story is emplotted in
its mature phase.[19] Through such an analysis, the problem of totality would
arise once again. For, while striving to be hospitable, comprehensive, and
ostensive, literary history inevitably finds itself endorsing a meta-narrative
which requires the subjugation, even elimination from view, of some unruly

element – writing about science, writing by lesbians, evangelical hymns, shilling-shockers, or whatever. A meta-narrative is simply the micro-narrative which has succeeded in climbing higher than all the others like it. It is, if you like, an ascendancy and a betrayal rather than a genealogy or aristocracy. When Seamus Deane refers to 'the power of the English canonical tradition to absorb a great deal of writing that, from a different point of view, can be reclaimed for the Irish tradition', he goes a long way towards unveiling the older sense of tradition as *mis*appropriation.[20]

But it is not primarily in the literary domain that the concept of totality remains problematic. The unexamined axiom in the Field Day enterprise is Ireland, for this constitutes the assumed totalizing vantage point (cf. 'world history' in orthodox Marxism) from which invitations to the hospitalizable are sent out. Thus, Ireland functions in the argument sometimes as a cultural entity, sometimes as a political one, sometimes even as a geographical one. If one accepts the first of these, then the culture of that geographical space known as Scotland should properly be treated because, for much of the historical period covered by the early pages of the *Anthology,* the oral or literary culture of the two places were interactive in a most intimate manner. Why then – considerations of expense, length etc., aside – is early Scottish literature omitted? Perhaps the implication that Gaelic Scotland constituted an instance (not wholly unique) of Irish colonizing activity was politically inadmissable.[21] The counterargument, that events in the eighth century (or earlier) hardly compromise the integrity of twentieth-century independent Ireland, is forceful – suspiciously so, if one recalls that Yeats's first play about Cuchulain, *On Baile's Strand* (1904), crucially depends on kinship and antagonism bridging the North Channel. The same Cuchulain presides in the General Post Office to commemorate the insurrection from which independence stemmed, represented by the statue so disgracefully embraced by Beckett's Neary. The nation, conceived historically, is no more and no less than a totality made up of all totalities subordinated to it and is (at the same time) overdetermined by totalities of a higher complexity.[22] In contrast, any notion of Ireland as 'self-identical whole' stems (whether it likes it or not) from the Prussian side of Hegel's system.

This last option generously afflicts both Field Day and its principal critics. Ireland as geographical entity is transcribed into a theory of representation in which fictional setting regulates the canon, especially in relation to nineteenth-century fiction. This process of selection is overdriven, however, by another, participation in Ireland as nation or proto-nation. Thus, until very recently Trollope's Irish-set novels were as predictably excluded from discussion as were Le Fanu's English-set ones. And now that Trollope has been grudgingly admitted, Godwin threatens to pose even more unsettling problems. For if *Mandeville* or *Caleb Williams* were to be admitted, the list might end in exotic scandal – with *The Holy Sinner* by Thomas Mann, for example, or with Raymond Queneau's (naturally) untranslated novel about bonking in the GPO, at Easter-tide 1916. It is true that *Dracula* has been admitted into the Field Day canon, yet an even greater best-seller – E. L. Voynich's *The Gadfly* – has yet to be trapped.

Literary history, if it is to avoid the impoverishment which is entailed in its systematic emplotment, betrays what the emplotters would set up as the nation or class or credo which is identical with itself. Only on these terms can it effect a critique of its own procedures and so make possible its renewal and self-betrayal. No one would want to argue that the social conditions required for the propagation of such thinking pertained in Hungary, certainly not in the period between the beginning of 1949 and the death of Stalin in 1953. But those who stigmatize Lukács as an unwavering (which is to say, wavering or inconsistent) endorser of the party line rarely allude to the even longer period of fascist rule during which culture was rigorously policed, political opposition outlawed and, ultimately, the Nazi programme of genocide facilitated.[23] Cold War logic has disgraced itself on both sides of its daggers-drawn equation mark; what may be needed is a recovery of that realization, so poignant in Benjamin, of the brutalization of civil life in Central Europe which followed from the Great War. That annihilation of experience was re-armed in the 1930s, and remained pervasive in a post-fascist phase which may not have concluded.

These concluding unscientific meditations on Hungarian history do not rely on, or presume, any intrinsic merit in that society and its culture. In so far as I am competent to make a judgement, it seems that literary criticism in Hungary is heavily sentimental, lodged in a *belle-lettriste* celebratory mode. Lukács may have been, as Agnes Nemes Nagy energetically insisted, a murderer.[24] Yet literary history, as practised in or about Ireland, can derive much from the comparative exercise. For example, Mary Gluck's *Georg Lukács and his Generation* documents a nineteenth-century social history in which a middle-class commercial minority acquired rural estates and noble titles, and yet these 'liberal fathers' begot a generation of 'illiberal children'. The difference-and-resemblance of this might be examined by historians of Victorian and Edwardian Ireland, not only for its insight into the delay-action relationship between minority and illiberalism but also for the opportunity provided to examine the construction of the modernist 'generation' of Yeats, Synge, and Joyce. Such an undertaking would not remain passively comparative, a kind of pen-friendship between parties who never meet, for any confrontation with the relationship of money and culture in nineteenth-century Ireland must soon lead to a questioning of the material basis on which Lissadel and Coole Park were erected.[25] The Hungarian poet, Endre Ady (1877 – 1919), if his indolent Anglo-phone translator were ever to finish the task of making his work accessible, could have a similar impact on the petrified argument about Irish Protestantism, for the Calvinism of Ady's upbringing pervades his poems of love and hatred with an intensity unparalleled in Irish writers' genteel encashment of their inheritance.[26] Finally, consideration of Hungary's vernacular languages from 1800 onwards could shed light on the virtual monolingualism of Ireland. But that is to look beyond the properly limited horizon of literary history.

What does lie within the proper boundaries of literary history, with regard to Ireland, at the close of the twentieth century? If the procedures of the present book have been rightly selective, is it a presupposition or conclusion of the argument that nothing of consequence for the literary historian has been written after the body of work signally conditioned by the Second World War? On the surface, the answer to the second question must surely be negative, for an impressive literature flourishes today, in succession not only to the generation of Beckett and Bowen (and Clarke and O'Faolain) but also in effective dialogue with figures who have not been mentioned in these pages.

Yet the choice of *Endgame* and *Eva Trout* for discussion does involve an admission of terminal crisis. Even from so oblique an angle as that struck by Anglo-Irish writers against the monstrosity of the Second World War, it was clear that culture – literature in particular – could not simply be resumed, taken up from where it had left off during the last Golden Age of Innocence. Beckett's too famous words – 'I can't go, I'll go on'[27] – should not be attributed exclusively to some individual character, even an unnamable one: they brokenly reflect or refract the conjuncture of impossibility and obligation, exhaustion and need, necessity and freedom in which the writer was situated (in Adorno's words) 'after Auschwitz'. If this seems a remote point of reference in a discussion which should quickly move on to the foundation of the Dolmen Press, the achievements of Michael McLaverty and Edna O'Brien, the rebuilding of the Abbey, then one should recall Denis Johnston's testimony to the victims of Buchenwald in *Nine Rivers from Jordan* (1953), the penetrating study of contaminated loyalty in Bowen's *The Heat of the Day* (1949), and the more morally unstable witness of Francis Stuart in *The Pillar of Cloud* (1948) and *Redemption* (1950). Thomas Kinsella's early poem, 'Downstream' (1962, revised 1964), is an attempt to navigate a passage into a new literature while yet preserving the full memory of what had passed remotely away.

Perhaps it should be emphasized that the business of the literary historian does not commence with the singling out of good poetry, fiction and drama, but rather with the elucidation of the appropriate concepts through which 'the good' (in aesthetic terms) might be evaluated. These concepts may in the end be analytical, but in the first instance they are likely to be symptomatological; or to be necessary portmanteau terms trading between these functions. Ascendancy and tradition have been the principal concepts under which a literature, produced between the French Revolution and the Second World War, has been analysed: these are not analytical terms but an effort has been made to employ them ultimately as symptomatological ones. Betrayal, in contrast, has come closer to acting as a term of analysis.

Our questions can finally be rephrased and left for others to consider. What are the significant concepts under which post-war Irish literature has been generated, or under which it can be revealingly criticized? Answers cannot simply be found by scanning the anthologies or totting up the prize money. They cannot be found by the application of 'taste' by the individual reader. (Who could, even now, recommend *Purgatory* or *Endgame* on such grounds?) The question involves historical as well as literary sensitivity, and may resist full articulation within the immediate period when inquiry and production co-exist. Whatever about the formalist critic or political commentator, the literary historian is not ready for Paul Durcan. This is not said in any sense to discourage critics from commendatory responses to poetry written this year or last: it is simply said to distinguish between the historical and literary domains, in terms of the contemporary.

The relevant concepts may not be visible at the same time as the work ultimately treated in their light is produced. Nor is it necessarily the case that the authors whom future literary historians will discuss shall be seen to stand in unbroken succession with those now large on our horizon. Even today, when we begin to locate major figures such as John McGahern or Seamus Heaney in a historical perspective, we are more aware of the discontinuities than of any supportive tradition. The concept of feminism looks certain to figure among the analytical instruments future literary historians will need, precisely because its symptomatological register is so strikingly negative. But will post-modernism, or ethnicity, or fideism, challenge for attention?

And what of Ireland? Is it a concept or a confusion? Is it a place, a location, in which intellectual inquiry will have value?

NOTES AND REFERENCES

1 Samuel Beckett, *Molloy, Malone Dies, the Unnamable* (London: Calder and Boyers, 1959), p. 293.

2 For an unusual perspective of Lukács as personal influence, see the Glaswegian Lionel Gossman's *Between Literature and History*, (Cambridge, Mass.: Harvard University Press, 1990).

2 Thomas Mann, *The Magic Mountain*, trans. Helen Lowe-Porter (New York: Knopf, 1945), pp. 508-9.

4 A discreet version of this scandal is discernible in Lóránt Czigány's account of Balázs: 'The great potentialities which Lukács thought he had discovered in Balázs remained potentialities only, and perhaps his disappointment over Balázs's failure to become a genuinely epoch-making creative writer contributed to Lukács's loss of interest in contemporary literature, or rather to his careful reluctance to acknowledge new talents.' *The Oxford History of Hungarian Literature* (Oxford: Clarendon Press, 1984 (corrected text of 1986)), p. 269.

5 For the (often heated) discussion of modernism by the Frankfurt critical theorists, see Ernst Bloch, György Lukács, Bertolt Brecht, Walter Benjamin, Theodor Adorno, *Aesthetics and Politics* (London: New Left Books, 1977). The general background is richly documented and exhaustively described in Rolf Wiggershaus, *The Frankfurt School: its History, Theories and Political Significance* (Cambridge: Polity Press, 1994).

6 For a discussion of Benjamin which takes account of unevenness and inconsistency, see Marshall Berman, *All That is Solid Melts into Air: the Experience of Modernity* (London: Verso, 1983), pp. 146-7 etc. See also Richard Wolin, *Walter Benjamin: an Aesthetic of Redemption* (New York: Columbia, 1982). The chapter on Lukács in Fredric Jameson, *Marxism and Form: Twentieth-Century Dialectical Theories of Literature* (Princeton: Princeton University Press, 1971) is still valuable for its demolition of the safety barriers erected between 'early Lukács' and 'mature Lukács' or, from the opposing perspective, between the mystic and the Bolshevik.

7 György Lukács, *Soul and Form*, trans. Ann Bostock (London: Merlin Press, 1971), p. 113.

8 Walter Benjamin, *Illuminations*, trans. Harry Zohn, (London: Cape, 1970), p. 255.

9 Andrew Benjamin and Peter Osborne, *Walter Benjamin's Philosophy: Destruction and Experience* (London: Routledge, 1994), p. 251.

10 Charles Rosen 'The Ruins of Walter Benjamin' in Gary Smith (ed.), *On Walter Benjamin: Critical Essays and Recollections* (Cambridge, Mass.: MIT Press, 1991), p. 170.

11 David Perkins, *Is Literary History Possible?* (Baltimore: Johns Hopkins University Press, 1992), p. 9. Cf. the programme of reception aesthetics in H.R. Jauss 'Literary History as a challenge to Literary Theory' in Timothy Bahti (ed.), *Towards an Aesthetic of Reception*, (Minneapolis: University of Minnesota Press, 1982).

12 See Marilyn Butler, *Maria Edgeworth: a Literary Biography* (Oxford: Clarendon Press, 1972), *Jane Austen and the War of Ideas* (Oxford: Clarendon Press, 1975), and *Romantics, Rebels and Revolutionaries* (Oxford University Press, 1981); Jerome McGann, *A Critique of Modern Textual Criticism* (Chicago: University

Press, 1981); Jerome McGann, *A Critique of Modern Textual Criticism* (Chicago: University of Chicago Press, 1983), *The Beauty of Inflections: Literary Investigations in Historical Method and Theory* (Oxford: Clarendon Press, 1985), *Social Values and Poetic Acts: the Historical Judgement of Literary Work* (Cambridge, Mass.: Harvard University Press, 1988) and *Towards a Literature of Knowledge* (Oxford: Clarendon Press, 1989.)

13 McGann, *The Beauty of Inflections*, op. cit., pp. 90, 341.

14 See 'The Poverty of Theory', or, an Orrery of Errors' (pp. 193-406) in Thompson, *The Poverty of Theory and Other Essays* (London: Merlin Press, 1978). See pp. 21-3 above for earlier comments on the significance of Thompson's polemic.

15 W. J. McCormack, *The Dublin Paper War of 1786–1788; a Bibliographical and Critical Inquiry, including an Account of the Origins of Protestant Ascendancy and its 'Baptism' in 1792* (Dublin: Irish Academic Press, 1993), pp. 50-6.

16 For the earlier estimate, see G. C. Bolton, *The Passing of the Irish Act of Union* (London: Oxford University Press, 1966). The revised figure is based on a preliminary survey made by the present writer in the spring of 1994, in preparation for a detailed presentation of the material.

17 Perkins, *Is Literary History Possible?*, p. 13, emphasis added.

18 'General Introduction, by Seamus Deane' in Deane et al., eds., *The Field Day Anthology of Irish Writing* (Derry: Field Day, 1991), vol. 1, p. xix.

19 See Hayden White, *Tropics of Discourse*, (Baltimore: University of Johns Hopkins Press, 1978), pp. 58-110.

20 Deane, loc. cit.

21 See Donnchadh Ó Corráin, *Ireland before the Normans* (Dublin: Gill and Macmillan, 1972), p. 69 etc.

22 This formulation draws on a speech delivered by Lukács in Milan in December 1947 and published as *A marscista filozófia feladatai az ui democráciában* in Budapest the following year, a crucial transitional moment in post-war Hungarian politics. See István Mészáros, *Lukács' Concept of Dialectic* (London: Merlin Press, 1972), pp. 61-91, & 103. For a rather less respectful analysis see Fredric Jameson, *Late Marxism: Adorno, or the Persistence of the Dialectic* (London: Verso, 1990), pp. 26-7.

23 See Jorg K. Hoensch, *A History of Modern Hungary 1867–1936* (London: Longman, 1988).

24 Consideration of distinguished writers etc. who have killed another human being deliberately is a nervous undertaking, one not designed to reassure admirers of Constance Gore-Booth, George Orwell, Samuel Beckett - to name but three. In contemporary Ireland, the difficulty revolves round the failure of the killers (or the vast majority of them) to write. In the end, Nemes Nagy's accusation misses the point, the point Hubert Butler neatly encapsulated in the term 'desk-murderer' - which opens a pandora's box.

25 Mary Gluck, *Georg Lukács and his Generation 1900–1918* (Cambridge, Mass.: Harvard University Press, 1985). See Neil McKendrick, John Brewer, J. H. Plumb, *The Birth of Consumer Society: the Commercialization of Eighteenth-Century England* (London: Hutchinson, 1983) for some examples of what might be done.

26 Though Vivian Mercier's *Modern Irish Literature: Sources and Founders* (Oxford: Clarendon Press, 1994) must be treated carefully in that it is a posthumous and

unfinished work, its extensive treatment of Irish Protestantism is based almost exclusively on the Church of Ireland. The neglect of non-conformity is all the more remarkable given Mercier's professed interest in evangelicalism which can be found in a wide variety of ecclesiastical communities – the Baptist churches, Methodism, and (from the early nineteenth century onwards) in the officially Calvinist Presbyterian Church in Ireland, not to mention the refugee Protestant groups (Huguenot and Palatine) from which Mercier himself was descended.

27   Beckett, *Molloy, Malone Dies, The Unnamable*, p. 418.

Index

453

George II, 83
George III, 60, 114, 130
George V, 236
George, Lloyd, 312
Germany, 10, 18, 28, 281, 341, 342, 362, 364, 366-7, 368, 387, 389, 399, 411, 412, 418, 419
Giffard, John, 70, 72-3, 85, 91n, 113, 117, 140, 153, 158, 159, 363
Gilbert, Stuart, 275
Gillespie, R, 382
Gladstone, William Ewart, 196-8
Glanmore, Co. Wicklow, 251
Glasheen, Adeline, 279
Glenavy, Beatrice, 158
Glendalough, Co. Wicklow, 249
Glengall, earl of, 149
Glenmacnass, Co. Wicklow, 245, 251
Glenmalure, Co. Wicklow, 246
Gluck, Mary, 446
Glorious Revolution, 31, 81, 87, 146
Godwin, William, 2, 54, 94, 97, 98, 105, 106, 109, 123, 206, 446
   Caleb Williams, 99-106, 107, 108, 316
Goering, Hermann, 397, 398, 429n
Goethe, J. W. von, 28, 305, 330, 360
Goethe-plakette, 390
Gogarty, O. St J., 315, 316, 421
Goldmann, Lucien, 220, 342
Goldsmith, Francis, 326
Goldsmith, John, 324, 326, 327
Goldsmith, Miss, 327
Goldsmith, Oliver, 9, 11, 13, 40, 83, 206, 305, 311, 319, 321, 324-8, 329, 333
Gonstarski, Stan, 396
Gossman, Lionel, 449n
Government of Ireland Act, 6, 380
Gowan, John Hunter, 113, 135,
Grattan, Henry, 59-60, 61-2, 70, 71, 74, 77, 78-9, 80, 82, 83, 86, 110, 137, 146, 166, 170, 171, 212, 307, 310, 311-2, 318, 329
Grattan, Henry Jnr, 61
Graves, Robert, 2, 145

Gray, Thomas, 53
Great War, 295, 346, 376, 401, 402, 407, 411, 431n, 435, 436, 446
Green, Alice Stopford, 316-7
Greenan, Co. Wicklow, 247, 251
Gregg, Tresham Dames, 165, 167, 168, 169, 170, 171, 197
Gregory, Augusta Isabella, Lady, 7, 8, 10, 126, 154, 159, 210, 233, 234, 253, 310, 326, 346, 352, 362, 369, 375, 376, 392
Gregory, Robert, 153
Gregory, Sir Wm, 352
Grene, Nicholas, 246
Greville, C. T., 51, 53
Grey, Lord Deputy, 251
Greystones, Co. Wicklow, 249
Griffin, Gerald, 142, 165, 181
Griffin, M. J., 313
Griffiths, Trevor, 443
Grohmann, Willi, 390

Habermas, Jürgen, 17, 116, 340n, 368
Hackett, Francis, 377, 427n
Hamilton, Dacre, 192, 204n
Hamilton, William Rowan, 208
Hardiman, James, 139, 140
Hardy, Thomas, 267
Harmon, Maurice, 90n
Harris, Daniel, 159
Hartnett, Michael, 376
Hastings, Warren, 88
Haughton, Samuel, 208
Hayden, Henri, 421
Healy, Patrick, 174
Heaney, Seamus, 100, 120n, 448
Heath, Edward, 21
Hegel, G. W. F., 32, 226, 323, 419, 420, 424, 425, 426, 437, 445
Heidegger, Martin, 12, 305-6, 336n, 366, 368, 417
Heller, Erich, 17
Henn, T. R., 9-10, 360
Henry II, 50
Herder, Johann Gottlieb von, 225, 228